Theoretical Perspectives
on Cognitive Aging

THEORETICAL PERSPECTIVES ON COGNITIVE AGING

TIMOTHY A. SALTHOUSE
Georgia Institute of Technology

LEA LAWRENCE ERLBAUM ASSOCIATES, PUBLISHERS
1991   Hillsdale, New Jersey   Hove and London

Lawrence Erlbaum Associates, Inc., Publishers
365 Broadway
Hillsdale, New Jersey 07642

Library of Congress Cataloging in Publication Data

Salthouse, Timothy A,
  Theoretical perspectives on cognitive aging / Timothy A. Salthouse.
    p.   cm.
  Includes bibliographical references and indexes.
  ISBN 0-8058-1170-2
  1. Cognition—Age factors.   2. Memory—Age factors.   3. Aging—Psychological aspects.   I. Title.
  BF724.55.C63S24   1991
  155.67—dc20   91-12732
                                                                      CIP

Printed in the United States of America
10 9 8 7 6 5 4 3 2

Contents

Preface

If older people do, in fact, tend to perform at lower levels in assorted cognitive tasks than young people, why is this the case? What is responsible for the frequently discussed, sometimes doubted, but invariably feared, mental declines reputed to be associated with increased age? The primary purposes of this book are first to review the evidence of age-related differences in cognitive functioning, and then to evaluate the major explanations proposed to account for the negative relations between age and cognition that have been established.

Two important restrictions should be acknowledged at the outset to minimize misunderstanding about what is to be covered in this book. First, the emphasis is on normal, or at least non-pathological, aging. It is often difficult to determine whether the behavioral differences observed across people of varying ages are attributable to pathological or to non-pathological factors. However, the influence of diseases and other assorted pathologies known to be more prevalent with increased age can be presumed to be reduced by emphasizing research involving comparisons of people less than about 80 years of age who generally report themselves to be in moderate to excellent health. Most of the empirical results to be described are therefore derived from research involving research participants possessing these characteristics.

The second restriction on the current coverage is that the explanations to be examined are limited to those relying upon psychological, rather than physiological or neurological, mechanisms. Ultimately, of course, a complete explanation of any aging phenomenon will require detailed understanding of age-related influences on the structure and functioning of the biological system. Whether the biological processes are considered the principal causes of the behavioral phenomena, or merely the physical medium in which those causes happen to be implemented, the contribution of biological factors to age-related differences in cognition can't be ignored. However, at the current time there appears to be relatively little evidence linking findings at the neurological or physiological level to such complex behavioral phenomena as performance on cognitive tests. It is consequently for this reason, rather than any presumption that biological factors are irrelevant for cognitive functioning, that a comprehensive evaluation of this category of explanation is not attempted in the present volume.

Many of the theoretical interpretations to be discussed can be traced back at least 50 to 70 years. Despite this moderately long history, there has apparently never been a systematic appraisal of the evidence relevant to the various theoretical perspectives proposed to account for cognitive aging phenomena. One possible reason for the absence of detailed evaluations of the major theoretical perspectives in the past is that as researchers have developed enthusiasm for a particular perspective, they have tended to become immersed in the details of investigating various methodological issues, or in the further exploration of findings discovered incidentally in the course of their investigations. As a consequence, these researchers, and others who read their reports in the literature, may sometimes lose track of, or perhaps even interest in, the original goal of explaining why age differences occur in various measures of cognitive functioning. The opportunistic style of research is often an exciting way of exploring the domain of interest and of discovering new phenomena. However, it is seldom the most direct means of answering a specific question, or of accomplishing a particular goal. It is occasionally desirable, even in the most flexible and unconstrained explorations, to make periodic 'compass checks' to ensure that one does not get lost. It is in this spirit of monitoring progress towards the important goal of understanding cognitive aging phenomena that it is hoped that the present book will prove useful.

The book contains nine chapters, with the first consisting of a relatively general introduction, and a discussion of theoretical dimensions and levels of scientific theorizing assumed to be helpful in understanding, and evaluating, alternative theoretical perspectives on cognitive aging. The second chapter is devoted to documenting the phenomena to be explained by theories of cognitive aging. Chapters 3 through 8 examine major theoretical perspectives attributing age differences in cognitive functioning to changes in the external environment (chapter 3), to patterns of disuse (chapter 4), to qualitative shifts in processing (chapter 5), to specific or localized deficits in aspects of memory, reasoning, or spatial functioning (chapters 6 and 7), and to relatively general impairments in processing (chapter 8). The final chapter is comprised of observations about the progress that has been made in explaining cognitive aging phenomena, and recommendations for research practices that might contribute to greater progress in the future.

ACKNOWLEDGMENTS

A project such as this reflects the contributions of a great many people. Not only am I grateful to the staff at Lawrence Erlbaum Associates for easing the transition from manuscript to book, but also to many students and colleagues who have convinced me of the importance of attempting a rigorous examination of theoretical perspectives on cognitive aging. Special gratitude is due two colleagues who devoted precious time to critiquing early drafts of the manuscript—Paul Baltes and Reinhold Kliegl. This is not the book that either of them would write, but it is certainly better than what I would have written without benefit of stimulating interactions with them. I would also like to acknowledge the hospitality they both exhibited while I worked on this book as a Visiting Scientist at the Max Planck Institute for Human Development and Education in Berlin. And last, but not least, I want to thank my family—Twila, Christopher, and Courtney —for their support and encouragement throughout the duration of this project.

Timothy A. Salthouse

1 The Need for, and Requirements of, Theories of Cognitive Aging

... [M]uch of what we have learned consists of detailed, low-level, empirical observations, lacking system and explanation. It is not sufficient merely to observe that certain age changes take place; we need to know why they take place.

—Bromley (1974, p. 372)

It is clear that simply listing the observations is not enough—the facts of observation do not speak for themselves, they have to be spoken for; and they are spoken for by a theory which imposes upon them a pattern of meaning, a logical structure.

—Bromley (1970, p. 77)

INTRODUCTION

The research literature concerned with the relations between aging and cognitive functioning is increasing so rapidly that it is becoming extremely difficult to assimilate all the new results, or even to discern whether progress is being made in the understanding of fundamental issues. In fact, because research activity in the area of cognitive aging is expanding in so many directions, there is probably little consensus concerning the identity of the fundamental issues, and still less with respect to whether they are getting close to being resolved.

Because the field of cognitive aging now seems to include virtually any research involving the collection of behavioral information from people over about 25 years of age, some restriction of scope is necessary to allow adequate discussion of the relevant research literature. One means by which this can be accomplished is to define the phenomena of interest very explicitly, and then to concentrate only on theoretical perspectives that attempt to provide explanations for those specific phenomena.

For the purposes of this book, therefore, the topic of cognitive aging will be circumscribed by operationally defining it in terms of the decrease in performance on various measures of cognitive functioning associated with

1

increasing age in the adult portion of the lifespan. As with all operational definitions, this particular definition has both advantages and disadvantages. The principal advantage is that it serves to focus the discussion, and may therefore minimize potentially endless debates about how the relevant constructs are to be defined. That is, in the present context cognition can be considered to be what is measured by selected cognitive tests, and age will be interpreted in terms of elapsed time since birth. Both of these constructs could obviously be elaborated and refined, but modifications of the constructs would only be considered pertinent if they contributed to greater understanding of the target phenomenon.

A disadvantage of operational definitions is that one can always raise the objection that the proposed method of defining the construct is too narrow, and does not do justice to the breadth and richness inherent in the term. This criticism can quite legitimately be directed against the interpretation of cognitive aging in terms of the negative relation between age and cognitive performance. For example, it could be objected that concentrating exclusively on this issue may give the misleading impression that increased age is associated with a decline in all aspects of cognition, and might serve to perpetuate unfavorable stereotypes about older adults.

There are, however, several good reasons why it seems desirable to restrict one's focus in a book of this type. One reason is pragmatic: Limitations of space preclude comprehensive coverage of all potentially relevant topics. The tradeoff in introductory books usually favors breadth rather than depth, but at the cost of providing relatively superficial discussion of each topic. In contrast, books intended to explore issues in depth must necessarily sacrifice a certain degree of breadth if the topics of primary interest are to receive sufficient discussion.

Given that it is sometimes desirable to have a narrow focus, why is the present focus on decline rather than on stability or growth? Ultimately, of course, one would hope that each major topic within a field would receive an equivalent amount of scrutiny. However, the greatest amount of empirical research in the field of cognitive aging has been concerned with phenomena of decline. As a consequence, negative relations between age and cognition are now very well established, but with little consensus about how they are to be explained. Moreover, other types of age-cognition relations are either not well documented (e.g., growth), or do not seem to require an explanation (e.g., stability).

The possibility of cognitive growth in adulthood has been the subject of considerable speculation, but this interest has not yet been translated into much directly relevant empirical evidence. Even advocates of this position acknowledge that "... very little presently is known about how adult cognition may improve with age" (Perlmutter, 1988, p. 261), and that the phenomenon of cognitive growth may be restricted to a few individuals in select domains (J. Smith & P.B. Baltes, 1990). The lack of knowledge about age-related improvements in cognition may be a consequence of the difficulty of investigating very complex aspects of cognition, such as wisdom and good judgment, which are frequently mentioned candidates for growth in the adult years. Alternatively, it is possible that the only cognitive growth that occurs during the adult years is that attributable to increments in accumulated knowledge acquired as a consequence of experience. If the latter is the case, then the relevant research may fall more within the purview of research on general learning rather than the study of aging and cognition, per se. Regardless of the reason for the limited empirical literature, however, it is clearly difficult to attempt to evaluate the adequacy of alternative theoretical interpretations for a phenomenon when the quantity of research relevant to that phenomenon is so sparse.

Because stability refers to constancy, or the absence of a difference, it can be argued that there is nothing to explain when no age-related differences are observed. That is, a finding of stability across the adult years presumably means that there is no change with age in the relevant behavioral characteristic, and if nothing has changed, then there may be no need for anything to be explained. Of course, there are cases in which stability is interesting because it is unexpected, or because it contrasts with decline or growth evident on other measures. The important point, however, is that stability is not always interesting, or deserving of explanation, because explanations are generally sought to account for the presence of effects and not for their absence.

A strong argument can also be made that despite the unpopularity of age-related declines, particularly in the realm of cognitive abilities, the greatest practical consequences of research on aging are likely to derive from attempts to learn about the causes for the negative aspects of aging. As Welford (1958) stated in his classic book: " ... it is not by glossing over or neglecting older people's difficulties but by seeking to understand them that we can best open the way to their removal" (p. 3). While it may therefore be more comforting in the short term to emphasize aspects of human cognition that either remain stable or improve as a function of age, the most important long-term benefits will probably result from research focusing on understanding the causes of the aspects of cognition that decline with age.

The primary focus in this book therefore will be on possible answers to the question of why increased age is often associated with lower levels of performance on certain measures of cognitive functioning. This is obviously not the only interesting question regarding aging and cognitive functioning, but the intention in this book is neither to conduct a complete inventory of cognitive deficiencies and competencies, nor to evaluate the balance between the assets and the liabilities of cognitive aging to estimate some type of net worth. Instead the goal is to concentrate on the presumed deficiencies or liabilities in an attempt both to specify their exact nature, and to identify their major causes. While not all of what might reasonably be included in the field of cognitive aging will therefore be represented in the subsequent chapters, the restriction of scope will allow a more concentrated and coherent discussion than otherwise possible of what is arguably the most important question in the area of aging and cognition at the present time—namely, what is responsible for the negative relation between age and certain measures of cognitive performance?

WHY A THEORETICAL APPROACH?

Most authors of review articles and textbooks rely on some kind of organizational scheme to provide a framework within which results from many different research projects can be integrated. Without a basis for integrating research findings and for identifying which of the many results are the most important, there is a very real danger of becoming overwhelmed by the vast quantity of seemingly unrelated facts. This, in turn, may result in the neglect of earlier findings, and of the channeling of future research efforts in tangential or unproductive directions.

Similar concerns about the dangers of an over-reliance on raw observations were expressed by Royce (1965) in the following passage:

> A solid observational base is absolutely essential for the growth and development of a young science. But, if it stakes too much of its future on naive empiricism, it runs the same risk of extinction which befell the dinosaur, which could not survive because of an overload of bodily bulk. (p. 447)

While there is no magical panacea that automatically organizes and supplies insight into complex phenomena, both organization and direction are primary functions, or at least major goals, of scientific theories. That is, theories are designed to provide a coherent framework within which a large number of observations can be assimilated, and to provide direction for research by imposing a set of priorities about the importance of different topics and issues. It therefore seems reasonable that the research literature would be more easily assimilated by relying on a theory to furnish the organizational framework for interpreting research findings.

A primary rationale for the present book is the assumption that if a single theory is useful for organizing a portion of the research literature in a field, then one might expect to get a fairly comprehensive coverage of the most important findings in that field by examining several different theoretical perspectives. Of course, consideration of several alternative theoretical perspectives does not guarantee that certain areas of research will not be omitted. However, if it is indeed the case that the neglected research is not relevant to any of the major theoretical positions, then such omissions might even be justified on the grounds that the omitted research does not address theoretically important issues.

Much of the research in the area of cognitive aging seems to have been motivated primarily by a desire to find out whether age differences exist in certain kinds of cognitive behavior. For example, a researcher might read about an intriguing result based on research with children or college students, and simply wonder whether older adults differ from young adults with respect to that behavioral characteristic. Results from research motivated in this fashion have contributed to a vast accumulation of observations or facts, some of which are quite interesting. However, not all results derived from this type of atheoretical curiosity are necessarily very important. Decisions concerning the importance of research findings are, admittedly, always somewhat subjective. Nevertheless, relevance to one or more theories appears at least as defensible a criterion for evaluating importance as any other, and may be the most compelling justification for choosing to engage in a particular type of research. (It certainly seems preferable to two justifications that have recently appeared in the research literature; namely, that the research was undertaken because not much is known about the topic [a fact which is true of a nearly infinite quantity of topics], or because the literature on the topic is small enough that it is relatively easy to keep up with the new publications [as though personal convenience rather than advancement of scientific understanding was the paramount consideration]).

Reliance on the criterion of relevance to major theoretical perspectives should therefore ensure that the research is important in the sense that it addresses issues concerning how age differences in cognitive functioning are to be interpreted. Other research can be considered secondary to this major question, elaborations on earlier themes, or concerned with minor issues which, even if resolved, would probably not alter fundamental understanding.

A second advantage of relying on an examination of leading theoretical perspectives as the basis for organizing a review of research in the area of cognitive aging is evaluative. That is, because each of the theories is intended to focus on the same general phenomenon, determination of their strengths and weaknesses provides one means of assessing the progress that has been made toward answering the question of why age differences occur in measures of cognitive functioning. No explicit comparisons of alternative perspectives is attempted in the chapters that follow, and the intent is not to identify (nor formulate) the single best theory of cognitive aging phenomena. Nevertheless, impressions of the viability of each perspective, or at least of its underlying assumptions, can be expected to emerge as the relevant evidence is reviewed.

There are also some disadvantages to a focus on theoretical perspectives. For example, one possible criticism is that many of the most important questions about the elderly are practical rather than theoretical. Advocates of this view might thus argue that devising methods of helping the impaired elderly should have a greater priority than attempting to discriminate among speculations about the causes of those impairments. This position was recently expressed by Kausler (1989b), in the context of research on memory, as follows: "Gerontological memory research needs less emphasis on theoretical issues and greater emphasis on the conditions that enhance memory performance of elderly adults" (p. 67). The primary rebuttal to this criticism is that, as noted above, books such as this must necessarily be limited in scope. Therefore while there may indeed be a need for books with a practical orientation, the focus of this particular book is not on how the cognitive functioning of the elderly can be enhanced, but rather what is responsible for the negative relations frequently observed between age and measures of cognitive performance. It is also important to note that there is considerable truth in the saying "There is nothing so practical as a good theory," because the design of effective remediations of a phenomenon usually requires adequate understanding of the causes of that phenomenon.

Another disadvantage of an emphasis on theoretical perspectives is that any attempt to determine the strengths and weaknesses of theoretical perspectives inevitably involves some subjectivity. Indeed, nearly all theoretical discussions can be considered somewhat biased or one-sided because they are usually presented by proponents, who naturally stress the positive aspects of the theory, or by opponents, who tend to emphasize the deficiencies of the theory. Although it may be unrealistic to expect to eliminate all bias and subjectivity in discussions of theoretical issues, a major goal in this book is to provide a probing, but balanced, assessment of the positive and negative aspects of each theoretical perspective through the careful evaluation of arguments of both advocates and critics.

Another source of subjectivity in the assessment of theoretical perspectives is related to the fact that because the theoretical perspectives seldom exist in a fully formulated or articulated form, they must be extracted and abstracted from the literature. This necessarily involves some rather arbitrary decisions concerning the interpretation of theoretical positions, and their attribution to specific individuals. It is therefore possible for disputes or confusion to arise because the ideas have been misinterpreted, because the original authors may not have realized all the implications of their arguments or assumptions, or because the authors have changed their positions over the course of their careers. Regardless of the proponents at the current time, however, the theoretical perspectives to be examined in this book appear to be the dominant ones in the field, and consequently they warrant careful consideration if one is interested in understanding the present state of knowledge regarding the reasons increased age is often associated with lower levels of cognitive functioning.

To reiterate, the goals of this book are to review the empirical literature relevant to the phenomenon of age-related decline in measures of cognitive functioning by means of an examination of the dominant theoretical perspectives proposed to account for this phenomenon. This will entail: (a) specifying the level of explanation provided, or at least attempted, by the theoretical perspectives; and (b) making explicit the assumptions of the major theoretical perspectives, and identifying implications of those assumptions. The remainder of this chapter is devoted to providing background information relevant to these aims. The first section elaborates on the different possible levels of theoretical analysis or explanation, and the second briefly describes some of the important dimensions along which theories of developmental phenomena might differ. The third and final section focuses on the special requirements of theories intended to account for developmental (i.e., change-oriented) phenomena.

LEVELS OF THEORETICAL DISCOURSE

There seems to be considerable agreement that theories within a given discipline are hierarchical in nature, with multiple levels of analysis and explanation. However, little consensus is currently evident in the scientific community with respect to the number of levels of theory that should be distinguished, or concerning the labels to be used in referring to those levels. Although admittedly somewhat arbitrary, six levels of theoretical discourse will be distinguished here, ranging from the extremely broad and generally unrecognized assumptions comprising one's world view, to the actual observations corresponding to the phenomena to be explained. A schematic outline of the six levels is portrayed in Figure 1.1.

World View

World views, also known as world hypotheses, scientific paradigms, and meta-models, are general beliefs and assumptions about the nature of reality and of mankind. These implicit orientations or biases are seldom explicitly recognized or acknowledged by practicing scientists, but they are nevertheless likely to influence the nature of the problems to be studied and the approaches employed for the investigation of those problems. The two world views that have received the most discussion by philosophers and

LEVELS OF THEORETICAL DISCOURSE

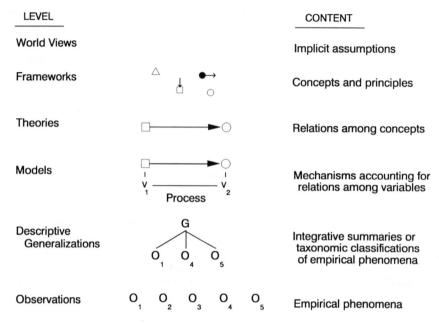

LEVEL	CONTENT
World Views	Implicit assumptions
Frameworks	Concepts and principles
Theories	Relations among concepts
Models	Mechanisms accounting for relations among variables
Descriptive Generalizations	Integrative summaries or taxonomic classifications of empirical phenomena
Observations	Empirical phenomena

Figure 1.1. Schematic illustration of six hierarchical levels of theoretical discourse.

philosophically oriented psychologists are mechanism and organicism. The mechanistic world view tends to conceptualize the world as a very elaborate machine; researchers working within this world view thus often attempt to determine the forces operating on entities in the world, and to specify the consequences of those forces. The organismic world view is based on the metaphor of the living organism with an emphasis on active, purpose-oriented behavior rather than reactive, externally driven behavior. Researchers working within the organismic world view thus frequently see their goal as that of trying to identify the evolving structure of dynamic entities, with only a peripheral interest in external forces and their consequences.

Because world views correspond to implicit orientations rather than to sets of explicit hypotheses about observable variables, they are not subject to direct empirical verification or falsification. Therefore, though they may influence the type of theoretical explanations considered plausible, and can affect the kinds of research problems deemed worthy of investigation, they are not themselves capable of being evaluated in terms of truth or falsity. The inability to distinguish among alternative world views on the basis of empirical observations has led some researchers to dismiss their importance in scientific theorizing. While perhaps understandable, this attitude is probably somewhat naive because these implicit assumptions can exert considerable influence on the direction of research in a given field by emphasizing the value or importance of some research questions, and deemphasizing the value or importance of other questions. Furthermore, as P.B. Baltes and Willis (1977) point out, world views may be especially important in a young field such as the psychology of aging because the meta-theoretical biases of the early pioneers are likely to determine the manner in which the field is initially defined.

Frameworks

Frameworks are intermediate in the hierarchy of theoretical discourse between world views and theories, and basically consist of a loose collection of concepts and principles. These concepts and principles are thought to be useful in understanding particular classes of phenomena, but unlike theories, they are not necessarily linked in specific causal relations. In a sense, therefore, frameworks can be considered analogous to the words and grammatical rules comprising a language; they consist of the elements and tools that can be used to construct structures with substantive content, but they have little meaning in and of themselves.

Frameworks are similar to world views in that the absence of direct linkages with empirical observations means that frameworks cannot be evaluated on the basis of truth or falsity, but rather must be judged according to criteria such as fertility or usefulness. Replacement of one framework by another is consequently not determined by an accumulation of contradictory evidence, but instead tends to occur gradually as a majority of researchers come to prefer the concepts and explanatory principles of the new framework over those of the old framework. An example of such a shift in framework within experimental psychology occurred in the 1960s when the associationism framework, with concepts such as elementary units or ideas and associations, was gradually replaced by the information-processing framework, with its emphasis on storage structures and processing operations. The life-span development and the contextualism frameworks are viewed by some observers as possible contenders to eventually replace information-processing as the dominant framework within the field of cognitive aging.

Theories

Theories, at a minimum, consist of sets of relations among concepts. Most of the concepts and types of interrelations are derived from a higher level framework. However, because at least some of the concepts are defined in an operational fashion, theoretical speculations can, at least in principle, be linked to empirical observations. It is this property that allows theories to be evaluated on the basis of truth or falsity because predicted (theoretical) relations can be compared against actual (empirical) observations.

Models

Models refer to applications of theories to specific sets of phenomena, often generated to account for behavior within a particular assessment situation such as a cognitive test or task. Models are frequently necessary as supplements to theories in order to specify the correspondence of empirical observations to theoretical concepts, and to indicate the mechanisms by which the postulated relations occur. However, because models often incorporate additional assumptions necessary to allow the theory to be applied in a particular context, a single theory is capable of generating numerous models.

Descriptive Generalizations

Descriptive generalizations are essentially a form of meta-description or meta-observation. Because descriptive generalizations are attempts to summarize or integrate patterns of empirical results, they are sometimes treated as though they were theoretical in the sense of being explanatory. Descriptive generalizations are nevertheless distinct from theories and models because they generally do not contain explanatory concepts or mechanisms, and are primarily labels for, or quantitative formulations of, empirical patterns. Although not addressing the questions of why or how the particular phenomena occur, these integrative summaries of empirical observations nevertheless serve a potentially valuable function by capturing regularities and systematic patterns in the phenomena to be explained by theories and models.

Descriptive generalizations are obviously useful only if they are valid, and this is one respect in which descriptive generalizations may differ from empirical observations. By convention, observations are assumed to be accurate or valid. However, descriptive generalizations are not necessarily valid because, for example, they might be based on small or unrepresentative samples of observations.

Many of the attempts to develop taxonomic categories for the classification of cognitive abilities that decline or remain stable across the adult years, (some of which are summarized in Table 1.1), are probably most accurately characterized as descriptive generalizations. Quantitative expressions of the relations between measures of the speed of performance of young adults and measures of the speed of performance of older adults

TABLE 1.1
Characteristics hypothesized to be associated
with differential aging effects

Greatest Age Effects	Smallest Age Effects	Source
mechanics of intelligence	pragmatics of intelligence	P.B. Baltes, Dittmann-Kohli, & Dixon (1984)
ability to acquire information	previously learned or stored information	Birren (1952)
psychomotor skills and perceptual-integrative abilities	verbal abilities and stored information	Botwinick (1967)
perceptual-motor and speed functions	verbal functions	Botwinick (1977)
capacity to acquire new concepts or to apply existing concepts quickly and accurately to complex situations	intellectual attainments	Bromley (1974)
unspecialized abilities	specialized abilities	Bromley (1974)
nonverbal information, speeded responses, novel situations	verbal information, nonspeeded responses, familiar situations	Burger, Botwinick, & Storandt (1987)
fluid ability, discriminate and perceive relations	crystallized ability, long-established habits	Cattell (1943)
create and interpret new programs	rely on previously compiled and well-practiced programs	Charness (1985b)
unfamiliar and difficult tasks	familiar and easy tasks	Cornelius (1984)
untrained or unpracticed abilities	optimally trained or optimally exercised abilities	N.W. Denney (1982)
immediate problem solving ability	previously accumulated experience	K. Fitzhugh, L. Fitzhugh, & Reitan (1967)
adaptability and rapid adjustment	accumulated experience	Foster & G.A. Taylor (1920)

(Cont.)

11

TABLE 1.1
(Continued)

understand new methods of thinking, adopt new methods of working, adjust to new situations	recall acquired information	Foulds & J.C. Raven (1948)
adaptability to new situations	functions within own environment	Fozard & J.C. Thomas (1975)
integrate new data and form new associations	receive new impressions	Gilbert (1952)
spatial abilities	verbal abilities	Halpern (1984)
intellectual power	intellectual products	Hebb (1942)
capacity to develop new patterns of response	functioning of already developed patterns of response	Hebb (1942)
learning capacity	utilize factors already acquired	Hollingworth (1927)
perceive relations and form abstractions	knowledge, awareness of collective intelligence of culture	J.L. Horn (1970)
ability to organize information, to ignore irrelevancies, to concentrate, to maintain and divide attention	use of knowledge to deal with problems and form new knowledge	J.L. Horn (1982)
functioning of current abilities	effects of earlier learning	H.E. Jones (1955)
problem solving, adaptation and the flexible use of mental resources	accumulation of verbal or factual inventory	H.E. Jones (1955)
abstract intelligence	accumulated experience	H.E. Jones (1959)
basic intelligence	acquired abilities	H.E. Jones & Conrad (1933)
process	structure	Kinsbourne (1974)
ability to solve novel problems	draw upon the fund of acquired knowledge	Kinsbourne (1974)
capacity to understand and acquire new knowledge	intellectual attainments as a result of intellectual activity in the past	Orme (1957)

(Cont.)

TABLE 1.1
(Continued)

flexibility and elasticity	routine or accustomed work	Proctor (1873)
capacity to acquire a new way of thinking	recall acquired information	J.C. Raven (1948)
immediate adaptive ability	stored memory	Reed & Reitan (1963)
operations or transformations on memory contents	simple access to accumulated knowledge	Salthouse (1988b, 1988c)
current processing efficiency	accumulated products of prior processing	Salthouse (1988c)
speed or efficiency in dealing with difficult and novel relationships	leniently timed "knowledge inventories"	Spieth (1965)
flexible handling of data	static knowledge based on prior experience	Verhage (1965)
demands on organic capacities	demands on knowledge and experience	Welford (1958)
mental agility	ordered knowledge	Welford (1962)
abstract reasoning, novel material, speeded responding	overlearned, well-practiced abilities	Willis (1987)

(Cerella, 1985, 1990; Cerella, Poon, & D. Williams, 1980; S. Hale, Myerson, & Wagstaff, 1987; Myerson, S. Hale, Wagstaff, Poon, & G.A. Smith, 1990; Salthouse, 1985a), when not accompanied by explanatory concepts or mechanisms, also appear to be descriptive generalizations rather than theories or models.

Empirical Observations

The level of empirical observation consists of systematic (i.e., organized and coherent) descriptions of behavioral phenomena. Observations are thus a selective and abstract representation of a portion of the behavior, and not the totality of the behavior. Examples of observations are the quantitative measures of performance on a particular cognitive test. Most qualitative descriptions of behavior would also be considered empirical observations because the process of description requires some selectivity and abstraction, and hence the descriptions are not completely isomorphic with the behavior itself.

Summary

It should be clear from this brief description of the different levels of theoretical discourse that the levels are all interdependent. That is, certain world views make it more likely that particular frameworks will be adopted, and these in turn influence the kind of theoretical assumptions considered reasonable, and the nature of the observations thought to be relevant. A complete understanding of a particular theoretical perspective thus requires some appreciation of the many ways in which that perspective is, or at least can be, manifested.

There are at least two implications of the existence of multiple, but interrelated, levels of theoretical discourse. The first is that it may be much more difficult than commonly assumed to test a theoretical perspective because any given perspective consists of a core theory plus numerous assumptions associated with the theorist's world view, the framework within which he or she is working, and the validity of the descriptive generalizations considered relevant to the theory. A discovery that a particular theoretical prediction was false therefore implies that one or more of the assumptions in the perspective was incorrect, but there is seldom any means of determining how important or critical the invalid assumption is for the perspective as a whole. Recognition of this difficulty has led some philosophers of science (e.g., Lakatos, 1970) to suggest that the popular falsification criterion for evaluating scientific theories may be too restrictive.

The second implication of the multiple levels of theoretical discourse is that while all these levels of theoretical discourse contribute to a theoretical perspective, they are not necessarily equally important for scientific progress. Specifically, a theoretical perspective would be very incomplete, and likely to be of limited scientific value, if theories and models have not been articulated to specify the linkages between concepts and observations. Frameworks and descriptive generalizations are useful, and perhaps even essential, levels of theoretical discourse, but they are not substitutes for the specification of how the theoretical concepts are related both to one another and to empirical observations. These latter functions are served by theories and models, and consequently a theoretical perspective must contain speculations at the level of theories and models if it is to be considered a viable explanation for the phenomena of interest.

DIMENSIONS OF VARIATION

The theoretical perspectives considered in the subsequent chapters attribute the source of age-related differences in cognition to a number of different factors. Specifically, age differences have been postulated to be due to: (a) changes occurring in the external environment, that is, outside the individual (chapter 3); (b) changes in the nature or frequencies of particular experiences (chapter 4); (c) qualitative alterations in the manner in which a task is performed, or in the meaning of the measures of performance (chapter 5); (d) changes in the efficiency or effectiveness of discrete processing components (chapters 6 and 7); and (e) changes in characteristics of processing resources assumed to be relevant for the efficient functioning of a large number of cognitive processes (chapter 8).

One of the principal ways in which these theoretical perspectives vary is with respect to the assumptions they make about the nature of aging, or about age-related influences. A foundation for understanding the theoretical perspectives can therefore be provided by discussing what appear to be the major substantive dimensions along which developmental theories can differ. (For the current purposes, the term development will be interpreted broadly to refer to both positive and negative changes associated with age at any period in the lifespan.) An overview of the discussion is presented in Table 1.2, in which the approximate positions of each theoretical perspective on the relevant dimensions are summarized.

A total of seven dimensions will be considered, although no claim is made that the dimensions are either exhaustive or mutually exclusive. The dimensions are also intended to represent only approximate continua, and not rigid and absolute dichotomies. Despite these limitations, the following collection of dimensions seem to represent most of the important conceptual distinctions serving to differentiate among the theoretical perspectives that have been, or could be, proposed to account for phenomena of age-related cognitive decline.

Intrinsic or Extrinsic

What is probably the most fundamental theoretical distinction for developmental theories concerns whether the hypothesized source of the developmental phenomena is endogenous (i.e., due to internal factors originating from within the organism), or exogenous (i.e., due to external factors originating from outside the organism). Although both internal (maturational) and external (environmental) factors are clearly necessary for development, and almost certainly interact in many complex ways, theories can still differ substantially in the relative emphasis placed on intrinsic as opposed to extrinsic determinants. A key issue in evaluating the

TABLE 1.2
Tentative Positions of the Major Theoretical Perspectives
on Seven Substantive Dimensions

	Theoretical Perspectives				
	Environmental Change	Disuse	Qualitative Differences	Localization of Specific Effects	Reduced Resources
Substantive Dimensions					
Extrinsic(+)/ Intrinsic(-)	+	+	?	?	?
Primary(+)/ Secondary(-)	-	-	-	?	?
Universal(+)/ Probabilistic(-)	?	?	?	?	?
Proximal(+)/ Distal(-)	-	-	?	+	?
Permanent(+)/ Modifiable(-)	-	-	?	?	?
Quantitative(+)/ Qualitative(-)	?	?	-	+	+
Breadth(+)/ Specificity(-)	+	+	?	-	+

degree of emphasis placed on exogenous factors is whether specific kinds of experience are assumed to be important in producing age-related differences. If they are, then the theory can be interpreted as postulating that extrinsic or exogenous factors make a major contribution to the developmental phenomena. That is, exogenous factors would be considered important in the theory because the age-related phenomena might not be expected to occur with other kinds of experiences, or under alternative exogenous conditions. However, if the theory postulates that age-related phenomena are not restricted to particular kinds of experiences or specific sets of extrinsic conditions, and would be expected to occur in virtually all situations, then it could be inferred that exogenous or extrinsic determinants were assumed to be relatively unimportant in that theory.

Exogenous factors can be further distinguished according to whether the environmental characteristics are stable and typical of all historical periods, or are changing and specific to particular historical periods. In Cattell's (1970) terminology, the former are termed *ecogenic* because they reflect the normal ecology, and the latter are termed *epogenic* because they represent epoch-specific events. Although both types of exogenous factors could contribute to the existence of age differences, they do so in different ways. That is, ecogenic influences are likely to contribute to age differences by altering the age-specific ecology, which in turn affects the pattern of experiences encountered at different ages. However, because ecogenic factors are stable, these types of age-specific experiences would not be expected to vary across historical time. In contrast, epogenic influences reflect characteristics of the environment that change from one generation to the next. Differences in cognitive performance between adults of different ages may therefore originate because the environment that one group of individuals experienced as they were maturing was quite different from that experienced by another, later-born, group of individuals. Age differences could thus be a consequence of everyone having different experiences at different ages (ecogenic influences), or of each generation having different experiences at the same age (epogenic influences).

It is important to point out that the contrast between intrinsic and extrinsic causes is not simply equivalent to a distinction between biological and environmental determinants. In fact, a distinction between biological and environmental determinants is often meaningless because the fact that humans are biological organisms implies that all causes of behavior must ultimately be represented biologically (i.e., physiologically or anatomically). That is, only one who is a firm mind-body dualist would be likely to deny that all manifestations of mind are channeled through, and hence have some form of physical realization in, the body. At a certain level, therefore, even extrinsic or environmental determinants must be mediated by, or based upon, biological changes. This point is evident in the speculation of J.L. Horn and Cattell (1966) that age-related declines in certain measures of cognitive performance are due to cumulative damage to the central nervous system produced by small effects of "... carbon monoxide poisoning, lead poisoning, high fever, blows to the head, anoxia resulting from a variety of causes, etc." (p. 213). Note that most of these possible determinants are extrinsic in the sense that they originate outside the organism, and yet any behavioral consequences of them are mediated through biological mechanisms or processes (i.e., through alterations in the central nervous system).

Theoretical perspectives with an extrinsic emphasis are usually easy to identify because the attribution of the cause of the age-related differences to factors outside the organism is often a salient feature of the theoretical perspective. Examples are the theories attributing age-related cognitive differences to systematic (epogenic) changes in characteristics of the external environment (discussed in chapter 3), or to changes in the pattern of one's experiences (discussed in chapter 4). In contrast, it is often difficult to determine whether a theory has a primarily intrinsic emphasis because several of the theories without an extrinsic emphasis are focused at a different level of analysis, with no strong position on the intrinsic-extrinsic issue. Examples are the theoretical perspectives focusing on qualitative differences (discussed in chapter 5), or emphasizing quantitative differences that are either specific (discussed in chapters 6 and 7), or general (discussed in chapter 8). It is sometimes assumed that these perspectives imply that the causes of either the qualitative or the quantitative differences were intrinsic, but there is seldom any necessary reason why the origin of the differences must have been either intrinsic or extrinsic.

Perhaps the theoretical perspectives with the strongest intrinsic or endogenous emphasis are those based on biological metaphors such as inhibition and neural noise, although even these hypothesized mediators might initially have been caused by exogenous rather than endogenous factors. The inhibition and neural noise concepts have been the topic of much speculation (e.g., concerning inhibition—Birren, 1956, 1959, 1960; Hasher & Zacks, 1988; Hebb, 1978; W.R. Miles, 1931; and concerning neural noise—Cane & Gregory, 1957; Crossman & Szafran, 1956; Gregory, 1957; Welford, 1956, 1958, and almost all his subsequent articles), but they have led to surprisingly little empirical research (although see Cremer & Zeef, 1987, and Salthouse & Lichty, 1985, for two exceptions in the case of neural noise). The absence of a substantial body of research directly implicating intrinsic factors in age-related cognitive declines makes it premature to attempt an evaluation of theories of this type at present, and thus there is no theoretical perspective with a strong, or necessary, intrinsic emphasis represented in this volume.

The lack of a theory based on intrinsic determinants may be considered a rather surprising omission in a book concerned with theoretical perspectives in cognitive aging because there seems to be a tendency to assume that most, if not all, age-related behavioral differences are attributable to intrinsic or endogenous factors. That is, for many people the implicit assumption is that most age-related differences have intrinsic causes, and all other interpretations are viewed as alternatives to this default position. There appear to be at least two possible explanations of the apparent paradox that intrinsic determinants are widely assumed to be important, and yet there is no clearly articulated representative of this perspective in the contemporary research literature. One explanation may be that most of the research inspired by an assumption of intrinsic determinants is encompassed within what is classified here as the localization perspective. That is, the goal of much of the analytical or localization research has been to determine whether specific aspects of cognitive functioning are susceptible to age-related influences. Although the choice of which aspects of cognition to investigate may indeed be guided by assumptions of intrinsic or endogenous change, it is rarely the case that those aspects could not have originated from extrinsic or exogenous causes. Research focused on the localization of age-related cognitive deficits therefore does not appear to imply a definite position on the intrinsic-extrinsic dimension because there is generally no necessary connection between the specific nature of the impairment and the cause of that impairment. This is true even when the localization is at the level of anatomical structures or physiological processes rather than cognitive components, although this degree of localization is likely to place greater constraints on the ultimate causes of the observed behavioral differences.

A second possible explanation for the paucity of theories explicitly based on endogenous or intrinsic determinants of cognitive aging phenomena is that linkages between biological and psychological characteristics are still very tenuous, and many of the relevant speculations are at, or even beyond, the boundaries of the discipline of psychology. With respect to the first point, Owens (1956) noted:

> Since aging so patently and undeniably involves organic and physiological changes, it would seem to be important to know the extent to which such changes condition performance on each of a variety of intellective tests. However, with the concept of organismic age as ill-defined as it is as present, an attempt to determine its psychometric correlates would still seem to be, as Lashley so aptly put it, an adventure in correlating the mysterious with the unknown. (p. 157)

This is not to say that progress has not been made in unraveling the mysteries and clarifying the unknowns, nor that research in both areas should not be pursued as vigorously as possible. What it does suggest, however, is that it may not yet be feasible to expect anatomical and physiological explanations for phenomena as complex as performance on the various subtests in intelligence batteries.

As an example of the issue of disciplinary boundaries, Cerella (1990), in a speculative discussion about the role of neural noise in the form of loss of neuronal connections in age-related slowing, suggested that ideas of this type were more compatible with the field of neurophysiology than with cognitive psychology. To the extent that reductionistic explanations cannot be evaluated within the context of the discipline in which the to-be-explained phenomena are evident, therefore, the relevance or meaningfulness of the theory within that discipline may be severely limited. It is thus possible that many developmental psychologists have viewed purely intrinsic or endogenous theories as representing the default explanation for age differences in behavior, and have perceived their primary goal as that of trying to evaluate the possible contribution of various kinds of extrinsic or exogenous determinants.

Primary or Secondary

Another potentially important theoretical dimension is that distinguishing between primary and secondary causes of developmental phenomena. Primary processes are those that are essential to development, whereas secondary processes are those that are frequently associated with development, but which are not fundamental or basic. For example, the occurrence of many diseases is often referred to as a secondary aging factor because it is at least theoretically possible for individuals to age without acquiring the diseases. In a certain respect, primary aging processes can be considered to represent the necessary or core aspects of aging, while secondary processes correspond to all the other factors often associated with increased age, and that frequently contribute to the observed levels of cognitive performance, but which are not inevitable consequences of aging.

Although primary aging frequently is considered to correspond to intrinsic or endogenous aging processes, the primary-secondary dimension is not simply equivalent to the intrinsic-extrinsic dimension. Not only could both primary and secondary processes be attributable to extrinsic causes, but secondary processes conceivably could also be a consequence of intrinsic factors such as the occurrence of a particular genetically determined disease.

The distinction between competence and performance, which is discussed in chapter 5, seems closely related to the primary-secondary distinction. That is, factors that prevent an individual from performing at his or her maximal level of competence are often postulated to be due exclusively to secondary aging processes, whereas the individual's actual level of competence is usually assumed to be determined by both primary and secondary aging processes.

The primary-secondary distinction is also relevant to theoretical perspectives emphasizing experiential influences, such as the environmental change and disuse perspectives discussed in chapters 3 and 4, respectively. Because it is presumably possible for people to age without undergoing substantial changes in the nature or frequency of what are hypothesized to be critical experiences, experiential determinants would probably be classified as secondary rather than primary.

Universal or Probabilistic

The universal-probabilistic dimension essentially refers to whether or not aging processes are assumed to affect all members of the species. As used here, universal means that the effects are inevitable and pertain to everyone without exception, whereas probabilistic merely indicates that there is a non-zero relation between age and the proportion of individuals exhibiting the effects.

Distinguishing between universal and probabilistic processes can be expected to be difficult because even universal processes are likely to have effects that vary both in degree, and in time of onset. As a consequence, universal processes in which there are individual differences in magnitude and onset may resemble probabilistic processes. Moreover, discriminating between these kinds of processes will almost certainly require very expensive and time-consuming longitudinal data from large samples of individuals. Perhaps because of the pragmatic difficulty of differentiating between them, the contrast between universal and probabilistic developmental processes does not appear to be a critical feature in any of the major theoretical perspectives currently proposed to account for age differences in cognitive functioning.

It is sometimes implied, however, that there is a necessary linkage between the magnitude of observed age differences, and the universality of the processes responsible for those differences. For example, it has been suggested that a discovery that almost no older adults perform at or above the mean level of young adults can be interpreted as indicating that the factors contributing to these age-related differences may be universal in nature. Although this interpretation is possible, arguments of this sort are best considered as speculative hypotheses rather than logical necessities because overlap in the distributions of characteristics for young and old adults could occur with either universal or probabilistic processes. Only if the assumption of universality is supplemented by assumptions that (a) the magnitude of aging effects is large, and (b) the within-age variability is small relative to the between-age variability, would one definitely expect non-overlapping distributions of behavioral characteristics in samples of young and old adults.

Proximal or Distal

The proximal-distal dimension refers to how far removed the hypothesized causal factors are from the to-be-explained phenomena. This distance can be temporal, as in the contrast between concurrent and historical influences discussed by P.B. Baltes and his colleagues (P.B. Baltes, 1973; P.B. Baltes, Reese, & Nesselroade, 1977; P.B. Baltes & Willis, 1977). Or the distance can be conceptual, as when a lengthy chain of explanatory steps intervenes between the hypothesized cause and the observed (or inferred) consequence. For example, explanations attributing age-related differences in cognitive performance to concurrent differences in self-efficacy beliefs require a sequence of intermediate steps, corresponding to a moderate conceptual distance, to link the systems of beliefs to observable measures of performance. With either the temporal or the conceptual interpretation of distance, explanations are proximal when the causes are immediate or direct, and they are distal when the causes are mediated or indirect.

Theories postulating that important determinants of phenomena observed in late adulthood are events occurring in childhood or early adulthood, such as the amount or type of education to which one had been exposed, typically rely on explanatory sequences that are distal in both the temporal and the conceptual senses. That is, in order for events to exert an influence across a span of 40 or more years it is usually necessary to postulate an extensive sequence of mediating relations to link the early causes to the later consequences. The environmental change (chapter 3) and disuse (chapter 4) perspectives are therefore likely to rely primarily on distal explanations because the relevant experiences presumably occurred years or even decades earlier.

Theories based on proximal explanations usually incorporate hypotheses about direct relations between two concurrent variables. Examples of proximal explanations are those in which performance differences on a given cognitive task are explained in terms of deficiencies in a specific processing component presumed to be important for successful performance in that task (chapters 6 and 7).

Permanent or Modifiable

This dimension refers to whether the developmental changes are assumed to be permanent and irreversible, or whether they are assumed to be capable of modification, and possibly even of complete reversal. Although the research literature concerned with aging and cognition contains frequent references to the terms permanent and irreversible, the more meaningful contrast may be between patterns of age differences that are either relatively easy, or relatively difficult, to modify. That is, permanence or irreversibility are characteristics that should probably be inferred to exist only after repeated failures to establish modifiability.

There is a tendency in some theoretical discussions to link the property of permanence to intrinsic sources. For example, Macht and Buschke (1984) claimed that Birren's speculation about age-related slowing "... suggests that such cognitive slowing should be an inherent characteristic of human aging and therefore irreversible" (p. 439). That these dimensions are not necessarily related to each other, or to the primary-secondary dimension, is evident in the following quotation from Birren (1964):

> While the slowing of psychomotor behavior with age seems to fit a concept of normal psychophysiological change ... [t]here is no reason to believe that, once the process is understood, psychomotor slowing cannot be modified in the time and rate of appearance in the individual, even if the underlying changes have a genetic basis. (p. 127)

If one interprets normal as equivalent to primary, and genetic as corresponding to intrinsic, then this passage indicates that it is possible to think of aging processes as being potentially modifiable even if they are both intrinsic and primary.

It also seems important to maintain a distinction between the concept of modifiability, which is used here to refer to relations between the performance of people of different ages, and the concept of plasticity, which can be interpreted as indicating the range of performance achievable by individuals of a given age. The question of modifiability is therefore not identical to the question of plasticity because it is possible for adults of any age to have substantial improvement in performance (i.e., plasticity) without necessarily altering the relations between age and performance (i.e., no modifiability). Stated somewhat differently, plasticity is a necessary, but not a sufficient, condition for modifiability. A discovery that the absolute level of performance in one or more age groups can be altered with a particular manipulation thus does not automatically imply that the manipulation would lead to the modification of any age differences that might exist in performance. This latter outcome would occur only if the plasticity is greater among older adults than among young adults, such that the initial performance differential between the two groups was eliminated as a consequence of the manipulation designed to investigate the degree of plasticity in adults of different ages.

Theoretical perspectives based on experiential determinants of development, such as changing environment (chapter 3) and disuse (chapter 4), are likely to favor a modifiability position because the patterns of experience could presumably be altered. The perspectives focusing on qualitative differences (chapter 5), or quantitative differences that are either specific (chapters 6 and 7) or general (chapter 8), do not appear to imply a position on the modifiability versus permanence issue. That is, because the question of whether the qualitative or quantitative differences can be altered is not a necessary or essential feature of these perspectives, the modifiability-permanence distinction is not pertinent unless the basic perspectives are supplemented by additional assumptions.

Quantitative or Qualitative

Quantitative variations are those in which there are varying amounts of the same attribute. Qualitative variations, in contrast, are those in which the differences are evident in several distinct attributes, such that there is a change in the overall structure, and not simply in the magnitude measured along a single dimension. Perhaps the most dramatic examples of qualitative developmental changes are the transitions of a tadpole into a frog, or a caterpillar into a butterfly, in which there is little resemblance between the morphological structures characteristic of different periods in the lifespan.

Although there is a tendency to treat qualitative differences as radical, and perhaps even mysterious, alterations, qualitative differences can often be interpreted as multidimensional quantitative differences. For example, Reese (1973) suggested that changes in height or weight represented quantitative variations, whereas changes in physique, a concept involving a number of interrelated dimensions, corresponded to qualitative variations. Another way of characterizing the quantitative-qualitative distinction was described by P.B. Baltes and Willis (1977), who suggested that quantitative variations referred to more or less of a given attribute, whereas qualitative or structural variations corresponded to different sets of attributes or to differing interrelations among attributes.

Theoretical perspectives based on the notion of qualitative change in adult development are discussed in chapter 5, and those emphasizing quantitative change in specific or general processes are the focus of chapters 6, 7, and 8. No explicit position on the qualitative versus quantitative dimension seems to be inherent in either the changing environment or disuse perspectives discussed in chapters 3 and 4.

Breadth or Specificity

Still another dimension along which theoretical perspectives can vary is with respect to the number or range of phenomena intended to be addressed by the theory. Some theories are narrow in that they are designed to account for phenomena observed within a very limited set of tasks or activities, whereas other theories are presumed to be broad enough to explain results from many different tasks or collections of activities.

Almost inseparable from the dimension of breadth, at least among contemporary theoretical perspectives of cognitive aging, is the dimension of precision or vagueness. That is, narrow and specific theories often contain quite detailed models of the relations among variables, sometimes expressed in a quantitative fashion. Most cognitive aging theories, however, tend to be rather vague because they are based on relatively general and imprecise assumptions about the relevant developmental concepts, and they lack detailed models of the mechanisms by which those concepts influence potentially observable variables. Only the localization perspective discussed in chapters 6 and 7 clearly belongs at the narrow and specific end of this dimension because the goal in that perspective is to identify the particular components of processing responsible for the age differences observed in specific cognitive tasks. All the remaining perspectives presumably have broader scope, but the vagueness with which they have been articulated makes it difficult to evaluate the degree to which they can actually account for any given set of phenomena.

Summary

The seven conceptual distinctions just discussed do not capture all the differences among the theoretical perspectives proposed to account for age-related cognitive declines, but they do seem to represent most of the major dimensions of variation. In this respect they can be interpreted as corresponding to the primary substantive assumptions distinguishing contemporary theories of cognitive aging from one another. Understanding the relations among the theoretical perspectives should thus be enhanced by an awareness of the similarities and differences among the perspectives at these fundamental levels. Moreover, recognition that certain assumptions are common to several different theoretical perspectives should also allow inferences about the validity of the underlying assumptions to be derived on the basis of the pattern of empirical evidence relevant to each perspective.

It is worth noting that, because there is little variation among existing theoretical perspectives with respect to certain of the dimensions, many alternative perspectives could be generated with different combinations of assumptions even without postulating new theoretical dimensions. The currently available theoretical perspectives should therefore be viewed as merely a subset of those that could be formulated to account for cognitive aging phenomena.

It is also noteworthy that expectations about the nature of the age trends have not been included as a substantive dimension. Some authors have suggested that hypotheses about the pattern of age-related differences are often implicit in an investigator's choice of a research design, and hence might be considered as potentially important theoretical assumptions. Schaie (1973), for example, has claimed that the three most popular assumptions or 'models' are irreversible-decrement, stability, and decrement-with-compensation. These characterizations are not treated as substantive assumptions here because they seem to reflect either generalizations about observed relations between age and performance (e.g., decrement vs. stability), or combinations of more fundamental theoretical assumptions (e.g., irreversibility vs. compensation). Furthermore, as F.H. Hooper and Sheehan (1977) pointed out:

> ... [T]hese models of the aging process are taxonomic descriptions or 'labels' for the phenomena at issue. They seldom tell us anything concerning the underlying determinants of aging. (p. 243)

SPECIAL REQUIREMENTS FOR DEVELOPMENTAL THEORIES

Theories designed to account for developmental phenomena differ from other behavioral theories in that they must account for changes in behavior, and not merely the behavior itself. This difference in focus appears to have contributed to a substantial amount of confusion regarding the nature of theories of developmental phenomena. Two of the issues that have been the most controversial in connection with the requirements of developmental theories are what should, and what should not, be included within a theory intended to account for developmental phenomena. These topics are discussed in the following sections.

Need for a Change Mechanism

Because a primary goal of theories of development is to specify the factors responsible for age-related changes in behavior, it is essential that developmental theories incorporate some type of change mechanism indicating why or how the changes occurred (P.B. Baltes, Reese, & Nesselroade, 1977; Bromley, 1974; Salthouse, 1982, 1985b). In fact, it can be argued that the necessity of incorporating an explanation for change is what primarily distinguishes developmental research from individual differences research. That is, developmental researchers are interested in the transition from one developmental state to another, and not simply in characterizing the nature of the differences that might exist across various categories of individuals. This point was clearly illustrated by Wohlwill (1973) in a contrast of the study of age differences with the study of sex differences. Although in both cases it is desirable to obtain comprehensive descriptions of any behavioral differences that might exist between the various groups, researchers interested in age differences additionally want to know why and how the characteristics associated with individuals at one age shifted to those evident among individuals at a later age. The study of development is therefore the study of *change*, and not simply the study of difference. It is true that the changes are never observed directly, and when the observations are derived from cross-sectional comparisons the inference of change requires an assumption that the individuals would have been equivalent in important respects had it been possible to assess them when they were all at the same age. The key point, however, is that it is not merely the nature of the differences that is of interest to developmental theorists, but also the origin and evolution of those differences.

Figure 1.2 portrays the role of developmental theory, and of change mechanisms, in accounting for age-related differences. The top panel contains histograms illustrating the profile of behavioral competencies

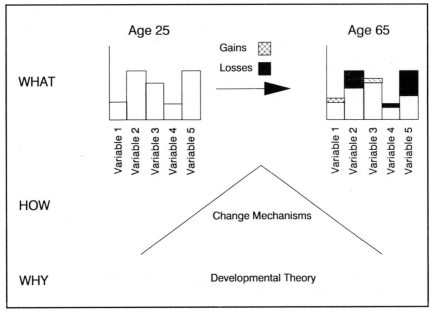

Figure 1.2.   Representation of the primary questions to be addressed by a developmental theory; what is the nature of the difference, how does it occur, and why does it occur?

across the same set of dependent variables at two different ages. Some, or possibly even all, of the variables in this diagram could reflect parameters derived from theoretical models of performance within a specific cognitive task. From a developmental perspective, however, the dependent variables simply provide descriptions, at varying levels of precision, of *what* it is that has to be explained. A developmental theory is needed to explain *why* the age-related differences occur, and to specify change mechanisms indicating *how* they occur.

The preceding discussion, and the relations illustrated in Figure 1.2, may help in understanding the controversy associated with the use of theories and models from cognitive psychology (and other nondevelopmental branches of psychology) in developmental research. One position, which has been strongly represented among researchers in cognitive aging, is that cognitive psychology supplies a rich set of concepts and models within which age-related differences can, and should, be interpreted. An explicit statement of this perspective was provided by Giambra and Arenberg (1980) in the context of a review of research on aging and problem solving:

On a bicycle, the back wheel must follow the front wheel. The geropsychology of problem solving and concept learning is the back wheel to the front wheel of the psychology of problem solving and concept learning. One might define the geropsychology of problem solving and concept learning as the study of the influence of age on theories, principles, and laws of problem solving and concept learning in the adult ... [Adherence to this view] ... would have geropsychologists attempt to replicate with older adults those experiments and procedures that have proven most fruitful in leading to coherent and relatively general theories of problem solving and concept learning in the young adult. (p. 257)

Although many cognitive aging researchers seem to have implicitly accepted some variant of this position, it is vulnerable to a number of potentially important criticisms. Among the objections raised against the "aging-as-back-wheel" position are: (a) that it relegates developmental research to a second-class status in which developmental researchers merely follow pathways explored initially by researchers in other subdisciplines (Welford, 1976); (b) that different-aged individuals are simply treated as quantitative variations in theoretical parameters rather than as manifestations of a phenomenon worthy of investigation in its own right (P.B. Baltes & Willis, 1977; Birren, 1959); (c) that models of the average young adult may fail to incorporate relevant dimensions along which important age-related differences might occur (Birren & W.R. Cunningham, 1985; Bromley, 1974; Rabbitt, 1982; Salthouse, 1980, 1982); and (d) that no explanation is provided for why or how the differences originate (Salthouse, 1982, 1985b). It is this last characteristic that is perhaps the most serious limitation of relying on existing cognitive models for the interpretation of developmental phenomena because those phenomena cannot be considered to be fully explained unless there is an account of why and how the differences occurred.

Theories and models formulated to account for the behavior of the average adult often provide an elaborate set of distinctions that could allow very refined descriptions of the pattern of behavioral differences across age groups. However, while these theories and models frequently lead to more precise descriptions of exactly what it is that appears to have changed, they seldom indicate why or how those changes occurred. It is in this sense that theories and models borrowed from research on "average" adults (typically 20-year-old college students) may have limited value as explanations for developmental phenomena. They are concerned primarily with describing the observed differences, and not with explaining the inferred changes.

It is important to note that what constitutes a satisfactory explanation clearly depends on one's primary focus. For example, researchers working in the subdiscipline within which a nondevelopmental theory originated can justifiably claim that the developmental phenomena were explained if they can be predicted, or accounted for, by variations in one or more parameters of the theory. However, the essence of the developmental approach is the emphasis on change, and thus a truly developmental explanation should indicate not only which parameters have changed, but why and how they changed.

Another way of understanding the difference between developmental theories and the extension of theories based on average adults to account for developmental phenomena is through consideration of the status of the age variable in each approach. In many theories originally formulated to account for the behavior of average adults, age is treated as an independent variable affecting one or more theoretical parameters. In contrast, an important characteristic of the developmental approach is that age is not simply viewed as an independent variable, but rather as an index of the effects of the processes of primary interest. This view was clearly articulated by Birren and Renner (1977):

> ... [A]ge must be approached in research as a variable that ultimately must be eliminated. That is, so long as age is used as the independent variable to array data, research remains at the descriptive state, despite the refined or experimental character of the data gathering process. (p. 26)

In other words, developmental psychologists tend to view age and time merely as dimensions along which the causal variables exert their influence, and not as causes of anything by themselves. Wohlwill (1970) elaborated this distinction by referring to the use of the age variable in developmental studies as analogous to the variable of time in studies of dark adaptation. Age and time are both dimensions without intrinsic causal significance, and the goal of the researcher is to attempt to explain what is occurring across the intervals of age or time to account for the relevant phenomena. From a developmental perspective, therefore, age is merely a surrogate, or a carrier, for the cumulative and aggregate effect of many different variables, each of which must be identified and isolated before developmental phenomena can be considered to be explained.

Because it is not really age, but rather the processes associated with age, that are of greatest interest to developmental researchers, it is generally preferable to refer to developmental observations as age-*related* differences rather than as age differences. That is, the term age differences has an undesirable connotation of direct causality that should be avoided whenever possible. However, in order to minimize unnecessary and awkward redundancy, the shorter "age differences" term will be used in this book. Unless otherwise stated, it should be interpreted as referring to age-related differences, and not as implying that the differences are caused by age or aging, per se.

Need for Nondevelopmental Explanations

While interpretations of age differences in cognitive functioning are sometimes deficient for failing to incorporate developmental change mechanisms, they can also suffer by trying to incorporate too much into their theoretical systems. This problem arises if a researcher attempts to account for all the observed individual differences with developmental mechanisms when only a relatively small portion of the interindividual variance is actually related to age. To illustrate, because correlations between age and measures of cognitive performance seldom exceed .5, less than 25% of the total variance in a dependent variable typically needs to be explained by a developmental theory. Nondevelopmental mechanisms are thus required to account for a greater proportion of the total variance because the remaining variance is not developmental, in that it is not systematically related to age.

A failure to appreciate the fact that only a rather small percentage of the total individual differences at any age are likely to be associated with developmental factors may have contributed to some of the enthusiasm associated with the practice of using age-homogeneous samples to investigate aging processes. Krauss (1980), for example, suggested that:

> Determining the contributing causes of the large individual differences among the elderly will provide valuable information on both the origins of decrements associated with aging and the factors contributing to successful aging. (p. 549)

Note that Krauss's argument seems to be based on the implicit assumption that much, if not all, of the individual differences observed among elderly individuals are attributable to individual differences in age-related processes. This assumption would only be reasonable if there were either no individual differences at earlier ages, or if the range of interindividual differences increased appreciably with increased age. The first condition is clearly false, and the available research evidence (discussed in chapter 2) is far from consistent regarding systematic increases with age in measures of interindividual variability of cognitive performance. It is, of course, entirely appropriate to study elderly adults in order to understand the behavior of the aged, but some type of age comparison seems necessary if one is interested in understanding the processes of aging or change. (See P.B. Baltes, Reese, & Nesselroade, 1977, and Hertzog, 1985, for further discussion of the problem of disentangling preexisting variance and change-related variance in developmental comparisons.)

This issue of the relevance of research based on age-homogeneous samples for inferences about processes of aging is also discussed in chapter 4 in the context of the interpretation of results from experiential manipulations. For the present purpose, the major point is that only a portion of the individual differences on any behavioral measure can be assumed to be associated with variations in age-related processes, and hence, attempts to account for all individual differences in behavior must incorporate nondevelopmental mechanisms as well as developmental ones.

SUMMARY

The distinctions among possible assumptions and levels of explanation or analysis discussed in this chapter are intended to provide a foundation to help understand some of the differences among theoretical perspectives identified as addressing the same phenomena. An important implication of the preceding discussion is that what superficially appear to be quite distinct theoretical perspectives are not necessarily in conflict, or even mutually exclusive. For example, two theoretical systems might have equivalent positions on most or all substantive dimensions, but appear to differ because they tend to vary with respect to their emphasis on different assumptions. Theoretical perspectives can also appear to differ because they correspond to different levels of analysis, with some focusing on specification at the model level, and others at the theory, or possibly even the framework, level.

Of course, this does not mean that there are no differences among the various perspectives, because they obviously differ in a number of important ways. What it does mean, however, is that a complete understanding of a theoretical perspective requires a thorough examination of the assumptions and implications of that perspective. This goal, as well as that of examining the evidence relevant to each perspective, is pursued in chapters 3 through 8, after first documenting the principal phenomenon to be explained in chapter 2.

2 What Needs to Be Explained?

A satisfactory explanation is not likely to be forthcoming where there is no agreement about what requires explanation. Obviously, a first step is to establish the necessary data ...

—Kay (1959, p. 614)

INTRODUCTION

As discussed in the previous chapter, a major goal of this book is to examine the strengths and weaknesses of alternative explanations of cognitive aging phenomena. Before different theoretical perspectives can be adequately evaluated, however, it is first necessary to clarify precisely what it is that they should be expected to explain. Specifying the exact nature of the criterion phenomenon is particularly important in the field of cognitive aging because of the enormous complexity of cognition, and a surprising lack of agreement about the fundamental phenomenon, namely, the relation between age and cognitive functioning. An indication of the diversity of views about the age-cognition relation is evident in the sample of quotations contained in Table 2.1.

Many of the characterizations in Table 2.1 are clearly contradictory, and thus it is desirable to achieve an accurate description of the relations between age and cognition before attempting to examine alternative explanations of those relations. The primary purpose of the present chapter is therefore to review descriptive research on age differences in cognitive functioning in order to characterize as clearly and unambiguously as possible the phenomena to be explained by theories of cognitive aging.

One approach that might be pursued in attempting to evaluate alternative theoretical perspectives is to identify one or two well established sets of results, and then to examine the adequacy of different explanations of those results. Comparing each interpretation with respect to exactly the same narrowly defined phenomenon would presumably allow the most objective basis for discriminating among rival explanations. Unfortunately,

TABLE 2.1
When Does Cognitive Aging Begin?

"All the age trends ... begin early and are usually progressive from the middle twenties onward." (Welford, 1966, p. 5)

"... the decline is continuous rather than abrupt and thus the loss of intellectual ability may be as important a consideration in a comparison of 50-year-olds with 30-year-olds, as it is in a comparison of 70-year-olds with 50-year-olds." (Salthouse, 1982, p. 82)

"... the abilities by which intelligence is measured ... decline with age ... and ... this decline is systematic and after age 30 more or less linear." (Wechsler, 1958, p. 142)

"Cross-sectional studies point to age forty as a time which some marked ... cognitive decline[s] ... begin to' occur." (Emery, 1985, p. 16)

"... the steady decline ... commencing in the middle twenties apparently slows down in the sixties." (Orme, 1957, p. 412)

"Intelligence ... matures very quickly ... and stays on a level until the early twenties. Then ... ability ... is gradually lost in the next sixty years, with the larger portion of the decrements coming in the forties and sixties." (Lawton, 1943, p. 14)

"... loss of capacity associated with age seems to occur at certain critical stages, particularly at about 40 and again at about 60 years, rather than to progress at a continuous rate." (Talland, 1968, p. 126)

"... relatively little decline in performance occurs until people are about 50 years old." (M.S. Albert & Heaton, 1988, p. 15)

"... data on rates of cognitive ageing ... suggest that a rapid rise to peak performance in the third and fourth decades of life is followed by a 'continuous decline' which is slight over the fifth and sixth decades and thereafter rapidly accelerates." (Rabbitt, 1990, p. 227)

"... all available objective data on cognitive ageing suggest that cognitive decline is slight up to the age of 50." (Rabbitt & Abson, 1990, p. 11)

"Most of adulthood ... appears to be characterized by increases and stability; decrements in most cases appear to be a characteristic of the post-retirement phase." (Labouvie-Vief, 1977, p. 237)

"... most intellectual abilities begin to decline in the 60s." (W.R. Cunningham, 1987, p. 126)

"... it is rather clear that, beginning around age 60, naturally occurring decline ... becomes more likely for more people and for more classes of intellectual functioning." (P.B. Baltes, Dittmann-Kohli, & Dixon, 1984, p. 38)

"The developmental pattern is best described as a sharp decline after 60 years of age, rather than a steady decline across the adult years." (Lehman & Mellinger, 1986, p. 179)

"... the major age-related decrements in cognitive performance ... [occur] ... in the sixties and seventies." (Fozard, Nuttall, & Waugh, 1972, p. 36)

"... tendency for intellectual function to decline beginning in the seventh or the eighth decade, with a more pronounced decline in the ninth decade." (Hochanadel & E. Kaplan, 1984, p. 231)

"On average, there is a gain until the late 30s or early 40s are reached, and then there is stability until the mid-50s or early 60s are reached." (Schaie, 1990b, p. 296)

(Cont.)

TABLE 2.1
(Continued)

"... most abilities tend to peak in early midlife, plateau until the late fifties or sixties, and then show decline, initially at a slow pace, but accelerating as the late seventies are reached." (Schaie, 1989b, p. 66)

"... limitations of mental functioning occurs precipitiously in individuals over the age of 65 or 70 and is closely related to health status." (Birren, 1968, p. 19)

"... intellectual decrement and decline in problem-solving abilities within individuals, when occurring before the late fifties, is pathological rather than normal." (Schaie, 1980b, p. 279)

this strategy is not always feasible because theoretical perspectives frequently differ not only in the nature of the explanations for a given finding, but also according to the phenomena or issues considered important enough to warrant an explanation. This clearly creates a problem because if theoretical perspectives vary with respect to the particular aspects of a phenomenon they are attempting to address, or even in terms of the specific phenomena considered to fall within the scope of the theory, then it may be inappropriate to attempt to evaluate them against a single criterion.

At some level, however, the various theories must be concerned with a similar set of empirical findings or else there would be no reason to consider them as rivals or alternatives. A useful strategy might therefore consist of identifying a set of core phenomena that are defined broadly enough to encompass the various aspects of primary concern in each of the different theoretical perspectives, and only then examining the degree to which each perspective accounts for those phenomena.

A variant of this latter strategy is employed in this chapter. Some of the major empirical results concerned with age differences in cognition will be described in order to indicate what must eventually be explained by a theory of cognitive aging. However, because cognition is an extremely broad concept, it is first necessary to introduce a few restrictions. Narrowing the scope of investigation is essential because without such restrictions, cognition may be so vague as to preclude meaningful investigation. As an example, consider the difficulty of examining cognition as defined by Perlmutter (1988) as "... the psychological ability that accounts for all of mental life" (p. 250).

For the current purposes, cognition will be defined as the collection of abilities measured in psychometric tests of intelligence. There are, of course, disadvantages associated with this particular way of conceptualizing cognition. In fact, two major criticisms can be directed against the reliance on psychometric tests as a means of examining cognition. One objection is that the lack of a theoretical rationale for most psychometric tests often leads to an emphasis on evaluating the products of cognition, rather than analyzing the processes responsible for creating those products. Because many tests are primarily designed to establish the relative position of the examinee within a population, they seldom provide any information relevant to how he or she achieved the observed level of proficiency. This is generally not a problem when the tests are used for applied purposes, such as prediction, but it can be a limitation if one is interested in specifying the causes of abnormal levels of performance.

A second criticism of existing psychometric tests is that potentially important and interesting aspects of cognition are not adequately assessed by current tests of intelligence. For example, wisdom, sagacity, judgment, insight, effective application of one's capacities, social cognition, long-range planning, and numerous other potentially important cognitive skills are not evaluated in any of the traditional psychometric intelligence batteries. Concerns have also been expressed that what is measured in psychometric tests is largely unimportant for, or irrelevant to, criteria such as life fulfillment or competent functioning in everyday activities.

Although these disadvantages are real, they are nonetheless more than balanced by several major advantages. As an example, one desirable feature of psychometric intelligence tests is that they are designed to reflect a broad range of cognitive abilities, and particularly when tests from several different test batteries are considered in combination, they can provide a much more comprehensive assessment of cognitive functioning than would be possible with any single test. Furthermore, because psychometric tests have been widely used since before the 1920s, there is an extensive body of relevant data, much of it based on representative samples across the entire adult age range. This allows much more precise determination of the nature of age trends on measures of cognitive functioning than would be possible with studies involving small numbers of individuals from only two or three age groups.

It is also important to emphasize that, for the present purposes, there is little interest in interpreting the results from psychometric intelligence tests as providing an accurate and valid assessment of intelligence, per se. That is, scores on the various subtests of intelligence batteries are not being used as indicators of either single or multiple types of intelligence, but instead as illustrations of the kind of phenomena that need to be explained by theories of cognitive aging. Furthermore, no claim is made that scores from psychometric tests of intelligence are the best measures of intelligence or cognition, nor that they necessarily reflect constructs of great practical importance.

This limited usage of intelligence tests therefore weakens the criticism that most intelligence tests were originally developed for purposes of academic selection in children and adolescents, and consequently may not be valid for adults in nonacademic settings (P.B. Baltes & G. Labouvie, 1973; P.B. Baltes & Willis, 1979; D. Cohen & Wu, 1980; Cornelius & Caspi, 1987; Demming & Pressey, 1957; H.E. Jones & O.J. Kaplan, 1945;

Lorge, 1957; Willis & P.B. Baltes, 1980). The issue of the validity of intelligence tests for adults is not a simple one because tests with established validity at one period in the lifespan may be more likely to be valid at other periods than tests for which no validity, and often no reliability, information is available. Furthermore, positive correlations in samples of middle-aged and older adults have been reported between intelligence scores and criteria such as performance on measures of everyday skills (Willis & Schaie, 1986a), success in learning to use a computer spreadsheet program (Garfein, Schaie, & Willis, 1988), and effectiveness as a manager 20 years later (Bray & A. Howard, 1983), implying that psychometric intelligence tests are not completely lacking in validity during the adult years. Nevertheless, debates about the validity or meaning of intelligence test scores are only of minor interest when those scores are merely used to define the phenomena that theoretical perspectives in cognitive aging should explain.

To summarize, then, standardized tests of intelligence have been used in many studies involving large and representative samples of adults across a wide range of ages, and as a consequence, have yielded an extensive amount of information about the relations between age and cognitive functioning. Existing psychometric intelligence tests do not assess all aspects of cognition, and there are legitimate questions regarding what scores on the tests actually represent. Results from such tests nevertheless appear to provide an impressive amount of information, both in terms of sampling from the domain of cognition and sampling from the population of individuals, relevant to the phenomena to be explained by theories of cognitive aging.

REVIEW OF AGE DIFFERENCES
IN PSYCHOMETRIC TESTS OF INTELLIGENCE

One of the earliest major studies examining age differences in intellectual tests was reported by Foster and G.A. Taylor (1920). These investigators administered a battery of 20 tests, similar to those used earlier by Binet, to 315 adults between 20 and 30 years of age, and to 106 adults between 50 and 84 years of age. The Foster and Taylor study was innovative in at least four important respects. First, Foster and Taylor were among the earliest researchers to document adult age differences in cognition using standardized assessment instruments. Second, comparisons of the performance of young and old adults were conducted after matching the two groups on total score, thereby revealing the existence of differential patterns of deficit across ability tests. It is also interesting that the differential patterns were similar to those reported in many later studies: The tests found to exhibit the greatest age differences favoring young adults were rearranging words to make sentences, visual memory, and producing as many words as possible in three minutes; older adults performed better on tests of comprehension, detection of absurdities, and providing definitions of abstract terms.

The third innovative aspect of Foster and Taylor's study was the idea of introducing age corrections to allow comparisons of an individual's performance with that of his or her age contemporaries. In other words, it was explicitly proposed that older adults had "... two possible standards of comparison, namely their supposed former ability (or that of average normal young person) and the average ability of their contemporaries" (Foster & Taylor, 1920, p. 54). The use of age adjustments in determining an individual's level of intellectual ability was subsequently incorporated into the Wechsler scales, which have become the most widely used of the contemporary intelligence batteries for adults. (The practice of adjusting scores according to age is not without controversy, however: Jarvik, 1988, has suggested that altering the criteria used to assign IQ scores based on the examinee's age may induce a complacency that cognitive functioning remains stable, and hence stifle research into the causes of any declines that may occur.)

Finally, and most interesting from the standpoint of theoretical interpretations, Foster and Taylor discussed three possible reasons for the age-related declines observed in some of their cognitive tests. Each is strikingly similar to contemporary speculations. For example, one of their hypotheses was that it is possible that "... given sufficient incentive and practice ... an older person may equal the performance of his juniors. The difficulty is that the common incentives such as praise, approval, etc., which are so effective with children, are of little avail with the old" (p. 54). Another suggestion was that "If we consider the tests in which the older subjects are superior we find them to be the ones which are more like the problems which arise in the daily life of adults and which could be answered best by persons who had had the accumulated experience of years" (p. 54).

Although the study was pioneering in many respects, the results from the Foster and Taylor study were probably limited in their influence because the battery of tests was somewhat idiosyncratic, and was apparently not used by other researchers in comparisons involving adults of different ages. In order to emphasize the results with the largest amount of data on age-cognition relations, the remainder of this chapter will focus on the major psychometric tests or batteries used in research with adults over a wide range of ages.

Army Alpha

The Army Alpha group intelligence test was developed during 1917 when a committee of psychologists (chaired by Yerkes, and including such eminent scientists as Boring, Terman, Thorndike, L.L. Thurstone, and Woodworth) was formed to determine how psychology could contribute to the efforts of the United States in World War I. One of the areas in which they felt they could make a real contribution was personnel evaluation and selection, primarily by using mental tests to eliminate the mentally unfit from induction into the army. The committee therefore decided to develop a test suitable for group assessment of individuals from a wide range of ability levels. Work progressed very rapidly, with an initial meeting in April of 1917, and a complete battery of tests, mostly adapted or modified from existing tests, assembled by May of 1917. This battery was administered to 400 individuals in June, and then revised and administered to another 4,000 individuals in July and August. Within six months of the original idea, the first group-administered battery of intellectual tests had been developed, tested, and revised. This is a remarkable achievement, particularly because, with few precedents for group testing, many of the testing and scoring procedures also had to be devised during this period.

Two versions of the selection tests were developed, one designed for the assessment of literate adults, termed the Army Alpha, and the other including only non-verbal items and designed for those who could not read English, which was designated the Army Beta. A total of 1,726,966 men were administered one of these two versions between September, 1917 and January, 1919. Because this mass testing effort required the employment of large numbers of psychologists, it is sometimes considered one of the most important events in the development of psychology as a profession (Dubois, 1970). However, the ambiguity of the status of professional psychologists as the field was first being established was reflected in the fact that the psychologists working on the testing project were commissioned in the Sanitation Corps of the United States Army!

The committee responsible for developing the Army classification tests identified seven criteria that were to be satisfied by the new test battery: The first requirement was that the tests had to be appropriate for group administration because the individual examination methods used at that time were impractical for testing large numbers of people. The second criterion was that the tests had to have demonstrable validity in the sense that the scores were correlated with existing tests of intelligence, or with observer ratings. Both of these forms of validity were considered acceptable because the Army Alpha scores were found to correlate .81 with scores on the Stanford-Binet intelligence battery, and were reported to correlate .50 with officers' ratings of intelligence (Yerkes, 1921). Another explicit criterion for the new test battery was that the tests should be designed to assess native ability rather than the results of school training. The remaining criteria were that the tests should be sensitive across a wide range of ability levels, the scoring should be objective and rapid, the tests should not require much time to administer, and the tests should be interesting.

Sample items from the eight tests ultimately incorporated in the Army Alpha are illustrated in Figure 2.1. In the Following Directions test a total of 12 directions were presented which were presumed to require oral comprehension, memory, and serial ordering of actions. The Arithmetic Reasoning test consisted of 20 arithmetic word problems to be completed within 5 minutes. The Common Sense test (sometimes termed Practical Judgment) appears to have involved both comprehension and general knowledge, and consisted of 16 items with a time limit of 1.5 minutes. The Antonym-Synonym test contained 40 word pairs which were to be classified as meaning the same or the opposite; one and a half minutes were allowed for the completion of 40 word pairs in this test of word knowledge. Disarranged Sentences required word strings to be rearranged into a meaningful sentence, and then categorized as true or false; a total of 24 sentences were presented with a time limit of 2 minutes. The Number Series Completion test required the examinee to determine which two numbers would continue the sequence. Twenty problems were presented with a time limit of 3 minutes. Three minutes were also allowed for the completion of 40 problems in the Verbal Analogies test, which required both reasoning abilities and knowledge of word meanings. Finally, 40 multiple-choice general knowledge questions were presented in the General Information test, with a time limit of 4 minutes.

The time allowances in the tests were deliberately selected such that only about 5% of the examinees could finish all the items in each test, thereby introducing a substantial speed component into the tests. In addition, the items in many of the tests were of ascending difficulty so that people reaching later items in each test were confronted with progressively more difficult problems. Perhaps because of this variation in item difficulty, the correlation between scores obtained under normal conditions and those obtained with double the standard time allowances was found to be .97 (Yerkes, 1921).

One of the most interesting results of the Army Alpha project from the perspective of research on aging and cognition was that a relatively strong negative relation was found between total score and the examinee's age. Because the range of ages for enlisted personnel was quite small, the data most relevant to the examination of age-cognition relations were based on tests administered to officers. Figure 55 and Table 366 in the comprehensive monograph (Yerkes, 1921) describing the complete military testing project indicate that scores decreased monotonically from the middle 20s through the 60s for 15,385 officers: Median scores for

Following Directions

When I say GO draw a line from circle 1 to circle 4 that will pass above circle 2 and below circle 3.

Arithmetic Reasoning

If a train goes 200 yards in 10 seconds, how many feet does it go in a fifth of a second?

Common Sense

The cause of echoes is: (a) the reflection of sound waves; (b) the presence of electricity in the air; (c) the presence of moisture in the air.

Antonym - Synonym

asunder - apart : same or different?

Disarranged Sentences

Rearrange these words to make a sentence, and classify it as true or false.

pays cautious it be to often

Number Series Completion

Complete the following sequence:

16 12 15 11 14 10 ___ ___

Verbal Analogy

ocean : pond :: deep - sea well shallow steep

General Information

The U.S.S. Michigan is a: a) destroyer; b) monitor; c) submarine; d) battleship

Figure 2.1.   Illustrative problems for the eight subtests of the Army Alpha.

examinees in their 20s were about 145, whereas those for examinees in their 30s, 40s, and 50s were 133, 125, and 120, respectively.

Despite these moderately large and monotonic age trends, the authors of the final report of the project were reluctant to interpret the results as indicating that intelligence declined with age. Instead they suggested that selection factors may have been responsible for the observed age relations. Yerkes (1921) expressed this position as follows:

> If ... among the older men only the poorer professional men could leave their businesses to enter the Army or were industrially unessential so that they were forced into the Army, then ... a relation ... would arise entirely as a result of selection in the Army and be utterly factitious as an indicator of a dependence of intelligence on adult age in general. ... The most reasonable surmise is that older officers are selected more on the basis of their specific experience and training, professional or military, and less on native intelligence than are younger officers who have as yet little valuable experience. (p. 813)

The hypothesis of differential representativeness as a determinant of the negative relations between age and cognitive performance in the Army Alpha tests was investigated in a later study by H.E. Jones and Conrad (1933). These researchers attempted to sample the entire population within several rural New England communities, encouraging participation by offering free movies as an incentive to participate in the research project. This recruitment strategy was apparently successful because the participation rates were quite high, an outcome which Jones and Conrad attributed to the fact that "... in these thrifty New England communities a free show proved a dependable means of gaining popular interest and support" (p. 234). The Army Alpha tests were eventually administered to a total of 1191 individuals between 10 and 60 years of age, with 678 of those in the range of 19 to 60 years of age.

Mean scores at each adult age range for the eight subtests of the Army Alpha from the Jones and Conrad (1933) project are displayed in Figure 2.2. Each of the scores is expressed in terms of the standard deviations from the distribution of scores of young adults between 19 and 21 years of age. This particular method of representing the scores allows direct comparisons of the performance at any given age relative to the performance of young adults because the units are immediately interpretable in terms of the distribution of scores in this standard, or comparison, group. For example, reference to a statistical table indicating the proportions of a normal distribution above a given standard deviation score can be used to determine the percentage of young adults performing above the average level of a group of adults of any given age. (Measures of the percentage of overlap as a function of the standard deviation index

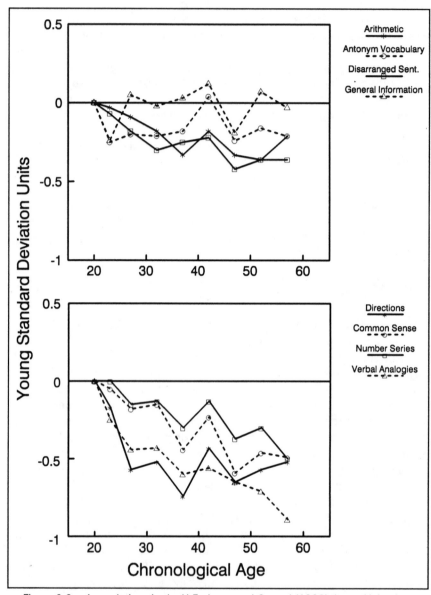

Figure 2.2   Age relations in the H.E. Jones and Conrad (1933) Army Alpha data expressed in units of standard deviations of young adults.

of effect size are also presented in J. Cohen's, 1988, Table 2.2.1. Sample values of the percentage of observations in one distribution that are above 50% of the observations of another distribution are 69.1% for an effect size of .5 standard deviations, 84.1% for an effect size of 1 standard deviation, and 93.3% for an effect size of 1.5 standard deviations.)

It is apparent in the results displayed in Figure 2.2 that the age trends vary across the different subtests of the Army Alpha. Small age-related effects are evident in the Arithmetic, Antonym-Synonym, Disarranged Sentences, and General Information tests, but more pronounced age differences occur with the Following Directions, Common Sense, Number Series, and Verbal Analogies tests. A generally similar ordering of the tests in terms of the magnitude of the age trends is available in the correlation coefficients between age and subtest score reported by McCrae, Arenberg, and Costa (1987). The relevant correlations, for 708 males between 17 and 101 years of age, were: Arithmetic = -.08, Antonym-Synonym = -.07, Disarranged Sentences = -.16, General Information = -.25, Following Directions = -.33, Common Sense = -.16, Number Series = -.39, and Verbal Analogies = -.48.

The Jones and Conrad (1933) study is exemplary with respect to its careful consideration of several alternative explanations for the results. Among the rival interpretations considered, and the reasons for rejecting them, were the following: (a)   Differential motivation: The tests and the testing situation were designed to be interesting, and the older individuals appeared as earnest as the young; (b) sensory loss: The age trends were similar among those individuals tested in large groups and those tested in their homes under special conditions, and the age differences were not restricted to tests with high auditory or visual demands; (c) remoteness from formal schooling: the Arithmetic Reasoning test is the most closely related to schooling and hence might be expected to exhibit large age-related declines, but the age trend on this test is actually quite small; (d) disuse of functions: The Following Directions and Common Sense tests are similar to frequently performed activities, and yet age-related declines are found on these tests; (e) speed: If lower scores among older adults are due to slower rates of performance, then the age differences might be expected to be smaller for measures of the number of items answered correctly than for measures of the number of items attempted, but this was not always the case; (f) failure to understand instructions: The magnitudes of the age trends were not related to the apparent difficulty of the test instructions.

Several other investigators have also reported age-related declines on other assessments based on the Army Alpha test. For example, Lorge (1936) reported a correlation of -.41 between total Army Alpha score and age in a sample of 143 adults between 20 and 70 years or older. A spiral omnibus version of the test battery, in which items from different subtests were intermixed in a progressively more difficult sequence, has been found to yield age correlations of -.35 (Bingham & W.T. Davis, 1924), -.46 (Lorge, 1936), and from -.39 to -.44 in samples differing in years of education (C.C. Miles & W.R. Miles, 1932).

Wechsler Scales

David Wechsler developed the first Wechsler-Bellevue Scale to fill a perceived need for an individual adult examination of intelligence that could be useful for clinicians in making psychological diagnoses. The test was initially standardized in 1939, and was standardized again with slight revisions in 1955 (as the Wechsler Adult Intelligence Scale, WAIS; Wechsler, 1955) and in 1981 (as the Wechsler Adult Intelligence Scale - Revised, WAIS-R; Wechsler, 1981). The standardization sample consisted of 1,071 adults from 17 to 70 years of age in 1939, 1,300 adults between 20 and 64 years of age plus an additional 475 adults from 60 to 75 or older in 1955, and 1,480 adults between 20 and 74 years of age in 1981. Each sample was intended to be representative of the general population with respect to education and occupation. Although the 1939 sample was restricted to urban residents from the New York City area, the 1955 and 1981 samples were drawn from across the United States and were designed to balance representation of rural and urban residents.

The general composition of the Wechsler battery has remained the same in the different revisions, although specific items have been modified and the Vocabulary test was changed from an optional to a standard test with the introduction of the 1955 WAIS version. The Information test consists of short-answer question such as, "What does the heart do?" It is intended to assess the individual's range of available information or knowledge. The Comprehension test is similar to the Army Alpha Common Sense test, and appears to measure practical information and ability to use past experience. Word knowledge is assessed in the Vocabulary test, which requires the examinee to provide the definitions of words. Criteria are specified for assigning partial scoring for incomplete answers. The Arithmetic Reasoning test is similar to the Army Alpha test of the same name and is designed to evaluate ability to reason quantitatively with practical calculations. The Similarities test is a type of verbal reasoning test in which the examinee is asked to state how two words are alike. Scoring is based on criteria established to award partial credit depending on the quality of the answer. The Digit Span test assesses memory with the forward digit span, requiring reproduction of a sequence of digits in the original order of presentation, and with the backward digit span, requiring reproduction of the digits in the reverse order of presentation.

The remaining five tests are non-verbal, and closely resemble tests from the Army Beta. Each of these involves some type of pictorial or spatial information, and includes a temporal component either by specifying time limits, or by awarding scoring bonuses for rapid responding. The Picture Arrangement test consists of a series of comic-strip pictures which are to be placed in the correct sequence to present a meaningful story. Perceptual closure and attention to details are assumed to be measured by the Picture

Completion test, which requires the examinee to discover and name the missing part of a picture. The Block Design test involves arranging colored blocks to match a displayed pattern, and is hypothesized to measure visual analysis and synthesis abilities. Synthesis abilities are also required in the Object Assembly test, which is a type of form-board test in which the task is to put pieces together into a familiar configuration much like a jigsaw puzzle. The Digit Symbol Substitution test consists of a page containing a code table, and vertical pairs of boxes with digits in the top box and nothing in the bottom box. The examinee is required to write or substitute the symbols associated with the digits, according to the displayed code table, as rapidly as possible.

Age trends on the subtests from the WAIS and WAIS-R standardization samples are displayed in Figure 2.3. These values were derived from the data for scaled score equivalents at each age reported in Tables 21 through 28 of the WAIS (Wechsler, 1955) and Table 21 of the WAIS-R (Wechsler, 1981) manuals. All scores were converted to standard deviation units by determining the raw score corresponding to the age group mean, and then converting this raw score into scaled score units for adults between 20 and 24 years of age, and finally into standard deviation units for the distribution of scores in this reference group.

It is apparent in Figure 2.3 that the tests in the top two panels, characterized as comprising the Verbal scale, exhibit much smaller age-related effects than those in the bottom two panels, which are referred to as comprising the Performance scale. Age correlations for 933 of the individuals in the 1955 sample, reported by Birren and Morrison (1961), and for all 1,480 individuals in the 1981 sample, derived from data reported by A.S. Kaufman, Reynolds, and McLean (1989) were, respectively: Information = -.07 and -.10, Comprehension = -.08 and -.10, Vocabulary = -.02 and -.09, Arithmetic = -.08 and -.13, Similarities = -.19 and -.27, Digit Span = -.19 and -.18, Picture Arrangement = -.37 and -.42, Picture Completion = -.28 and -.38, Block Design = -.32 and -.41, Object Assembly = -.28 and -.41, and Digit Symbol = -.46 and -.54.

Primary Mental Abilities

One of the criticisms frequently directed against intelligence test batteries such as the Army Alpha and the Wechsler scales is that each of the component tests assesses a confusing mixture of different cognitive abilities. L.L Thurstone and T.G. Thurstone (1941, 1949) were therefore motivated to develop a test battery based on a factor-analytic investigation of 60 tests. Five factors were found to account for a relatively large proportion of the variance in these tests, and a new test battery was developed by selecting one test to represent each factor. Examples of the types of items from the

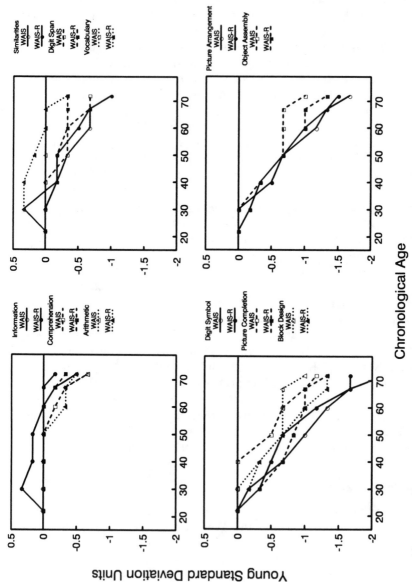

Figure 2.3.   Age relations in the WAIS (Wechsler, 1955) and WAIS-R (Wechsler, 1981) standardization data expressed in units of standard deviations of young adults.

46

five tests forming the Primary Mental Abilities (PMA) battery are illustrated in Figure 2.4.

The Verbal Meaning test is a multiple-choice vocabulary test, with 50 items to be answered in 4 minutes. The Space test requires the examinee to determine which geometric figures are the same as the target figure, but

Verbal Meaning

HAPPY

a. Sad b. Young c. Small d. Glad

Space

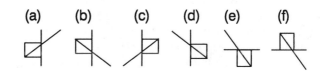

Reasoning

d e y f g y h i y j k y __

b m l y x

Number

26
18
53
81
———
178
R W

Word Fluency

Write as many words as you can
which begin with the letter S.

Figure 2.4.   Illustrative problems for the five subtests of the Thurstone Primary Mental Abilities (PMA) Tests.

merely rotated in the picture plane. Each problem contains six alternative figures, and there are 20 problems to be completed in 5 minutes. The Reasoning test is a letter series completion test in which the examinee is to discover the rule relating the letters in the sequence, and then use that rule to identify the letter that would best continue the sequence. A total of 30 problems are presented with a time limit of 6 minutes. The Number test consists of simple, two-digit addition problems, with the examinee instructed to mark the answer as right or wrong. Six minutes are allowed to solve 70 problems. In the Word Fluency test examinees are allowed 5 minutes to write as many words as possible that begin with the letter S.

Schaie has administered the PMA battery to large samples of adults every seven years since 1956. Means and standard deviations for each age group with each subtest for the over 2,800 adults ranging from 22 to 84 years of age tested between the years 1956 and 1977 are reported in Table 1 of Schaie (1985). These values have been converted into units of standard deviations for the distribution of scores for adults between 22 and 28 years of age, and are displayed in Figure 2.5.

The results illustrated in Figure 2.5 age appear quite similar to those from the Army Alpha and Wechsler tests. Small age-related declines are evident in the Number test, which resemble the results with the Arithmetic

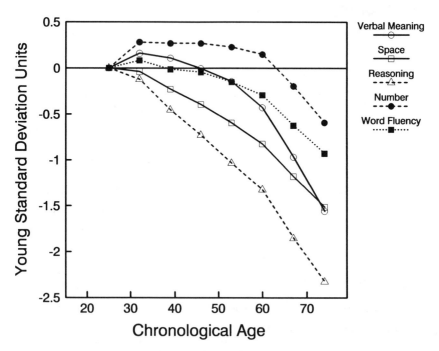

Figure 2.5.   Age relations in the Schaie (1985) PMA data expressed in standard deviations of young adults.

tests in the Army Alpha and Wechsler batteries. In contrast, the age trends are more pronounced with the Space and Reasoning tests, which is like the pattern for the tests of reasoning and spatial abilities in the Army Alpha and Wechsler batteries.

General Aptitude Test Battery

Another test battery developed on the basis of factor analyses of a large number of tests is the General Aptitude Test Battery used by the United States Employment Service. This battery consists of 12 short tests, which are often combined to yield nine factors. Several large-scale studies have been conducted which allow an examination of age-related effects on these tests, and most have revealed age-related declines similar to those described with the Army Alpha, Wechsler, and Primary Mental Abilities Tests (Droege, Crambert, & Henlein, 1963; Fozard & Nuttall, 1971; Hirt, 1959; Stein, 1962). As an illustration, Hirt (1959) reported age correlations, in a sample of 400 adults between 25 and 83 years of age, of -.21 for scores on a test of numerical computation, and -.56 for scores on a test of spatial perception or visualization.

Raven's Progressive Matrices

Although only a single test, the Raven's Progressive Matrices is often used in the assessment of general intelligence because it was designed to measure what Spearman (1927) considered the essence of intelligence, namely, the perception and abstraction of relationships. Each item in the test consists of a matrix of geometric patterns. The examinee is instructed to determine the relations among elements in the rows and the columns, and then to select the pattern that best completes the matrix. The test can be administered under timed or untimed conditions.

The Raven's test has been extensively used in Great Britain since the late 1930s, and a considerable amount of data was collected from military personnel during World War II. The data from two very large samples of males applying for, or serving in, the Navy (Vernon, 1947) and the Army (Slater, 1948) were analyzed in terms of the relations between age and performance. Both studies covered a range of only 18 to 42 years of age, but there were over 89,000 individuals in the Navy sample, and the 2,500 individuals in the Army sample were selected to be equally distributed across this age range and matched on years of education. Mean scores for these two groups, and for 300 males and 240 females tested by Heron and Chown (1967), are displayed in Figure 2.6. The data from each of these groups represent performance with 20-minute time limits, but the data of 2,972 American veterans reported by H.R. Burke (1985), which are also

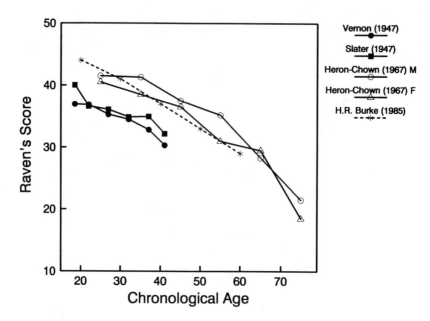

Figure 2.6.   Age relations in the Raven's Progressive Matrices Test from data by
H.R. Burke (1985), Heron and Chown (1967), Slater (1947), and Vernon (1947).

shown in Figure 2.6, indicate that similar trends are evident with untimed
administrations.

Each of the functions in Figure 2.6 indicates that increased age is
associated with monotonic declines in performance. Correlations between
age and Raven's performance are generally in the moderate to large range,
with reported values of -.27 (H.R. Burke, 1972), -.49 (Wetherick, 1966),
-.55 (Edwards & Wine, 1963), -.61 (F.H. Hooper, J.O. Hooper, &
Colbert, 1984), and -.62 (T.R. Wilson, 1963).

GENERALIZATIONS FROM PSYCHOMETRIC RESULTS

Large Individual Differences

One point that should be obvious from the results reviewed above is that
the differences in cognitive performance associated with aging are small
relative to the total range of individual differences. This fact was noted by
the earliest researchers in the field (W.R. Miles, 1933; Thorndike,
Bregman, Tilton, & Woodyard, 1928; Weisenburg, Roe, & McBride,
1936), and is evident both in the comparisons of performance in terms of
young-adult standard deviation units, and in the magnitude of the

correlation coefficients. Figures 2.2, 2.3, and 2.5 reveal that the means at older ages are almost always within one or two standard deviations of the mean of adults in their early 20s, and therefore even at the oldest ages there are likely to be some individuals whose level of performance exceeds that of the average 20-year-old. The correlation coefficients provide another indication of the relative magnitude of the age relations because the square of the correlation indicates the proportion of the total variance in the measures of cognitive performance associated with chronological age. There is a considerable range in the magnitude of the correlations, but only a few of them exceed -.4. This indicates that generally less than 16% of the total variance in these measures of cognitive performance is systematically related to chronological age.

The observations that there is considerable overlap in the scores of people of different ages, and that age is associated with a relatively small percentage of the total variance in cognitive performance, can be interpreted in two quite different ways. On the one hand, they can be viewed as indicating that age differences are too small to be of practical significance, and may also be of only limited theoretical importance. It certainly does seem to be the case that the age relations are much too small to allow accurate prediction at the level of individuals. On the other hand, while the age relations are small in absolute magnitude, they are large relative to other predictors of cognitive performance. That is, an individual's age may be the most valuable piece of information about that individual for the purpose of predicting his or her level of cognitive performance because variables such as gender, personality type, and ethnic origin generally account for even smaller percentages of variance in measures of cognitive functioning. Moreover, according to J. Cohen (1988), correlations among variables in the behavioral sciences should be considered of medium magnitude when they are in the range of .3, and should be considered large when they are in the range of .5. In the context of behavioral research, therefore, age-cognition relations are generally medium to large. (It may also help place these effects in perspective by noting that R. Rosenthal, 1990, has recently pointed out that correlations of less that .1 are often interpreted as reflecting dramatic effects in biomedical research.)

Gradual Age Relations

A second generalization from the results summarized in Figures 2.2, 2.3, 2.5, and 2.6 is that many of the age-cognition functions appear to be roughly linear, with little indication of abrupt transitions from stable to declining performance. There are some exceptions to this pattern because performance plateaus or periods of stability are apparent in the Wechsler Information, Comprehension, Arithmetic, and Vocabulary tests, and in the

PMA Verbal Meaning, Number, and Word Fluency tests. For other tests, however, increased age appears to be associated with gradual but monotonic declines in the average levels of performance.

Although not of immediate theoretical interest, the existence of gradual and largely monotonic age-related declines has at least two potentially important methodological implications. The first implication is that the magnitude of the age relations is likely to be underestimated in samples with limited age ranges. That is, to the extent that age effects are continuous across the adult years, then estimates of those effects are likely to be attenuated when the range of ages is restricted. One should therefore be cautious in interpreting results derived from samples with a relatively narrow age range, such as 50 to 80, as reflecting the total impact of age-related influences.

The second methodological implication of the gradual age trends evident in many cognitive tests is that labeling of individuals as young or old apparently cannot be justified on the basis of age-performance functions. In the absence of discrete transitions in level of performance at particular ages, classifications such as young, middle-aged, old—or the increasingly popular but oxymoronic term, young-old—may be almost completely arbitrary. Fortunately, conventions have apparently served to induce some regularity in the assignment of labels to particular age ranges. For example, Camp, West, and Poon (1989) have reported that researchers working in the area of cognition and aging have been fairly consistent in referring to adults between 18 and 30 years of age as young, to those between 39 and 58 as middle-aged, and to those from 62 to 90 as old. There are nevertheless still many cases of ambiguity in the labeling of people from different age ranges. A particularly striking example of the confusion that can result from the lack of consistent labeling practices is evident in two studies by the same investigator, one in which adults with a mean age of 42.2 years were described as older adults (Buschke, 1974), and the other in which adults with a mean age of 44.7 years were designated as younger adults (Buschke & Grober, 1986).

Differential Decline

A third generalization from the results summarized above is that the age relations vary dramatically across different cognitive tests. Relatively little, or late occurring, age-related decline is evident in tests such as the General Information and Antonym-Synonym tests from the Army Alpha, the Information, Comprehension, and Vocabulary tests from the Wechsler scales, and the PMA Number test. In contrast, pronounced, and early occurring, declines are evident in the Following Directions and Verbal Analogies tests from the Army Alpha, in the Wechsler Digit Symbol Substitution, Picture Completion, Picture Arrangement, Object Assembly, and Block Design tests, in the PMA Reasoning and Space tests, and in the Raven's Progressive Matrices Test.

This differential susceptibility of tests to age-related effects has been recognized since the very first investigations of aging and cognition (Foster & G.A. Taylor, 1920; Gilbert, 1935; Hollingworth, 1927; H.E. Jones & Conrad, 1933; W.R. Miles, 1933, 1935; Thorndike, et al., 1928; Weisenburg, et al., 1936; Willoughby, 1927), and has led to many speculations about factors that might be responsible for different age trends across cognitive tests. Some of the characteristics hypothesized to differentiate between activities or tasks with large, and with small, susceptibility to age-related effects are listed in Table 1.1.

Although several of the entries in Table 1.1 were apparently intended by their authors to represent theories or explanations, they are probably more appropriately considered as descriptive generalizations. That is, few of the taxonomies are stated precisely enough to allow a priori classification of the measures of performance, and virtually all fail to specify change mechanisms that might account for the developmental trends present in one class of measures but absent in the other class of measures.

There is another reason the speculations listed in Table 1.1 should be interpreted cautiously—namely, that the across-test comparisons from which most of the distinctions are derived confound a great many factors. Not only do the tests vary with respect to content of the material, but they also differ in the type or quantity of manipulations or transformations required, the nature and speed requirements of the response, etc. In fact, even items within the same test may not be homogeneous in terms of these characteristics because there may be different age trends across items within the same tests (L.P. Sands, Terry, & Meredith, 1989).

The fact that many psychometric tests have arbitrary difficulty levels may result in confoundings of amount of processing with type of processing. That is, items from different tests frequently differ in how much processing is required to answer the items, as well as in the content of the material and the nature of the operations to be performed. To illustrate, panel A in Figure 2.7 displays a linear relation between age and ability superimposed on three levels of task demands. Each horizontal line is intended to represent the amount of ability necessary to achieve near-maximum performance for that level of task demand. The three functions in panel B of Figure 2.7 will then result if one makes the additional assumption that performance is proportional to ability when the task demands exceed one's level of ability. That is, performance will be invariant across most of the age range when the task requires low amounts of ability, but the age trends will become apparent at younger ages as the demands of the task increase.

An implication of the argument summarized in Figure 2.7 is that quite different age-performance functions may be produced even if there is a single linear relation between age and the actual or true level of cognitive ability. At least some of the variation in age relations observed across different cognitive tests may therefore be attributable to differences in task demands or processing requirements, and not simply to differences in the content of the items. Although this argument is merely speculative at the present time (but see chapter 8 for further discussion), the possibility that measures of cognitive functioning differ on dimensions other than substantive content should make one cautious about accepting the validity of interpretations of the apparently different patterns of age relations evident in various measures of cognitive performance.

ARTIFACTUAL INTERPRETATIONS

The major theoretical explanations proposed to account for the relations between age and cognition evident in Figures 2.2, 2.3, 2.5, and 2.6 will be described, and thoroughly examined, in later chapters. At this point, however, it is desirable to consider several interpretations which, if valid, would greatly alter the nature of the phenomena to be explained.

Differential Representativeness

As noted above, the possibility that age differences in cognitive performance might be attributable to differences in selectivity or representativeness of individuals at different ages was raised by Yerkes (1921) in his discussion of results from the Army Alpha testing in World War I. This interpretation was made less plausible by H.E. Jones and Conrad (1933) in their finding of similar age trends in a nearly exhaustive sample of several New England communities, and in results from other studies with representative samples (Wechsler, 1955, 1981). Legitimate concerns can nevertheless still be raised about the representativeness of participants in most studies examining relations between age and cognitive functioning.

Two general questions seem particularly germane to the representativeness issue. These are: (a) What percentage of the population of possible participants agrees to participate in research projects assessing relations between age and cognitive functioning?; and (b) Do those who agree to participate differ with respect to their performance on cognitive tests from those who do not participate? Interpretations of the relations between age and cognitive performance may be compromised if the answers to one or both of these questions vary as a function of the age of the individual.

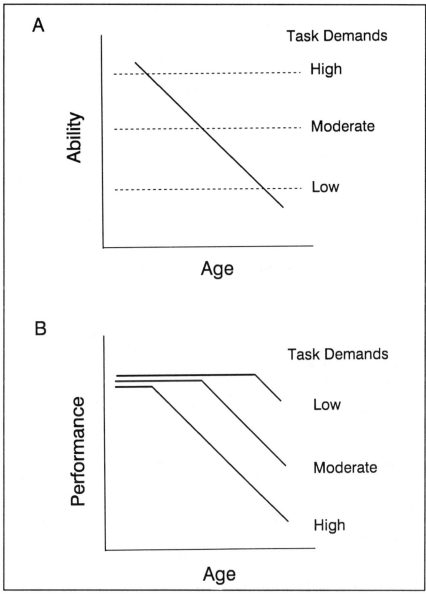

Figure 2.7.   Illustration of how a linear age decline in ability (Panel A) can result in different patterns of age relations depending upon the demands of the task (Panel B).

Several researchers have reported information about the response rates for people asked to participate in research projects on aging and cognition. For example, N.W. Denney (1980), Lovelace and Cooley (1982), and Sinnott and Guttmann (1978) all claimed that approximately 50% of the older adults who were contacted were willing to participate in their projects. Herzog and Rogers (1989) found that 57% of the individuals in a stratified probability sample across a wide range of ages were willing to be interviewed in a study involving assessment of memory functioning. Amount of education is probably an important factor influencing response rate. Perlmutter (1978) reported that 53% of PhDs between 60 and 65 years of age were willing to participate in a research project, but only 11% of the non-PhDs within that age range agreed to participate. C.L. Rose (1965) also reported that individuals volunteering to participate in a research project concerned with aging had more years of education than nonvolunteers. In an earlier study involving only college faculty members, Sward (1945) found that a high percentage (70.3%) of current or retired college faculty members between 60 and 79 years of age were willing to participate in the research project. Little age difference in participation was noted in this study because it was also reported that 76.3% of faculty members between 21 and 42 years of age who were approached agreed to participate.

Detailed information about participation rates as a function of age and monetary incentive have been reported by Gribbin and Schaie (1976). Invitations to participate in a research project were mailed to 2,466 members of a health maintenance organization. Half of the individuals received a letter mentioning payment of $10, and half received a letter with no mention of monetary payment. Interested individuals responded by returning a stamped postcard indicating their willingness to participate. The percentages of positive responses (i.e., indications of willingness to participate) are displayed in Figure 2.8 as a function of age and incentive condition. Also illustrated in this figure are the participation rates reported by Schaie (1959) for the 2,818 individuals invited to participate in an earlier assessment of the same type.

The data in Figure 2.8 suggest that participation rates do not differ much across most of the adult years. Neither age nor incentive condition were significant determinants of participation rate. (There were also no significant effects associated with the incentive manipulation on performance in the PMA cognitive tests.)

Another investigation of volunteering rates at different ages has been reported by R. Lachman, J.L. Lachman, and D.W. Taylor (1982). These researchers sent letters to school teachers in three different age ranges asking them to participate in a research project. Slightly more than 25% of the teachers between 21 and 25 years of age agreed to participate, but only 15.5% of the 41-to-45-year-olds, and 15.2% of the 61-to-70-year-olds, responded positively to the letter. Follow-up telephone calls to individuals who did not respond to the letters yielded 23.7%, 13.2%, and 12.3% agreements to participate for ages 21 to 25, 41 to 45, and 61 to 70, respectively. Todd, K.E. Davis, and Cofferty (1983-84), in a study concerned with social relationships, reported volunteering rates in these age groups of 16.1%, 19.6%, and 13.3%.

This brief review indicates that the results on the relation between age and participation rates are somewhat inconsistent. Absolute volunteering rates range from less than 15% to over 50%, and some studies have found older adults to be less willing to participate in research projects than young adults while no age differences were reported in other studies.

R. Lachman, et al. (1982) also attempted to determine whether the performance levels of volunteers and nonvolunteers differed in samples of young and old adults. Volunteers were identified as those individuals agreeing to participate on the basis of an initial letter. Because it is impossible to force true nonvolunteers to participate, reluctant individuals who had originally refused to participate in the project were contacted again and offered an attractive incentive ($80) to change their minds and participate. Those who only agreed to participate under these conditions

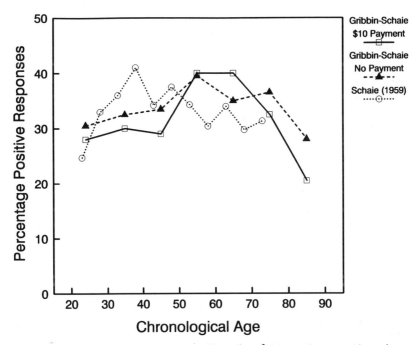

Figure 2.8.   Percentage of people willing to participate in research projects concerned with aging, based on data from Gribbin and Schaie (1976) and Schaie (1959).

were designated nonvolunteers. Actual compensation was equated in all groups for those individuals who eventually participated in the project.

One of the most interesting findings from the R. Lachman, et al. (1982) study was that the volunteer status of the participants had no significant effect on any of the 19 performance measures examined. Young adults had significantly higher scores on seven measures of speed and memory, and older adults had significantly higher scores on five measures related to knowledge, but neither the main effect of volunteer status nor its interaction with age was statistically significant on any of the measures.

The available results are more equivocal than one would like concerning the issue of differential representativeness as a factor contributing to the age differences observed in measures of cognitive functioning. It seems likely that participants in research projects are positively biased relative to the general population with respect to amount of education and socioeconomic status, and this bias may be somewhat greater with increased age because it appears that a smaller percentage of older adults than younger adults may be willing to participate in research projects concerned with age and cognition. Whether the people who participate differ in interesting dimensions of cognitive functioning from those who refuse to participate cannot be definitively determined at the present time, but the results of R. Lachman, et al. suggest that any differences that do exist may be relatively small. Moreover, if it is really the case that the older participants are more select than younger participants in level of education and socioeconomic status, then any bias in the assessment of age differences in cognitive performance would probably result in an underestimate of the true relation between age and cognition. To the extent that differential representativeness contributes to the pattern of age differences observed in measures of cognitive functioning, therefore, it seems likely that the direction of the influence is a reduction rather than an enhancement of the true age differences.

Health Status

There are well documented declines with increased age in health status, with the latter defined broadly as freedom from debilitating diseases. Because cognition, as with all forms of behavior, is ultimately dependent upon the condition of the biological substrate, it is natural to ask whether changes in health status mediate some or all of the age differences observed in measures of cognitive functioning. This type of influence is clearly plausible because the incidence of many diseases increases with age, and at least some of those diseases are known to impair various aspects of cognition.

Although it seems highly likely that health factors could contribute to age differences in cognition, it does not necessarily follow that they are responsible for all, or even most, of the cognitive differences frequently observed between adults of different ages. As an example, a causal relation would not be implicated if either the incidence of the debilitating diseases is very low, or if there is little impairment of cognition until the disease is in a very advanced state.

A straightforward method of determining whether age differences in cognitive functioning are mediated by health factors consists of examining the magnitude of relations between age and cognition among adults known to be healthy and free of nearly all potentially debilitating diseases. If the age-related effects in this sample are greatly attenuated compared to a typical or unselected sample, then it would be reasonable to infer that aspects related to health probably do contribute to the influence of age on those measures of cognitive functioning. In contrast, little influence of health would be inferred if the age trends in the healthy sample were found to be similar to those obtained in unselected samples. Unfortunately, because of the difficulty associated with assessing health status, this method is not as simple as it appears.

Two general methods have been used to assess the health status of research participants in studies of cognitive aging. One consists of a variety of objective examinations by physicians or other trained medical personnel. For example, a general physical examination might be administered, sometimes followed by more rigorous screening for specific diseases. Medical examinations are fairly expensive, however, and thus most researchers with a primary interest in relations between age and cognition have relied upon self-ratings to assess health status.

Of crucial importance when considering the use of self-ratings to evaluate an individual's health status is the question of their validity. Three types of correlations have been cited as evidence that subjective assessments of one's health along a simple continuum ranging from excellent to poor have at least some validity. These consist of significant relations between measures of self-reported health and (a) physician assessments of overall health (Heyman & Jeffers, 1963; LaRue, Bank, Jarvik, & Hetland, 1979; Maddox, 1962, 1964; Maddox & Douglass, 1973; Suchman, B.S. Phillips, & Streib, 1958); (b) reported medical problems or number of prescription medications (Fillenbaum, 1979; G.A. Kaplan & Camacho, 1983; Liang, 1986; B.S. Linn & M.W. Linn, 1980; Mossey & Shapiro, 1982; Pilpel, Carmel, & Galinsky, 1988; Salthouse, Kausler, & Saults, 1990; Tissue, 1972); and (c) longevity or survival (Botwinick, West, & Storandt, 1978; Heyman & Jeffers, 1963; G.A. Kaplan & Camacho, 1983; LaRue, et al., 1979; Mossey & Shapiro, 1982; Pfeiffer, 1970; Singer, Garfinkel, S.M. Cohen, & Srole, 1976; Suchman, et al., 1958).

Although these patterns of relationships lend credibility to the measures of self-rated health, they do not mean that self-ratings of health are necessarily accurate indices of objective health. For example, Maddox and

Douglass (1973) reported that self-ratings are more optimistic than assessments based on physician examinations or medical histories, and several researchers have found little influence of age on self-reported health despite increases with age in reported medical problems or number of prescription medicines (Kosnik, Winslow, D. Kline, Rasinski, & Sekuler, 1988; Perlmutter, 1978; Salthouse, Kausler, & Saults, 1990). In the Salthouse, Kausler, and Saults analysis, for example, the correlations with age were .03 for self-rated health (on a scale ranging from 1 for excellent to 5 for poor), but .30 for number of prescription medicines being taken, and .27 for reports of treatment for high blood pressure.

These discrepancies between self-ratings and more objective indicators of health suggest that self assessments probably incorporate a subjective component in addition to an objective appraisal of health. The subjectivity may reflect the use of one's age peers as the reference group, and therefore incorporate an expectation of lower standards of health with increased age. It may also represent the extent to which health factors actually limit one's activities, rather than the mere presence or absence of certain symptoms. Still another possibility is that self-ratings are influenced by personality characteristics such as depression or neuroticism as well as by objective health status. In any case, however, the available evidence seems to suggest that self-ratings have at least some validity as indicators of objective health status.

A strong prediction from the health-as-mediator perspective is that age differences in measures of cognitive performance should be greatly reduced, and possibly even eliminated, when age comparisons are conducted in samples known to be free of virtually all serious diseases. It could, of course, be argued that one can never be certain that an individual is perfectly healthy, but careful medical screening can be used to ensure there are at least no obvious symptoms of any major diseases.

Several studies have been reported in which extensive examinations were used to exclude any individuals suspected to be suffering from potentially debilitating diseases. One of these studies was conducted at the National Institutes of Health, and was reported by Botwinick and Birren (1963). The research participants in this study underwent a two-stage screening process. An initial general medical examination was used to eliminate people with obvious health problems. A second more intensive series of medical tests was then used to separate the remaining participants into those suspected to have some type of cardiovascular disease and those who, as far as could be determined, were in optimal health. This latter group consisted of 27 males with an average age of 71 years. Comparisons revealed that even the performance of this optimally healthy group of older adults was substantially below that of average (i.e., unselected) young adults on several cognitive tests. For example, the mean performance, in standard deviation units of young adults, was -2.7 for the Raven's Progressive

Matrices test, -1.3 for the Wechsler Digit Symbol Substitution test, and -0.7 for the Wechsler Block Design test. The two major conclusions from this study were:

> (1) Healthy men over 65 do better on psychological tests than men unselected for health, and (2) age differences in patterns of abilities were found even in a population devoid of apparent disease. (Botwinick & Birren, 1963, p. 100)

Several studies involving pilots and air traffic controllers are also relevant to the issue of health as a potential mediator of age differences in cognition. Birren and Spieth (1962) and Spieth (1964, 1965) were able to administer a battery of perceptual-motor and cognitive tests (e.g., Wechsler Digit Symbol Substitution and Block Design tests) to pilots and air traffic controllers at the time they were taking the physical examinations required for their certification. A clear pattern of declining performance with increased age was evident in this sample, even among the individuals classified as strictly healthy because of the absence of any evidence of neurological or cardiovascular pathology. It is important to note that pilots and air traffic controllers, besides being healthier, probably have a higher level of education and of socioeconomic status than members of the general population. Furthermore, most of the participants in the Birren and Spieth (1962), and Spieth (1964, 1965) projects were less than 60 years of age. These factors can be expected to reduce the likelihood of finding significant age relations, and thus the presence of age-related declines in these studies appears particularly convincing.

A recent study of "optimally healthy" adults was reported by M.S. Albert, Duffy, and Naeser (1987; see also M.S. Albert, Wolfe, & LaFleche, 1990). The 100 30-to-85-year-old males participating in this study were considered healthy because:

> The selection criteria excluded individuals with hypertension, coronary artery disease, lung disease, kidney disease, cancer, alcoholism, psychiatric illness, learning disabilities, severe head trauma, or epilepsy. (p. 143)

Unfortunately, only a limited number of cognitive tests known to be sensitive to age-related effects were administered to the research participants in this project. Nevertheless, typical age differences were reported on several tests. As an example, mean performance of 70-year-olds, in standard deviation units of 30-year-olds, were -2.21 on a naming task, -1.69 on a proverbs task, -1.05 on a fluency task, and -0.88 on a visual-verbal concept task.

Research participants can also be categorized with respect to health status on the basis of their self-ratings of health. That is, those individuals who rate their health as excellent can be considered to be healthy, and age trends among these individuals can be contrasted with the age trends observed in unselected adults. Results of this type from two recent projects, with composite measures of cognitive functioning, are illustrated in Figure 2.9.

Each variable in Figure 2.9 represents the average z-score for two measures of cognitive performance, and the results are expressed in standard deviation units from the distribution of scores across the entire sample. (The reference distribution was the entire sample and not just the young adults in order to facilitate examination of the main effects of health status as well as those of age.) The data in the top three panels are based on the results from 362 adults performing the computer-controlled tasks described in Salthouse, Kausler, and Saults (1988a). The speed variable reflects performance on a digit symbol test and a number comparison test, the memory variable corresponds to accuracy of reporting identities (verbal information) and locations (spatial information) from a matrix, and the paired associate variable reflects accuracy on two trials of a paired associate task. The data in the bottom three panels are based on results from 383 adults reported in Salthouse and D.R. Mitchell (1990). The paper-and-pencil tests used to measure each variable were Number Comparison and Finding A's for speed, Paper Folding and Surface Development for spatial, and Shipley Abstraction and Letter Sets for reasoning.

The striking characteristic of all the results portrayed in Figure 2.9 is that the age trends were virtually identical among the subsamples reporting themselves to be in excellent health, and in the entire sample. The apparent implication is that, at least for people who volunteer to participate in research projects of this type, self-reported health status seems to be relatively unimportant as a determinant of the magnitude of age differences in cognition.

This conclusion concerning the minimal influence of health variations on age differences in cognitive performance is supported by research in which statistical control procedures are used to equate people of different ages on various measures of health status. A particularly interesting study of this type was reported by E.H. Schludermann, S.M. Schludermann, Merryman, and B.W. Brown (1983). These investigators were able to examine interrelations among medical and cognitive measures in a sample of 558 males between 24 and 85 years of age. Most of the participants in this project submitted to two days of medical and psychological examinations as part of a preventive health program. Many physiological measurements were obtained from each participant, with a particular emphasis on measures of cardiovascular functioning.

One of the major results of the E.H. Schuldermann, et al. study was that the correlation between age and a measure of inductive reasoning (Halstead Category Test) was -.43, and it was only reduced to -.29 after statistically controlling a variety of potentially important physiological

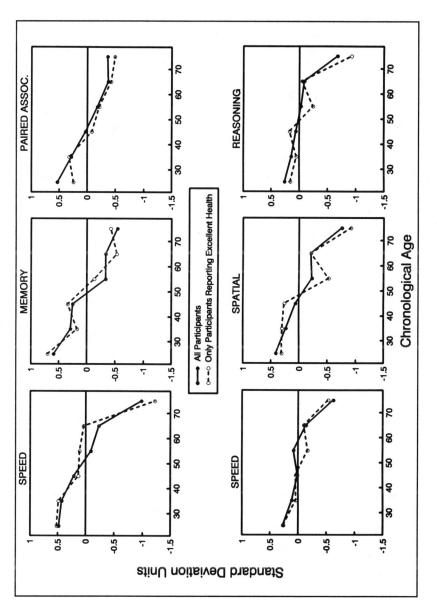

Figure 2.9. Age relations in composite measures of cognitive performance for all individuals and only for individuals reporting themselves to be in excellent health. Data in the top three graphs from Salthouse, Kausler, and Saults (1988a), and those in the bottom three graphs from Salthouse and D.R. Mitchell (1990).

measures. The conclusions reached by the authors were very similar to those reached 20 years earlier by Botwinick and Birren (1963):

> The analyses reported in this chapter have suggested some age decrements in cognitive functions, some age-related deterioration in health, and some relationship between cognitive and physiological age changes. However, this relationship has not been shown to be high enough to attribute *most* cognitive changes to deteriorating health. (E.H. Schuldermann, et al., 1983, p. 128)

At least three additional studies have reported data indicating that the age-related effects on inductive reasoning are not greatly attenuated by statistical control of an index of health in the form of systolic blood pressure. Because complete correlation matrices were reported, partial correlations can be computed between age and cognitive performance after adjusting for systolic blood pressure. The original and partial correlations were -.42 and -.39 for PMA Space performance, and -.49 and -.40 for PMA Reasoning performance in a study by J.W. Clark (1960); -.64 and -.55 (Males) and -.51 and -.46 (Females) for Raven's Progressive Matrices performance in a study by Heron and Chown (1967); and -.57 and -.45 for performance on the Cattell Culture-Fair test in a study by R.R. Powell and Pohndorf (1971).

Relatively modest attenuation of the age-cognition relation has also been found when self-ratings are used as the measure of health status. Results from several recent projects with a variety of different cognitive measures are summarized in Table 2.2. Notice that even though a decline in self-rated health was reported in several of the studies, statistical control of the health variable resulted in only slight reductions of the correlation between age and the measures of cognitive performance.

Longitudinal analyses of the interrelations among age, health, and cognition have been reported in two studies. Hertzog, Schaie, and Gribbin (1978) classified 156 43-to-73-year-old participants in the Seattle Longitudinal Study according to their cardiovascular health status on the basis of medical histories, and then examined their performance on the PMA tests across a 7-year interval. Although individuals with cardiovascular disease were less likely to continue to participate in the project, the longitudinal age differences in the measure of cognitive functioning did not vary markedly as a function of cardiovascular disease. A few of the age-by-disease interactions were statistically significant, but they were quite complex (e.g., one was apparently attributable to people with hypertension improving their level of performance over the 7-year interval). It is likely that some may have occurred by chance because they were reported in the context of 360 statistical comparisons.

Field, Schaie, and Leino (1988) reported analyses of data from 57 adults tested in 1969 when their mean age was 69, and again in 1983 when their

TABLE 2.2
Correlations between age and cognition before and
after statistical control of self-rated health.

Measure	Zero-Order Correlation	Partial Correlation	Age-Health Correlation	Source
Digit Span	-.31	-.30	.25	Botwinick & Storandt (1974)
Serial Learning	-.51	-.49	"	"
Logical Paragraphs	-.42	-.40	"	"
Following Instruct.	-.49	-.47	"	"
Visual Organ. Test	-.59	-.57	"	"
Forward/Backward Digit Span Composite	.03	.02	-.15	Perlmutter & Nyquist (1990)
Digit Symbol/Block Design Composite	-.78	-.78	"	"
Digit Symbol	-.54	-.54	.03	Salthouse, Kausler, & Saults (1988a)
Number Comparison	-.36	-.36	"	"
Verbal Memory	-.38	-.38	"	"
Spatial Memory	-.43	-.43	"	"
Paired Assoc. 1	-.30	-.30	"	"
Paired Assoc. 2	-.38	-.38	"	"
Computation Span	-.46	-.43	.26	Salthouse, D.R. Mitchell, Skovronek, & Babcock (1989)
Integrative Reasoning	-.53	-.51	"	"
Paper Folding	-.53	-.52	"	"
Paper Folding	-.37	-.37	.10	Salthouse & D.R. Mitchell (1990)
Surface Development	-.30	-.30	"	"
Letter Sets	-.26	-.26	"	"
Shipley Abstraction	-.25	-.25	"	"
Finding A's	-.17	-.17	"	"
Number Comparison	-.30	-.30	"	"

(Cont.)

TABLE 2.2
(Continued)

Digit Span	-.34	-.33	.22	Salthouse & Babcock (in press)
Word Span	-.42	-.39	"	"
Computation Span	-.48	-.46	"	"
Listening Span	-.52	-.50	"	"

Note: Cognitive measures are scaled such that higher values indicate better performance, and ratings of health are scaled such that higher values indicate poorer health.

mean age was 83. The Wechsler Verbal and Performance scales were used as the measures of cognitive functioning, and health was evaluated with a composite measure based on answers to questions about health limitations, perceived changes in health, and so on. Declines on both the Verbal and Performance scales were observed across the 14-year interval, and both variables had moderate (i.e., .23 to .40) correlations with the health index at each measurement occasion. Health status, however, was not a significant predictor of cognitive change. That is, the 1969 health measures were not significantly related to the 1983 cognitive performance measures, and there was no significant relation between changes in cognitive measures and changes in health measures. The authors suggested on the basis of descriptions of several case studies that health factors may contribute to some of the observed cognitive changes, but the reported statistical analyses provide little indication that declining health mediates the cognitive declines in the group as a whole.

The available research on the interrelations of age, health, and cognition suggests that, contrary to intuition and popular opinion, there is little evidence that declines in cognitive performance associated with increased age are mediated by declines in health status. This does not mean that health factors have no influence on cognitive functioning, nor that age-related effects in certain cognitive measures may not be accelerated among individuals experiencing particular diseases. What it does suggest, however, is that the people who agree to participate in cognitive psychological research projects exhibit similar influences of age regardless of their health status. It is likely that these people are positively biased with respect to health, and greater health-related effects may therefore be evident in a more representative sample of the population. For the present purposes, however, the important point is that the age trends in a variety of measures of cognitive functioning appear to be independent of either the self-rated, or the objectively assessed, health status of the participants. More sensitive assessments may eventually reveal greater influence of health factors, but the currently available research seems to indicate that age-related declines in health status are not responsible for most of the age-related declines in cognitive functioning commonly observed among adults recruited from samples of convenience.

Limited Impact

Another interpretation of the age trends summarized in Figures 2.2, 2.3, 2.5, and 2.6 is that they reflect rather dramatic declines for a small segment of the population, with most people maintaining stable levels of cognitive performance throughout this age range. In other words, the fact that there is a decline in the average level of performance does not necessarily mean that there are equivalent declines in performance for every individual, or even that most individuals experience some degree of decline.

There are at least two methods of investigating the plausibility of this limited-impact interpretation of the age differences in cognitive functioning. One consists of examining the relation between age and measures of interindividual variability, and the other involves examining the stability of cognitive performance in longitudinal studies.

If aging effects are restricted to a small proportion of adults, then measures of the across-individual variability of cognitive performance should be expected to increase with increased age. In fact, it is commonly assumed that this is the case because cognitive performance is often believed to be influenced by health and experience factors that do not have uniform impact on all individuals (M.S. Albert, 1988; P.B. Baltes, Reese, & Lipsitt, 1980; P.B. Baltes & Willis, 1977; Botwinick, 1967; Bromley, 1974; Charness, 1982; Clarkson-Smith & A.A. Hartley, 1989; Donahue, 1956; Hertzog, 1985; W.J. Hoyer, 1974; Kausler, 1982; Perlmutter, 1988; Rabbitt, 1982; Schaffer & Poon, 1982; Schaie, 1983, 1988, 1989b; Schonfield, 1974; Wechsler, 1952; Welford, 1957, 1958, 1959; Willis, 1985, 1989b).

Despite the plausibility of the assumption that increased age is associated with greater variability of cognitive performance, several reviewers have suggested there is still little convincing evidence that interindividual variability is consistently greater with increased age (Bornstein & Smircina, 1982; Camp, et al., 1989; Kinsbourne, 1980; R. Lachman & J.L. Lachman, 1980; R. Lachman, et al., 1982). Problems of obtaining comparable samples, and measurement artifacts such as scores approaching a lower floor or an upper ceiling that may distort the observed variances, serve to complicate interpretations. This is particularly true for measures of speed of performance in which there is an absolute minimum, but no maximum, so that variability tends to increase with increases in the mean (S. Hale, Myerson, G.A. Smith, & Poon, 1988; Salthouse, 1985a).

As a means of examining the relation between age and interindividual variability, Figures 2.10, 2.11, and 2.12 illustrate the ratio of variances at each age to the variance at the youngest age for the H.E. Jones and Conrad (1933) Army Alpha data (Figure 2.10), the WAIS (Wechsler, 1955) and WAIS-R (Wechsler, 1981) data (Figure 2.11), and the Schaie (1985) PMA data (Figure 2.12). A clear prediction from the assumption that individual differences increase with age is that these ratios should become progressively larger as a function of age. It is apparent in these figures, however, that there is little consistent trend between age (in the range between about 20 and 70 years) and interindividual variability. Moreover, comparisons of the WAIS and WAIS-R Picture Completion, Picture Arrangement, and Similarities tests reveal that variability does not even increase or decrease uniformly as a function of age within the same test.

Some of the past confusion regarding age and variability may have been due to a failure to distinguish between conceptually distinct sources of variability. As an example, Wechsler (1958, pp. 96-97) combined scores across several different tests in his analysis of age and variability, a procedure that mixes within-test and between-test variability. The age-related increases in variability he observed may therefore have reflected the existence of different age trends across the component tests, and not increases in interindividual variability within any given test.

The data in Figures 2.10, 2.11, and 2.12, together with those from Figures 2.2, 2.3, and 2.5, indicate that the mean level of performance can decrease without concomitant increases in variance. This pattern is evident in several of the Wechsler Performance tests, and in most of the Army Alpha and PMA tests. An implication of these data is that it is apparently not the case that some people remain stable while others decline markedly, because that would result in increases in variance that are not observed. Instead the results seem to suggest that, at least in these samples, the entire distribution is shifted toward lower levels of performance with increased age.

Another aspect of individual differences in susceptibility to age-related influences concerns variability in the rate of change from one age to another. Several studies have reported information about the magnitude of test-retest correlations in longitudinal assessments, which can be used as an indication of the relative stability of performance across the intervening years. Owens (1966) reported the correlations across measurements in 1919, 1950, and 1961 for the Army Alpha tests. The correlations for individual tests ranged from .30 to .83, but the total score had correlations of .79 between 1919 and 1950, .92 between 1950 and 1961, and .78 between 1919 and 1961. Schwartzman, D. Gold, Andres, Arbuckle, and Chaikelson (1987) also reported a test-retest correlation of .78 for 259 males across a

40-year interval with a test battery reported to correlate .80 with composite score on the Army Alpha.

Longitudinal test-retest correlations of .86 and .83, respectively, were reported by Field, et al. (1988) with the WAIS Verbal and Performance

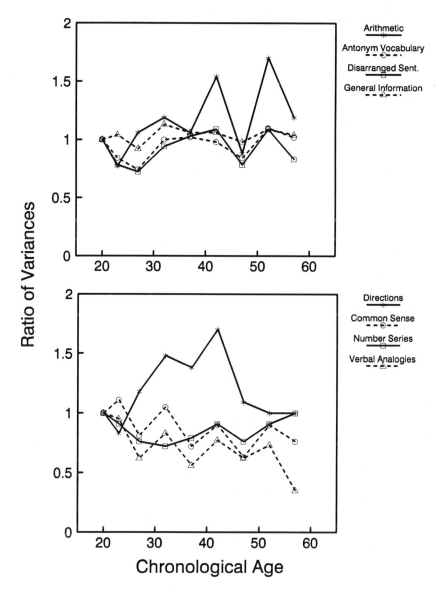

Figure 2.10.   Ratio of variances at each age to the variance in young adults for the H.E. Jones and Conrad (1933) data from eight Army Alpha subtests.

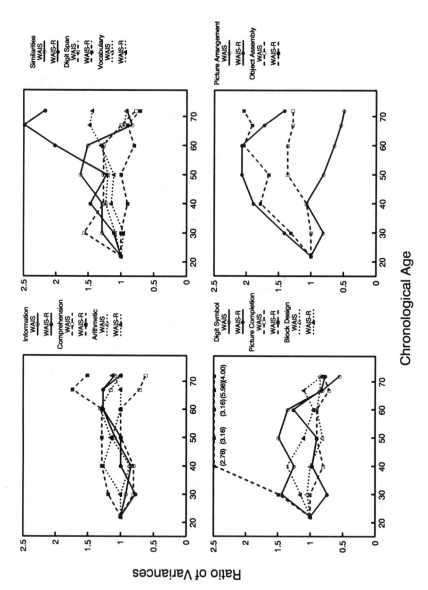

Figure 2.11. Ratio of variances at each age to the variance in young adults for the WAIS (Wechsler, 1955) and WAIS-R (Wechsler, 1981) data from 11 subtests.

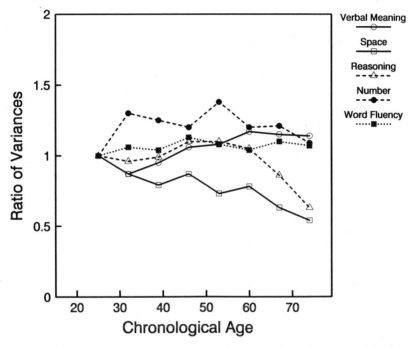

Figure 2.12.   Ratio of variances at each age to the variance in young adults for the Schaie (1985) Primary Mental Abilities data from five subtests.

scales across a 14-year interval. Rank-order correlations over a comparable interval were reported by Maddox and Douglass (1974) to be .93 and .85 for the Verbal and Performance scales, respectively. Retest correlations for the full-scale scores across intervals ranging from 6 to 16 years were all above .92 in a study reported by Green and Reimanis (1970).

A correlation of .85 for the PMA Reasoning test across a 5-year interval was reported by M.E. Lachman and Leff (1989). Test-retest correlations for all the PMA tests were reported in Table 13 of Schaie (1985). The medians across subtests were .81 for 7-year intervals, .78 for 14-year intervals, and .78 for 21-year intervals. A composite measure of intellectual aptitude had test-retest correlations of .88, .85, and .86 for 7-, 14-, and 21-year intervals, respectively. Hertzog and Schaie (1986, 1988) analyzed the stability of another composite intelligence measure derived from the PMA scores, and found that it also had very high stability across a 14-year interval. Correlations across measurement occasions separated by 14 years for this measure were reported to be at or above .9.

These high correlations between performance at two occasions of measurement suggest that people tend to preserve their relative positions across time, even though the average level of performance is often declining. Stated somewhat differently, the finding of high stability of the relative orderings of performance seems to imply that individual differences in the rate of change are relatively small. It is still possible that some people could have declined substantially while others preserved their abilities, but the relatively high stability coefficients indicate that one's later performance could be predicted with reasonable accuracy from his or her performance at an earlier time.

Still another type of analysis is also relevant to the issue of interindividual variability in patterns of age-related cognitive decline. This consists of categorizing individuals as having remained stable or having declined in a given cognitive ability according to whether the magnitude of their longitudinal performance change exceeded one across-individual standard error of measurement. Schaie (1984b, 1988, 1989a, 1990b) has reported that only a small percentage of people exhibit decline according to this criterion.

The sensitivity of this particular method of analysis appears questionable, however, because of the unknown relation between across-individual variability, reflected in the between-person standard error of measurement, and within-individual variability, which should ideally be used to evaluate within-individual change. The classification of individuals as having remained stable or having declined is therefore likely to be imprecise if, as is almost certainly the case, the within-individual variability is not identical to the between-individual variability (see Salthouse, 1989b).

Researchers using longitudinal designs currently seem to be in a somewhat paradoxical position; They are presumably interested in individual aging trends, and yet the amount of data available from any given individual is seldom sufficient to allow reliable assessment of trends at the level of a single individual. The problem is that unless there is some means of determining that the change experienced by an individual across several measurement occasions is large relative to his or her own variability at each measurement occasion, then it may be impossible to infer that the magnitude of change is significantly greater (or less) than zero, or that it is significantly different from that experienced by another individual. Moreover, without considerably more information about the relations between across-individual and within-individual variability, measures of across-individual variability may be poor substitutes for measures of within-individual, within-occasion variability that would allow accurate statistical evaluation of longitudinal comparisons at the level of individuals.

There is not yet much research on the relations between age and interindividual variability, but the results that are available appear inconsistent with expectations based on the assumption that average age trends are a consequence of a few individuals declining in performance, with most others maintaining their original levels of performance. If the aging effects were of this type then one would expect increases in interindividual variance with increased age, and relatively low stability coefficients in longitudinal assessments of cognitive performance. Neither of these patterns is evident in the existing data, and therefore the limited-impact interpretation seems to have little empirical support at the current time.

Educational Differences

It is sometimes claimed that age differences in measures of intellectual performance are an artifact of differences in quantity or quality of education. For example, Bandura (1989) asserted that:

> The major share of age differences in intelligence seems to be due to differences in educational experiences across generations rather than to biological aging. It is not so much that the old have declined in intelligence but that the young have had the benefit of richer intellectual experiences enabling them to function at a higher level. (p. 734)

No research evidence was cited in support of this claim, but it is probably true that many of the studies examining relations between age and cognitive functioning have confounded age and average amount of education. Lorge (1956) provided one of the clearest descriptions of this potential problem in the following passage:

> In World War I, the correlation between Alpha and the highest school grade reached was 0.65. In World War II, the correlation between AGCT [Army General Classification Test] and highest school grade reached was also about 0.65. Schooling makes for a difference in intelligence test scores. The greater the amount of schooling, the higher the intelligence test performance. It is well known that the older adults in the population have had much less formal schooling than those persons born in the last twenty years. Since there is a positive correlation between schooling and intelligence test score, it must follow that the older members of the population are at some disadvantage not only because of their remoteness from formal schooling but also because they had less of it. (p. 133)

One of the key phrases in the preceding passage is the claim that "Schooling makes for a difference in intelligence test scores." Although this is clearly the interpretation favored by Lorge, it is not the only possible interpretation of the correlation between amount of education and intelligence test score. As most students learn in introductory statistics courses, correlations merely indicate that a relation exists, and by themselves are not informative about the direction of that relation. The ambiguity inherent in correlations between amount of education and level of cognitive functioning has been pointed out numerous times by researchers in aging (Birren & Morrison, 1961; Botwinick, 1978; Heaton, I. Grant, & Matthews, 1986; Salthouse, 1982; Welford, 1985; Willis, 1985). The problem is that, on the one hand, more education could be considered a cause of higher cognitive ability in that additional education may increase intellectual capacity, or maximize the opportunity for individuals to reach their potential. On the other hand, it is also possible that amount of education is at least partly a consequence of level of cognitive ability, because progressively higher levels of cognitive functioning are presumably required to benefit from additional amounts of education. Some of the ambiguity may originate because the same variable—a measure of cognitive ability—is assumed to reflect the beneficial effects of exposure to environmental stimulation in the form of education, and also functions as a selection criterion used to control access to that stimulation.

A basic issue relevant to the role of education and cognitive functioning concerns the exact status of the education variable. Is it analogous to the role of nutrition on physical health, in that it can be assumed to exert a major causal influence? Or is it more like income, which is meaningful in across-time comparisons only after adjusting for inflation? Lorge's (1956) claim that it is a logical necessity that older adults are disadvantaged by a lower average level of education is clearly based on the former, education-as-cause, interpretation. However, only if it is assumed that opportunities to acquire additional education are largely unrelated to cognitive ability would it be reasonable to interpret the education-cognition relation as evidence that amount of education was a major causal factor influencing level of cognitive ability. Green (1969) argued that this was the case until recently in Puerto Rico, but presented no evidence to document this assertion.

The most reasonable position at the current time is probably that there are reciprocal or interactive effects between amount of education and level of cognitive functioning (Blum & Jarvik, 1974; Kesler, N.W. Denney, & Whitely, 1976; Schaie & Willis, 1986; Willis, 1985). Increased educational exposure is likely to maximize the opportunities for an individual to achieve his or her optimum level of functioning by providing a stimulating environment, but because selectivity in admission and promotion policies are likely to favor those with higher cognitive abilities, level of ability can also be assumed to influence the amount of education to which one is exposed.

For the reasons just discussed, the argument that all age differences in cognition are an artifact of educational differences should not be considered as logically necessary. Nevertheless, the possibility that amount of education might influence level of cognitive functioning, together with the historical changes in the proportion of the population pursuing advanced education, clearly could contribute to artifactual age differences in measures of cognitive functioning. It is therefore important to determine the extent to which the potential confounding between age and education is responsible for the observed relations between age and cognition.

What would seem to be the most straightforward method of examining the potential confounding influence of education on the relation between age and cognitive functioning is to restrict the comparisons to individuals with equivalent amounts of education. Unfortunately, there are two complications with this procedure. One is that a year of education may not have had the same meaning at different periods in history because of changes over time in educational quality (Birren, 1959; Birren & Morrison, 1961; Camp, et al., 1989; Granick & Friedman, 1967; Krauss, 1980; R. Lachman, et al., 1982; Matarazzo, 1976; Perlmutter, 1978; Poon, Krauss, & Bowles, 1984; Salthouse, 1982, 1989a; Welford, 1985). If the quality of education has been improving over time, then young adults may be advantaged relative to older adults even when everyone has the same number of years of education. Of course, the opposite might be true if educational quality has been deteriorating over time. Opinions differ drastically on this issue, but there is little empirical evidence available to allow definitive resolution of the controversy about the direction of changes in educational quality.

The second complication of trying to match on quantity of education is that there may have been historical changes in the opportunities to acquire more education. If the attainment of high levels of education was differentially dependent in the past than at the current time on factors such as intellectual ability, motivation, or family income, then adults of different ages will likely vary on important characteristics besides amount of education. This argument was first outlined over 50 years ago (Gilbert, 1935), and is frequently mentioned as a problem with the strategy of matching adults of different ages on the basis of education (Flynn, 1984; Krauss, 1980; R. Lachman, et al., 1982; Salthouse, 1982, 1989a). Because it is generally assumed that there are more opportunities to receive advanced education now than in the past, balancing adults of different ages on educational quantity may result in the sample of older adults being more select or elite relative to their age peers than the sample of young adults.

Although possible differences in educational quality and access to extended education make attempts to control for variations in amount of education problematic, results from analyses attempting to control for differences in education can still be informative. The findings from several studies in which research participants were matched on the basis of years of education, or in which statistical control procedures were used to examine age effects after adjusting for differences in amount of education, have generally been consistent in indicating that age differences are still evident when educational differences are controlled. An early example of this finding was reported by C.C. Miles and W.R. Miles (1932), using the Otis Intelligence Test. The correlations between age and total score were -.39 for adults with 0 to 8 years of education, -.40 for those with 9 to 12 years of education, and -.44 for those with 1 to 10 years of college.

Similar results of nearly equivalent age trends in groups with different amounts of education have been reported in tests such as the PMA (Schaie, 1959), the General Aptitude Test Battery (Droege, et al., 1963; Fozard & Nuttall, 1971; Stein, 1962), the Raven's Progressive Matrices (Guttman, 1981, 1984; F.H. Hooper, et al., 1984; Panek & Stoner, 1980; Slater, 1947), and the Wechsler Scales (Birren & Morrison, 1961; Heaton, et al., 1986; A.S. Kaufman, et al., 1989). As an example, correlations of WAIS subtest scores with age before and after partialling out self-reported years of education, reported by Birren and Morrison (1961), are displayed in Figure 2.13. Notice that adjusting for educational differences in this fashion causes the age trends on several of the verbal tests to become positive rather than negative, but otherwise tends to reduce, and not eliminate, the age relations.

There is one apparent exception to the general pattern of matching on education resulting in similar, but somewhat attenuated, age relationships. This is a study by Green (1969) based on analyses of data from the Spanish-language standardization sample for the WAIS. Much smaller age relations were found when the age groups were balanced for amount of education compared with the age relations apparent in a sample in which the average amount of education decreased with increased age. However, the individuals in Green's samples had very low amounts of formal education, with averages of 8.36 years for ages 25 to 29 and only 3.96 years for ages 55 to 64. The educational effects in his study may therefore have limited generalizability to the higher levels of education typical of most studies comparing adults of different ages. In fact, a recent study by A.S. Kaufman, et al., (1989) found results similar to those of Green (1969) only in the group with 0 to 8 years of education, but not in any groups with more years of education.

It is still not clear whether positive correlations between amount of education and level of cognitive functioning in samples of adults are best interpreted as indicating that education is the cause, or the consequence, of level of cognitive ability. Attempts to adjust for variations in education in the examination of age trends in measures of cognitive performance are also hampered by the possibility of historical changes in the quality of, or access to, education. Despite these complications, the available research seems to suggest that moderate to large relationships exist between age and many measures of cognitive functioning both when adults of different ages

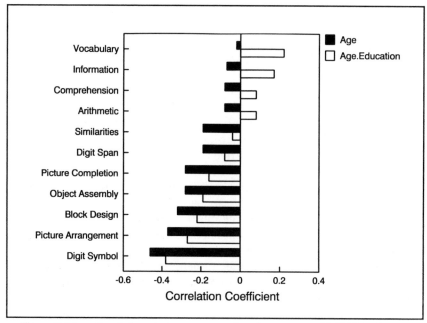

Figure 2.13.   Correlations between age and performance on 11 WAIS subtests before and after statistical control of years of education. Data from Birren and Morrison (1961).

are matched in amount of education, and when statistical control procedures are used to adjust for differences in education. At the present time, therefore, it does not appear that variations in education can account for more than a small proportion of the age differences observed in certain measures of cognitive functioning.

Speed

Over 50 years ago, when some of the first major studies concerned with the relations between age and performance on intellectual tests were being reported, Lorge (1936) claimed that:

> The reported deterioration is more apparent than genuine. It lacks genuineness in the sense that the test used to measure mental ability is not a genuine test of mental power. Contaminating power with speed measurements among older adults obscures the true relationship of intellectual power to age. The inference of mental decline is an unfortunate libel upon adults. (p. 110)

A few years later Goldfarb (1941) suggested that:

> ... while the older adult is not able to work as fast when he grows older, he probably retains almost unimpaired his capacity to solve mental problems of equal difficulty to those he could solve when younger. (p. 66)

A key aspect of these arguments seems to be the notion that older adults perform poorly on some mental tests because the time limits on the tests are too short to allow optimum assessment of mental power in older adults. It is clearly true that many cognitive tests are speeded, in the sense that they are designed so that very few examinees are able to attempt all items. If the rate of perceiving or responding slows down with increased age, then it is possible that at least some of the age-related declines in measures of cognitive functioning may be attributable to largely uninteresting peripheral processes rather than to true declines in cognitive power. In support of this argument are the findings of substantial negative relations between age and measures of clerical-perceptual speed, including the speed of transferring answers to response forms (Bellucci & W.J. Hoyer, 1975; Hertzog, 1989; F.W. Hoyer, W.J. Hoyer, Treat, & P.B. Baltes, 1978-79). Someone who achieved a low score on a speeded test merely because of an inability to write rapidly would probably not be considered intellectually inferior, and consequently it may be unfair to evaluate older adults with speeded tests when they are known to be slower than young adults in aspects of perceptual and motor functioning that seem independent of intellectual power.

While the preceding argument is plausible, it needs to be evaluated in terms of the empirical evidence before concluding that the validity of all reported relations between age and measures of cognitive performance are necessarily threatened. At least three different approaches are available for investigating this peripheral speed interpretation of the age differences in measures of cognitive functioning, but each has problems which either limit the applicability of the procedure, or which complicate the interpretation of results obtained from it.

One procedure is that employed by Lorge (1936). He attempted to separate speed and power contributions by matching adults of different ages on the basis of scores on a power test, and then examining age trends in tests suspected to have varying amounts of speed involvement. Large age differences in the Army Alpha and several other test batteries were still found even when individuals were matched according to performance on another test administered without time limits. This led Lorge to infer that many of the age-related declines reported in measures of cognitive functioning are attributable to uninteresting reductions in the speed with which the individual could work, and not to any real losses in intellectual power.

A weakness of Lorge's (1936) procedure is that cognitive tests vary in terms of their age sensitivity for many reasons, and therefore it cannot be concluded that people matched on the basis of scores on one test were necessarily equivalent in all relevant cognitive abilities. A more desirable procedure, employed in a number of studies, is to examine age trends in the same tests administered under normal and relaxed time limits. Relaxing or removing the time limits should reduce the speeded aspect by allowing all the items to be attempted, but it probably does not otherwise alter the nature of the test.

The major disadvantage of the altered time-limit procedure for removing the influence of peripheral speed processes is that with certain tests, eliminating the time limits may greatly reduce the range of scores. That is, some tests are designed to assess efficiency rather than power, and the items are of such low levels of difficulty that few errors would be made if no time limits were imposed. It is also possible that altering the time limits on a speeded test may reduce the validity of the measures, although this is less of a concern in the present context in which test scores are not being used to predict effectiveness in other situations.

Results from four studies are consistent in revealing that age differences in performance were reduced, but not eliminated, by allowing examinees to work as long as they desired. C.C. Miles (1934) reported this result in a study with the Otis Test; Schaie, F. Rosenthal, and Perlman (1953) with the PMA tests, and Klodin (1976) and Storandt (1977) with various Wechsler tests.

A possible exception to the tendency for age differences to be reduced with extended time limits occurs with the Raven's Progressive Matrices test. Heron and Chown (1967) found very similar age trends with 20-minute and 40-minute administrations, and several researchers have reported large age differences when this test was presented under untimed conditions (H.R. Burke, 1972, 1985; Cerella, DiCara, D. Williams, & Bowles, 1986; W.R. Cunningham, Clayton, & Overton, 1975; Foulds & J.C. Raven, 1948; F.H. Hooper, et al., 1984; Ruth & Birren, 1985).

The third procedure that could be used to determine age-related effects on measures of cognition after removing effects associated with slower perceptual-motor processes consists of attempting to adjust for, or statistically remove, influences of peripheral speed. The assumption is that more accurate estimates of cognitive power will be obtained if the differences associated with the speed of perceiving and responding are eliminated.

The major problem with this procedure is that measures of the speed of even very simple clerical-perceptual processes may reflect the contribution of central or cognitive factors. In fact, although tasks such as comparing numbers and canceling letters seem to involve few cognitive demands, some researchers have interpreted performance on them as reflections of cognitive speed (Hertzog, 1989). The distinction between measures of peripheral or sensory-motor and central or cognitive speed is not yet clear, and the issue is further complicated by the fact that very simple and highly speeded tests are actually included in several intelligence test batteries (e.g., Wechsler Digit Symbol Substitution and PMA Word Fluency).

The uncertainty about whether important aspects of cognition are also being controlled when the contribution of speed of perceptual-motor processes is removed by statistical means necessarily results in a certain amount of ambiguity. Nevertheless, statistical control procedures appear to provide one of the best methods currently available for examining the influence of speed factors on age differences in cognitive performance. One study (Goldfarb, 1941) from which relevant data are available involved the administration of the Wechsler-Bellevue Scale, three choice reaction time tasks, and three paper-and-pencil perceptual speed tests, to 168 adults between 18 and 64 years of age. Reliability of each of the speed measures was high, with estimated reliabilities ranging from .89 to .98. From the published correlations it was possible to compute the partial correlations between age and Wechsler test scores after controlling for reaction time or perceptual speed. The averages of these partial correlations across the three measures of each type of speed, and across males and females, are displayed in Figure 2.14.

The generally similar pattern of correlations with and without control of the speed measures suggests that, at least in these data, many of the age relations are largely independent of age differences in sensory and motor slowing as assessed by perceptual speed and reaction time measures. However, the degree to which age effects are attenuated by control of perceptual speed factors is likely to vary as a function of the nature of the cognitive tests and the measures of perceptual-motor speed. For example, J.W. Clark (1960) administered a battery of tests including the PMA Space and PMA Reasoning tests as well as letter cancellation and reaction time speed tests to 102 adults between 20 and 70 years of age. The correlations between age and PMA Space score were -.42 with no adjustment, -.32 after partialling out letter cancellation speed, and -.19 after partialling out reaction time. The age correlations with PMA Reasoning score were -.49 for the zero-order correlation, -.33 after partialling letter cancellation speed, and -.34 after partialling reaction time.

Schaie (1989c) and Hertzog (1989) recently reported analyses of the relations among age, paper-and-pencil perceptual speed measures, and PMA performance, in considerably larger samples. Both studies found that a sizable proportion of the age differences in the PMA tests could be eliminated by statistical control of measures of perceptual speed. Schaie's (1989c) results are illustrated in Figure 2.15. (The values in this figure are based on corrected data reported by Schaie, 1990a, because there were errors in the data reported in the original article.) Notice that the age relations were actually reversed for the Verbal Meaning, Number, and Word Fluency measures after the influence of perceptual speed was statistically controlled, and that the age effects were also greatly attenuated for the Space and Reasoning measures. A possible reason perceptual-speed factors may be so important in the age relations in these data is that the PMA tests were originally developed for use by adolescents between 11 and 17 years of age, and hence the levels of difficulty may be lower than those in tests designed explicitly for adults (Hertzog, 1989).

The evidence just described is consistent with the idea that some of the lower scores on cognitive tests with increased age are attributable to a slowing down of perceptual and motor processes. There is still considerable controversy about whether the slowing is merely a peripheral factor that limits the expression of one's abilities, or is an intrinsic component or determinant of one's level of cognitive ability. Regardless of the ultimate resolution of this issue, however, substantial age relations are still evident

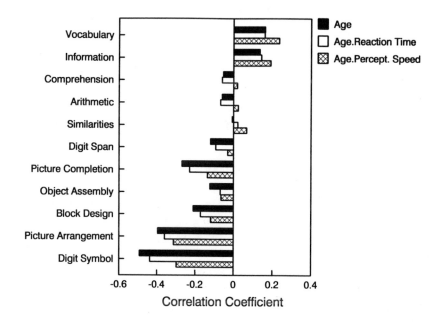

Figure 2.14.   Correlations between age and performance on 11 Wechsler-Bellevue subtests before and after statistical control of reaction time and perceptual speed. Data from Goldfarb (1941).

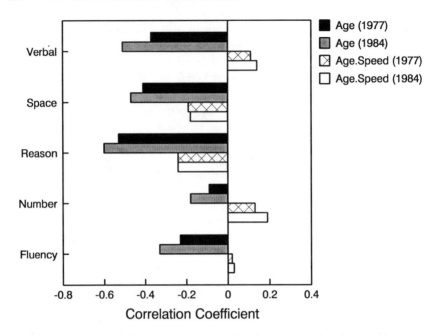

Figure 2.15   Correlations between age and performance on five Primary Mental Abilities subtest before and after statistical control of perceptual speed. Data from Schaie (1983).

in many measures when time limits are removed or attempts are made to eliminate effects associated with variations in perceptual-motor speed. Therefore speed of peripheral perceptual and motor processes is apparently not the only factor responsible for age differences in measures of cognitive performance.

SUMMARY

The purpose of this chapter was to review findings from psychometric tests of intelligence as a means of documenting the phenomena to be explained by theories of cognitive aging. Both the advantages and the disadvantages of relying upon standardized mental tests to examine the relations between age and cognitive functioning were discussed. Although intelligence tests have been quite controversial, many of the issues of contention do not appear relevant to the current focus of attempting to understand the causes for the relations between age and cognitive functioning. As Wechsler (1958) stated:

One may allow that our present tests are not altogether suited for adults and even concede that they do not measure what has been defined as intelligence. But whatever it is that the tests measure, the argument advanced does not controvert the fact that the abilities involved alter with the aging process. (p. 139)

Among the generalizations that appear warranted from the research reviewed in this chapter, and which are in need of explanation by theories of cognitive aging, are the following: (a) Little or no negative effects associated with increased age seem to be evident in most measures of accumulated knowledge or previously acquired information such as several of the Wechsler Verbal tests; (b) age-related declines accounting for 10% to 20% of the total variance, and corresponding to differences between 20-year-olds and 65-year-olds of between .5 to 1.5 young adult standard deviations, are often found with measures of the efficiency of current processing, such as several of the Wechsler Performance tests; (c) age relations vary across different measures of cognitive functioning, with some of the variation perhaps attributable to differences in the type of cognition being assessed, and some of it possibly due to differences in either the amount of processing required or in the importance of speed factors; and (d) although quite plausible arguments can be constructed attributing some or all of the age differences to artifacts related to differential representativeness, health, impact on only a limited segment of the population, education, and perceptual-motor speed, the bulk of the available evidence seems to suggest that these factors are not sufficient to account for all the observed age trends.

3 Environmental Change

... [I]t is frequently more plausible to argue that people of different ages differ on a given characteristic because they belong to a different generation, rather than because they differ in age.
—Schaie (1975, p. 113)

People do not grow older in a vacuum, but in a complex environment that is also changing over time. Because an increase of one year in age is necessarily accompanied by an increment of one year in historical time, and because aspects of the environment relevant to cognitive functioning could change over time, a serious confounding may exist between effects attributable to age-related endogenous changes and effects attributable to exogenous changes in the environment.

A major theoretical perspective in developmental psychology, and particularly in the psychology of adult development, claims that what appear to be consequences of changes originating from within the organism are actually attributable to changes occurring in the external environment. Proponents of this view maintain that many age differences are more appropriately characterized as obsolescence effects induced by rapid environmental change, and are not true reflections of deterioration occurring within the individual (G.V. Labouvie, 1973; Labouvie-Vief, 1976, 1977, 1985; Labouvie-Vief, W.F. Hoyer, M.M. Baltes, & P.B. Baltes, 1974; Schaie, 1974, 1975, 1980a, 1980b, 1984a; Schaie & Labouvie-Vief, 1974; Schaie & Strother, 1968b). That is, it has been argued that older adults appear deficient only relative to younger adults growing up in more recent periods of time, but have not deteriorated in comparison to their own earlier levels of performance.

Although the particular aspects of the environment that might be responsible for time-related changes in cognitive performance are still a matter of speculation, it is beyond dispute that the environment has changed tremendously over the last 50 to 100 years. Changes have been evident in broad dimensions such as health-related practices, attitudes, social roles, economic opportunities, and retirement policies, as well as in

84

very specific measures such as the percentage of single-parent families, and the average number of hours per week spent watching television. As noted in chapter 2, there have also been frequent references to changes in educational practices and/or standards, although the absence of widely-accepted measures of quality and quantity of education has made many of these assertions difficult to document.

In addition to social and cultural changes, environments also change in biological and physical characteristics. For example, approaches to the prevention and cure of medical problems and sensitivity to the importance of balanced nutrition have changed dramatically over the past 50 years, with the consequence that general health and physical well-being are more likely to be maintained until older ages in recent times than in the past. Judging from concerns expressed about reductions in environmental quality due to increased air pollution, water pollution, and noise pollution, these aspects of the environment have also changed over time. Furthermore, every few months new information seems to be released about the growing dangers associated with increasing or decreasing levels of another physical characteristic of the environment such as alar, asbestos, carbon monoxide, dioxin, lead, ozone, radiation, radon, and so on.

Moreover, while it is difficult to predict the effects of single and isolated changes, it is impossible to predict the cumulative effect of many simultaneous changes. Even when changes in certain variables might reasonably be expected to result in positive benefits on cognitive functioning, and others could plausibly be argued to lead to detrimental consequences, the total effect cannot be anticipated when several influences are operating concurrently. J.L. Horn and Donaldson (1980) provided a good example of this problem in a discussion of the difficulty of trying to predict the combined effects on cognitive functioning of two time-related environmental changes: an increase in the average amount of education (which might be expected to contribute to higher levels of functioning), and an increase in the concentration of smog (which might be expected to contribute to lower levels of functioning).

In light of the extremely large number of environmental characteristics undergoing change, and the very small amount of knowledge currently available about determinants of cognitive functioning, it is impossible on a priori grounds to dismiss the potential contributions of exogenous, environmental changes on the relation between age and measures of cognitive functioning. The focus in this chapter will therefore be on the examination of research relevant to what will be termed the changing-environment perspective of cognitive aging. The two major goals will be: (a) to evaluate evidence concerning the possibility that changes in the environment contribute to age differences in cognitive functioning, and (b) to assess the importance of influences of this type relative to influences that might originate from within the individual.

TIME-LAG COMPARISONS

A first step in investigating the environmental change perspective is to determine whether relatively short-term (i.e., occurring within an interval of less than 50 years) changes in the biophysical or sociocultural environment do, in fact, influence level of cognitive performance. Perhaps the simplest method of determining the consequences on cognitive functioning of changes in the external environment is to examine measures of cognitive performance as a function of the time of measurement among individuals within a limited range of ages. This strategy of comparing same-age individuals at different points in time is illustrated in Figure 3.1. Note that each diagonal line represents people born in a different year, and that

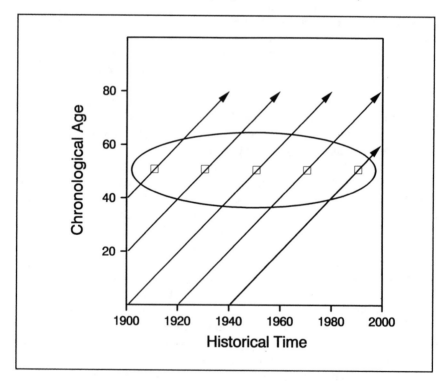

Figure 3.1.   Schematic illustration of time-lag comparisons (circled squares) when chronological age is increasing with historical time (i.e., people are represented by diagonal lines).

the horizontal slice corresponds to people of the same age at different points in historical time. If time-related changes in the environment do affect level of cognitive functioning, comparisons of the performance of people of equivalent ages who are assessed at different points in time should reveal systematic effects of the time at which the measurement occurs.

The value of these kinds of time-lag comparisons for the interpretation of age differences was illustrated by Borkan, Hults, and R.J. Glynn (1983) with the measure of physical stature or height. Borkan, et al. found adults in their 20s to be taller than adults in their 70s, a phenomenon often attributed to compression and atrophy of the disks in the spinal column. By obtaining height measurements at two different periods separated by an interval of 10 years, it was then possible to determine that people of the same age, but born (and measured) 10 years later, were taller than their predecessors. Borkan, et al. therefore inferred that a sizable proportion of the age-related height difference found in cross-sectional comparisons may be due to changes in exogenous, environmental, factors such as improvements in nutrition and health care.

The Borkan, et al. study is interesting because it not only provides a model of the type of informative outcome possible from time-lag analyses, but it also serves to emphasize the point, discussed in chapter 1, that it is not always meaningful to attempt to distinguish between biological and environmental determinants of development. That is, the presumed cause of an observed developmental phenomenon may be intrinsic (endogenous) or extrinsic (exogenous), but it is necessarily represented biologically. An individual's height is obviously a biological characteristic, but the Borkan, et al. results suggest that it may be influenced by both endogenous (i.e., maturational) and exogenous factors (in this case, probably related to changing patterns of nutrition).

Several informal time-lag comparisons have been discussed in the domain of cognitive functioning. For example, Kausler (1982, 1985) suggested that time-lag effects may be relatively small because measurements of perceptual span, memory span, and reaction time have yielded similar absolute values over the approximately 100 years in which systematic psychological research has been conducted. The representativeness of the subject populations in these different periods is not known, however, and few, if any of the studies involved identical stimulus materials and procedures. Furthermore, in none of the studies were there direct statistical comparisons of the level of performance across the different times of measurement. It is probably prudent, therefore, not to attempt to reach a conclusion on the basis of these informal and unsystematic observations. Fortunately, several relatively well-controlled studies with direct comparisons across a range of time periods have been reported. These results will be discussed in the context of the specific tests used to assess cognitive functioning.

Army Alpha

One of the earliest of the major time-lag studies involving adults was reported by Tuddenham (1948), who compared the scores on the Army Alpha of 768 enlisted soldiers tested in 1944, during World War II, with the scores of 48,102 enlisted soldiers tested in World War I. Although the number of soldiers tested in World War II was much smaller than that tested in World War I, special sampling procedures were used to ensure that the participants were representative of the total pool of inductees. The result of primary interest from this study was that the World War II soldiers achieved much higher scores than the World War I soldiers. Median performance of the soldiers in 1944 was equivalent to performance at the 83rd percentile of the scores from the 1918 examinees, and the median score in World War I soldiers corresponded to the 22nd percentile of the scores from World War II. Assuming that the scores were normally distributed, these results lead to estimates that the soldiers in 1944 performed an average of about .96 standard deviations higher than the soldiers in 1918. The apparent increase in measured intelligence due to time-lag effects is therefore .037 standard deviation units per year.

Although at first glance these results appear reasonably convincing, several characteristics of the Tuddenham study raise questions about whether the time-lag differences may have been spurious. For example, the two samples may not have been equally representative of the respective populations at the time of testing because, as mentioned in chapter 2, there could have been an under-representation of higher levels of ability among soldiers in World War I. In addition, the version of the Army Alpha administered in World War II was slightly different from that used in World War I; Tuddenham himself pointed out that this may have resulted in somewhat higher scores among the 1944 examinees. Conditions of testing probably also differed in the two situations because the World War I testing was almost certainly less organized and more chaotic than that in World War II because neither the examinees nor the examiners could have had much prior experience with group-administered tests during those initial assessments. Finally, the soldiers in World War II had recently taken a similar test battery—the Army General Classification Test—and hence, they had recent practice with a group-administered intelligence test before taking the Army Alpha. Each of these differences could have contributed to higher levels of performance among the individuals in the World War II sample, and thus at least some of the observed time-lag difference may be due to factors other than changes in the external environment.

Fortunately for the sake of resolving ambiguity, two later studies using the Army Alpha have reported qualitatively similar, albeit somewhat smaller, time-lag improvements in cognitive performance (W.R. Cunningham & Birren, 1976; Owens, 1966). The study by Owens (1966) consisted of a comparison of the scores of 96 male college freshmen tested in 1919 with the scores of 101 male college freshmen tested in 1961. Examinees in 1961 performed an average of .44 standard deviation units higher than those in 1919, yielding an estimated annual gain of .010 standard deviation units over the 42-year period. An additional feature of the Owens study was that the time-lag effects were reported for each subtest. The time-related effects varied substantially across subtests, with minimal gains and even losses for the Antonym-Synonym subtest (.00), the General Information subtest (-.03), and the Arithmetic subtest (-.31), but sizable gains for the Series Completion (.63) and Analogies (.90) reasoning tests.

W.R. Cunningham and Birren (1976) compared the scores of 32 college undergraduates tested in 1944 with those of 32 college undergraduates tested in 1972. Performance was higher in the 1972 testing, with an increase of about .5 standard deviations for a verbal factor identified in a factor analysis and an increase of about 1.0 standard deviations for a number factor.

Wechsler Scales

The Wechsler intelligence tests have undergone several revisions since their original introduction, and consequently few time-lag comparisons are available in which the identical test was administered to people of the same age at different points in time. However, indirect inferences about time-related performance improvements are still possible because several studies have been reported in which the same individuals were administered both the old and new versions of the tests.

The logic of these comparisons is based on the following assumptions: (a) The samples used to provide the norms for each test are representative of the general population; (b) the distribution of scores in both samples is normal, with known means and standard deviations; and (c) both tests are assessing the same general construct(s). Given these assumptions, the individuals taking both tests can be used as a basis for calibrating the scores of one normative group in terms of the scores of the other normative group. As an example, Wechsler (1981) reported that 72 adults between 35 and 44 years of age received an average IQ of 111.3 on the WAIS, but an average IQ of 103.8 on the WAIS-R. This difference leads to the inference that intellectual ability within the population increased from 1953-1954 (WAIS standardization) to 1978 (WAIS-R standardization) by about 7.5 IQ points, or .5 standard deviation units, given that the standard deviation of IQ scores is fixed at 15.

After various adjustments for differences in sample variances, biases in samples, and aggregation across several studies, Flynn (1984) used these types of comparisons to estimate that there has been an annual increase in the U.S. population over the last 40 to 50 years of about .333 IQ points, or .022 standard deviation units. Roughly similar estimates of annual gains of .25 IQ points, or .017 standard deviation units, were derived by K.C. Parker (1986) on the basis of slightly different analyses and results from a different combination of published studies.

Parker (1986) also claimed that the time-lag improvements were greater for adults than for adolescents, and suggested that this might account for the apparent tendency for the peak performance to occur at later ages in more recent revisions of the Wechsler tests. However, Parker's evidence for age-differential time-lag effects does not appear very compelling because his comparisons were based on a very restricted range of ages (i.e., 15-17 for adolescents and 17-44 for adults). Furthermore, Flynn (1984) has reported, in direct contradiction to Parker's claim, that the estimated time-lag gains were of comparable magnitude for children, teen-agers, and adults.

Primary Mental Abilities

Some of the most detailed information about time-lag effects comes from Schaie's Seattle Longitudinal Study (Schaie, 1983, 1988). The same five subtests of the Primary Mental Abilities were administered to both new and old participants on five occasions between 1956 and 1984. Because the T-score values for the 3,442 first-time participants have been reported by Schaie (1988, Table 8.1), it is possible to use this information to plot the scores of participants within a given range of ages as a function of the year in which they were first tested. (It should be noted that the scores have been scaled to T-scores on the basis of the total sample of 3,442 individuals, and not with respect to the distribution of scores at the first time of measurement for individuals within a limited age range. The estimates of the magnitude of time-lag effects are therefore likely to be attenuated relative to those reported in other comparisons discussed in this section because the standard deviation from the total sample incorporates across-age, across-time, and within-time variability, and not simply within-time variability as in the other comparisons.)

Figure 3.2 illustrates the time-lag functions from 1956 to 1984 at age 25, 46, and 67 for each of the five Primary Mental Ability subtests. Notice that most of the functions have a positive trend, with an average annual gain across all the displayed data of .07 T-score units. It is also apparent in

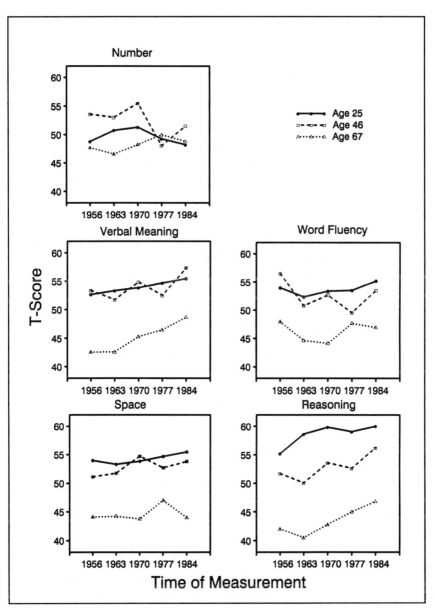

Figure 3.2. Time-lag relations for the five Primary Mental Abilities subtests at three ages. Data from Schaie (1983).

Figure 3.2 that the positive time-lag gains are much greater for the Reasoning subtest than for the Number subtest, a pattern consistent with that reported by Owens (1966) in his analysis of time-lag effects on the Army Alpha.

Raven's Progressive Matrices

Very convincing evidence for positive time-lag effects with the Raven's Progressive Matrices test has been presented by Flynn (1987), using data compiled from records of military draft examinations in The Netherlands, Belgium, France, and Norway. In each case, the samples were large and quite representative because they consisted of over 75% of the relevant population of male 18- or 19-year-olds. The data from The Netherlands spanned a 30-year period, with scores from 65,363 individuals in 1952, and 57,897 individuals in 1982. One measure of performance in these two samples was the percentage of examinees answering more than 24 of the 40 items correct. This value was 31.2% in 1952, and 82.2% in 1982. Assuming that the performance distributions are approximately normal and have similar variances, one can infer that the scores increased about 1.41 standard deviation units over the 30-year interval, for an annual gain of approximately .047 standard deviation units.

The data from Belgium were based on 45,700 individuals tested in 1958, and 56,700 individuals tested in 1967. Scores were reported separately for French-speaking and Dutch-speaking examinees, but similar time-lag improvements of .43 and .52 standard deviation units were found across the nine-year interval for both comparisons. The corresponding annual gains are therefore .048 and .058 standard deviation units.

Data from France were obtained in 1949 and 1974, with the 50th percentile score in 1949 found to correspond to the 5th percentile of the scores in 1974. This represents an increase of about 1.67 standard deviation units over 25 years, or an estimated annual gain of .067 standard deviation units. The Norwegian data were collected in 1954 and 1980, with the latter scores approximately .76 standard deviation units higher than the former, or an estimated annual gain of .029 standard deviation units.

Summary

Most of the results just described are consistent in revealing systematically higher levels of intellectual performance at more recent times of testing. The estimated gains across a 40-year interval average about 2.8 T-score units in the PMA data, and range from .4 to as much as 2.8 standard deviation units for the other measures. Effects on cognitive performance associated with time-related changes in the environment therefore appear to be substantial, and clearly lend credibility to Flynn's (1984) suggestion that "Allowing for obsolescence in intelligence testing is just as essential as allowing for inflation in economic analysis" (p. 44).

What is Responsible for Time-Lag Effects?

The factors contributing to the time-lag effects on cognitive functioning have not been isolated, but several categories of interpretation have received serious consideration. For example, one possibility is that the increases in cognitive performance are not actually attributable to environmental changes, but are due to genetic improvements in the tested population across the interval between successive measurements. This interpretation was advanced as a partial explanation for time-related improvements in measures of intelligence observed in Japan on the theory that increased rural-to-urban migration and more extensive intermarriage may have contributed to greater genetic diversity (A.M. Anderson, 1982). Average levels of intelligence might also increase for genetic reasons if fertility rates were greatest among individuals at the highest levels of ability. However, genetic changes seem unlikely as a viable explanation for most of the time-lag effects reported above because of the short intervals within which the changes would have to have occurred, the apparent stability of many of the populations, and the absence of convincing evidence of a positive relation between level of intelligence and number of offspring.

A second conceivable interpretation of time-lag effects is that they are produced by progressive changes in either the representativeness of the samples, or in the procedures used in the administration or scoring of the cognitive assessments. One example of a potential time-by-representativeness bias was mentioned by McCrae, et al., (1987) in describing changes in recruitment criteria for a multiple-entry longitudinal study that resulted in positively-biased early participants. Very misleading conclusions could have resulted had time-lag comparisons been conducted in this project because of the progressive selection bias. Progressive instrumentation changes are often difficult for people not associated with the project to detect, but Schaie (1983; Schaie & Hertzog, 1985, 1986) has suggested that factors related to instrumentation changes may have contributed to some of the time-lag effects observed in the Seattle Longitudinal Study. Although these factors are potentially powerful, it seems unlikely that they were operating, and in a consistently positive direction, in each of the comparisons described.

Another explanation for time-related improvements in cognitive performance that appears unlikely is that the increases are simply attributable to a greater accumulation of factual knowledge. While it is intuitively plausible that many of the time-related gains might be associated with increases in learned content or general knowledge, the sizable time-lag effects in the Raven's Progressive Matrices scores indicate that many of the gains have occurred in measures of abstract problem solving ability. The data of Owens (1966) and Schaie (1988) also indicate that time-lag gains were as great or greater for fluid or process tests of spatial and reasoning ability as for crystallized or product tests of vocabulary, general information, and numerical skills. Furthermore, Flynn (1987) actually reported smaller time-lag effects for measures of learned content than for measures of abstract problem solving, and he claimed that a similar pattern was evident in data from the Wechsler tests: he estimated that time-lag gains were about twice as large for the scores on Performance tests as for the scores on Verbal tests. This same pattern is also evident in the time-lag research reviewed by Lynn and Hampson (1986). If anything, therefore, the evidence seems to suggest that, contrary to a number of speculations (Cattell, 1972; J.L. Horn & Donaldson, 1976; H.E. Jones & Conrad, 1933; Kausler, 1982), later generations are achieving higher scores because of superior levels of abstract reasoning, not because of a greater accumulation of factual information.

It could be argued that acquired knowledge is still involved in the time-lag improvements in measures of fluid or process abilities, but that the knowledge is abstract and procedural rather than specific and factual. The primary difficulty with this argument is that the nature of the knowledge that would allow one to perform better on a wide variety of tests of fluid or process aspects of cognition has not yet been specified in enough detail to allow this speculation to be empirically investigated.

One of the most frequently mentioned hypotheses proposed to account for time-related improvements in measures of cognitive ability attributes them to changes in educational practices. For example, Tuddenham (1948) pointed out that there were moderate to large correlations between years of education and Army Alpha score in both the World War II and World War I samples, and that the average number of years of education in the 1918 sample was 8 while that in the 1943 sample was 10. After adjusting for this difference in average amount of education, Tuddenham reported that about half of the time-lag difference was eliminated. He also suggested that all the difference might have been accounted for if it had also been possible to adjust for increases in length of the school year, improvements in facilities, and better preparation of teachers.

Changes in the nature, as well as in the quantity, of instruction would also have to have occurred in order to account for the pattern in which time-lag improvements are apparently greater for measures of abstract reasoning than for measures of general knowledge. Very little evidence is available to document this speculation, but several researchers (P.B. Baltes

& Schaie, 1974; Botwinick, 1967; Rabinowitz, Ackerman, Craik, & Hinchley, 1982; Schaie & Zelinski, 1979) have claimed that, relative to earlier times, schools currently emphasize abstraction, generalization, and inferential reasoning to a greater extent, and rote memorization to a lesser extent. (An interesting implication of this argument, for which there is apparently no positive evidence, is that if there are lasting effects of these early educational experiences, then older adults exposed to previous pedagogical practices might be expected to perform better than young adults on tasks requiring rote memorization.)

Evidence interpreted as consistent with an educational influence is the finding by Teasdale and Owen (1989) that the time-lag improvements in intelligence performance among Danish draftees have primarily been in the lower regions of the distribution of intelligence. That is, scores at the 10th and 25th percentiles increased substantially from the 1950s to the 1980s, but very little shift occurred in scores at the 90th percentile. The authors claimed that because educational changes over this interval largely benefitted the least able individuals, most of the time-lag gains, and particularly the differentially greater gains at lower ability levels, were attributable to historical changes in educational practices. However, this conclusion should be considered tentative because a more complex pattern was reported by Lynn and Hampson (1986). These investigators found that the time-lag gains were greater for individuals in the lower portion of the distribution for children between 11 and 15 years of age, but were greater for individuals in the higher portion of the distribution for children between 6 and 11 years of age.

Although the idea that changes in educational practices are responsible for many time-lag effects is plausible in many respects, one rather fundamental expectation from the educational interpretation of time-lag improvements has apparently failed to receive empirical support. This is the assumption that if time-lag improvements are attributable to changes in educational practices, then the magnitude of the time-lag effects should become progressively larger as cumulative exposure to the educational system increases. In other words, time-lag improvements should be very small for young children who are just beginning formal schooling, but should increase as one spends more time in the improved educational system. The consequences of educational improvements might therefore be expected to be proportional to the length of time the individuals were exposed to the educational system, with the magnitude of the time-lag effects increasing continuously from about age 6 to about age 20. No such trend was evident in the results reported by Flynn (1984, 1987). Instead, Flynn's analyses suggest that the time-lag effects are roughly uniform in magnitude from about age 2 to at least middle adulthood. Other researchers have also reported sizable positive time-lag effects in children between 9 and 13 years of age (Emanuelsson & Svensson, 1986; Lynn & Hampson, 1986; Lynn, Hampson, & Mullineux, 1987), and thus it appears that the relevant environmental changes are either operating in the period before the start of formal schooling, or during the very early school years.

One rather dramatic exception to the positive time-lag effects with measures of intellectual ability is the well-publicized decline in Scholastic Aptitude Test (SAT) scores that occurred in the United States between about 1963 and 1981. These negative time-lag effects raise obvious questions about the reliability and meaning of the positive time-lag effects evident in other tests of intellectual abilities. The reasons for this discrepancy between increases in intelligence test scores and decreases in SAT scores are not yet known, but Flynn (1984) has offered an interesting speculation. His basic assumption was that the SAT primarily reflects academic achievement rather than intellectual ability. He suggested that the positive time-lag effects on intelligence tests were due to increases over time in intellectual ability, while the negative time-lag effects on the SAT reflected decreases in non-intellectual factors such as motivation, study habits, and self-discipline. Flynn elaborated on these ideas (Flynn, 1987) by emphasizing a distinction between abstract problem solving ability and acquired knowledge, suggesting that the former can be assumed to be measured by many intelligence tests, and can be postulated to have increased over the years, whereas the latter is presumed to be assessed in the SAT, and seems to have decreased over time.

Many other factors are also still viable as potential determinants of time-lag improvements in cognitive functioning. For example, temporal changes in test sophistication, nutrition, public health practices, and general cultural stimulation by means of television, books, educational toys and games, magazines, and newspapers, might all be expected to result in higher levels of cognitive performance at more recent times of testing. It is possible that the relative importance of at least some of these factors to the time-lag effects in cognitive performance might be determined by contrasting the magnitude of the time-lag effects on different kinds of variables. As an example, Teasdale and Owen (1989) examined the time-lag effects on measures of intelligence, and on measures of height. They found that the increase in physical height has slowed in recent years, but that the increase in measured intelligence has continued. Teasdale and Owen therefore argued that although nutritional factors, which were presumably responsible for the increase in height, may have contributed to some of the time-lag effects in intelligence, they are probably not responsible for all of them.

Much more research with an analytical focus is clearly desirable in order to make it possible to specify the exact source of the environmental change effects manifested in higher levels of performance across successive times of measurement. Regardless of the specific causes, however, the evidence from the available time-lag studies clearly indicates that performance on many of the variables of interest to cognitive psychologists has increased systematically across historical time. It seems highly likely, therefore, that changes in various aspects of the external environment can influence the level of performance on cognitive tests, and thus environmental change must be seriously considered as a possible cause of at least some of the observed age differences in cognitive functioning.

IMPLICATIONS OF TIME-LAG EFFECTS

Acceptance of the conclusion that performance on intellectual tests has increased systematically over the past 40 to 50 years for same-aged individuals raises two issues of fundamental importance for interpretations of cognitive aging phenomena. These are: (a) whether the generalizability of age differences in cognitive functioning is necessarily limited to the particular time, and environmental conditions, in effect when the measurements were obtained; and (b) whether the validity of age comparisons of cognitive performance is seriously jeopardized because of confoundings between age and specific environmental conditions.

It is clear that the existence of substantial time-lag effects threatens the generalizability of *absolute* levels of performance to different measurement periods. However, despite the assertions of some authors (P.B. Baltes & G.V. Labouvie, 1973; P.B. Baltes & Schaie, 1976; P.B. Baltes & Willis, 1979; Flynn, 1987; Perlmutter & List, 1982; J. Raven & Court, 1989; Schaie, 1965, 1967, 1980a, 1980b; Willis & P.B. Baltes, 1980), it is not obvious that generalizability of *relative* differences is also limited. That is, similar patterns of age differences may or may not be found when performance on cognitive tests is improving over time. As will be demonstrated later, this question depends upon the status of a number of additional assumptions, and is not a logical necessity, as sometimes implied.

Actually, the consistency with which age trends have been reported across different temporal intervals and cultural contexts allows a relatively powerful case to be made that the presence of environmental change does not limit the generalizability of age comparisons in cognitive performance. The brief historical review in chapter 2 indicated that roughly similar patterns of age-related cognitive differences have been found over a period of almost 70 years (i.e., 1920 to 1990). Although the range of cultural contexts is not great, age differences similar to those reported from studies in the United States, Canada, and Great Britain have been reported in studies conducted in China (data by Zhang reported in J. Raven & Court, 1989), Columbia (Ardila & Rosselli, 1989), France (Pacaud & Welford, 1989), Germany (K.F. Riegel, R.M. Riegel, & G. Meyer, 1967), India (Ramalingaswami, 1975), Israel (Guttman, 1981, 1984), The Netherlands

(Dirken, 1972; Verhage, 1965), Puerto Rico (Green, 1969), and Sweden (Helander, 1967). The discovery that comparable patterns of age differences in cognitive performance have been reported despite a moderate variety of biophysical and sociocultural environmental conditions therefore suggests that these patterns are not restricted to a very narrow range of environmental characteristics.

The issue of the validity of age comparisons in light of established positive time-lag effects is quite complex, and depends both on the type of research design used to make age comparisons, and on the nature of the impact of the environmental changes. It is therefore appropriate to consider this issue in the context of a discussion of differences between cross-sectional and longitudinal designs.

Cross-Sectional and Longitudinal Designs

It is often implied that a major reason for discrepancies between cross-sectional and longitudinal studies is the existence of factors related to environmental change, and hence that comparisons of results from cross-sectional and longitudinal designs would be informative about the contribution of environmental change effects. For example, Blum, Jarvik, and E.T. Clark (1970), Kleemeier (1962), Krauss (1980), Perlmutter (1988), and Rabbitt (1983) have all implied that results from cross-sectional designs confound age and environmental change effects, but that results from longitudinal designs can be interpreted as representing relatively pure age effects. The situation is not that simple, however, as revealed by careful consideration of Figure 3.3.

It should be clear from this figure that because increases in age are associated with increments in historical time, any age comparison (vertical axis) necessarily involves different amounts of exposure to a potentially changing environment (horizontal axis). Whether the contrasts are longitudinal and comprised of different points along the same diagonal line (representing people born in a given year), or are cross-sectional and based on points at the same period in time from different diagonals (representing different people at different ages), increased age (vertical axis) is inevitably associated with increased environmental exposure (horizontal axis). Both designs are therefore "contaminated" by positive associations between age and cumulative exposure to an environment that may be changing in important respects.

Because results from both types of research designs can be influenced by time-lag effects, the consequences of time-lag effects in either cross-sectional or longitudinal studies can be predicted only if one is willing to make several important assumptions. Particular combinations of these assumptions can be considered as corresponding to distinct models of the

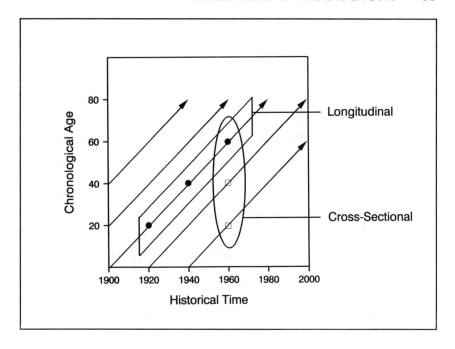

Figure 3.3.   Schematic illustration of how both longitudinal and cross-sectional comparisons involve a confounding between increasing age (vertical axis) and elapsed time during which the environment could be changing (horizontal axis).

nature of environmental change. In the following discussion, three prototypical models will be differentiated on the basis of their assumptions about the age of greatest susceptibility to relevant aspects of environmental change, and about the existence, and relative position, of an asymptote on the effects of environmental change. For the sake of simplicity, it will be assumed in describing the models that there are *no* endogenous or maturational influences on performance, and that the relevant aspects of the environment are in a steady state of continuous change in the direction leading to improved levels of cognitive functioning. All the relations between age and performance in the models to be discussed are therefore due to exogenous changes in the environment, and not to any endogenous changes originating within the individual.

Model 1 postulates that environmental change factors have their greatest impact in the childhood years, and that there is a relatively early asymptote on the effects of these factors. This model is consistent with speculations that it is the early years of life, and especially the period of formal schooling, when changes in the environment are likely to have the maximum influence (Anastasi, 1958; Fozard & J.C. Thomas, 1975;

Welford, 1958). Kuhlen (1963) provided one of the most extensive arguments for why children would be expected to exhibit the greatest susceptibility to environmental changes. His reasoning was as follows:

> ... [A]t least in the American culture, there are massive efforts to transmit the culture to the young through formal education. Thus, the young get the quick advantages of new advances in knowledge ... [and] ... older people, as compared with younger, tend not to experience so directly the impact of cultural change ... because of reduced need or motivation to learn (reflecting the decreased demand of the culture that they learn), ... because of pressure of the work-a-day world, which denies the adult opportunities to interact with his broader environment, and ... because of the tendency of older persons to insulate themselves psychologically from new features of their environment. (pp. 118-119)

The expected relations between age and performance given the assumptions of Model 1 are illustrated in Figure 3.4. Panel A in this figure indicates that the time lag effects are assumed to be greatest during the childhood years, represented here at age 10, with little or no systematic effects during the adult years. The three functions in panel B illustrate the consequences of this pattern of time lag effects for individuals born in three different years, with their age at the time of measurement indicated by the filled circles. Notice that because the time lag effects are positive, later-born individuals are expected to achieve successively higher asymptotic levels of performance. The assumption that the environmental change effects are concentrated in the childhood years means that no further influence of environmental change will be experienced once adulthood is reached, and hence cognitive performance will remain stable at the asymptotic level throughout the adult years. As indicated in panel C, these assumptions imply that there will be no relation between adult age and performance when using a longitudinal design, but that increased age will be associated with a decrease in performance when a cross-sectional design is used. According to Model 1, then, the results of cross-sectional studies will be misleading with respect to the relation between performance and intrinsic or endogenous determinants of development across the adult years.

Model 2 is based on the assumption there are no asymptotes on the effects of environmental change and that, perhaps because of a lifetime accumulation of effects, the consequences of environmental change are greatest in the later adult years. This perspective has been favored by numerous investigators (P.B. Baltes & Reese, 1984; Barton, Plemons, Willis, & P.B. Baltes, 1975; Flavell, 1970; Kausler, 1982; Schaie, 1984a, 1986), apparently in part because of a belief that maturational factors dominate as determinants of early development, and hence environmental

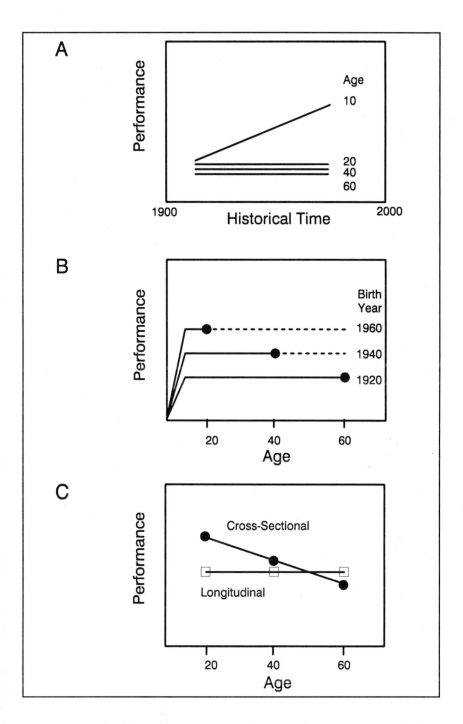

Figure 3.4   Illustration of assumptions of Model 1 concerning time-lag effects at different ages (Panel A), projected patterns of performance at each age (Panel B), and expected trends in cross-sectional and longitudinal comparisons (Panel C).

101

factors are likely to make their greatest relative contribution in the period of later development. What appear to be functionally equivalent models were discussed by P.B. Baltes (1968) and Willis (1985). P.B. Baltes' (1968) model, which was actually a hypothetical example used to illustrate an argument, was based on the suggestion that time-related gains accelerate from generation to generation, thereby resulting in the greatest generational differences, and hence the largest time-lag differences, in the period of late adulthood. Willis' (1985) proposal was somewhat more complex in that she suggested that "Although these effects probably originate in childhood, their consequences are probably most debilitating in old age" (p. 827). However because one can only be certain that effects exist at the point at which they are observed, the predictions from her interpretation appear indistinguishable from those based on a model assuming that late adulthood is the period in which both the manifestations of, and also the susceptibility to, environmental changes are greatest.

Expectations concerning age-performance relations based on the assumptions of Model 2 are illustrated in Figure 3.5. As in Figure 3.4, panel A portrays the assumptions concerning time-lag effects; in this case they are that the time-lag effects are greater at older ages. The consequences of progressively increasing time-lag effects for individuals born in three different years are represented in panel B, with their ages at the time of measurement indicated by the filled circles. It can be seen that, consistent with the pattern of time-lag effects in panel A, the differences between the three individuals would have been smallest had it been possible to measure them all in early adulthood, and would have been largest had it been possible to measure them all in late adulthood. The nature of the results from a cross-sectional assessment depend upon the specific parameters of the positively accelerating functions relating age to performance, but one potential outcome is represented in panel C. Notice there are age-related increases with a longitudinal design, and increases followed by decreases with a cross-sectional design. If the assumptions of Model 2 are valid, therefore, the influence on developmental trends of exogenous changes in the environment may be greater, and more systematic, with longitudinal assessments than with cross-sectional assessments.

Although Models 1 and 2 have received the most discussion in the developmental literature, the simplest model may be that in which the effects of environmental change are assumed to be equivalent in magnitude throughout most of the lifespan. A model of this type seems to have been implicit (and sometimes explicit, e.g., Schaie & Strother, 1968b, 1968c) when Schaie (1970; 1988; Schaie, G.V. Labouvie, & Buech, 1973; Schaie & Labouvie-Vief, 1974; Schaie & Strother, 1968b, 1968c) constructed composite longitudinal gradients by sequencing together longitudinal

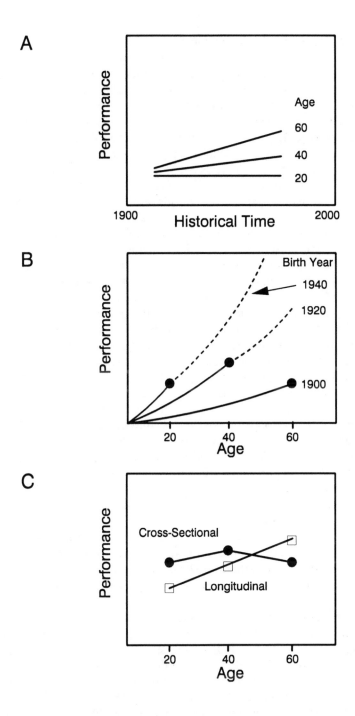

Figure 3.5.   Illustration of assumptions of Model 2 concerning time-lag effects at different ages (Panel A), projected patterns of performance at each age (Panel B), and expected trends in cross-sectional and longitudinal comparisons (Panel C).

103

changes derived from different ages to produce a single function. That is, only if one assumed that the time-lag effects were comparable at different ages would it be meaningful to link time-related changes obtained from people of different ages together as a unified representation of within-individual change. If the time-lag effects were not equivalent across the age range of interest then the value of these composite gradients would be quite limited because the age axis could not be interpreted as reflecting a constant mixture of endogenous and exogenous determinants. Age-performance relations expected from this model, Model 3, are illustrated in Figure 3.6.

The assumption that the time-lag effects are equivalent throughout the adult years is represented by parallel functions relating performance to historical time in panel A. Because when the rate of change is constant the consequence of the change is a linear function of the duration of exposure, the functions in panel B indicate that performance would be expected to be directly related to the number of years the individual has experienced the changing environment. The predicted pattern of age relations under the assumptions of Model 3 are illustrated in panel C. Note that these assumptions lead to the expectations that increased age will be associated with progressively higher levels of performance with both cross-sectional and longitudinal assessments. Positive relations between age and performance, even in the absence of any intrinsic or endogenous determinants of development, would therefore be evident in both types of assessments if the assumptions of Model 3 are valid.

Many other models could obviously be imagined with different combinations of assumptions, but the three described above suffice to illustrate the range of potential distortions of age trends that could be produced by the existence of positive time-lag effects. It should be emphasized again that all the predictions were derived with the assumption of no intrinsic or endogenous effects, and thus the patterns in Figures 3.4 through 3.6 will be superimposed on any intrinsic or maturational effects that might exist. They can therefore be interpreted as representing possible exogenous (environmental change) confounds of endogenous (maturational) effects.

One means of discriminating among the models just described is on the basis of the relative magnitudes of the time-lag effects at different ages in adulthood. That is, Model 1 postulates that the effects should be approximately zero for all ages once maturity is reached, Model 2 postulates that the effects should increase more or less monotonically with increased age, and Model 3 assumes that positive time-lag effects of comparable magnitude would be evident at all ages.

As noted earlier, Flynn (1984, 1987) has suggested that the time-lag effects appear to be invariant across a wide range of ages in both childhood

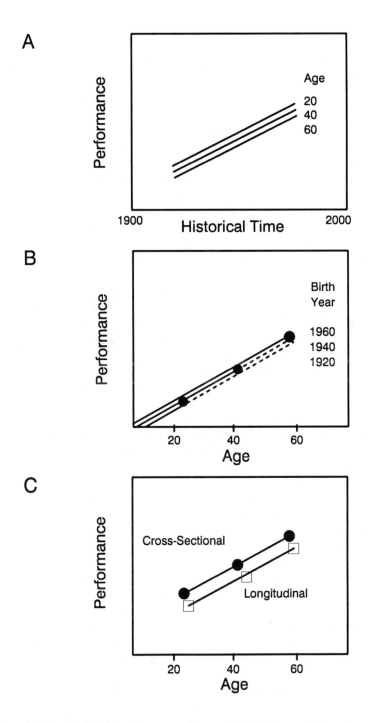

Figure 3.6.   Illustration of assumptions of Model 3 concerning time-lag effects at different ages (Panel A), projected patterns of performance at each age (Panel B), and expected trends in cross-sectional and longitudinal comparisons (Panel C).

105

and adulthood. Quantitatively similar time-lag effects for adults between the 20s and the 70s have been reported by Arenberg for measures of problem solving (Arenberg, 1982a) and visual memory (Arenberg, 1982b). The PMA data of Schaie, illustrated in Figure 3.2, also seem consistent with the view that time-lag effects are roughly equivalent in magnitude across much of the adult life span. However, the Arenberg and Schaie data reveal there is considerable variability in the time-lag effects, both across and within age groups. It is therefore possible that there are systematic relations between age and the magnitude of time-lag effects, but that those relations have been difficult to detect because they are obscured by large variability. Although this possibility cannot be dismissed, most of the currently available results suggest there are little or no age differences in the susceptibility to time-lag influences, and thus the data appear more consistent with Model 3 than with either Models 1 or 2.

The conclusion that Model 3 may be the most plausible of the models discussed leads to a rather surprising implication. This is that because both cross-sectional and longitudinal research designs result in age-related increases in performance under the assumptions of this model, any detrimental effects associated with endogenous maturational factors may be *underestimated* and *not overestimated* by both data collection procedures. That is, contrary to the suggestions of many previous authors (M.S. Albert, 1988; Schaie, 1979, 1988; Schaie & Hertzog, 1983; Schaie & Labouvie-Vief, 1974; Schaie & Strother, 1968b, 1968c), the existence of substantial environmental change effects operating in a positive direction, if they are cumulative and operating to an equivalent extent throughout the life span, seems likely to minimize rather than to exaggerate the contributions of maturational or endogenous influences. This is obviously a conclusion that should be considered quite tentative until supported with additional evidence. Nevertheless, the mere fact that it is plausible should make one skeptical of claims that all, or even most, observed age differences favoring young adults are attributable to exogenous (environmental) factors rather than endogenous (maturational) factors.

To summarize, while convincing evidence is available indicating that performance on numerous cognitive tests has improved over historical time, there is still relatively little understanding of the implications of these time-related changes on the relations between age and cognitive functioning. Under certain combinations of assumptions, changes in relevant aspects of the environment can lead to negative age-performance relations with cross-sectional comparisons, but under other sets of assumptions the environmental changes can lead to positive age-performance relations with longitudinal comparisons. Still other mixtures of assumptions lead to predictions that environmental changes will produce positive age-performance relations in both types of assessments. At the present time, therefore, it does not appear possible to specify the exact nature of the consequences of positive time-lag effects on age differences in cognitive performance. What does seem clear, however, is that it is probably too simplistic to claim that all the age differences observed in measures of cognitive performance are attributable to changes in the external environment.

COHORT AND ENVIRONMENTAL CHANGE

Although cross-sectional and longitudinal designs do not differ with respect to the simple presence or absence of susceptibility to effects of environmental change, they do differ in terms of cohort membership. The term cohort generally refers to people entering a particular system together, and thus sharing common environmental experiences at similar periods relative to their entry into the system (P.B. Baltes, Cornelius, & Nesselroade, 1979; Kosloski, 1986; Rosow, 1978; Schaie, 1984a; Schaie & Hertzog, 1982). In the context of developmental psychology, the time of one's birth is usually interpreted as marking the entry into the "system" of life. Longitudinal comparisons are based on assessments of people who entered the system at the same time, but who are then measured at different periods. The relevant data therefore consist of within-cohort contrasts. Cross-sectional designs, on the other hand, are based on between-cohort contrasts because they involve comparisons at the same period of people of different ages, and hence also of different times of entry into the system.

The idea that cohort membership might be an important determinant of developmental phenomena was first seriously investigated in the 1960s. At about that time results from a number of studies seemed to suggest that age trends in measures of cognitive functioning from longitudinal studies were much smaller than those typically observed in cross-sectional studies. It was therefore hypothesized that much of this discrepancy might be attributable to the existence of cohort differences. In the strongest version of this interpretation (Labouvie-Vief, 1976, 1985; Labouvie-Vief, et al., 1974; Schaie, 1975, 1980b; Schaie & Labouvie-Vief, 1974; Schaie, G. Labouvie, & Buech, 1973), it was proposed that no age-related changes in intellectual ability occurred after the attainment of maturity. Age differences observed in cross-sectional studies were hypothesized to be determined by progressively higher levels of performance achieved by later generations, with little or no within-generation change across the adult years. Because the adult years were postulated to be characterized by stability of performance, and all age differences were presumed to be due to different asymptotic levels of functioning reached during adolescence and early adulthood, this interpretation is obviously similar to Model 1 described above.

In order for the cohort interpretation to be considered plausible, a substantial portion of the difference in results between cross-sectional and longitudinal studies should be found to be associated with cohort differences. However, in addition to differing in cohort membership, cross-sectional and longitudinal studies also differ in other potentially important respects such as amount of practice, susceptibility to selective attrition, and potential for instrumentation changes associated with test administration and scoring procedures. Amount of practice is a potentially critical factor because longitudinal assessments are necessarily repeated assessments and therefore, unlike cross-sectional studies, the amount of prior testing experience will be positively correlated with the age of the individual being tested. Selective attrition refers to the possibility that the participants who remain in a longitudinal study may no longer be representative of the individuals initially recruited to participate in the study. There are now numerous reports (P.B. Baltes, Schaie, & Nardi, 1971; Botwinick, 1977; Cooney, Schaie, & Willis, 1988; McCarty, Siegler, & Logue, 1982; Riegel, et al., 1968; Schaie, 1988; Schaie, G. Labouvie, & T.J. Barrett, 1973; Siegler & Botwinick, 1979; E.V. Sullivan & Corkin, 1984) that continuing participants in longitudinal studies are positively biased; that is, returnees generally have higher levels of many intellectual abilities than the individuals who do not continue their participation. Several researchers have also noted that procedural changes in administration or scoring is a potentially serious problem in longitudinal studies (Botwinick & Birren, 1965; Schaie, 1983; Schaie & Hertzog, 1985, 1986).

Of the three differences just described, practice and selective attrition can definitely be expected to minimize age differences in longitudinal studies relative to those in cross-sectional studies because they will tend to inflate the performance of older individuals more than that of younger individuals. The contribution of cohort factors to the discrepancy in results between cross-sectional and longitudinal studies can therefore be accurately evaluated only after the effects of practice and selective attrition have been taken into account.

There appears to be only one data set with all the necessary characteristics for conducting the desired comparisons of age-related effects within and between cohorts—Schaie's Seattle Longitudinal Study (Schaie, 1983, 1988). This is one of the few large-sample studies in which the same measures were examined both longitudinally and cross-sectionally. It is also one of a very limited number of studies in which performance was examined in independent samples of the same birth cohort at different points in time. Results from independent samples of individuals within the same birth cohort are extremely informative for the purpose of investigating cohort interpretations of age differences because they share one of the primary advantages of longitudinal studies without suffering from the two major disadvantages. That is, as in the longitudinal study, the individuals are all members of the same birth cohort. However, because different people are tested at different times, their performance cannot be affected by prior practice, and it also seems less likely that the sample could have become unrepresentative through selective attrition. The hypothesis that most of the age differences observed in cross-sectional studies are attributable to differences between cohorts, and that there is little or no age change within a given cohort, can therefore be directly investigated by examining age- and time-related performance differences in this same-cohort independent-sample comparison.

All the necessary data for making the relevant comparisons have been published in Schaie (1983), where complete results of the Seattle Longitudinal Study from 1956 through 1977 are summarized. (Data through 1984 are presented in Schaie, 1988, but without the results from the important same-cohort independent-samples comparisons.) Because the interval between successive measurement occasions was 7 years, results from each type of data collection method will be expressed in terms of performance differences across a 7-year interval. That is, the scores indicate the magnitude of change inferred or observed across an interval of 7 years, and thus roughly correspond to the slope of the function relating age to performance. All values are expressed in T-score units based on the distribution of 2,810 scores at first test.

Cross-sectional data for first-time participants are derived from Schaie's (1983) Table 4.5. Averages across the four measurement occasions were computed, and then differences between each 7-year age grouping were determined. The resulting values therefore represent the cross-sectional differences between groups separated by 7 years in age at an average measurement occasion between 1966 and 1967.

In order to obtain the greatest amount of longitudinal data, 7-year change scores were derived from the data of 1,601 individuals summarized in Schaie's (1983) Table 4.8. The resulting values therefore correspond to the average changes in performance for participants tested in 1956 and again in 1963, for those tested in 1963 and again in 1970, and for those tested in 1970 and again in 1977. Across the entire data set, the average year for the first measurement occasion was 1963, and the average year for the second measurement occasion was 1970.

Data for the same-cohort independent-sample comparison are presented in Schaie's (1983) Table 4.12. These values consist of differences between the scores of 2,151 individuals tested at one point in time, and the scores of 2,083 different individuals who were 7 years older and tested 7 years later. As with the longitudinal data, the average year for the initial measurement was 1963 and the average year for the later measurement was 1970.

Average 7-year time-lag differences can also be computed to estimate the magnitude of the performance difference associated with environmental change factors. The values are derived, using data in Schaie's (1983) Table 4.5, by determining the slope of the regression equation relating performance to year of testing, and then multiplying the slope by 7 to estimate the average time-lag change across a 7-year interval.

The functions relating each of these estimated 7-year differences to chronological age for the five PMA subtests are illustrated in Figure 3.7. Because the displayed values represent estimates of the amount of change over a 7-year interval, positive values correspond to improved levels of performance, negative values correspond to lowered levels of performance, and values of zero indicate that performance did not systematically differ across the interval.

There are three important points to note about the results displayed in Figure 3.7. The first is that most of the between-age (cross-sectional, longitudinal, same cohort) differences tend to become progressively more negative with increased age. This is consistent with the negatively accelerated age relations for these measures illustrated in Figure 2.5.

The second important point to note from Figure 3.7 is that the estimated differences from cross-sectional comparisons are generally larger than those from longitudinal or same-cohort comparisons. This seems to suggest that the cross-sectional differences occur earlier, and are larger in magnitude, than the differences from either longitudinal or same cohort comparisons. However, this interpretation is complicated by the third important characteristic of the data in Figure 3.7—that many of the estimated time-lag differences are positive. The longitudinal and same-cohort differences are therefore likely to be inflated by the generally favorable environmental changes occurring between the first and second measurement intervals. Because all the observations are collected at the same average measurement occasion in the cross-sectional method, estimates derived from this method are not subject to inflation by positive time-lag effects.

In light of the positive time-lag effects for many of the variables, the most meaningful comparisons of results from the three research designs may be those in which the estimated differences in longitudinal and same-cohort contrasts are adjusted for the age-specific time-lag differences occurring between the two measurement occasions. That is, if it is assumed that cohort membership exerts an influence independent of the time-lag effects indexing environmental change, then the time-lag effects should first be removed from the values derived from the temporally spaced longitudinal and same-cohort contrasts. Estimates of the 7-year differences "corrected" in this manner by subtracting the time-lag differences from the

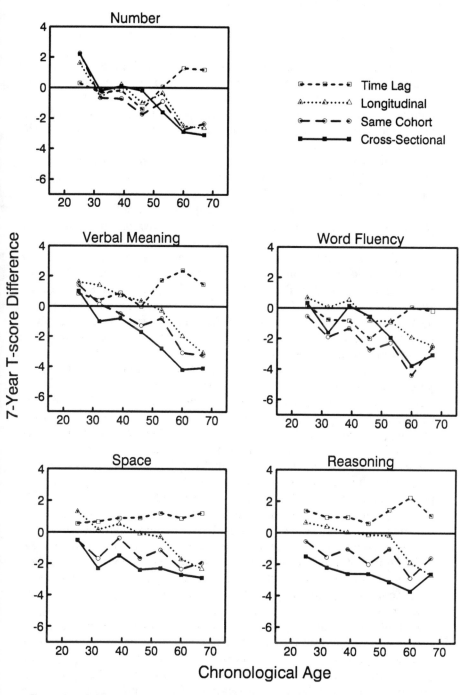

Figure 3.7. Differences in T-score units for the five PMA subtests across seven years from time-lag, longitudinal, independent samples from the same cohort, and cross-sectional comparisons. Data derived from Schaie (1983).

longitudinal and same-cohort differences at each age are displayed in Figure 3.8.

The most striking feature of the data illustrated in Figure 3.8 is the very similar pattern evident in the cross-sectional and same-cohort comparisons. The functions based on longitudinal comparisons tend to be elevated relative to the other functions, which may reflect effects associated with practice and/or selective attrition. Of particular importance, however, is the discovery that very similar relations between age and cognitive performance are apparent in the same-cohort and the mixed-cohort (cross-sectional) comparisons after making adjustments for practice, selective attrition, and environmental change.

The results just described are obviously based on only a limited set of cognitive measures, and are derived from a particular subpopulation of individuals. They are nonetheless important because they seem to provide little support for the claim that results from cross-sectional studies are misleading due to a confounding of age differences with cohort differences. To the extent that the results of Schaie's Seattle Longitudinal Study provide an accurate reflection of cognitive functioning in adulthood, therefore, these analyses suggest that cohort membership, per se, may have relatively little effect on either the direction or the magnitude of age differences in cognitive performance.

The suggestion that factors related to cohort membership exert minimal influence on relations between age and cognitive performance is quite different from the conclusions previously reached by Schaie and his colleagues in numerous reports based on these same data (Schaie, 1983; Schaie & Gribbin, 1975; Schaie, et al., 1973; Schaie & Labouvie-Vief, 1974; Schaie & Strother, 1968b, 1968c). It is thus desirable to consider how the same results could have led to virtually opposite conclusions regarding the importance of cohort factors in age differences in cognition. One potentially important difference in the two sets of analyses is that many of the earlier analyses by Schaie and his colleagues were based on only a portion of the currently available data. In fact, stronger evidence of cohort-independent age effects is apparent in more recent reports of the data, in which some of the earlier claims regarding the importance of cohort influences were qualified (Schaie, 1988, 1989b; Schaie & Hertzog, 1983). The methods used to evaluate the contribution of cohort factors to the relations between age and cognitive performance also differed in the two sets of analyses. Schaie generally investigated cohort effects in analyses of variance which allowed the detection of irregular or nonsystematic effects in addition to systematic ones. Furthermore, in some of the analyses the range of cohort variation was much larger than the range of age variation, thereby spuriously inflating the magnitude of cohort effects relative to age effects (Adam, 1977; Botwinick & Arenberg, 1976). Finally, whereas the

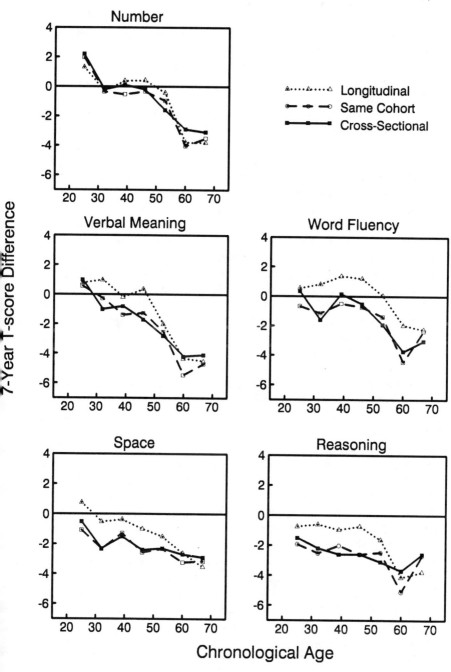

Figure 3.8. Differences in T-score units for the five PMA subtests across seven years for longitudinal, independent samples from the same cohort, and cross-sectional comparisons after subtracting the age-specific time-lag effects from the longitudinal and independent sample-same cohort comparisons. Data derived from Schaie (1983).

113

independent-samples same-cohort data were introduced in part to control for the influence of subject attrition and prior practice, there was apparently no attempt to remove the time-lag effects from the within-cohort comparisons in any of Schaie's analyses. This last feature may be particularly important because an examination of Figures 3.7 and 3.8 reveals that the independent-groups same-cohort function and the cross-sectional function differ by an amount nearly identical to the positive time-lag effects occurring across the 7-year interval.

Both the analyses described above and the analyses performed by Schaie can be considered to involve confoundings of cohort effects, as indexed by year of birth, and environmental change effects, as indexed by year of measurement. In Schaie's analyses, cohort effects were confounded with time of measurement (in what he termed a cohort-sequential design), and thus the effects could not be unambiguously interpreted as reflections of cohort factors instead of environmental change factors. In the analyses just reported the time-lag estimates can be postulated to represent a mixture of environmental change and cohort factors because people of the same age but tested at different times (i.e., the time-lag contrasts) are necessarily from different cohorts. Subtracting time-lag estimates from the same-cohort and longitudinal difference scores may therefore not only remove the environmental change effects, but also some of the effects associated with cohort variation.

A key factor in how the results of the various analyses are to be interpreted concerns the relation between the environmental change and cohort factors. Based on the relative amounts of discussion devoted to each topic in the literature, many researchers apparently feel that cohort factors are either more important, or possibly more fundamental, than factors related to environmental change. This is rather surprising because changes in the environment are a prerequisite for the existence of distinctive cohorts: If there are no changes in any aspect of the environment, then there is no reason to expect that different generations will vary in the nature of their experiences. Of course, successive cohorts could contribute to some of the changes that occur in the environment. However, while changes in the environment are both necessary and sufficient for the existence of distinct cohorts, differences in cohorts may be sufficient, but do not appear necessary, to produce environmental change. In terms of causal priorities, therefore, environmental change could plausibly be argued to be the more fundamental concept because all the differences between cohorts presumably originate from changes in the biophysical or sociocultural environment whereas the reverse is not the case.

Re-examination of the Cohort Concept

It is desirable, regardless of the nature of the empirical evidence concerning age differences in within-cohort and between-cohort comparisons, to review the status of the cohort concept as a possible causal factor in the age differences in cognitive performance. Even a superficial perusal of the research literature reveals there is considerable confusion regarding the nature of a cohort. Evidence of the perplexity is apparent by considering some of the methods proposed as controls for cohort-related factors in research on adult development: matching on years of education (G. Cohen, 1979; Parks, D.B. Mitchell, & Perlmutter, 1986) or socioeconomic status (Anooshian, Mammarella, & Hertel, 1989); using measures based on games in which the basic rules of play have not changed for centuries (Charness, 1981a); or restricting comparisons to the best performers in each age group (Gottsdanker, 1980); or to full-time students (Jacewicz & A.A. Hartley, 1979), or to individuals above a minimum age, such as 50 (J.T. Hartley, 1989; Rabbitt & McInnis, 1988). Quite different conceptions of the nature of a cohort must obviously have been held by these researchers to lead to such a mixture of possible "solutions" to the "cohort problem." Some authors have even complained that the cohort concept is so vague that "Currently, every ambiguity of data, method, or occasion is eligible to be nominated as a potential cohort difference or cultural change" (Birren, W.R. Cunningham, & Yamamoto, 1983, p. 542).

An informative discussion of the cohort concept was provided by P.B. Baltes, et al., (1979), in which three usages or interpretations of the cohort concept were distinguished. The three interpretations were cohort as error or disturbance, cohort as a dimension of generalization, and cohort as a theoretical variable contributing to developmental change. Although each of these ways of conceptualizing cohorts is potentially useful, only the interpretation emphasizing the role of cohort as a potential determinant of age-related declines in measures of cognitive functioning appears directly relevant to the study of possible causes of age differences in cognitive performance. That is, cohort influences are only of marginal interest in the present context if they are considered to correspond to unsystematic perturbations of developmental functions, or if they are assumed to affect the representativeness of particular developmental comparisons.

In order to analyze the causal influence that cohort factors might have on age differences in cognitive performance, it is first desirable to consider exactly what it means to belong to one cohort as opposed to another. It was mentioned earlier that a cohort is generally defined as a group of people sharing common environmental experiences at similar periods. A cohort is therefore not simply determined by factors related to age or to the changing environment, but instead is a specific product of the interaction of these two factors. Cohorts defined in terms of year of birth thus consist of potentially unique configurations of specific environmental experiences at particular chronological ages.

Conceptualizing cohorts as particular configurations of experiences and ages reveals that different cohorts are not necessarily ordered in any systematic fashion. For example, veterans of World War I born in 1900 and veterans of World War II born in 1924 may be more similar to one another with respect to many defining characteristics of a cohort than either is to nonveterans born between those years, say in 1912. In fact, because cohorts can be defined as qualitative constellations of age-specific experiences, the existence of an orderly relation across successive cohorts could even be interpreted as an indication of the operation of other presumably more fundamental factors, in which case the cohort categorization might be considered superfluous, and possibly even misleading.

The absence of a systematic ordering of cohorts is a major problem if cohort factors are postulated to contribute to the age differences in cognitive performance. That is, because the age differences in cognition are systematic, and nearly always monotonic if not linear, the causes of those differences must presumably be at least as systematic and monotonic as the phenomena they are intended to explain. Because successive cohorts are distinguished from one another in qualitative rather than quantitative respects, it is difficult to see how they could be responsible for the orderly quantitative relations between age and cognitive performance frequently observed.

The qualitative nature of the cohort concept also raises the issue of whether cohort effects can, in principle, ever be replicated. The same kinds of observations can obviously be repeated on the same individuals, but this might more appropriately be considered repetition rather than replication. In order to replicate a phenomenon one should be able to demonstrate that the same pattern occurs when using different methods, different occasions, or different samples. A fundamental problem with the cohort concept as a potential cause of developmental phenomena is that the ambiguity of cohort membership makes it difficult to determine whether new cohorts differ from one another in the same ways in which the original cohorts differed from each other, or even whether the new research participants actually belong to different cohorts than those tested earlier.

It is also not obvious what pattern of results should be considered as replicating a finding of cohort differences. For example, if Cohort 1 differs from Cohort 2 by X units on some measure of performance, should Cohorts 3 and 4 also be expected to differ by X units? Without knowing more about the nature of each cohort, it is possible that a close replication would be achieved by obtaining no difference between the groups, or a difference of Y or Z units instead of X units. Because each cohort is potentially unique, and defined primarily by qualitative rather than quantitative characteristics, there may be no basis for determining whether two patterns of results should be considered successful or unsuccessful replications of one another.

Although not necessarily a disadvantage when cohort is simply used as a descriptive concept, the ambiguity of cohort identity, and the implications of this for replicability, is a serious limitation when the concept of a cohort is used as a causal factor in age differences in cognitive performance. The difficulty arises because it is impossible to investigate hypotheses about the influence of cohort factors when those factors cannot be consistently identified or replicated.

A number of developmental psychologists have tried to circumvent some of the complications associated with cohort identity by defining cohorts solely in terms of the individuals' year of birth. This practice, however, has led to new problems (Kosloski, 1986; Rosow, 1978). Three of the problems were clearly described by Rosow (1978), and have been labeled the boundary problem, the distinctive experience problem, and the differential effects problem. The boundary problem exists because the coherence of a cohort rests on commonality of experiences, and it is unlikely that individuals will be meaningfully grouped with respect to common experiences when they are classified according to arbitrary temporal boundaries. The distinctive experience problem is related to the idea that not all experiences are presumed to be relevant, and there is no assurance that individuals classified together on the basis of year of birth all share the critical experiences. Finally, because the impact of experiences may not be uniform among individuals born within specified temporal intervals, relying upon birth year to define cohorts also leads to the problem of possible differential effects of critical experiences among individuals treated as equivalent.

One of the most serious analytical problems with using year of birth to classify cohorts is that cohort defined in this manner is not independent of other important developmental determinants such as endogenous maturation, indexed by age, and exogenous environmental change, indexed by time of measurement. That is, when all three concepts are indexed by temporal variables, the values of two of them are sufficient to determine the value of the third. Both the implications of this lack of independence, and the value of statistical models designed to assess the contribution of each developmental determinant, have been the subject of enormous controversy over the past 25 years. However, most authors currently seem to agree that one cannot separate the effects associated with maturation, environmental change, and cohort by purely statistical means (Schaie, 1986; Schaie & Hertzog, 1983, 1985). Thus, much of the debate concerning the value or usefulness of Schaie's (1965) General Developmental Model now appears to be primarily of historical interest.

To reiterate, serious questions have been raised about the meaningfulness of the cohort concept as a potential cause of age differences in cognition. Some years ago, Schaie and P.B. Baltes (1975) defended the cohort concept by claiming that: "Logically, the status of cohort is the same as that of other variables such as social class or sex except for its inherent time component" (p. 386). As suggested above, every aspect of this statement can be challenged when cohort is interpreted as a causal variable because: (a) the time component is not "inherent" but almost completely arbitrary; (b) qualitatively determined cohorts lack a systematic ordering such as that implied by social class; and (c) unlike sex, members of different cohort categories cannot be readily distinguished on the basis of critical, or defining, characteristics.

Many of the problems associated with both the cohort and the environmental change concepts are attributable to the fact that, like age (see chapter 1), they are not meaningful influences themselves, but instead refer to combinations of influences which in the aggregate are correlated with the passage of time. The global contribution of these causal factors can be indexed by the relation between time and certain measures of cognitive performance, but time, like any other index, provides a very crude and indirect indication of the operation of the relevant variables. As many authors (P.B. Baltes, 1968; P.B. Baltes, et al., 1979; Birren, et al., 1983; Charness, 1985a; Kosloski, 1986; Nesselroade & E.W. Labouvie, 1985; Rosow, 1978; Schaie, 1984a, 1986, 1989b; Willis, 1989a) have pointed out, these conglomerate constructs must be unpacked or decomposed to achieve a reasonable level of understanding. This will almost certainly involve replacing time as an index of the combined effects of a mixture of many different variables with direct measurements of the variables presumed to be critical. Only when relevant variables have been identified and quantified will it be possible to determine what is actually responsible for time-related effects on cognitive performance. Identification and measurement of the critical variables is also essential to allow replication and prediction, two prerequisites for scientific progress.

Schaie (1984, 1986) has recently proposed one strategy for decomposing relevant aspects of the social and cultural environment. His suggestion involves identifying salient historic events, technological innovations, and so forth, and estimating the extent to which each event affected the general population at each point in time. Measures of the density and significance of historical events could then be used as predictors of relevant measures of cognitive performance. Similar analyses might also be conducted to yield measures representing biological and physical characteristics of the environment that are hypothesized to contribute to time-related cognitive differences.

An additional advantage of identifying the critical variables currently embedded in the cohort and environmental-change constructs is that relevant research could then be conducted within short time frames by comparing existing groups known to differ on the dimensions presumed to be relevant. Eckensberger, Krewer, and Kasper (1984) pointed out that this strategy effectively treats "... cross-cultural differences (determined at a given point of historical time) as a simulation of socio-historical and cultural change, that is, as indicants of the same mechanisms that also underlie social-cultural change" (p. 74). Appropriate comparisons might be found in subcultures within the same society, as well across samples from different societies. In either case, the analyses might make it possible to disentangle the vague concepts of cohort and environmental change from the also vague, but nonetheless conceptually distinct, concept of maturation or endogenous change.

CONTROLLED ENVIRONMENT COMPARISONS

Another means of investigating the environmental change interpretation of age differences in cognitive functioning involves comparing the performance of individuals of different ages in environments that have not changed appreciably across multiple generations. If significant relations between age and measures of cognitive performance are found in samples from stable environments, then it could be concluded that at least some of the age differences are not attributable to changes occurring in the external environment.

It is probably impossible to find human populations where all potentially relevant aspects of the environment have remained constant throughout much of an individual's lifespan, but this goal may be more attainable by focusing on organisms with much shorter lifespans. Age comparisons in animals may therefore provide some of the most meaningful evidence relevant to the hypothesis that changes in the external environment are responsible for age differences observed in humans. Certain environmental characteristics, such as air quality or levels of chemical contaminants in food or water, may not remain invariant even in animal studies. However, the greater degree of environmental control possible in animal research relative to that possible in research with humans allows the investigator to be certain there have been no changes in educational practices, and probably also no time-related changes in cultural stimulation that could complicate the interpretation of any age differences that might be observed.

The greatest limitation of research with animals is that, because of a more restricted behavioral repertoire, many of the available measures are only of marginal interest to cognitive psychologists. Although there is clearly no equivalent of the WAIS-R for rats or monkeys, inferences about relative levels of memory functioning in nonhuman organisms are nevertheless possible based on results from several experimental paradigms.

One experimental procedure in which very consistent results have been reported is the one-trial passive avoidance paradigm. This procedure consists of placing an animal in one chamber of a two-chambered apparatus, and waiting until it enters the second chamber. As soon as the animal enters the second chamber an electric shock is delivered, and the animal is removed from the apparatus. At some later period the animal is returned to the original chamber and the time to enter the second chamber, where it was previously shocked, is recorded.

If the animal remembers the aversive event during the interval between successive placements in the apparatus, then it would be expected to avoid entering the shock chamber. However, if the aversive event is forgotten, then the animal is likely to re-enter the shock chamber when returned to the apparatus. Either the probability of entering the shock chamber, or the amount of time intervening between placement in the apparatus and entering the critical chamber, can therefore be used as a measure of memory for discrete events.

One of the best-documented findings in the literature on age differences in animal behavior is that older animals, when placed in the apparatus a second time, either enter the shock chamber more frequently, or have a shorter latency to enter it, than younger animals. This evidence of an age-related memory deficit has been found in numerous studies involving both mice (Bartus, Dean, Goas, & Lippa, 1980; Dean, Scozzafava, Goas, Regan, Beer, & Bartus, 1981) and rats (P.E. Gold, McGaugh, Hankins, R.P. Rose, & Vasquez, 1982; Lippa, 1980; McNamara, V.A. Benignus, G. Benignus, & A.T. Miller, 1977; Soffie & Giurgea, 1988; Winocur, 1988; Zornetzer, R.F. Thompson, & Rogers, 1982).

A second experimental procedure useful for assessing memory in nonhuman organisms involves a radial maze apparatus in which each arm contains either a food or a water reward. After consuming the reward in a given arm, the rat is returned to the center of the apparatus without replacing the consumed reward. Most animals, with a moderate amount of experience in the situation, learn to explore new arms of the maze with each successive placement in the apparatus. However, if the animal has difficulty remembering which pathways it had already traversed, it would be expected to make errors by continuing to select old (but now nonrewarding) pathways in the maze.

A well replicated finding is that older rats are less efficient (i.e., make more repetitions of earlier pathways) in this type of apparatus relative to young rats (Barnes, 1979; Barnes & McNaughton, 1985; Barnes, Nadel, & Honig, 1980; Gallagher, Bostock, & R. King, 1985; Ingram, London, & Goodrick, 1981; Soffie & Giurgea, 1988; J.E. Wallace, Krauter, & B.A. Campbell, 1980). As with the passive avoidance results, these findings suggest that pronounced age-related memory deficits are evident even in animals raised in highly controlled environments.

Although the results from the passive avoidance and radial maze procedures appear relevant to human cognition, there are likely to be fewer problems in extrapolating findings when studying a species more closely related to humans. Research with monkeys or other nonhuman primates should therefore prove extremely valuable in understanding processes of cognitive aging. Unfortunately, only a few age-comparative studies involving primates have been reported.

One experimental paradigm used by several investigators (which is very similar to a procedure frequently used with humans) involves testing visual short-term memory with matrix stimuli. The primate version of the task consists of the presentation of a display containing one or two illuminated cells in a matrix, followed by a variable delay. At the end of the delay interval the matrix is re-presented without any illuminated cells and the monkey is rewarded for touching the previously illuminated cells.

Results from several projects (Bartus, 1979; Bartus & Dean, 1979; Medin, 1969; Medin, O'Neal, Smeltz, & R.T. Davis, 1973) reveal that older monkeys tend to perform poorer than younger monkeys in this delayed spatial memory procedure. Flicker, Bartus, T.H. Crook, and Ferris (1984) have pointed out that this result closely resembles the finding of lower accuracy with increased age in a very similar task performed by humans. (See chapters 6 and 7 for additional citations to reports of human age differences in the accuracy of reproducing target positions from a spatial matrix.)

The three procedures described above are obviously only a very small sample of the experimental manipulations that have been administered to animals of different ages. However, they are sufficient to indicate that the phenomenon of age differences in cognitive performance is apparently not restricted to humans living in rapidly changing environments. It therefore seems reasonable to infer that not all age differences in cognitive functioning can be attributed to changes extrinsic to the individual.

EVALUATION OF THE ENVIRONMENTAL
CHANGE PERSPECTIVE

It is indisputable that many potentially relevant aspects of the environment change as people age. It is therefore quite plausible to speculate that at least some of the observed age differences in cognitive functioning may be attributable to changes occurring outside the individual, and are due to exogenous rather than to endogenous factors. Moreover, the discovery that the average level of performance in many cognitive tests has increased across successive generations, as revealed by time-lag comparisons, is clearly consistent with this hypothesis. However, it is not yet possible to predict the consequences of time-lag effects on adult age differences in cognition because of uncertainty regarding assumptions such as the age of maximum susceptibility to the influence of environmental change, and whether there is an asymptote on the cognitive effects of environmental changes. In fact, under what might be considered the most reasonable assumptions on the basis of the available data, the distortion of the age-cognition relations caused by positive time-lag effects appears to be in the direction of a bias in favor of older individuals, implying that observed age differences actually provide underestimates of the influence of endogenous determinants of development. Furthermore, other results, such as patterns of age differences observed among animals living in relatively stable environments, suggest that changes in the external environment probably cannot account for all the cognitive differences reported across individuals of different ages.

The vagueness of the environmental change perspective, and particularly the absence of explicit hypotheses regarding the particular aspects of the changing environment that might be responsible for different levels of cognitive performance, suggests that, at the present time, the perspective is more of a framework than a theory or model. That is, the environmental change perspective seems to consist primarily of a loose collection of ideas about the importance of exogenous changes in the environment. As it currently stands, therefore, the environmental change perspective provides the hint of an answer to the question of the *why* of developmental phenomena, but offers little that is relevant to the questions of the *what* and *how* of development. In order to convert these ideas from the status of a framework to that of a true theory, hypotheses must be offered to indicate the particular environmental dimensions that influence specific aspects of cognition, and to describe how those influences are mediated.

4 Disuse Interpretations

A decrease in test ability among adults probably is caused by the fact that adults, as they grow older, exercise their minds less and less with the materials found on psychological tests.

—Sorenson (1933, p. 736)

The disuse perspective attempts to account for age differences in cognitive functioning in terms of changes in the nature of the activities performed by people of different ages. Irrespective of possible changes in the external environment, it is hypothesized that there are changes with age in the pattern and frequency of daily experiences, and that these experiential variations are responsible for many of the age differences observed in measures of cognitive functioning. Versions of the disuse perspective have been discussed from the time of the first studies concerned with age and cognition (Foster & G.A. Taylor, 1920; Thorndike, et al., 1928), and have been incorporated into the general culture in the form of slogans such as "Use it or lose it," and "He who lives by his wits dies with his wits." The disuse perspective has been quite popular, at least in part because amount or type of experience is presumably under the individual's control, and thus the possibility is raised that at least some age differences in cognitive functioning might be amenable to remediation or prevention.

Three broad categories of research are relevant to the disuse perspective of cognitive aging. One consists of contrasts across activities or tasks presumed to differ in familiarity, a second involves comparisons across groups of people postulated to vary with respect to the amount of experience they have had with specific activities, and the third is comprised of attempts to manipulate the amount of relevant experience through the provision of practice or training. Each of these is examined in turn.

ACROSS ACTIVITY COMPARISONS

It is almost certainly true that there are large variations in the frequency with which different activities or tasks are performed, and it is often speculated that there may be shifts in the patterns or distributions of these frequencies with increased age. If the amount of experience with certain activities influences proficiency on cognitive tasks related to those activities, and if that experience varies across the adult years, then it follows that experiential factors may contribute to age differences in cognitive functioning.

Unfortunately, although the preceding argument is plausible, there have been very few empirical observations of the actual frequencies of different activities. The absence of detailed information about the types and frequencies of activities performed at different ages has often been lamented (Arbuckle, D. Gold, & Andres, 1986; Birren, 1959; Dennis, 1953; J.T. Hartley, Harker, & D.A. Walsh, 1980; Kuhn, Pennington, & Leadbeater, 1983; Salthouse & Kausler, 1985; Scheidt, 1981), but to little avail because the desired information is still lacking. As Landauer (1989) recently suggested, "The kind of attention that has been lavished on the social life of children and apes also needs to be applied to the intellectual life of adults" (p. 122).

A convincing argument that variations in experience with particular activities contribute to the age differences observed in measures of cognitive performance requires two steps: First, differences as a function of age in the quantity or type of experiences must be documented. And second, the variations in experience must be shown to influence the magnitude of the age differences in cognitive performance. The evidence relevant to these issues is discussed in the following sections.

Experiential Differences

Although there are no complete, and apparently not even any partial, inventories of the activities performed by representative adults of different ages, several studies have collected information at different periods in adulthood either on perceived intellectual or cognitive demands, or on the estimated frequency of performing selected activities. For example, Perlmutter and her colleagues (Perlmutter, 1978; Parks, et al., 1986; Perlmutter, Metzger, Nezworski, & K. Miller, 1981) asked young and old adults to rate their memory or cognitive demands on a 10-point scale. All of these studies reported cognitive performance differences favoring young adults, but none found significant age differences in the self-assessments of mental demands. Prohaska, E.A. Leventhal, H. Leventhal, and Keller (1985) did report significant age differences in self-reported activity levels, but in the direction of an increase with age in ratings of agreement with the statement "I stay mentally alert and active." At least from these two types of self-report information, therefore, it does not appear that older adults generally perceive themselves to be living in cognitively unstimulating environments.

Most of the studies concerning the frequency of various activities at different periods in adulthood have focused on the activity of reading. Furthermore, the dominant finding has been that the number of hours per week devoted to reading newspapers or magazines (or other types of nonprofessional material) tends to increase with increased age (Pfeiffer & G.C. Davis, 1971; Ratner, Schell, Crimmins, Mittelman, & Baldinelli, 1987; Rice, 1986a, 1986b; Rice & B.J. Meyer, 1985, 1986; Salthouse, et al., 1988a; Surber, Kowalski, & Pena-Paez, 1984). The average number of hours per week reported to have been devoted to reading has varied from 8 or 9 (Pfeiffer & G.C. Davis, 1971; Salthouse, et al., 1988a) to 15 or more (Rice, 1986a; Rice & B.J. Meyer, 1985), with correlations between age and the number of hours of reading per week ranging from .20 to .31 (Rice & B.J. Meyer, 1986; Salthouse, et al., 1988a). The fact that increased age is apparently associated with more, rather than less, reading activity makes it unlikely that age-related reductions in cognitive performance could be mediated by changes in the frequency of reading.

Ratings of the familiarity of cognitive tests by adults of different ages may also be relevant to the issue of possible age differences in the frequency of various activities. As expected from the disuse perspective, Cornelius (1984) found that there was a significant decrease with age in the rated familiarity of cognitive tests (e.g., Letter Series, Letter Sets, Matrices) in which older adults generally perform the poorest compared with young adults. While these results are interesting, the basis for the familiarity judgments was not clear (e.g., recognition of the specific test, or experience with processes involved in those kinds of activities), and it is possible that the ratings may have been influenced by perceptions of level of performance because they were generated after the subjects performed the tasks. For both of these reasons, therefore, one should be cautious about interpreting the Cornelius (1984) results as indicating that lack of familiarity is a major cause of the poorer performance of older adults in the cognitive tests.

Rice (1986a) attempted to estimate the frequency of different activities on the basis of analyses of special diaries kept by adults of different ages. This approach is promising, but large and representative samples of research participants are probably necessary before one can attempt to draw conclusions about age relations in patterns of activities from data of this type. It also seems desirable to provide some method of evaluating the validity of the diary records if this method of investigation is to be pursued in the future.

It is unfortunate that more information is not available about the distribution of various activities at different ages because, in the absence of empirical data, assessments of the representativeness of various activities must be based on subjective judgments. Furthermore, when subjectivity influences decisions, considerable differences of opinion are likely to occur. An illustration of the diversity of views on the issue of the representativeness of specific cognitive tasks or activities is shown in Table 4.1. Entries in the top of the page consist of activities or tasks that have been considered representative, meaningful, or realistic, while entries in the bottom of the page have been considered unrepresentative, meaningless, or unrealistic.

Many of the classifications in Table 4.1 are probably idiosyncratic, and a few are clearly contradictory because the same task appears in both sections (e.g., prose memory). At least some of this inconsistency and confusion may be attributable to a failure to distinguish between the superficial tasks or activities, and the processes or components constituting those tasks or activities. For example, paired associate learning tasks with unrelated words or nonsense syllables are unlikely to occupy a large portion of anyone's daily routine. However, association processes may be used frequently in many common activities such as associating names with faces, objects, places, streets, events, and so on. (For related arguments see Kausler, 1985, 1989a; Kausler & Lichty, 1988; Salthouse, 1985b; Salthouse & Kausler, 1985). To the extent that tasks or activities can be analyzed into more elementary processes or components, the most appropriate determination of prevalence or frequency may be at this molecular or componential level rather than at the level of the superficial task or activity.

Because there is very little information about the frequency of performing different activities, and virtually no information about the frequency of using important cognitive processes, one cannot verify the accuracy of judgments about the representativeness of various activities. Claims that certain tasks or dependent measures are more representative or ecologically valid than others should therefore be viewed with skepticism until appropriate empirical evidence is available to document the hypothesized differences in frequency of occurrence.

Despite these reservations about the validity of claims of ecological validity, it is still useful to review the results from age-comparative studies involving tasks that have been argued to be more meaningful or representative than traditional tests or tasks used to measure cognitive functioning. On the one hand, if the age differences in these tasks are smaller than those usually found with other types of tasks, and if amount of experience is the critical feature distinguishing these tasks from more

TABLE 4.1
What activities are ecologically valid?

Activity	Source
Representative, Meaningful, or Realistic	
absolute frequency judgments	Kausler (1985)
associating names and faces	T.H. Crook & West (1990); Devolder, Brigham, & Pressley (1990); Hulicka (1965)
digit span tasks	Erickson, Poon, & Walsh-Sweeney (1980)
drawing lines indicating the level of water in filled bottles	M.M. Akiyama, H. Akiyama, & Goodrich (1985)
games	Charness (1985b)
indicating preferences for pocket notebooks	Capon, Kuhn, & Gurucharri (1981)
knowledge actualization tasks	Perlmutter (1980)
memory for appointments	Devolder, Brigham, & Pressley (1990)
memory for conversations	Kausler & Hakami (1983)
memory for discrete actions	Backman (1989); Kausler & Lichty (1988)
memory for organized spatial information	Sharps & Gollin (1987); Waddell & Rogoff, (1981, 1987)
memory for prose material	Backman (1989); Devolder, Brigham, & Pressley (1990); Gilbert & Levee (1971); S.K. Gordon & W.C. Clark (1974); J.T. Hartley (1986); J.T. Hartley, Harker, & D.A. Walsh (1980); Hultsch & Dixon (1984); Hultsch, Hertzog, & Dixon (1984); Peak (1968); Rice, B.J. Meyer, & D.C. Miller (1989); Zelinski, Gilewski, & L.W. Thompson (1980)
memory for proverbs or adages	Wood & Pratt (1987)
memory for spatial locations	Park, Puglisi, & Lutz (1982); Sharps & Gollin (1987)
memory for shopping list information	McCarthy, Ferris, E. Clark, & T.H. Crook (1981)
memory for simultaneously displayed information	Mueller, Rankin, & Carlomusto (1979)
memory for television show content	Backman (1989)
paired associate learning	Belbin & Downs (1966); Kausler (1982, 1989a)
performing more than one activity at a time	Wingfield & Sandoval (1980)

(Cont.)

127

TABLE 4.1
(Continued)

problem solving	Charness (1985b)
processing of senseless sounding directions, endless forms, and uninteresting information	C.C. Adams & Rebok (1983)
recall of a sequence of events	Hashtroudi, M.K. Johnson, & Chrosniak (1990); Padgett & Ratner (1987); Spilich (1985)
self-generated activities	Lichty, Bressie, & Krell (1988)
semantic integration tasks	D.A. Walsh & Baldwin (1977); D.A. Walsh, Baldwin, & Finkle (1980)
subject-performed tasks	Backman & Nilsson (1984)
tasks with three-dimensional stimuli	Puglisi (1986)
trivia information about Canada and Canadians	McIntyre & Craik (1987)
understanding oral directions	Price (1933)
vocabulary, reading, spelling, and arithmetic tasks	Weisenburg, Roe, & McBride (1936)

Unrepresentative, Meaningless, or Unrealistic

active, strategic remembering	A.D. Smith (1980a)
backwards digit span	Dennis (1953)
free-recall memory	Kausler (1982)
immediate recall of single-presentation items	Talland (1968)
intentional memory for list content	Kausler (1985)
memory for experimental activities	Knopf & Neidhardt (1989)
memory for printed words and photographs of faces	T.H. Crook & West (1990)
memory for prose material	J.T. Hartley (1989); Rice (1986a,b)
memory for unrelated words	J.T. Hartley, Harker, & D.A. Walsh (1980); Poitrenaud, Malbezin, & Guez (1989); Waddell & Rogoff (1981); Zelinski, Gilewski, & L.W. Thompson (1980)
paired associate learning and digit span	N.W. Denney & D.R. Denney (1982)
paired associate learning with lengthy lists	Kausler (1989a)
perspective-taking tasks	Kirasic & G.L. Allen (1985)
psychometric tests of intelligence	Rybash, Hoyer, & Roodin (1986)
quantitative word problems	Sternberg & Berg (1987)

(Cont.)

TABLE 4.1
(Continued)

recall of simple, unstructured, material over very brief periods of time	Rabbitt & McInnis (1988)
recognition memory for conversations	Kausler (1985)
relative frequency judgments	Kausler, Hakami, & R.E. Wright (1982)
rote learning of verbal materials	Backman & Nilsson (1984)
remembering to mail postcards	Sinnott (1986, 1989)
skills tapped by the digit symbol substitution test	Fozard & J.C. Thomas (1975); Poitrenaud, Malbezin, & Guez (1989)
spatial psychometric tests	Kirasic & G.L. Allen (1985)
tests of vocabulary and general information	Rybash, Hoyer, & Roodin (1986)
thinking in terms of geometric symbols	Brozek (1951)
use of similarity classifications or constraint-seeking strategies	N.W. Denney & D.R. Denney (1982)

traditional tasks, then the results would be consistent with the disuse interpretation. On the other hand, interpretations based on the disuse principle would fail to be supported if the performance differences between young and old adults on tasks assumed to be performed frequently are similar in magnitude to those observed in more traditional laboratory tasks.

Ecologically Valid Tasks

It is widely accepted that accuracy of prediction increases as the assessment tasks more closely resemble the criterion activity for which performance is to be predicted. If one's goal is to predict functioning in everyday situations, therefore, it is reasonable to attempt to study tasks with the greatest resemblance to the activities encountered in natural situations. Versions of this basic argument have been used by many researchers to advocate greater investigation of ecologically valid cognitive tasks. For example, Charness (1982) claimed that "... to provide valid generalizations about aging, it is necessary to use the tasks that people engage in on a day to day basis" (p. 22).

Although there has been considerable interest in the concept of ecological validity, it is not yet clear whether research based on this notion has made a substantial contribution to the understanding of adult age differences in cognition. One fundamental problem is that the defining criteria for an ecologically valid task or activity have never been explicitly identified (Hultsch & Dixon, 1990; Salthouse, 1990; Salthouse & Kausler,

1985). Perhaps the closest approximation to such a set of criteria was provided by West (1989), who suggested that a practical or everyday memory task should have:

> (1) content that is practical (e.g., real people are introduced, not slides), (2) encoding conditions that are practical (e.g., a grocery list is written down before making a trip to the store, rather than a list of test items read by an experimenter), (3) retrieval conditions that are practical (e.g., the person walks back through the building to find the exit, and does not draw the path on a piece of paper), and (4) motivations that are practical (e.g., the individual needs to know what he has done, rather than simply trying to remember to pass a memory test). (p. 575)

West acknowledges, however, that very few tasks satisfy more than two of her criteria, and thus there may be no activities for which the claim of ecological validity is not subject to challenge.

It is also worth noting that ecologically valid activities should not be automatically assumed to be performed at higher levels, or to exhibit smaller age differences, than typical laboratory tasks. As Rabbitt and Abson (1990) point out, some characteristics of traditional laboratory tasks may be more favorable to older adults than ecologically valid or real-life activities:

> Unlike real-life demands, laboratory tasks are experienced under conditions of minimal distraction and stress. They are typically very brief and so do not require sustained attention. Most importantly, they do not test the efficiency with which people can switch back and forth between competing activities without forgetting their last actions, remember and use plans to control complex sequences of behavior, or continuously update the large bodies of semantic and procedural knowledge upon which they must momentarily draw in order to manage their lives. (p. 2)

Many of the abilities mentioned in this passage have been hypothesized to be negatively associated with increased age. Age differences might therefore be expected to be larger in realistic situations than in typical laboratory assessments if these characteristics are more common in real-life activities than in laboratory tasks.

A second major problem with the notion of ecological validity is that, as noted above, very little information is currently available concerning the frequencies of natural activities. The entries in Table 4.1 indicate that this has led to arbitrary, and occasionally contradictory, claims about whether a given task is representative of everyday life. Scheidt (1981) has implied that a tendency to focus on superficial characteristics of the activities may be responsible for some of this confusion:

Too many of the ecologically-oriented studies conducted in the cognitive area represent demonstrations of techniques with ecologically-cosmetic features. Too many researchers have opted for quick, convenient 'real world' representations of tasks, stimuli, situations, and rules, settling upon these efforts as somehow being more ecologically valid than traditional research operations. (p. 227)

Another potential limitation of tasks presumed to be ecologically valid is the possibility that an emphasis on tasks with superficial resemblance to natural activities may actually tend to weaken, rather than strengthen, generalizability to other activities. The number of natural activities is clearly too large to permit each to be investigated, and the tailoring of a task to a specific situation in order to maximize superficial aspects of ecological validity may reduce the likelihood that the task is predictive of performance in other tasks or situations. Performance in naturalistic tasks may therefore have a sizable proportion of task- or situation-specific variance compared with more artificial and abstract tasks in which the crucial or relevant mechanisms are isolated, and attempts are made to control extraneous and irrelevant sources of variation. Consequently, it has been argued (Banaji & Crowder, 1989; Kausler & Lichty, 1988; Mook, 1983, 1989; Salthouse & Kausler, 1985), that the greatest generalizability is likely to be associated with tasks in which the most control can be exerted because only then can one be confident that basic mechanisms, that is, those that are presumably common to many different tasks, have been identified.

Lockhart and Craik (1990) relied upon similar reasoning to claim that:

... an ecologically valid approach to the study of memory does not demand the abandonment of laboratory experimentation. Rather, it imposes the requirement that laboratory paradigms capture and preserve those features of remembering that are important to everyday adaptive cognitive functioning. (p. 89)

The somewhat surprising implication of the preceding argument is that relatively contrived and artificial situations may be required to ensure maximum generalizability because of the vast number of uncontrolled factors contributing to performance variations in natural situations, and the impossibility of incorporating all of them in the limited tasks or activities to be investigated. N.W. Denney (1989) and Nesselroade and E.W. Labouvie (1985) have also pointed out that the use of what are presumed to be more natural tasks or stimuli does not necessarily mean that the resulting measures are any more reliable or valid with respect to the assessment of important theoretical constructs than those derived from traditional laboratory tasks.

Perhaps the greatest complication associated with the interpretation of results from ecologically valid tasks is that if the tasks are truly representative of daily situations, then the amount of cumulative experience with them is likely to be positively correlated with chronological age. This introduces a potentially serious confounding because, to the extent that performance on the tasks is favorably influenced by experience, the factors responsible for the relations between age and performance would be difficult to interpret due to the greater cumulative experience on the part of older adults. In other words, the age differences could be smaller because the activities have not been subject to disuse, but they might also be smaller because older adults have had the benefit of much more relevant experience than young adults. Instead of eliminating a disuse bias against older adults, therefore, assessment of cognitive functioning by means of commonly performed activities might be introducing a cumulative experience bias against young adults. Indeed, this latter argument has been used to suggest that tests of general information and vocabulary are not appropriate in age comparisons of cognitive functioning because increased age is associated with more opportunities for the acquisition of the relevant material, and hence older adults may have an unfair advantage over young adults (Conrad, 1930; Conrad, H.E. Jones, & Hsiao, 1933; H.E. Jones, 1956, 1959).

It is rather ironic that one of the reasons many researchers in cognitive aging have been enthusiastic about ecologically valid tasks is that they were assumed to provide fairer and more meaningful assessments of the capacities of older adults than traditional psychometric tests or laboratory tasks. However, if this naturalism and meaningfulness is gained only at the expense of creating a bias against young adults who have not had as many opportunities to acquire the relevant experience, then the use of ecologically valid tasks may still fail to provide fair assessments for adults of all ages. The ecological validity issue is complicated, and the importance of ecological validity clearly depends on whether one's primary goal is to predict functioning in specific situations, or to explore theoretical distinctions among experience and other age-related factors as determinants of cognitive functioning. Nevertheless, the procedure of using novel tasks and stimuli, although often disparaged by proponents of the ecological validity approach, still appears to be a viable method of minimizing both the negative (disuse) and positive (cumulative experience) confoundings of age and experience in assessments of cognitive performance.

It should be mentioned that another potential advantage of ecologically valid tasks is that they may be more interesting to some research participants than more traditional laboratory tasks. For example, several researchers (T.H. Crook, 1979; Erickson, Poon, & Walsh-Sweeney, 1980; Flicker, Ferris, T.H. Crook, & Bartus, 1987; Hulicka, 1965; Hulicka &

Rust, 1964; E.D. Hybertson, Perdue, & D. Hybertson, 1982; Kausler, 1982; Kirasic & Allen, 1985; Nesselroade & E.W. Labouvie, 1985) have suggested that more meaningful or naturalistic tasks may increase the motivational level of older adults. This argument is plausible, but Birren (1964) has provided an equally plausible counterargument that unfamiliar laboratory tasks "... may elicit a greater curiosity about the materials and a greater desire to manipulate them" (p. 173). Unfortunately, there doesn't seem to be any evidence that would allow resolution of the issue of whether motivation to perform well is affected by the apparent familiarity of the tasks at this time.

As discussed above, a finding of no age differences in measures of performance from tasks presumed to resemble familiar activities would be equivocal because of the difficulty of distinguishing between the effects associated with increased age and those associated with greater cumulative experience. However, a finding that young adults perform at higher levels than older adults in such tasks might be informative because an outcome of this type would suggest that the largely negative age-related effects are apparently more powerful than the presumably positive contributions associated with more extensive experience. For this reason, if none other, therefore, it is of interest to determine whether age differences are evident in tasks that have been hypothesized to be similar to frequently performed activities.

A sample of tasks that might be considered to be ecologically valid, and in which young adults have been found to perform at significantly higher levels than older adults, is listed in Table 4.2. Of course, there is no objective evidence that the activities represented by these tasks are truly frequent, or representative of daily life for adults of any age. Nevertheless, the fact that age differences roughly similar to those reported with traditional laboratory measures are evident in these measures presumed to be realistic and meaningful suggests that the phenomenon of age-related declines in certain aspects of cognitive functioning is not restricted to artificial and contrived laboratory situations.

Recall of prose or discourse material has also been treated as an ecologically valid task because it involves meaningful material and familiar operations (S.K. Gordon & W.C. Clark, 1974; J.T. Hartley, 1986; Hultsch, Hertzog, & Dixon, 1984; Peak, 1968; Zelinski & Gilewski, 1988). Furthermore, the results on reading behavior summarized earlier indicate that the presumably relevant activity of reading is frequent at all ages, and possibly even more common among older adults than among young adults. It might therefore be expected that age differences would be small to non-existent on measures of performance on tasks involving prose memory.

While some authors have suggested that age differences are minimal in memory tasks involving prose material (Labouvie-Vief, 1981; Labouvie-

TABLE 4.2
Presumably meaningful or ecologically valid tasks
in which age differences favoring young adults
have been reported.

Task	Source
accuracy of discriminating paintings from different artists	Hess & Wallsten (1987)
accuracy in eyewitness identifications of details from a simulated event	G. Cohen & Faulkner (1989a), Yarmey & Kent (1980)
accuracy in reporting information from street signs	Belbin (1956), Manstead & J.S. Lee (1979)
cohesion of diary entries	Kemper (1990)
comprehension and memory of prescription drug information	Morrell, Park, & Poon (1989, 1990)
concept identification in the context of determining which food is poisoned	Arenberg (1968b), A.A. Hartley (1981), Hayslip & Sterns (1979)
creativity in writing a story	Alpaugh, Parham, Cole, & Birren (1982)
effectiveness in solving practical or everyday problems	N.W. Denney & A.M. Palmer (1981), N.W. Denney, Pearce, & A.M. Palmer (1982)
learning to interpret fares and bus routes	Neale, Toye, & Belbin (1968)
learning to use a word-processing system or other computer packages	Egan & Gomez (1985), P.K. Elias, M.F. Elias, Robbins, & Gage (1987), M. Gist, B. Rosen, & Schwoerer (1988); A.A. Hartley, J.T. Hartley, & S.A. Johnson (1984); Zandri & Charness (1989)
memory for bridge hands by bridge players	Charness (1979)
memory for chess positions by chess players	Charness (1981a,b), Pfau & M.D. Murphy (1988)
memory for common objects (e.g., penney, telephone dial)	Foos (1989)
memory for conversations	Kausler & Hakami (1983)
memory for digits when entering responses on a telephone dial	T.H. Crook, Ferris, McCarthy, & Rae (1980)
memory for faces	J.C. Bartlett, Leslie, Tubbs, & Fulton (1989), T.H. Crook & West (1990), Ferris, T.H. Crook, E. Clark, McCarthy, & Rae, (1980), Flicker, Ferris, T.H. Crook, & Bartus (1989), S.E. Mason (1986), Moscovitch (1982), A.D. Smith & Winograd (1978)

(Cont.)

TABLE 4.2
(Continued)

memory for familiar environments	G.W. Evans, Brennan, Skorpanich, & Held (1984), Rabbitt (1989)
memory for grocery items	McCarthy, Ferris, E. Clark, & T.H. Crook (1981)
memory for location of objects	Bruce & J.F. Herman (1986), T.H. Crook, Ferris, & McCarthy (1979), Flicker, Bartus, T.H. Crook, & Ferris (1984), Flicker, Ferris, T.H. Crook, & Bartus (1987), L.L. Light & Zelinski (1983), Ohta (1983), Perlmutter, Metzger, Nezworski, & K. Miller (1981), Pezdek (1983), Zelinski & L.L. Light (1988)
memory for movies	Conrad & H.E. Jones (1929), H.E. Jones, Conrad, & A. Horn (1928)
memory for odors	Stevens, Cain, & Demarque (1990)
memory for proverbs or adages	Wood & Pratt (1987)
memory for recently performed activities	Bromley (1958), R.L. Cohen, Sandler, & Schroeder (1987), Guttentag & R.R. Hunt (1988), Kausler & Hakami (1983), Kausler, Lichty, & R.T. Davis (1985), Kausler, Lichty, Hakami, & Freund (1986), Kausler & P.L. Phillips (1988), Lichty, Bressie, & Krell (1988), Lichty, Kausler, & Martinez (1986), Peak (1968, 1970), Randt, E.R. Brown, & Osborne (1980), Salthouse, Kausler, & Saults (1988a)
memory for recently performed actions in an athletic competition	Backman & Molander (1986)
memory for recipes or action sequences	Hashtroudi, M.K. Johnson, & Chrosniak (1990), Padgett & Ratner (1987), Ratner, Padgett, & Bushey (1988), Taub (1975)
memory for simulated news broadcasts	R.D. Hill, T.H. Crook, Zadek, Sheikh, & Yesavage (1989); Stine, Wingfield, & Myers (1990)
memory for songs	J.C. Bartlett & Snelus (1980)
memory for source of factual information	Dywan & Jacoby (1990), McIntyre & Craik (1987)
memory for what one previously said or wrote	Koriat, Ben-Zur, & Sheffer (1988), Taub (1979)

(Cont.)

TABLE 4.2
(Continued)

memory for what one was recently asked	Herzog & Rodgers (1989)
memory for whether an action was performed (or a word read) or imagined	G. Cohen & Faulkner (1981, 1989a), Guttentag & R.R. Hunt (1988), Hashtroudi, M.K. Johnson, & Chrosniak (1989, 1990), Rabinowitz (1989a)
paired associate learning with name and face material	T.H. Crook & West (1990), Devolder, Brigham, & Pressley (1990), Ferris, T.H. Crook, Flicker, Reisberg, & Bartus (1986), Hulicka (1967a,b), J.P. Robertson (1957)
reasoning problems with meaningful content	Burton & Joel (1945), G. Cohen (1981), Friend & Zubek (1958), F.H. Hooper, J.O. Hooper, & Colbert (1984), Pacaud & Welford (1989), Rimoldi & Vander Woude (1969), Sinnott (1975)
recognizing environmental scenes from different perspectives	Bruce & J.F. Herman (1983)
remembering to perform an intended action	Cockburn & P.T. Smith (1988), Dobbs & Rule (1987)
speech reading ability	Farrimond (1959)
syntactic complexity of speech	Kemper & Rash (1988), Kynette & Kemper (1986)
syntactic complexity of writing	Kemper (1987a), Kemper & Rash (1988)
twenty-questions in the context of a detective game	E.D. Hybertson, Perdue, & D. Hybertson (1982)

Vief & Schell, 1982; Poon, 1985), many studies suggest that older adults frequently perform at lower levels than young adults (for recent reviews see G. Cohen, 1988; J.T. Hartley, 1989; B.J. Meyer, 1987; B.J. Meyer & Rice, 1989; B.J. Meyer, C.J. Young, & B.J. Bartlett, 1989; Spilich, 1985; and Zelinski & Gilewski, 1988). Objections could still be raised that few people have much experience recalling prose passages in the manner in which they are required in psychological research projects. Nevertheless, most researchers would probably agree that the use of meaningful materials and unstructured recall conditions seems closer to most real-life situations than traditional laboratory tasks involving verbatim recall of unrelated words. The discovery that older adults generally recall less information from prose passages than young adults therefore suggests that abstract and unfamiliar tasks are not necessary to produce age differences on measures of cognitive performance.

A number of psychometric tests have also been designed to assess cognitive abilities in a more meaningful, or ecologically valid, manner than that used in traditional intelligence tests. For example, special versions of the PMA Reasoning and Space tests were created by Schaie (1985) to increase the meaningfulness of the materials for older adults. The new versions employed ordered sequences of words (e.g., days of the week) instead of letters in the series completion Reasoning test, and drawings of familiar objects instead of abstract figures in the spatial rotation Space test. Changing the nature of the stimulus materials apparently had little effect, however, because scores on the two versions of each test were found to be highly correlated (i.e., r = .73 and r = .83 for the Reasoning and Space tests, respectively), and very similar age relations were evident in the traditional and the special versions of each ability test.

A project conducted by Willis and Schaie (1986a; Willis, 1987; Schaie, 1987, 1988) was explicitly designed to investigate practical or everyday problem solving by means of the ETS Basic Skills Test. This test consists of questions concerned with practical situations such as: "... understanding of labels on household articles, reading a street map, understanding charts/schedules, paragraph comprehension, filling out forms, reading newspaper and phone directory advertisements, understanding technical documents, and comprehending newspaper text" (Willis & Schaie, 1986a, p. 245).

Three results from this project are of interest in the present context. One important finding concerned ratings from older adults (60 to 88 years of age) of the frequency with which activities represented in the test were performed. Five of the activity categories were reported to be performed at least weekly, another category of activities was reported to be performed about once a month, and only two activities were reported to be performed rarely. The second finding relevant to the disuse perspective was that scores on the ETS Basic Skills Test were moderately correlated with measures of cognitive performance from traditional psychometric tests (Willis & Schaie, 1986a). This suggests that, contrary to some speculations (Rybash, W.J. Hoyer, & Roodin, 1986), similar factors may be contributing to individual differences in the proficiency of real-life or everyday activities and to individual differences in the performance of typical psychometric cognitive tests. The third important result was the discovery of significant age-related performance declines on the Basic Skills Test (Schaie, 1988). Scores were relatively stable from the 20s through the 40s, but declines accelerated such that there was only a 42% overlap in the distributions of scores from 25-year-olds and 74-year-olds. Significant negative correlations between age and a composite score on a subset of items from this test have also been reported by Perlmutter, M. Kaplan, and Nyquist (1990). Despite the presumably high ecological validity of these measures, the pattern of correlations and age differences suggest that performance on the ETS Basic Skills Test is influenced by many of the same factors that affect performance on more traditional tests of cognitive functioning.

Another category of evidence relevant to the disuse perspective derives from self-reports of cognitive changes. These self-appraisals are of interest because they can be assumed to reflect experience with a wide range of activities, and not just those that are seldom encountered and thus potentially most subject to disuse. Although not universal (for exceptions see Bennett-Levy & G.E. Powell, 1980; Jackson, Bogers & Kerstholt, 1988; Sunderland, Harris, & Baddeley, 1984; and Tenney, 1984), many investigators have found that older adults report more problems with, or greater declines in, memory and other cognitive abilities than young adults (Cavanaugh, Grady, & Perlmutter, 1983; G. Cohen & Faulkner, 1984, 1986; T.H. Crook & Larrabee, 1990; Dixon & Hultsch, 1983; Dobbs & Rule, 1987; Herzog & Rodgers, 1989; Hulicka, 1982; Hultsch, Hertzog, & Dixon, 1987; Hultsch, Hertzog, Dixon, & Davidson, 1988; Niederehe & Yoder, 1989; Perlmutter, 1978; Perlmutter, et al., 1981; Prohaska, Parham, & Teitelman, 1984; Rebok, Offermann, Wirtz, & Montaglione, 1986; Riege, 1983; P. Roberts, 1983; Zelinski, Gilewski, & L.W. Thompson, 1980). The apparent implication, assuming that these self-reports are valid (see Rabbitt & Abson, 1990, for a recent discussion of this issue), is that age-related declines in cognitive functioning are not confined to infrequent and unnoticed activities, but instead are salient and pervasive enough to be perceived and reported by many adults.

Summary

One implication of the disuse perspective is that if age differences in cognitive performance are caused by lack of relevant experience, then much smaller, and perhaps even no, age differences should be expected when cognitive functioning is assessed with measures based on frequently performed activities. Although the basic argument is plausible, this hypothesis has been difficult to test in a rigorous fashion. The two major problems are: (a) that there is not yet any consensus regarding the frequency of different activities, or even at which level of analysis the evaluation of frequencies should be conducted; and (b) that if the activities are performed at high levels of frequency then the cumulative experience invariably favors older adults such that experience is positively correlated with, and hence potentially confounded with, increased age.

These problems clearly complicate interpretations of results from activities with different frequencies. However, the currently available evidence suggests that young adults tend to perform at higher levels than older adults in a variety of tasks presumed to resemble common or frequent activities. The research results based on across-activity comparisons therefore do not appear very consistent with the disuse perspective, but in the absence of definitive information about the frequencies of various activities or processes, this conclusion should be considered only tentative at the present time.

ACROSS-PERSON COMPARISONS

Experience with cognitive activities also varies across people because people differ considerably in the type and frequency of activities in which they engage. Some of these experiential variations may be associated with the individual's status as a student, or with his or her occupation, but others are simply characteristics of the person's lifestyle. Regardless of the source of the experiential variations, if they are important determinants of age relations in cognitive performance then one might expect different age trends for people with different amounts of relevant experience. That is, people who have extensive experience with relevant activities should exhibit little or no age differences on selected measures of cognitive performance, whereas people with lesser amounts of experience should have moderate to large performance declines because of factors related to disuse.

Three categories of research are relevant to the question of whether people with varying amounts of experience have different patterns of age-related cognitive differences. These consist of studies examining the role of student status, studies involving people from the same occupation, and studies attempting to determine the relations between level of experience with relevant activities and the magnitude of age differences in cognitive functioning.

Does Student Status Make a Difference?

The type of experience most frequently mentioned in connection with the disuse hypothesis is that associated with formal schooling (Craik & Rabinowitz, 1984; Eisdorfer, 1969; Hanley-Dunn & McIntosh, 1984; J.T. Hartley, 1986; H.E. Jones, 1959; Kausler, 1985; C.E. McFarland, Warren, & Crockard, 1985; Monge, 1969; Monge & Gardner, 1976; Perlmutter & D.B. Mitchell, 1982; Poon, Fozard, & Treat, 1978; Rabinowitz, Ackerman, Craik, & Hinchley, 1982; Schaie & Zelinski, 1979; Schmitt, M.D. Murphy, & R.E. Sanders, 1981; A.D. Smith, 1980; Sorenson, 1933, 1938; Zelinski, et al., 1980; Zivian & Darjes, 1983). A clear statement of what might be termed the student status hypothesis was provided by Parks, et al. (1986):

... [W]e suggest that being a student demands the use and practice of cognitive processes that optimize experimental cognitive task performance, and because student demands tend to be confounded with age in adulthood, a student status difference previously has been inappropriately interpreted as a developmental effect. (p. 250)

The primary expectation from the student status hypothesis is that age differences should be much smaller, and perhaps even eliminated, when age and student status are separated by restricting comparisons either to only students, or to only nonstudents. There is considerable evidence contradicting the part of this prediction concerned with nonstudents because most of the participants in nearly all large-scale studies involving adults across the entire adult age range have been nonstudents, and, as reviewed in chapter 2, many of those studies have revealed substantial age differences on a variety of measures of cognitive effectiveness. It is nevertheless still possible that comparisons limited to students of different ages might reveal somewhat different age trends than those found in studies involving only nonstudents, or mixtures of students and nonstudents.

Unfortunately, several problems complicate the interpretation of comparisons involving students of different ages. One potentially severe problem is that older students may be more select members of their age group than young students are of their age group. That is, because the normative pattern is for young adults to attend college and for middle-aged and older adults to pursue their occupations or other noneducational interests, the middle-aged and older adults who are attending school may differ in important respects from their age peers who are not attending school. This selectivity may be manifested in ambition, motivation, curiosity, or general intellectual ability, but, regardless of how it is expressed, if it is not present to the same extent in young adults, then a confounding may exist between age and these selection characteristics.

Another limitation associated with comparisons of students at varying ages is that there may be differences in either the number or type of courses taken by people of different ages. If the older students are taking fewer courses, are taking primarily elective courses rather than those required for an academic degree, or are taking courses in evening or special programs, then the cognitive demands of their school experiences may not be equivalent to those of the typical young adult college student.

Still other problems that complicate comparisons of students of different ages are that several potentially relevant studies compared only young and middle-aged adults (Jacewicz & A.A. Hartley, 1979; Nolan, Havemeyer, & Vig, 1978; Zivian & Darjes, 1983), or had samples with as few as 10 individuals in each group (Jacewicz & A.A. Hartley, 1979; Zivian & Darjes, 1983). These features result in very low power to detect any age differences that might exist.

Despite these complications, which could either exaggerate or minimize age trends depending on how they are combined and their relative levels of importance, results from several studies are consistent in indicating that young college students generally perform better than older college students on a variety of cognitive tasks. Age differences in comparisons restricted to students have been reported with assorted reasoning tasks (Arenberg & Robertson-Tchabo, 1985; F.H. Hooper, et al., 1984; Persaud, 1987), prose memory tasks (S.K. Gordon & W.C. Clark, 1974; J.T. Hartley, 1986; Ratner, et al., 1987), paired associate learning and block design tasks (Parks, et al., 1986), and miscellaneous learning or memory tasks (R.L. Cohen, Sandler, & Schroeder, 1987; Thorndike, et al., 1928; Sorenson, 1938).

An alternative strategy for investigating effects on cognitive performance associated with student status was described by Salthouse, et al., (1988a). The basic idea was that if being a student conferred special advantages (or disadvantages) beyond those associated with a given age, then the performance of students should be underestimated (or overestimated) on the basis of linear regression equations relating age and performance in samples of nonstudents. A total of 27 measures of cognitive performance were examined in the Salthouse, et al. study. For most of the measures the performance of young college students was found to be predicted accurately from the regression equations relating performance to age among nonstudent, but comparably educated, adults. Only with a measure of the accuracy of reconstructing the order in which different tasks were performed were the college students found to be more accurate than expected from the predictions.

Although there are problems of interpretation with each of the methods of investigating the student status hypothesis, the results from the different procedures appear quite consistent. Comparisons involving only nonstudents, only students, or predictions of student performance from nonstudent regression equations, all suggest that few cognitive differences appear to be associated with student status, per se. It is possible that other measures of cognitive functioning might reveal somewhat different results, but the student status hypothesis has not been supported on the basis of currently available data.

Within-Occupation Comparisons

Age comparisons of measures of cognitive performance among individuals from the same occupation can be quite informative because the samples are often homogeneous with respect to potentially important variables such as education, income, and social class. Of particular interest in the present context is that members of the same occupation can also be expected to be similar to one another in terms of their patterns of experience with different activities, and thus there may be less of a confounding between age and experience in these individuals than in more heterogeneous samples.

The degree to which experience is relevant probably varies according to the specificity of the match between the occupation and the particular measure of cognitive functioning employed. That is, studies in which individuals are simply categorized according to occupational class are likely to have the weakest relations between experience and cognition, studies in which everyone is a member of the same occupation but there is no obvious relation between the occupation and the measures of cognitive performance are intermediate, and studies in which everyone is a member of an occupation with clear relevance to the measures of cognitive performance can be expected to have the strongest relations between experience and measures of cognitive performance. While these different kinds of studies vary in terms of their relevance to the issue of the role of experience on age differences in cognition, it is nevertheless useful to examine results from each of these categories of research.

An early study by Vernon (1947) reported that the magnitude of the age differences on the Raven's Progressive Matrices Test varied across different occupational groups. Little information about the sampling procedures was provided, however, and consequently one cannot determine whether selection biases may have operated such that the older members of the occupations might not have been as representative of their age group as were the younger members.

Heron and Chown (1967) also found that occupational class was related to the magnitude of age differences on the Raven's. Adults from higher-status occupations were reported to have smaller age differences in reasoning performance than those from unskilled or manual labor occupations. This finding is somewhat ambiguous, however, because an additional analysis was conducted attempting to control for overall level of mental ability by matching people from different occupations on the basis of their score on a vocabulary test. Much smaller occupational differences in the age trends were evident in this second analysis, suggesting that the initial results may have been attributable to level of mental ability, and not to occupation, per se.

The most extensive investigation of occupational class on age trends in cognitive performance was reported by Fozard and Nuttall (1971). A total of 1,146 men between 28 and 83 years of age were administered the General Aptitude Test Battery (GATB), and assigned occupational classifications based on their current, or most recent, occupations. Performance on each of the GATB tests was expressed in standard scores, with a mean of 100 and a standard deviation of 20. Scores for the five

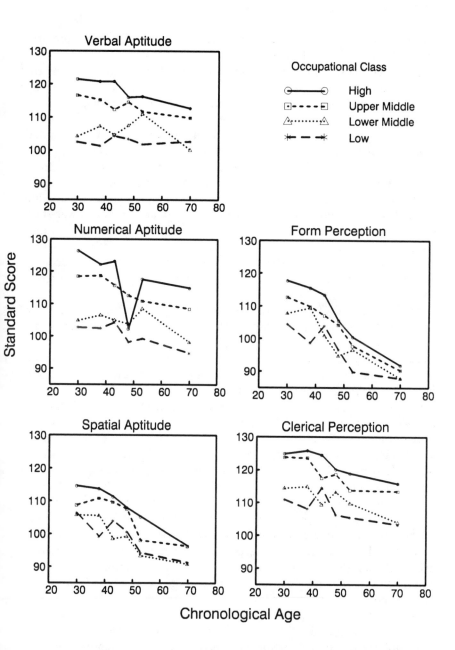

Figure 4.1. Age relations on five subtests of the General Aptitude Test Battery at four different levels of occupational status. Data from Fozard and Nuttall (1971).

cognitive tests in the battery are displayed in Figure 4.1 as a function of age and occupational class.

Three points should be noted about the results in Figure 4.1. The first is that, as is often the case (see chapter 2), the magnitude of the age differences varies across cognitive measures. In particular, small age differences are evident in the antonym-synonym measure of verbal aptitude, but the differences are more pronounced with the arithmetic reasoning measure of numerical aptitude, the perceptual comparison measures of form perception, and the spatial visualization measure of spatial aptitude. The second point is that each performance measure is sensitive to occupational class, with members of higher-status occupations generally performing at higher levels than members of lower-status occupations. Finally, and perhaps most important, the age and occupational class effects were additive rather than interactive. That is, the functions relating age to performance were nearly parallel for the different occupational classes, and do not appear to systematically diverge or converge with increased age.

Salthouse, et al., (1988a) also reported data in which the joint effects of age and occupational status can be examined. Although not analyzed in terms of occupational status in the original report, the research participants can be categorized in this manner because all subjects reported their own or their spouse's occupation. Participants were classified in terms of occupational level according to Hollinghead's (1957) system as high (n = 77 in categories 5, 6, and 7), medium (n = 157 in categories 3 and 4), and low (n = 70 in categories 1 and 2); relations between age and performance for each group are displayed in Figure 4.2. The scores in each graph are composites based on the average z-score for two independent measures. The paired associate score is based on two trials with different pairs of words, the memory score is based on the accuracy of recalling identities of letters and the accuracy of recalling positions of target items, and the speed score is based on the speed of performing computer-administered versions of the Digit Symbol Substitution Test and the Number Comparison Test. (Note that because the paired associate and memory scores are based on accuracy and the speed score is based on time, better performance corresponds to higher values for the first two measures and to lower values for the speed measure.)

The results of the Salthouse, et al. (1988a) project are similar to those of Fozard and Nuttall (1971). In particular, although there appear to be some main effects of occupational status (e.g., with the memory and speed variables), there is little evidence of any age-by-occupational status interactions because parallel age relations are apparent across the three occupational class categorizations.

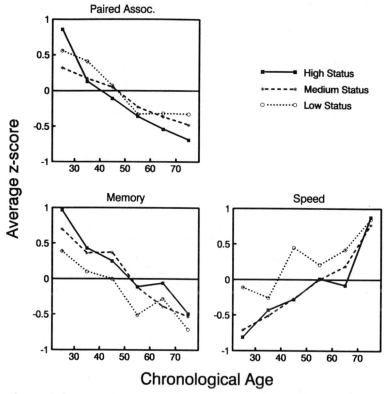

Figure 4.2.   Age relations on three composite measures of cognitive performance at three levels of occupational status. Data from Salthouse, Kausler, and Saults (1988a).

Relations between age and measures of cognitive functioning in members of different occupations were also examined in two studies by Avolio and Waldman (1987, 1990). Results from the first study were interpreted as indicating that the age relations were smaller among those in more skilled occupations. However, several characteristics of the study suggest that this conclusion may be premature. Not only were most of the 131 participants in the Avolio and Waldman (1987) study rather young (with a mean age of 30.5), but the average amount of experience at their current job was reported to be less than 2 years. It is also not obvious why electricians and mechanics (who were reported to exhibit smaller age effects) would necessarily be expected to use spatial visualization, numerical, verbal, and mechanical reasoning abilities more than truck drivers and equipment operators (who were found to have larger age effects on measures of these abilities).

The second study involved a much larger sample of adults (21,646), with a slightly greater average age (32.5 years), and more average years of experience (6.2 years). Age correlations for a composite measure of general intellectual ability and for a measure of numerical ability are displayed in Figure 4.3 for the 10 occupational categories analyzed in their project. Sample sizes for the occupational categories ranged from 724 to 4,145, and thus the correlations can be assumed to be fairly stable.

The data summarized in Figure 4.3 clearly indicate that the magnitude of the age relations varies across occupational categories. However, it is not obvious how these differences can be interpreted in terms of variations in patterns of experience. For example, the requirements of health care or inspection jobs do not appear less cognitively demanding than those of clerical or small assembly jobs, and yet people in the former jobs exhibited much stronger negative relations between age and cognitive performance than those in the latter jobs. An additional analysis based on ratings of job complexity failed to reveal differential age patterns as a function of the complexity of the job, and thus the occupational differences are apparently also not attributable to variations in job complexity. The different age trends observed in the Avolio and Waldman (1990) study may have been a consequence of differing degrees of selective attrition occurring in various

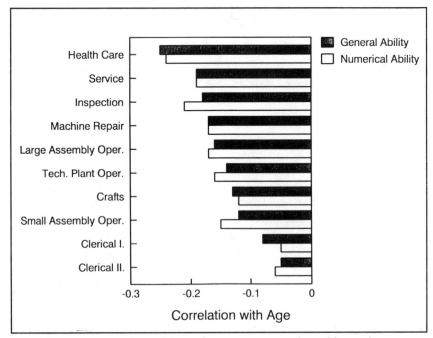

Figure 4.3.   Correlations with age for two measures of cognitive performance across 10 occupational categories. Data from Waldman and Avolio (1989).

occupations, but unfortunately this possibility could not be evaluated from the reported data.

Clement (1969) also claimed that "... teachers showed less fall with age than did ... factory workers in various measures of physical, intellectual and social performance" (p. 64). No statistical analyses were reported in support of this conclusion, however, and members of the different occupational groups also differed in overall intellectual level. Any differential age trends that may exist could therefore be due as much, or more, to initial intellectual ability differences as to occupational differences.

Another study sometimes cited in support of an experiential influence on age-related effects in cognition was reported by Cijfer (1966). This study was a replication of an exploratory study by Allan, described in Welford (1958). Both studies involved a reasoning task in which a series of statements were presented which the individual was to read, and then he or she answered a set of questions concerning the compatibility of the statements with one another, the conclusions that could be drawn, and so on. Furthermore, in both studies, participants took the materials home and were allowed several days to return the answers. No mention was made in either report whether the instructions specified that the participants were to work on the problems themselves, or that there should be any limit on the amount of time they spent working on the problems.

The main result leading Cijfer to suggest that experiential factors influenced the magnitude of age differences on reasoning performance was a different pattern of age differences in his study, in which the research participants were physicians, than in the study originally reported by Welford (1958). In the original study young adults were reported to have made more deductions than older adults, but no such age difference was evident among the Dutch physicians in the Cijfer replication study. This apparent difference, which was not evaluated statistically, is a very tenuous basis on which to reach a conclusion because potentially important procedural differences may have existed between the two studies, particularly considering that the materials and instructions apparently had to be translated from English to Dutch. Furthermore, although physicians might be expected to have more experience with reasoning problems than people from clerical or management occupations, it is not obvious why they should also be superior to individuals drawn from university teaching and research staff, from which one of the samples described in Welford (1958) was recruited.

Results interpreted as supporting an experiential moderation of the influence of age on cognitive functioning have also been reported by Crosson (1984). The participants in this project were members of the same avocation—creative artists and writers. The measure of cognitive performance used was the time to find targets in an embedded figures test, the assumption being that "... writers and artists of all ages ... actively practiced removing either words or forms from their usual context" (p. 169). Correlations between age (with a range of 23 to 77 years) and time to locate targets on the embedded figures tests were .28 for 88 artists, and .33 for 78 writers. Because these correlations were smaller than that found in a previous study involving unselected adults (r = .50 in J.A. Lee & Pollack, 1978), Crosson suggested that her results were consistent with the hypothesis that age effects were minimal with continuously exercised skills. Although it is conceivable that there are smaller age effects on embedded figures performance among samples of writers and artists, it is also possible that chance sampling variability could have contributed to the apparent differences between Crosson's (1984) results and those of J.A. Lee and Pollack (1978). In fact, two other studies with embedded figures tests have reported correlations between age and measures of embedded figures performance intermediate between those found in these two studies: correlations of .40 in Botwinick and Storandt (1974), and .37 in Chown (1961). Smaller age differences in a sample of creative adults compared with a sample of unselected adults were also reported by Crosson and Robertson-Tchabo (1983), but the measure of creativity in that study was based on preference ratings, and consequently may be more reflective of stylistic differences than of true differences in creative ability.

One of the most interesting of the occupationally homogeneous studies was an early investigation in which young and old college professors were contrasted on a battery of cognitive tests (Sward, 1945). Although other studies have been reported in which younger faculty members were found to be superior to older ones on various measures of cognitive functioning (Macht & Buschke, 1984; Perlmutter, 1978; R.R. Powell & Pohndorf, 1971; J.M. Thomas & Charles, 1964; Traxler, 1973), the Sward (1945) study is unique in several respects. First, the 45 young (ages 21 to 42) and 45 old (ages 60 to 79) faculty members were matched with respect to academic discipline, and were found to be comparable in characteristics such as academic honors and parents' occupational level. Second, a broad range of cognitive tests were administered, with the total battery requiring three to four hours across three separate sessions. And third, considerable attention was paid to the procedures and analyses, with both the reliability and the intercorrelations of the measures reported in each group. The major results from this project, with performance of older adults expressed in units of young adult standard deviations, are illustrated in Figure 4.4.

Perhaps the most striking feature of the results in Figure 4.4 is how closely they resemble the patterns found in many other studies in which different cognitive tests have been administered to adults of various ages (see chapter 2). As is frequently the case, the performance differences were either very small or favoring older adults rather than young adults on

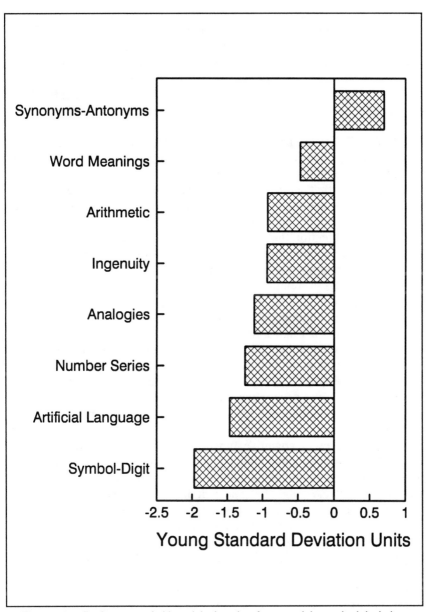

Figure 4.4.   Performance of older adults in units of young adult standard deviations for eight cognitive tests administered to young and old college faculty members. Data from Sward (1945).

measures of verbal information or word knowledge, but the differences were larger and favored young adults on measures of abstract reasoning and speeded substitution. (It should be noted that only the Artificial Language and Symbol-Digit tasks were administered with time limits.) The results of this study, therefore, appear very similar to those frequently found in unselected samples comprised of people from a variety of different occupations.

In addition to the studies described above, a number of studies have been conducted in which comparisons by age were reported on measures of cognitive performance from individuals who were members of the same occupation. These studies, all of which reported significant differences favoring young adults on one or more measures of cognitive functioning, are listed in Table 4.3. The number and diversity of entries in Table 4.3 clearly indicate that age differences in cognitive performance are often apparent even when all research participants are members of the same occupation.

A possible objection that could be directed against many of the studies with occupationally homogeneous samples is that, even though everyone in the sample may have had similar experiences, there might not be any reason to expect a relation between the activities performed in the occupation and proficiency on the aspects of cognition assessed in the study. Klein and Shaffer (1986) did suggest that because their research participants were all English teachers they could be considered skilled in remembering words from sentences, but this argument is not particularly compelling without additional information concerning the actual activities performed by English teachers. In most of the other studies involving members of the same occupation the researchers did not even attempt to relate occupational experiences to the aspects of cognition being assessed.

In an effort to provide a more powerful test of the effects of experience on age differences in cognitive functioning, Salthouse, Babcock, D.R. Mitchell, Skovronek, and Palmon (1990) measured spatial visualization performance among practicing architects and an age-matched sample of unselected adults. As might be expected, older architects were found to be superior to unselected age peers on several measures of spatial visualization ability (e.g., paper folding, surface development, visual synthesis, form board, block design). Two distinct interpretations of these differences were considered. One was termed *differential preservation*: The two groups may have differed in terms of how well their spatial abilities were preserved with increased age. That is, architects might have maintained high levels of spatial abilities because these abilities were used continuously in their work, but spatial abilities may have declined in unselected adults because of disuse. The second interpretation, termed *preserved differentiation*, was that the architects and unselected adults may always have differed in spatial

TABLE 4.3
Studies revealing age differences favoring young adults
with samples from the same occupation.

Occupation	Task	Source
Teachers	divergent thinking	Alpaugh & Birren (1977)
"	inductive reasoning	Garfield & Blek (1952)
"	intentional word recall	Klein & Shaffer (1986)
"	word memory and digit symbol substitution	R. Lachman, J.L. Lachman, & D.W. Taylor (1982)
"	prose memory	Moenster (1972)
Nuns and Parochial School Teachers	memory for words	Erber (1974)
"	prose memory	Ulatowska, Cannito, Hayashi, & Fleming (1985)
"	perceptual closure	Wentworth-Roth, Mackintosh, & Fialkoff (1974)
Pilots and Air Traffic Controllers	digit symbol substitution and block design	Birren & Spieth (1962)
"	miscellaneous psychometric tests	Glanzer & Glaser (1959)
"	choice reaction time	Szafran (1970)
"	spatial visualization and inductive reasoning	Cobb, Lay, & Bourdet (1971), Trites & Cobb (1964)
Nurses	rod-and-frame	Gruenfeld & MacEachron (1975)
"	memory for words	Kriauciunas (1968)
Factory Employees	semantic categorization reaction time	Dirken (1972)
"	miscellaneous psychometric tests	Helander (1967)
Food Service Employees	digit span and Everyday Life Skills Test	Perlmutter, M. Kaplan, & Nyquist (1990)
Business Executives	concept formation	E.H. Schludermann, S.M. Schludermann, Merryman, & B.W. Brown (1983)
"	lists of words	T.L. Rose & Yesavage (1983)

(Cont.)

TABLE 4.3
(Continued)

Business Executives	name recall	Yesavage & T.L. Rose (1984)
"	special version of Army Alpha	Bingham & W.T. Davis (1924)
"	word recall and digit-letter substitution	Poitrenaud, Malbezin, & Guez (1989)

visualization ability, and these initial differences were merely preserved as the individuals grew older.

Another study in the Salthouse, Babcock, D.R. Mitchell, Skovronek, and Palmon (1990) project attempted to discriminate between the differential preservation and preserved differentiation interpretations. The reasoning was that if the differential preservation view were correct, then little or no age difference would be expected in comparisons restricted to architects because, with those skills continuously in use, there would have been no opportunity for spatial visualization abilities to decline due to disuse. Three measures of spatial visualization ability were obtained in this study: number of items answered correctly on a surface development test, accuracy of paper folding decisions, and accuracy of visual synthesis decisions. Significant age-related performance declines were found on each measure, and the age trends for the surface development and paper folding measures were nearly identical to those found among unselected adults. (No comparison of architects and unselected adults was possible with the measure of visual synthesis accuracy.) These results thus favor the preserved differentiation interpretation because the initial ability differences were preserved across the adult years, and not that the architects maintained their abilities while unselected adults did not.

The preceding review reveals that results from age-comparative research involving members of the same occupation have been fairly consistent, but surprising. The predominant pattern has been a finding of typical (i.e., consistent with results from unselected samples) age-performance relations even when all research participants belong to the same occupation, and presumably share many common experiences. This outcome is surprising because it might reasonably have been expected that age differences would be smaller when increased age is associated with greater amounts of relevant experience. However, the currently available results suggest that the magnitude of the relations between age and measures of cognitive performance are similar regardless of the nature of one's occupation, and by inference, of one's pattern of experiences.

Activity Analyses

One version of the disuse perspective postulates that at least some of the cognitive deficits associated with increased age are attributable to a decrease with age in the range of activities one performs. Two examples of this type of argument are contained in a recent edited volume on the topic of everyday cognition. The first example was provided by G. Cohen and Faulkner (1989b) in a discussion of an experiential interpretation of age differences in memory:

> ... [E]lderly individuals are less exposed to novel perceptual events. With a less mobile existence, events are more routine, and the environment is more unchanging. Because the real external events that make up daily life for the older person are liable to be familiar, routine, frequently repeated, they will produce memory traces that lack distinctiveness. (p. 228)

Later in the same volume, Kausler (1989a) suggested that age-related deficiencies in concept-name associations might originate because:

> The relatively passive life style of many elderly adults is likely to carry with it a reduction of conversational activity, a reduction that could be sufficient to result in some degree of atrophy of the ability to retrieve concept-to-name associations. (p. 493)

Although perhaps reasonable with respect to institutionalized individuals, and possibly some retired adults, arguments based on activity restrictions seem much less compelling for people in their 50s and 60s who are still working and leading active lives. Because age-related cognitive differences are frequently reported in samples of research participants within these age ranges, explanations based on a general reduction in overall activity level have limited applicability in accounting for age trends evident across most of the adult years. It may still be plausible, however, to suggest that certain age differences originate because of age-related changes in the frequency of specific activities.

Several methods are available for investigating possible relations between different kinds of experience and the magnitude of age-associated effects on cognitive functioning. One method consists of simply examining correlations between measures of experience with different activities and measures of cognitive performance in a sample of older adults (Arbuckle, et al., 1986; Correll, Rokosz, & Blanchard, 1966; Craik, Byrd, & Swanson, 1987; DeCarlo, 1974; M. Williams, 1960). The implicit assumption in this kind of research seems to be that the experiential variation may have contributed to some of the differences in performance evident among older adults. As discussed in chapter 1, however, this assumption is not necessarily valid because variations in experience are but one of several possible determinants of an individual's current level of cognitive functioning. Furthermore, the causal direction of the experience-cognition relation is ambiguous when the two variables are examined at a single point in time (or within a narrow range of ages). To illustrate, high levels of cognitive functioning may be a prerequisite for certain kinds of experiences, in which case the correlation would reflect the effects of cognition on experience, rather than the effects of experience on cognition. The preserved differentiation interpretation discussed earlier in connection with the Salthouse, Babcock, D.R. Mitchell, Skovronek, and Palmon (1990) study on architects might be considered an example of this sort of cognition-experience influence.

A preferable procedure for examining the role of differential experience on the relation between age and cognitive functioning involves collecting data on both experience and cognitive variables for individuals throughout the entire adult age range. Data of this nature allow two potentially informative analyses to be conducted. One consists of comparisons of the magnitude of the experience-cognition relation at each of several age ranges. These comparisons are relevant to the disuse interpretation because, if it is really the variations in the patterns of lifelong experience that contribute to the individual differences observed within a sample of older adults, then little or no relation between the measures of experience and the measures of cognition would be expected within a sample of young adults who have not yet had much of an opportunity to accumulate the benefits of those experiences.

The second analysis possible when the experience and cognitive performance measures are available from adults across the entire adult age range consists of attempts to use statistical procedures to determine the magnitude of the age-cognition relation after adjusting for variations in experience. The rationale is that if most of the age differences in cognition are mediated by differences in experience, then statistical control of the experience variables should reduce, or possibly even eliminate, the negative relation between age and measures of cognitive performance.

Both of these methods of analysis can be illustrated with results from a study by Rice and B.J. Meyer (1986). This study involved a total of 422 adults who completed a questionnaire about reading habits, and also performed a prose recall task. Responses to the questionnaire items were subjected to a factor analysis to identify coherent groupings of items, and then correlations between the factor scores and measures of prose recall performance were computed.

Three of the factors from the questionnaire responses were found to be significantly related to either age or to prose recall performance. One factor, termed Read for Need, was based on the number of hours per week spent reading (required) textbooks, and on the frequency of constructing outlines when reading. A factor labeled Read News was based on the number of hours per week spent reading newspapers and magazines. The third factor was designated Read Lots because it was derived from self ratings of how often the individual read, and how much enjoyment he or she derived from reading.

Significant positive correlations between prose recall and the Read for Need (r = .19) and Read Lots (r = .25) factors were found in the sample of 159 adults between 62 and 80 years of age. These results cannot be used to infer that variations in reading habits were necessarily responsible for age differences in prose recall, however, because roughly similar correlations were apparent in samples of 117 adults between 40 and 54 years of age (r = .07 and .29, respectively), and of 146 adults between 18 and 32 years of age (r = .12 and .20, respectively).

The overall correlation between age and prose recall performance in the Rice and B.J. Meyer (1986) study was -.24. Correlations between age and the reading factors were -.37 for Read for Need, .31 for Read for News, and .09 for Read Lots. The correlations between prose recall performance and the reading factors were .20 for Read for Need, .07 for Read for News, and .22 for Read Lots. The resulting partial correlations between age and prose recall performance were -.18 after control of Read for Need, -.28 after control of Read for News, and -.27 after control of Read Lots. With two of the three experience variables, therefore, equating adults of various ages with respect to relevant experience resulted in larger, rather than smaller, relations between age and recall performance.

A similar pattern was evident in a later study by Rice, B.J. Meyer, and D.C. Miller (1988) in which 54 adults were asked to record the amount of time devoted to different types of activities over a 5-week period. The correlation between age and prose recall performance in this sample was -.41, and that between prose recall performance and the total number of hours per week spent reading was .32. The correlation between age and amount of reading per week was not reported in this study, but it was probably positive based on the findings of the earlier Rice and B.J. Meyer (1986) study, and of a study by Salthouse, et al., (1988a). The correlation between age and recall would therefore increase, rather than decrease, if adjustments were made for variations in amount of reading experience.

Another project in which interrelations of age, experience, and cognitive performance were examined was recently conducted by Salthouse and D.R. Mitchell (1990). The cognitive variables of primary interest in this project were measures of spatial visualization ability (i.e., scores on paper folding and surface development tests). The experience variables were based on responses to a series of questions about experience with activities presumed to require spatial visualization abilities. The major results of this study were very similar to those of Rice and B.J. Meyer (1986). Correlations between experience and cognitive performance were similar for young, middle-aged, and old adults (e.g., the correlations between the spatial visualization measure and an experience component labeled Spatial Perspective were .17, .10, and .17, respectively), and the correlation between age and spatial visualization performance was -.37 before statistical control of the experience components, and -.35 after the variance associated with the relevant experience components had been removed.

The best method of evaluating the effects of different types of experiences on the relation between age and cognition undoubtedly involves longitudinal comparisons. However, as mentioned in chapter 2, the stability of many cognitive measures is often quite high. This high stability implies that the interval between successive measurements must be moderately long, and the sample size reasonably large, in order to be able to detect relations between experiential variables and rates of longitudinal change. It is therefore not surprising that there are not many longitudinal studies relevant to experiential influences on cognitive change.

Several studies have attempted to identify significant predictors of individual differences in the changes of cognitive performance observed across successive measurement occasions, but few of the variables that have been examined have reflected experience with cognitive activities. For example, Gribbin, Schaie, and Parham (1980) and Owens (1966) investigated lifestyle variables such as income, urban or rural residence, marital status, and so on. Siegler (1983) was interested in physical activity as a predictor of individual change, and Shichita, Hatano, Ohashi, Shibata, and Matuzaki (1986) and Schwartzman, et al., (1987) relied upon composite activity measures based on a mixture of physical, social, recreational, and cognitive activities. Green and Reimanis (1970) attempted to extract a measure of cognitive activity from patient records of residents of a Veterans' Administration domiciliary, but the validity of this activity measure is not known. In any case, it was not found to correlate with amount of longitudinal change in full-scale score from the Wechsler tests.

One of the most intriguing studies of experiential influences on cognitive functioning was conducted from a sociological perspective. Kohn and Schooler (1978, 1983) examined the relation between concepts which they labeled the *substantive complexity of work* and *ideational flexibility*. Substantive work complexity was intended to represent the degree to which the activities performed during a job required thought and independent judgment. Ideational flexibility was postulated to represent flexibility in coping with intellectual demands in complex situations. Both theoretical constructs were assessed by means of multiple indicators; the particular measures used in the assessment of each construct are listed in Table 4.4.

Although the ideational flexibility measure bears little resemblance to traditional psychometric tests, the fact that it is based on a diverse set of

TABLE 4.4
Measures used in the assessment
of ideational flexibility and substantive complexity of work
in the Kohn and Schooler (1983) study.

Ideational Flexibility

1. Goodenough intelligence estimate from Draw-A-Person Test.

2. Witkin sophistication-of-body-concept from the Draw-A-Person Test.

3. Embedded Figures Test.

4. Interviewer's appraisal of respondent's intelligence.

5. Frequency of agreement in responding to agree-disagree questions.

6. Rating of the adequacy of answer to "What are all the arguments you can think of for and against allowing cigarette commercials on TV?"

7. Rating of the adequacy of the answer to "Suppose you wanted to open a hamburger stand and there were two locations available. What questions would you consider in deciding which of the two locations offers a better business opportunity?"

Substantive Complexity of Work

1. Rated Complexity of Work with Data (e.g., Low = no use of data, or follow specific instructions; High = use data to coordinate actions and synthesize knowledge).

2. Estimated time working with data.

3. Rated Complexity of Work with Things (e.g., Low = no use of things, or move or carry objects; High = operating or repairing equipment).

4. Estimated time working with things.

5. Rated Complexity of Work with People (e.g., Low = no work with people, or serve people; High = negotiating with, instructing, or advising people)

6. Estimated time working with people

7. Appraisal of overall complexity of work (e.g., Low = routine, or minimal thought; High = complex problem solving, setting up systems with numerous interrelated variables)

---

variables with a certain amount of face validity as reflections of intelligence suggests that it may share considerable variance with intelligence measures derived from conventional tests. Moreover, the finding by K.A. Miller and Kohn (1983) that the ideational flexibility measure had correlations of .75 or greater with measures of the intellectuality of leisure activities, as represented by the number of hours watching television or reading books, the intellectual content of magazines, and so forth, indicates that it probably has at least some validity as an index of level of cognitive functioning.

The results from the Kohn and Schooler project most relevant for the current purpose are the 10-year longitudinal data from 687 men between

26 and 64 years of age at the beginning of the study. The correlation between the substantive complexity measure at the two assessment periods was .77, and that between the ideational flexibility measure at the beginning and end of the 10-year interval was .93. Despite this high stability of ideational flexibility, both age and current level of substantive complexity of work were found to be significant predictors of the Time 2 ideational flexibility score after controlling for the Time 1 ideational flexibility score. The standardized regression coefficients in predicting the Time 2 ideational flexibility measure were .71 from Time 1 ideational flexibility, .17 from Time 2 substantive complexity of work, and -.14 from age at Time 2.

The Kohn and Schooler (1978, 1983) findings therefore suggest that there is a positive relation between the cognitive demands of an individual's work and the amount of incremental change in cognitive functioning occurring over a 10-year interval. The negative coefficient for age indicates that, independent of both prior cognitive level and the nature of work, there is a decrease in the amount of gain (or perhaps even a loss) at older ages. When considered in combination, therefore, these findings present a mixed picture for the disuse interpretation: Although there is evidence of an experiential influence on the level of cognitive functioning, the age-related influences are of nearly the same magnitude and in the opposite direction.

Summary

Research based on across-person comparisons is relevant to the disuse perspective if people vary in terms of the amount of experience they have with specific kinds of cognitive activities. That is, if age-related declines are caused by lack of experience with relevant activities, then the magnitude of the relations between age and measures of cognitive performance should be expected to vary as a function of the amount of experience the individuals have with relevant activities.

Attempts to investigate this implication of the disuse perspective have yielded largely negative results. Studies based on global categorizations of activity, such as student status and occupational level, have generally found age differences comparable to those reported with unselected samples. Results from research including more direct measures of specific experience have been mixed, with most indicating little or no effects of experience on the magnitude of the age trends. The primary exception is the study of Kohn and Schooler (1978, 1983) in which it appears that both age and type of experience influence the amount of cognitive change. No firm conclusions can therefore be reached at the present time regarding the role of experiential factors as moderators of the susceptibility to age-related influences in cognitive functioning. It must be acknowledged, however, that the bulk of the currently available evidence appears more negative than positive.

EFFECTS OF ADDED EXPERIENCE

One of the most popular methods of investigating the disuse interpretation of age differences in cognitive functioning has involved manipulations of experience by means of training or practice. The primary hypothesis has been that if lack of relevant experience is the cause of many age differences in cognition, then one might expect to eliminate at least some of the age differences by providing everyone with appropriate kinds of experience. Although certain outcomes of manipulated-experience studies could be informative about the disuse perspective, research of this type has been the focus of considerable controversy.

Much of the debate associated with the status of manipulated-experience studies as they relate to the disuse perspective has been based on logical, rather than empirical, issues. That is, the empirical results have generally been quite consistent, but there have been many disputes regarding the relevance of research involving manipulations of experience to the disuse perspective. Even the rationale for studying the effects of added experience can be questioned because of concerns about the validity of the underlying reasoning. This problem can be illustrated by analyzing the argument behind the use of experiential manipulations. The basic hypothesis seems to be that if the disuse perspective is true then age differences should be eliminated with added experience. In abstract form, the hypothesis is: IF A, THEN B, where A refers to the disuse perspective and B refers to the elimination of age differences with experience. When expressed in this manner it can be seen that the primary outcome relevant to the validity of the disuse perspective (A) would be a failure to eliminate age differences in experience (not B). That is, the valid form of the argument is: IF A, THEN B; NOT B, THEREFORE NOT A (modus tollens), whereas reasoning of the form: IF A, THEN B; B, THEREFORE A, is not valid (but is so common that it is known as the Fallacy of Affirming the Consequent). Strictly speaking, therefore, the only outcome of manipulated-experience studies that would be truly informative about the status of the disuse perspective would be a finding that the age differences were *not* eliminated with added experience, and that would presumably lead to the inference that the disuse perspective was wrong.

Controversy has also been associated with interpretations of the finding that the performance of older adults on various cognitive tests improves after an assortment of training experiences. This result has led some researchers to conclude that most, or possibly even all, age differences in cognitive functioning are attributable to experiential deficits (W.J. Hoyer, G.V. Labouvie, & P.B. Baltes, 1973; Labouvie-Vief & Gonda, 1976; Plemons, Willis, & P.B. Baltes, 1978; Schaie, 1984b; Willis, Blieszner, & P.B. Baltes, 1981; Willis, Cornelius, Blow, & P.B. Baltes, 1983), or that a finding of this nature implies that performance differences between young and old adults are reversible (Labouvie-Vief & Gonda, 1976; J.A. Sanders, Sterns, M. Smith, & R.E. Sanders, 1975; Sterns & R.E. Sanders, 1980). Others have suggested that experiential factors are implicated in age-related decrements because of the ease with which performance can be improved in older adults (Crovitz, 1966; N.W. Denney, 1979; N.W. Denney & D.R. Denney, 1974; Hornblum & Overton, 1976; Kleinman & Brodzinsky, 1978; Perlmutter, 1988; Reese & Rodeheaver, 1985), although the basis for evaluating the ease or difficulty of producing the performance improvements has never been clearly specified.

Each of these arguments has been criticized on the grounds that a demonstration that the cognitive performance of older adults can be improved does not necessarily address the question of the cause of the initial age differences on those measures of performance (Arenberg, 1982a; Botwinick, 1978; N.W. Denney, 1979; Donaldson, 1981; A.A. Hartley & J.W. Anderson, 1986; J.L. Horn, 1979; J.L. Horn & Donaldson, 1976, 1977; P. Roberts, 1983; Salthouse, 1982, 1985b, 1987b, 1987c, 1989b). The reasoning behind many of the criticisms is that the discovery that a manipulation is effective in improving the performance of one group of individuals does not automatically allow one to conclude that the processes affected by that manipulation are responsible for the performance differences between that group and some other, higher-performing, group of individuals. Comparisons of the magnitude of training gains with age-related declines may therefore be of little value unless there is evidence that the same mechanisms are involved in both the performance gains and the performance declines.

This point has been elaborated in discussions of the possible effects of prosthetic devices such as corrective lenses (Birren & Renner, 1977; Salthouse, 1985b, 1987c), and hearing aids (Arenberg, 1982a). Although clearly unrelated to experiential factors, provision of these sensory supplements could be considered an intervention that is likely to improve the performance of older adults because many older individuals suffer from a variety of sensory impairments. If the basis for claiming that cognitive decline has been remediated is simply an improvement in the level of performance, therefore, then virtually any manipulation—whether it involves the administration of training, the provision of sensory aids, or merely the elimination of the difficult items in the test—could be claimed to be effective in remediating decline. What is necessary, but often lacking, in research involving manipulations of experience is evidence that the processes altered by the experiential intervention are isomorphic or homologous to those associated with developmental changes (P.B. Baltes, et al., 1977).

Perhaps the greatest controversy associated with experiential intervention research concerns the value of that research for the purpose of understanding processes of aging when it only involves samples of older adults. There appear to be at least seven valid reasons why training or other manipulated-experience studies with age-homogeneous samples might be valuable:

1. They can allow the researcher to determine whether traditional modes of performance assessment reflect the individual's optimum capacities, or whether he or she is capable of performing at higher levels with different conditions of assessment, or after greater amounts of experience. That is, examination of the level of performance before and after experiential interventions can indicate whether traditional (i.e., single-session) assessments should be assumed to be measuring fixed and absolute capacities, or are merely a somewhat arbitrary point on a function relating level of performance to amount of experience.
2. Training studies can be useful for determining which kinds of experiential interventions are most effective in leading to improvements in cognitive performance.
3. Careful analyses of the nature of training-related performance improvements may allow one to identify the particular aspects of performance responsible for improved levels of functioning.
4. Individuals exhibiting varying amounts of benefit from training can be contrasted to determine the individual characteristics associated with differential training gains.
5. Successful training interventions might serve to challenge accepted beliefs that some individuals or groups are incapable of learning, as reflected in the cliche, "You can't teach an old dog new tricks."
6. Measures of the rapidity of improvement with practice or training might serve as an index of either the severity, or the importance, of individual differences in measures of cognitive performance (Charness, 1989).
7. Training research can have important practical consequences if the performance of minimally-functioning individuals can be improved through training to reach a basic level of competence or achievement.

Although all these justifications for age-homogeneous training (or other manipulations of experience) research are legitimate, only the third and fifth justifications appear directly relevant to the goal of understanding the processes of aging, and even then the contribution seems rather weak. That is, training research might be helpful in identifying mechanisms responsible for changes in performance, as suggested in the third justification, but those change mechanisms must then be treated as mere hypotheses about developmental processes that need to be investigated in age-comparative research in the same manner as any other hypotheses. With respect to the fifth justification, a discovery that the performance of older adults can be improved with a training intervention is certainly more consistent with the disuse perspective than a failure to find any benefits of training. However, as noted in chapter 1, a finding of behavioral plasticity in one group of adults is only a necessary, and not a sufficient, condition for inferring modifiability of age relations. Moreover, most of the more extreme unfavorable stereotypes about age and behavioral plasticity that could be challenged by training research involving only older adults seem to have been discarded years ago. For example, although negative views about the learning capabilities of older adults were expressed a century ago by William James (1893), many reviewers since then have concluded that there is little evidence that older adults are completely incapable of learning (Arenberg & Robertson-Tchabo, 1977; Gilbert, 1952; Kausler, 1982; W.R. Miles, 1942; W.R. Miles & C.C. Miles, 1943). Instead of asking whether older adults have complete or absolute impairments, therefore, most contemporary researchers have been interested in whether they have relative impairments, and if so, what the causes of those impairments might be (N.W. Denney, 1982; Salthouse, 1985b, 1987c).

The importance of including some type of age comparison if the research is intended to address issues relevant to aging is implicit in a description by P.B. Baltes, et al. (1977) of the reasoning involved in making inferences about age differences on the basis of intervention studies. Their hypothetical example involved attempting to determine whether age differences in a measure of dart-throwing accuracy might be attributable to different amounts of practice.

> ... [A]ccording to the hypothesis that practice is the explanatory variable, the assertion would be that 20-year-olds are more accurate because they have experienced the most preexperimental practice in dart throwing; and 50-year-olds ... have less preexperimental practice ... Accordingly, one would hypothesize that short-term treatments involving practice in dart throwing ... would lead to a significant performance increment in ... older adults. Young adults, on the contrary, would benefit comparatively little from this experience, since their preexperimental life history contained a level of practice in dart throwing that brought them close to their asymptotic level of

performance in that behavior. ... [T]he assertion is that—due to life-history differences—different age groups respond *differentially* to the same treatment. (pp. 180-181)

This passage makes it clear that the fundamental prediction from the disuse perspective is not simply that older adults will improve with practice or training, but that they will have greater magnitudes of improvement than will young adults. Without a group of adults of a different age against which the improvements of older adults can be compared, therefore, it may be impossible to conclude anything about the nature of age differences on the cognitive tasks or on other activities of interest.

Willis (1985, 1987, 1989a; Willis & P.B. Baltes, 1981) has argued that a sample of young adults provides an inappropriate basis of comparison for assessing the training benefits of older adults. Among the reasons offered by Willis (1987) for suggesting that young adults are not the proper comparison are that variability is considerable in the performance of older adults, and that young adults are not necessarily at the peak level of cognitive functioning. These arguments do not appear very compelling, however, because whenever two groups differ in mean level of performance there is a difference to be explained, and if that difference is attributable to something that can be remediated by intervention then it seems reasonable to examine the possibility of differential benefits of experiential interventions. The existence of large individual differences in the performance of older (and young) adults therefore seems irrelevant to the question of whether the observed age differences are attributable to disuse, as is the suggestion that young adults may not be at their peak level of functioning, unless it is additionally assumed that the reason they are not at their peak is lack of relevant experience.

Perhaps the most important reason why Willis has objected to the inclusion of young adults in training studies is a belief that young and old adults differ in many respects besides age, and in particular, are not equivalent with respect to factors related to cohort membership. This is a puzzling argument because if cohorts are postulated to differ primarily in terms of their patterns of experiences (see chapter 3), then cohort effects should be found to be even more amenable to experiential intervention than effects due to maturationally based (endogenous) differences. That is, it is precisely when one assumes that the differences are of experiential (exogenous) origin that training or practice that modifies relevant experience should be found to be most beneficial (Salthouse, 1989b).

On the other side of these arguments against the value of young-adult samples in training studies are two reasons why, if one's primary goal is increased understanding of the processes of aging, they are meaningful, and probably essential. One reason is that, as is implicit in the P.B. Baltes, et al. (1977) passage cited previously, some sort of age comparison seems necessary in order to draw inferences about developmental mechanisms. Only if one were to make very strong, and probably unsubstantiated, assumptions that most individual differences among older adults were attributable to differential patterns of aging, would it be reasonable to reach conclusions about the processes of aging from the study of a single age group (see chapter 1).

The second important reason for including multiple age groups in training studies is that there may be a variety of consequences of training, and comparisons across age groups might be helpful in distinguishing among them. For example, several researchers have suggested that performance improvements associated with experience can be of several types, ranging from remediation or reactivation of prior levels of competence to various kinds of acquisition of new skills in the form of compensation, accommodation, and so on (P.B. Baltes, Kliegl, & Dittmann-Kohli, 1988; P.B. Baltes & Lindenberger, 1988; N.W. Denney, 1979; Salthouse, 1984, 1987b, 1987c; Schaie & Willis, 1986; Willis, 1987, 1989b; Willis & Schaie, 1986b). These various consequences of training are potentially distinguishable when the training is administered to people of different levels of current ability and different experiential histories, because only those individuals whose abilities have declined from disuse would be expected to benefit from remediation, whereas everyone might benefit from opportunities to acquire new skills. Administration of the training procedure to individuals whose abilities have not declined (e.g., young adults), as well as to those whose abilities have declined (e.g., older adults), therefore provides a basis for evaluating the extent to which training benefits in older adults can be attributed to remediation of disuse. Comparisons can be either quantitative, in the form of the magnitude of the training-related improvement, or qualitative, in terms of analyses of the specific processes associated with the performance improvements. In each case, however, training-related benefits evident in the group of young adults cannot be attributed to the remediation of disuse-mediated decline if this group has experienced neither disuse nor decline. Results of the training manipulations in young adults can therefore be used to help evaluate how much of the training benefit apparent in older adults might be due to remediation of disuse-mediated declines as opposed to the acquisition of new skills.

In fact, however, even the comparisons of the magnitude of training effects across adults of different ages are not necessarily informative because older adults might fail to exhibit greater training benefits than young adults either due to inferior learning abilities, or due to the difficulty of reversing the cumulative effects of prolonged disuse. That is, if training effects are conceptualized as consisting of both the restoration of old skills and the learning of new skills, and if young adults are superior in the efficiency of new learning, then they may have equivalent or greater net training benefits than older adults even if there is some remediation of disuse among the older adults. It is also possible that, despite being of experiential origin, the extensive period of disuse may have resulted in a relatively permanent difference that cannot easily be modified through moderate, or even extensive, amounts of additional experience (J.E. Anderson, 1956b; Birren, 1960, 1970; Sorenson, 1938; Willis, 1985).

The preceding discussion implies that there is only one outcome from training studies that would be consistent with the possibility that experiential factors contribute to age differences in cognitive functioning. This is the finding that when young and old adults receive the same training intervention, the benefits of that intervention are greater among older adults than among younger adults. The likelihood of obtaining this result may be small if there are age differences in the efficiency of learning, or if young adults are not already close to their optimal or asymptotic level of functioning at the pretraining assessment. Furthermore, as suggested earlier, it is not valid on the basis of evidence of this type to conclude that the disuse perspective is correct, but only that it has survived one possible test in which a critical prediction could have been falsified. Nonetheless, because all other possible outcomes of training research would be ambiguous, this seems to be the only result from training studies that could be considered even moderately supportive of the disuse interpretation of age differences in cognitive functioning. The available training research will therefore be reviewed to determine the frequency with which this particular finding has been reported.

A number of age-comparative studies with experiential manipulations have been conducted; those examining obviously cognitive measures are summarized in Table 4.5. Excluded from this listing are studies in which the primary dependent variables were measures of speeded performance, but the results from such studies are generally consistent with the findings summarized in Table 4.5, in that most have found that the age differences remained roughly constant across practice, particularly after the first few sessions (Berg, Hertzog, & E. Hunt, 1982; Madden, 1982; Madden & Nebes, 1980; Plude, et al., 1983; Salthouse & Somberg, 1982b).

The results summarized in Table 4.5 are quite consistent, but any conclusions must be qualified because all of the studies suffer from several limitations. For example, most of the studies have relied upon small samples (usually less than 20 adults per age group), restricted amounts of practice or experience (generally fewer than 10 hours of actual on-task experience), and narrow (typically single variable) assessment of the theoretical constructs. The weaknesses in this research preclude reaching definitive conclusions, despite the absence of any evidence indicating

TABLE 4.5
Results of age-comparative studies across multiple sessions

Task	Sessions	Practice Effect	Source
digit symbol substitution	5	Y > O	Beres & A. Baron (1981)
mental computation	6	Y = O	Charness & J.I.D. Campbell (1988)
Primary Mental Abilities tests	4	Y > O, Y = O	Kamin (1957)
serial recall	20	Y > O	Kliegl, J. Smith, & P.B. Baltes (1989)
recognition memory	7	Y = O	LeBreck & A. Baron (1987)
prose memory	5	Y = O	B.J. Meyer, C.J. Young, & B.J. Bartlett (1989)
serial recall	3	Y = O	Rebok & Balcerak (1989)
serial recall	3	Y > O	T.L. Rose & Yesavage (1983)
block design	3	Y = O	Salthouse (1987e)
concept formation	2	Y = O	E.H. Schludermann, S.M. Schludermann, Merryman, & B.W. Brown (1983)
memory span	4	Y = O	Taub (1973)
memory span	5	Y > O	Taub & Long (1972)
name-face memory	2	Y > O	Yesavage & T.L. Rose (1984)

greater improvement on the part of older adults as expected from the disuse perspective.

One of the most ambitious projects involving manipulations of experience was reported by Schaie and Willis (1986; Willis & Schaie, 1986b, 1988). These researchers used longitudinal data to classify older adults as having remained stable or having declined on reasoning or spatial abilities (as assessed by the PMA Reasoning and Space tests), and then administered training programs designed to increase one of the two abilities. Because there was no basis for evaluating the magnitude of performance change with respect to each individual's own level of variability, the between-individual standard error of measurement was used as the basis for classifying people as having declined or remained stable. Those people whose scores decreased more than one between-individual standard error of measurement over a 14-year interval were classified as having declined in that ability, while those with a change of less than this amount were classified as having remained stable in the ability. As mentioned in chapter 2, the accuracy of this classification may be suspect because of the unknown relations between across-individual variability and within-individual variability.

Four groups of older adults, age 64 to 95, participated in the Schaie and Willis study. There were between 51 and 67 subjects in each of four training groups: reasoning training for stable and declining individuals, and space training for stable and declining individuals. Each research participant completed a battery of psychometric tests before and after the five 1-hour training sessions. These tests allowed assessment of abilities at the level of theoretical constructs, with three or four indicators of each of five abilities: inductive reasoning, spatial orientation, perceptual speed, numeric, and verbal abilities.

Separate analyses of variance for each of the ability factors were reported by Willis and Schaie (1986b). These analyses revealed that performance improved on each of the abilities from the pretest to the posttest, but that the interaction between training and measurement occasion was significant only for the target abilities of reasoning and space. Of greatest relevance for the disuse perspective are the interactions of measurement occasion (pretest vs. posttest) by status (stable vs. decline), training (reasoning vs. space) by status, and training by status by measurement occasion. None of these interactions was significant for either the reasoning or the space ability factor scores. The apparent implication is that people classified as having declined in a particular ability exhibited no greater (or lesser) gains as a function of training than people classified as having remained stable in the ability.

An illustration of the gain scores (posttest minus pretest) for the four reasoning measures and the four space measures as a function of type of training and longitudinal status is displayed in Figure 4.5. The successive clusters represent performance on different tests of the trained ability, with Test 1 representing the PMA criterion test (Reasoning or Space) around which the training program was designed. Tests 2, 3, and 4 in each cluster differed with respect to the nature of the stimulus material, but required the same operations (i.e., series completion for reasoning and spatial rotation for space) as the target test.

Three points should be noted about the results in Figure 4.5. The first is that the training programs were apparently effective because performance gains were observed in nearly all contrasts. The second interesting point is that although it appears that the individuals classified as having declined in the trained ability may have had a slightly greater training-related gain on the target test than the individuals classified as

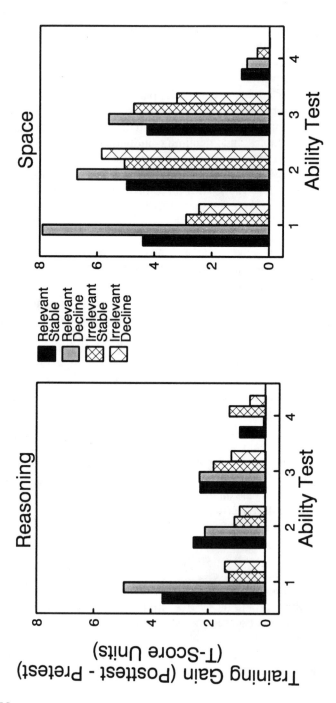

Figure 4.5. Change scores for Reasoning and Space training programs across four measures of each ability as a function of longitudinal status (stable or decline) and type of training program. Data from Willis and Schaie (1986b).

168

having remained stable, this advantage did not hold for the closely related tests designed to assess the same construct. And finally, the results suggest that the training gains for several of the spatial ability tests were nearly as great for the individuals receiving irrelevant training as for those receiving relevant training. This seems to imply that some of the benefits of the training programs may not have been ability-specific, but were more general in nature.

The Schaie and Willis project has been described in some detail because the authors have interpreted the results as providing strong support for a disuse perspective on cognitive aging. For example, Willis (1989b) stated:

> We interpret these findings as lending support to the notion of the plasticity of behavior into late adulthood and suggesting that for at least a substantial proportion of the community-dwelling elderly, observed cognitive decline is not irreversible. Part of what has been termed "decline" is likely attributable to disuse and can be subjected to environmental manipulations involving relatively simple educational training techniques. (p. 557)

As mentioned above, there are logical difficulties with concluding that an intervention has reversed or remediated a deficit when the benefits of the intervention are evident even among individuals not exhibiting the deficit. Because what is arguably the most important finding of the Schaie and Willis project was that the amount of training-related improvement for individuals classified as having remained stable in the ability was statistically indistinguishable from that for individuals classified as having declined in the ability, no claims of differential benefit appear justified. Moreover, because there was apparently no decline that could be remediated for the individuals classified as having remained stable in the relevant ability, the nature of the training benefits for both groups are presumably related to new learning rather than to the restoration of skills that have deteriorated through disuse.

Therefore, while the Schaie and Willis training project is important, the results appear too equivocal to allow strong conclusions about the mechanisms responsible for age-related declines in cognitive performance. The fact that very little information was provided regarding the equivalence of processes involved in the developmental losses and the training gains, and that the finding that the training benefits were not restricted to those individuals whose abilities were assumed to have declined, seems to preclude an interpretation that the training intervention actually remediated or reversed the observed declines.

Summary

It is frequently assumed that if lack of experience is responsible for the existence of age differences in measures of cognitive functioning, then the provision of relevant experience should result in the elimination, or at least the attenuation, of those differences. Although experiential interventions have been quite popular, the rationale for this kind of research has been questioned because of its dependence on several implicit assumptions that may not be correct (e.g., that the disuse has not resulted in permanent alterations, that young adults are close to an asymptote with respect to the effects of experience, and that there are no age differences in the efficiency of new learning). Whether what is incorrect is the disuse perspective, or one or more of these auxiliary assumptions, the results from age-comparative studies involving manipulations of training or practice have consistently failed to reveal any greater gains for older adults than for young adults. Research based on manipulations of experience therefore does not yet appear to have provided convincing support for the disuse perspective of cognitive aging.

EVALUATION OF THE DISUSE PERSPECTIVE

Over 30 years ago, J.E. Anderson (1956b) posed three fundamental questions relevant to the disuse perspective of cognitive aging:

> Does active participation in intellectual activity preserve intelligence? ... Can we modify the downward changes in older age by providing stimulating environments and promoting opportunities for participation? ... (and) ... When does the effect of use begin to diminish and how rapidly? (pp. 268-269)

Unfortunately, it still appears impossible to provide definitive answers to any of these questions.

Despite the plausibility of the fundamental assumption that loss of ability is attributable to lack of use, there currently seems to be little convincing evidence that people of different ages differ in the frequency of using various cognitive processes. Furthermore, sizable age differences have been reported in many tasks hypothesized to be ecologically valid (and therefore presumably of high naturally occurring frequency) and in a variety of tasks among students and members of the same occupation, who can be assumed to have similar kinds of experiences. Gains in performance associated with additional experience through the provision of training or practice also have not been found to be greater for older individuals, or for individuals who have declined in their abilities, compared to those who are younger or whose abilities appear to have remained stable. The available evidence therefore provides little concrete support for the view that variations in experience contribute to the age differences frequently observed in measures of cognitive performance.

A puzzling question for the disuse perspective is why age differences in cognitive functioning are as large as they are in light of the considerable experiential diversity that seems to exist across the adult population. Even the analyses of variability in performance (e.g., Figures 2.11, 2.12, and 2.13) do not reveal the systematic age-related increases in interindividual variance one might expect if amount or type of experience were a major determinant of cognitive functioning. At least three interpretations can be proposed to account for the surprising absence of evidence for experiential influences on the magnitude of age differences in cognitive performance. One interpretation is that naturally occurring experience has little direct effect on most measures of cognitive performance, and instead exerts its influence primarily on the quality or quantity of knowledge one possesses (Bray & A. Howard, 1983; Schmidt, J.E. Hunter, & Outerbridge, 1986). According to this view, experiential effects should not be expected on measures of the proficiency of basic cognitive processes, but only on measures reflecting an individual's accumulated knowledge. A second possible interpretation is that the degree of variation in relevant aspects of experience is really rather small for most people. That is, the extent, or the importance, of individual differences in amount or type of experience may have been overestimated relative to the vast similarities. It is conceivable, for example, that the experience most adults have with many cognitive activities is so extensive as to approach the point at which the effects of experience on cognitive abilities are at a nearly asymptotic level. Still another possibility is that experiential effects are extremely specific to particular materials and processes. Under this latter interpretation, little or no effect of experience would be expected on most cognitive measures because those effects do not operate at the level of ability constructs, but only at the level of very narrow and specific measures of performance.

It is interesting to note that although each of the preceding interpretations seems plausible, none of them appears consistent with the disuse perspective of cognitive aging. That is, the age declines in many measures of cognitive functioning cannot be attributed to factors related to disuse if: (a) experience does not directly alter the efficiency of basic cognitive processes; (b) virtually all adults have acquired near-asymptotic levels of experience; or (c) the benefits of experience are restricted to very specific measures, and do not extend to broader theoretical constructs such as cognitive abilities. These and other interpretations must be thoroughly investigated if the disuse perspective is to remain viable as a possible explanation of cognitive aging phenomena.

As with the changing environment perspective, the disuse perspective appears to be more of a loose collection of vague ideas rather than a clearly specified set of relations between explicitly defined concepts. In the terminology of theoretical levels discussed in chapter 1, the disuse perspective is more like a framework than a theory or model. At least three requirements need to be satisfied before the concept of disuse can be rigorously evaluated. First, the level (e.g., activity, task, process) at which the use or disuse is to be analyzed must be specified. Second, the actual amounts of use, at the level of analysis considered most informative, must be documented for each of the age ranges of interest. And third, detailed models must be provided of the mechanisms by which disuse is presumed to contribute to lower levels of cognitive functioning.

With respect to the third requirement, models of disuse-mediated loss of ability may require completely new formulations, or they may simply be based on adaptations of existing models. As an example, if disuse is interpreted as the opposite of use, then models of learning and skill acquisition might account for both gains and losses in performance but with the mechanisms merely assumed to operate in reverse in the case of disuse-mediated deterioration of performance. Alternatively, disuse phenomena could be viewed as explainable in terms of theories of forgetting, perhaps by relying upon concepts such as decay and interference or displacement. Whatever the nature of the mechanisms, however, some answers to the questions of the *how* of development appear necessary before the disuse perspective can be considered a complete theory of cognitive aging.

5

Qualitative Differences: Structure, Strategies, and the Relation Between Competence and Performance

> ... [I]t is still not certain that some differences in the cognitive
> behavior of young and old are primarily a matter of deficit, since it
> is possible that adulthood and aging bring qualitative changes that
> may mimic decrements but in fact signal adaptive reorganization.
> —Labouvie-Vief (1985, p. 519)

It is an old cliche that apples can't be compared with oranges because they differ in qualitative, and not simply quantitative, dimensions. A frequent concern in research on individual differences is that people may differ from one another in qualitative respects, and hence that the scores on cognitive tests may not reflect the same characteristics in all people. There are many reasons why the meaning of a score might not be the same in different individuals, and yet only if it is assumed that there are little or no qualitative differences could quantitative comparisons be interpreted as indicating variations along the same dimension.

Among researchers interested in the relations between aging and cognition, there is a long tradition of questioning the appropriateness of cognitive tasks or mental tests for assessing older adults (Demming & Pressey, 1957; Foster & G.A. Taylor, 1920; Gardner & Monge, 1977; Hollingworth, 1927; Lorge, 1956; Sorenson, 1933). A primary concern is that there may be a change with age in the way certain tasks or activities, and particularly cognitive tests, are perceived and/or performed. Perhaps because of changing experiences or social demands, or because different stages of life are associated with different goals or purposes, what is ostensibly the same task or activity may require different kinds of abilities, or different adaptations or integrations of the same abilities, at various periods in adulthood. If such a qualitative shift does occur, then many of what appear to be age deficits might be more appropriately considered as mere age differences, without any pejorative connotations.

The perspective that age differences may reflect qualitative rather than quantitative factors, and may be less informative about capacities than about styles, stages, or adaptations, has been discussed by many

173

researchers (Cavanaugh, Kramer, Sinnott, Camp, & Markley, 1985; Labouvie-Vief, 1980, 1982, 1985; Labouvie-Vief & Blanchard-Fields, 1982; Labouvie-Vief & Chandler, 1978; Perlmutter, 1988; Perlmutter, et al., 1987; Perlmutter, et al., 1990; Rybash, et al., 1985; Schaie, 1977-78). Unfortunately, as Ceci and Cornelius (1990) and Sternberg and Berg (1987) point out, few of these speculations have been supported by convincing empirical evidence, nor have they typically been accompanied by suggestions about the type of research that might provide such support. Moreover, the focus of many of the discussions has not been on the causes of the well-documented negative relations between age and certain measures of cognitive functioning, but rather on attempting to describe a broader context within which those differences might be considered relatively unimportant, or possibly even adaptive. Even if eventually found to be valid, therefore, it is not clear that these conjectures would contribute to greater understanding of the origin and nature of age differences in the type of cognition assessed by existing psychometric tests.

Despite the pretheoretical status of many of the speculations, it is nevertheless important to consider research evidence relevant to the possibility that increased age is associated with qualitative shifts in the nature of cognition. Bromley (1972) noted that many interesting and theoretically important cognitive changes in children were overlooked when the focus was exclusively on quantitative measures, and were only revealed when researchers such as Piaget examined qualitative differences in the structure and function of cognition at different ages. For the same reasons that it may be inappropriate to characterize children as quantitatively impoverished adults, therefore, it might also be misleading to characterize older adults as quantitatively diminished relative to young adults.

The goal in this chapter will be to review research in five topic areas, each of which is related to the broad issue of whether cognitive performance measures have the same meaning in adults of different ages. The first section concerns research on the distinction between performance and competence, because scores may not represent the same ability constructs in all individuals if performance is more limited by ability-extraneous factors in some age groups than in others. The second section reviews research from experimental studies on the organization or structure of verbal information in long-term memory. This is relevant to the general issue of measurement equivalence because if there is evidence that knowledge is structured differently in adults of different ages, then performance measures based on that knowledge may differ for qualitative or structural reasons and not simply because of variations along quantitative dimensions. One of the most powerful ways of determining the meaning of a variable is to examine the pattern of correlations it has with other variables; thus, research based on correlational analyses of data from adults of different ages is reviewed in the third section. The fourth section of the chapter focuses on the question of whether there are age differences in the types of strategies used to perform cognitive tasks. This research is relevant to the issue of qualitative differences because one cannot be confident that the task is measuring the same characteristic at all ages if people of varying ages differ in the manner in which they perform the task. The final section of the chapter is devoted to the topic of metacognition because a low level of cognitive performance may reflect qualitative deficiencies in metacognitive or executive processes as much, or perhaps even more, than limitations in quantitative aspects of cognitive ability.

PERFORMANCE AND COMPETENCE

An individual's competence level is what he or she is capable of achieving under optimal evaluation conditions. In contrast, what the individual actually does in a given assessment situation corresponds to his or her measured level of performance. Although performance is used to infer competence, the two concepts are not necessarily identical because the expression of competence may be limited by ability-extraneous factors.

There are two basic reasons the performance-competence distinction is important in developmental research. One reason is that estimates of the *absolute* limits of performance may be erroneous and misleading if relatively minor changes in assessment conditions allow an individual's level of performance to more closely approximate his or her actual competence. That is, scores on psychometric and cognitive tests could not be interpreted as indicating true competence if ability-extraneous factors are operating to suppress performance below competence. The second reason the performance-competence distinction is important is that invalid inferences may be reached about *relative* comparisons if the performance-competence gap is larger in some individuals than in others. If the performance of older adults is more limited by a variety of ability-extraneous factors than is the performance of young adults, for example, then the results from comparisons of adults of different ages will not provide accurate indications of the relations between age and underlying competence.

The greatest interest in the performance-competence distinction among researchers in aging and cognition has focused on the second issue concerning the possibility that the gap between performance and competence becomes larger with increased age. This interest is most frequently manifested in the form of an hypothesis considered deserving of investigation (P.B. Baltes, Dittmann-Kohli & Dixon, 1984; P.B. Baltes & G.V. Labouvie, 1973; Barton, et al., 1975; Birkhill & Schaie, 1975; Hornblum & Overton, 1976; H.E. Jones, 1956, 1959; Labouvie-Vief, 1977;

Labouvie-Vief, et al., 1974; Reese & Rodeheaver, 1985). Occasionally, however, there is an implication that the hypothesis has already been confirmed, as revealed by the following quotations:

> These findings suggest that, if these [ability-extraneous] factors were eliminated, young and old adults could perform alike. There is no age difference in intellectual competence. (Datan, Rodeheaver, & Hughes, 1987, p. 166)

> Adults of all ages have been known to have trouble understanding instructions, coordinating responses on answer sheets, combating fatigue during testing, or finding meaning in particular tasks required on tests. Elderly adults are more likely to experience these difficulties because of their relative inexperience in taking tests, susceptibility to visual and physical fatigue, and insufficient motivation to excel. (Kirasic & G.L. Allen, 1985, p. 197)

That the issue is not as simple as implied by these authors is evident from the writings of other researchers who have suggested that ability-extraneous factors may actually be more detrimental to young adults than to older adults. Kliegl, J. Smith, and P.B. Baltes (1986, 1989), for example, have speculated that age differences on certain measures of cognitive functioning might be magnified after extensive training, implying that older adults are less disadvantaged than young adults by typical, single-session conditions of assessment. J.L. Horn (1982) has also reported that the age differences on various measures of cognitive functioning increase, rather than decrease, when ability-extraneous factors such as persistence and carefulness are statistically controlled.

The dramatic differences of opinion on the question of whether age-related processes merely influence performance or also affect competence indicate that the relevant research literature must be carefully examined to evaluate both the existence, and the direction, of possible relations between age and the magnitude of the performance-competence gap. The following sections therefore review research addressing the relation between age and each of several potential performance-limiting, or ability-extraneous, factors.

Greater Cautiousness

One of the most frequently mentioned performance-limiting factors is cautiousness, or hesitancy about making responses that may be incorrect. It is often hypothesized that one of the reasons older adults might achieve lower scores than young adults on a variety of cognitive tests is that they are more reluctant to venture a response unless they are confident that it is correct. The reasoning behind this argument can be clarified by considering the following hypothetical example. Assume that both young and old adults know the answers to 50% of the items on a given test, are somewhat confident about the answers to 30% of the items, and don't know the answers to the remaining 20% of the items. Furthermore, assume that the probability of a correct answer is 1.0 when the answer is known, that it is .5 when there is some confidence in the answer, and that it is .2 when the answer is not known and the response is merely a guess. If older adults only answer items for which they are very confident, then their scores will be $(1.0 \times 50\%) = 50\%$. However, if young adults respond to all items, then their scores will be $([1.0 \times 50\%] + [.5 \times 30\%] + [.2 \times 20\%])$ $= 69\%$. An age difference in performance would therefore result on the basis of differences in cautiousness, despite equivalent levels of competence (i.e., percentage of known items) in the two groups.

Several types of research have been considered relevant to the cautiousness interpretation of age differences in cognition. For example, a number of studies have compared young and old adults in their willingness to make decisions in life scenario situations with different likelihoods of success. However, the relevance of these measures to performance on cognitive tests is not clear because there is apparently no evidence that the factors affecting preferences in these semi-realistic life situations are similar to those influencing response tendencies in cognitive tasks. In any case, it appears there are no age differences in the decision preferences in this kind of task when the research participants are always required to select a response, and are denied the option of not responding (Botwinick, 1969).

Age differences in cautiousness have also been investigated by determining the level of problem difficulty the individual is willing to attempt. For example, vocabulary items can be selected such that there are different probabilities that an individual will be successful at answering the items. Risk preference can then be assessed by allowing the individual to choose the difficulty level at which he or she is to work. Tasks of this type seem to measure level of aspiration more than reluctance to make a response in a cognitive test, and therefore it is not obvious that this research is pertinent to performance on cognitive tests. Definitive conclusions regarding age trends on this measure of cautiousness are also not possible because the pattern of age trends in the available research has not been consistent (Okun, 1976; Okun & C.S. Elias, 1977; Okun & Siegler, 1976; Okun, Siegler, & George, 1978; Okun, Stock, & Ceurvorst, 1980).

Signal detection analyses of response bias are also sometimes interpreted as providing an indication of cautiousness levels. Once again, however, questions can be raised about the extent to which these measures, which are usually obtained from sensory or memory tasks, should be considered equivalent to the hypothesized tendency to want more certainty before committing to a response on a cognitive test. Moreover, there is apparently not yet any evidence that cautiousness as reflected in response bias measures from signal detection tasks is a stable, task-independent, characteristic of an individual. The only age-comparative study examining response bias measures from several different tasks in the same people (A. Baron & LeBreck, 1987) had extremely small sample sizes (i.e., 10 young adults and 10 older adults), and therefore correlational analyses, which might have been helpful in evaluating whether the measures represent a common construct, would not have been very powerful.

The types of analyses that are probably the most pertinent to the differential cautiousness interpretation of adult age differences in cognitive performance are comparisons within actual cognitive tasks of the proportion of omission responses, comparisons of the percentage of attempted items answered correctly, and comparisons of decision accuracy when responses are required on all items. With respect to omission responses, older adults might be expected to omit responding to a greater proportion of items than young adults if, relative to young adults, they are less likely to respond in cognitive tests unless they are quite confident that their answer is correct. Unfortunately, a finding of a greater proportion of omission responses with increased age cannot always be interpreted as indicating that confidence factors are involved. Omissions may also result simply from a lack of ability or knowledge because a reasonable reaction if one does not know the answer to an item is to skip it and try the next item. Analyses of the proportion of omission responses may therefore be informative about cautiousness interpretations only when there are no age differences in the relative frequency of omissions, in which case one would presumably infer that any age differences in level of performance were probably *not* mediated by age differences in cautiousness.

Less equivocal evidence relevant to the lack-of-confidence hypothesis might be available from accuracy comparisons on items for which responses were produced. Comparisons of this sort might be possible either by restricting analyses to items with an overt response, or by requiring a response to all items. Age differences might be expected to be smaller with either of these methods compared to those observed under more traditional assessment procedures if an unwillingness to venture a response that might be incorrect is the source of a substantial proportion of many observed age differences. That is, since the analyses are based only on responses that have been emitted, the influence of any reluctance to emit a response should be minimal, and consequently the magnitude of the age differences might be reduced. In several recent studies this expectation has not been confirmed because fairly typical negative relations between age and accuracy in a variety of cognitive tasks have been found when performance is analyzed in one or both of these ways (Salthouse, 1988e; Salthouse, Babcock, Skovronek, D.R. Mitchell, & Palmon, 1990; Salthouse, et al., 1988a; Salthouse & D.R. Mitchell, 1990; Salthouse, D.R. Mitchell, Skovronek, & Babcock, 1989).

This brief review suggests that differential cautiousness does not appear to be a major factor contributing to age differences in cognitive performance. Evidence establishing that older adults are generally more cautious than young adults is still equivocal, and it has not yet been demonstrated that cautiousness is an important determinant of either the existence, or the magnitude, of age differences in cognitive performance. The explanation for the age differences, as Birren (1964) suggested, does not seem to be that older adults are less likely than young adults to respond at the same level of confidence, but rather that they are less likely to achieve the same level of confidence.

Loss of Self-Efficacy

Related to the greater cautiousness hypothesis is the view that there may be a decrease with age in one's beliefs concerning the likelihood that he or she will be successful in a task. This lack of confidence in one's own abilities, or loss of self-efficacy, may lead to lower performance on cognitive tasks either because a perception of futility reduces the amount of effort invested in the task, or because a fear of failure increases the level of debilitating anxiety.

There are two aspects of the self-efficacy hypothesis as it pertains to cognitive aging. The first is the assumption that self-appraisals of one's own level of ability decrease with age; that is, that self-efficacy beliefs are lower among older adults than among young adults. Evidence on this issue is fairly consistent. As early as 1945, Sward reported that older adults made more self-deprecating comments in cognitive testing situations than young adults. Later studies involving more systematic data collection on this issue have also reported that there is often a decrease with age in self-assessed ratings of cognitive ability, or in ratings of expected success on a variety of cognitive tasks (J.M. Berry, West, & Dennehey, 1989; Cavanaugh, 1986-87; Cavanaugh & Poon, 1989; G. Cohen & Faulkner, 1984; Cornelius & Caspi, 1986; Dixon & Hultsch, 1983; Dobbs & Rule, 1987; Hanley-Dunn & McIntosh, 1984; Herzog & Rodgers, 1989; Hultsch, et al., 1987; M.E. Lachman & Jelalian, 1984; Prohaska, Parham & Teitelman, 1984; Rebok & Balcerak, 1989; Salthouse & D.R. Mitchell, 1990; Zelinski, et al., 1980).

The second aspect of the self-efficacy hypothesis concerns the causal status of self-efficacy beliefs on the relations between age and cognitive performance. One interpretation is that a decrease with age in appraisals of one's own abilities leads to reductions in cognitive performance because of diminished levels of self-confidence and motivation. From this view, therefore, reductions in self-efficacy beliefs with increased age may be the cause of at least some of the age-related declines in cognitive performance. An alternative interpretation is that changes in self appraisals follow reductions in cognitive ability, and hence are consequences, rather than causes, of the diminished levels of ability. The negative relation between age and beliefs in one's own capabilities, according to this frame of reference, originates from an accurate realization that one's cognitive abilities have declined.

Only a limited amount of empirical evidence relevant to the interpretations of self-efficacy as cause or as consequence of age-related ability declines is available. Consistent with the causal interpretation are results suggesting that young and old adults are equally sensitive to manipulations designed to alter self-appraisals. That is, both young and old adults have been found to exhibit improvements in measures of cognitive performance following positive, confidence-building feedback (Bellucci & W.J. Hoyer, 1975; Mergler & W.J. Hoyer, 1981), and similar decrements in performance after negative, confidence-decreasing feedback (Prohaska, et al., 1984). These results suggest that the mechanisms relating self-appraisal to cognitive performance continue to function throughout most of the adult age range, but they do not necessarily imply that age-related declines in self-efficacy beliefs are responsible for age-related declines in cognitive performance.

Several studies have examined the self-efficacy-as-consequence interpretation of the relation between self-efficacy beliefs and cognitive ability by attempting to predict age differences in self-efficacy from measures of cognitive ability. For example, Cornelius and Caspi (1986) collected measures of self-efficacy beliefs and measures of inductive reasoning performance from adults between 35 and 79 years of age, and then statistically controlled inductive reasoning score before determining the relation between age and self-efficacy. There were significant declines in self-efficacy with increased age when the measure of intellectual ability was not controlled for, but there were no significant age effects on the self-efficacy variable after controlling for the ability measure. The findings were therefore interpreted by the authors as being consistent with the view that declines in cognitive self-efficacy are a consequence, rather than a cause, of the age-related declines in cognitive ability. M.E. Lachman and Jelalian (1984) also found older adults to be comparable to young adults in initial self-efficacy beliefs but less accurate in the performance of an inductive reasoning task, thus suggesting that low levels of self-efficacy beliefs are not necessary for poor cognitive performance among older adults.

Two longitudinal studies are also relevant to the issue of the causal role of self-efficacy beliefs on age differences in cognitive performance. Both studies included measures of cognitive ability and self-efficacy, but unfortunately the retest intervals in these studies were only 2 years (M.E. Lachman, 1983) and 5 years (M.E. Lachman & Leff, 1989), and in neither study were there significant changes over these intervals in the mean levels of either self-efficacy or cognitive ability. There was also very high stability of the measures of cognitive ability, indicating there was relatively little variability across individuals in the magnitude of cognitive change over the test-retest interval. The self-efficacy measures had lower stabilities, however, and thus cognitive ability at the first measurement occasion was used to predict individual differences in self-efficacy change from the first to the second measurement occasion. In both the 1983 and the 1989 studies, the initial level of cognitive ability was found to be a significant predictor of the longitudinal changes in self-efficacy beliefs.

Although the M.E. Lachman (1983) and M.E. Lachman and Leff (1989) results appear consistent with cognitive ability as the cause rather than as the consequence of age differences in self-efficacy, this interpretation should probably be considered quite tentative. One reason for caution in accepting this view is that in neither study were there significant age-related changes in the mean level of either cognitive ability or self-efficacy. This is a potentially serious problem if one is interested in making inferences about development because there seems to be no reason to expect that the processes responsible for fluctuations of individuals around the same mean (i.e., lack of stability) are necessarily equivalent to the processes involved in the age-related declines in mean levels of self-efficacy beliefs documented in many other studies. A second limitation of the M.E. Lachman studies is that only unidirectional comparisons (i.e., ability as a determinant of self-efficacy) were possible because of the high stability of the cognitive ability measures across the test-retest interval. In other words, the absence of appreciable variability in the magnitude of the longitudinal changes in cognitive ability precluded a test of the alternative hypothesis that changes in self-efficacy beliefs mediate changes in cognitive ability.

The status of self-efficacy beliefs as a potential mediator of age differences in cognition is difficult to evaluate at the present time. It does appear that increased age is associated with a decline in confidence regarding one's own abilities, but little evidence exists to indicate that the relations between age and self-efficacy beliefs are the cause, and not the consequence, of the negative relations between age and cognitive functioning.

Increased Anxiety

Another performance-limiting factor often mentioned as a possible cause of lower cognitive performance among older adults is a heightened level of test or situational anxiety. It is sometimes asserted that older adults are more anxious in testing situations than young adults, and that this greater anxiety somehow contributes to, or possibly exacerbates, their poorer performance on cognitive tests (T.H. Crook, 1979; T. Hunt, 1989; R.A. McFarland & O'Doherty, 1959; Yesavage, Lapp, & Sheikh, 1989). This speculation is clearly plausible, but Birren (1964) has pointed out that it may be just as reasonable to propose that test anxiety decreases with age because older adults might be less concerned than young adults about how they are viewed by other people. Anxiety may also be lower among older adults if, as Avorn (1982) has argued, there is a decrease with age in "... the need to prove oneself or succeed in a university-based testing situation" (p. 326).

Virtually all the research on age and test anxiety has assessed anxiety by means of a series of questions answered before or after performing one or more cognitive tests. Most of the results have been consistent in revealing similar levels of reported anxiety for young and old adults (Erber, Abello, & Moninger, 1988; LaRue & D'Elia, 1985; Monge & Gardner, 1976; Mueller, Kausler, & Faherty, 1980; Mueller, Kausler, Faherty, & Oliveri, 1980; Mueller & M.J. Ross, 1984; Perlmutter, 1978; E. Ross, 1968). However, in support of Birren's (1964) suggestion, young adults have been found to report higher levels of test or situational anxiety than older adults in some studies (Cavanaugh & N. Murphy, 1986; Mueller, Rankin, & Carlomusto, 1979; J.P. Robertson, 1957). To the extent that these self-report measures are valid reflections of the individual's level of anxiety, the results of the available studies are clearly inconsistent with the hypothesis that greater levels of anxiety are responsible for the age differences in measures of cognitive functioning.

Decreased Motivation

The idea that age-related reductions in cognitive functioning might be at least partially attributable to diminished levels of motivation was raised by two of the prominent pioneers in psychology. William James (1893) claimed there was a loss of curiosity after age 25, and Edward Thorndike (Thorndike, et al., 1928) suggested that by 25 most adults had satisfied their need for learning. It is not surprising in view of the eminence of these early advocates that the hypothesis of decreased motivation is frequently mentioned as a possible cause of adult age differences in cognitive functioning.

The basic argument underlying the motivation interpretation is that most people don't perform at their optimum in activities in which they have little interest, and therefore some of the age differences in cognitive performance may be due to older adults having a lower level of motivation to do well on cognitive tests than young adults. As with most complex behavior, however, the explanation is probably not so simple. In particular, the relation between motivation and performance is unlikely to be unidirectional because people are also generally not interested in activities in which they don't perform well (Bromley, 1974; J.L. Horn, Donaldson, & Engstrom, 1981; H.E. Jones, 1959). This point was noted by Donald Hebb, who, when reflecting on his own aging, suggested that "The real change ... is a lowered ability to think ... [T]he loss of interest ... is secondary to that" (Hebb, 1978, p. 20). If relations between age and level of motivation were to be found, therefore, it would still remain to be determined whether the lower motivation is the cause, or the effect, of lower performance on cognitive tests.

There are apparently no objective and direct methods for assessing motivation in cognitive testing situations, and consequently either subjective or indirect evidence must be used to evaluate the motivation hypothesis. With respect to the subjective evidence, several researchers have noted that it is their impression that older adults are at least as motivated as young adults when participating in cognitive studies (D.R. Davies & Griew, 1965; Friend & Zubek, 1958; H.E. Jones & O.J. Kaplan, 1945; Kay, 1955; M.D. Murphy, R.E. Sanders, Gabriesheski, & Schmitt, 1981; Schonfield, 1980; Welford, 1957, 1958). According to many of these observers, decreased motivation manifests itself primarily in a reluctance to participate in research projects, but once they have agreed to participate, the effort or interest among older adults does not appear any less than that among young adults.

There are also various categories of indirect evidence that are relevant to the motivation hypothesis. One is the report by Monge and Gardner (1976) that a measure of the need to achieve was larger with increased age, implying that general or non-specific motivation may actually be greater among older adults than among young adults. Age differences in cognitive performance have also been found when all research participants are believed to be highly motivated (Ganzler, 1964; Schaie & Strother, 1968a, 1968d). Particularly convincing in this respect are the results of Trembly and O'Connor (1966) in which age-related declines in cognitive performance were found among people who paid a fee to take a battery of tests for purposes of occupational guidance. Because the General Aptitude Test Battery is also used extensively for employment selection, the findings of decreases with age in many of the subtests in this battery (Droege, et al., 1963; Fozard & Nuttall, 1971; Hirt, 1959; Stein, 1962) also cannot be attributed to diminished motivation. The research on ecologically valid tasks discussed in chapter 4 is also relevant to the motivation hypothesis because virtually everyone might be expected to have reasonably high levels of motivation for meaningful and naturalistic activities. As reported earlier, young adults are frequently found to perform at higher levels than older adults on these types of tasks, and thus the motivation interpretation of age differences in cognitive performance is again not supported.

Finally, there are a few experimental studies in which the performance of young and old adults has been compared under normal conditions, and in conditions in which some kind of reward was offered for high performance. If older adults perform worse than young adults because of lower levels of motivation, then one might expect the age differences to be eliminated, or at least substantially reduced, when all participants are performing under conditions of high motivation. Although it is not known whether the rewards were equally motivating to adults of all ages, it is noteworthy that young and old adults have been found to exhibit equivalent effects of reward in three independent studies involving quite different measures of cognitive performance (E.A. Grant, Storandt, & Botwinick, 1978; J.T. Hartley & D.A. Walsh, 1980; F.W. Hoyer, W.J. Hoyer, et al., 1978).

No single source of evidence is compelling by itself, but when taken in combination, the preceding findings appear to provide little support for the hypothesis that lower levels of motivation on the part of older adults are responsible for their relatively poor performance on cognitive tests.

Lack of Familiarity

Another factor often mentioned in connection with older adults not performing at their optimum level is lack of familiarity with the tasks or stimulus materials used in cognitive testing situations. If performance is generally higher with familiar activities, and if older adults are less familiar than young adults with the types of tasks or materials used in cognitive assessments, then it is clearly possible that a lack of familiarity might contribute to the age differences observed on various measures of cognitive performance.

Because the research with activities hypothesized to be ecologically valid has revealed that young adults often perform at higher levels than older adults even with what are assumed to be highly familiar activities, it seems unlikely that a differential familiarity interpretation can account for all the age-related cognitive differences. The findings that age differences in cognitive tasks tend to persist across moderate to extensive amounts of practice (see Table 4.5) also suggests that lack of familiarity is probably not a major determinant of age differences in cognitive performance.

Despite this negative evidence, there is still considerable interest in the differential familiarity interpretation of the relation between age and measures of cognitive functioning. Two sets of observations appear to have contributed to this interest. One is the impression that young adults are more accustomed to the procedures and materials used in cognitive tests than are older adults, at least in part because of the prevalence of various kinds of cognitive assessment during the period of formal schooling which usually ends in young adulthood. In support of this assumption is the finding by Cornelius (1984) that cognitive tests were rated to be less familiar by older adults than by young adults. While it is probably true that recent experience with many types of tests is greater for young adults than for older adults, it does not necessarily follow that experience with the cognitive processes or components presumed to be assessed by those tests is also greater. As discussed in chapter 4, the most important factor may be the frequency of the processes required by the task, and not simply the frequency of superficial characteristics of the materials, or of the particular manner in which the effectiveness of relevant processes is evaluated. Without information about frequency or familiarity at the level of basic or fundamental processes, therefore, it may be impossible to do more than speculate about the relations between age and familiarity with the processes required by different cognitive tests.

The second set of observations often considered consistent with the differential familiarity interpretation are derived from studies using generationally-biased stimulus materials. Howell (1972) was apparently the first investigator to manipulate the familiarity of the stimulus material such that some stimuli were more familiar and meaningful to young adults, and other stimuli were more familiar and meaningful to older adults. The major finding in her study was that the age differences were largest with the stimulus materials most familiar to young adults, and were smallest with stimulus materials most familiar to older adults. This result was replicated by Poon and Fozard (1978), and there are now many studies in which similar interaction patterns have been reported. The predominant finding has been that older adults tend to perform best with dated stimulus materials (e.g., pictures from 1906 mail-order catalogs, names of actors, musicians, or politicians from the 1930s, words like poultice or fedora, etc.), and young adults perform best with contemporary equivalents of these items (Backman, Herlitz, & Karlsson, 1987; Backman & Karlsson, 1985; T.R. Barrett & Watkins, 1986; T.R. Barrett & M. Wright, 1981; Erber, Galt, & Botwinick, 1985; Hanley-Dunn & McIntosh, 1984; Hultsch & Dixon, 1983; Worden & Sherman-Brown, 1983).

Although the results have been fairly consistent, there is controversy about how the findings from studies with generationally-biased stimulus materials should be interpreted. One position was stated by Poon, et al., (1986) as follows:

... [T]he use of some neutral or unfamiliar stimuli may exaggerate the degree of memory difficulty for older people and ... therefore the observed deficit could be the result of the stimuli employed rather than an indication of a flawed memory process. (p. 6)

The claim that neutral stimuli may exaggerate the problems of older adults implies that the fairest assessment of an individual's memory functioning would involve stimulus materials with which he or she is highly familiar. However, an alternative interpretation of the results from studies with stimuli of varying degrees of familiarity is that they are simply another manifestation of the well-established principle that memory is enhanced by the use of familiar and meaningful material. From this latter perspective, therefore, the use of generationally-biased stimulus materials confounds age and familiarity, and hence results from studies employing such materials are likely to be of limited value for the purpose of understanding the nature of age differences in cognition. Unfortunately, it does not appear possible to distinguish between these two interpretations on the basis of the available empirical evidence.

Two studies with paired-associate tasks are also relevant to the issue of the role of familiarity in age differences in cognition. Both studies attempted to create same-generation and cross-generation paired-associate lists, and then compared the performance of young and old adults with each list. Wittels (1972) created the lists by asking young and old adults to generate associations to stimulus terms, and Winn, J.W. Elias and Marshall (1976) relied on meaningfulness norms from 1928 and 1960 to produce generationally-appropriate pairs. Although one can plausibly argue that the materials in each study are specially suited to either young or old adults, young adults were found to have higher levels of performance on both sets of material in both studies.

The research just summarized suggests there is only limited support for the hypothesis that the competence of older adults is not adequately reflected in performance on cognitive tests because they are less familiar than young adults with the stimulus materials and testing procedures. The research reviewed in chapter 4 indicated that age differences are present in many familiar and everyday cognitive activities, and that they persist across at least moderate amounts of practice. Adults at any age perform better on tasks involving stimulus materials with which they have at least some familiarity, but the relevance of this observation to the well-documented findings of age differences on tasks using equally familiar or equally unfamiliar stimulus materials has not yet been established.

Sensory Loss

Because increased age is often accompanied by a variety of sensory impairments, it is sometimes hypothesized that difficulties on the part of older adults in seeing or hearing either the instructions or the stimulus materials contribute to their relatively poor levels of performance on cognitive tests. Although significant correlations between visual or auditory sensitivity and cognitive performance have been reported in groups of older adults (Granick, Kleban, & A.D. Weiss, 1976; Schaie, P.B. Baltes, & Strother, 1964), there is apparently little evidence at the present time that sensory factors actually mediate the age relations found on many cognitive measures.

One result that might be convincing in supporting a sensory-mediated interpretation would be a finding that the age differences were eliminated when the tasks or materials were presented in a manner such that the influence of sensory factors was minimized. Two studies have been conducted in which visual stimulus materials were presented to young and old adults in normal and enlarged formats (Storandt & Futterman, 1982; J.M. Thomas & Charles, 1964). In neither study was there a significant interaction between age and display format, thus suggesting that the age differences were relatively independent of sensory factors within the range of sensory variation investigated.

It is obvious that cognitive performance will be impaired if sensory limitations prevent relevant stimulus information from ever being registered. It is also true that the prevalence of many sensory problems tends to increase with increased age. However, the sensory deficiencies experienced by most adults up to their 60s or 70s are apparently not severe enough to be responsible for a substantial proportion of the age differences frequently reported in cognitive tasks. Of course, one reason for the lack of evidence that sensory factors contribute to the age differences in cognitive performance may be that not much research has addressed this issue, and hence any conclusions about the interrelations of age, sensory limitations, and cognitive performance should be considered merely tentative until additional research becomes available.

Greater Susceptibility to Fatigue

A final performance-limiting factor to be considered is susceptibility to fatigue. Furry and P.B. Baltes (1973) reported that the performance of older adults on several PMA tests was more negatively affected than the performance of young adults by a potentially fatiguing pretest activity (i.e., cancelling letters for 20 minutes). This result was interpreted as suggesting that one reason older adults may perform at lower levels than young adults is that they are more easily fatigued by prior activity. Although the Furry and P.B. Baltes results are consistent with this interpretation, two subsequent studies (W.R. Cunningham, Sepkoski, & Opel, 1978 and Furry & Schaie, 1979) failed to find significant fatigue effects in samples of older adults. Little compelling evidence therefore exists at the present time to indicate that older adults perform worse than young adults on cognitive tests because they are more susceptible to the detrimental effects of fatigue.

Summary

The research reviewed in this section generally supports the idea that most cognitive assessments do not represent the optimum performance of which an individual is capable. For most people, therefore, it can probably be concluded that performance in conventional assessment situations is an underestimate of their absolute level of competence. Although a considerable gap may exist between performance and competence, there is little evidence in the available research of a systematic relation between the magnitude of this gap and adult age. At least on the basis of the existing research, therefore, it appears that the cognitive competence of adults of all ages is assessed equally well (or equally poorly) by psychometric tests and experimental tasks.

STRUCTURE OF INFORMATION IN MEMORY

A potentially important determinant of cognitive functioning is the manner in which information is organized in the individual's knowledge system. If two groups of people were found to have a qualitatively different way of organizing available information, then their performance on tasks requiring the use of that information should probably not be interpreted as simply reflecting quantitative variation along the same dimension. It is for this reason that it is important to evaluate evidence relevant to the possibility of qualitatively different ways of organizing or structuring information among adults of different ages. Although it is obviously impossible to directly examine the organization of information in an individual's brain, evidence relevant to the structure of information in memory is available from a variety of indirect procedures.

Word Associations

Word associations are often considered to provide an indication of the way information is organized because the associates given in response to a stimulus word are likely to have representations in memory that are close, at least functionally if not anatomically, to that of the stimulus word. The discovery that young and old adults are similar in the type and the variability of word associations produced (Bowles, D. Williams, & Poon, 1983; D.M. Burke & Peters, 1986; D.V. Howard, 1980; Lovelace & Cooley, 1982; Puglisi, Park, & A.D. Smith, 1987; Scialfa & Margolis, 1986) suggests little or no age differences in the way information is represented in memory. As Lovelace and Cooley (1982) noted, these results imply:

> ... that any differences in the performance of young and older adults on tasks involving linguistic materials are not likely to be attributable to any differences in the associative structure of the internal lexicon. (p. 437)

Priming

Another method used to infer cognitive structure is the priming procedure in which processing of a target item is facilitated by the prior presentation of related material. Because the facilitation only occurs if the prior materials (e.g., sentences and words) are related to the target words, the priming phenomenon has been interpreted as reflecting relations that exist among items in long-term memory. Different patterns of facilitation in priming studies among young and old adults would therefore be expected if they have different structural organizations of information in memory. However, a consistent result has been that young and old adults have similar patterns of priming facilitation across a broad range of contextual materials and target words (Balota & Duchek, 1988, 1989; Bowles & Poon, 1985, 1988; D.M. Burke, H. White, & Diaz, 1987; D.M. Burke & Yee, 1984; Chiarello, Church, & W.J. Hoyer, 1985; G. Cohen & Faulkner, 1983b; Hasher & Zacks, 1988; D.V. Howard, 1983; D.V. Howard, Heisey, & Shaw, 1986; D.V. Howard, McAndrews, & Lasaga, 1981; D.V. Howard, Shaw, & Heisey, 1986; L.L. Light & Albertson, 1988; Madden, 1986b, 1988, 1989; Nebes, Boller, & Holland, 1986; Rabbitt, 1984). The implication of these results is that the organization of lexical information, at least with respect to many associative relations, is similar in adults of different ages.

Frequency Effects

Another aspect of the structure of information in memory concerns the representation of items with different frequencies of occurrence. High-frequency items should be more accessible than low-frequency items for speeded decisions, but they might also be expected to be less discriminable, and hence lead to poorer recognition memory performance, than items with lower frequencies. Several studies have reported that both young and old adults exhibit these patterns to nearly equivalent degrees whether the measure is response latency (Bowles & Poon, 1981; E.O. Clark, 1980; D.B. Mitchell, 1989; Poon & Fozard, 1980; J.C. Thomas, Fozard, & Waugh, 1977), or recognition memory accuracy (Bowles & Poon, 1982; E.O. Clark, 1980). To the extent that the patterns of latencies and accuracies reflect how the information is represented, then, these results suggest that words of varying frequencies are organized in a similar manner by both young and old adults.

Typicality Effects

Just as decisions are expected to be faster for items that have a greater frequency of occurrence, so might decisions be expected to be faster for items that are better or more typical members of a category. That is, if categorical information is organized along some sort of gradient with the best or most typical members situated closest to the category name, then decisions about category membership should be fastest for typical category exemplars and slowest for atypical exemplars. However, young and old adults may not exhibit the same advantage of typicality if there is a qualitative shift with age in how categorical information is organized. No support is available for this qualitative-difference expectation; indeed, at least six studies have reported similar patterns of typicality effects in young and old adults (Byrd, 1984; Eysenck, 1975; Mueller, Kausler, Faherty, & Olivieri, 1980; Nebes, et al., 1986; Petros, Zehr, & Chabot, 1983; Reder, Wible, & J. Martin, 1986).

Picture-Superiority Effects

For reasons that are not yet completely understood, but which may relate to how information is represented in memory, items presented as pictures are generally remembered better than the same items presented as words. The finding that both young and old adults exhibit picture-superiority effects (Craik & Byrd, 1982; Keitz & Gounard, 1976; Park & Puglisi, 1985; Park, Puglisi, & Sovacool, 1983; Puglisi, Park, A.D. Smith, & Dudley, 1988; Waugh & Barr, 1989; and in one of two experiments by Rissenberg & Glanzer, 1986; and in two of three experiments by Winograd, A.D. Smith, & E.W. Simon, 1982) are consistent with an assumption of similar organization of information in memory across much of adulthood.

Script Effects

A final category of evidence relevant to the issue of possible qualitative differences in the organization of information in memory concerns effects related to scripts or stereotyped event sequences. The existence of scripts can be inferred by differential recall for events that are consistent or inconsistent with a script theme, or simply by asking individuals to generate the sequence of events associated with a given activity. Both sets of procedures have revealed that young and old adults appear to use similar kinds of scripts for common activities, such as going to a restaurant (Hess, 1985; Hess, Vandermaas, Donley, & S.S. Snyder, 1987; L.L. Light & P.A. Anderson, 1983; Zelinski & Miura, 1988). It has also been reported that young and old adults exhibit similar advantages in memory performance of greater knowledge about the topic of a to-be-remembered passage (Arbuckle, Vanderleck, Harsany, & Lapidus, 1990), and that both groups make more confusion errors for incorrect items compatible with the same mental model as the presented target items (Radvansky, Gerard, Zacks, & Hasher, 1990). These results, and comparable findings in a pictorial analog of a script called a scene schema (Azmitia & Perlmutter, 1988), suggest that the general organization of information about events and objects are similar in adults of different ages.

Summary

The procedures discussed in the preceding section represent attempts to derive information about the structural organization of cognitive information in a manner analogous to how a telephone caller might be able to make inferences about the organization of books in a library on the basis of various types of questions (Salthouse, 1988b). In both cases indirect procedures are necessary, but ample opportunities exist for potential differences in organizational structure to be revealed. The sensitivity of the procedures employed thus far is probably not great, but the available evidence provides little indication that the structure or organization of long-term information differs across the adult life span.

CORRELATIONAL ANALYSES

Nesselroade (1977) pointed out that a finding of age differences in the mean score on a test immediately raises the question of what has changed with age—the people, or what the test is measuring. This is a critical issue in developmental research because the use of the same test or task does not necessarily ensure that performance is determined by the same psychological processes in all individuals. It is at least conceivable that people of different ages may rely upon different combinations of processes or abilities to perform what is ostensibly the same task. To the extent that this is the case, quantitative comparisons might be meaningless because the scores would reflect the functioning of qualitatively different processes.

Some method of evaluating what is being measured in samples of adults of different ages is therefore necessary to ensure that a variable has the same meaning at each age. Analysis of the pattern of correlations that a variable has with other variables is a particularly powerful way of assessing this type of measurement equivalence. Just as it is possible to learn a lot about the characteristics of an individual on the basis of information indicating how that person is similar to, or differs from, other people, so also is it possible to learn what a variable represents by examining its pattern of correlations with other variables. It can be inferred to measure processes similar to those assessed by other variables with which it is correlated, and to measure something different from the processes assessed by other variables with which it is not correlated.

The primary procedure used to analyze patterns of correlations is some version of factor analysis. Groups of variables with moderate to high intercorrelations with one another are identified as comprising distinct factors, and the strength of the relation between a variable and a factor is represented by the loading or weight of the variable on the factor.

Five schematic representations of possible outcomes of factor analyses are illustrated in Figure 5.1. The boxes in these diagrams represent scores on observed variables, and the circles indicate the inferred factors or theoretical constructs. Solid lines indicate a strong relation, and weak relations are portrayed by dotted lines.

Assume that scores on variables A, B, C, and D were obtained from samples of young and older adults, and that scores on variable A, which is the variable of primary interest, are significantly lower in older adults than in young adults. Can we infer that older adults have smaller quantities of the processes responsible for the scores on A than young adults? Although this is the most frequent interpretation of such a finding, it is only reasonable if the same processes are responsible for performance in each age group. That is, only if young and old adults have equivalent relations among variables and factors (i.e., are represented by the same factor diagram), would it be meaningful to interpret the differences as primarily representing quantitative, and not qualitative, variations.

Each configuration in Figure 5.1 corresponds to a somewhat different pattern of relations among variables and factors. Outcomes 1, 2, and 3, for example, are qualitatively distinct and indicate a lack of configural equivalence because the variables exhibit different patterns of interrelations with each other. Variable A seems to reflect a relatively general construct in Outcome 1, and is more specific in Outcomes 2 and 3, but with greater similarity to variable C in Outcome 2, and greater similarity to variable B in Outcome 3.

Outcomes 3, 4, and 5 share the same basic configuration and are thus configurally equivalent, but they vary in the strength of the relations either

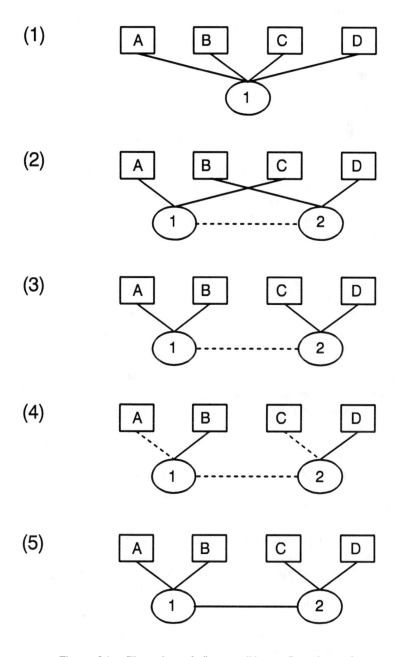

Figure 5.1. Illustration of five possible configurations of performance measures (in squares) and inferred factors (in circles) that might result from factor analyses.

between constructs, or between variables and constructs. Outcomes 3 and 4 differ in the extent to which the variables are related to their respective constructs or factors. Factor analytic representations of correlational patterns that differ in this fashion are said to lack metric equivalence because, although the factors are determined by the same variables, the metric or weighting of variables to factors is not identical.

Outcomes 3 and 5 differ only with respect to the strength of the relation between the inferred factors or constructs. Patterns such as these are configurally equivalent (because the factors are determined by the same variables), and metrically equivalent (because the weightings of variables to factors are similar), but are still not identical.

Although the conceptual distinctions among the factor-analytic outcomes illustrated in Figure 5.1 are reasonably clear, it has proven rather difficult to determine whether, and if so precisely how, the factor solutions based on data of adults of various ages are different from one another. One problem is that accurate determination of factor structure requires considerable information from each of many individuals. For example, it is often recommended that each hypothesized factor be represented by at least three measures, and that data be available from 100 or more individuals in each sample for which factor analyses are to be conducted. Age-comparative research with three hypothesized factors is therefore likely to require data from 9 variables from a minimum of 200 individuals. Because relatively few studies have collected this much data from this many adults of different ages, the number of data sets suitable for age comparisons of factor structures is very limited.

A second problem associated with developmental comparisons of factor structure relates to the difficulty of distinguishing among alternative factor-analytic outcomes. The complications arise because many different factor-analytic procedures can be used, and the type and number of factors, as well as the relations among them, are highly dependent on the particular analytic procedures employed. In fact, many of the analyses reported before about 1980 have been criticized because of the arbitrariness of certain of the procedures, and the failure to conduct tests of the equivalence of the factor solutions derived from data of adults of different ages (W.R. Cunningham, 1978, 1987; Hertzog, 1987).

Factor-analytic investigations are also limited in their ability to detect differences in factor structure by the particular combination of measures included in the assessment battery. That is, a shift in a measure from one construct to another is not detectable unless measures of both constructs are represented in the test battery. To illustrate, consider the hypothesis that a particular measure, in addition to reflecting its primary construct, is influenced by impulsiveness among young adults but by reflectivity among older adults. This kind of shift in what the variable is measuring would not be detectable if measures corresponding to impulsiveness and reflectivity were not included in the assessment battery preventing these constructs from emerging in the factor analysis.

For the reasons listed above, the number of age-comparative factor-analytic studies is not great, and only a fraction of those that have been conducted used procedures that are currently considered acceptable. It is nevertheless encouraging that most of the recent studies involving cognitive variables have yielded fairly consistent results. The predominant finding has been that the factor structures of young and old adults seem to be both configurally and metrically equivalent, but with somewhat larger factor correlations among older adults than among young adults (Cowart & McCallum, 1984; W.R. Cunningham, 1980; Hertzog & Schaie, 1986; K.C. Parker, 1983; Schaie, Willis, Jay, & Chipuer, 1989; Stricker & Rock, 1987). In terms of the outcomes portrayed in Figure 5.1, young and old adults appear to differ in a manner corresponding to the contrast between outcomes 3 and 5, with stronger relations between factors (Outcome 5) for older adults.

Summary

The important point to be noted from this brief discussion of age-comparative factor-analytic studies is that there is little current evidence to indicate that there is a qualitative difference in the factor structure of cognitive abilities across different ages. Additional research is still needed, particularly including variables suspected to reflect factors that might be hypothesized to change in meaning across the adult years. It is also desirable to explore hypotheses about why correlations among cognitive factors appear to increase with increased age. On the basis of the available correlational evidence, however, it appears that many measures of cognitive functioning are assessing the same general constructs across most of the adult life span.

STRATEGY DIFFERENCES

A popular interpretation of age differences in cognitive performance attributes those differences to the use of ineffective strategies by older adults. Some of the ways in which this hypothesis has been expressed are listed in Table 5.1.

The sample of quotations contained in Table 5.1 clearly indicates there is considerable interest (and occasionally confidence) in the hypothesis that age differences in cognitive functioning are at least partially attributable to age differences in the use of effective strategies. However, in order to

TABLE 5.1
Statements concerning the influence of strategic factors on age differences in cognitive performance

"... it appears that a metacognitive strategy difference is in part responsible for the deficits in problem solving in later life." (C.C. Adams & Rebok, 1982-83, p. 278)

"Age differences in recall are interpretable as reflecting differences in the use of suitable strategies." (P.B. Baltes, Reese, & Lipsitt, 1980, p. 85)

"... memory growth and decline do not reflect merely increasing and decreasing efficiency of performing a fixed set of encoding, storing, and retrieving processes, but rather reflect the development of qualitatively different processes (operations) for encoding, storing, and retrieving." (P.B. Baltes, Reese, & Lipsitt, 1980, p. 86)

"As age advances, the individual shifts from strategies which are intellectually demanding (but accurate and logically efficient) to strategies which are less demanding (but relatively inaccurate and inefficient)." (Bromley, 1974, p. 173)

"... in laboratory list-learning experiments the evidence supporting [age-related] decreases in strategies is considerable." (Cavanaugh, Kramer, Sinnott, Camp, & Markley, 1985, p. 165)

"... age-related changes in memory performance result, in part, from age-related changes in the use of deliberate mnemonic strategies." (Guttentag, 1985, p. 57)

"Older adults are less likely than younger adults to generate optimal strategies." (A.A. Hartley & J.W. Anderson, 1986, p. 657)

"... the development with practice of appropriate strategies of task performance can diminish and even reverse effects of ... [irreversible deterioration in the central nervous system]." (M. Martin, 1986, p. 69)

"... the aged often appear deficient in spontaneously producing appropriate and effective memory strategies when asked to remember, even though these strategies are helpful if older adults are induced to use them." (M.D. Murphy, R.E. Sanders, Gabriesheski, & Schmitt, 1981, p. 185)

"Especially with laboratory-type memory tasks, older adults tend to show poorer memory performance and fail to produce the kinds of effective strategies that young adults adopt spontaneously." (M.D. Murphy, Schmitt, Caruso, & R.E. Sanders, 1987, p. 331)

"... adult age differences in memory may be related to older adults engaging in less efficient strategic processing." (Perlmutter, 1978, p. 332)

"... an important factor contributing to age differences in memory performance is change in the use of effective strategies." (Perlmutter & D.B. Mitchell, 1982, p. 136)

"Young adults tend to use kinds of cognitive strategies that are more effective for problem solving than the kinds elderly adults and young children tend to use." (Reese & Rodeheaver, 1985, p. 476)

"The older adults have the requisite capabilities but, for some reason, fail to produce spontaneously an appropriate strategy in the context of the memory task." (Schmitt, M.D. Murphy, & R.E. Sanders, 1981, p. 336

"... the decline in old age is most severe on memory tasks that require the use of effortful or active encoding and retrieval strategies." (Zacks, 1982, p. 203) evaluate the empirical evidence relevant to this hypothesis, one must first specify exactly what is meant by a strategy. For the current purposes a strategy can be defined as one of several alternative methods for performing a particular cognitive task. While seemingly quite simple, this definition incorporates four assumptions that are critical in understanding the concept of a strategy. These assumptions are: (a) that strategies are specific to particular tasks, (b) that all the people being compared are equally capable of executing the strategies, (c) that variations in strategies have consequences for level of performance on the task, and (d) that the evidence used to infer the existence of strategy differences is distinct from that used to indicate the level of performance.

The first aspect of this definition of a strategy is that it is linked to a limited set of cognitive tasks. This restriction is necessary in order to allow a distinction between strategies, which are postulated to pertain to specific tasks, and metacognitive or executive processes, which are hypothesized to affect the selection and monitoring of strategies for a wide range of cognitive tasks. Task-specific strategies are discussed in the present section, and the topic of age differences in metacognition is discussed in the final section of this chapter.

A second aspect of the current definition of a strategy is that it is an optional method of performing the cognitive task. That is, the method must be within the capability of the individual or it cannot be considered a strategy for him or her even though it may be a strategy for other individuals. The relation between strategy and ability has been the source of much confusion and controversy. A major problem is that it is difficult to determine the extent to which strategies are truly optional methods of deploying one's abilities (i.e., are causes of observed performance), or are more appropriately considered reflections of each individual's adaptation to his or her own level of abilities (i.e., are consequences of level of ability). An illustration of the first position is evident in the following:

> ... [S]trategy selection at a specific point in time is determined by one's experience, what one knows, one's personality, beliefs about one's abilities, level of motivation, the particular task at hand, and social constraints. (Cavanaugh, et al., 1985, pp. 162-163)

What is particularly noteworthy in this passage is that although many other determinants of strategies are mentioned, there is no direct reference to the actual abilities of the individual. The apparent implication is that virtually everyone has the option of selecting among the same set of strategies, regardless of his or her level of ability.

In contrast to the strategy-as-cause position, a number of authors have argued that certain strategies are only effective if relevant cognitive abilities exceed some minimum level. For example, several researchers (Bromley,

1970; Charness, 1985b; G. Cohen, 1988; Guttentag, 1985; A.A. Hartley & J.W. Anderson, 1983a; Rabinowitz, et al., 1982; Salthouse, 1985b, 1988c, 1988d, 1988e) have stressed that some strategies place heavy demands on memory or other cognitive resources, and hence they may be beyond the capabilities of older adults, who are impaired in these respects relative to young adults.

A study by Reder, et al., (1986) can be used to illustrate the difficulty of ensuring that what is inferred to be an optional strategy is actually within the capability of all research participants. These researchers distinguished two strategies for making decisions about previously presented information. The *direct retrieval* strategy involved searching memory for a specific fact, while the *plausibility* strategy consisted of "... using available information to infer or reason that a statement is true" (p. 73). Notice that, according to these definitions, an individual could be considered to be using the plausibility strategy whenever he or she is unable to remember the target information and merely makes a reasonable guess about the answer. Only if the respondent refuses to venture a rational guess, and effectively discontinues participation in the experiment, would he or she apparently not be credited with the use of one of these two "strategies."

The authors acknowledged that what they referred to as the plausibility strategy was probably easier and less demanding than the remembering strategy. They also stated that there was "... no evidence that older subjects could use the direct retrieval strategy effectively if they wanted to" (Reder, et al., 1986, p. 80). The combination that one strategy is apparently inferred to be operative whenever another is not, that the strategies differ in ease of use, and that older adults may not be able to execute one of the strategies, raises serious doubts about the meaningfulness of the Reder, et al. (1986) interpretation of age differences in strategies.

Welford (1958) has also discussed the idea that what appears to be a different approach to a task may actually be an adaptation to an inability to perform the task in the required manner. For example, in a logical reasoning task older adults might comment on the material, rather than draw logical deductions as requested, not because they have a different strategy for performing the task, but because a comment allows some type of answer to be provided even when the correct answer cannot be determined. Reports that older adults are more likely to react to the content of propositional statements rather than to their logical relations (Friend & Zubek, 1958; M.L. Young, 1966) should therefore not necessarily be interpreted as a reflection of the use of a different strategy until there is some assurance that these individuals are as capable as young adults of executing the task in the requested manner.

The third assumption implicit in the concept of a strategy is that variations in strategies should lead to detectable differences in some aspect of either the quality or the efficiency of performance. An assumption of this nature seems imperative to rule out considering minor variations in the manner in which a task is performed (e.g., whether one is smiling or frowning when engaged in the task) as reflections of different strategies. Of course there may be situations in which presumably different strategies lead to equivalent levels of performance. The important point, however, is that distinctions between purported strategies may be meaningless if the strategies are functionally equivalent in the sense that there are no situations in which strategic variations correspond to different performance consequences.

A recent study of complex decision-making in young and old adults (M.M.S. Johnson, 1990) illustrates the problem of inferring differences in strategy when there is no information about accompanying differences in the efficiency or effectiveness of performance. One of the interesting findings in this study was that older adults were apparently more likely than young adults to examine information by focusing on the same attributes from different decision alternatives, whereas young adults were more likely to examine information by concentrating on different attributes within the same decision alternatives. Although these apparent differences in information acquisition patterns may reflect genuinely different strategies, the consequences of these differences on the quality of decision-making could not be determined because no optimum decision was specified against which each individual's responses could be evaluated. It is therefore not obvious that the patterns of information acquisition should be considered as representing distinct strategies, or merely different styles of gathering functionally equivalent information. Interpretation of this particular study is further complicated by the fact that the young adults requested almost twice as much information as the older adults, and the manner in which information is requested may depend upon the total amount of information already available, or planned to be requested.

The fourth assumption incorporated in the current definition of a strategy is that the evidence leading to the inference of different strategies should be distinct from the actual measures of performance. That is, there is no basis for attributing differences in performance to differences in strategies if the same evidence used to establish the performance differences is also used to infer the existence of the strategy differences hypothesized to account for the performance differences. In order to consider variations in strategy as distinct from, and perhaps responsible for, variations in performance, the evidence relating to strategy use should be independent of the evidence concerning level of performance. This does not appear to be the situation in the 20 Questions task frequently cited as demonstrating an age-related strategy deficiency (N.W. Denney, 1980, 1985; A.A. Hartley & J.W. Anderson, 1983a, 1986; E.D. Hybertson, et al., 1982). In this task, it is impossible to achieve high levels of performance without using an efficient strategy because performance is assessed in terms of the efficiency or information value of the sequence of questions (i.e., strategy) used to identify the target item. The 20 Questions task may therefore be too simple to allow an examination of the role of strategy differences in cognitive performance because type of strategy and level of performance cannot be distinguished.

Another example of the difficulty of separating measures of strategy from measures of performance is evident in a study reported by Zacks (1982). The task in this study was to report the identity of the most recently presented member of a probed category. Young adults were found to be generally more accurate than older adults, and they exhibited less of a serial position effect across the six input items than did older adults. An additional finding was that the relation between report accuracy and input position was similar in young and old adults when the young adults were instructed to repeat each item aloud until the next one appeared. Zacks suggested that the presence of a pronounced serial position effect indicated that older adults were less likely to use active encoding strategies than young adults, and that the requirement to vocalize each item reduced the likelihood or effectiveness of active encoding in young adults. However, an alternative interpretation is that the serial position differences were a consequence of the lower overall level of performance. That is, older adults, and young adults required to engage in repetition rehearsal, may simply have been more likely to forget the earlier information, but the most recently presented information was probably still available and could be accurately reported, thus giving rise to a typical serial position function.

Objections can obviously be raised against some of the criteria proposed as defining characteristics of a strategy. However, it seems essential that criteria similar to these be adopted, and the related issues be addressed, if the notion of strategic variation is to be considered meaningful as a potential determinant of age-related differences in cognitive performance.

A convincing argument that age differences in cognitive performance are at least partially attributable to age differences in the use of effective strategies seems to require two kinds of evidence. The first relates to the issue of whether young and old adults do in fact differ with respect to patterns of strategy usage in cognitive tasks. The second concerns whether, if there are age differences in the frequency of using different strategies, these strategic differences actually mediate some of the age differences in cognitive performance.

Evidence for Age Differences in Strategy Use

Perhaps the simplest way of determining if adults of different ages use different strategies is to ask them to report the strategy they used after they have completed performing a cognitive task. The validity of these reports is usually unknown because there is seldom any means of verifying the accuracy of self reports. Nevertheless, self-reports provide one source of information relevant to the hypothesis that young and old adults use different strategies, and that at least some of the age differences in cognitive performance are due to these strategic differences.

One of the earliest studies to collect reports from young and old adults of the strategies used on cognitive tasks was conducted by Cimbalo and Brink (1982). Three types of strategies were identified as having been used in an immediate memory task. An association strategy was reported equally often by young and old adults, but young adults reported using grouping and rote repetition strategies somewhat more frequently than older adults. Note that while grouping is generally considered to be an effective rehearsal strategy, rote repetition is not. The fact that young adults reported more of both types of strategies therefore precludes any general conclusion about age and strategy effectiveness from the results of this study. Another study in which somewhat surprising age differences in the frequency of different types of strategies were reported involved memory for locations on a map (J.L. Thomas, 1985). Young adults were most likely to report using a verbal labeling strategy, while the majority of the older adults reported using a spatial or structural strategy, which might have been expected to be more effective.

Little or no age differences in self-reported memory strategies have been reported by S.M. Glynn, Okun, Muth, and Britton (1983), Lichty, Bressie, and Krell (1988), Rankin, Karol, and Tuten (1984), Rice and B.J. Meyer (1986), and Wood and Pratt (1987). Similar distributions of reported strategy usage among young and old adults were also reported by G. Cohen and Faulkner (1983a) in mental rotation and linguistic verification tasks. This particular null result should probably be interpreted with some caution, however, because only 12 individuals were tested in each age group, and hence the power to detect any age differences that might have existed was quite low.

A recent attempt to investigate possible age differences in the strategy or style of remembering information from stories was reported by C. Adams, Labouvie-Vief, Hobart, and Dorosz (1990). Although the authors suggested that older adults rely more on an integrative or interpretative style of recall than young adults, the evidence in support of this speculation appears rather weak. Not only were the percentages of responses classified as integrations or interpretations small in both young and old adults, but the mean levels of either kind of response were not significantly different in the two age groups.

Several studies have investigated possible age differences in strategy usage in the context of free recall memory tasks. These tasks are presumed to be very amenable to strategic variation because the research participant is allowed to recall the items in any order, and certain recall orders (e.g., recall of last-presented items first, or recall grouped according to categorical membership) tend to lead to higher levels of recall than other recall orders. The strategy of recalling the latest items first is generally effective in increasing recall because the most recently presented items are still in a high state of availability when recall begins. Both Parkinson, Lindholm, and Inman (1982) and R.E. Wright (1982) found that older adults were as likely as young adults to begin their recall with the latest presented items, suggesting that use of this particular strategy does not differ across young and old adults.

R.E. Sanders, M.D. Murphy, Schmitt, and K.K. Walsh (1980) instructed young and older adults to think aloud as they studied items in a free recall task, and then analyzed tape recordings of these verbalizations for evidence of differential strategy use. The 10 young adults in this condition were found to rehearse the items in categorical groups to a greater extent than the 10 older adults performing in the same condition. This age difference was statistically significant, but questions can be raised about the generality of the results because other studies have been inconsistent in the extent to which young and old adults appear to rely on categorical clustering in memory tasks (see chapter 6).

Another method of inferring strategy usage is based on analyses of the time allocated to each portion of a sequential task. The distribution of these times forms a profile of processing durations which can be considered a reflection of the strategy used by the individual in performing the task. That is, the amount of time allocated to each portion of a task can be interpreted as an indication of the individual's strategy because different strategies are likely to lead to different allocations of processing effort across various portions of the task. The time spent studying each successively presented element in a series completion task was analyzed by Salthouse and Prill (1987). The qualitative pattern of study times across successive elements was very similar in young and old adults, particularly for problems eventually answered correctly (see Figure 5.2). Similar allocations of study times by adults of different ages have also been found with successively presented portions of a geometric analogies task (Salthouse, 1987d), with a successively presented integrative reasoning task (Salthouse, Legg, Palmon, & D.R. Mitchell, 1990), and with word-by-word reading in a sentence memory task (Stine, 1990).

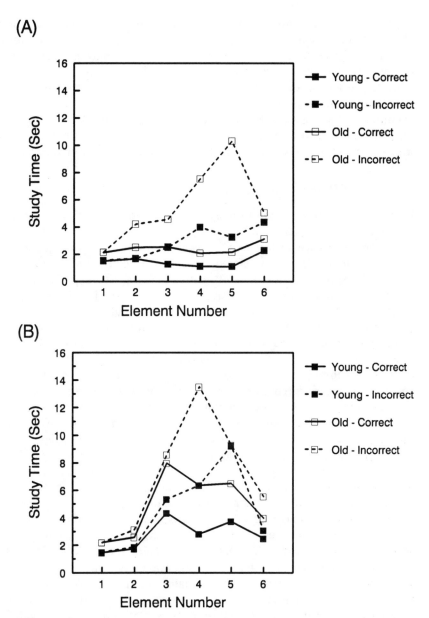

Figure 5.2. Profiles of study times as a function of age, element number and eventual decision accuracy in series completion problems. Data from Salthouse and Prill (1987).

This evidence reveals mixed support for the hypothesis that young and old adults differ with respect to the type of strategies used to perform various cognitive tasks. Some results suggest there may be age-related strategic differences, but the absence of age differences on measures such as recall order or the distribution of processing times that might be expected to reflect the use of different strategies, is inconsistent with this hypothesis. No strong conclusion therefore appears possible at the present time with respect to whether adults of different ages vary in the extent to which they employ effective strategies for performing cognitive tasks.

Strategy as Cause or as Consequence

If reliable age differences in strategy usage were to be found, the question would then arise whether those differences were the cause of the age-related performance differences, or were themselves a consequence of some other more fundamental factor. Because strategies can be considered another form of behavior, it is ultimately necessary to explain why age differences in strategies might exist. An important issue in this connection is whether older adults are as capable as young adults at using effective strategies, but simply do not use them as frequently or as spontaneously as young adults (i.e., a production deficiency). If this were the case, then age differences in measures of cognitive performance might be expected to be reduced or eliminated when everyone is using the same strategy. In contrast, if age differences in strategy use originate because the most effective strategies are too demanding for older adults (i.e., a processing deficiency), then age differences in cognitive performance would be expected even when all individuals were using the same strategies.

At least three procedures could be used to determine whether strategic differences might be responsible for age differences in cognitive performance. One procedure involves obtaining independent measures of strategy, such as output order in free recall or profiles of processing durations in reasoning or spatial tasks, and then comparing the performance of young and old adults only for those individuals found to be using the same strategy. As noted above, there was little evidence of strategic differences in several memory and reasoning tasks in which young adults were found to perform substantially better than older adults. If confirmed in additional research, these results would imply that strategic differences are not necessary to produce age differences in cognitive performance.

A second possible method of investigating the contribution of strategy factors to age differences in cognitive performance consists of examining age-related effects in tasks that are performed incidentally, and thus presumably without active or deliberate strategies. Although it seems reasonable to assume that strategy usage is minimal when the tasks are performed without conscious awareness or intention, a robust finding in many studies has been that young adults are generally superior to older adults in a variety of assessments of incidentally acquired information (Azmitia & Perlmutter, 1988; J.C. Bartlett & Leslie, 1986; Bromley, 1958; Charness, 1979, 1981a, 1981b; Farrimond, 1969; J.L. Horn, et al., 1981; H.E. Jones, Conrad, & A. Horn, 1928; Kausler & Lair, 1965, 1968; Lair, Moon, & Kausler, 1969; Mergler, Dusek, & W.J. Hoyer, 1977; Naveh-Benjamin, 1987; Nebes & Andrews-Kulis, 1976; Peak, 1968, 1970; Randt, E.R. Brown, & Osborne, 1980; Salthouse, et al., 1988a; Thorndike, et al., 1928; Willoughby, 1929, 1930). Unfortunately, while these and other studies are consistent in indicating the presence of age differences when the information was acquired under incidental conditions (see the section on depth of processing in chapter 6), the relevance of the findings to the issue of the role of strategies in age differences in memory remains somewhat ambiguous. The difficulty is that strategies may be involved whenever memory for the information is tested, and therefore age differences might have existed in the effectiveness of strategies used at the time of test even if there were no differences in strategic involvement when the material was initially presented. Although this possibility means that interpretations must be qualified, the results of studies with incidental memory tasks nevertheless do suggest that age differences in memory are probably not attributable to variations in strategies related to the acquisition or encoding of subsequently tested information.

The third procedure that can be used to determine whether age differences in strategies are responsible for age differences in cognitive performance consists of providing extensive training to ensure that everyone is using the same strategy. For example, in two recent projects the evidence that similar strategies were being used by all research participants was particularly convincing because the ultimate level of performance achieved seems unlikely to have been possible without using the trained strategy (or one very closely related to it). One of these projects required remembering lists of up to 30 words in their original order of presentation (Kliegl, et al., 1989); in the other, participants had to square two-digit numbers mentally (Charness & J.I.D. Campbell, 1988). Both of these tasks are beyond the capabilities of most untrained adults, and therefore one can be reasonably confident that everyone was using special, and quite likely the instructed, strategies to perform the tasks. Despite what can be presumed to be equivalent methods of performing the tasks, young adults were faster at mental calculation (Charness & J.I.D. Campbell, 1988), and were able to remember more items at short stimulus presentation rates (Kliegl, et al., 1989), than comparably experienced older adults. It is implausible in these studies, therefore, that the age differences in the available measures of cognitive performance could be attributable to young and old adults using different strategies to perform the tasks.

Summary

It is almost certainly true that, for most cognitive tasks, different levels of performance can result from the use of different strategies. Nevertheless, the hypothesis that many of the age differences in cognitive performance might be attributable to differences in strategy usage currently lacks convincing empirical support. There is still relatively little evidence that adults of different ages use different strategies when performing cognitive tasks, and it appears that strategic differences are not necessary to produce age differences in cognitive performance. It is too soon to dismiss the possibility that at least some age differences in cognitive functioning are attributable to the use of less effective strategies on the part of older adults. However, the hypothesis must be treated as merely an interesting speculation until additional research is conducted investigating the relations between ability and strategy use at all ages, and examining additional methods of inferring the existence of strategy differences independent of measures of performance.

METACOGNITION

Metacognition is a very broad term, with numerous connotations. In a general sense it refers to the operation of executive processes presumed to be responsible for control and monitoring of all aspects of the cognitive system, including selection and execution of strategies for the performance of specific cognitive tasks. Metacognition is potentially important in cognitive development because quantitative comparisons involving adults of different ages may be meaningless if people of different ages vary in the nature or efficiency of these executive or control processes.

Most of the adult developmental research on metacognition has focused on the domain of memory, and is therefore referred to as metamemory. Three topics are frequently discussed as falling within the scope of metamemory: self-evaluations of one's memory abilities, knowledge about memory in general, and monitoring the functioning of one's own memory. Much of the research on self-assessments of memory ability was discussed in connection with the topic on self-efficacy, and can be succinctly summarized by stating that there is frequently a decrease with age in ratings of one's own ability to memorize.

Knowledge about Memory

Interest in the knowledge an individual possesses about general memory functioning has been motivated by the concern that memory performance might be impaired because of lack of fundamental knowledge about how the memory system works. Several researchers have therefore asked adults of different ages questions about the relative effectiveness of different remembering strategies, about the ease of remembering different types of information, and so on. Most of the published studies have found little or no age differences in this kind of general knowledge about memory functioning (Anooshian, et al., 1989; Cavanaugh & Poon, 1989; Hultsch, et al., 1987; Perlmutter, 1978; but not Dixon & Hultsch, 1983). Of course, the knowledge assessments have not been exhaustive, but the currently available evidence seems to suggest that age differences in basic understanding of how memory functions are minimal to non-existent.

Memory Monitoring

Age-comparative research on memory monitoring has focused on the investigation of possible age differences in awareness of one's own memory functioning. The assumption is that optimum performance in a memory task is dependent upon accurate monitoring of the availability of information in one's memory, and on timely evaluation of the relative effectiveness of different strategies. It has therefore been hypothesized that age differences in the performance of certain memory tasks may be at least partially attributable to a reduction with age in the accuracy of monitoring the contents of one's memory, or in the effectiveness of the processes used to operate on those contents.

One measure proposed as an index of memory monitoring is the amount of time allocated to studying the to-be-remembered material. As an example, M.D. Murphy, et al., (1981) suggested that older adults were deficient relative to young adults in monitoring their recall readiness because they were found to spend less time studying the materials than young adults. The validity of study time as a reflection of memory monitoring processes is still not established, but, in any case, numerous other studies (Bruce, Coyne, & Botwinick, 1982; Erber, et al., 1985; Lovelace & Marsh, 1985; McDowd & Botwinick, 1984; Perlmutter, 1978, 1979; Perlmutter, et al., 1981; and Rabinowitz, 1989b), including one by several of the original investigators (M.D. Murphy, Schmitt, Caruso, & R.E. Sanders, 1987) have failed to replicate this finding.

Another method of investigating memory monitoring accuracy consists of asking research participants to indicate the confidence or feeling-of-knowing they have regarding each to-be-answered or to-be-remembered item. Precision of memory monitoring is indicated by the strength of the relationship between the feeling-of-knowing rating and the ultimate answer or recall accuracy of the item. If older adults have less memory monitoring ability than young adults, then, compared to young adults, they should have smaller differences in accuracy between items with a strong feeling-of-knowing and those with a weak feeling-of-knowing. In contrast, the two groups should have similar relations between the feeling-of-knowing ratings and the levels of performance if young and old adults are equivalent in this sort of memory monitoring.

Results from studies with a variety of different stimulus materials suggest that the second hypothesis is more likely to be correct. This is reflected in a consistent finding that there are no significant differences between young and old adults in the relations between measures of performance and feeling-of-knowing judgments (Anooshian, et al., 1989; Backman & Karlsson, 1985; Butterfield, T.O. Nelson, & Peck, 1988; J.L. Lachman, R. Lachman, & Thronesberry, 1979; R. Lachman & J.L. Lachman, 1980; R. Lachman, et al., 1982).

A related procedure for evaluating memory monitoring involves asking the research participant to make predictions about how many items will be recalled, or about the probability of recalling specific items. The general finding in most studies has been that young and old adults are more similar to one another in their predictions of recall than they are in their actual levels of recall (Brigham & Pressley, 1988; Bruce, et al., 1982; Coyne, 1985; Lovelace & Marsh, 1985; M.D. Murphy, et al., 1981; Perlmutter, 1978; Rabinowitz, Ackerman, Craik, & Hinchley, 1982; Rebok & Balcerak, 1989; Shaw & Craik, 1989; but see Devolder, Brigham, & Pressley, 1990, and Hertzog, Dixon, & Hultsch, 1990, for exceptions). Because recall performance is usually lower for older adults than for young adults, this pattern means that, in an absolute sense, older adults tend to overestimate their performance, whereas young adults tend to underestimate their performance. However, relative prediction accuracy seems to be about equal in the two groups because both young and old adults alter their predictions appropriately with variations in imagery value and word frequency (Bruce, et al., 1982), item relatedness (Rabinowitz, et al., 1982), presentation rate (Coyne, 1985), type of encoding and recall cue (Shaw & Craik, 1989), and according to whether the item was eventually recalled successfully (Lovelace & Marsh, 1985; Rabinowitz, et al., 1982; Shaw & Craik, 1989).

Some of the complexities associated with age-comparative research on metacognition are illustrated in a study reported by Brigham and Pressley (1988). A primary purpose of this study was to investigate possible age differences in the ability to monitor the effectiveness of alternative strategies. The task consisted of learning definitions of unfamiliar words with either a key-word strategy ("Think of a mediator and incorporate it in a sentence") or a semantic-context strategy ("Make up a sentence containing the word"). Three categories of data were obtained from each of the young and old research participants. One category consisted of measures of actual performance in terms of the number of words learned with each strategy. The second set of data consisted of stated preferences for the two strategies before, and after, attempting to use them to learn the words. And finally, the research participants were also asked to state the reasons they preferred one strategy over the other.

Based on results of earlier research, Brigham and Pressley hypothesized that the key-word strategy would be more effective than the semantic-context strategy. They therefore evaluated effectiveness of strategy monitoring by determining the preference for this strategy after everyone had used both strategies to perform the task. Only 42% of the older adults, compared to 98% of the young adults, preferred the key-word strategy in the post-experimental evaluation. Brigham and Pressley interpreted these findings as indicating that older adults may be less effective at monitoring the relative success of the two strategies than young adults. However, three additional results suggest that this interpretation may be premature. First is the finding that more young adults than older adults also had a preference for the key-word strategy before using it to perform the task (i.e., 65% vs. 40%). Not all the differences in preference observed at the end of the experiment can therefore be attributed to monitoring differences because fairly substantial age differences were apparently evident before either strategy was used. The second complicating result is that the advantage of the key-word strategy in learning word meanings was actually greater for young adults than for older adults. Because the benefits of the strategy were objectively greater for young adults than for older adults, there is less compelling evidence to justify a preference for it among older adults than among young adults. Finally, when asked the reasons for preferring one strategy over another, only 47% of the older adults, compared to 93% of the young adults, mentioned a criterion of utility or effectiveness in increasing memory performance.

When considered in combination, therefore, the results of the Brigham and Pressley (1988) study do not appear to warrant strong conclusions concerning relations between age and the metacognitive skill of monitoring strategy effectiveness. Young adults do have a greater preference for the more effective strategy than older adults, but they also favor it somewhat more before comparing it with the other strategy, the objective advantage of the strategy is greater for them than for older adults, and they are more likely than older adults to use a criterion of superior recall as the basis for making their preference decisions. This overall pattern is interesting, but probably too complex to justify an inference that young and old adults differ in the accuracy of monitoring the effectiveness of different strategies.

A later study by Devolder, et al., (1990) also investigated metacognitive monitoring abilities in young and old adults. Participants in this project made estimates of their level of performance either before or after completing each of several cognitive tasks. Of primary interest were the age by time-of-estimation interactions because they were presumed to "... signal a developmental shift in monitoring ability, with one age group more competent than the other in on-line monitoring of memory performance" (p. 292). Only one of nine interactions was statistically significant: Young adults were much worse than older adults at estimating their ability to keep appointments before participating in the task, but were similar in their performance estimates after participation. The general failure to find evidence of age differences in performance monitoring was apparently discouraging to the authors because they concluded their article stating "... more may be learned about adult metacognition and cognition by studying individual monitoring differences within ages and between tasks than by additional research on age differences per se" (p. 302).

Several additional studies have been reported in which young and old adults have been asked to indicate their preference for or the judged usefulness of different strategies, but these studies also seem limited with respect to the conclusions that can be reached. For example, Zivian and Darjes (1983) asked 10 young adults and 10 older adults to rate 20 memory strategies in terms of their "usefulness" in remembering lists of words. The rank-order correlation between the two sets of ratings was .29, but it is difficult to evaluate the meaning of this correlation with such small samples, with no information about the reliability of the ratings, and in the context of such vague rating instructions.

A.A. Hartley and J.W. Anderson (1986) obtained ratings from 12 young adults and 12 older adults of "how good" various strategies were for solving a version of the 20 Questions task. Older adults were found to rate the most efficient "halving" strategy lower than young adults, leading the authors to suggest there may be a decline with age in the ability to evaluate the effectiveness of optimal strategies. It is important to note, however, that the key (and indeed the only) principle in the 20 Questions task is that the number of remaining alternatives should be reduced by the maximum amount with each question. If young and old adults differed in their understanding of this fundamental principle, then the age differences in strategy ratings may have reflected different criteria for what "goodness" meant in the experimental context, and not different evaluations of the degree to which each strategy implemented the principle.

Summary

Because measures of the efficiency of component processes are not necessarily meaningful if those processes are organized or used in different ways, it is important to consider the possibility that adults of different ages might vary in metacognitive, or executive, functioning. Research on this topic is relatively recent, but results from the available studies do not appear to provide much support for the hypothesis of age differences in metacognitive functioning. Little or no age differences have typically been reported in measures of general knowledge about memory, and most studies have found young and old adults to be fairly similar in measures of memory monitoring effectiveness. The concept of metacognition is still rather new, however, and hence the amount of relevant research is still quite limited. As Devolder and Pressley (1989) suggested, the study of metacognitive factors should be broadened and expanded before definitive conclusions can be reached regarding the influence of metacognition on age differences in cognitive functioning.

EVALUATION OF QUALITATIVE-DIFFERENCE INTERPRETATIONS

It has been suggested that many of the attempts to interpret age differences in cognitive functioning in terms of qualitative differences are based more on hope than on fact. Conrad (1956) expressed this view in stating:

> Students of maturity and old age generally develop a kindly bias toward the subjects of their study, tending to place the blame for lack of motivation among the aged on, say, the lack of opportunity; or to view a decline in learning-ability with reservations about a "speed factor," "lack of realistic problem appeal," "unfavorable social competition;" etc. This optimistic bias if it may be so called is natural perhaps only human but it is scientifically dangerous ... We need to recognize and emphasize the disabilities of old age, as well as its competencies and potentialities. (p. 183).

More recently, Botwinick (1967, p. 202) claimed that it was "ostrich-like" to ignore age-related cognitive deficits, and Kausler (1982, p. 5) characterized as counterproductive the "Pollyanna" position that denies the existence of negative relations between age and cognitive functioning. These opinions should not constrain speculations and hypotheses about the causes of cognitive aging phenomena, but they do serve as reminders that a phenomenon cannot be dismissed as a relatively uninteresting consequence of qualitative changes without empirical evidence documenting the existence, and causal importance, of the hypothesized qualitative differences.

Perhaps appropriate questions for revealing qualitative differences have not yet been asked, or possibly the methodological procedures employed in past investigations have been deficient in important respects. What is relatively clear from the available research, however, is that young and old adults do not appear markedly different in what the measures of cognitive performance actually reflect. There is little evidence of a greater performance-competence gap in older adults than in young adults, a variety of measures of cognitive structure reveal similar organization of information across the adult years, the recent factor-analytic studies seem to indicate that young and old adults have similar patterns of correlations among variables, and convincing evidence of age differences is not yet available in measures of strategy use or metacognitive effectiveness.

The qualitative difference perspective is a mixture of ideas loosely organized around the theme that the age differences observed in many measures of cognitive performance may reflect changes that are qualitative, and not just quantitative. Most of the ideas therefore seem to be at the level of a theoretical framework; in only a few cases were the speculations formulated in sufficient detail to allow investigation of specific predictions. An important priority for future research relevant to the qualitative differences perspective should be the exploration of alternative, and ideally more explicit, conceptualizations of qualitative differences which explain both *why* there are age-related changes in structures, styles, or strategies, and *how* those changes contribute to lower levels of cognitive performance. It is essential that neither of these aspects be neglected because there seems to be a tendency among some theorists and researchers interested in the qualitative difference perspective to concentrate on the discovery of gains or changes in other aspects of the individual (e.g., wisdom, self-concept, social intelligence, etc.), and to dismiss as unimportant or unworthy of explanation the negative relations between age and cognition that have already been established. From the vantage point of attempting to understand the origin of cognitive age differences, the existence of age differences in characteristics postulated to reflect a qualitative shift in the individual as he or she grows older are only interesting to the extent that they can help explain the primary phenomenon of age differences in cognitive functioning. Therefore while it is desirable that new ways of examining the possibility that increased age is associated with qualitative changes be explored, it is also important that the goal of explaining how the qualitative differences might account for the frequently observed age-related declines in cognitive functioning not be displaced nor forgotten in the process.

6

Analytical Approaches to Localization: I. Memory Abilities

It is implicit that the goal is to localize the primary age changes along the sequence of events beginning with a stimulus (input) and ending with a response (output).

—Birren (1956, pp. 102-103)

The theoretical perspective to be discussed in this chapter and the next differs from the perspectives discussed in previous chapters in that the explanatory focus is more proximal than distal. That is, the goal of analytical approaches generally is not to indicate the ultimate source or origin of the observed age differences, but instead to specify as precisely as possible the particular processes or components of cognition that are impaired with increased age.

The terms analytical and localizational are used to characterize this approach because the primary goal has been to analyze cognitive behavior into its constituent elements, and then to try to localize the age-related effects to a particular subset of these elements. Most of the attempts to localize the proximal sources of age differences in cognition rely on analytical models designed to explain phenomena observed within the context of specific experimental tasks or paradigms. The models vary considerably in precision, and some are not much more than vague metaphors. However, almost all models postulate distinctions among theoretical constructs such as structures, stages, processes, or components. Consequently, researchers applying these models in the field of aging have attempted to identify which of the hypothesized entities is, or are, primarily responsible for the age-related deficits reported in various measures of cognitive performance. In order to be effective in localizing age-related influences, age differences should be small or non-existent on measures of certain components, and large and robust on measures reflecting other components. Research evidence will therefore be examined to determine the extent to which several proposed classification systems differentiate between variables exhibiting small and large amounts of sensitivity to age-related effects.

Because most analytically oriented models were designed to account for phenomena within relatively narrow domains of cognition, the research conducted from this perspective is easy to compartmentalize according to the type of cognition under investigation. The majority of the age-related research conducted from the analytical perspective has focused on memory abilities, with some also addressing reasoning abilities and spatial abilities. The current chapter will review analytically oriented research concerned with memory abilities, and the following chapter will focus on both reasoning abilities and spatial abilities. A fundamental question to be addressed in each chapter is what, or where, is the proximal locus of the age differences in the relevant cognitive ability.

INTERFERENCE INTERPRETATIONS

One of the oldest hypotheses concerning age differences in learning and memory attributes those differences to an increase with age in susceptibility to various types of interference. H.E. Jones (1959) captured one aspect of this position in the statement that "Old people seem more forgetful partly because they have so much more to forget ..." (p. 731). The assumption implicit in H.E. Jones' characterization seems to be that there is a finite capacity for remembering (or perhaps merely for storing what is remembered), and that because older adults have remembered so much more information over their lifetimes than have young adults, they are operating closer to their capacity limits than are young adults. The memory functioning of older adults may therefore be less reliable than that of young adults because their storage systems have less residual volume. Another metaphor compatible with the interference interpretation is that the memory system is something like a chalkboard. That is, it is a very effective medium for temporary storage when it is new (or young) because the chalkboard can be easily written on and easily erased. However, with age and cumulative use it gradually loses some of its effectiveness because it becomes harder to deposit new records on the surface, and those that are deposited are less distinguishable in the context of earlier, incompletely erased, markings. The interference from prior usage can thus be viewed as having contributed to a reduction in functional effectiveness of the storage, or memory, system.

At least three conceptually distinct types of interference can be identified. Pre-experimental interference is that attributable to prior learning or already existing habits that may hinder (and sometimes facilitate) performance in experimental situations. Interference can also originate within an experiment because of activity that either occurs before, or after, the initial exposure to the to-be-remembered material. Age-comparative research within each of these categories will be reviewed to evaluate the hypothesis that a greater susceptibility to interference is a primary locus, or source, of age differences in memory.

Pre-experimental Interference

The hypothesis that older adults are more affected than young adults by disruption of pre-existing habits was first tested by Ruch (1934) in an important early study on aging and cognition. Each individual participated in a battery of five tasks, two perceptual-motor tasks and three paired-associates tasks. The paired-associates tasks differed with respect to the type of stimulus material employed. The easiest material involved familiar and meaningful associates with pairs of words such as MAN and BOY. A second type of material, consisting of nonsense equations such as $L \times B = D$, was expected to be more difficult because it would have no prior associations. The third type of material consisted of false equations, such as $6 \times 3 = 5$, and was expected to present the greatest difficulty because it had no previous positive associations and actually conflicted with prior knowledge. Performance on each task was represented by the number of paired associates answered correctly across 15 repetitions of 10 pairs. The major findings in this study were that the age differences were greater when the material was unfamiliar (i.e., nonsense equations) than when it was familiar, but contrary to Ruch's hypothesis, there was no additional impairment for older adults when the material directly conflicted with information from past experience (i.e., false equations).

Results generally similar to Ruch's have been reported in many subsequent studies in which pre-experimental familiarity was manipulated by means of the association value of items in paired-associate learning tasks. *Association value* in this context refers to the extent to which the two items in the pair are familiar or natural according to past experience; it can be systematically determined either by ratings, or by analyses of the frequency of generating specific associates of target items. Examples of pairs with high associative strength are BREAD-BUTTER and KING-QUEEN, whereas pairs such as BREAD-KING or BUTTER-QUEEN have low associative strength. A well replicated finding has been that age differences in paired-associate learning or cued recall are greater when the pairs have low associative strength than when they have high associative strength (Botwinick & Storandt, 1974; Canestrari, 1966; Kausler & Lair, 1966; Lair, et al., 1969; Rabinowitz, 1986; Rabinowitz & Ackerman, 1982; Rabinowitz, Craik, & Ackerman, 1982; E. Ross, 1968; Shaps & Nilsson, 1980; Zaretsky & Halberstam, 1968; but see Rabinowitz, Ackerman, Craik, & Hinchley, 1982, for an exception). Because low associative strength items are, by definition, less consistent with past experience, this result is in line with the expectation that age deficits are greatest when the learning fails to coincide with past experiences.

Although generally similar results have been found in most studies investigating pre-experimental interference, the interpretation of these results has been somewhat equivocal because of an apparent confounding between consistency with past learning and the amount of new learning required. In other words, material that is not consistent with past experience is likely to involve the greatest amount of new learning, whereas material that is consistent with past experience seems to require the least new learning (Welford, 1958). It is therefore conceivable that what was actually being manipulated in these studies was the amount of current processing required in the task, and not the amount of interference with prior learning. Unfortunately, it does not appear possible to distinguish among these alternatives on the basis of available research.

Interference from Prior Activity

Interference effects can also be studied by manipulating what occurs before or after the presentation of the to-be-remembered information. Disruption produced by prior activity can be assessed by determining the relation between performance on a given cognitive task and the amount of prior experience with the same, or similar, tasks involving different stimulus materials. Because memory performance generally declines as a function of the amount of previous related experience, this is often termed proactive (or forward acting) interference.

One of the simplest methods of assessing susceptibility to proactive interference consists of comparing performance on similar types of material across successive trials or exposures to a task. If the level of performance declines more across successive trials in older adults than in young adults, one might infer that there is an age-related increase in the susceptibility to proactive interference. Although the procedure seems straightforward, results from age-comparative studies of proactive interference have been mixed. For example, some researchers have found similar magnitudes of performance declines across successive free-recall lists for young and old adults (Craik, 1968a, 1968b; R.E. Sanders, et al., 1980), while others have reported that older adults have greater performance reductions than young adults (J.T. Hartley & D.A. Walsh, 1980).

Diverse results have also been reported from studies in which sets of similar items (e.g., words from the same semantic category) are presented with a period of distracting activity interpolated between the presentation and recall of each set of items. A common finding with this procedure is that accuracy decreases across successive trials, presumably because of some sort of build-up of interference or inhibition. However, the magnitude of these progressive interference effects are sometimes reported to be greater for older adults than for young adults (Schonfield, Davidson, & H. Jones, 1983), are sometimes reported to be equal in magnitude for young and old adults (Fozard & Waugh, 1969; Keevil-Rogers & Schnore, 1969; Lorsbach, 1990; Moscovitch & Winocur, 1983), and are sometimes inconsistent, with both patterns evident in one or more conditions of an experiment (C.S. Elias & Hirasuna, 1976; Mistler-Lachman, 1977).

No definitive conclusion can therefore be reached from the available evidence concerning age differences in sensitivity to interference from previous activity. It is possible that more detailed analyses might help resolve some of the discrepancies among the existing studies. For example, comparisons of patterns of intrusion errors from prior trials might be informative about the influence of confusion from earlier presented information as a potential source of proactive interference. On this particular issue, however, the available evidence again does not allow a firm conclusion because some studies have reported more intra-experimental intrusion errors for older adults than for young adults (J.T. Hartley & D.A. Walsh, 1980; Rankin & Collins, 1985; Taub, 1966), but other studies have reported that young and old adults do not differ significantly in the frequency with which they make these kinds of errors (Craik, 1968a; Moscovitch & Winocur, 1983; Winocur & Moscovitch, 1983).

Interference from Subsequent Activity

Memory performance can also be disrupted by activity intervening between the presentation of, and the test on, the relevant information. This kind of interference is sometimes referred to as retroactive (backward acting) interference because the later activity can impair the retention of previously presented information. A greater susceptibility to interference from subsequent activity among older adults relative to young adults might indicate that, with increased age, there is a decrease in the stability or an increase in the fragility of stored information.

It is useful to think of interference from subsequent activity both in terms of the nature of the activity performed, and in terms of its temporal pattern (i.e., how long, and when) it is performed. Four kinds of interpolated activity have been investigated: (a) similar tasks, (b) additional stimulus material in the same task (input interference), (c) responses in the same task (output interference), and (d) different tasks or activities. In addition, each kind of interference can be examined with respect to the onset and the duration of the interpolated activity.

Studies investigating the effects of intervening activity with the same task generally involve a sequence of three events: one or more trials devoted to set 1 materials, one or more trials with set 2 materials, and then some type of test with set 1 materials to determine the effects of the interpolated activity. Performance on the test of set 1 materials is either compared with performance on a test of the same materials before the interpolated activity, or with performance after a similar sequence of events involving different kinds of set 2 materials. An illustrative study was reported by Query and Megran (1983), in which a total of 677 adults between 15 and at least 70 years of age participated in seven free-recall trials. The first five trials and the seventh trial involved the same stimulus material, but the sixth trial involved a different set of stimulus items. The percentage of correct responses in the fifth and seventh trials, as well as the initial trial with the same material, is displayed in Figure 6.1 as a function of age of the respondent.

The nearly parallel functions for performance in the fifth and seventh trials in Figure 6.1 suggests that the interference associated with an interpolated trial involving different stimulus material was nearly identical across the adult life-span. While the Query and Megran results appear fairly clear, other studies have produced somewhat different results. For example, Worden and Meggison (1984), using a procedure similar to that of Query and Megran (1983), reported a greater decline in accuracy for older adults than for young adults when a second set of materials was presented between the initial and subsequent test of the original materials. Examining the research literature further, one finds some reports of more disruption from interpolated tasks in older adults (Arenberg, 1968a; Kay, 1951; Suci, Davidoff, & Braun, 1962; Traxler, 1973; Wimer & Wigdor, 1958), and other reports of similar interference in young and old adults, at least under certain conditions (Arenberg, 1967; Gladis & Braun, 1958; Hulicka, 1967a). Hulicka (1967a) suggested that some of the discrepancies in the results reported may be attributable to variations in the amount of initial learning, but several of the studies in which older adults were found to have greater interference than young adults required all research participants to reach the same criterion of initial learning before performing the second activity (Suci, et al., 1962; Wimer & Wigdor, 1958). Inadequate initial learning, then, is apparently not the complete explanation for the different patterns of results in studies of interpolated interference.

A limitation of the procedure of examining interference in terms of intervening tasks is that the manipulation may be too coarse to provide meaningful information about the nature of any interference effects that might be observed. With few exceptions, the studies have merely contrasted performance with and without, or before and after, the interpolated task, and have not attempted to examine the consequences of systematic manipulations of potentially relevant variables.

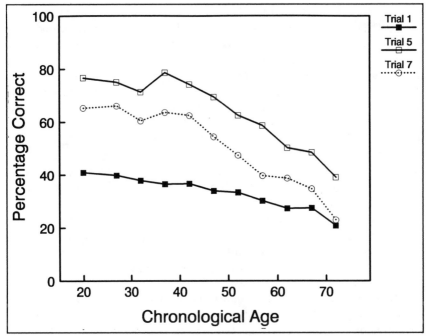

Figure 6.1.   Age relations on three trials of the same list of words with an intervening list of different words on trial 6. Data from Query and Megran (1983).

One theoretical distinction that has proven useful in more detailed analyses of interference effects is that between input interference and output interference. Input interference is the reduction in performance associated with the presentation of additional input items; output interference is the reduction in performance associated with the production of responses. A simple method of determining whether there are age differences in susceptibility to input interference is to examine memory performance as a function of the number of items in the list. If older adults are more affected by input interference than young adults, then their recall performance would be expected to decline more than that of young adults as the number of list items increases. This particular method of examining input interference has not proven very successful, however, because neither old nor young adults have shown appreciable declines in performance when additional items are presented in memory tasks (Craik, 1968a; Erber, 1974; A.D. Smith, 1976, 1979; Taub, 1968b; but see Taub & Long, 1972, for an exception). Furthermore, variations in how much performance increased with increases in the length of the list could be attributable to a variety of factors unrelated to interference (such as difficulty of search and retrieval as suggested by Craik, 1968a), and therefore cannot be interpreted exclusively in terms of differential susceptibility to input interference.

A.D. Smith (1975a) designed an experiment to investigate age differences in both input and output interference. In Smith's procedure, which was based on earlier research by Tulving and Arbuckle (1966), eight digit-word pairs were presented; subjects were then cued with each digit for recall of the appropriate word. In order to understand how input and output interference can be distinguished in this task, consider a trial involving the following three pairs: 1-tree, 2-home, and 3-dog. If the probe items consisted of 1=? and 3=?, then the first item would have zero items of output interference (because there were no prior responses), and two items of input interference (because two additional pairs, 2-home and 3-dog, were presented before the probe). The second item would have one item of output interference (the response to the 1=? probe) and zero items of input interference (because no additional pairs were presented before the probes). By orthogonally combining input order and output order, it was thus possible to investigate the effects of both input interference and output interference.

The major findings of A.D. Smith's (1975a) study were that increasing the number of prior input or output items resulted in lower levels of recall for adults in all three age groups (young, middle-aged, and old), but that the amount of performance decline was nearly equivalent for each group (i.e., there was no interaction of age and either number of input or number of output items). Another study by A.D. Smith (1974), based on a somewhat different experimental procedure, also found no age differences in the magnitude of output interference.

Evidence that could be interpreted as consistent with an age difference in susceptibility to output interference derives from dichotic listening tasks, or visual analogs of the dichotic listening task, in which two sets of material are presented simultaneously and the research participant is instructed to recall one set before the other. A reliable finding with both auditory presentations (Caird, 1966; L.E. Clark & Knowles, 1973; Craik, 1965; Inglis & Ankus, 1965; Inglis & Caird, 1963; Mackay & Inglis, 1963) and visual presentations (Taub, 1968a; Taub & Grieff, 1967) is that of substantial age differences in the material recalled second. Age differences were almost always smaller for the material recalled first, and in many of the studies the age differences in the first-recalled material were not statistically significant. Because the set of items to be recalled first is randomly selected, the differentially poorer performance on the second set can be assumed to be attributable to some type of interference associated with recalling items from the first set. These results, then, are compatible with the idea that there may be an increase with age in susceptibility to output interference, at least across relatively short intervals.

A popular research paradigm for the investigation of interference in memory involves presenting the to-be-remembered material, requiring the research participant to perform an unrelated activity, and then asking him or her to recall the original material. This is generally referred to as the Brown-Peterson paradigm, after the researchers who reported research with versions of this procedure in the late 1950s (J. Brown, 1958; L.R. Peterson & M.J. Peterson, 1959). It might be more accurate to refer to it as the Cameron paradigm, however, because results from a version of this procedure were reported by D.E. Cameron in 1943. Cameron's (1943) implementation of the task involved the presentation of a 3-digit number either with no activity during a retention interval, or with the participant instructed to spell words backwards. Older adults with diagnosed memory problems were found to perform at a level equivalent to that of young adults when no activity was required during the retention interval, but their performance was much worse than that of young adults when the distracting activity (backward spelling) had to be performed during the retention interval.

Several age-comparative studies have employed versions of this paradigm manipulating the length of the interval during which the distracting activity had to be performed. The dominant finding, reported in most of the studies, has been that adults of different ages exhibit parallel declines in accuracy with increased duration of distracting activity (Charness, 1981b; Dobbs & Rule, 1989; Keevil-Rogers & Schnore, 1969; Kriauciunas, 1968; Puckett & Lawson, 1989; Puckett & Stockburger, 1988; E. Ryan & Butters, 1980; Talland, 1967). There are some exceptions to this pattern, but they do not seem to threaten the validity of the basic conclusion. For example, Rabinowitz and Craik (1986) reported an interaction of age and duration of the distracting activity, but close examination of their results indicate that this was apparently attributable to superior performance of the older adults with the shortest retention interval. Sampling fluctuations may therefore have been responsible for the anomalous finding in this study. Interactions of age and retention interval were also reported by Inman and Parkinson (1983) and Parkinson, Inman, and Dannenbaum (1985), but in both cases there were also age differences favoring young adults before the initiation of the distracting activity. When Parkinson, et al. (1985) adjusted the number of repetitions of the material to equate young and old adults on performance with no distracting activity, the interaction disappeared.

The available research on retroactive or subsequent interference seems to indicate that adults of different ages are not differentially susceptible to these effects, except perhaps when the intervening activity occurs immediately after the presentation of the items. Based on the results of studies with two simultaneous auditory or visual presentations, it is possible that activity related to responding may be more detrimental, and particularly so for older adults relative to young adults, than that associated with the presentation of additional input.

Summary

Attempts to explain adult age differences in memory in terms of interference mechanisms appear to have had only limited success. Age differences are generally smaller when the items to be remembered have higher pre-existing associations, but this does not necessarily imply that interference processes are involved, because it may simply be a reflection of less demanding processing. Furthermore, studies of the influence of previous and subsequent activity on memory performance have been inconsistent with respect to whether or not the manipulations altered the magnitude of the age differences. With the possible exception of greater susceptibility with increased age to output interference within short intervals, the available research seems to suggest that interference-associated processes are not responsible for many of the age differences in memory.

PRIMARY, SECONDARY, AND TERTIARY MEMORY

Distinctions are frequently made among various kinds of memory on the basis of the apparent duration of the stored information. For example, the term *sensory store* generally refers to information persisting for a second or less, *primary* or *short-term memory* refers to information preserved up to perhaps 30 seconds, *secondary* or *long-term memory* refers to information maintained from minutes to years, and *tertiary* or *remote memory* refers to information remembered for from years to decades. Although there is a moderate amount of age-comparative research concerned with sensory storage, it is not of immediate interest in the present context because there is apparently little evidence that characteristics of sensory storage are related to higher-order aspects of cognition.

Of the three remaining categories of memory, there is nearly universal agreement that secondary memory is impaired with increased age, but controversy exists regarding the effects associated with age on primary and tertiary memory. Popular positions on these issues were initially expressed many years ago. For example, Thorndike, et al., (1928) claimed that immediate or "temporary" memory was stable across most of the adult years. Regarding remote memory, Proctor (1873) quoted a Dr. Carpenter as stating:

The impairment of the memory in old age commonly shows itself in regard to new impressions; those of the earlier period of life not only remaining in full distinctness, but even it would seem increasing in vividness ... (p. 550)

In this section, research concerned with age differences in primary and remote memory is reviewed. Research on secondary memory will not be explicitly discussed because, as noted above, it is widely acknowledged that there are age differences in secondary memory. Distinctions among types of memory are only helpful in understanding relations between age and memory if the various types of memory are differentially affected by increased age. Therefore the major question concerning the hypothesized storage systems is whether age differences are not evident, or at least are considerably less pronounced, on measures of primary or tertiary memory.

Primary Memory

As just mentioned, the belief that there are little or no age differences in primary memory dates back at least to Thorndike, et al. (1928). This opinion has been endorsed with slightly different terminology by many researchers since that time (Craik, 1968a, 1968b, 1977; Fozard, 1985; Gilbert, 1935, 1941; Kaszniak, Poon, & Riege, 1986; Poon, 1985; R.E. Sanders, et al., 1980; Welford, 1980).

Before attempting to examine evidence relevant to the claim that primary memory is largely unaffected by increased age, it is important to emphasize that primary memory is defined as information in current awareness. In Craik's (1977) words, "Primary memory is involved when the retained material is still 'in mind,' still being rehearsed, still at the focus of conscious attention" (p. 392). Because information that resides in primary memory is, by definition, immediately accessible, the most meaningful question to ask about primary memory concerns its capacity, and not the availability of its contents. In other words, individual differences may exist in the probability that a particular item is in primary memory, but there should be little or no variation in the availability of information that is in primary memory because a defining characteristic of information in primary memory is that it is immediately accessible and in conscious awareness.

One of the simplest methods of measuring the capacity of primary memory is by using span tasks designed to assess the maximum number of unrelated items that can be repeated immediately. Although it is frequently claimed that tasks such as forward digit span exhibit little or no decline across the adult years (Bromley, 1958; Craik, 1968a, 1977; Fozard, 1985; Kaszniak, et al., 1986; Welford, 1980; Wingfield & Stine, 1989), small to moderate age-related declines are often found. For example, the following correlations between age and forward digit span have been reported in studies involving adults across most of the adult age range: -.16 (M.S. Albert, H.S. Heller, & Milberg, 1988), -.31 (Botwinick & Storandt, 1974), -.13 (Dirken, 1972), -.31 (Hayslip & Kennelly, 1982), -.27 for males and -.19 for females (Heron & Chown, 1967), -.18 (F.H. Hooper, et al., 1984), -.25 (Potvin, et al., 1973), and -.12 (Robertson-Tchabo & Arenberg, 1976).

A recent study by Salthouse and Babcock (in press) measured forward memory spans for both digits and words in a sample of 462 adults between 18 and 87 years of age. Their data, with each decade represented by between 52 and 103 individuals, are illustrated in Figure 6.2. Notice that there is a nearly monotonic decline with age in both digit span and word span, such that adults in their 60s are performing between about .6 and .8 standard deviations below the level of adults in their 20s. Correlations with age in the Salthouse and Babcock sample were -.27 for digit span, and -.39 for word span. Similar age trends in forward digit spans and forward spans for visual sequences (i.e., reproducing the order in which shapes were designated) are evident in data from the Wechsler Memory Scale - Revised (Wechsler, 1987), which are also displayed in Figure 6.2.

Span tasks may not be ideal for measuring primary memory capacity

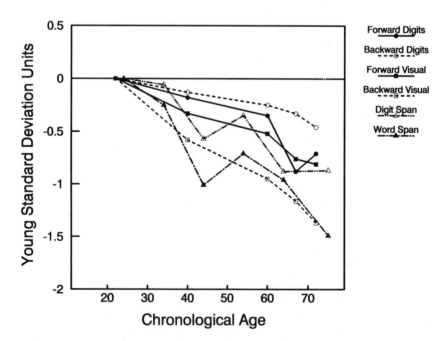

Figure 6.2.   Age relations on measures of memory span expressed in units of young adult standard deviations.   Data from Wechsler Memory Scale - Revised (Wechsler, 1987) for forward and backward span tasks, and from Salthouse and Babcock (in press) for digit and word span tasks.

because it is sometimes suggested that they reflect the contribution of secondary memory processes, in addition to those of primary memory (e.g., Craik, 1977). Alternative methods of assessing the capacity of primary memory are therefore desirable to provide a more complete or accurate determination of the relations between age and primary memory capacity. One such method (actually a collection of slightly different methods) is based on analyzing the accuracy of recall from the last few input items in a free-recall task. The assumption is that recall of the most recently presented items is likely to be based on material still contained in primary memory, and hence measures of the number of items recalled from the last positions in a list can serve as an indication of the capacity of an individual's primary memory.

Estimates of primary memory capacities derived in this fashion from young and old adults in six independent experiments are summarized in Table 6.1. Although not all the individual comparisons were statistically significant, it can be seen that young adults had larger estimated primary memory capacities than older adults in every contrast.

The research summarized above indicates that age differences favoring young adults are frequently reported in measures of memory span, and in measures of recall from terminal positions in a free-recall list. Furthermore, similar findings of age differences on these and other measures of primary

TABLE 6.1
Estimates of primary memory capacity from free-recall tasks.

Recall from last 4 (or 5) input positions

Young	*Old*	*Young/Old*	*Source*
2.36	1.56	1.51	Arenberg (1976)
1.7	1.3	1.31	J.T. Hartley & D.A. Walsh (1980)
2.70	2.09	1.29	Parkinson, Lindholm, & Inman (1982)
3.7	3.2	1.16	D.A. Walsh & Baldwin (1977)
3.46	2.87	1.21	D.A. Walsh, Baldwin, & Finkle (1980)

Recall with no more than 7 intervening (input and output) items

Young	*Old*	*Young/Old*	*Source*
1.4	1.2	1.17	J.T. Hartley & D.A. Walsh
2.86	2.28	1.25	Parkinson, Lindholm, & Inman (1982)
2.80	2.56	1.09	R.E. Wright (1982)

memory capacity have been reported by J.L. Horn, et al., (1981), Moscovitch (1982) and Robertson-Tchabo and Arenberg (1976). To the extent that these span and recency measures are accurate reflections of the capacity of primary memory, therefore, it can apparently be inferred that, contrary to frequent assertions, there is a slight to moderate decrease with age in the number of items that can be retained in primary memory.

Tertiary or Remote Memory

It is common folklore that as people grow older they may lose the ability to remember new information, but they are as effective as ever at remembering information from the remote past. However, this belief is largely based on anecdotal observations that are of questionable validity because (a) the accuracy of the recalled information cannot be easily verified, and (b) there is little or no control of the number of times the material has been recalled (or rehearsed) since the original events. Concerns have therefore been raised about whether the information being reported is accurate, and whether the duration of the memory is from the original event or merely from the time of the last recollection (Botwinick, 1967; Craik, 1977; Erber, 1981; Poon, Fozard, Paulshock, & J.C. Thomas, 1979; Salthouse, 1982; Schonfield & Stones, 1979; Squire, 1974; Warrington & H.I. Sanders, 1971; Welford, 1958). There are also some indications that subjective reports of information from long-term memory may not be as resistant to age decrements as popularly believed. For example, although in neither case was the accuracy of the reports verified, Schonfield (1972) reported that fewer older adults than young adults were able to recall names of former school teachers, and Yarmey and Bull (1978) reported older adults less able than young adults to recall what they were doing when they learned that President John Kennedy had been assassinated.

In an attempt to obtain assessments of memory for objectively verifiable information, several researchers have used questionnaires to evaluate memory for public events, or for names and faces of prominent people. Two assumptions are critical in this approach to the assessment of remote memory. One is that the various events or people were all at least moderately salient or newsworthy, such that a large proportion of the relevant population would have been exposed to the events at the time of their occurrence, or in the case of names or faces of people, in their period of prominence. The second important assumption is that very few opportunities have been available to acquire the information since the original event or period of prominence. This latter requirement is essential in order to be confident that the memory is as old as the actual event, and does not simply date from the last encounter with the information.

One strategy for assessing the likelihood that the information could have been encountered subsequent to the actual event involves determining the level of performance achieved by individuals who were born after the event, and thus could not possibly have experienced it first-hand (Howes & Katz, 1988; Squire, 1974; Warrington & H.I. Sanders, 1971). If the individuals whose only opportunity to acquire the information was from historical or retrospective accounts perform at a chance level, then the items may be appropriate for assessing old memories. However, if performance is above chance for individuals who were not even alive when the events occurred, then at least some of the information is likely to have been acquired or rehearsed since the original events, and consequently the memories probably should not be assumed to be as old as the actual events.

Perhaps because of differences in the degree to which the relevant assumptions have been satisfied, a mixed pattern of results has been reported from studies examining remote memory in people of different ages. Some studies have found older adults to be superior to young adults on measures assumed to reflect remote memory (Perlmutter, 1978; Poon, et al., 1979; Stuart-Hamilton, Perfect, & Rabbitt, 1988), others have found them to be inferior (Squire, 1974; Warrington & H.I. Sanders, 1971), and still others have reported small or unsystematic age effects (Botwinick & Storandt, 1974, 1980; Howes & Katz, 1988; Perlmutter, Metzger, K. Miller, & Nezworski, 1980; Storandt, E.A. Grant, & B.C. Gordon, 1978).

Age differences in remote memory have also been investigated with variants of the public events questionnaire procedure. For example, two studies have reported age-related declines in memory for old songs (J.C. Bartlett & Snelus, 1980), and for old television shows (Squire, 1989). In the latter study, adults with a mean age of 30 selected the correct title of 74.4% of television shows occurring in a single season from 0 to 5 years ago, compared with an accuracy of 66.7% for adults with a mean age of 54.

An intriguing series of studies concerned with memory for very old information has been conducted by H.P. Bahrick. In different reports the focus has been on memory for names and faces of high school classmates (H.P. Bahrick, P.O. Bahrick, & Wittlinger, 1975), names and locations of buildings and streets from one's college campus (H.P. Bahrick, 1979, 1983), and vocabulary, grammar, and comprehension of a foreign language studied years earlier (H.P. Bahrick, 1984).

A similar method of testing for the relevant material, and collection of miscellaneous background information, has been employed in most of Bahrick's studies. For example, a test of foreign language might be administered followed by questions about the number of language courses taken and the grades received in each, the frequency of using the language in the intervening interval, etc. This information was then used in multiple regression analyses to adjust the forgetting curves for degree of initial learning and amount of rehearsal during the retention interval. For most of the materials investigated, memory was found to decline rather steeply across the first 3 to 5 years and then to remain relatively stable for 30 years or more. Although Bahrick's procedure involves a confounding of age of the individual with age of the memory (because most of the events occurred at about the same age), this does not necessarily present a problem of interpretation when the results indicate, as they do in many of his studies, that memory performance remains stable across long periods of time. That is, if accuracy of the information had declined over the interval then it would have been difficult, and perhaps impossible, to determine whether the decline was attributable to the age of the memory or to the age of the individual. However, because most of the loss of information appears to occur within the first few years, Bahrick's results suggest that neither the duration of the information nor the age of the individual is a major factor influencing the preservation of information across intervals between 5 and 30 to 40 years.

Summary

The research summarized above indicates that the primary-secondary-tertiary taxonomy of memory systems has not led to unequivocal localization of the age differences in memory. Research on remote or tertiary memory has been plagued with methodological problems, and, although there is some evidence that very old information might be maintained equally well by adults of different ages, other evidence suggests that older adults are less accurate than young adults in recalling old information. Furthermore, although it is frequently claimed that primary memory processes are unaffected by increased age, several sets of results appear consistent in indicating that young adults have slightly larger memory spans, and greater recall from recency portions of free recall lists, than older adults. It is possible that the magnitude of the age-related effects are greater in most measures of secondary memory than in most measures of primary or tertiary memory, but these kinds of comparisons are complicated when the various memory systems are presumed to differ in their salient properties (e.g., capacity versus availability), and if the measures being compared are not equivalent in discriminating power (see the Appendix to chapter 7). For all these reasons, therefore, it seems premature at this time to conclude that age differences in memory are limited to secondary memory processes.

ENCODING, STORAGE, AND RETRIEVAL

Memory is frequently partitioned into processes of *registration*, *retention*, and *recall*, or in slightly different terminology, into stages of *encoding*, *storage*, and *retrieval*. A large amount of research involving adults of different ages has been based on this classification. Much of this research was clearly motivated by an attempt to determine which of the three hypothesized aspects of remembering was most susceptible to age-related impairments. Unfortunately, efforts at localizing age deficits in one of these mnemonic stages have been complicated by the intrinsic interrelations among the processes. For example, if the material is not adequately encoded then it may not be stored, and if it is not stored then it can't possibly be retrieved. Despite the difficulties associated with studying a single component in a complex system, the relevant literature will be examined to evaluate the possibility that age differences might be greater in certain stages of remembering than in others.

Encoding

The term encoding is seldom precisely defined, but instead has been used broadly to refer to a variety of processes ranging from those associated with early sensory and perceptual analyses, to the extensive elaboration and organization of information in conjunction with one's existing knowledge. Perhaps because of a failure to distinguish among these potentially quite different conceptualizations of encoding, there has been little consensus regarding exactly what should and what should not be considered encoding from the perspective of research on memory. It is therefore not surprising that an assortment of different approaches have been used to investigate the possibility of adult age differences in encoding efficiency or effectiveness.

One method of investigating age differences in encoding has focused on association or elaboration processes by examining the extent to which adults of different ages use imagery mediators, or benefit either from imagery instructions or from the presence of materials conducive to enhanced performance through the use of imagery. This has been considered a promising avenue of investigation because association processes have long been suspected to be a major problem for older adults: It was more than 50 years ago when Gilbert claimed that forming new associations was the kind of learning that was the most difficult for older adults (Gilbert, 1935).

Several studies have found that imagery mediators are reported to be used less often in paired-associate tasks by older adults than by young adults (Hulicka & Grossman, 1967; Hulicka, Sterns, & Grossman, 1967;

Rowe & Schnore, 1971). However, apparently this is not the entire explanation for age differences in memory, because young and old adults have also been found to exhibit performance differences on trials when either self-reports (Hulicka & Grossman, 1967; Hulicka, et al., 1967), or the explicit presentation of a mediator (Canestrari, 1968), suggest that the same kind of mediator was used by both groups. It might be hypothesized that there would be qualitative differences in the nature of the mediators used by adults of different ages, but little or no structural differences in the nature of the descriptions of the mediators produced by young and old adults have been found by Marshall, et al., (1978) or by Nebes and Andrews-Kulis (1976).

Several studies have also been reported in which young and old adults were compared before and after imagery instructions. Comparisons of this sort are sometimes complicated because of measurement artifacts such as young adults performing at or near a ceiling level, or because of confounds with processing requirements due to the added difficulty of trying to remember and implement instructions to form images while also trying to remember the relevant information. Perhaps because of variations in one or both of these respects, results from research on the effects of imagery instructions have been mixed, with equivalent benefits for young and old adults reported in some studies (Rabinowitz, Craik, & Ackerman, 1982; Yesavage & T.L. Rose, 1984), greater benefits for young adults reported in other studies (Kliegl, et al., 1989; S.E. Mason & A.D. Smith, 1977; T.L. Rose & Yesavage, 1983), and greater benefits for older adults reported in still other studies (Poon & Walsh-Sweeney, 1981; Treat, Poon, & Fozard, 1981; Treat & Reese, 1976).

One reasonably consistent finding has been that older adults exhibit memory advantages similar to those of young adults when concrete or high-imagery items are used as stimulus materials rather than abstract or low-imagery items (Bruce, et al., 1982; Rowe & Schnore, 1971; Whitbourne & Slevin, 1978; Witte & Freund, 1976; but see Rissenberg & Glanzer, 1986, for an exception). These results seem to suggest that aging does not alter the ability to benefit from imagery if the stimulus materials are conducive to its use.

Another method of investigating age differences in encoding has concentrated on the analysis of organizational processes inferred from the pattern of recall. The underlying assumption is that the order in which items are recalled can be informative about the relations that have been formed among the items, which is often assumed to have occurred at the time of encoding. Two types of recall organization are usually distinguished: input-output organization, in which the recall order corresponds either to the order in which the items were presented or to the categories to which the items belong, and output-output organization in which the correspondence is between the recall orders on successive trials. Unfortunately, neither type of recall organization has been found to exhibit easily interpretable patterns of age differences. Some studies have reported that young adults exhibit more input-output organization than older adults (Craik & Masani, 1969; D.V. Howard, et al., 1981; Hultsch, 1974; R.E. Sanders, et al., 1980; A.D. Smith, 1980; Witte, Freund, & Sebby, 1990; Worden & Sherman-Brown, 1983), while others have reported unsystematic trends or no significant age differences (Cavanaugh & Poon, 1989; Eysenck, 1974; Guttentag & R.R. Hunt, 1988; Hertzog, et al., 1990; Hultsch, et al., 1990; Luszcz, T.H. Roberts, & Mattiske, 1990; Hultsch, 1971; Park, A.D. Smith, Dudley, & Lafranza, 1989; Tubi & Calev, 1989; Weinert, Schneider, & Knopf, 1988; Zivian & Darjes, 1983), or even more organization for older adults than for young adults (Guttentag, 1988). Young adults were reported to have higher levels of output-output organization in studies by Hultsch (1974), Macht and Buschke (1983), Rankin, et al., (1984), and Witte, et al. (1990), but no differences across age groups were found by S.K. Gordon (1975) or Laurence (1966). Although there have been speculations about the reasons for these diverse patterns of results, there is not yet a consensus concerning the basis for the inconsistencies, and the lack of uniformity appears to preclude a definite conclusion concerning age-related influences on organizational processes in memory at the current time.

More consistent findings have been reported on several indirect measures of encoding effectiveness. For example, results from a release-from-proactive-interference paradigm suggest that little or no age differences may occur in the sensitivity to a variety of potentially encodable dimensions of the stimulus. This paradigm can be used to determine whether research participants are sensitive to particular stimulus dimensions by presenting several stimuli within the same general category, and then determining whether level of recall performance improves with a shift in the nature of the stimulus material to a different category. If it does, then one can infer that the property distinguishing items from different categories corresponded to a salient encoding dimension for those individuals. The important finding in the present context is that both young and old adults have been found to exhibit similar performance improvements with shifts in taxonomic, rhyme, letter-digit, or male name-female name categories (C.S. Elias & Hirasuna, 1976; Mistler-Lachman, 1977; Moscovitch & Winocur, 1983; Puglisi, 1980).

Another category of indirect evidence suggesting that encoding effectiveness may be similar in young and old adults is available in the findings, described further on, that there are little or no age differences in the benefits of repetition of the same stimulus. The reasoning relating repetition effects to quality of encoding has been summarized by R.L. Cohen, et al., (1987):

> ... [I]f elderly individuals do not encode a word as well as the young adults on its first presentation, it is reasonable to expect them to encode it more poorly on its second occurrence as well. On this basis, the encoding problems of the elderly should be compounded by a second presentation, and word repetition could be expected to magnify the aging effect. (p. 280)

The discovery that young and old adults are often found to derive equivalent benefits from stimulus repetition can therefore be interpreted as indicating that encoding processes are relatively unaffected by increased age.

Quite a few studies have also been reported in which the speed or accuracy of decisions was facilitated in both young and old adults by the previous presentation of related material (Balota & Duchek, 1988, 1989; Bowles & Poon, 1988; D.M. Burke & Harrold, 1988; D.M. Burke, et al., 1987; D.M. Burke & Yee, 1984; Cerella & Fozard, 1984; Chiarello, et al., 1985; G. Cohen & Faulkner, 1983b; Hasher & Zacks, 1988; D.V. Howard, 1983; D.V. Howard, et al., 1981, 1986; L.L. Light & Albertson, 1988; Madden, 1986b; Nebes, Boller, & Holland, 1986; Rabbitt, 1982; Rabinowitz, 1986). These priming effects are relevant to stimulus encoding because they suggest that certain aspects of a target stimulus may be activated in a similar manner by young and old adults. Although some researchers seem to have assumed that amount of priming is a direct reflection of the degree of encoding, the relation between the priming phenomenon and mnemonic encoding is still not well understood. Both the magnitude of priming and the degree of encoding can be influenced by numerous factors, and there is apparently not yet any evidence documenting the nature of the correspondence between the two constructs. Nevertheless, the existence of priming does seem to imply that some form of stimulus activation has occurred, and the finding of qualitatively similar priming in both young and old adults suggests that roughly comparable kinds of stimulus activation processes are evident at all ages.

At least from the measures based on release-from-proactive-interference and on priming procedures, therefore, it appears that there may be little or no age differences in certain aspects of stimulus encoding. This inference should be considered quite tentative because these measures are indirect, and consequently the statistical power to detect any differences that might exist may be low. Furthermore, young adults have sometimes been reported to function at higher levels than older adults when the tasks are amenable to the use of associational or organizational processes.

Storage

Storage as a component of memory generally refers to the preservation of information between the initial presentation, or input, and the time of test, or output. Research on retroactive interference, in which distracting activities are performed between the presentation and test of the material, is obviously relevant to the issue of possible age differences in information storage. Unfortunately, as discussed earlier in this chapter, the evidence concerning age-related effects in the susceptibility to retroactive interference is rather mixed, with a possibility that older adults might have somewhat more output interference than young adults over brief intervals, but no clear pattern apparent with longer intervals.

Another seemingly straightforward method of investigating age differences in storage processes consists of examining the effects, in adults of different ages, of varying the retention interval between the presentation and test of the relevant information. Although the method appears simple, conclusions from this research are complicated because somewhat different results have been reported from studies with short (seconds to hours) retention intervals, and those with long (days to months) retention intervals.

Effects of storage over short retention intervals are often investigated by a continuous recognition procedure in which a long series of items is presented, and the research participant is periodically asked to decide whether a given item had been presented earlier in the sequence. At least eight independent experiments have found that young and old adults exhibit nearly parallel rates of forgetting as a function of the interval between presentation and test (Craik, 1971; Erber, 1978; Ferris, T.H. Crook, E. Clark, McCarthy, & Rae, 1980; Flicker, Ferris, T.H. Crook, & Bartus, 1989; LeBreck & A. Baron, 1987; Lehman & Mellinger, 1986; Poon & Fozard, 1980; Wickelgren, 1975). This finding must be qualified somewhat because no age differences are usually reported with very short intervals, but the items are probably still in primary memory with brief intervals and forgetting rates are only meaningful when the information is no longer in conscious awareness.

Young and old adults have also been found to produce similar functions relating recall accuracy to retention interval when the interval is filled with a distracting activity (see citations earlier in this chapter). This research with the Brown-Peterson (or Cameron) paradigm is usually interpreted in the context of interference interpretations of memory, but it is also relevant to the issue of storage if it is assumed that the primary function of the distracting activity is to prevent rehearsal. The discovery that young and old adults lose information at a comparable rate in the absence of rehearsal can therefore be interpreted as suggesting that adults of different ages are equivalent in preserving information across short intervals without rehearsal.

Results of four tasks with both immediate and approximately 30-minute delayed memory tests are displayed in Figure 6.3. These data are derived from the stratified representative sample used in the standardization of the 1987 revision of the Wechsler Memory Scale (Wechsler, 1987). Notice that with each task the age trends are fairly similar for both the immediate performance and performance after a 30-minute delay. The patterns are thus compatible with the results just discussed in that the loss of information across short intervals of time does not appear to vary as a function of age.

The picture is much less clear when the retention interval has been extended to 24 hours or more. One study in which performance was assessed on several tasks both immediately and after a 24-hour delay was conducted by Randt, et al., (1980). A total of 200 adults were administered a battery of memory tasks, including free recall of unrelated words and paired-associate learning. Both tasks were presented using a procedure in which incorrect trials were repeated until a correct response was made to each stimulus item. The initial memory assessment occurred after a few

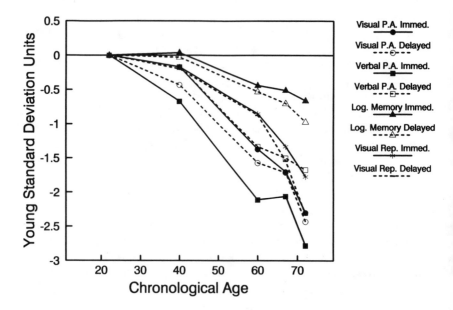

Figure 6.3.   Age relations on four memory measures for immediate and 30-minute delayed tests, expressed in units of young adult standard deviations. Data from the Wechsler Memory Scale - Revised (Wechsler, 1987).

minutes of another activity. Incorrect trials were then repeated until the response was correct, and after a delay of 24 hours the memory test was presented again. Results from the two memory tasks, expressed in units of standard deviations of young adults, are displayed in Figure 6.4.

It is apparent from the data of Figure 6.4 that the pattern of age differences varies across tasks and across retention interval. That is, the age trends appear to be greater for the delayed test than for the immediate test in the recall task, but are greater for the immediate test than for the delayed test with the paired-associates task. The inconsistency evident in this single study has been mirrored in conflicting results across studies, as revealed in the different patterns of age differences with varying retention intervals listed in Table 6.2. Unfortunately, the factors that might be responsible for these variations in results have not yet been identified. It therefore appears impossible at the current time to reach any firm conclusions concerning possible age differences in the effectiveness of retaining information across intervals extending beyond a few hours.

Another source of evidence relevant to possible age differences in storage processes comes from studies examining the effects of repetition on

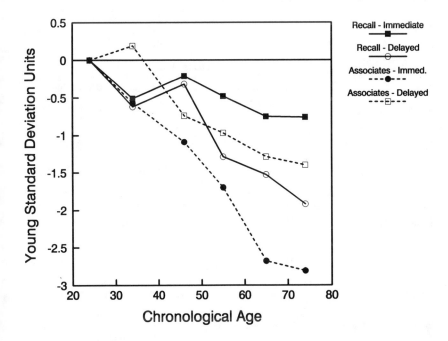

Figure 6.4.   Age relations on two memory measures for immediate and 24-hour delayed tests, expressed in units of young adult standard deviations. Data from Randt, E.R. Brown, and Osborne (1980).

TABLE 6.2
Results from studies with retention intervals of 24 hours or greater

Retention Intervals	Stimulus Material	Source
Similar Rates of Loss for Young and Older Adults		
Immediate - 3 weeks	words	Backman & Mantyla (1988)
15 minutes - 1 week	words	Desroches, Kaiman, & Ballard (1966)
3 days	script actions	Hess (1985)
3 days	script actions	Hess, Donley, & Vandermaas (1989)
20 minutes - 1 week	name-face pairs	Hulicka (1965)
5 minutes - 1 week	design-name pairs	Hulicka & R. Weiss (1965)
Immediate - 1 week	prose	Hultsch & Dixon (1983)
Immediate - 1 month	prose	Hultsch, Hertzog, & Dixon (1984)
2 weeks	prose	B.J. Meyer, C.J. Young, & B.J. Bartlett (1989)
Immediate - 3 weeks	line drawings	D.B. Mitchell, A.S. Brown, & D.R. Murphy (1990)
10 minutes - 2 days	line drawings	Rybarczyk, Hart, & Harkins (1987)
Greater Losses for Older Adults		
3 days	word pairs	Belbin & Downs (1965)
1 day	words	Bruning, Holzbauer, & Kimberlin (1975)
1 week	prose	G. Cohen & Faulkner (1984)
1 month	drawing	Harwood & Naylor (1969)
1 week	word or picture pairs	Howe & M.A. Hunter (1986)
15 minutes to 1 week	nonsense equation	Hulicka & Rust (1964)
4 months	binary arithmetic	Jamieson (1971)
7 days	words	L.L. Light, Singh, & Capps (1986)
1 month	pictures and line drawings	Park, Puglisi, & A.D. Smith (1986)
Immediate to 1 month	line drawings	Park, Royal, Dudley, & Morrell (1988)
45 minutes to 1 month	word pairs	Wimer (1960)

memory performance. The reasoning is that repetition benefits can only occur if some aspects of the earlier experience had been effectively stored. Age differences in the effectiveness of mechanisms concerned with storage can therefore be investigated by examining the relations between memory performance and the number of repetitions of the same material. In examining repetition effects it is important to distinguish between effects at the level of discrete stimuli, and effects on aggregate measures of performance which might reflect the influence of organizational or retrieval strategies in addition to storage effectiveness. A frequent finding has been that young adults exhibit greater improvements in overall performance across successive trials involving the same material than do older adults. One illustration of this phenomenon can be seen in a comparison of performance on Trials 1 and 5 from the Query and Megran (1983) study displayed in Figure 6.1. These data clearly show a decrease with age in the gain from the first to the fifth trial in this task. A similar finding of larger trial-to-trial improvements for young adults compared with older adults has been reported in other studies (Bleecker, Bolla-Wilson, & J.R. Heller, 1985; T.H. Crook & West, 1990; Drachman & Leavitt, 1972; S.K. Gordon, 1975; S.K. Gordon & W.C. Clark, 1974; Koriat, Ben-Zur, & Sheffer, 1988; Macht & Buschke, 1983; Mueller, et al., 1979; Rankin & Firnhaber, 1986; Taub & G.E. Kline, 1978; Worden & Sherman-Brown, 1983), although there are a few exceptions (Furchtgott & Busemeyer, 1979; Hultsch, 1974; Keitz & Gounard, 1976; Rankin, et al., 1984), and even some cases where both patterns have been reported (Witte, et al., 1990).

In contrast to the pronounced age differences in the degree to which repetition improves overall performance, young and old adults have been reported to derive nearly equivalent benefit from repetitions of discrete stimulus events (Balota, Duchek, & Paullin, 1989; Byrd, 1984; R.L. Cohen, et al., 1987; Flicker, et al., 1989; D.B. Mitchell, 1989; D.B. Mitchell, A.S. Brown, & D.R. Murphy, 1990; Moscovitch, 1982; Rabbitt, 1982, 1984; Rabinowitz, 1989a; Salthouse & Prill, 1988) or of successful retrievals (Rabinowitz & Craik, 1986). Repetition of the same stimuli has also been found to result in equivalent performance improvements among young and old adults when the repetitions are surreptitiously introduced without informing research participants about them (Caird, 1966; Heron & Craik, 1964; Talland, 1968). Because the gains in performance associated with repetitions of individual stimulus items have been similar for young and old adults, it can apparently be inferred that the two groups were equally effective at preserving discrete stimulus information across the interval from the first to the second presentation.

One interpretation of the findings that young and old adults appear similar in the rates at which information is lost through forgetting, or gained through repetition, is that there are little or no age differences in the effectiveness of retaining information over short intervals. This interpretation is complicated, however, by the mixed pattern of results with retention intervals of 24 hours or more, and by the fact that in certain circumstances young adults exhibit greater overall performance improvements from one trial to the next than older adults. Some of the assessments across long retention intervals may have failed to ensure that all participants had encoded the information equally well, and non-storage processes (e.g., deliberate rehearsal or retrieval strategies) may have been involved in the improvements based on aggregate performance measures. Until the discrepancies among these results are resolved, however, no firm conclusion can be reached concerning the presence or absence of age differences in the effectiveness of mechanisms related to storage.

Retrieval

Retrieval refers to the processes associated with making previously encoded and stored information available for current processing. If memory is considered analogous to the preserving of information in storage cabinets, then retrieval corresponds to the activity of locating and extracting the relevant files.

The primary investigative procedure used to examine age differences in the retrieval stage of memory consists of determining whether the magnitude of age differences in memory performance is varied by alterations in the retrieval requirements of the situation. Although they appear simple, these comparisons can be quite complicated because reducing the retrieval requirements almost always reduces the overall processing demands of the task as well. There are at least two senses in which the processing demands can be considered to be reduced by minimizing the retrieval requirements. The first is that a memory task with diminished retrieval requirements often involves fewer, or less demanding, processing operations than the standard version of the task (Botwinick, 1978; Salthouse, 1982). That is, a version of a task in which the retrieval component requires lesser amounts of processing is generally easier than a version without that processing reduction. The second sense in which processing demands are reduced is that decreasing the retrieval requirement also tends to decrease the amount of information needed to perform the task successfully. Absolute levels of performance may therefore improve because partial, rather than complete, information is sufficient to select correct responses (Drachman & Leavitt, 1972; McNulty & Caird, 1966, 1967). Results from studies attempting to manipulate the retrieval requirements of a task may thus be equivocal if the task versions with reduced retrieval demands involve fewer total processing operations, less demanding processing, or require smaller amounts of information in order to be performed effectively.

Another reason for questioning the assumption that recall and recognition tests are distinguished simply by the necessity of retrieval in recall relates to the recognition failure phenomenon. This phenomenon suggests that successful memory performance is determined by the compatibility of cues at encoding and recall, and not simply by the presence of response alternatives in recognition. The recognition failure effect occurs when words that are not recognized are later recalled successfully. This should be impossible if recall and recognition differ only by the requirement to retrieve information in recall, and yet many studies, including several in which adults of different ages were contrasted (Rabinowitz, 1984; Shaps & Nilsson, 1980), have confirmed the basic phenomenon.

It has long been noted that age differences in memory seem smaller when tested with recognition procedures than with recall procedures (C.C. Miles, 1934). Although this observation has been frequently reported, it is

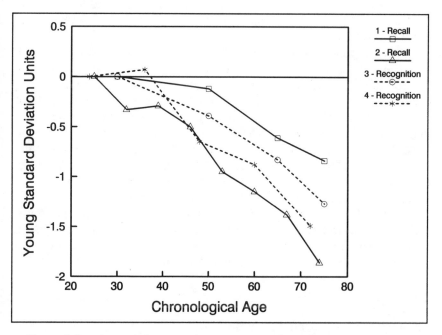

Figure 6.5.   Age relations on two measures of recall memory and two measures of recognition memory, expressed in units of young adult standard deviations. Data from (1) Herzog and Rodgers (1989), (2) Schaie (1988), (3) Herzog and Rodgers (1989), and (4) Trahan, Larrabee, and Levin (1986).

not always true, as illustrated by the data in Figure 6.5. This figure portrays results of: (1) recall of topics of earlier conversations (Herzog & Rodgers, 1989); (2) free recall of unrelated words (Schaie, 1988); (3) recognition of previously presented questions (Herzog & Rodgers, 1989); and (4) recognition of pictures (Trahan, Larrabee, & Levin, 1986). Notice that the tasks requiring recall result in both the smallest, and the largest, age-related declines.

Ideally, of course, comparisons of recall and recognition should involve the same materials, and the tasks should vary only with respect to the retrieval requirement. Unfortunately this degree of control is seldom possible. A fundamental problem is that there is no standard version of a recognition task against which performance on recall tasks can be compared because quite different performance levels can be produced by manipulating the number, or the similarity, of the alternatives in the recognition test. Variations in the nature of the recognition tests have probably contributed to some of the discrepancies apparent in previous studies, which have sometimes found age differences in recall tests but not in recognition tests (Craik & McDowd, 1987; Schonfield & E.A. Robertson, 1966; Shaps & Nilsson, 1980), and other times have found young adults to be superior to older adults in tests of both recall and recognition (Einstein & McDaniel, 1990; Erber, 1974, 1978; Rabinowitz, 1984; N. White & W.R. Cunningham, 1982).

Inferences about possible age differences in retrieval have also been based on comparisons of cued recall and free recall because the presentation of a cue at retrieval presumably minimizes the necessity for, or at least the extent of, retrieval. Several studies have been carried out with adults of different ages, but as with the recall-recognition comparisons, the results have been mixed. When the cue at recall is the first letter of the word there are apparently equal (but often small) benefits for both young and old adults (Drachman & Leavitt, 1972; Rankin & Hinrichs, 1983; E. Simon, 1979; A.D. Smith, 1977). When the recall cue is the name of a category, however, the age differences have either been unsystematic (Hultsch, 1975), non-existent (Macht & Buschke, 1984; Rankin & Hinrichs, 1983), in the direction of greater benefits for older adults than for young adults (Erber, 1984; Laurence, 1967; A.D. Smith, 1977), or in the direction of greater benefits for young adults than for older adults (E. Simon, 1979).

Summary

Although there has been a great deal of research devoted to determining whether the encoding, the storage, or the retrieval component of memory presents the greatest difficulties for older adults, few unequivocal conclusions can be reached on the basis of the available data. Age-related effects on measures presumed to reflect the functioning of a specific component have been quite variable, and even when there is moderate agreement concerning the nature of the results, there are almost always debates about whether those results can be interpreted as indicating a deficit in a specific processing component.

EPISODIC AND SEMANTIC MEMORY

Not all the information stored in memory is of the same type, but rather, it varies with respect to dimensions such as personal significance, specificity, and number of prior opportunities for learning. Most research on memory has used material deliberately selected to be relatively meaningless, fairly specific rather than general, and with restricted opportunities for prior learning. Recognition that only a limited aspect of memory had been studied in these laboratory research investigations led Tulving (1972, 1983) to introduce a distinction between episodic and semantic memory. Episodic memory was postulated to consist of memory for the episodes that happen in one's life, including characteristics of the artificial events created in psychological experiments. In contrast, semantic memory was postulated to consist of the body of organized, general, and highly overlearned information comprising an individual's declarative knowledge system. If the episodic memory system is considered similar to a diary, then the semantic memory system may be analogous to the contents of a combined mental dictionary and mental encyclopedia. That is, semantic memory includes lexical or dictionary information such as word names and meanings, and factual information of the kind usually found in an encyclopedia.

The episodic-semantic distinction has been influential in research concerned with cognitive aging because it is widely assumed age differences in memory are confined to measures of episodic memory, and measures of semantic memory processes are largely unaffected by increased age. One reason for this belief is that there are well-documented age differences in many laboratory tests of memory, but few systematic age-related effects in measures of general information or vocabulary knowledge derived from tests in intelligence batteries (as in the Army Alpha and Wechsler batteries discussed in chapter 2). Young and old adults have also been reported to produce similar patterns of word associations (Bowles, et al., 1983; D.M. Burke & Peters, 1986; Byrd, 1984; D.V. Howard, 1980; Lovelace & Cooley, 1982; Puglisi, et al., 1987; Scialfa & Margolis, 1986), and show similar facilitative effects on processing related information (e.g., the studies of priming cited earlier). As discussed in chapter 5, these latter two sets of findings have been interpreted as suggesting that the organization of semantic information probably remains intact across the adult years.

Although certain measures assumed to reflect semantic and episodic memory do appear to exhibit somewhat different age trends, the reasons for the varying age relations are not yet clear. One possibility is that semantic information is highly overlearned relative to most episodic information. In other words, the dissimilar patterns of age differences in episodic and semantic measures may be attributable to degree of learning if people are repeatedly exposed to the information preserved in semantic memory, but have limited opportunities to acquire episodic information. To the extent that amount of learning is the critical variable, many comparisons of semantic and episodic memory processes may confound age and amount of experience because increased age is associated with greater amounts of experience, and hence more opportunities to learn the relevant information (see the discussion of ecologically valid tasks in chapter 4).

Another difference between many of the tasks used in the assessment of episodic and semantic memory functioning is that semantic memory tasks often involve speeded decisions about highly overlearned material, while episodic memory tasks are generally designed to evaluate the degree to which new material has been learned. For example, the findings of similar priming effects among young and old adults in decisions about whether a letter string is a word, or whether a word is related to earlier material, has led to inferences that semantic memory is preserved across the adult years. Some of these same studies have also led to conclusions that episodic memory is impaired because older adults have been found to perform at lower levels than young adults in remembering which items had been presented earlier (Balota & Duchek, 1989; D.M. Burke, H. White, & Diaz, 1987; D.M. Burke & Yee, 1984; E.O. Clark, 1980; Dorfman, Glanzer, & J. Kaufman, 1986; D.V. Howard, 1983; D.V. Howard, Heisey, & Shaw, 1986; D.V. Howard, et al., 1981; L.L. Light & Albertson, 1988; Madden, 1986b; Rabinowitz, 1986). These kinds of comparisons obviously confound a number of variables, and are not easily interpreted without eliminating at least some of the potential confounds. For example, in order to interpret the results just described it would be desirable to know whether priming benefits are also evident with material residing in episodic memory, and whether memory failures can occur with information assumed to exist in semantic memory. Fortunately evidence is available concerning both of these contrasts.

Evidence that young and old adults exhibit equivalent priming of episodic information has been reported by D.V. Howard (1988a; D.V. Howard, Heisey, & Shaw, 1986), Rabinowitz (1986), and Balota and Duchek (1989). In the D.V. Howard experiments, sentences were presented followed by words that were to be classified as having been presented in the earlier sentences or not. Even though the words in the sentences were selected to be unrelated to one another, the time needed to make a decision about whether a word had been presented earlier was faster if it was immediately preceded in the test by the word that preceded it in the sentence. The relation between the two words was therefore episodic in nature because it was established only in the context of the previous sentence, but it was apparently sufficient to lead to substantial priming. Furthermore, the magnitude of the priming was comparable for young and old adults, although it did appear to be somewhat weaker for older adults when the original sentences were only presented once. The experiment by Rabinowitz (1986) was very similar, but involved pairs of words instead of sentences. As in the D.V. Howard, Heisey, and Shaw (1986) study, decision times in the recognition test were faster when the target word was preceded by the other member of the pair, and the magnitude of this priming effect was as large for older adults as for young adults. Target words in the Balota and Duchek (1989) experiment were presented in paragraphs, and priming was assessed by comparing the relative speed of old/new recognition decisions when the target words were preceded by words that had, or had not, been presented previously. Once again, nearly identical patterns of priming facilitation were reported for young and old adults.

The D.V. Howard, Heisey, and Shaw (1986), Rabinowitz (1986), and Balota and Duchek (1989) results are thus consistent in demonstrating that young and old adults derive similar benefits from priming even when the relevant information was recently presented, and hence can be assumed to be in episodic memory. An implication of these findings is that equivalent priming for young and old adults apparently cannot be considered an exclusive property of semantic memory.

Two categories of evidence are pertinent to the issue of the existence of age differences in the accessibility of information stored in semantic memory. One consists of self-reports of the difficulty experienced remembering the names of things or people. At least when the things and people are familiar, these names can be assumed to exist in semantic memory, and thus semantic memory processes are apparently affected when the information is temporarily unavailable. Several studies employing memory questionnaires (Cavanaugh & Poon, 1989; G. Cohen & Faulkner, 1984; T.H. Crook & Larrabee, 1990; Hultsch, et al., 1987; M. Martin, 1986) or diaries (Cavanaugh, et al., 1983) have found that older adults report more difficulties than young adults in remembering names. More detailed investigations of specific failures to recall the names of objects, or of people one knows, have also been reported by D.M. Burke, Worthley, and J. Martin (1988) and G. Cohen and Faulkner (1986). In both studies, older adults were found to report more temporary blockages of lexical information than young adults.

A related category of evidence consists of laboratory investigations of the ability to provide the names of objects or concepts on the basis of drawings or definitions of the words. Significant age-related declines in the accuracy of naming objects illustrated in drawings have been reported by several groups of investigators using the Boston Naming Test (M.S. Albert, et al., 1987, 1988; Borod, Goodglass, & E. Kaplan, 1980; Nichols, Obler, M. Albert, & Goodglass, 1985). There have also been a number of reports that young adults are more accurate than older adults in identifying a word from its definition (Bowles, 1989; Bowles & Poon, 1985; Maylor, 1990; and unpublished studies described in N.W. Denney, 1984, and in Schonfield & Stones, 1979). An exception to this pattern was reported by Rissenberg and Glanzer (1987) in which the performance of young and old adults was found to be equivalent in a task requiring the identification of words from definitions. It is noteworthy, however, that the older adults in the Rissenberg and Glanzer study had higher scores on a traditional vocabulary test than the young adults, and hence age-related difficulties in accessing semantic information may have been obscured because the older adults were more likely to have the items in semantic memory than young adults in the first place.

Summary

The research just described suggests that, at least when evaluated with respect to priming and memory failure criteria, episodic and semantic memory are not easily distinguished in terms of their general sensitivity to age-related influences. Age differences often seem to be smaller when tasks involve semantic rather than episodic information, but because it is not yet clear what the critical distinction between the two types of memory is, only very tentative conclusions concerning the degree of age sensitivity to tasks requiring semantic or episodic information appear justified at this time.

DEPTH OF PROCESSING

An alternative to the view of memory as a set of distinct structures or storage systems is based on the idea that memory can be conceived of as the act of carrying out processing operations (Craik & Lockhart, 1972; Lockhart & Craik, 1990). This approach to memory is more dynamic than structural in that greater emphasis is placed on processes than on either products or the storage systems where those products are preserved. A salient characteristic of this perspective is the assumption that some processing operations are more effective than others because they are either more intensive (deeper), or more extensive (broader). One way of thinking about memory from the depth-of-processing perspective is that it is analogous to the formation of roots in a tree. Just as the stability of a tree is enhanced by deeper and broader roots, so the durability of memory is assumed to be greater when the initial processing is deep and elaborate rather than superficial and shallow.

Age differences in memory within the depth-of-processing perspective can be attributed to variations in either the quality, or the quantity, of the processing operations carried out at the time of presentation of the to-be-remembered material. People not using effective operations, or using them infrequently, would be expected to exhibit a variety of symptoms of impaired memory such as poorer retention of individual items, reduced organization or elaboration, and less integration of items with specific contexts.

Two distinct versions of the depth-of-processing hypothesis have been applied to research on aging. The *production deficiency* version postulates that older adults are less likely than young adults to use effective processing operations spontaneously, but that they are still capable of using them when instructed, or otherwise induced, to do so. Because it is assumed that older adults are still capable of using the more effective operations, this interpretation proposes that the age-related limitation is merely one of production, and not of capability or potential. The *processing deficiency* version, on the other hand, postulates that older adults are not as capable as young adults at executing the most effective processing operations. Some presumably more fundamental age-related changes must therefore be assumed to have occurred resulting in a diminished ability to carry out the processing operations that are the most beneficial for successful performance in memory tasks.

One means by which the production deficiency and processing deficiency interpretations have been investigated is through attempts to control the nature of the processing carried out at the time of stimulus presentation. However, predictions about the consequences of these manipulations on adults of different ages depend upon specific assumptions about the effects of the efforts to control processing. On the one hand, processing could be controlled by guiding the nature of the processing operations to be performed, thereby inducing the same type of processing in everyone. On the other hand, processing could be controlled by decreasing the amount of processing that must be initiated and/or performed by the research participant. For example, instructing the individual as to the type of processing to be performed on the stimulus materials eliminates the necessity to choose encoding operations, and the designated processing may also be more efficient than that which would have been spontaneously selected. Unfortunately, it is not easy to distinguish between the processing-guidance and the processing-reduction interpretations because few measures are available to assess the quality or the quantity of stimulus processing independent of the observed level of memory performance.

The situation is fairly simple in the case of the production deficiency version of the depth-of-processing perspective. If, as is postulated by this account, age differences in memory performance are attributable to inappropriate processing by the poorer-performing individuals, then those differences would be expected to be eliminated when young and old adults carry out the same processing operations. Whether the manipulations designed to ensure that everyone is executing similar operations also result in quantitative reductions in the amount of required processing should be irrelevant. If adults of different ages do not differ in the type of processing because they are carrying out the same operations, then the production deficiency version of the depth-of-processing hypothesis seems to lead to a prediction of no age differences in memory performance.

Evidence concerning this prediction is overwhelmingly negative. Many studies have found that young adults recall (and often recognize) at higher levels than older adults when members of both age groups perform the same operations on the materials at the time of original presentation. This is true in most of the studies investigating effects of different orienting tasks (described later), and the same pattern of nearly constant age differences has also been reported in several other studies in which attempts were made to ensure equivalent initial processing of the stimulus materials either by requiring some kind of generation of the stimulus materials (Dick, Kean, & D. Sands, 1989; McDaniel, E.B. Ryan, & C.J. Cunningham, 1989; C.E. McFarland, et al., 1985; D.B. Mitchell, R.R. Hunt, & Schmitt, 1986; Rabinowitz, 1989a), or by using a variety of special procedures (Buschke, 1988; Dorfman, et al., 1986; Macht & Buschke, 1983, 1984). As long as the scores are not constrained by artifacts such as measurement floors or ceilings, the results of many studies suggest that age differences in memory performance remain relatively invariant across different kinds of encoding operations. Because of the variety of encoding manipulations examined, it seems unlikely that none of these manipulations was successful in inducing qualitatively similar processing among young and old adults. It therefore appears reasonable to conclude that the production deficiency version of the depth-of-processing hypothesis is probably not viable as an explanation for most of the age differences observed in measures of memory functioning.

There are two quite different predictions from the processing deficiency hypothesis, depending upon whether the manipulations designed to control processing at the time of stimulus presentation are assumed to guide, or to reduce, the processing of the to-be-remembered information. On the one hand, if the control of processing merely guides processing but does not reduce the overall processing requirements, then the age differences might be expected to be largest in the conditions with the greatest processing demands. The reasoning is that older adults can be assumed to be less capable than young adults at carrying out effective processing, and therefore their deficiencies should be most pronounced when the largest amount of processing is required. On the other hand, if the processing requirements are reduced by the procedures designed to control processing, then the age differences might be expected to be smallest in the conditions which result in the greatest reduction in processing demands. That is, older adults may benefit more than young adults when the orienting or encoding instructions result in a large decrease in the amount of self-initiated or self-determined processing, thus making previously demanding conditions more within the limited capabilities of older adults. Compared with a control condition, therefore, a manipulation assumed to involve a deeper and more effective type of processing could plausibly be expected to lead either to larger, or to smaller, performance differences between young and old adults, with the direction of the effect varying according to whether the manipulation is assumed to guide, or to reduce, processing of the stimulus items.

Although opposite in direction, the two predictions from the processing deficiency version of the depth-of-processing hypothesis are not easily distinguished because of the difficulty of determining the precise nature of the effects induced by the processing manipulations. It is even conceivable that the manipulations intended to control processing have different effects in different individuals (D.M. Burke & L.L. Light, 1981; Craik & E. Simon, 1980; E. Simon, 1979), or that both outcomes occur to varying degrees within the same people. It is perhaps not surprising in view of this ambiguity about whether control of processing exerts its effects through the guidance or reduction of processing that results from studies with manipulations of processing during stimulus presentation have been inconsistent. No interactions between age and encoding or orienting task have been reported by some investigators (Backman & Mantyla, 1988; Backman, Mantyla, & Erngrund, 1984; T.R. Barrett & M. Wright, 1981; Buschke & Macht, 1983; Craik & Rabinowitz, 1985; Erber, et al., 1985; Guttentag, 1988; D.B. Mitchell & Perlmutter, 1986; Rankin & Collins, 1985; A.D. Smith & Winograd, 1978; Zelinski, D.A. Walsh, & L.W. Thompson, 1978). Other investigators have reported greater age differences in conditions inducing deep semantic processing (Duchek, 1984; Erber, T.G. Herman, & Botwinick, 1980; Eysenck, 1974; L.L. Light & Singh, 1987; S.E. Mason, 1979; Rankin & Collins, 1986). And still other researchers have reported smaller, and sometimes even nonexistent, age differences in conditions with deep or semantic processing, often in conjunction with the presentation of a cue at the time of recall (Moscovitch, 1982; Rankin & Hyland, 1983; Shaw & Craik, 1989; A.D. Smith, 1977; Till, 1985).

It is obviously difficult to draw conclusions about the processing-deficiency version of the depth-of-processing perspective in the face of these conflicting results. Moreover, it seems likely that progress in evaluating both versions of the depth-of-processing hypothesis will continue to be slow until methods become available to assess the effects actually induced by the various manipulations intended to control stimulus processing.

Another approach employed to investigate the depth-of-processing perspective has involved trying to infer the kind of processing from the pattern of errors in a recognition test, or from the effectiveness of different types of recall cues. Error analyses have been conducted on the assumption that the proportions of different kinds of errors may be informative about the extent to which particular kinds of processing were carried out at encoding. False recognition responses to items that are either acoustically or semantically related to the target items have been investigated most often in this connection. Unfortunately, mixed results have been reported in age-comparative studies with these procedures. A.D. Smith (1975b) found that older adults had a greater proportion of false-positive responses to semantic distractors than young adults, and Rankin and Kausler (1979) found older adults had higher proportions of errors to both semantic and acoustic distractors than young adults. However, no age differences in proportions of errors to different kinds of distractors were reported in three other studies (Coyne, J.F. Herman, & Botwinick, 1980; Dick, et al., 1989; Rankin & Hyland, 1983).

Examination of the effectiveness of different types of recall cues in young and old adults has been motivated by the hypothesis that older adults may derive less benefit than young adults from specific and precise cues because their shallower processing results in more general and superficial encoding (Craik & Byrd, 1982; Craik & Rabinowitz, 1984; Rabinowitz & Ackerman, 1982). Support for this hypothesis was provided by studies by Perlmutter (1979) and Rabinowitz, et al., (1982) in which young adults benefitted more than older adults when cued by their own associates of the target words, compared to being cued by more general cues. However, this interaction pattern was not replicated in a subsequent study by Guttentag and Siemens (1986). In the later study no significant age differences were found in either the specific or general cue conditions, although both young and old adults recalled more words when cued with their own associates. Young and old adults were also found to benefit equally from generating distinctive or precise, rather than common or imprecise, elaborations in two related studies (Rankin & Firnhaber, 1986; Hashtroudi, E.S. Parker, Luis, & Reisen, 1989).

Summary

The depth-of-processing perspective has inspired a considerable amount of research, and has led to increased emphasis on the activity of the individual as a potentially important determinant of memory performance. However, few strong conclusions about the nature of age differences in memory functioning appear to have emerged from research motivated from the depth-of-processing perspective due to inconsistent outcomes across studies. A likely reason for the poor replicability is the lack of well-accepted procedures for assessing either the type, or the amount, of processing induced by different orienting or encoding tasks. This omission also contributes to logical problems because, without independent evidence regarding the processing actually carried out by adults of different ages, there is a clear risk of circularity in attributing age differences in memory to age differences in type of processing.

AUTOMATIC AND EFFORTFUL PROCESSING

In the last 15 years or so there has been considerable interest in the idea that mental operations vary with respect to their attentional requirements. Operations or processes that can be executed with little or no demands on attention have been termed automatic, while those that can only operate when supplied with, or monitored by, attention are designated as effortful. The distinction between automatic and effortful processes was extended to aging phenomena by Hasher and Zacks (1979), who essentially argued that age-related declines were confined to effortful or attention-demanding processes such as those involved in the use of imagery, organization, and rehearsal. Only "limited developmental trends" were postulated to be evident with automatic processes.

The Hasher and Zacks speculations have been controversial because one of the criteria they proposed for determining whether a process was automatic was developmental invariance. By incorporating an assumption about age relations as one of the defining criteria of the phenomenon, it was virtually impossible to investigate the validity of the hypothesis of no age differences in automatic processes. That is, if age differences were found in a measure suspected to be automatic, then all the criteria would not be satisfied, and the processes contributing to that measure might no longer be considered automatic.

Many researchers were unwilling to accept all of Hasher and Zacks' criteria for automaticity, however, and extensive research has been conducted investigating age differences in processes hypothesized to be automatic. Much of this research has attempted to determine whether there are age differences in processes that satisfy other important criteria of automaticity, such as the lack of an effect of intentionality on task performance. Automatic processes are presumed to be independent of attention or conscious control, and therefore performance on them should be as effective when the processes are executed intentionally as when they are executed unintentionally. Thus, one research strategy used for investigating the hypothesis of age invariance in automatic processes has been to determine whether there are age differences in tasks in which there are no effects associated with being informed that one's memory for the relevant information is to be tested. The contrast between intentional and unintentional or incidental memory is sometimes equivocal because research participants are usually aware that their memory will be tested for some aspects of the stimulus material, and they are uninformed only with respect to the specific aspect to be tested (Kausler & Hakami, 1982; Kausler, Lichty, & Hakami, 1984). Nevertheless, the absence of an effect of intentional remembering instructions is consistent with the hypothesis that the processes in the task may be automatic, and therefore it is of interest to determine whether age differences would be found in tasks in which there were no effects of intentionality.

A relatively large number of memory studies have been reported in which there was no significant difference between performance under intentional and unintentional conditions, but significantly higher levels of performance for young adults compared with older adults. This pattern has been found with tasks involving memory for recently performed activities (Kausler & Hakami, 1983; Kausler, Lichty, & Freund, 1985; Kausler & P.L. Phillips, 1988; Lichty, Kausler, & Martinez, 1986), memory for frequency-of-occurrence information (Hasher & Zacks, 1979; Kausler, Hakami, & R.E. Wright, 1982; Kausler, Lichty, & Freund, 1985; Kausler, Lichty, & Hakami, 1984; Kausler, R.E. Wright, & Hakami, 1981), memory for conversations (Kausler & Hakami, 1983), memory for modality of presentations (Lehman & Mellinger, 1984), memory for lateral orientation of pictures (J.C. Bartlett, Till, Gernsbacher, & Gorman, 1983), and memory for temporal order information (Kausler, Lichty, & R.T. Davis, 1985; Kausler & P.L. Phillips, 1988).

Hasher and Zacks (1979) also hypothesized that processes likely to be automatic are those concerned with "... fundamental aspects of the flow of information, namely, spatial, temporal, and frequency-of-occurrence information" (p. 356). Much research has therefore been directed at investigating possible age differences in these processes. With few exceptions, the research has revealed significantly better performance in young adults than in old adults.

Three studies (Attig & Hasher, 1980; Kausler & Puckett, 1980; R.E. Sanders, Wise, Liddle, & M.D. Murphy, 1990) reported that young and old adults performed at equivalent levels in frequency judgment tasks. However, at least 11 studies have been reported in which young adults were found to be more sensitive than older adults to variations in frequency of occurrence in at least some conditions (Ellis, R.L. Palmer, & Reeves, 1988; Freund & Witte, 1986; Hasher & Zacks, 1979; Kausler & Hakami, 1982; Kausler, et al., 1982; Kausler, Lichty, & Freund, 1985; Kausler, et al., 1984; Kausler, Salthouse, & Saults, 1987; Kausler, et al., 1981; Kellogg, 1983; Warren & S.A. Mitchell, 1980).

Results of research on memory for temporal order of information have revealed either small but non-significant advantages for young adults (McCormack, 1981; Perlmutter, et al., 1981), or significantly higher levels of performance for young adults relative to older adults (Kausler, Lichty, & R.T. Davis, 1985; Kausler & P.L. Phillips, 1988; Kausler, Salthouse, & Saults, 1988; Waugh & Barr, 1982, 1989).

Although not all were designed to investigate hypotheses concerning age invariance of automatic processes, quite a few studies have been reported in which adults of different ages were compared on memory for the spatial position of target items. A variety of stimulus displays have been used in this research, ranging from variations in the position of words on a piece of paper to different locations of objects in three-dimensional cubicles and rooms. The dominant finding in most of the studies has been that young adults were more accurate than older adults in reproducing the locations of previously presented stimulus material (Bruce & J.F. Herman, 1986; Cherry & Park, 1989; Flicker, et al., 1984; Flicker, et al., 1987; L.L. Light & Zelinski, 1983; Naveh-Benjamin, 1987; Park, Cherry, A.D. Smith, & Lafranza, 1990; Park, Puglisi, & Lutz, 1982; Park, et al., 1983; Perlmutter, et al., 1981; Pezdek, 1983; Puglisi, Park, A.D. Smith, & G.W. Hill, 1985; Salthouse, 1987a, 1988e; Salthouse, et al., 1988a; Schear & Nebes, 1980; J.L. Thomas, 1985; Zelinski & L.L. Light, 1988).

There are some exceptions to this general pattern. For example, McCormack (1982) reported two studies in which spatial memory was tested by asking subjects about the locations of words on cards. Although young adults were somewhat more accurate than older adults at recalling the word locations in both studies, in neither case was the age difference statistically significant. Age differences in spatial memory were also not evident in certain conditions of the studies by Sharps and Gollin (1987) and Waddell and Rogoff (1981, 1987). Both groups of investigators used stimulus displays consisting of organized panoramas or elaborate maps and actual rooms, and they suggested that age differences might be minimized with the use of such naturalistic stimuli. However, it should be noted that the power to detect age differences in these studies may have been weak because the age range was only about 25 years between the middle-aged and older adults tested in the Waddell and Rogoff (1981, 1987) studies, and the sample sizes in each age-by-condition cell in the research design were only 10 and 8 in the Waddell and Rogoff studies, and 14 and 7 in the two experiments in Sharps and Gollins (1987). Furthermore, the absence of age differences in several of the conditions in the second Sharps and Gollin experiment conflicts with the results of at least six other experiments (Bruce & J.F. Herman, 1986; L.L. Light & Zelinski, 1983; Park, Cherry, A.D. Smith, & Lafranza, 1990; Perlmutter, et al., 1981; J.L. Thomas, 1985; Zelinski & L.L. Light, 1988), suggesting that unusual procedures or samples may be responsible for their atypical results.

Summary

Hasher and Zacks' (1979) suggestion that automatic processes are immune from age-related effects has inspired a considerable amount of research, but most of the results of that research have been unfavorable with respect to their proposal. It is still possible that the basic hypothesis is valid, but that none of the measures examined thus far have been truly, or fully, automatic. For example, many of the memory tests have involved the recall or reproduction of the relevant information, and hence effortful processes may be needed to demonstrate the existence in storage of information that might have been automatically encoded. In other words, a task may exhibit age differences if it includes at least one non-automatic component, despite the existence of other potentially age-independent automatic processes. The difficulty with this line of argument is that it may make the entire hypothesis untestable if it is impossible to assess the functioning of automatic processes without the operation of at least some effortful processes.

EXPLICIT AND IMPLICIT ASSESSMENTS OF MEMORY

Inspired primarily by research findings on amnesics, several researchers have been exploring a distinction between explicit and implicit assessments of memory in comparisons of young and old adults. As D.V. Howard (1988b) pointed out, this distinction pertains to testing conditions in a manner analogous to the distinction between intentional and incidental remembering applies to presentation conditions. That is, just as material can be presented to individuals without intentional instructions for remembering, so might its retention be tested without deliberate attempts to remember.

Most assessments of memory are considered to be explicit because they require processes of conscious recollection in the form of overt responses of recall or recognition. Effects of prior experience are demonstrated implicitly or indirectly by differential performance in situations which, at least superficially, do not appear to involve memory. To illustrate, a popular procedure for the implicit assessment of memory involves the initial presentation of a set of words, often in the guise of collecting ratings for a later purpose. A second, purportedly unrelated, task is then introduced in which research participants are asked to complete word stems (e.g., ST_ _ _), or word fragments (e.g., F_ _GM_ _T_), to spell homophones (e.g., right or write), or to identify perceptually degraded words (e.g., WORDS). An effect of prior experience is inferred when the probability of completion, spelling, or identification of the critical items is greater for items that were presented earlier than for similar items not previously exposed in the experimental situation. If items presented earlier have higher response probabilities in these situations than otherwise similar items which were not presented earlier, then it can be inferred that there was an effect of prior experience in the task (i.e., that some information had been preserved in memory).

Several other phenomena are also often discussed in the context of implicit memory assessments. Among these are repetition effects associated with the prior presentation of identical items, and priming effects induced by the prior presentation of related material. In both cases the speed or accuracy of decisions to the target items are frequently facilitated by the earlier presentations, indicating that some record of the earlier information was available at the time of the decision even though that information was not explicitly assessed.

There are currently two major interpretations of the basis for the implicit-explicit distinction, and each has its proponents in the area of cognitive aging. One position is the structural or systems view, in which it is hypothesized that performance in implicit assessments is based on a structurally different memory system than that involved in explicit assessments (D.B. Mitchell, 1989; D.B. Mitchell, et al., 1990). The alternative, processing-based, interpretation hypothesizes that implicit and explicit assessments involve different types of processing, with explicit memory perhaps determined by a conscious recollection process in addition to the automatic activation process presumed responsible for performance on implicit assessments (D.V. Howard, 1988b; L.L. Light, 1988).

Although the factors responsible for the difference between explicit and implicit assessments are still not well understood, the implicit-explicit distinction has attracted considerable interest among researchers in cognitive aging because a number of findings suggest that age differences may be absent, or at least much reduced, for implicit measures of memory compared with explicit measures of memory. This has been reported not only in the priming and repetition phenomena discussed earlier, but also in measures based on tasks requiring stem completion (L.L. Light & Singh, 1987), fragment completion (L.L. Light, Singh, & Capps, 1986), spelling bias (D.V. Howard, 1988b), and perceptual identification (L.L. Light & Singh, 1987; but see Abbenhuis, W.G.M. Raaijmakers, J.G.W. Raaijmakers, & vanWoerden, 1990).

Results from several studies in which values of the implicit memory measures were reported for both young and old adults are summarized in Table 6.3. Few of the age comparisons in this table were statistically significant, but it is important to note that the measures obtained from young adults were higher than those from older adults in 14 of the 18 comparisons. Furthermore, in 3 of the 4 contrasts in which young adults did not have higher scores, the magnitude of the implicit memory effect in young adults was less than .10, or 10%. Results from these contrasts may therefore be suspect because comparisons of the magnitude of an effect in different age groups are not very meaningful when the effect is apparently not very robust in the standard, or reference, group.

It should also be noted that few of the studies listed in Table 6.3 reported the reliabilities of the performance measures, or the statistical power of the age comparisons. L.L. Light and Albertson (1989) and L.L. Light and Singh (1987) indicated that the power to detect as significant differences as large as those observed in their studies was less than .3, but Chiarello and W.J. Hoyer (1988) reported power of .78 in a study in which significant age differences were found in measures of implicit memory. It is thus conceivable that some of the failures to find significant age differences in memory when assessed by implicit procedures may be attributable to low statistical power.

How are these results, suggesting the possible existence of small age differences in implicit memory measures, explained by proponents of the hypothesis that age differences are absent in implicit assessments of memory? One argument is that these implicit assessments may be influenced by the other type of memory (i.e., a process of conscious recollection, or the episodic memory system). While the suggestion that many implicit assessments are contaminated by explicit remembering or episodic processes preserves the original hypothesis, it does so only at the risk of introducing an uncomfortable circularity. That is, age differences are presumed to be present because the tasks include conscious recollection or the episodic system, but the tasks are apparently inferred to include conscious recollection or the episodic system because age differences are present. As when any hypothetical construct is postulated, some

TABLE 6.3
Performance of Young and Old Adults
in Implicit Measures of Memory

(Presented Items)		(Not Presented Items)		Implicit Memory Measure		Source
Young	Old	Young	Old	Young	Old	
Word-Stem Completion						
						Chiarello & W.J. Hoyer (1988)
.45	.35	.12	.13	.33	.22	Non-semantic
.51	.42	.12	.11	.39	.31	Semantic
.57	.48	.15	.11	.42	.37	Dick, Kean & D. Sands (1989)
.30	.22	.06	.05	.24	.17	Experiment 1 - Non-semantic
.37	.31	.08	.07	.29	.24	Experiment 1 - Semantic
.36	.27	.08	.07	.28	.20	Experiment 2
						D.V. Howard (1988b)
-	-	-	-	.08	.08	Experiment 1
-	-	-	-	.08	.08	Experiment 2
Spelling Bias						
						D.V. Howard (1988b)
-	-	-	-	.45	.27	Experiment 1
-	-	-	-	.30	.34	Experiment 2 - Immediate
-	-	-	-	.33	.16	Experiment 2 - Delayed
-	-	-	-	.13	.09	Experiment 3 - Immediate
-	-	-	-	.05	.13	Experiment 3 - Delayed
.37	.32	.25	.36	.12	-.04	T.L. Rose, Yesavage, R.D. Hill, & Bower (1986)
Identification under Degradation						
						Light & Singh (1987)
.24	.16	.13	.07	.11	.09	Non-semantic
.30	.19	.14	.07	.16	.12	Semantic
Category Exemplar Generation						
.30	.26	.12	.13	.18	.13	Light & Albertson (1989)
Word-Fragment Completion						
.58	.53	.45	.43	.13	.10	Light, Singh, & Capps (1986)

independent means of establishing its existence seems necessary to minimize reliance upon assumptions whose validity cannot be verified.

Although the explicit-implicit distinction currently appears promising with respect to differentiating between memory measures with varying degrees of age sensitivity, a number of important questions remain unanswered. Important priorities for future research should be to document the reliability of the measures and the statistical power of the comparisons, and to examine the relations among a variety of different implicit measures. These steps are desirable to establish that the apparent differences between explicit and implicit measures of memory are not artifacts of differential reliability or statistical power, and to determine whether proficiency in implicit assessments of memory is a unitary construct that can be considered a stable trait-like characteristic of an individual, or whether it is more appropriately considered as specific to particular tasks or assessment methods.

Summary

Although still quite recent and not yet fully explored, the status of the explicit-implicit distinction as a basis for interpreting age differences in memory seems much like the automatic-effortful and depth-of-processing taxonomies. Some evidence is available that can be considered as supporting localization of the age differences, but there is also a certain amount of inconsistent evidence. The discrepancies have been addressed with post-hoc interpretations, but convincing arguments will probably require independent evidence that the theoretical constructs operate in the hypothesized manner.

SUMMARY OF ATTEMPTS
AT MEMORY LOCALIZATION

A general evaluation of the localization perspective is presented at the end of the next chapter; the discussion in this section is therefore restricted to the research concerned with localizing age differences in memory. The seven memory taxonomies reviewed in this chapter reflect distinctions based on: competition or displacement (interference); storage systems (primary-secondary-tertiary); quality or quantity of processing (encoding-storage-retrieval, depth-of-processing, and automatic-effortful); type of stored information (episodic-semantic); and methods of assessment (explicit-implicit). Other theoretical distinctions have also been investigated, but many may merely be special cases of one or more of the preceding taxonomies. For example, several memory researchers have attempted to investigate the possibility that older adults are deficient in the integration of to-be-remembered information with various aspects of its context (D.M. Burke & L.L. Light, 1981; Craik & Rabinowitz, 1984; Park, 1988; E. Simon, 1979). Contextual integration appears to be an outcome of processing, however, and therefore it is probably best viewed as a symptom of the efficiency of processing at either study or test, and not as a principal cause of memory performance in and of itself.

Although each of the taxonomies has been intensively investigated, none appears to have been completely successful in partitioning memory phenomena according to the degree of age sensitivity of the relevant measures. A major problem hampering these localization efforts is that many of the empirical results have failed to be replicated, even at the gross level of the qualitative pattern of age differences. As a consequence, few strong conclusions seem possible regarding the proximal locus of age differences in memory on the basis of currently available research.

There are at least two distinct interpretations of the relative lack of success in the prior attempts to localize age differences in memory within specific components, structures, or processes. One possibility, which tends to be favored by the advocates of a particular perspective, is that the studies yielding results incompatible with the hypotheses either have methodological flaws, or else have employed unusual procedures or atypical samples of research participants. Given the present limited knowledge about memory functioning, it is certainly conceivable that results from different studies have not been consistent because important, and perhaps not-yet-identified, variables have not been adequately controlled.

An alternative interpretation of why it has been difficult to localize age differences in memory is that none of the previous distinctions has been successful in capturing the salient dimension (or dimensions) along which age differences are most evident. Of course, the viability of this possibility cannot be established until dimensions with more powerful discriminating capabilities have been identified. For this reason, if none other, therefore, it is important to continue to explore new analytical taxonomies that might result in a more accurate and coherent organization of the research literature concerned with relations between age and memory.

Although still vague and not yet systematically investigated, one dimension that may eventually prove important in helping to understand the relations between age and memory is that related to the amount of processing required in the task. Because there are not yet any direct evaluations of how much processing is actually required in a given task, judgments about processing requirements must be subjective and rather imprecise. The basic idea, however, is that memory (and other cognitive) tasks vary with respect to the processing demands placed on the individual, and that the performance differences between young and old adults tend to be largest when the overall demands are greatest. This notion is obviously related to, but somewhat more general, than distinctions such as automatic-effortful, implicit-explicit, and depth of processing.

Craik (1983, 1984, 1986; Craik, et al., 1987) has referred to a continuum of self-initiated activity, or its converse, environmental support, as a means of characterizing the amount-of-processing dimension. Backman (1989) has included both contextual and cognitive support as factors that tend to minimize the magnitude of age differences in memory tasks. The common concept in both Craik's and Backman's proposals is that age differences seem to be smallest when the task situation either: (a) provides more support in the form of guided encoding, or minimal requirements of retrieval; (b) requires less total processing of whatever type; or (c) ostensibly requires the same amount of processing, but with fewer demands associated with choice or selection because the processing is more constrained. In each case, the suggestion is that the magnitude of the age differences is attenuated with a reduction in what the individual is required to do on his or her own to perform the task successfully. Little can be said about this dimension at the present time, but the notion that age differences may be determined by the overall demands on a few relatively general factors is elaborated in the discussion of processing resources in chapter 8.

7

Analytical Approaches to Localization: II. Reasoning and Spatial Abilities

> *If tasks could be classified in terms of the extent to which various components are involved and the pattern of age effects in each task ascertained then we would be on our way to success in localizing age deficits in particular portions of the information-processing system.*
> —R. Lachman, J.L. Lachman, & D.W. Taylor (1982, p. 293)

It is somewhat surprising, in light of the well-documented findings from psychometric tests of age-related differences in reasoning and spatial abilities, that there have been relatively few analytical studies of the nature of these differences. One factor contributing to this lack of process-oriented research is that until recently cognitive psychologists have not exhibited much interest in either reasoning abilities or spatial abilities. As a consequence, few theoretical taxonomies or models of performance in specific tasks have been developed to guide research, or to aid in its interpretation. Nevertheless, several attempts have been made to identify the aspects of reasoning or spatial tasks that present the greatest problems for older adults. This research is therefore analytical in orientation, even though it is seldom based on models as explicit as those available in the memory literature.

One of the major issues in age-comparative research on reasoning and spatial abilities is whether there are age-related impairments in these abilities, independent of any age differences that might exist in relevant aspects of memory. Because age-related declines in memory seem to be well established, it has been considered important to determine the extent to which memory factors might contribute to any observed performance differences before postulating the existence of specific deficits in reasoning or spatial abilities. What might therefore be considered the default hypothesis for analytical research on age differences in reasoning and spatial abilities was stated in the context of research on reasoning and problem solving as follows:

> Close examination of the data reveals ... no evidence of a change with age in the actual capacity to make the intellectual 'leaps' or insights required.

Rather it would appear that limitations for the older subjects lie in the gathering and holding in mind of the data on which such insights depend. (Welford, 1958, p. 223)

The goal of the present chapter is to examine analytically oriented research on age differences in both reasoning abilities and spatial abilities, with a special emphasis on the role of memory as a potential mediator of those differences. Following the sections discussing the research in each of these abilities is an evaluation of the analytical localization perspective discussed in this and the previous chapter. Finally, an appendix to the chapter consists of a brief discussion of limitations of the analysis-of-variance interaction procedure, which is the most commonly used method to identify specific processing deficits associated with increased age.

REASONING ABILITIES

Reasoning can be defined as the integration and interpretation of information in order to reach decisions. Ability to reason can therefore be assessed with tasks as simple as sentence comprehension, to as complex as those involving creativity and problem solving. It is probably unrealistic to attempt to review all categories of research that might involve reasoning, but much of the literature can be encompassed within four topics: reasoning during comprehension, integrative reasoning, inductive reasoning, and abstract reasoning.

Comprehension

The area of comprehension is quite broad, and includes aspects related to sensory analysis and syntactic parsing, as well as those concerned with integration and inference. In this section only research emphasizing the higher-order aspects of comprehension will be considered. However, comprehension will not be interpreted as broadly as in the test of that name in the Wechsler intelligence batteries because the items in that test appear to assess general knowledge as much as, and possibly even more than, basic reasoning.

The Following Directions test from the Army Alpha can be considered to assess comprehension because the examinee is required to demonstrate understanding of a sentence by executing the specified actions. Although this and other similar tests appear to require only minimal interpretation of information, it is nevertheless noteworthy that young adults are often found to perform significantly better than older adults in these types of assessments. For example, the H.E. Jones and Conrad (1933) results illustrated in Figure 2.2, and the -.33 correlation with age reported by

McCrae, Arenberg, and Costa (1987), indicate that increased age is associated with lower levels of performance on the Army Alpha Following Directions test. Age-related declines in the accuracy of carrying out simple actions according to oral instructions have also been reported by Botwinick and Storandt (1974), O.B. Emery (1985), Feier and L.J. Gerstman (1980), and Lesser (1976). An early study by Price (1933, described in more detail in Sorenson, 1938) found significant age differences in comprehension when it was assessed by the accuracy of immediate recall of moderately complex directions. According to Sorenson, one set of directions concerned details about the delivery of a parcel, including when and where it was to be delivered, what to do if no one was home, and how to obtain a receipt for the delivery. The correlation between age and a measure of successful recall of these kinds of directions, for 655 adults between 25 and 90 years of age, was -.51.

The fact that substantial age differences are found even when a series of statements merely has to be reported or paraphrased suggests that memory factors may be involved in some of the comprehension difficulties associated with increased age. Further support for this interpretation is evident in the results of studies in which the syntactic structure of target sentences has been manipulated. Certain sentence structures, such as this one in which there is an embedded clause, can be assumed to place greater demands on memory than simpler sentences without embedded clauses. Furthermore, right-branching sentences, which have two successive clauses, require less temporary storage of information than left-branching sentences, in which an embedded clause interrupts the main clause. Consider these two examples:

(1) Mary was pleased because John's team won the game.
(2) Because John's team won the game, Mary was pleased.

Sentence (1) is right-branching because the subordinate clause follows the main clause. This ordering is reversed in the left-branching version represented in sentence (2). According to Kemper (1987b), left-branching sentences require more processing and storage because the embedded clause must be retained while the main clause is being comprehended. Consistent with the suggestion that memory factors contribute to the age differences in comprehension are the findings by Bergman (1980) and Kemper (1987b) that older adults experience greater difficulties than young adults in recalling sentences with centrally embedded or left-branching clauses. Kemper and her colleagues have also reported significant decreases with age in the use of syntactically complex structures, such as left-branching sentences, in diaries (Kemper, 1987a), in spontaneous speech (Kemper & Rash, 1988; Kynette & Kemper, 1986), and in the detection and correction of grammatical errors (Kemper, 1986).

The aspect of comprehension that probably has the greatest relevance to traditional tests of reasoning concerns the generation of pragmatic or implicit inferences. L.L. Light and Albertson (1988) defined a pragmatic inference as occurring "... when an utterance leads the hearer or reader to expect something that is neither explicitly stated nor logically implied, but which nevertheless seems likely on the basis of prior experience or general world knowledge" (p. 134). These inferences can be considered a form of reasoning because the presented information is integrated with already existing knowledge to lead to a new expectation or awareness.

One of the first studies to compare adults of different ages in their ability to carry out this type of automatic or implicit reasoning was reported by G. Cohen (1979). The stimulus materials in her study were sets of related sentences, such as a description of a woman going to the park to feed ducks. Immediately after the oral presentation of the passage the research participants were asked questions based on explicitly presented information, and based on information that was only implicit in the passage. For example, a question of what was fed to the ducks would require explicit information because the fact that bread was given to the ducks was clearly stated in the passage. A question requiring an implicit inference might ask whether the woman went to the park today, given the information in the passage that she went to the park every day the weather was nice, and that it has been raining the past three days. Although not logically necessary, it is reasonable to infer that the woman did not go to the park today because, based on one's world knowledge, most people do not enjoy going to parks when it is raining.

Cohen (1979, Experiment 1) found that although older adults made somewhat more errors than young adults in responses to both explicit and implicit questions, the age difference was greater for questions requiring implicit inferences. These findings were replicated in a later study by Cohen (1981, Experiment 2), and similar results indicating larger age differences for implicit than for explicit information were reported in studies by L.L. Light, Zelinski, and M.M. Moore (1982), Zacks and Hasher (1988), and Zacks, Hasher, Doren, Hamm, and Attig (1987). L.L. Light, et al. (1982) included an important feature in their project by also reporting analyses of the accuracy of implicit inferences conditional upon the accuracy of decisions concerning the relevant factual information. In two independent studies, it was found that the implicit inferences of young adults were more accurate than those of older adults even when the two groups had equivalent recall of relevant facts. These results suggest that there may be age-related deficits in implicit reasoning above and beyond any age differences that might exist in processes of memory.

There are some exceptions to the tendency for age differences to be greater for questions requiring implicit than explicit information. Belmore

(1981), for example, found the opposite pattern with slightly larger age differences for questions concerning explicit information than for those based on implicit information. Overall accuracy was nearly the same for explicit and implicit questions in the Belmore study, however, and thus the distinction between the two kinds of questions may have been too small to have provided a sensitive test of the magnitude of age effects on measures of explicit and implicit information.

Three additional studies have relied upon indirect evidence to conclude that young and old adults were equivalent in processing implicit information. Burke and Yee (1984) found that both young and old adults were significantly faster at deciding that a target was a word when it was an instrument of the preceding sentence than when it was unrelated. For example, the sentence "The cook cut the meat" resulted in faster decisions for the word "knife" as the target than for the word "key" as the target. These results are therefore consistent with the interpretation that both young and old adults were activating implicit information while comprehending the sentence. In a later study, Burke and Harrold (1988) found that the decision times to verify properties of objects were affected by the preceding sentence context for both young and old adults. For example, verification that 'oranges are round' was faster when preceded by the sentence "The oranges rolled off the uneven table." than when preceded by the sentence "The oranges quenched the thirst of the hot children." In both the Burke and Yee (1984) and Burke and Harrold (1988) studies, therefore, it appears that young and old adults were similar in rapidly accessing and integrating stored knowledge during the process of comprehension.

The third study with indirect evidence about age differences in implicit inferences was reported by Hess and Arnould (1986), who used a false recognition procedure to investigate the existence of implicit inferences. This procedure requires the research participant to inspect a series of sentences, and then later decide whether test sentences had been presented in the earlier inspection series. Because young and old adults were similar in the proportion of implicit target sentences falsely recognized as having been previously presented, it was concluded that adults in both age groups incorporate implicit information into their memory representations at the time the sentence is encoded. However, it is not clear that this is the only, or even the simplest, interpretation of the absence of age differences in the measure of false recognitions. Because the instructions stated that recognition decisions should be based on whether the targets had been explicitly presented, there are at least two factors that could be contributing to the existence of false recognitions. On the one hand, as Hess and Arnould (1986) suggested, both young and old adults may have activated implicit information that is integrated with the memory representation. On the other hand, it is also possible that the older adults were merely poorer than the young adults in discriminating whether the information had been previously presented. If older adults are less sensitive at discriminating between old and related new information, then they would be expected to have high false recognition rates for related new information even if they have less activation of implicit information. Reder, Wible, and J. Martin (1986), in fact, have reported that older adults are less accurate than young adults at discriminating whether plausible statements had been presented in an earlier passage. Because of this difficulty of separating the relative contributions of integration and discrimination processes, the false recognition procedure is probably not optimal for determining the nature of the processing at the time of comprehension.

L.L. Light (L.L. Light, 1988; L.L. Light & Albertson, 1988; L.L. Light & P.A. Anderson, 1988) has recently suggested that many of the discrepancies evident in research on the relations between age and either the extent, or effectiveness, of implicit inferences during comprehension may be attributable to differential involvement of working memory. For example, L.L. Light and Albertson (1988) claimed "... that older adults are just as likely to draw inferences as young adults *except* when they cannot remember relevant facts, a problem that occurs when memory load is high" (p. 150). Although this interpretation is consistent with results from several studies by L.L. Light and her colleagues investigating the accuracy of judgments about the reference of pronouns (L.L. Light & Capps, 1986), it is not clear that it can account for all the existing results. In particular, the findings that age differences are larger for questions assessing implicit information than for questions assessing explicit information (G. Cohen, 1979, 1981; Zacks & Hasher, 1988; Zacks, et al., 1987), and that age differences were still evident when the accuracy of inferences was conditionalized on accurate recall of relevant facts (L.L. Light, et al., 1982), appear incompatible with an interpretation based exclusively on memory deficiencies.

Integrative Reasoning

A study by Nehrke (1972) was one of the first to investigate a specific hypothesis about the causes of age differences in reasoning. Nehrke's hypothesis was that older adults might perform at lower levels than young adults in syllogistic reasoning because, when evaluating the validity of an argument, they are more influenced than young adults by the emotional content of premises and conclusions. He therefore presented syllogisms with either emotional content (e.g., the justification of political repression) or non-emotional content (e.g., the identity of geometric figures). Although accuracy of judging the validity of emotional syllogisms was much lower than that for non-emotional syllogisms, similar age trends were evident with both types of material. The hypothesis of a greater emotional influence with increased age was consequently not supported. Results from the 247 males and 293 females, all with more than 12 years of education, are displayed in Figure 7.1.

Substantial age trends are clearly apparent in Nehrke's data, but the age effects may actually be smaller than those found on other tests of reasoning because the problems were presented in a written format, with no time limits. G. Cohen (1981, Experiment 1), for example, found that oral presentation of reasoning problems results in larger age differences than written presentation. Furthermore, the presence of time limits is often assumed to be especially disadvantageous to older adults, if for no other reason than that their perceptual-motor processes associated with reading and writing are slower than those of young adults.

Adults of different ages have also been compared with respect to their performance on linear ordering problems in which a series of premises describing the relations between two terms are presented, followed by some type of response designed to indicate whether the information had been integrated into a linear sequence. In a number of comparisons, young adults have been found to be more accurate than middle-aged or older

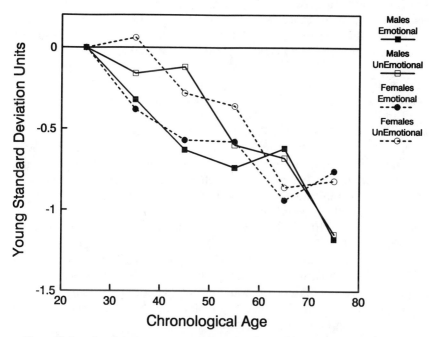

Figure 7.1. Age relations on a measure of syllogistic reasoning for problems with emotional and unemotional content, expressed in units of young adult standard deviations. Data from Nehrke (1972).

adults in these linear-ordering tasks (Arenberg & Robertson-Tchabo, 1985; Foos, 1989; Fullerton, 1983, 1988; L.L. Light, et al., 1982, Experiment 3; Salthouse, Legg, Palmon, & D.R. Mitchell, 1990; Salthouse, D.R. Mitchell, Skovronek, & Babcock, 1989).

A primary issue in many of these studies has been the role of memory factors in the apparent age-related declines in integrative reasoning performance. One manipulation used to examine the involvement of memory in the age differences in integrative reasoning tasks consists of comparing adults of different ages on the accuracy of verifying previously presented information relative to the accuracy of confirming inferences derived by integrating information. The logic of these comparisons is that performance on questions regarding previously presented information can be interpreted as reflecting memory effects, while performance on questions requiring integration can be interpreted as indicating the additional effects associated with a component of integration or reasoning. The first study of this type was reported by L.L. Light, et al., (1982, Experiment 3). Three premises (e.g., relating terms C and D, relating terms B and C, and relating terms A and B) were presented, followed by questions about explicitly presented information (e.g., the relation between terms B and C), and about information requiring across-premise integration (e.g., the relation between terms A and C). Although older adults were found to be somewhat less accurate than young adults with both types of questions, the age differences were larger for the questions requiring integration (reasoning and memory) than for those not requiring integration (memory only).

A similar procedure was used by Fullerton in two studies comparing young and old adults (Fullerton, 1983), or comparing young and middle-aged adults (Fullerton, 1988). The older adults in the 1983 study performed at near chance levels in all conditions so comparisons of the relative magnitude of the age differences with explicitly presented and with integrative items were not very informative in this study. Both young and middle-aged adults performed above chance in the 1988 study, however, and the results replicated those of L.L. Light, et al. (1982, Experiment 3) with respect to the existence of age differences on both types of questions, but with larger differences for the questions requiring integration of information. The finding that the age differences were greater when integration was required suggests that increased age is associated either with specific impairments in integrative reasoning, or with greater susceptibility to increases in the amount of required processing (because the requirement to integrate and remember can be presumed to involve more processing than only remembering).

What at first impression appears to be a different pattern of results was reported by Arenberg and Robertson-Tchabo (1985). These investigators found that the age differences were similar in magnitude for questions based on previously presented information, and for questions requiring integration of information. An important procedural difference may be responsible for the apparent discrepancy from the results of other researchers. This relates to the fact that the questions about previously presented information in the Fullerton (1983, 1988) and L.L. Light, et al. (1982) studies were in the same format as that in which the information was originally presented (e.g., David was taller than James - David was taller than James), but in the Arenberg and Robertson-Tchabo (1985) study the verification questions were presented in a new format (e.g., David was taller than James - James was shorter than David). Although still assessing previously presented information, the rearranged questions probably required additional processing of the information to obtain a correct answer (i.e., A>B has to be transformed to B<A). This extra processing may have more nearly equated the processing requirements for questions assessing explicit and integrative information, and thereby contributed to the elimination of differential age effects.

Further support for the view that age differences are more pronounced when stored information must be transformed in some manner is provided by Salthouse, Legg, Palmon, and D.R. Mitchell (1990) and Salthouse, D.R. Mitchell, Skovronek, and Babcock (1989). The tasks used in these studies consisted of premises expressing the relation between pairs of terms (e.g., A and B do the SAME), followed by questions concerning the relation between pairs of the same or different terms (e.g., If A INCREASES what will happen to B?). Note that, as in the Arenberg and Robertson-Tchabo (1985) study, the information is originally presented in one format, but the questions probe the information in a different format. One, two, three, or four premises were presented, followed by a question requiring no integration across premises (because both terms were originally described in a single premise), or by a question requiring integration of information across two, three, or four premises.

The most interesting comparison for the current purpose is that between accuracy of the decisions concerning information contained in only one of the presented premises, and accuracy of the decisions concerning information that had to be integrated across all the presented premises. The former can be interpreted as reflecting the contribution of memory factors, while the latter represents the influence of memory for the relevant information plus the effectiveness of integrating information across premises. To the extent that increased age is associated with difficulties in integrating information across multiple premises, therefore, the age differences should be larger for questions requiring across-premise integration than for those in which all the relevant information was presented in a single premise. Values of these measures for the 20 adults in each decade in the Salthouse, D.R. Mitchell, Skovronek, and Babcock (1989) study are displayed in Figure 7.2.

The first point to be noted about the data illustrated in Figure 7.2 is that substantial age differences were evident in all conditions. The age relations are less pronounced with the easiest (one premise) and most difficult (four premise) conditions, presumably because of measurement ceilings and floors, respectively, but accuracy is consistently lower for adults in their 60s and 70s than for those in their 20s and 30s with each number of premises. The second finding of interest is that in each case, the age differences were of nearly the same magnitude for the questions requiring no across-premise integration (portrayed by dotted lines) as for those in which the information had to be integrated across all the presented premises (portrayed by solid lines). Another result, reported in Salthouse, Legg, Palmon, and D.R. Mitchell (1990), was that although decision accuracy did not vary as a function of the number of relevant premises, decision time did increase systematically with the number of premises containing relevant information that had to be integrated. Taken in combination, therefore,

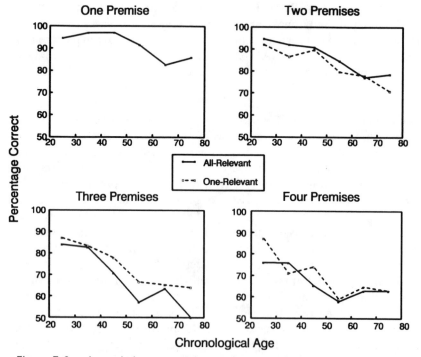

Figure 7.2.   Age relations on an integrative reasoning task with different numbers of premises for problems with all premises relevant to the solution and for problems with only one relevant premise. Data from Salthouse, D.R. Mitchell, Skovronek, and Babcock (1989).

these two sets of results suggest that across-premise integration is a time-consuming process, but that its effectiveness is apparently invariant across much of the adult life-span. Nearly all the age differences in the relatively simple integrative reasoning tasks used in the Salthouse, D.R. Mitchell, Skovronek, and Babcock (1989) and Salthouse, Legg, Palmon, and D.R. Mitchell (1990) studies, therefore, seem to be attributable to differences in the availability of the relevant information, and not to differences in the effectiveness of integration, per se. The findings by Arenberg and Robertson-Tchabo (1985) and L.L. Light, et al. (1982), that there were no age differences in reasoning accuracy when all the information was simultaneously available, are also compatible with this conclusion. Another result consistent with the memory interpretation of age differences in integrative reasoning is the discovery by R.E. Wright (1981) that young and old adults did not differ in the accuracy of simple reasoning except when severe memory demands were imposed by the requirement of simultaneously remembering a list of digits while trying to solve the reasoning problems.

Several investigators have also examined age differences in complex integrative reasoning tasks containing many elements, and several different kinds of interrelations. For example, the Logical Apparatus Device used by Arenberg (1974, 1988), Jerome (1962), and M.L. Young (1966) involves 10 elements from three categories (initial, intermediate, and goal) and 10 interrelations, also of three types (facilitating, inhibiting, and combining). The task for the participants in these studies was to determine the nature of each of the connections between elements, and then to devise a sequence of connections to link an initial element to the goal element. As might be imagined with this many elements and relations, the task can become quite complicated. In fact, between 40 and 120 minutes were often devoted to instructions and practice problems, and up to 150 minutes were required for the solution of from one to three problems. Perhaps in an attempt to make the task less intimidating, in most of the studies the research participants were allowed to proceed at their own pace, and to take notes whenever desired.

Two results have consistently been found with this task: a decrease with age in the number of successful solutions, and an increase with age in the number of redundant or uninformative inquiries (Arenberg, 1974, 1988; Jerome, 1962; M.L. Young, 1966). A similar tendency for an increase with age in the collection of redundant information was noted by Welford (1958), who attributed it to memory limitations because the outcomes of earlier requests were presumably forgotten and had to be repeated. The enormous complexity of the Logical Analysis tasks makes it difficult to identify a single critical variable responsible for the age differences in performance, if for no other reason than that the long time required for solution may lead many people to lose patience, or become bored, and consequently abandon serious attempts to solve the problems. The increase with age in the number of redundant or uninformative inputs is nonetheless consistent with the view that memory factors may contribute to at least some of the age differences in these tasks.

Another integrative reasoning task in which increased age has been found to be associated with more redundant and less efficient functioning is the 20 Questions task. There are numerous variants of this task, but most require the research participant to identify a target item by using the fewest number of questions. Some type of information integration is necessary to generate the optimum sequence of questions, such that each question eliminates half the remaining alternatives and the outcome of the prior question determines the nature of the following question. There is apparently a decrease with age either in the ability to recognize this efficient principle, or in the ability to execute it successfully, because a consistent finding has been that older adults require many more questions to identify the target items in 20 Questions tasks than do young or middle-aged adults (Charness, 1987; N.W. Denney, 1980; D.R. Denney & N.W. Denney, 1973; N.W. Denney & D.R. Denney, 1982; N.W. Denney & A.M. Palmer, 1981; N.W. Denney, Pearce, & A.M. Palmer, 1982; A.A. Hartley & J.W. Anderson, 1983a, 1983b, 1986; J.L. Horn, et al., 1981; E.D. Hybertson, et al., 1982; Kesler, N.W. Denney, & Whitely, 1976; Rimoldi & Vander Woude, 1969).

Inductive Reasoning

Inductive reasoning is similar to integrative reasoning in that different pieces of information have to be integrated, but it differs in that the relation among those pieces must also be abstracted. Several procedures have been used to measure abstraction or induction ability, and each can be considered to represent a different type of inductive reasoning task. For example, concept identification tasks generally require the research participant merely to identify the abstract relation, while other inductive reasoning tasks require the individual to demonstrate awareness of the relation by using it to classify elements into groups (classification tasks), to select an item sharing the same relation (analogy tasks), to continue a sequence (series completion tasks), or to identify a missing element in a matrix (matrix tasks).

Age differences favoring young adults have consistently been reported on a variety of inductive reasoning tasks. As noted in chapter 2, moderate to large negative relations between age and performance have been reported in the Army Alpha Series Completion Test, in the Primary Mental Abilities Reasoning Test, and in the Raven's Progressive Matrices Test.

There are other tests in intelligence batteries that require induction, but they also seem to involve a substantial knowledge component and thus probably do not provide unambiguous assessments of either inductive reasoning or knowledge. Examples are the Army Alpha Verbal Analogies Test and the Wechsler Similarities Test. In both of these, low performance could be a consequence of either poor induction ability or incomplete knowledge of word meanings.

Sizable age differences have also been reported on several other tests of inductive reasoning. For example, the Shipley Abstraction Test (Shipley, 1986) consists of 20 series-completion items with various kinds of stimulus material. Among the studies reporting significant age differences favoring young adults on this test are: Belmore (1981), Bromley (1963), Garfield and Blek (1952), J.T. Hartley (1986, 1988, 1989), F.H. Hooper, et al., (1984), Kraus, Chalker, and Macindoe (1967), C.F. Mason and Ganzler (1964), Salthouse and D.R. Mitchell (1990), and Shelton, Parsons, and Leber (1982). The Halstead Category Test (Halstead, 1947) is a concept identification task widely used in neuropsychological assessment. Significantly better performance on the Category Test by young adults compared with either middle-aged or older adults has been reported in numerous studies (Aftanas & Royce, 1969; Bigler, Steinman, & Newton, 1981; Blusewicz, Schenkenberg, Dustman, & Beck, 1977; M.F. Elias, Robbins, Schultz, & T.W. Pierce, 1990; Golden & Schlutter, 1978; Heaton, et al., 1986; Hochla & Parsons, 1982; Mack & Carlson, 1978; T.W. Pierce, et al., 1989; Prigatano & Parsons, 1976; Reed & Reitan, 1963; Reitan, 1962; E.H. Schludermann, et al., 1983; Vega & Parsons, 1967). Significant age differences, again with young adults performing at higher levels than older adults, have also been reported in miscellaneous tests of inductive reasoning (Arvey & Mussio, 1973; Bilash & Zubek, 1960; Cobb, Lay, & Bourdet, 1971; Cornelius, 1984; Gilbert, 1935; Guttman, 1984; A.A. Hartley, 1981; Hayslip & Sterns, 1979; Helander, 1967; Hess & Slaughter, 1986; F.H. Hooper, et al., 1984; J.L. Horn & Cattell, 1966; J.L. Horn, et al., 1981; W.J. Hoyer, Rebok, & Sved, 1979; Kausler, et al., 1982; Kausler & Puckett, 1980; M.E. Lachman & Jelalian, 1984; Salthouse, 1988e; Salthouse, et al., 1988a; Salthouse & D.R. Mitchell, 1990; Salthouse & Prill, 1987; Sorenson, 1938; Sward, 1945; Trembly & O'Connor, 1966; West, Odom, & Aschkenasy, 1978; Wetherick, 1975).

Illustrations of the relations between age and performance on concept identification (Arenberg, 1988), geometric analogies (Salthouse, et al., 1988a), and series completion (Salthouse & D.R. Mitchell, 1990) tests are presented in Figure 7.3. It is apparent that there are appreciable age-related declines in performance on each of these tests, despite the fact that the concept identification and geometric analogies tests were administered without time limits in a self-paced format. The age correlations were -.45

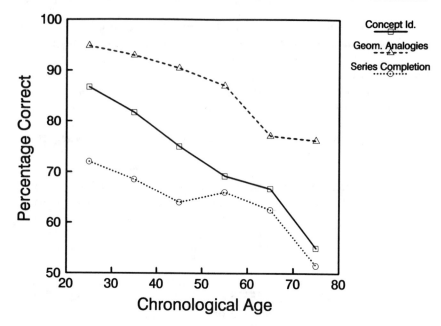

Figure 7.3.   Age relations on three measures of inductive reasoning. Data
for concept identification from Arenberg (1988), for geometric analogies from
Salthouse, Kausler, and Saults (1988a), and for series completion from
Salthouse and D.R. Mitchell (1990).

for the 830 adults with the concept identification measure, -.43 for the 233
adults with the geometric analogies measure, and -.33 for the 379 adults
with the series completion measure. Similar correlations in the range of
-.26 to -.44 between age and measures of inductive reasoning have been
reported by other investigators (Aftanas & Royce, 1969; Cornelius, 1984;
F.H. Hooper, et al., 1984; W.J. Hoyer, et al., 1979; Kraus, et al., 1967;
C.F. Mason & Ganzler, 1964; T.W. Pierce, et al., 1989; E.H.
Schludermann, et al., 1983).

Although the existence of age differences in inductive reasoning is very
well-documented, there are only a handful of studies that have attempted
to identify the reasons for these differences. Results from several of the
available studies seem to implicate memory factors as a major determinant
of the age differences in inductive reasoning. For example, Salthouse
(1987d) found that the magnitude of age differences in the accuracy of
solving geometric analogy problems increased with an increase in the
number of elements in each term in the analogy. Additional elements can
be expected to place greater demands on memory, and therefore the
discovery, in three independent experiments, that older adults had greater
reductions in accuracy when the problems contained more elements is

consistent with the view that age differences in memory contribute to the age differences in reasoning. Another finding in one of the experiments was that the age differences also increased when a 5-sec delay was introduced between the first two (i.e., A:B) and the second two (i.e., C:D) terms in the analogy problem. Again the interaction of age with a manipulation presumed to increase demands on memory supports the interpretation that age differences in inductive reasoning are at least partially attributable to age-related memory deficiencies.

It should be noted that an earlier study by Brinley, Jovick, and McLaughlin (1974) did not find significantly greater age differences in inductive reasoning accuracy with more elements per term, or with successive rather than simultaneous displays of the stimulus material. The discrepancy between the Salthouse (1987d) and Brinley, et al. (1974) results may be attributable to the relative strength of the manipulations in the two studies. Both main effects were significant in the Salthouse study, but neither was significant in the Brinley, et al. study. The experimental manipulations in the Brinley, et al. study may therefore have been too weak to have revealed age differences in susceptibility to their effects.

Rather surprising age differences in concept identification tasks have been reported by Arenberg (1968b, 1988). The results are surprising because the task was framed in the context of an interesting detective game of trying to identify the poisoned food in a collection of meals. Research participants were allowed as much time as necessary to solve the problems, and were also encouraged to take notes while performing the task. Different procedures were used in the two studies, but in both cases, young adults were found to perform at higher levels of accuracy than older adults. There was also evidence in each study suggesting that memory factors may have been involved in the age differences in performance.

A reception procedure, in which the experimenter determines the combination of stimulus attributes (i.e., foods in the meal) to be presented on each trial, was used in Arenberg's 1968 study. Memory factors were implicated in the age differences on this task by the finding that older adults experienced more difficulty than young adults on trials when all the stimulus information was redundant with what had been presented earlier. Older adults, to a greater extent than young adults, apparently failed to recognize that no new information was being presented in the redundant trials, and consequently treated them as involving new, and thus potentially confusing, information. The 1988 study involved a selection procedure in which the research participant was allowed to select the combination of stimulus attributes to be examined on each trial. Measures of the efficiency of selecting informative (i.e., non-redundant) combinations of attributes were found to have correlations of between -.37 and -.40 with chronological age. In both Arenberg studies, therefore, the age-related deficiencies in concept identification tasks were accompanied by age-related impairments in certain aspects of memory.

Further evidence of the involvement of memory in the age differences in inductive reasoning is provided by two studies using modified versions of a concept identification task. The first was a study by Offenbach (1974) involving a procedure that allowed identification of the hypothesis used by the research participant on each trial. This, in turn, allowed analyses of the probability of retaining or discarding an hypothesis on successive trials as a function of the type of feedback received. As might be expected, young adults retained the previous hypothesis on most (88%) of the trials in which the feedback was positive, and seldom (9.4%) retained it after negative or disconfirming feedback. In contrast, older adults were less likely to retain the previous hypothesis after positive feedback (50%), and were more likely to retain it after negative feedback (20%). The older adults were therefore functioning as though they had little or no memory for the previous hypothesis, with the consequence that their attempts to solve the concept identification task were less systematic and more random than those of young adults.

The interpretation that older adults are less effective in concept identification tasks at least in part because of memory limitations received additional support in a later study by Kellogg (1983). Participants in this study were occasionally asked to report the hypothesis they had used in the previous trial. In keeping with the deficient-memory view of the Offenbach (1974) results, Kellogg (1983) found that young adults were more accurate than older adults at recalling their prior hypotheses.

It cannot yet be concluded that all age differences in inductive reasoning are mediated by age differences in memory because there is some evidence that other factors are also involved in the decline in inductive reasoning performance associated with increased age. One such result is the finding by W.J. Hoyer, et al., (1979) that the performance of older adults was more affected than that of young adults by increasing the number of irrelevant stimulus dimensions in a classification task. It is therefore possible that increased age is associated with poorer abstraction because of a decrease in the efficiency of discriminating relevant from irrelevant information. Rebok (1981) failed to replicate these results in a study involving middle-aged and older adults, however, and thus this interpretation should be considered tentative at this time.

Abstraction processes in series completion tasks were investigated more directly in two studies by Salthouse and Prill (1987). Special problems were created which varied in the degree of abstraction necessary to identify the invariant relation among elements in the series. First-order problems were those in which the elements of the sequence increased or decreased by a constant amount, such as 2-4-6-8-10-?. These problems were expected to be relatively easy because the invariance in the problems is apparent in the difference between adjacent elements (i.e., +2 in the preceding example remains constant across the sequence). Second-order problems were expected to be more difficult because the amount of increase or decrease from one element to the next varied across successive elements. For instance, a possible second-order sequence is 2-4-7-11-16-??, in which the rule is "Add a constant (2), and then increment that constant by another constant (1) with each successive element." In other words, the sequence is produced by: 2, 2+(2) = 4, 4+(2+1) = 7, 7+(2+2)=11, 11+(2+3)=16, and 16+(2+4)=22.

Two separate experiments were conducted, with the first-order and second-order problems presented in either paper-and-pencil format, or on a computer. In both studies young and old adults were nearly equivalent in the accuracy of solving first-order problems, but accuracy of solving second-order problems was much lower for older adults than for young adults.

The second experiment in the Salthouse and Prill (1987) project involved a condition in which the elements in the sequence were displayed successively on a computer screen. The research participants were allowed to inspect each series element as long as desired, but they could only examine one element at a time because the preceding element was removed when the next element was presented. An advantage of this unusual presentation format is that it allowed an examination of the time spent studying or processing each element in the sequence. Profiles of these processing durations for the samples of young and old adults in this study are illustrated in Figure 5.2A for first-order problems, and in Figure 5.2B for second-order problems.

Notice that although the older adults generally devote more time to the processing of all elements than young adults, the age difference for second-order problems is particularly pronounced in the middle of the sequence. A second noteworthy aspect of the data in Figure 5.2 is that both young and old adults spend more time on problems eventually answered incorrectly than on problems answered correctly, and that this increased processing is most apparent for elements in the middle of the sequence. Taken in combination, these two findings suggest that the study-time measures are sensitive reflections of on-line processing, and that older adults experience greater difficulty than young adults at the point in the sequence (i.e., the third element) where higher-level abstraction is required. That is, second-order problems are not differentiated from the simple progression of first-order problems until the presentation of the third element, and consequently that is when alternative relations among elements must first be considered.

A conclusion implied from the results just described is that adult age differences in series completion induction problems are at least partially attributable to age-related difficulties in achieving the necessary level of abstraction. Not only are the age differences in solution accuracy larger on problems in which the elements are linked by second-order rather than by first-order relations, but the duration profiles reveal that the greatest differences in study time occur at the position in the sequence at which higher-order abstraction first becomes necessary.

Another reason for suspecting that increased age might be associated with difficulties in detecting and abstracting relations is that adult age differences are often found in the efficiency or fluency of generating alternative classifications of stimulus elements. This is evident indirectly in measures of performance on variants of the 20 Questions task discussed earlier, and more directly in assorted measures of conceptual flexibility or divergent thinking (Alpaugh & Birren, 1977; Alpaugh, Parham, Cole, & Birren, 1982; W.R. Cunningham, 1980; McCrae, et al., 1987; Ruff, R.H. Light, & R.W. Evans, 1987; Schultz, Kaye, & W.J. Hoyer, 1980). Bromley (1956, 1967), for example, found that there was a decrease with age, even among adults matched on overall Wechsler intelligence score, in the number of different arrangements of wooden blocks that could be generated. At least some of the age differences in inductive reasoning tasks may therefore be attributable to failures to detect relations among elements because of a decreased ability to conceptualize alternative classifications or arrangements of the stimuli.

Abstract Reasoning

Abstract reasoning is similar to both integrative and inductive reasoning, but also requires awareness of an underlying principle that transcends the specific context or situation. One means of assessing abstract reasoning is with tests requiring the interpretation of proverbs. Bromley (1957) used both multiple-choice and free-response methods with proverb materials to assess age differences in the ability to think in abstract terms. Significant age-related declines were found on both types of measures in young, middle-aged, and older adults matched on overall Wechsler intelligence score. In a later source, Bromley (1974) interpreted these results as indicating that:

> The old person is more literal, more concrete, more concerned with tangible and immediate impressions, less able to detach himself from the particular example and consider the general class or principle, less able to ignore the individual fact in order to think in hypothetical terms. It is in these respects that the thinking of the older person becomes less abstract. (p. 189)

Superior performance by young adults relative to older adults in the Gorham Proverb Interpretation Test has been reported by Aftanas and Royce (1969), M.S. Albert, et al., (1987, 1990), and Hamsher and Benton (1978). The Wechsler Similarities Test can also be viewed as a type of abstract reasoning test because the relation between the terms for which a similarity is to be identified is often rather abstract. As noted in chapter 2, significant age-related declines have been reported on this test. Unfortunately, there is, at present, no analytical research in which hypotheses about the reasons for these age differences in abstract reasoning have been investigated.

Summary of Research on Reasoning Abilities

There is abundant evident that increased age is associated with poorer performance on several types of reasoning tests, but it has not yet been determined whether this is primarily a manifestation of impaired memory processes, or whether it also reflects a deficiency in processing components more specific to reasoning. It is clearly difficult, if not impossible, to integrate information or abstract relations if all the relevant information is not simultaneously available due to limitations of memory. Moreover, impairments of memory could be responsible for the unsystematic and unorderly solution attempts of older adults that have been noted (Arenberg, 1974, 1982a; Jerome, 1962; Maule & Sanford, 1980; Offenbach, 1974; Sanford, 1973; Welford, 1958; M.L. Young, 1966). However, despite the plausibility of arguments concerning the influence of memory factors on reasoning, and the existence of a certain amount of supporting evidence, it is still too soon to conclude that most age differences in reasoning are mediated by age differences in various memory processes. A worthy goal for future research is the specification, in sufficient detail to allow systematic investigation, of the precise mechanisms by which memory limitations impose constraints on the performance of different kinds of reasoning tasks.

SPATIAL ABILITIES

Spatial abilities are assessed by tasks that involve memory for, and/or some type of manipulation of, spatial information. One or more tests of spatial ability are generally included in most intelligence test batteries. The Army Alpha is a notable exception because spatial tests formed the major portion of a special version of the test battery, the Army Beta, created for illiterate examinees. Four of the Wechsler tests (Block Design, Object Assembly, Picture Arrangement, and Picture Completion) involve spatial information, as does the Space test from the Primary Mental Abilities battery.

Age-related research on spatial abilities can be roughly grouped into studies focusing primarily on memory for spatial information, and studies concerned with manipulations such as the segmentation, integration, or transformation of spatial information. The limited analytical research on spatial abilities is therefore reviewed in sections devoted to memory for, and manipulation of, spatial information. Within each topic the research literature documenting the existence of age differences in the relevant aspect of performance is briefly described, followed by a discussion of the available studies attempting to specify the factors that might be responsible for those differences.

Memory for Spatial Information

Many different procedures have been used to assess age differences in spatial memory, and in most of them the average level of performance has been found to be significantly higher for young adults than for older adults. As an example, a large number of studies have reported significant age differences in the accuracy of recognizing or reproducing geometric designs (Aftanas & Royce, 1969; Arenberg, 1977, 1978, 1982b, 1987; Blusewicz, Dustman, Schenkenberg, & Beck, 1977; Cowart & McCallum, 1984; A.D. Davies, 1967; Dustman & Beck, 1980; Ferris, et al., 1980; Gilbert, 1935, 1941; Gilbert & Levee, 1971; Grundvig, Ajax, & Needham, 1973; Hamsher & Benton, 1978; Harker & Riege, 1985; Heron & Chown, 1967; Kear-Colwell & M. Heller, 1978; Kendall, 1962; Quattlebaum & W.F. White, 1969; Riege & Inman, 1981; Riege, Kelly, & Klane, 1981; Rybarczyk, Hart, & Harkins, 1987; Shelton, et al., 1982; Sterne, 1973; Trembly & O'Connor, 1966).

Significantly higher accuracy for young adults than for older adults has also been reported in measures of memory for spatial location (Bruce & J.F. Herman, 1986; Cherry & Park, 1989; L.L. Light & Zelinski, 1983; Naveh-Benjamin, 1987; Park, Cherry, A.D. Smith, & Lafranza, 1990; Park, et al., 1982; Park, et al., 1983; Perlmutter, et al., 1981; Pezdek, 1983; Puglisi, et al., 1985; Zelinski & L.L. Light, 1988), including reproduction of the positions of target cells in a matrix (Adamowicz, 1976; Flicker, et al., 1984, 1987; Salthouse, 1987a, 1988e; Salthouse, et al., 1988a; Schear & Nebes, 1980). Superior performance by young adults relative to older adults has also been reported in miscellaneous other measures of memory for spatial information (Botwinick & Storandt, 1974; Bromley, 1958; Hess, 1982; Ludwig, 1982; T.E. Moore, Richards, & Hood, 1984; Muhs, E.H. Hooper, & Papalia-Finlay, 1979-80).

An illustration of the relations between age and spatial memory is presented in Figure 7.4. These data represent the means at each decade for

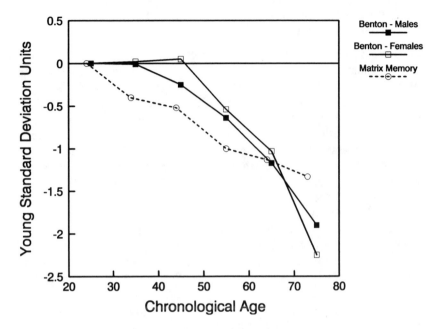

Figure 7.4.   Age relations on two measures of spatial memory expressed in units of young adult standard deviations.   Data for Benton Visual Retention Test from Robertson-Tchabo and Arenberg (1989) and for matrix memory from Salthouse, Kausler, and Saults (1988a).

846 college-educated men and 272 college-educated women on the Benton Visual Retention Test involving geometric designs (Robertson-Tchabo & Arenberg, 1989), and for a total of 362 men and women on a measure of the accuracy of reproducing the positions of target positions in a matrix (Salthouse, et al., 1988a). Age correlations for these and other measures of spatial memory have ranged from about -.20 to -.60 (Aftanas & Royce, 1969; Arenberg, 1978; Botwinick & Storandt, 1974; Grundvig, et al., 1973; Riege & Inman, 1981; Salthouse, et al., 1988a).

It is rather surprising, and also disappointing, that there have apparently been no studies in which hypotheses about the specific processes responsible for these age differences in spatial memory have been investigated. As a consequence, even speculations are currently lacking concerning the processes or components contributing to the poorer performance of older adults relative to young adults on spatial memory tasks.

Segmentation, Integration, and Transformation of Spatial Information

A wide assortment of tests and procedures have been used to assess various spatial transformation abilities. In most studies in which the performance of adults of different ages has been contrasted, young adults have been found to perform at higher levels than older adults. For example, embedded or hidden figures tests have been used in several studies to determine whether there is a relation between age and the speed or accuracy of segmenting complex patterns to identify target stimuli. The common finding is that older adults are slower and/or less accurate than young adults (Axelrod & L.D. Cohen, 1961; G.V. Barrett, Mihal, Panek, Sterns, & R.A. Alexander, 1977; Basowitz & Korchin, 1957; Bogard, 1974; Botwinick & Storandt, 1974; Capitani, Della Sala, Lucchelli, Soave, & Spinnler, 1988; Chown, 1961; M.N. Crook, et al., 1958; Crosson, 1984; Eisner, 1972; Guttman, 1984; A.A. Hartley, 1989; Helander, 1967; J.A. Lee & Pollack, 1978; Panek, 1985; Panek, G.V. Barrett, Sterns, & R.A. Alexander, 1978; Prohaska, et al., 1984; Schultz, W.J. Hoyer, & Kaye, 1980; Schwartz & Karp, 1967).

Age differences have also been reported on tasks requiring the integration of spatial information. One test of spatial integration ability is the Hooper Visual Organization Test, in which the task is to identify the object represented by jumbled jigsaw pieces. Numerous studies have reported that increased age is associated with lower performance on this test (Aftanas & Royce, 1969; Botwinick & Storandt, 1974; Cerella, et al., 1986; C.F. Mason & Ganzler, 1964; Potvin, et al., 1981; Sterne, 1973; Tamkin & Jacobsen, 1984; Wentworth-Rohr, Mackintosh, & Fialkoff, 1974), as well as on assorted form-boards tests requiring the assembly of pieces into a whole (Bilash & Zubek, 1960; Demming & Pressey, 1957; Heston & Cannell, 1941; J.L. Horn & Cattell, 1966; Salthouse, Babcock, Skovronek, D.R. Mitchell, & Palmon, 1990; Weisenberg, et al., 1936). In addition, substantial age differences in either the accuracy or the speed of identifying degraded or incomplete figures have frequently been reported (Basowitz & Korchin, 1957; Cremer & Zeef, 1987; M.N. Crook, et al., 1958; Danziger & Salthouse, 1978; Dirken, 1972; Glanzer & Glaser, 1959; Kinsbourne, 1974; D.W. Kline, Culler, & Sucec, 1977; D.W. Kline, Hogan, & Stier, 1980; L.L. Light & Singh, 1987; Puglisi & Park, 1987; Read, 1987; Salthouse, 1988c; Salthouse & Lichty, 1985; Salthouse & Prill, 1988; J.M. Thomas & Charles, 1964; Verville & N. Cameron, 1946; J.G. Wallace, 1956; Wasserstein, Zappulla, J. Rosen, L. Gerstman, & Rock, 1987).

Tasks requiring rotation or folding transformations have also been found to yield significant age differences favoring young adults. This is evident in several tests of paper folding requiring the visualization of spatial transformations (Prohaska, et al., 1984; Salthouse, 1988e; Salthouse, et al., 1988a; Salthouse & D.R. Mitchell, 1990; Salthouse, D.R. Mitchell, Skovronek, & Babcock, 1989; Salthouse, Babcock, Skovronek, D.R. Mitchell & Palmon, 1990), and in numerous tests involving rotation or other transformations (Adamowicz & Hudson, 1978; Berg, et al., 1982; Cerella, Poon, & Fozard, 1981; Clarkson-Smith & Halpern, 1983; Cobb, et al., 1971; G. Cohen & Faulkner, 1983a; Gaylord & Marsh, 1975; Guttman, 1984; Helander, 1967; J.F. Herman & Bruce, 1983; J.L. Horn & Cattell, 1966; Jacewicz & A.A. Hartley, 1987; K. Pierce & Storandt, 1987; Puglisi & Morrell, 1986; J.R. Wilson, et al., 1975). More complex transformations, such as those required to decide what a scene would look like when viewed from a different perspective, have likewise been found to present greater difficulty for older adults than for young adults (Bruce & J.F. Herman, 1983; Del Vento Bielby & Papalia, 1975; J.F. Herman & Coyne, 1980; Kirasic, 1989; Looft & Charles, 1971; Ohta, 1983; Ohta, D.A. Walsh, & Krauss, 1981; Rubin, 1974).

The relation between age and performance on three spatial manipulation tests is displayed in Figure 7.5. The data are based on results from 379 males and females on the Paper Folding and Surface Development tests (Salthouse & D.R. Mitchell, 1990), and from 175 females on the

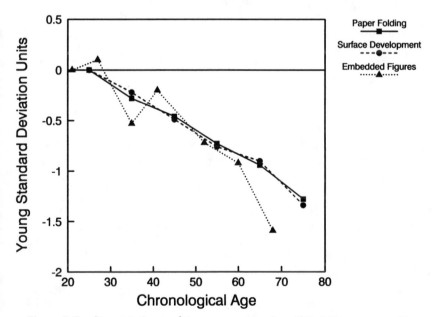

Figure 7.5.   Age relations on three measures of spatial ability expressed in units of young adult standard deviations. Data for paper folding and surface development from Salthouse and D.R. Mitchell (1990), and for embedded figures from Panek, Barrett, Sterns, and Alexander (1978).

Embedded Figures Test (Panek, et al., 1978). Representative correlations between age and assorted measures of spatial ability are listed in Table 7.1.

The primary focus in the few analytical age-comparative studies of spatial manipulation abilities has been on determining whether there are age differences in specific spatial processes. However, before discussing the results of these studies it is important to consider the possibility that age differences in spatial abilities might simply be attributable to the fact that many of the tests of spatial abilities are speeded, and therefore may penalize older adults merely because their peripheral perceptual and motor processes are probably slower than those of young adults. At least three sets of results suggest that this interpretation is unlikely as the complete explanation for the age differences observed in various spatial tasks. One set of results are those by Klodin (1976), Spieth (1964), and Storandt (1977) indicating that the age differences in several of the spatial tests in the Wechsler battery are still pronounced when the tests are administered with no time limits, and bonuses for rapid responding are eliminated. A second relevant finding is that significant age differences have been reported when the duration of peripheral perceptual-motor processes are subtracted from the measures of spatial performance (Royer, Gilmore, & Gruhn, 1984), or when individual differences in perceptual speed are statistically removed from the measures of spatial ability (Salthouse & D.R. Mitchell, 1990). Third, and perhaps most convincing, substantial age differences are evident on many measures of spatial performance when the items are individually presented and examinees are allowed as much time as necessary to respond (Salthouse, 1987a, 1987e; Salthouse, et al., 1988a; Salthouse & D.R. Mitchell, 1989; Salthouse, D.R. Mitchell, & Palmon, 1989; Salthouse, D.R. Mitchell, Skovronek, & Babcock, 1989; Salthouse, Babcock, Skovronek, D.R. Mitchell, & Palmon, 1990).

Age-related difficulties in segmentation processes appear to be implicated in the age differences found in various hidden or embedded figures tests where the required skill is the isolation or segmentation of targets from their contexts. One of the few studies with an experimental manipulation of segmentation difficulty was conducted by Royer, et al., (1984) using a task based on the Wechsler Block Design test. These investigators varied the perceptual cohesiveness of the to-be-reproduced stimulus designs by manipulating the number of edges between blocks that shared the same color. It can be assumed that designs with greater perceptual cohesiveness (i.e., designs containing fewer block boundaries marked by color changes) are more difficult to segment into distinct blocks because the block boundaries are not immediately visible. As expected if segmentation difficulties increase with age, adults over the age of 49 were more affected by increasing the perceptual cohesiveness of the designs than were adults under 30.

TABLE 7.1
Correlations between age and measures of spatial ability

Correlation	Measure	Source
-.36	Hooper VOT	Aftanas & Royce (1969)
-.28	Embedded Figures	G.V. Barrett, Mihal, Panek, Sterns, & R.A. Alexander (1977)
-.59	Hooper VOT	Botwinick & Storandt (1974)
-.37	Embedded Figures	Chown (1961)
-.34	Folding and Visualization	Cobb, Lay, & Bourdet (1971)
-.20	Embedded Figures	Crosson (1984)
-.29	Perceptual Closure	Dirken (1972)
-.33	Identification of Degraded Objects	Glanzer & Glaser (1959)
-.50	Embedded Figures	J.A. Lee & Pollack (1978)
-.43	Embedded Figures	"
-.38	Hooper VOT	C.F. Mason & Ganzler (1964)
-.45	Hooper VOT	"
-.33	Block Assembly	W.R. Miles (1935
-.44	Block Assembly	"
-.20	Perceptual Closure	Salthouse, Kausler, & Saults (1988a)
-.28	Paper Folding	"
-.53	Paper Folding	Salthouse, D.R. Mitchell, Skovronek, & Babcock (1989)
-.40	Paper Folding	Salthouse, Babcock, D.R. Mitchell Skovronek, & Palmon (1990)
-.37	Surface Development	"
-.54	Cube Comparison	"
-.22	Form Boards	"
-.38	Paper Folding	Salthouse & D.R. Mitchell (1990)
-.30	Surface Development	"
-.42	Hooper VOT	Sterne (1973)
-.50	"	Tamkins & Jacobsen (1984)
-.49	Perceptual Closure	Wassertein, Zappulla, J. Rosen, R. Gerstman, & Rock (1987)
-.67	"	"
-.28	Hooper VOT	Wentworth-Rohr, Mackintosh, & Fialkoff (1974)
-.37	"	"
-.69	"	"

Note: All variables are scaled such that negative correlations indicate poorer performance with increased age.

Age differences in integration processes have also been investigated in the context of either perceptual closure tasks or mental synthesis tasks. Although age differences have been found to be significant in memory for both closure or completion tasks (Salthouse & Prill, 1988) and synthesis tasks (Ludwig, 1982) after adjustment for age differences in memory, the nature of the hypothesized integration deficit is still not clear. One result consistent with the involvement of memory processes in the age differences is the finding that, relative to young adults, older adults have greater increases in decision time, and greater decreases in decision accuracy, with an increase in the number of required integration operations (Salthouse, 1987a; Salthouse & D.R. Mitchell, 1989). However, it has also been reported that the magnitude of age differences remains relatively constant across variations in the information value of the stimulus fragments (Danziger & Salthouse, 1978, Experiment 3), the completeness of the stimuli (Cremer & Zeef, 1987; Salthouse, 1988c), the number of line segments in the composite stimulus (Salthouse, 1987a; Salthouse & D.R. Mitchell, 1989), the type of response or decision required (Danziger & Salthouse, 1978, Experiments 1 and 2; Salthouse & Prill, 1988, Experiment 1), the presence or absence of redundant information displays (Salthouse, D.R. Mitchell, & Palmon, 1989), and moderate levels of practice (Salthouse & Prill, 1988, Experiment 2). At least some of these experimental manipulations (e.g., stimulus completeness, number of segments, redundant displays) might have been expected to alter dependence on memory, and thus the lack of differential effects of the manipulations on young and old adults appears inconsistent with a mediating role of memory in the age differences in spatial integration. This assortment of findings does place constraints on plausible interpretations of the phenomenon of age differences in spatial integration, but by themselves they are not sufficient to indicate which single hypothesis provides the most plausible proximal-level explanation of those differences.

Effectiveness or efficiency of spatial transformation processes has been investigated with a variety of procedures. For example, Salthouse (1987e) created a computer-administered version of the Wechsler Block Design test that allowed assessment of the efficiency of block manipulation processes, independent of individual differences in motor speed or manual dexterity. The task in this test was to use the keys on a computer keyboard to rotate an isometric representation of a block so that the target pattern was visible on the front surface of the block. Older adults were generally slower than young adults at performing the task, but they were also less efficient in that they did not select the optimum sequence of block rotations as frequently as young adults. The age differences in manipulation efficiency were particularly pronounced when the target pattern was not on one of the visible surfaces (top, front, and right) of the block, thereby leading to the inference that older adults may be impaired in generating or accessing, as well as manipulating, spatial representations. That is, compared with young adults, the older adults seemed to have less information about the contents of surfaces not currently visible, as well as greater difficulty in selecting the optimum sequence of rotations. The extent to which these differences might be consequences of memory limitations could not be determined, but the basic results are apparently robust because the same general pattern was obtained across three sessions of practice, and across two different formats for presenting stimuli and registering responses.

Tasks requiring the visualization of a sequence of paper-folding operations have also been used in the investigation of age differences in the speed and accuracy of spatial transformations. Two studies with paper-and-pencil (Salthouse, 1988e) and computer-administered (Salthouse, D.R. Mitchell, Skovronek, & Babcock, 1989) paper-folding tasks found that older adults were more sensitive than young adults to increases in the number of required folding operations. This greater sensitivity was evident in larger decreases in decision accuracy, and larger increases in decision time, as a function of the number of folds presented prior to the display of a hole punched through the folded paper.

The contribution of memory factors to these apparent age differences in transformation efficiency was investigated in the Salthouse, D.R. Mitchell, Skovronek, and Babcock (1989) study by comparing performance on trials in which all the displayed folds were relevant to the decision, with performance on trials in which only a single fold was relevant. The logic of these comparisons is identical to that described earlier in the context of the integrative reasoning task performed by these same individuals because the reasoning and paper-folding tasks were designed to be structurally identical. The data from the paper-folding task are illustrated in Figure 7.6.

Although, for reasons not yet understood, accuracy was unusually high in trials when only one of three folds was relevant to the decision, the data in Figure 7.6 are generally similar to those from the verbal reasoning task illustrated in Figure 7.2. The same conclusion therefore seems appropriate —namely, that most of the age-related decrease in accuracy with multiple operations (in this case folds of the paper) appears attributable to an inability to preserve the relevant information, and not to difficulties in integrating the products of those operations.

Several investigators have contrasted the performance of young and old adults in the mental rotation paradigm introduced by Shepard and his colleagues (e.g., Shepard & Metzler, 1971). In at least six independent studies, older adults, compared with young adults, were found to have larger slopes of the function relating decision time to angular orientation,

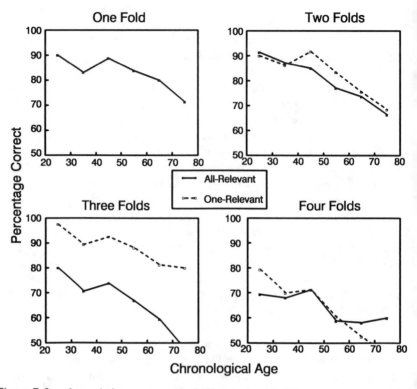

Figure 7.6. Age relations on a paper folding task with different numbers of folds for problems with all folds relevant to the solution and for problems with only one relevant fold. Data from Salthouse, D.R. Mitchell, Skovronek, and Babcock (1989).

indicating a slower rate of mental rotation (Berg, et al., 1982; Cerella, et al., 1981; Clarkson-Smith & Halpern, 1983; Gaylord & Marsh, 1975; Jacewicz & A.A. Hartley, 1987; Puglisi & Morrell, 1986). Older adults were also reported to have higher error rates than young adults in each study, although the age differences in accuracy were not always statistically significant. Only Berg, et al. (1982) reported data on error rates at each angle of orientation. It appears from their data that, at least in the first experimental session, there was a greater increase in error rate with orientation discrepancy for older adults than for young adults. This suggests that some rotation transformations may become less effective, in addition to being less efficient, with increased age. Whether the age differences in the efficiency or effectiveness of mental rotation are influenced by age differences in memory processes cannot be determined from the available data.

Memory factors were assumed to have played a role in the age differences found in a recent study of perspective-taking by Kirasic (1989). There were two conditions in this experiment, both of which required the research participant to specify the direction and distance between two objects. In one condition the objects were pictures of unfamiliar buildings in a novel spatial array; in the other condition the objects were familiar buildings matching the arrangement in the small town in which the participants lived. No direct comparison of performance across the two conditions was reported, but the data clearly suggest that the age differences were larger in the novel arrangement (i.e., directional errors of 44.9° for older adults and 28.3° for young adults) than in the familiar arrangement (i.e., directional errors of 12.9° for both young and old adults). Kirasic interpreted this pattern of results in terms of the greater memory demands in the novel array because knowledge of the familiar locations could presumably be accessed from long-term memory. An implication of this interpretation is that there may be no age-related difficulty in the effectiveness of spatial transformations such as perspective-taking or mental rotation when the relevant spatial information is readily available in long-term memory. This intriguing possibility should be investigated further with special attention to ensuring that the same kinds of transformations are actually required with both familiar and unfamiliar spatial arrays.

Summary of Research on Spatial Abilities

Not much can yet be said about the reasons for age differences on measures of spatial ability. Increased age has consistently been found to be associated with poorer performance in tests of spatial memory, and in tests requiring various sorts of spatial manipulations or transformations. However, little analytical research has been conducted in the area of spatial cognition. The extent to which memory or other factors might contribute to the age differences observed in measures requiring spatial transformations therefore is not yet known, nor are the specific components responsible for the age differences in spatial memory.

EVALUATION OF THE ANALYTICAL, LOCALIZATION, PERSPECTIVE

Most of the research described in this and the preceding chapter was designed to provide information about the specific aspects of cognitive functioning most affected by increased age. The underlying assumption has been that cognitive performance can be analyzed into distinct components, and that age differences in measures of overall performance can be explained or understood in terms of the relative effectiveness of those components.

A fundamental prerequisite for the success of the analytical perspective is the ability to isolate the age differences to one or more components. If the age differences cannot be localized with respect to specific processes or structures, then this approach appears to have no advantage over less analytical approaches. The research reviewed in chapter 6 and in the current chapter suggests that unequivocal evidence that the adult age differences in cognition can be localized in, or isolated to, a few critical components is still quite limited. Although each of the taxonomies of memory examined in chapter 6 was proposed as a means of organizing the research literature, none was found to provide a completely satisfactory partitioning of tasks according to the presence or absence of age differences because young adults have been found to perform at higher levels than older adults in at least some measures of nearly all hypothesized components of memory. There is much less analytical research on reasoning and spatial abilities, but the research that is available provides only weak evidence that age differences are restricted to specific processing components.

It is still too early to determine whether the analytical approach will eventually prove successful in the localization of adult age differences in cognitive functioning. What may be appropriate at this time, however, is to consider several substantive and methodological issues related to the analytical or localization perspective in cognitive aging. The substantive issues are addressed in the present section, and methodological reservations about the primary investigative strategy used by analytically-oriented researchers—namely, searching for age-by-treatment interactions—are discussed in the appendix to this chapter.

One important issue regarding the analytical approach concerns the validity of the fundamental assumption that age differences can be localized in one or two "critical" processes or components. A basic question is whether it is reasonable to claim that age differences have been isolated when there is little assurance that there has been an exhaustive examination of all relevant processes or components. That is, other processing components sensitive to the effects associated with increased age could also exist but may not have been identified in a given study because they were: (a) omitted from the model used to guide the investigations of task performance; (b) included in the model but not measured in the study; or (c) included and measured but not found to reveal significant age effects because of low statistical power. These concerns regarding inferences that age differences have been isolated or localized are potentially serious because it is generally not feasible to be exhaustive in the investigation of processing-related determinants of age differences in a given cognitive task, and there are almost no attempts to establish that the sensitivity to detect age differences was equivalent for every measure examined (e.g., see the discussion of discriminating power in the appendix of this chapter).

A second reservation about the analytical, process-oriented approach in adult developmental research is that the combined results of many studies seem to suggest that there are many age-sensitive processes or components. This has contributed to a proliferation of purportedly "critical" processes or components, and leads to doubts about the ultimate parsimony of the localization perspective. One can obviously question whether progress is being made toward integrative understanding when the number of phenomena in need of explanation is apparently increasing rather than decreasing. An illustration of this tendency toward greater numbers of purportedly more specific "explanations" of age differences is evident in a list of hypothesized localizations of adult age differences in cognition extracted from an unsystematic survey of the research literature by Salthouse (1985b). A total of 47 interpretations relying on what are at least superficially distinct processing components were identified in this non-exhaustive review.

The lack of integration in the interpretations proposed to account for age differences across cognitive tasks is partly attributable to the diverse nature of the cognitive tasks being investigated. For example, even analyses conducted by the same investigator often fail to specify common age-sensitive elements across tasks such as block design (Salthouse, 1987e), digit symbol substitution (Salthouse, 1978b), geometric analogies (Salthouse, 1987d), integrative reasoning (Salthouse, Legg, Palmon, & D.R. Mitchell, 1990; Salthouse, D.R. Mitchell, Skovronek, & Babcock, 1989), paper folding (Salthouse, 1988e; Salthouse, D.R. Mitchell, Skovronek, & Babcock, 1989), perceptual closure (Danziger & Salthouse, 1978; Salthouse & Prill, 1988), series completion (Salthouse & Prill, 1987), and spatial integration (Salthouse, 1987a; Salthouse & D.R. Mitchell, 1989; Salthouse, D.R. Mitchell, & Palmon, 1989). Each of the cited projects compared adults of different ages in several theoretically distinct processing components, but few of the components were sufficiently similar to allow meaningful generalizations across tasks.

The tendency for analytically-oriented researchers to focus on narrow aspects of cognition, with little attempt at integration, has frequently been lamented as contributing to a fragmented and unintegrated literature on adult cognition (Birren & Renner, 1977; Salthouse, 1982, 1985b, 1988c, 1988d; Waugh & Barr, 1980). This concern was expressed very clearly by J.L. Horn (1986):

... [R]esearch deriving from these process-focused theories is netting improved insights concerning how humans comprehend and resolve intellectual difficulties. But there is a sense in which this work is not putting Humpty Dumpty back together again. Process-focused research does not address issues pertaining to the breadth of intellectual capacities. Instead, the work focuses on a particular kind of performance, usually that of a single test. It is hazardous to generalize that findings from such work indicate processes that are fundamental to most intellectual tasks. It is difficult to see the development of most intellectual abilities within the context of this research. When analysis becomes very refined, there can be great difficulty in realizing synthesis. (p. 43)

Collections of basic processing components or elementary information processes have been proposed by several information-processing theorists (Carroll, 1976; Newell & H.A. Simon, 1972; A.M. Rose, 1980), but most researchers apparently have not felt constrained to restrict their postulated processes to those included on one or more of these lists. In addition, very few attempts have been made to explore correlations among the measures presumed to reflect the same or different processing components from different tasks, or from similar tasks in different contexts. Although time-consuming and possibly quite expensive, research examining the correlations among measures of many theoretical components in samples with large numbers of individuals is highly desirable to avoid redundancy in characterizing cognitive constructs, and to minimize the confusion that exists when different components are assigned similar labels. Not only would results from this kind of research likely lead to a reduction in the number of processes or components presumed to be contributing to age differences in cognition, but they would probably also provide a meaningful basis for integrating findings from what seem to be quite distinct tasks.

A third concern about the ultimate value of localization approaches relates to the highly interrelated and interconnected nature of human cognition. Specifically, it seems unlikely that substantial changes in one aspect of processing would leave other aspects completely unaffected, particularly when the changes have occurred gradually across many years (J.E. Anderson, 1956a, 1956b, 1958; R. Lachman, et al., 1982; Schonfield & Stones, 1979; Welford, 1958). Indeed, Salthouse (1985b) suggested that "... the possible interactive effects among various aspects of the processing system are so great that it may be impossible to study individual differences in a single mechanism without making fairly strong explicit, or implicit, assumptions about the absence of differences in other mechanisms" (p. 74). Unfortunately, resolution of the problem of identifying the critical component(s) in complex interactive systems will probably have to wait until more sophisticated processing models, focused at the level of cognitive components, are developed to specify the consequences of an impairment of one component on a number of interrelated variables.

A fourth reservation about the contribution of localization-based approaches to the understanding of relations between adult age and cognition concerns the issue of whether process analyses are leading to actual explanations of the observed age differences in performance, or are simply providing more precise and refined descriptions of those differences. Description is obviously a prerequisite to explanation, and what is considered explanation as opposed to description depends both upon one's disciplinary orientation, and upon the level of theoretical analysis adopted (see chapter 1). Nevertheless, it does not seem particularly satisfying to attribute age differences to deficiencies in certain processing components without also specifying the causes of the age differences in those components. It is therefore legitimate to question whether age differences in hypothesized processing components should be regarded as *sources* of the age differences in performance, or merely as *symptoms* of some more fundamental age-related difficulty. Localization approaches seek to provide precise answers to the question of where or *what* the differences are, but they often seem to neglect the questions of *how* and *why* those differences originated. As discussed in chapter 1, interpretations of cognitive aging phenomena that fail to incorporate change mechanisms may not qualify as true developmental explanations.

To summarize, analytical approaches to the investigation of age differences in cognition have clearly provided more specific, and presumably more precise, characterizations of the nature of cognitive performance differences between young and old adults than those available from other research traditions. However, it has been argued that age differences cannot be claimed to have been isolated or localized unless (a) there has been an exhaustive assessment, with equivalent statistical power, of all relevant components; and (b) there is evidence that the total number of age-sensitive constructs is decreasing rather than increasing. Furthermore, even if the localization was successful, the status of localization as explanation or description might remain somewhat ambiguous until mechanisms are introduced to account for why, and how, the age differences in specific components originated.

APPENDIX
Reservations About the Reliance on the Methodology
of Age X Treatment Interactions in Analytical Research

The key concept in the analytical approach to cognitive aging is the notion of differential deficit. That is, if age-related performance deficits are found to be differential, and larger in some tasks or conditions than in others, then it has been considered reasonable to infer that some processes or components are more affected by age-related changes than are others. The assumptions implicit in this reasoning are schematically illustrated in Figure 7.7.

Notice that Variable 1 is assumed to be influenced by the efficiency or effectiveness of Process X, and that Variable 2 is assumed to be influenced by variations in the efficiency or effectiveness of both Process X and Process Y. Contrasts of the magnitude of age differences in Variables 1 and 2 can therefore be postulated to be informative about the effects of age on Process Y, the component hypothesized to be involved in Variable 2 but not in Variable 1. If the age differences are greater on Variable 2 than with Variable 1, then one can presumably infer that Process Y is more sensitive to age-related effects than Process X. This selective or differential pattern of impairment has been the primary source of evidence for age-related deficits in specific processes. Age X treatment (or age X process) interactions of this type are often implicitly inferred to exist, even if not explicitly tested, whenever a significant age difference is found with one variable but not with another. For example, most of the memory classifications discussed in chapter 6 have been investigated by examining interactions between age and variables reflecting postulated distinctions such as primary versus secondary, recognition versus recall, episodic versus semantic, shallow versus deep, automatic versus effortful, implicit versus explicit, and so on. Although the methodology of inferring a differential

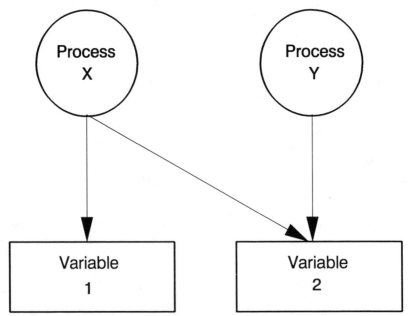

Figure 7.7.   Schematic illustration of logic underlying use of statistical interactions to infer specific deficits.

deficit on the basis of statistical interactions is potentially powerful, its success is dependent upon several important, but not widely recognized, assumptions. Three of these assumptions that seem particularly relevant to research in cognitive aging are briefly discussed in this appendix.

Validity of the Performance-Process Linkage

An initial, and extremely important, assumption is that the performance variables are valid reflections of the theoretical processes of interest. The issue here is whether the measures of performance (e.g., Variables 1 and 2) can be interpreted as representing the influence of the relevant theoretical processes (e.g., Processes X and Y), and not other factors that are either more specific, or more general, than the processes of interest. Only if the determinants of the two performance measures being compared are identical except for the critical processes would it be appropriate to attribute any differences that might be observed in the variables to differences in the hypothesized processes.

Attributions may be too general if the performance differences are caused by the particular method of implementing the added process, and not by the efficiency or effectiveness of the process itself. For example, the manipulation used to introduce Process Y may also alter the sensory requirements of the task, and therefore lead to greater changes in performance in one age group than in another for reasons unrelated to the efficiency or effectiveness of Process Y. Over-generalizations of this type can usually be minimized by relying on the principle of converging operations (D.T. Campbell & Fiske, 1959; Garner, Hake, & Ericksen, 1956) when evaluating the effects of a theoretical process or construct.

Attributions may be too specific if the interaction is interpreted as reflecting the operation of a particular process when it is really a consequence of more general factors. One theoretical perspective based on the notion of relatively general factors is discussed at length in chapter 8, but for the present purposes it should merely be noted that some interactions may result from the operation of a general factor that leads to greater impairments of performance whenever the number of cognitive operations, or the amount of processing required in the task, increases. That is, if there is some sort of general limitation on processing, and if for whatever reason this limitation becomes more pronounced with increased age, then the magnitude of the age differences would be expected to be largest on the measures reflecting the greatest amount of processing. In terms of Figure 7.7, age differences might be larger with Variable 2 than with Variable 1, not because of the involvement of Process Y, but because more total processing is required when two processing operations are involved (X+Y) than when only one operation is involved (X). It is therefore possible that interactions interpreted as evidence of selective deficits may actually reflect the influence of broader and more general factors.

The validity of variables as reflections of theoretical constructs is difficult to evaluate outside the context of a particular theoretical model. It is nevertheless important to recognize that inferences about differential deficits are only meaningful to the extent that the postulated linkages between observable aspects of performance and theoretical processes are accurate, and at the appropriate level of generalization.

Equivalent Discriminating Power

A second assumption critical for the appropriate interpretation of statistical interactions is that the relevant measures of performance are all equivalent with respect to discriminating power. Spurious interactions may result if the measures being compared vary in discriminating power such that the effects associated with group differences or experimental manipulations are more likely to be detected with some measures than with other measures.

There are two primary determinants of discriminating power: reliability and variability. Both of these properties affect the amount of variance in the measure that is available to be associated with other measures. Reliability is important because measures with low reliability have a smaller portion of systematic variance that can be related to other measures. Variability, which directly affects the amount of variance, is influenced by both the range of performance, and the region in the performance scale of the average level of performance. That is, variance generally increases as the range of scores increases, and it usually decreases as the average level of performance shifts away from the middle of the measurement scale.

Assessments of the variance and reliability of performance measures are likely to prove particularly informative in certain research areas, such as evaluating age-related influences on automatic and effortful processing, or on implicit and explicit measures of memory. As just noted, artifactual interactions may result if the various measures differ in their variances or reliabilities such that the age differences are attenuated on the measures of performance that have low reliability or small variability. This seems likely in the case of measures of truly automatic processes, which are sometimes postulated to exhibit little interindividual variation in efficiency (Hasher & Zacks, 1979), and with implicit measures of memory, which are frequently based on difference scores of unknown, but potentially low, reliability.

L.J. Chapman and J.P. Chapman (1973, 1978) have been so impressed by the potential influence of variations in discriminating power on statistical interactions that they have argued that inferences of differential deficit are warranted only if the relevant performance variables have first been matched on discriminating power. The method proposed by Chapman and Chapman (1973, 1978) for matching variables in discriminating power involves selecting pairs of items from the two tests (or tasks or conditions) with the same level of difficulty (e.g., average percentage correct), and with similar correlations of each item to the total score. This procedure not only results in the two sets of items having equivalent reliability, but both the reliability and variance of performance measures based on those items should also remain relatively constant across different levels of ability. The Chapman and Chapman method does not appear unduly cumbersome, and adopting it in future age-comparative research may minimize the occurrence of artifactual interactions produced because some dependent measures are more sensitive or discriminating than others.

Characteristics of the Process-Variable Relation

Meaningful interpretation of statistical interactions is also dependent upon several assumptions about the nature of the relation between the performance variables and the theoretical processes. For example, a common, but generally unrecognized, assumption about the process-variable relation is that it is monotonic and uniformly linear. In other words, it seems to be implicit in the reasoning of many researchers that a given increment in the theoretical process will result in the same magnitude of change in the performance variable across all levels of the process. The minimal assumption of monotonicity may be reasonable for many process-variable relations, but there is rarely any basis for distinguishing among more subtle forms of the process-variable function. As an example, each of the functions illustrated in Figure 7.8 appears plausible as a characterization of the relation between a theoretical process and a dependent variable. Panel (A) is the commonly assumed linear function, panel (B) is a negatively accelerated function of the type that might result if there is a saturation of the theoretical process, panel (C) is a positively accelerated function of the type that might result if a threshold is operating, and panel (D) is an ogive corresponding to a combination of (B) and (C).

The major point to note from the functions portrayed in Figure 7.8 is that although these alternatives can seldom be distinguished on the basis of explicit theoretical postulates or empirical evidence, the presence or absence of statistical interactions is critically dependent upon the particular form of the process-variable function. This is evident in the figure by the variation in the intervals between the performance variables (i.e., 1, 2, 3, and 4), despite equal intervals along the process axis (i.e., a, b, c, and d). To illustrate, the interval between 1 and 2 is equal to, greater than, or

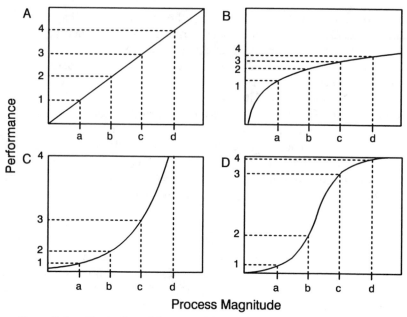

Figure 7.8.   Illustration of four possible relations between the magnitude of a theoretical process and the level of observed performance.

smaller than, the interval between 3 and 4 in panels A, B, and C, respectively. The interactions could therefore be absent, in the direction of larger differences between processes a and b than between processes c and d, or in the direction of larger differences between processes c and d than between processes a and b.

An implication of the dependence of interactions on the scale of measurement is that only cross-over or disordinal interactions, in which the direction of the age difference reverses from one variable to another, are unambiguous. All other interactions are somewhat capricious (i.e., dependent on specific assumptions about process-variable relations), and can be created or eliminated by suitable transformations of the measurement scale (A. Baron & Treiman, 1980; Bogartz, 1976; Loftus, 1978; Loftus, Truax, & W.W. Nelson, 1987; Salthouse, 1985a, 1985b; Winer, 1971). Confidence in inferences concerning differential deficit based on the existence of statistical interactions should therefore be tempered by recognition of the arbitrary nature of most interactions, and the realization that they can be made to appear or disappear by imposing transformations that can have quite plausible justifications.

It is worth noting that this issue, concerning the importance of measurement scales for the interpretation of interactions, is a generalization of the familiar problem of measurement floors or ceilings in which the slope of the process-variable function approaches zero. (Actually, however, measurement floors and ceilings are often more complicated than many researchers realize because they can be functional, as well as absolute, in that the dependent measures may cease to vary with changes in the theoretical process because they are limited by other processes, and not simply by the maximum or minimum possible score.) Measurement floors and ceilings clearly distort the process-variable relation because the dependent variable is completely insensitive to variations in the magnitude of the theoretical process when these artifacts of measurement occur. The primary point of the preceding discussion, however, is that distortions can also occur when the relative sensitivity of the variable to the process changes as a function of the level of either the variable or the process.

Some of the arbitrariness of response scales can be eliminated if the researcher has a theoretical justification for expecting one particular process-variable function, and its corresponding measurement scale, over another (Bogartz, 1976; Loftus, 1978). For example, if with temporal variables it is assumed that a manipulation simply lengthens the duration of the total task by the time required to execute an additional process, then the most meaningful comparisons may involve absolute values along a linear continuum. However, an alternative assumption is that the manipulation alters the probability that one or more existing processes could be successfully executed. The most appropriate measurement scale under this assumption might be some kind of proportional or ratio measure because the manipulation may affect the number of times certain processes must be repeated. Unfortunately, researchers are seldom explicit about the mechanisms by which manipulations (such as priming, or the presence or absence of a secondary task) exert their effects. As a consequence, this means of reducing the ambiguity inherent in the arbitrary scaling of dependent variables has seldom been employed.

Because few of the performance measures in cognitive psychological research are meaningful in an absolute sense, it is sometimes more informative to express performance in units of population variability rather than in the original units of measurement. This method of analyzing the results does not eliminate the ambiguity inherent in the original measures, but it does have the advantage of indicating the degree to which there is overlap in two or more distributions. The reference distribution in age-comparative research can either be the performance of young adults in each condition of interest, or the performance of each age group in a control or baseline condition. Statistical evaluation can then be conducted either by within-group analyses of variance or t-tests on the performance of older adults scaled in young standard deviation units, or by between-groups analyses of variance or t-tests on the performance of each group scaled in standard deviation units for that age group in the control or baseline condition.

A specific example is described to illustrate how comparisons might be conducted with performance expressed in units of population variability. An interesting feature of this example is that the alternative analyses appear to lead to strikingly different conclusions than those reached by the investigators based on analyses of scores in the original (but nevertheless arbitrary) units of measurement. This discrepancy serves to emphasize the limitations of reliance upon the interaction methodology when there is no strong theoretical or empirical rationale for preferring one measurement scale over another. The research to be described was reported by Park, et al., (1989). These investigators conducted two memory experiments in which the presence or absence of digit monitoring at both presentation and test of verbal stimulus materials was manipulated. Results of their experiments are summarized in Table 7.2.

TABLE 7.2
Alternative analyses of the Park, A.D. Smith, Dudley,
& Lafranza (1989) experiments

| | *Digit Monitoring at:* *Presentation/Test* | | | |
	No/No *Mean (SD)*	*No/Yes* *Mean (SD)*	*Yes/No* *Mean (SD)*	*Yes/Yes* *Mean (SD)*
Experiment 1				
(1) Young	22.06 (3.61)	15.50 (4.84)	13.69 (4.09)	10.81 (3.47)
(2) Old	17.81 (6.61)	15.13 (2.92)	8.06 (5.09)	5.73 (3.77)
(3) Old in Young SD units	-1.18	-0.08	-1.38	-1.46
(4) Young in Young No/No SD units	0	-1.82	-2.32	-3.12
(5) Old in Old No/No SD units	0	-0.41	-1.48	-1.83
Experiment 2				
(6) Young	20.25 (2.73)	16.44 (3.10)	13.44 (4.66)	12.94 (4.91)
(7) Old	15.62 (3.90)	12.31 (4.57)	7.00 (4.06	5.81 (3.88)
(8) Old in Young SD units	-1.70	-1.33	-1.38	-1.45
(9) Young in Young No/No SD units	0	-1.40	-2.49	-2.68
(10) Old in Old No/No SD Units	0	-0.85	-2.21	-2.52

Statistically significant interactions between age and digit monitoring at stimulus presentation were found in both of the experiments in Park, et al. (1989). In Experiment 1 the young adults remembered an average of 2.31 (i.e., 22.06 - 17.81 = 4.25 plus 15.50 - 15.13 = 0.37 divided by 2) more words than older adults when there was no digit monitoring at stimulus presentation, but they remembered an average of 5.36 (i.e., 13.69 - 8.06 = 5.63 plus 10.81 - 5.73 = 5.08 divided by 2) more words when digit monitoring was required during stimulus presentation. A similar interaction pattern in two separate experiments led the authors to conclude that the encoding stage of memory (assumed to be operative at the time of stimulus presentation) is more demanding for older adults than is the retrieval stage (assumed to be operative at stimulus test). They further suggested that "... the present data do not support any hypothesis that older adults suffer from a general deficiency in processing information" (p. 1190). Both conclusions can be challenged on the basis of alternative, but equally meaningful, analyses of their results.

Entries in rows 3 and 8 of Table 7.2 indicate the mean performance of older adults scaled in standard deviation units of the performance of young adults. If the experimental manipulations do indeed influence the magnitude of the age differences, then the values in the second, third, and fourth columns should be substantially greater (or smaller) than those in the first column. That is, if the two groups become more (or less) similar to one another as a function of the experimental manipulations, then the overlap in the distributions should increase (or decrease). Inspection of the table entries reveals that only in Experiment 1, with digit monitoring at test but not at presentation, was the age difference expressed in distributional overlap appreciably different from the control condition. Moreover, in this case the difference between groups was actually smaller (i.e., the overlap in distributions greater) than in the control condition.

The condition effects can also be expressed in terms of standard deviations of each group's performance in the control condition. If the experimental manipulations have greater effects in older adults than in young adults, then these measures of relative performance should be more negative (i.e., the differences between distributions should be greater) for older adults than for young adults. The entries in rows 4, 5, 9, and 10 indicate that this expectation was not confirmed, and if anything, the condition manipulations appear to have resulted in greater relative performance disruptions (as reflected in reduced overlap in distributions of performance in control and experimental conditions) in young adults than in older adults.

In neither of these comparisons based on performance differences scaled in units of variability is there convincing evidence that the age differences are differentially greater in some conditions than in others. The results just described could not be evaluated statistically because only mean values were reported in the published article, but the direction of the differences was generally opposite to that implied by the authors' conclusions. In other words, instead of the older adults experiencing greater performance impairments than young adults with the requirement to monitor digits during stimulus presentation, these data suggest that it may be the young adults who show the greatest performance declines.

It should be emphasized that the interpretational ambiguity just described is inherent in measurement scales and the methodology of statistical interactions, and does not reflect a defect unique to the Park, et al, (1989) study. The fact that there is seldom any strong basis for rejecting the imposition of transformations that can distort the existence, or the direction, of interactions should therefore make one very cautious whenever attempting to make inferences on the basis of the presence or the absence of statistical interactions.

These examples and the accompanying discussion are intended to illustrate that the interpretation of statistical interactions is quite complex, and cannot be used to infer the presence (or absence) of selective impairments or differential deficits without careful consideration of several potentially critical issues. Among these are the reliability and discriminating power of the dependent measures, the justification of assumptions concerning the particular form of the function relating theoretical processes to observed variables, and the meaningfulness of absolute versus distribution-referenced measures. Only when some consensus is reached on these vital matters will it be possible to have confidence in the interaction methodology as a basis for reaching inferences about patterns of selective (i.e., localized or specific) impairment. Until that time, researchers should exercise considerable prudence when drawing analytical conclusions based on the presence or absence of statistical interactions.

8 Reduced Processing Resources

It would seem that the principal function of psychological research on aging is to reduce the great variety of changes in behavior associated with age to a smaller number of concepts.
—Birren, Riegel, & Morrison (1963, p. 10)

The essence of the reduced processing resources perspective is the hypothesis that many age differences in cognitive performance may be attributable to age-related changes in a few relatively general factors or mechanisms. Most proponents of the processing resources perspective tend to accept the usefulness of analytical approaches, but they are also interested in determining whether many of the inferred differences in specific processing components might themselves be interpretable in terms of a limited number of comparatively broad mechanisms. Hypotheses about processing resources should therefore not be viewed as alternatives or substitutes for analytical processing models, but rather as supplements to or extensions of them. A schematic illustration of the principal differences between the localization perspective discussed in the last two chapters and the processing resources perspective to be discussed in this chapter is presented in Figure 8.1.

Notice that the key difference between the two perspectives is that the processing resources view postulates the existence of a small number of processing resources intervening between the age variable and the inferred processing components. There is still very little understanding of the exact nature of processing resources, but it is usually assumed that processing resources are limited in quantity, and relevant for the successful execution of many different processing components. They are therefore hypothesized to serve as a source of supply or support for processing because their existence is assumed to enable or enhance other aspects of cognitive functioning.

A fundamental assumption of the processing resources perspective is that m, the number of hypothesized resources, is considerably smaller than n, the number of age-sensitive processing components. In fact, the major

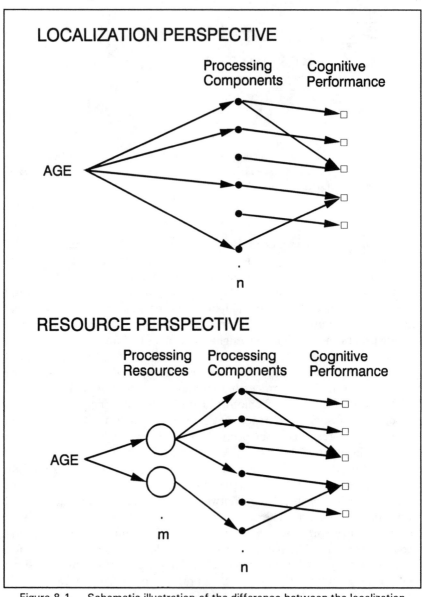

Figure 8.1.   Schematic illustration of the difference between the localization approach and the reduced resources approach to cognitive aging.

appeal of the processing resources perspective seems to have been that it might provide a more parsimonious and integrative explanation of cognitive aging phenomena than that possible with component-localization approaches.

Different versions of the resource perspective can be distinguished depending upon the nature of the assumptions about the value of m (i.e., the number of hypothesized resources), about the number of processes presumed to be affected by resource limitations (i.e., the universality of resource consequences), about the contribution of other factors to cognitive age differences (i.e., the exclusivity of resources as a determinant of cognitive age differences), and about the permanence of resource-performance relations (i.e., the modifiability of resource influences). The most extreme versions of the processing resources perspective, discussed more often by opponents than by proponents, are single resource ($m = 1$) models in which the unitary resource is postulated to be the sole, and immodifiable, determinant of all observed age differences.

Although probably not seriously believed by any contemporary theorist, a potentially useful investigative strategy has been to hypothesize that a single resource is responsible for most, if not all, observed age differences in measures of cognitive performance, and then to determine the proportion of the total age differences that can be attributed to age-related reductions in that single factor. One version of this strategy was termed "single parameter sufficiency analysis" by Salthouse (1988c), and was postulated to consist of two basic steps. The first involved the construction of detailed quantitative models to account for the performance of a sample of adults from a narrow range of ages on two or more cognitive tasks. The second step consisted of determining whether alteration of a single parameter common to the models from each task was sufficient to predict the level, and pattern, of performance of adults from a different range of ages. If successful, results from this research strategy might provide impressive support for the view that the processing resource represented by that single parameter is a major factor contributing to the performance differences between the two groups. Unfortunately, this strategy does not yet appear practical because there are few quantitative models of cognitive tasks, and even fewer in which the same parameters have been incorporated in models of different tasks.

In this chapter the focus will be on a moderate version of the processing resources perspective that postulates the existence of a few, relatively general, determinants of cognitive performance. This view is distinguished from the more traditional analytical information-processing perspectives primarily on the basis of the assumption that cognitive performance is determined by a few general entities, in addition to many specific components. That is, resources must be few or this perspective offers no advantages of parsimony over the component-localization perspective, and yet they must be moderately general in order to account for a wide range of phenomena.

The processing resources perspective is both more recent, and somewhat more abstract, than the other theoretical perspectives discussed in this book. As a consequence, the amount of relevant evidence is rather sparse. The discussion in this chapter reflects this early stage of development, and is more conceptual, with less reference to empirical findings, than the discussions in previous chapters.

Reservations About Resources

Hypothesizing the existence of general resources in addition to specific components can lead to the criticism that this adds an unnecessary level of complexity to the explanation of age differences in cognitive functioning. That is, objections can be raised that attributing age differences in cognitive performance to alterations in processing resources does not really explain the differences, but merely removes the proposed explanatory mechanism one step further from the actual observations. Ultimately, of course, the potency of this criticism will depend upon the success of the processing resources approach in accounting for empirical results. If age differences in a few general processing resources can account for many phenomena, then this perspective may reduce the number of explanations that are required, thereby resulting in simpler, rather than more complex, explanatory systems.

Another aspect of the processing resources perspective that has led to a certain amount of controversy is the tendency to view the hypothesis of diminished processing resources as a complete, and already verified, explanation for the age differences observed in a particular cognitive task. This practice has led to justifiable criticisms of circularity in that resources are inferred to be reduced because cognitive performance is impaired, but the cognitive impairments are then explained in terms of the diminished supply of processing resources (L.L. Light, 1988; L.L. Light & D.M. Burke, 1988; Salthouse, 1982, 1985b, 1988d, 1988e; Salthouse, D.R. Mitchell, Skovronek, & Babcock, 1989). Obviously what is necessary to escape this circular reasoning are attempts to examine the hypothesized linkages between adult age and indices of processing resources, and between the processing resource indices and measures of cognitive performance.

Still another concern about the processing resources perspective is that because these interpretations are based on the notion of quantitative deficits, it is sometimes assumed that they would be unable to account for qualitative differences in cognitive performance. This is not necessarily the case, however, because there appear to be several ways in which quantitative differences could contribute to qualitative variations. For example, changes in the strategy used to perform a task might emerge as a consequence of reduced resources because the resource demands of the most effective strategies exceed the available supply (Bromley, 1970; G. Cohen, 1988; Guttentag, 1985; Salthouse, 1985b, 1988c). Numerous speculations have been offered about how quantitative variations could produce what appear to be qualitative differences in performance. As an illustration, Salthouse (1982, 1985b, 1988c) and Welford (1958) have pointed out that much abstract thought is dependent on integrating, or detecting relations among, simultaneously available pieces of information. Quantitative reductions in the amount of information that can be kept active are therefore likely to impair the ability to achieve higher-level abstractions, which can be considered a qualitative phenomenon. Bromley (1967) has also argued that quantitative reductions in the rate of processing information will decrease the number of conceptual transformations that can be achieved, and hence also decrease the likelihood of unique or high-quality transformations. Finally, as noted in chapter 7, the complex interdependencies that exist throughout the human information processing system makes it likely that differences in one aspect will lead to adjustments and modifications in many other aspects. For all these reasons, therefore, even if the initial age-related changes were produced by quantitative differences, qualitative changes might easily emerge as a consequence of those quantitative differences.

Another controversial issue regarding the processing resources perspective has been the question of how many distinct types of processing resources are necessary to account for all the observed age differences in cognitive performance. Although this question will ultimately be important, there is still considerable debate about whether one or more resources are *sufficient* to account for *some* cognitive aging phenomena. The most salient question at the current time therefore seems to be whether the age differences observed in several different tasks, which presumably involve a variety of different processing components, can be explained in terms of age-related changes in a limited number of general mechanisms. Only if this question is answered in the affirmative does it then seem meaningful to try to determine the minimum number of these relatively broad mechanisms required to account for all the age differences observed in the performance of assorted cognitive tasks.

A final reservation about the concept of processing resources relates to how it is to be measured. This issue will be discussed in some detail in later sections, but for the present purpose it is important to recognize that a resource is considered to be something that is more fundamental than, and hence in some sense responsible for, the cognitive performance differences one is attempting to explain. The distinction between measures of cognitive functioning and indices of processing resources is not always clear, but it is theoretically quite important because there may be little value in learning that the age differences in a specific cognitive measure could be explained by, or interpreted in terms of, the age differences in another cognitive measure. Only if there were some reason to believe that the latter measure reflected a more basic or fundamental entity would results of this type be interesting from the processing resources perspective. As an example, research demonstrating that the age differences in specific measures of cognitive performance were eliminated by matching adults of different ages on general intelligence would not necessarily be relevant to the processing resource perspective. The construct of general intelligence is presumably more complex than a measure of performance on a specific cognitive task, and thus it may not be particularly meaningful to discover that age differences in certain elementary processes are attenuated after procedures are employed to minimize age differences in a measure of complex behavior comprised of those, and other, basic processes.

Fewer Resources, Diminished Effectiveness, More Demanding Processes, or Reduced Selectivity?

The simplest interpretation of the processing resources perspective is that the quantity of processing resources declines with increased age. However, functionally equivalent consequences might be produced from other kinds of alterations. For example, it is possible that the quantity of resources could remain constant, but that the level of cognitive performance might decrease because the resources become less effective due to decreases in either the reliability or consistency of deployment. That is, the peak capacity or optimum level of functioning may not change, but the maximum levels might be reached less frequently with increased age because high levels of resource expenditure cannot be sustained as long as was possible at younger ages.

Another possibility is that the supply of resources does not change, but instead increased age is associated with an increase in the demands on those resources. That is, the component processes could become less efficient with age in the sense that they require more resources for their successful operation. Cognitive performance will therefore be limited by the quantity of resources, but not because of age-related changes in the actual quantity of resources available. A key issue in this interpretation concerns the number of processing components assumed to have become less efficient with increased age. If the number is large then the interpretation resembles the view postulating a reduction in the quantity of resources, and if the number is small it is probably indistinguishable from the component-localization perspective.

A third interpretation that is functionally similar to, but nonetheless theoretically distinct from, the reduced resources interpretation is that the quantity of resources does not decline, but instead there is an age-related impairment in the selectivity or efficiency with which resources are allocated to processing components. Plude and W.J. Hoyer (1985), for instance, have suggested that older adults differ from young adults primarily in terms of the efficiency of allocating limited resources, and Hasher and Zacks (1988) have proposed that effective working memory capacity is reduced with increased age because a portion of the capacity is occupied by the intrusion of irrelevant information.

Although each of the preceding alternatives may lead to consequences similar to those that might result from a reduction in processing resources, they should ultimately be distinguishable if they are based on truly different theoretical assumptions. For example, the hypothesis of allocation deficiencies might be supported if age differences are reduced by controlling resource allocation through instructional or payoff manipulations. Furthermore, a reduction in working memory capacity caused by a failure to inhibit irrelevant information leads to expectations that increased age should be associated with more task-irrelevant thoughts, and to better performance on tests of incidental (and presumably irrelevant) information. Some evidence is relevant to these comparisons because little or no age differences have been reported in the amount of performance change associated with instructions or payoffs designed to alter resource allocation (Ponds, Brouwer, & van Wolffelaar, 1988; Salthouse, Rogan, & Prill, 1984; Somberg & Salthouse, 1982), and older adults have been reported to recall less rather than more incidental information (see citations in chapter 5). Contradictory results have been reported regarding whether older adults report more task-irrelevant thoughts than young adults (Giambra, 1989; Hashtroudi, M.K. Johnson, & Chrosniak, 1990). In general, however, the available research does not yet appear either sufficiently extensive or convincing to allow discriminations among the different versions of the processing resource perspective. For the sake of simplicity, therefore, all the subsequent discussion will refer to the diminished-quantity version of the processing resources perspective, but with the recognition that most of the discussion probably applies equally well to these related, but theoretically distinct, interpretations.

THE AGE-COMPLEXITY EFFECT

One important body of evidence relevant to the processing resources perspective is what has come to be known as the age-complexity effect, or the tendency for the magnitude of age differences in cognitive performance to increase with the complexity of the task. What may have been the first convincing demonstration of this phenomenon was provided by Clay (1954) in an experiment requiring research participants to place numbers in cells of a matrix in a manner such that the sums of the rows and columns equalled specified values. Complexity was varied by increasing the size of the matrix from 3x3, to 4x4, to 5x5, and finally, to 6x6. The research participants were allowed to work at their own pace, and each individual worked on only one problem. Despite these presumably optimal conditions for the assessment of maximum levels of functioning, adults between 55 and 78 years of age were generally less successful than adults between 18 and 24, and most importantly, the magnitude of the performance difference between the two age groups increased as the complexity of the problem increased. To illustrate, 94% of the young adults and 88% of the older adults produced correct solutions to the simplest, 3x3, problem, and 75% of the young adults but only 31% of the older adults were successful in the most complex, 6x6, problem.

The phenomenon that, relative to young adults, older adults appear to exhibit greater changes in performance with increased task complexity is quite robust, and has been noted many times (Arenberg & Robertson-Tchabo, 1977; Birren, 1956; Birren & Riegel, 1962; Birren, et al., 1962; Botwinick, Brinley, & Robbin, 1958; Crowder, 1980; J.L. Horn, 1970; W.J. Hoyer & Plude, 1982; H.E. Jones, 1959; Kay, 1959; Kinsbourne, 1980; Klatzky, 1988; Salthouse, 1982, 1985b, 1988a,1988c, 1988d, 1988e; Salthouse, D.R. Mitchell, Skovronek, & Babcock, 1989; Welford, 1958; Wingfield, Poon, Lombardi, & Lowe, 1985). This age-complexity phenomenon is important from the processing resources perspective because it is consistent with the view that many of the age differences in cognitive tasks originate because of limitations on a few general resources. That is, increases in task complexity can be assumed to increase the demands on processing resources, and the performance of older adults is affected more than that of young adults because they have smaller quantities of resources available.

Although a moderate amount of empirical evidence seems relevant to the age-complexity phenomenon, the phenomenon has been difficult to investigate in a rigorous fashion because of problems in defining exactly what is meant by task complexity. Birren (1956) and Crossman and Szafran (1956) raised the issue of the ambiguity inherent in the notion of complexity over 30 years ago, and there is still no consensus with respect to how complexity should be operationally defined (Craik & McDowd, 1987; J.L. Horn, 1970; Salthouse, 1985b, 1988a). One point does seem to be clear, however, and that is that not all variations in performance, even those observed within the context of a single task, should be interpreted as reflections of differences in processing complexity.

At a minimum, it seems desirable to distinguish the concept of complexity from a concept like difficulty or discriminability. For example, Salthouse (1985b, 1988c) used the term complexity to refer to the hypothesized number of processing operations required to perform a task, while the concept of difficulty was assumed to correspond to the duration, or the probability of error, associated with the execution of a given operation. Both of these usages are distinct from the psychometric meaning of difficulty based on the average level of performance. The actual level of performance that one observes may not only reflect the operation of theoretical constructs such as complexity or difficulty, but is probably influenced also by a variety of factors unrelated to these constructs. Unfortunately, distinctions among complexity, difficulty, and level of performance may be of limited interest unless it is possible to identify exactly which processing operations are involved in particular cognitive tasks, and to determine the efficiency or effectiveness of each operation. Nevertheless, the fact that these concepts can be distinguished at a theoretical level suggests that it is probably misleading to claim that the processing resources interpretation predicts larger age differences with any manipulation that contributes to a decrease in level of performance (Gick, Craik, & Morris, 1988), or that the age-complexity phenomenon is of little interest because it is tautological (Park, A.D. Smith, Morrell, Puglisi, & Dudley, 1990).

A necessary condition for the productive investigation of the age-complexity effect, and in particular its relation to the processing resources interpretation of age-related cognitive differences, is much more detailed information about what makes cognitive tasks complex. That is, in order for the phenomenon of larger age differences with greater task complexity to be considered convincing evidence for the involvement of processing resources, explanations should be provided for why more resources are required at high levels of complexity, and for why performance is impaired when the demands of the task exceed the resources available to the individual.

Although they do not provide direct answers to these questions, results from two recent projects nevertheless illustrate the relevance of the age-complexity phenomenon to the processing resource interpretation of cognitive age differences (Salthouse, 1988e; Salthouse, D.R. Mitchell,

Skovronek, & Babcock, 1989). Both of the projects were based on the assumptions summarized in Equation 1.

$$\text{Cognitive Performance} = f(\text{Resources},\text{Demands}) + \text{Other Determinants} \quad (1)$$

Equation 1 is obviously very crude, but it serves to emphasize two characteristics of the moderate version of the processing resources perspective. The first is that age differences are not universally expected because cognitive tasks are assumed to vary in the demands placed on the limited resources. If, for whatever reason, the demands on the resources are slight relative to the available resources, and there is a minor influence of age on the other determinants, then little or no age differences in performance might be expected. The second point evident in the assumptions represented in Equation 1 is that resources are not the exclusive source of age differences in performance because performance differences could also be attributed to non-resource or "other" determinants.

It is difficult to derive precise quantitative predictions without considerably more knowledge, or additional strong assumptions, about the interrelations among performance, resources, and task demands. Nevertheless, several qualitative predictions can be generated about the relation between performance and task demands, and the effects of age on this relation. For example, under many sets of assumptions an increase in processing demands will result in a decline in performance roughly proportional to the amount of available resources. Therefore, if increased age is associated with a reduction in the quantity of available resources, then one would expect older adults to exhibit larger decrements in performance than young adults as the processing demands became greater. This, of course, is the complexity effect already described.

The Salthouse (1988e) and Salthouse, D.R. Mitchell, Skovronek, and Babcock (1989) projects investigated the age-complexity phenomenon with quantitative variations in complexity produced by manipulating variables hypothesized to influence the number of processing operations necessary to perform the tasks. Both projects involved moderate numbers of research participants, with 100 young adults and either 40 or 100 older adults in each of two studies in the Salthouse (1988e) project, and 120 adults between 20 and 79 years of age in the Salthouse, D.R. Mitchell, Skovronek, and Babcock (1989) study. Each research participant performed at least two different cognitive tasks involving four levels of task complexity.

In the studies reported by Salthouse (1988e), the complexity manipulations consisted of varying the number of frames containing to-be-integrated line segments in a visual synthesis task, varying the number of folds prior to a display of a hole punch in a paper-folding task, and varying the number of elements or the number of transformations in two versions of a geometric analogies task. Complexity effects were assessed by computing the slope of the function relating error rate or decision time to the hypothesized number of required operations. As predicted from the processing resources perspective, older adults were found to have significantly larger complexity slopes than young adults in all 16 comparisons across the two studies, two dependent variables, and four tasks.

The study by Salthouse, D.R. Mitchell, Skovronek, and Babcock (1989) involved the administration of verbal integrative reasoning and spatial paper folding tasks to male college graduates. The two tasks (which were described in chapter 7) were structurally similar in that decisions were required after the presentation of one, two, three, or four pieces of information, with the information consisting of additional premises in the reasoning task, and additional folds of a piece of paper in the paper-folding task. In both tasks, complexity effects were assessed by the slope of the function relating decision errors to amount of information (i.e., number of premises or number of folds). These slopes had statistically significant, and nearly identical, correlations with age of .43 for the reasoning task, and .45 for the paper-folding task.

The evidence from these two projects is therefore consistent with the prediction that decrements in performance associated with additional processing demands become more pronounced with increased age. This phenomenon is not easily attributable to the operation of specific processing components because it is evident across a wide range of manipulations (e.g., involving verbal and spatial integration, transformation, and abstraction processes), and it occurs when the processing demands are varied by altering the number of times the same operation is required, and not simply by adding new operations.

A second qualitative prediction derivable from the assumptions embodied in Equation 1 is that the complexity effects from different tasks should be correlated with one another if each of the tasks makes demands on a common resource. This prediction is based on two premises. First, the magnitude of the complexity effect is hypothesized to be proportional to the quantity of available resources. And second, performance on each task is postulated to be limited by the same processing resource. It therefore follows that the performance reduction associated with additional processing demands in one task should be related to the performance reduction associated with additional processing demands in a second task. An important aspect of this prediction is that it need only be assumed that the complexity manipulations in the two tasks alter demands on a common resource, and not that task complexity is necessarily varied in the same manner.

Both of the projects described above also provide evidence relevant to this prediction. In the study in the Salthouse (1988e) project, 4 of 12 correlations (6 for young adults and 6 for older adults) between the slopes of the accuracy measures were significant, and 6 of the 12 correlations between the slopes for the time measures were significant. One factor hypothesized to be contributing to the relatively small correlations in the first study was low reliability of the slope measures. A second study was therefore designed to provide information about the reliability of the slope measures, in addition to allowing further examination of the correlation between measures. As suspected, the reliabilities of the slopes for the accuracy measures were low, averaging .19 for young adults and .43 for old adults. The reliabilities of the slopes for the decision time measures were in the moderate range, however, with averages of .70 and .76 for young and old adults, respectively. As might be expected in light of the differential reliabilities, in the second study none of the correlations between the accuracy slopes was significant, but all four (two for young adults and two for older adults) of the correlations between slopes for the time measures were significantly greater than zero.

Estimates of the reliability of the complexity slopes for the accuracy measures in the Salthouse, D.R. Mitchell, Skovronek, and Babcock (1989) study were .76 for the reasoning task and .42 for the paper folding task. The correlation between the two complexity slopes was .63, indicating that the relation between the two different complexity slopes was of about the same magnitude as the relation of each slope measure to itself.

Although the evidence is not extensive, and some of the measures are hampered by the low reliability often found with scores based on differences between observed variables, it appears that the second prediction from the processing resources perspective also has moderate support. An implication of these findings is that a common factor is apparently involved in what seem to be quite distinct cognitive tasks because, across different individuals, the amount by which performance declines as processing requirements are increased in one task is related to the amount by which performance declines as processing requirements are increased in the second task. This again is a result difficult to interpret from a perspective postulating deficits in specific processing components because it seems to imply that common factors are contributing to performance variations in different tasks, despite little apparent overlap in the identity of relevant processing components.

A third complexity-related prediction derivable from the processing resources perspective can be viewed as a combination of the first two predictions. That is, the initial assumption is that the greater performance decrements with increased task complexity reflect a smaller quantity of processing resources with increased age. The second assumption is that the same processing resources are involved across a range of different tasks. These two assumptions, together with Equation 1, therefore lead to the prediction that the resource-dependent performance of older adults should be a function of the resource-dependent performance of young adults, and of the differences in resource quantity between the two groups. The exact form of the function and its quantitative parameters will vary depending upon assumptions about how performance, processing resources, and processing demands are interrelated (e.g., Salthouse, 1985a, 1985b; 1988e). Whatever the nature of the function, however, if a major factor contributing to the existence of age differences in several cognitive tasks is a reduction in the quantity of general processing resources, then a systematic relation would be expected between the performance levels of young and old adults regardless of the identity or composition of the processing components involved in the tasks. In other words, an important determinant of the size of the age differences in many cognitive tasks is postulated to be the magnitude of the demands on a limited number of finite processing resources, and not merely the specific processes which might be affected by the manipulation of those demands. Most measures of cognitive performance are undoubtedly influenced by a variety of factors besides processing resources, and consequently they provide crude indices of the quantity of available processing resources. Furthermore, the particular combination of resource and non-resource influences is likely to vary across tasks, making systematic relations even more difficult to detect. Nevertheless, the possibility that a general relation may exist between the performance of young and old adults is sufficiently important to warrant examination, despite these and other problems that can be expected to limit the precision of the analyses.

Perhaps the simplest method of examining the prediction is to plot the performance of older adults as a function of the performance of younger adults. In other words, the time or error rate of older adults in a given experimental condition is plotted against the time or error rate of young adults in that same condition. Brinley (1965) initially expressed results from an aging study in this format for strictly empirical reasons, but the theoretical significance of these young-old plots was pointed out by Salthouse (1978a), and later elaborated by Cerella, et al., (1980), Cerella (1985, 1990), Myerson, S. Hale, Wagstaff, Poon, and G.A. Smith (1990), and Salthouse (1985a, 1985b).

A frequent finding with reaction time measures is that there is a very strong relation between the performance of young and old adults across tasks with a variety of different decision requirements. Analyses described in Salthouse (1985a, 1985b) reveal that the data from many studies can be characterized by nearly linear relations, with slopes of old times to young times ranging from about 1.2 to 2.0. Linear equations tend to represent the data reasonably well, with the r^2 values indicating that the proportions of predicted variance often exceed .95. Similar systematic relations have also been reported in meta-analyses based on mixtures of subjects, tasks, procedures, and ranges of reaction times (Cerella, 1985; Cerella, et al., 1980; S. Hale, et al., 1987; Myerson, et al., 1990), and with measures of the interval to escape backward masking (Salthouse, 1982, pp. 169-170). Attempts to determine the type of quantitative equation that best characterizes the age relations have not yet been very successful because most of the alternatives that have been investigated have each accounted for 85% or more of the variance (Cerella, 1990; Myerson, et al., 1990). At least with the data examined thus far, therefore, it appears that a variety of speculations are equally capable of describing the gross patterns of the empirical results. Greater discriminability might be possible if the data base is extended to encompass exceptions that have generally been ignored in the past (Salthouse, 1988a), and to address differences at the level of individuals rather than entire groups. Regardless of the specific form of the equation, however, it is clear that substantial relations are evident between measures of the speeded performance of young and old adults.

Most of the previous analyses, and all the meta-analyses, have focused on speeded measures of performance such as reaction time, or time to escape backward masking. The processing resources prediction is not necessarily restricted to speed measures, however, and similar systematic relations between the performance of young and old adults would be expected with any dependent measure reflecting demands on limited resources. It is more complicated to examine these relations with other dependent variables because the measures from different tasks are not necessarily comparable (e.g., what is the correspondence between a measure of percent correct decisions in a reasoning task and the number of words correctly recalled in a memory task?), and the range of meaningful performance is often restricted by artifacts of measurement floors and ceilings. Furthermore, the reliability of measures representing accuracy or quality-of-performance may be lower than that based on the same number of observations with measures of speed of performance. Despite these qualifications, the resources prediction should apply to performance measures other than speed, and thus it is of interest to determine whether systematic relations also exist between measures of performance accuracy for young and old adults.

As a means of addressing this issue, the data from the two studies in the project reported in Salthouse (1988e) are displayed in Figure 8.2. The top panels in each figure represent the relations between young and old adults on the measure of decision time, and the bottom panels represent the relations for the measure of error percentage. Notice that although the percentage of variance (r^2) accounted for by the linear equations is larger

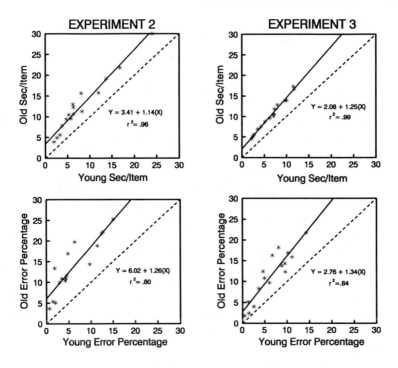

Figure 8.2.   Performance of older adults as a function of the performance of young adults in two experiments Salthouse (1988c). Data in the top two graphs represent speed of performance, and those in the bottom two graphs represent error percentage.

for the decision time measures, substantial relations between the performances of young and old adults are also present with the error percentage measures.

The implication of these relatively strong linear relations is that both the speed and the accuracy of older adults on a variety of different cognitive tasks can apparently be predicted with reasonably good precision simply by knowing the speed and accuracy of young adults on those tasks and the general relation between the performance of the two groups. No information about the specific processes presumed to be involved in any of the tasks seems to be required. Only if a data point deviates substantially from the remaining points in young-old plots such as those in Figure 8.2 would there be evidence that the processes contributing to that measure might be uniquely, or disproportionately, affected by age-related factors.

Although, in the terminology of the levels of theoretical discourse discussed in chapter 1, the age-complexity effect is only a descriptive generalization, it does suggest an alternative interpretation of many of the results previously considered as evidence for the existence of specific deficits. That is, processing components are frequently inferred to be age-sensitive because versions of a task including those components result in larger age differences than versions of the task without those components. However, if the version of the task with the components is more complex (i.e., involves more processing operations) than the version without the components, then larger age differences would be expected simply because of the tendency for age differences to be proportional to task complexity. The possibility that many of the differences attributed to specific deficits are a consequence of a more general impairment was mentioned in the discussion of reservations about the methodology of statistical interactions in the appendix of the previous chapter, and has been discussed previously by several researchers (Cerella, 1985; Cerella, et al., 1980; Crowder, 1980; Kay, 1959; Myerson, et al., 1990; Salthouse, 1978a, 1985a, 1988a).

Two attempts to use young-old plots to examine hypothesized age differences in specific components have been reported by Brinley (1965) and by McDowd and Craik (1988). Brinley was interested in determining whether there were age differences in processes related to rigidity, as measured by the speed of performing a mixture of processing operations relative to the speed of performing each of the operations separately. McDowd and Craik (1988) investigated the effects of age on divided attention processes by comparing young and old adults in their reaction times for tasks performed alone, and performed in combination. In both cases, all the relevant data appeared to fall along the same function relating the performance of older adults to the performance of young adults. The same conclusion was therefore reached in the two projects—namely, that the effects of the manipulations were consistent with an increase in overall task complexity, and not with a specific age-related impairment.

More analyses like these should probably be conducted in the future because the existence of a systematic relation between the performance of young and old adults makes it desirable that results that are hypothesized to reflect a specific processing deficit be evaluated in the context of the overall pattern of performance differences. Analyses in the future should also rely upon accepted statistical procedures to determine whether the equations characterizing the relations between the performance of young and old adults across different sets of data are significantly different from one another. This could be accomplished either by direct contrasts of the statistical significance of the difference in the parameters derived from alternative equations, or by determining whether the original equation must be significantly altered to accomodate the results from the new conditions. Regardless of the particular evaluation method employed, the role of subjective factors influencing interpretations would be minimized by using an objective criterion as the basis for inferring that certain data deviate from the general pattern.

To summarize, although the amount of relevant evidence is still small, that which is available seems to indicate that: (a) age differences in cognitive performance tend to be larger when more processing operations are required; (b) there are significant correlations between the magnitude of the performance differences associated with additional processing operations across several different tasks; and (c) across a relatively wide range of cognitive tasks and measures of performance, the average performance of older adults is predicted moderately well by the average performance of young adults. Although no single result is definitive by itself, this combination of results appears quite consistent with the assumptions of the processing resources perspective, and hence can be considered important evidence in support of that perspective.

INVESTIGATING THE PROCESSING RESOURCES PERSPECTIVE

One of the most controversial aspects of the processing resources perspective is whether, and if so, how, hypotheses related to processing resources can be investigated. The research on the age-complexity phenomenon described above represents one method of examining the implications of the processing resources perspective, but additional investigative procedures are clearly needed to provide a more complete evaluation. Four categories of research that have been, or could be, considered relevant to the investigation of the processing resources perspective are discussed in this section. The first consists of suggestions, which although plausible, do not appear to represent necessary implications of the processing resources view. The second is comprised of speculations about the reasons increased age is associated with a reduction in processing resources. Techniques based on experimental manipulations of processing resources are discussed in the third category, and finally the logic underlying attempts to use statistical control procedures is described.

Potentially Misleading "Predictions"

An initial step in the investigation of any theoretical perspective is the identification of predictions or implications of the perspective. In order for the predictions to be treated seriously, however, it should first be established that they do indeed follow from reasonable sets of assumptions. This requirement is particularly important in the case of the processing resources perspective because some of the implications purported to be derived from resource theories appear to have been based on overly simplistic or naive conceptualizations of the processing resources perspective.

One unrealistic "prediction" is the claim that if a general factor such as processing resources is postulated, then age differences favoring young adults should be expected on every measure of cognitive performance. In other words, it is sometimes argued that the existence of a general factor implies that there should be across-the-board, or universal, declines in every possible measure of cognitive performance. However, this argument is plausible only if one adopts an extreme view in which processing resources are assumed to affect all processing components, and are the exclusive determinant of the age differences in most cognitive tasks. As mentioned earlier in this chapter, a more reasonable position appears to be that processing resources may be relevant to many but not all processing components, and that there are other determinants of age differences in cognitive functioning besides limitations in processing resources.

A related, and also somewhat misleading, prediction is the idea that if many processes are influenced by a common factor, then all variables based on those processes should exhibit identical magnitudes or rates of age-related changes. Although this expectation may seem plausible, the prediction of equivalent rates of decline does not necessarily follow from the processing resources perspective because variables may differ in their degree of dependence on the common factor. That is, if there is a range in the extent to which performance measures are dependent upon a common resource, then there will almost certainly be variation in the rate and degree to which reductions in that resource are manifested in different measures.

Another interpretation of the processing resources perspective that does not inevitably follow is the claim that if many measures of cognitive performance are influenced by declines in a single factor, then those measures should be more closely related to one another in old age than during young adulthood. The problem with this prediction is that while a reduction in resources should contribute to lower levels of performance, there may be no reason to expect that the resource reduction would also alter the relative orderings of individuals on the relevant measures. Only if one made the additional assumption that there were large individual differences in either the rate, or the magnitude, of resource reduction would the processing resources perspective necessarily lead to an expectation of an age-related change in the magnitude of the correlations among variables. That is, correlations among resource-dependent performance measures might increase if resources declined by varying amounts in different individuals. However, since this additional assumption is not intrinsic to the processing resources perspective, predictions about changes in correlations with age should not be considered necessary or strong implications of the processing resources view.

Investigation of the Age-Resource Linkage

A question of obvious importance to the processing resources perspective is how the hypothesized age differences in processing resources originate. Most of the discussion of this topic in the research literature has not focused on whether the distal source of the reduction in resources is endogenous or exogenous, but rather on the proximal nature of the diminished resources. In this sense the issue of the nature of the resource reduction appears to be at or beyond the boundary of the discipline of psychology because processing resources are frequently viewed as an explanatory primitive, not further decomposable in terms of psychological concepts. Some type of limited reductionism, in which certain concepts are considered primitives in the discipline, seems necessary in order to avoid traps of circularity (in which the same phenomena are merely relabeled), and infinite regress (in which a satisfactory explanation is never achieved because progressively more primitive explanations are continuously introduced).

A variety of speculations about the proximal nature of resource reductions have been proposed, but most seem to share two characteristics. First, they are invariably quite abstract, in that they are seldom accompanied by citations of relevant neurophysiological evidence. And second, each can be considered to be broadly consistent with general age trends. Examples of such speculations are the ideas that age-related deficits might be attributable to losses of cortical tissue (Craik, 1982), a decline in glucose utilization (Craik, 1986), lower levels of systemic arousal or activation (Salthouse, 1988c), slower rates of propagation of activation (Salthouse, 1988c), less efficient transmission of information across successive neural steps (Myerson, et al., 1990), a reduction in the number of processing nodes or units that can be active simultaneously (Salthouse, 1988c; J.C. Thomas, et al., 1977), losses in synaptic density (Birren, Woods, & M.V. Williams, 1979), and decreased levels of neural connectivity (Cerella, 1990; Greene, 1983).

Although few researchers would deny the potential importance of efforts to specify the proximal nature of processing resources, opinions differ dramatically concerning the status of current speculations, and the direction for future behavioral research on this topic. For example, consider the contrasting positions expressed by Cerella (1990) and Salthouse (1988e) concerning age-resource relations. On the one hand, Cerella claimed that the speculations and data "... match exactly, qualitatively and quantitatively" (p. 219). Salthouse (1988e), on the other hand, suggested that the speculations and results were only "... compatible ... to at least a first degree of approximation" (p. 11). With respect to future priorities, Cerella argued that "What is wanting at this stage is not more data, but further consideration of the existing data" (p. 209). In contrast, Salthouse (1988c) suggested that "... it is impossible to derive precise predictions without making many unsubstantiated assumptions ... [and consequently what is needed is] ... additional research focused on the discovery of the mechanisms responsible for performance in specific cognitive tasks" (p. 14).

It is difficult in light of these rather dramatic differences of opinion to predict how future research on this topic will differ from that conducted in the past. The questions of why and how processing resources decline with increased age are extremely important, however, and thus it is desirable that research on this subject continue. Even if behavioral research is unable to identify the distal determinants of the proximal neurological or physiological concomitants of processing resources, more precise specification of the nature of processing resources, and how they are related to age, is likely to provide constraints on the range of viable explanations at both the proximal and distal levels.

Experimental Manipulation of Processing Resources

One of the most powerful methods of investigating the processing resources perspective is through experimental manipulation of the quantity of processing resources. Unfortunately it is difficult to achieve this degree of control because it is usually assumed that the quantity of processing resources is a relatively stable, trait-like characteristic of an individual, and is therefore likely to be resistant to modification. Two strategies have nevertheless been proposed that are relevant to the experimental manipulation ideal. Both strategies involve altering the resource requirements of the task or experimental situation, and thus are similar to the procedures used to investigate the age-complexity effect, in which all levels of the experimental manipulation are presented to adults of all ages. The procedures are more specific to the experimental investigation of processing resources, however, when tasks with higher resource demands are only administered to young adults (simulation strategy), or when tasks with lower resource demands are only administered to older adults (minimization-of-influence strategy).

The simulation strategy attempts to simulate or mimic the hypothesized resource limitation of older adults in a sample of young adults. If the simulation manipulation is successful, one would expect the performance of the young adults under the simulated conditions of reduced resources to be similar to that of older adults under normal conditions. However, because there are a great many ways in which quantitative levels of performance can be altered, results from attempted simulations are seldom very convincing unless the same qualitative pattern of preserved and impaired processes is evident among young adults in the conditions of simulated reduced resources, and among older adults under normal conditions. That is, it is not sufficient merely to demonstrate that the performance of young adults is impaired by a given manipulation, but it should also be demonstrated that the configuration of processes that are and are not affected by the manipulation resembles that normally found in contrasts of older adults with young adults. Furthermore, in order to provide the greatest amount of information, the processes should not vary only along a single continuum because the "qualitative" profile might then merely be a reflection of quantitative variations in processing demands or complexity.

An important assumption of the simulation strategy is that the consequences of a lower level of resources are the same regardless of the developmental history. In other words, it must be assumed that there have not been any long-term adjustments to the gradual loss of resources by older adults. If there has been an adaptation to the progressive loss of processing resources, such that older adults have gradually modified the way in which they perform certain activities, then the attempted simulation will likely be unsuccessful even though the original cause of the age differences in the relevant measures of cognitive performance may have been a reduction in processing resources.

A second strategy related to the experimental manipulation of resource quantity consists of attempting to minimize the influence of the critical resource among older adults. If the conditions of the task can be modified to reduce the dependence on the critical processing resource, then one might expect the performance of older adults to improve to a level closer to the normal level of younger adults. An example of this strategy might be allowing notes to be made during a problem-solving task (Arenberg, 1968b, 1974, 1988; E.D. Hybertson, et al., 1982; Jerome, 1962). This manipulation doesn't alter the quantity of resources related to an individual's working memory, but it may reduce the influence of that resource by eliminating the requirement that all intermediate products be stored internally. Another example of the minimization-of-influence strategy is what Craik (1986) has referred to as *environmental support* in memory. In his words, "... the provision of orienting tasks or retrieval cues does not inject processing resources into the system, and so these manipulations are better described as providing environmental support" (p. 413). To the extent that tasks providing environmental support require fewer processing resources than those without such support, one would expect age differences to be minimized because the reduced requirements are more likely to be within the capacities of older adults.

The likelihood that the minimization-of-influence strategy will be successful depends on the extent to which the experimental manipulation reduces all the influence of the relevant resource. If the manipulation affects only a few resource-dependent processing components, then it should probably not be expected to eliminate all the consequences of diminished resources. Unfortunately, both experimental manipulation strategies are hampered by lack of knowledge about the nature of processing resources, and about the mechanisms by which they influence the level of cognitive performance. Much more information is therefore needed concerning how resource quantity affects efficiency of cognitive processing in order to design appropriate minimization-of-influence manipulations or reduced-resource simulations.

Statistical Control of Processing Resources

Another approach to the investigation of the processing resources perspective consists of attempts to combine the two critical relations—that between increased age and diminished resources, and that between diminished resources and impairments of cognitive performance. This approach involves using statistical procedures to determine the proportion of the age differences in the measures of cognitive performance that can be accounted for by controlling, or adjusting for, the age differences associated with indices of processing resources.

The logic underlying these comparisons can be clarified by reference to Figure 8.3, in which the three primary constructs—age, cognitive performance, and processing resources—are represented by overlapping circles. The area of a circle corresponds to the total variance associated with that construct, and the regions of overlap indicate the proportions of common or shared variance. Of particular interest from the processing resources perspective are the relative sizes of the regions designated c and b because these correspond to the variance common to age and cognition that is, or is not, respectively, associated with processing resources. In other words, the sum of b and c corresponds to the variance shared between age and cognitive performance, and the ratio of c to b+c indicates the proportion of the variance common to age and cognitive performance that is also associated with processing resources.

One method of estimating the relative contribution of processing resources to age differences in cognitive performance involves the following four steps. First, the variance shared by age and cognition but not by

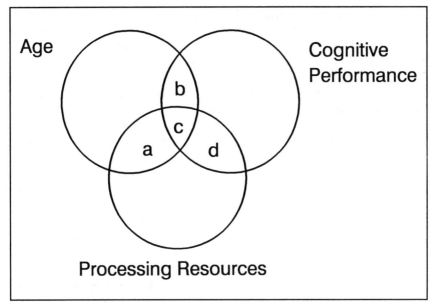

Figure 8.3.   Schematic illustration of the relations among the variance of age, measures of cognitive performance, and measures of processing resources.

processing resources (i.e., region b) is computed by determining the increment in R^2 in predicting cognitive performance from age after the variance associated with processing resources (region c) has been removed or controlled. Second, the total variance common to age and cognition (regions b and c) is determined by squaring the correlation between age and the measure of cognitive performance. Next, the proportion of the common variance not shared with processing resources (i.e., b/[b+c]) is estimated by dividing the first value by the second value. And finally, the proportion of the shared age-cognition variance also common to processing resources (i.e., c/[b+c]) is derived by taking the complement of the third value (i.e., 1-[b/(b+c)] = [(b+c)-b]/(b+c) = c/[b+c]).

This sequence of steps has been described in detail because analyses are sometimes reported in the context of investigations of resource hypotheses that appear to have little or no relevance to the processing resources interpretation. For example, a discovery that an index of processing resources accounts for a significant proportion of the variance in cognitive performance after the variance associated with age has already been accounted for is informative about the region labeled d, but not about regions b or c. Furthermore, comparisons of the magnitudes of the age-cognition (b+c) and resource-cognition (c+d) relations are not directly relevant to the issue of how much of the age-cognition relation is common to, and perhaps mediated by, processing resources (i.e., c relative to b+c).

An important requirement of these kinds of statistical-control analyses is that the assessments of the cognitive performance and processing resource constructs are both reliable and valid. Reliability can be evaluated with conventional methods of determining the consistency and stability of measurement. However, validity of hypothetical constructs such as processing resources can often be evaluated only by examining correlations among measures presumed to represent the same construct. It is therefore highly desirable that investigations relying upon statistical control procedures incorporate multiple measures of the hypothesized processing resources. The existence of multiple measures allows two potentially informative correlational analyses. On one hand, if the measures do not have moderately high correlations with one another then they may not represent the same construct, and thus reductions in the magnitude of the age-cognition relation could not be easily interpreted in terms of the influence of a single processing resources construct. On the other hand, if the correlations among measures are relatively high, then not only can one be more confident that they are measuring the same theoretical construct, but the assessment of that construct can also be expected to be more precise and reliable than when the assessment is based on single variables.

An assumption of most statistical control procedures is that there are linear relations between both age and resource quantity, and resource quantity and cognitive performance. Results from the procedures may therefore be misleading if the actual relations among these constructs are not linear. Some information about the nature of the relevant functions can often be derived from inspection of the data, but only if it is further assumed that there are linear relations between the unobservable resource quantity and the measures used to index that quantity (see the discussion of the process-variable relation in the appendix of chapter 7).

A second assumption critical to the statistical-control-of-resources technique is that a given level of resources has the same effect on cognitive performance regardless of the developmental history. This is essentially the same assumption discussed earlier in the context of the strategy of simulating reduced resources. Both procedures must assume that resources at their peak in young adulthood and resources that may have declined across the adult years, if the current levels are equivalent, produce identical effects on cognitive performance. Little or no adaptation to the gradually diminishing resources must therefore have occurred such that the consequences of having a particular level of resources are different at different ages.

Although not an assumption, another important requirement for the meaningful analysis of correlations, which is the basis for virtually all statistical control procedures, is a moderately large sample of relevant observations. No absolute minimum number of research participants can be specified, but results from studies with less than approximately 100 individuals may be of little value in attempting to derive accurate estimates of the proportion of variance attributable to different combinations of factors.

What are Processing Resources?

All the procedures currently available for the investigation of the processing resources interpretation seem to require considerable information before any results from those procedures could be unambiguously interpreted. Two issues appear to be of crucial importance. These concern the vagueness of the resource construct (i.e., What is it?), and ambiguity of the mechanisms (i.e., How do variations in processing resources affect cognitive performance?).

No definite answers can yet be provided to these fundamental issues because of the uncertainty about the exact nature of processing resources. It may nevertheless be possible to sharpen or refine speculations about the nature of the processing resources construct by examining different conceptualizations of processing resources. Salthouse (1985b, 1988c, 1988d, 1988e) suggested that most discussions of processing resources can be classified into three categories based on the dominant metaphor used for conceptualizing processing resources. These metaphors view resources as related to (a) limitations of time, in the form of rate of processing; (b) limitations of space, in the form of restrictions on working memory capacity; and (c) limitations of energy, in the form of attentional capacity. The following sections examine the speculations and evidence relevant to each of these ways of thinking about processing resources as they might contribute to age differences in cognitive functioning.

SPEED AS A PROCESSING RESOURCE

The notion that adult age differences in cognitive performance might be related to the speed with which an individual can carry out information-processing operations is not a single well-defined hypothesis, but is more appropriately considered as an assemblage of loosely related ideas. That is, many different assumptions are possible, and various combinations of assumptions lead to quite different predictions and interpretations. Perhaps the closest to a consensus position is the claim that: Slowing of all or some processes, by the same or varying amounts, due to one or several factors, affects a few or most cognitive tasks. The qualifications, of course, refer to alternative assumptions that have been, or could be, adopted in postulating that the speed of information processing is a potentially important determinant of age differences in cognitive performance. However, nearly all proponents of a speed-based interpretation seem to agree that more rapid execution of cognitive operations allows more, and possibly better, processing to be carried out. It is for this reason that the rate at which processing operations can be executed may be viewed as analogous to a processing resource.

One of the unique features of speed from the processing resource perspective is the idea that it might be productively conceptualized as an independent variable in addition to its more traditional usage as a dependent variable. This suggestion, originally introduced by Birren (1956, 1964, 1965, 1970, 1974), is based on the assumption that the world is not static, and that the information within it does not remain stable. Instead it is postulated that the environment is constantly changing such that information sometimes becomes obsolete, and that there is frequently a decrease in availability of information over time because of factors such as decay or displacement. Impairments in performance may therefore result from a slower rate of processing information if the products of early processing are lost during the execution of later processing. Some of the implications of a slower rate of processing have been explored more systematically, albeit very abstractly, by examining the consequences of altered rates of the propagation of activation in the form of a simple network simulation by Salthouse (1985b, 1988c).

A number of more concrete speculations have been offered concerning the possible consequences of different rates of processing information. For example, within the domain of memory it has been suggested that slower processing will result in shallower or less elaborate encoding of to-be-remembered information (Salthouse, 1980; Salthouse & Kail, 1983; Waugh & Barr, 1980; Wingfield, 1980; Wingfield & Stine, 1989), and lower levels of many types of mnemonic organization (Kirchner, 1958; Salthouse, 1980). There is also some evidence indicating that increased age is associated with a slower rate of rehearsal of information (Salthouse, 1980; R.E. Sanders, et al., 1980), a slower rate of scanning or retrieving information (Anders & Fozard, 1973; Anders, Fozard, & Lillyquist, 1972; Blumenthal & Madden, 1988; Eriksen, Hamlin, & Daye, 1973; Ford, Roth, Mohs, Hopkins, & Kopell, 1979; Madden, 1982, 1983; Madden, Blumenthal, P.A. Allen, & C.F. Emery, 1989; Madden & Nebes, 1980; Marsh, 1975; Plude & W.J. Hoyer, 1981; Plude, W.J. Hoyer, & Lazar, 1982; Puglisi, 1986; Salthouse & Somberg, 1982a, 1982b; Strayer, Wickens, & Braune, 1987; J.C. Thomas, Waugh, & Fozard, 1978), and longer time to access abstract codes (Guttentag & Madden, 1987; Lorsbach & Simpson, 1984, 1988; Madden, et al., 1989; Mueller, et al., 1980; Petros, et al., 1983).

Slower rates of processing have also been related to other cognitive phenomena. For example, difficulties in divided attention have been attributed to slower alternation between simultaneous activities (Talland, 1967, 1968), and problems in comprehension have been linked to slower rates of perceiving, accessing, and integrating new and stored information (Birren & Riegel, 1962; G. Cohen, 1979; Salthouse & Kail, 1983; Spilich, 1985; Stine, Wingfield, & Poon, 1986). There has also been speculation that slower processing may affect higher-order cognitive processes by reducing the likelihood that higher levels of integration and abstraction dependent upon the completion of earlier processing will ever be achieved (Alpaugh & Birren, 1977; Birren, 1955, 1964, 1974; Birren & Riegel, 1962; Bromley, 1967; Fozard & J.C. Thomas, 1975; Heron & Chown, 1967; H.E. Jones, 1956; Salthouse, 1982, 1985b, 1988c; Witt & W.R. Cunningham, 1979).

With few exceptions, the preceding arguments have relied upon appeals to plausibility rather than upon empirical evidence as the basis for persuasion. While many of the suggestions seem reasonable, the viability of the proposals will ultimately be determined by the amount and consistency of empirical support. It is for this reason that it is important to examine and evaluate the available evidence relevant to the speed version of the processing resources perspective.

Results from Experimental Manipulations

Very few studies have employed an experimental manipulation to investigate the possibility that speed or rate of processing might function as a processing resource. One study which attempted to simulate the effects of a slower rate of processing in a sample of young adults was reported by Salthouse (1980). The rationale in this study was that if a primary determinant of memory performance is the rate at which the relevant information can be rehearsed, and if the rate of rehearsal can be modified by increasing the number of syllables in the to-be-remembered words, then young adults might be expected to perform in a manner similar to older adults when they are required to remember words with a greater number of syllables. Both young adults and older adults were found to be slower at rapidly naming three-syllable words compared to one-syllable words, and thus there was some evidence that the number-of-syllables manipulation was successful in altering rate of rehearsal. As expected, overall level of recall was lower for older adults than for young adults, and both groups remembered more one-syllable words than three-syllable words. The qualitative patterns were also similar in that the serial position functions (i.e., primacy, recency, and asymptote segments) for young versus old age groups with one-syllable words differed in the same manner as did the serial position functions for young adults with one-syllable words versus three-syllable words.

Although the results from the Salthouse (1980) study were consistent with the expectations from the speed-of-processing interpretation, it seems unlikely that manipulations of the number of syllables in a word will prove to be an effective means of simulating the effects of a slower rate of processing in a very wide range of situations. Number of rehearsals is only one of the factors influencing memory performance, and other factors (e.g., organization, formation of associations, etc.) may be independent of the number of syllables in the to-be-remembered units.

Several authors have implied that the influence of a slower rate of processing should be minimized by increasing the duration of stimulus presentation, or by allowing more time for responding (D.M. Burke & L.L. Light, 1981; G. Cohen, 1979, 1981; Craik & Rabinowitz, 1984, 1985; Rabinowitz, 1989b; E. Simon, 1979). However, it is difficult to imagine that more than a few processing components would be affected by these manipulations, and therefore it is not clear that the performance of older adults should be expected to reach the performance level of young adults with alterations in stimulus duration or response interval even if rate of processing were the only factor responsible for the age differences. For example, increasing the duration of stimulus presentation would probably increase the likelihood that the stimulus was accurately registered, but it is not obvious that it would also alter the rate at which the material could be rehearsed, or the number of associations, elaborations, or alternative organizations that could be formed. In fact, if young adults are faster than older adults at these other processes, then extending the duration of stimulus presentation should allow them to execute more of the processes between each successive stimulus, and thus young adults would actually be expected to derive greater performance benefits with slower rates of presentation than older adults (e.g., Salthouse, 1988c).

Unfortunately, an unambiguous method of minimizing the influence of a slower rate of processing on cognitive performance does not yet appear to be available. Use of the minimization-of-influence strategy for investigating the speed version of the processing resources perspective will, therefore, probably have to be postponed until there is better understanding of the nature, and the consequences, of age-related slowing.

How Should Processing Speed be Assessed?

The central construct in the hypothesis that a slower rate of processing with increased age contributes to age differences in cognitive performance is obviously speed, or rate, of processing. It is therefore imperative for the effective investigation of this version of the processing resources perspective that appropriate measures of processing speed be identified.

Many researchers have relied upon measures of perceptual or clerical speed to assess an individual's rate of processing. Although plausible arguments can be made that these measures might be reasonable reflections of the average speed of executing cognitive operations (e.g., Bromley, 1974; Hertzog, 1989; Salthouse, 1985b), they are indirect, and probably impure, indices of the hypothesized rate-of-processing construct. That is, the theoretically most interesting aspect of rate of processing is the minimum time required to execute a variety of different internal cognitive operations, and not the input (sensory) and output (motor) times associated with perceiving and responding to materials. Because these latter processes are usually included in perceptual speed measures, it may be misleading to use the phrase "cognitive slowing" (Hertzog, 1989; Schaie & Hertzog, 1983) to refer to results from perceptual speed measures unless there is evidence that most of the age-related variance in those measures primarily reflects the duration of relevant cognitive processes, and not the contributions of the theoretically less interesting peripheral processes.

Researchers attempting to select an appropriate measure of processing speed in the context of age-comparative research are currently confronted by a paradox. On the one hand, there are many reports of systematic relations between the average speeds of groups of young and old adults across a wide range of experimental tasks (Bashore, Osman, & Heffley, 1989; Cerella, 1985, 1990; Cerella, Poon & Fozard, 1981; Cerella, et al., 1980, 1981; Charness & J.I.D. Campbell, 1988; S. Hale, et al., 1987; Madden, 1984, 1986b, 1988, 1989; McDowd & Craik, 1988; Myerson, et al., 1990; Puglisi, 1986; Salthouse, 1982, 1985a, 1985b, 1987d; Salthouse & Somberg, 1982a). The various studies have differed with respect to the specific values of the parameters relating the times of young and old adults, but they are quite consistent in finding high correlations (often greater than .9) between speed measures in the two groups. The existence of these orderly relations seems to imply that almost any speeded measure will suffice as an index of speed of processing because a large number of measures can apparently be characterized in terms of the same quantitative function.

On the other hand, if all speed measures represent the same construct, then one might expect them to be highly correlated with one another. Only a few age-comparative studies have reported correlations among speeded measures (Birren, et al., 1962; Laux & Lane, 1985; Madden, 1989; Salthouse, 1988e; D.A. Walsh, 1982), but the dominant finding in most of these studies has been that a relatively small amount of the reliable variance associated with each variable is shared with other variables presumed to assess the same construct. This may be a reflection of the existence of several somewhat independent speed factors (Bashore, et al., 1989; Birren, 1965; Birren, et al., 1979; Hertzog, 1989; Hertzog, Raskind,

& Cannon, 1986; Salthouse, 1985b; Strayer, et al., 1987; Welford, 1962; N. White & W.R. Cunningham, 1987), or it may simply mean that each measure is influenced by specific determinants in addition to the common speed factor. In either case, however, the lack of high intercorrelations among measures postulated to reflect speed of processing clearly presents problems for the measurement of the speed construct, and hence also for the investigation of the implications of the speed version of the processing resources hypothesis.

A worthy goal for future research would be to determine the interrelations among various measures used to index speed of processing both within, and across, age groups. Results from factor-analytic procedures in conjunction with age-complexity analyses in the form of young-old plots might then be used to determine the number of distinct speed factors involved in age-related slowing, and to identify the best measures of each factor. Both of these kinds of analyses were reported by Brinley (1965), but the speeded tasks in his project were all very similar and the first factor in the factor analysis accounted for more than five times as much variance as did any other factor in the data of both young and old adults. Outcomes of the analyses are likely to prove more informative if a greater diversity of speeded tasks were included so that several major factors could be identified in the factor analyses, and young-old regression equations could then be contrasted for the measures contributing to each factor.

Statistical Control of Speed

Several analyses have been reported in which relations between age and assorted cognitive measures have been examined before and after the statistical control of one or more measures of speed. A mixture of methods and measures has been employed, but a representative overview of both the variety of procedures and the range of results can be provided by considering three projects.

The first project, conducted by J.L. Horn (1982; J.L. Horn, et al., 1981), involved the administration of a collection of paper-and-pencil tests to two samples of 105 and 147 male prison inmates between 20 and 60 years of age. Cognitive performance was assessed by means of a composite of scores on matrices, letter series, and paper-folding tests; speed was measured by performance on clerical comparison or matching tasks, and by the time to solve various items from the cognitive tests. This latter measure may not be very meaningful as an index of processing speed, however, because it is likely to be influenced by factors such as ability and personal style, particularly when the primary emphasis in the task is on the accuracy of performance, rather than its speed.

Correlations between age and the clerical-perceptual speed measures in the two samples were -.41 and -.23, and the age-cognition correlations were -.20 and -.27, respectively. The speed-cognition correlations were .29 in the first sample and .31 in the second sample. J.L. Horn, et al. (1981) converted these values into estimated IQ units (scaled to a mean of 100 and a standard deviation of 15) of decline per decade, and estimated that the cognition decline was 3.19 IQ points per decade in one study, and 4.93 IQ points per decade in the other study. These values were reduced to 1.47 and 3.80, respectively, by using semi-partial correlation procedures to control for clerical-perceptual speed. It can therefore be inferred that 53.9% (i.e., [(3.19-1.47)/3.19]X100) and 22.9% (i.e., [(4.93-3.80)/4.93]X100) of the age differences in fluid measures of cognition were associated with age-related reductions in speed in the two studies.

The second project reporting analyses of the contribution of speed of processing to age differences in measures of cognitive performance was reported by Salthouse, Kausler, and Saults (1988b). Two samples of 129 and 233 adults between 20 and 79 years of age performed a battery of computer-controlled cognitive tasks. Among the tasks were series completion and geometric analogies reasoning tasks, paper folding and perceptual closure tasks, and paired associate learning tasks. The measures of speed of performance were median time to make digit symbol substitution decisions and median time to make number-comparison decisions. The speed measures had correlations with age of between .30 and .56, and the cognitive measures had an average correlation with age of approximately -.30.

Path analysis procedures were used to estimate the direct and indirect, or speed-mediated, effects of age on the measures of cognitive performance. The median absolute path coefficients for the indirect influence of digit-symbol speed on the relation between age and measures of cognitive performance was .09, and that for the indirect influence of number-comparison speed was .04. The ratio of indirect effects to total effects yields estimates that 32.1% (digit symbol) or 13.3% (number comparison) of the overall age differences in the measures of cognitive performance were associated with age differences in speed.

The most recent analysis of the contribution of speed factors to age differences in cognitive functioning was reported by Hertzog (1989). His data were based on the administration of a battery of paper-and-pencil cognitive tests to 592 adults between 43 and 78 years of age. Processing speed was assessed by paper-and-pencil tests of perceptual speed (e.g., Number Comparison, Identical Pictures, and Finding As), and also by measures of the time to transfer answers from the test form to the answer sheet.

Hertzog used hierarchical regression analyses and commonality analyses to estimate the effects of age and speed on cognitive performance. Based on the percentages of variance associated with age before and after control of the two speed indices, it can be inferred that statistical control of the speed variables reduced the age-related variance in cognitive performance by an average of 92.2%, with a range of 84.6% to 97.5%. These are obviously much higher values than those obtained in the other studies described, but they are in the range of those obtained (see Figure 2.15) in a very similar study by Schaie (1989c). A possible reason for these unusually high estimates of the role of perceptual speed in the age differences in the Hertzog (1989) and Schaie (1989c) studies is that all the cognitive measures in both projects were derived from speeded tests with brief time limits and low levels of item difficulty.

Several smaller-scale analyses have also been reported in which contributions of speed to age differences in cognition have been examined (Charness, 1987; J.T. Hartley, 1986, 1988; Salthouse, 1988e; see also the analyses reported in Salthouse, 1985b, using the Digit Symbol Substitution measure as the index of processing speed). However, the studies described above contain some of the largest samples, and illustrate the approximate range of outcomes, that have been reported. In general, the results of these studies seem to provide moderate support for the hypothesis that age differences in speed of processing are responsible for at least some of the age differences in cognitive tasks. The magnitude of the speed contribution appears to vary as a function of the nature of the cognitive measures (e.g., speed vs. power assessments), and according to the means by which processing speed was assessed. From 13% to 54% of the age-related variance may be attributable to speed factors for many cognitive measures, and up to 90% or more for measures from highly speeded tests containing items for which few errors would be likely to occur if unlimited time were available.

WORKING MEMORY AS A PROCESSING RESOURCE

Working memory is distinguished from other related memory concepts primarily because of its presumed role in a variety of cognitive tasks. As Baddeley (1986) put it, "The essence of the concept of working memory lies in its implication that memory processes play an important role in non-memory tasks" (p. 246). Unlike short-term or primary memory, therefore, working memory is of interest largely because it is explicitly hypothesized to be an important factor contributing to success in other cognitive tasks.

An informative description of the potential influence of working memory limitations was provided by Charness (1985b) in the context of mental multiplication. He suggested that working memory limitations become readily apparent when one tries to multiply two-digit numbers mentally, using neither paper and pencil or any calculating devices. The difficulty in such problems is not attributable to any particular step in the procedure, but it occurs because the combined storage and processing requirements exceed the capacities of working memory.

This notion is elaborated in Figure 8.4, which illustrates the sequence of steps, and intermediate products, that might be involved in trying to multiply 78 by 78 mentally. Notice that although the operations at each step can be easily accomplished, the problem as a whole is difficult because of the long sequence of steps that have to be executed while temporarily storing intermediate results. Contrasting the total problem with the subproblem of 8x78, represented by the first 5 steps, reveals at least three aspects that increase as the problem becomes more complex: (a) the number of processing operations (i.e., the number of entries in the left column); (b) the amount of information temporarily stored (i.e., the number of entries in the right column); and (c) the number of exchanges between, or coordinating steps of, storage and processing (i.e., the number of arrows between columns). As will be seen in the subsequent discussion, each of these aspects or dimensions has been proposed as a possible source of adult age differences in working memory.

It is apparent in the example in Figure 8.4 that older adults would be expected to have great difficulty with mental computation problems if there is a decrease with age in one or more of these aspects of working memory. In fact, two studies have reported that, as might be suspected from the analysis just described, age differences in mental arithmetic do appear to be related to limitations of working memory. An experiment by R.E. Wright (1981) found that young and old adults did not differ when arithmetic problems were presented visually, but that older adults made more errors than young adults when one or both numbers in the problem were presented auditorily, and hence more reliance had to be placed on working memory. Foos (1989) presented three problems involving pairs of two-digit numbers, and ensured working memory involvement by requiring all three problems to be solved before reporting the solutions to any of them. Older adults were generally less accurate than young adults, and there was also an interaction between age and serial position, with age differences greatest on the middle problem in the series. Foos interpreted the interaction as indicating a loss of information from working memory, but it might also reflect a tendency for older individuals to ignore the presentation of the second problem while they were trying to solve the first problem. Regardless of how the interaction in the Foos experiment is interpreted, however, the results from both the R.E. Wright (1981) and

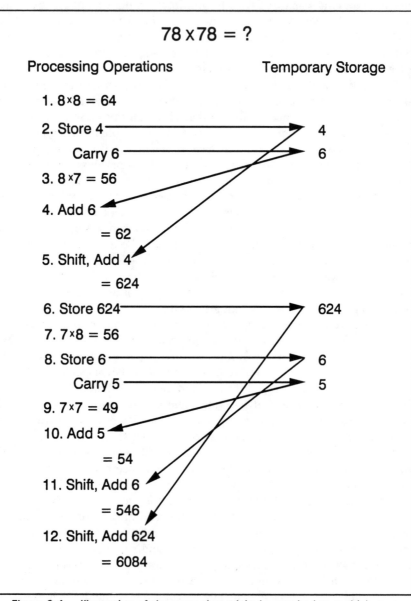

Figure 8.4. Illustration of the steps that might be required to multiply two numbers mentally.

Foos (1989) experiments seem consistent in suggesting that working memory factors contribute to the age differences in mental arithmetic.

Working memory factors have also been implicated in the age differences in a variety of other cognitive tasks. For example, Welford (1958, 1962, 1980) has been a strong advocate of the view that limitations on the ability to hold information while performing other mental operations is a major factor responsible for age differences in many measures of cognitive functioning. At various times he has suggested that it might be a key determinant of age differences in perceptual-motor skills (1958), learning and problem solving (1958), abstraction (1962), and thinking and fluid intelligence (1980). Arguments for the importance of working memory factors in age differences in language comprehension have also been outlined by G. Cohen (1988), Hasher and Zacks (1988), and L.L. Light (1990). Although the speculations have been plausible, very few studies have been conducted in which the age differences in cognitive functioning have been directly linked to age differences in working memory (but see chapter 7 for a review of some relevant research).

Results from Experimental Manipulations

Although there have been several attempts to simulate the effects of a smaller working memory capacity in young adults, and to minimize the influence of reductions in working memory in older adults, the results have not been very informative because of the lack of distinctive qualitative patterns that could be compared. That is, while several manipulations that result in quantitative variations in the absolute level of performance have been reported, detailed comparisons of the qualitative pattern of spared and impaired performance generally have not been conducted. It is therefore impossible on the basis of these studies to determine whether the shifts in performance observed in one group of adults across various levels of an experimental manipulation are attributable to the same processes hypothesized to distinguish the performance of young adults from that of older adults.

At least two studies have relied upon concurrent memory loads to simulate the effects of reduced working memory capacity in young adults. Both R.E. Wright (1981) and Morris, Gick, and Craik (1988) compared errors in reasoning when the reasoning task was performed alone, and when it was performed while also remembering a set of unrelated digits. As expected, performance was generally lower in both young and old adults with the concurrent memory load than without. However, in neither case were comparisons of qualitative patterns across age groups and concurrent memory load conditions very informative because results were reported from only two sentence types in Morris, et al. (1988), and in the R.E.

Wright (1981) study the performance measures were probably not very reliable because each research participant received only four trials with each of four sentence types.

How Should Working Memory be Assessed?

Working memory is a complex entity, and the optimal manner in which to assess it clearly depends on the particular aspect of working memory assumed to be most important for either the relations between age and working memory, or for those between working memory and cognition. As noted earlier, working memory can be conceptualized as involving requirements of storage, processing, and coordination. Each of these has been proposed by one or more investigators as a primary source of age differences in working memory. Parkinson (1982), for example, claimed that "... much of the literature on memory in the aged is explicable in terms of a reduction in storage capacity as indexed by digit span" (p. 90). In support of this assertion, Parkinson and his colleagues (Inman & Parkinson, 1983; Parkinson, 1982; Parkinson, et al., 1982, 1985; see also Puckett & Lawson, 1989) have reported that many of the age differences in more complex memory tasks are eliminated when subjects are matched on digit span. Hasher and Zacks (1988; Zacks & Hasher, 1988) have also implied that functional limitations of storage capacity, hypothesized to be caused by the intrusion of irrelevant information, are the primary cause of age differences in working memory. Other researchers have argued that the age differences in working memory capacity are largely attributable to age-related reductions in the efficiency of processing (Baddeley, 1986; Craik, 1977; Craik & Rabinowitz, 1984; Gick, et al., 1988; Morris, et al., 1988). Finally, it has also been suggested that a major factor contributing to age differences in working memory and other aspects of cognitive functioning is a difficulty in coordinating information (Kirchner, 1958; Talland, 1968; Taub, 1968a; Welford, 1958), or a failure to update and index information accurately (Rabbitt, 1981). Research results relevant to the effects of age on each of these different aspects of working memory have recently been reviewed by Salthouse (1990).

A central issue in research concerned with aging and working memory has been the relation between the amount of processing required in the tasks and the magnitude of the age differences in relevant measures of performance. As already noted, several researchers have suggested that the age differences in working memory originate because the necessity of carrying out processing while simultaneously storing information exceeds the limited processing or operational capacities of older adults. This view leads to the prediction that the magnitude of age differences should increase as the processing requirements in the task increase.

Perhaps the most common method of manipulating the processing requirements in simple memory tasks involves the contrast between forward and backward digit spans. Because the backward digit span task requires the items to be reported in the reverse order of the original presentation, the hypothesis that age-related impairments are attributable to limitations in processing leads to the expectation that the age differences should be much larger in this task than in the forward digit span task. This pattern has been found in some studies (Hayslip & Kennelly, 1982; A.R. Potvin, et al., 1973), but it is hardly consistent. In other studies the age differences were either larger with forward digit span (Charness, 1987; A.R. Potvin, et al., 1981) or the age differences were similar for forward and backward digit spans (Botwinick & Storandt, 1974; A.A. Hartley, 1989; Holtzman, Familitant, Deptula, & W.J. Hoyer, 1986; J.L. Horn, et al., 1981). Forward and backward span tasks involving digits and sequences of designated shapes are included in the Wechsler Memory Scale - Revised (Wechsler, 1987). Means from the 263 adults in the stratified standardization sample for the two tasks in this test battery are displayed in Figure 6.2. Notice that whereas the age differences are somewhat greater for the backward version of the visual sequence task, they are actually smaller for the backward version of the digit span task.

Results from 14 other studies in which at least 20 young (mean ages less than 35) and 20 older (mean ages above 60) adults were administered both forward and backwards digit span tasks were summarized by Babcock and Salthouse (1990). They found that although the age differences were generally larger with the backward digit span than with the forward digit span, the difference was not dramatic. On the average, young adults appeared to have approximately a 14% advantage over older adults with the backward digit span, but the advantage with the forward digit span was still an appreciable 8%.

The results of two studies in the Babcock and Salthouse (1990) article provide additional evidence that tasks with greater processing requirements do not invariably lead to larger age differences. The primary tasks in these studies were a forward digit span task and a computation span task in which research participants were required to solve a series of arithmetic problems while remembering the last digit in each problem. As expected because of the requirement to carry out processing while also remembering the digits, performance in the computation span task was lower than that in the digit span task for both young and older adults. Of greater interest, however, was the discovery that the magnitude of the age differences was similar in the two tasks. This was evident in two independent studies, both in comparisons of the absolute span estimates, and in comparisons of the performance of older adults expressed in young adult standard deviation units. To illustrate, the average performance of older adults on the minimal-processing digit span task was -1.63 young adult standard deviation units in one study and -1.61 in the other, while the averages on the more processing-intensive computation span task were -.82 in one study and -1.39 in the other study. Similar magnitude age differences in tasks requiring memory for words presented alone, or for words presented at the ends of sentences have also been reported in two additional studies (L.L. Light & P.A. Anderson, 1985; Gick, et al., 1988). An exception to this pattern is a study by Wingfield, Stine, Lahar, and Aberdeen (1988), in which age differences were larger when the to-be-remembered words were presented in the context of sentences than when they were presented alone.

Another task often interpreted as indicating that age differences increase as processing requirements increase is the n-back task of Kay (described in Welford, 1958) and Kirchner (1958). This task consists of the presentation of a continuous sequence of letters or digits, with the research participant instructed to respond with the item n items back in the sequence. When n is 0 the task is obviously quite easy because the response is to the current stimulus. However, working memory involvement increases as the value of n increases to 1, 2, or 3 because of the necessity of continuously updating information and replacing old items with new items. Kirchner's (1958) results clearly suggested that older adults had greater difficulty in this task than young adults, particularly as the value of n exceeded 1. Both young and old adults were above 99% correct in the 0-back condition, but accuracy dropped to 87% for older adults in the 1-back condition, and to 52% in the 2-back condition. In contrast, young adults were still at 99% accuracy in the 1-back condition and their accuracy dropped to only 90% in the 2-back condition.

Braune and Wickens (1985) have also reported that accuracy in the 2-back condition of the task decreased between 20 and 60 years of age. Unfortunately, they did not include other conditions to allow comparisons with different amounts of processing involvement. Dobbs and Rule (1989) measured performance in the 0-back, 1-back, and 2-back conditions in adults from 30 to over 70 years of age, but only a single trial of 10 to 12 digits was apparently presented in each condition. At least some of the poor performance of older adults in the 1-back and 2-back conditions in their study might therefore have been attributable to confusion about exactly what was required in the more complex version of the task.

Although some of the results from the n-back task appear convincing in indicating that older adults experience greater difficulties than young adults as the requirements for simultaneous processing and storage increase, somewhat conflicting results have been reported in a closely related task. This is the running memory span task in which lists of unpredictable length are presented with instructions to recall as many items as possible from the end positions in the sequence. Successful performance on this task thus seems to require the same type of continuous exchange of new and old information as that required in the n-back task because the last few items must be updated with the presentation of each successive item.

One might expect results from the running memory span task to be similar to those from the n-back task if the necessity of continuously updating the status of items in memory is a major factor contributing to age differences in working memory. However, two experiments by Talland (1968) suggest that age-related effects are relatively small in the performance of running memory span tasks. Accuracy of recall in different age groups as a function of the position of the item in the presentation sequence is displayed in Figure 8.5. Results from an experiment involving written responses are illustrated in the top panel of Figure 8.5, and those from an experiment involving oral responses are illustrated in the bottom panel. Forty males in each decade participated in the written response experiment, and 36 in each decade took part in the oral response experiment.

Both sets of results portrayed in Figure 8.5 indicate that, with the possible exception of the N-3 items with written responses, there was little age-associated effect on report accuracy for items in the last four positions of the list. Because the lengths of the lists could not be predicted, accurate performance requires monitoring and updating continuously changing information. The invariance across age in Talland's studies therefore seems to suggest that these abilities are largely unaffected by increased age.

In view of the apparently different age trends on the n-back and running memory tasks, the question naturally arises as to the correlations among the proposed measures of working memory. That is, at least some of these apparent discrepancies might be resolved if it were known that despite superficial similarities, the measures of performance in the n-back and running memory tasks were not correlated with one another. More generally, confidence that one's measures reflect a common construct increases when the correlations among them are at least moderate in relation to their reliabilities.

Unfortunately, there are few studies in which correlations among alternative measures of working memory have been examined. Several reports of correlations between forward and backward digit spans are available (Botwinick & Storandt, 1974; Dobbs & Rule, 1989; Hayslip & Kennelly, 1982; F.H. Hooper, et al., 1984; L.L. Light & P.A. Anderson, 1985; Perlmutter & Nyquist, 1990), with typical values averaging about .5. Correlations among other proposed measures of working memory are often lower (L.L. Light & P.A. Anderson, 1985; Salthouse, 1988e).

As is the case with the speed-of-processing construct, it would be advantageous if future research were to investigate interrelations among possible measures of working memory in large samples of individuals from different age ranges. The results of such projects would be particularly

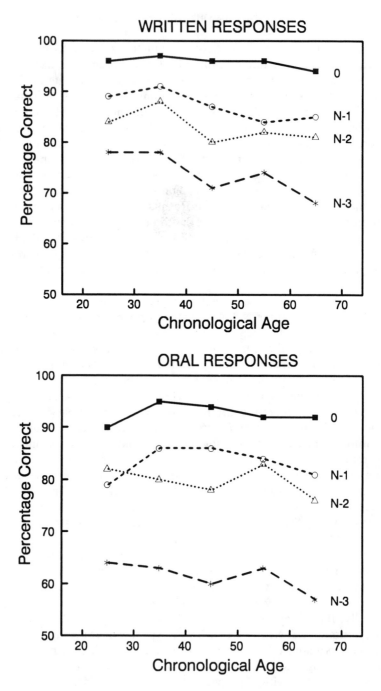

Figure 8.5. Age relations for running memory span tasks as a function of the serial position of the recalled items. Data from Talland (1968).

valuable if the set of tasks included measures reflecting different relative emphases on the storage, processing, and coordination aspects of working memory. The research that is currently available has not proven very informative regarding which of these aspects is primarily responsible for age-related decreases in working memory. Because there is controversy associated with the degree to which working memory is domain-specific, it would also be desirable if the tasks involved a mixture of materials and presentation modalities.

Statistical Control of Working Memory

It is somewhat surprising, considering the popularity of the working-memory version of the processing resource perspective, that few studies with moderate to large samples have examined the effects of statistical control of working memory indices on the magnitude of age differences in measures of cognitive functioning. There have been a number of small-scale studies, each with less than a total of 100 research participants across the entire adult age range (Charness, 1987; J.T. Hartley, 1986, L.L. Light & P.A. Anderson, 1985; Salthouse & Prill, 1987; Stine & Wingfield, 1987; Stine, Wingfield, & Myers, 1990). However, perhaps because of the instability of correlation-based parameters with small samples, those studies have yielded only weak and inconsistent results.

Several studies have also been reported in which, for various reasons, the analyses are of limited usefulness for the purpose of evaluating the contribution of working memory to age differences in cognitive functioning. For example, two studies by J.T. Hartley (1986, 1988) failed to find age differences in the working memory measure (reading span), and age differences in cognitive functioning cannot be expected to be mediated by age differences in working memory when there are no age differences in the measure of working memory. J.L. Horn (1982, J.L. Horn, et al., 1981) claimed to have assessed working memory with a construct (termed Short-Term Acquisition and Retrieval) based on a composite of measures of recency recall, primacy recall, paired-associates performance, digit span, and serial recall. Although these measures may reflect processes of short-term acquisition and recall, the mixture appears to lack theoretical justification as an index of working memory. Hultsch, Hertzog, and Dixon (1990) also assessed working memory with measures (i.e., variants of the n-back and reading span tasks) of questionable validity and unknown reliability.

One-hundred young adults (ages 18 to 25) and 100 older adults (ages 57 to 67) in a study by Salthouse (1988e) were administered paper-and-pencil tests of paper-folding, visual synthesis, and geometric analogies along with the backward digit span task. The mean percentage of variance common to age and cognitive performance, across eight measures of decision time and decision accuracy, was 25.0, and that common to age and backward digit span was 12.2. The mean age-associated variance after statistical control of the backward digit span index of working memory was 20.1. The results of this study therefore suggest that working memory, as assessed by the backward digit span measure, may have been responsible for approximately 20% (i.e., [(25.0-20.1)/25.0]X100 = 19.6%) of the age differences in the available measures of cognition.

Because participants in the Salthouse (1988e) study also performed the Digit Symbol Substitution test sometimes hypothesized to reflect perceptual or cognitive speed, it was possible to compare the relative strengths of processing speed and working memory contributions to the age differences in cognition. In this particular comparison, the speed interpretation was the more powerful: Statistical control of the digit symbol measure reduced the age differences in the cognitive measures by approximately 63%, compared to the less than 20% with the backward digit span measure. Furthermore, control of the digit symbol measure reduced the age differences in backward digit span by 95.1%, whereas control of the backward digit span measure reduced the age differences in digit symbol substitution by only 10.1%.

The study described earlier by Salthouse, D.R. Mitchell, Skovronek, and Babcock (1989) also involved measurement of each individual's computation span as an index of working memory capacity. The computation span variable correlated -.46 with chronological age among the 120 participants, correlated .48 with average accuracy in the verbal reasoning task, and correlated .38 with average accuracy in the spatial paper folding task. Both of these cognitive measures had correlations of -.53 with chronological age. Computations of the proportion of variance associated with age before and after statistical control of the computation span measure led to estimates that approximately 57% of the age differences in the reasoning task, and 43% of those in the paper-folding task, may have been mediated by age differences in working memory, as indexed by the computation span measure.

ATTENTION AS A PROCESSING RESOURCE

The idea that attention might serve as a sort of fuel or energy source for cognitive operations, and that age differences in certain measures of cognition might be attributable to reductions in the available supply of attention, has been discussed by several authors (Craik & Byrd, 1982; Hasher & Zacks, 1979; Plude & W.J. Hoyer, 1985). As with other resource conceptualizations, it is also assumed that processing operations vary in their requirements for attention, with some processing operations requiring considerable attention for their successful execution, and others functioning more or less automatically with minimal attention demands.

Also like other resource conceptualizations, differences of opinion exist concerning the characteristics of the resource, in this case, attention. For example, some researchers tend to view attentional capacity as a relatively fixed and stable property of an individual, while others have claimed that it may vary within, as well as across, individuals (e.g., Hasher & Zacks, 1979). There are also differences in assumptions about how the concept of attention is best measured. Plude and W.J. Hoyer (1985), for example, asserted that "... measuring attention consists of evaluating the selectivity of information processing" (p. 52). A.A. Hartley, Kieley, and Slabach (1990) have also emphasized the shifting or switching properties of attention in the assessment of attention. In contrast, D.M. Burke and L.L. Light (1981) virtually defined attentional or processing capacity in terms of divided attention in their statement: "A well-established finding in research on aging is that the elderly have diminished processing capacity in that they are less able than the young to divide attention between two tasks to be performed simultaneously" (pp. 528-529). Most researchers in the area of cognition and aging have tended to emphasize division of attention in their discussions of attention as a processing resource, and thus the current discussion will be restricted to that aspect of attention.

Although it is often claimed that older adults experience greater difficulties than young adults in divided-attention situations, the empirical results are rather mixed. Older adults have been found to perform at lower levels than young adults when two tasks are to be performed simultaneously in several studies (Broadbent & Heron, 1962; J.L. Horn, et al., 1981; McDowd, 1986; Peak, 1968; Ponds, et al., 1988; Salthouse, et al., 1984; Talland, 1962), but in other studies, young and old adults have exhibited similar divided-attention deficits (e.g., Baddeley, Logie, Bressi, Della Sala, & Spinnler, 1986; Braune & Wickens, 1985; McDowd & Craik, 1988; Morris, et al., 1988, 1990; Park, Puglisi, A.D. Smith, & Dudley, 1987; Peak, 1970; Somberg & Salthouse, 1982; Wickens, Braune, & Stokes, 1987). A satisfactory explanation is not yet available to account for these discrepancies, but they will have to be resolved, perhaps by means of studies with large samples and combinations of several different tasks, if the phenomenon of divided-attention deficits is to function as the basis for the attentional resource interpretation.

Results from Experimental Manipulations

The most popular method for simulating reduced quantities of the attentional resource in young adults has been to require them to perform a concurrent task to divert some of their attention from the primary task. To the extent that this manipulation successfully mimics the hypothesized reduced levels of attentional capacity among older adults, then the performance of young adults when performing a concurrent attention-demanding task would be expected to resemble that of older adults performing the task under normal conditions.

An early application of this procedure was described by Rabinowitz, Craik, and Ackerman (1982). The primary task in their study was a recall task in which target words were paired with either strong or weak associates at encoding (presentation) and at retrieval (test). Both young and old adults performed the task under normal conditions, and a second group of young adults performed the task while simultaneously monitoring auditory digits for the occurrence of consecutive odd digits. The general pattern of results across conditions was similar for all groups (i.e., highest recall with strong cues at both presentation and test, and lower recall with strong cues at presentation and weak cues at test). Of particular interest was the finding that older adults, and young adults performing under conditions of divided attention, recalled fewer items than the young adults performing under normal conditions. (The major findings of this study were replicated in a later study by Puglisi, et al., 1988.)

Rabinowitz, Craik, and Ackerman (1982) hypothesized that a common factor of reduced attentional resources was responsible for the similar qualitative patterns observed with divided attention, and with increased age. However, not all studies in which available attentional resources were manipulated by the requirement of concurrent digit monitoring have produced results consistent with the simulation of reduced resources expectation. For example, Park, et al., (1987) found that young adults performing under division of attention had lower levels of picture memory than young adults under normal (i.e., no digit monitoring) conditions, but no performance differences were found between young and old adults under normal conditions. These results are thus incompatible with the attentional hypothesis because the simulation interpretation would have predicted significant age differences when there was evidence that the amount of processing resources (as affected by the division-of-attention manipulation) influenced performance in the task. Guttentag (1988) also found that although the level of recall was similar for older adults and for young adults under conditions of divided attention, older adults exhibited much more clustering in recall than the young adults under divided-attention conditions. The qualitative patterns of older adults and young adults in the condition simulating a reduced quantity of resources were therefore not equivalent, despite similar levels of overall performance.

The status of concurrent digit monitoring as a means of altering the attentional requirements seems analogous to manipulations of rate of stimulus presentation and presence or absence of a concurrent memory load as methods of altering speed or working-memory resource requirements. In each case there is some evidence suggesting that the manipulation may be successful, but there is also a certain amount of conflicting evidence. As noted earlier, much more information about the nature of each type of processing resource, and how it exerts its influence on cognitive performance, will likely be required before more effective manipulations can be identified and implemented.

How Should Attentional Capacity be Assessed?

Largely because of the emphasis on divided-attention phenomena, most researchers interested in attention as a processing resource have assumed that an individual's attentional capacity could be measured in the context of a divided-attention or dual-task situation. The rationale for the use of dual-task procedures to assess attentional requirements has been compared to Archimedes' Displacement Principle (Salthouse, 1985b; Underwood, 1976). That is, just as the size of an object can be determined by measuring the amount of water displaced when it is immersed in a container of water, so might the attentional demands of a task be estimated by the amount of interference it produces when it is performed concurrently with another task.

Dual-task procedures have been widely used in comparisons of the attentional demands of different tasks, and it has often been assumed that this methodology could be extended to allow estimates of attentional capacity in different individuals. Quite a few studies therefore have been conducted in which young and old adults were compared when performing a primary task and a secondary reaction-time task. In almost all of these studies the disruption in secondary reaction time when performed concurrently with the primary task has been greater for older adults than for young adults (Craik & McDowd, 1987; Guttentag & Madden, 1987; Jennings, Nebes, & Yovetich, 1990; Lorsbach & Simpson, 1988; Macht & Buschke, 1983; Madden, 1986a, 1987; Madden, et al., 1989; McDowd, 1986; McDowd & Craik, 1988; Nestor, Parasuraman, & Haxby, 1989; Salthouse & Saults, 1987; Salthouse & Somberg, 1982b; but not Duchek, 1984, or Tun, 1989).

Although many of these researchers have inferred on the basis of their results that attentional capacity declines with age, (or equivalently, that attentional demands of processing increase with age), it is not clear that these conclusions are justified on the basis of the available data. One concern is that the relevant studies have relied exclusively upon reaction time as the index of attentional capacity. Because all the evidence that the attentional requirements of older adults are greater than those of young adults is based on results from a single dependent measure, it cannot yet be determined whether the phenomenon is generalizable to other dependent measures.

Another issue that must ultimately be resolved before results from secondary-task procedures can be interpreted unambiguously is how the capability of responding faster to a secondary-task probe stimulus translates into higher levels of functioning in a variety of cognitive tasks. The assumption has been that secondary-task reaction time is an index of the quantity of an attentional resource that is needed for many cognitive tasks. However, mechanisms must be specified, and investigated, to indicate how the same entity is responsible for facilitation of speed in responding to a probe stimulus, and for enhancement of the quality of processing in various cognitive tasks.

Perhaps the most serious problem with the use of dual-task procedures are the large number of untested assumptions that are necessary in order to make inferences about individual differences in attentional capacity. Many of these issues have been discussed elsewhere (Guttentag, 1989; Salthouse, 1982, 1985b, 1988d, 1988e; Somberg & Salthouse, 1982), and therefore the assumptions are merely summarized in Table 8.1. The fact that few attempts have been made to evaluate the validity of any of these assumptions clearly weakens the confidence one might have in the secondary task technique as a measure of attentional capacity.

Statistical Control of Attentional Resources

Lacking a consensus with respect to how attentional resources are to be measured, there have apparently been no studies in which age differences in cognition have been examined before and after statistical control of an index of attention. In fact, at present there doesn't even seem to be much evidence that available measures of attention are significantly related to measures of cognitive functioning.

TIME = SPACE = ENERGY?

Although it is convenient to categorize speculations about processing resources in terms of metaphors of time, space, and energy, these conceptualizations are not necessarily distinct and independent. Not only are the arguments for each resource based on similar reasoning, but the same results are sometimes interpreted as evidence for different resource conceptualizations. One striking example of this phenomenon is the study by Kirchner (1958) with the n-back task discussed earlier in the context of working-memory capacity (i.e., the space metaphor). Craik (1977) and

TABLE 8.1
Requirements of Dual-task Procedures for the Assessment
of Individual Differences in Attentional Capacity of Individuals

1. Performance is assessed on both tasks in single and dual-task conditions, and either (a) performance remains invariant in one task so that all differences are reflected in measures of the other task, or (b) attention-operating characteristics are generated to allow assessment of performance in a dual-task metric.

2. Performance in both tasks is equivalent for all individuals when each task is performed alone, or explicit assumptions are provided for why absolute, relative, or some other type of comparison is meaningful when baseline levels of performance are different.

3. Performance impairments associated with dual-task conditions are not attributable to structural interference (e.g., use of the same input or output "structures").

4. A common fixed-capacity attentional resource is required by processes in both tasks.

5. All individuals allocate attentional resources to the two tasks in an equivalent manner.

6. All individuals have identical functions relating resources to task performance, including locations of the points of transition between resource-limited and data-limited performance.

7. All individuals have identical overhead or concurrence costs associated with the joint performance of two tasks.

8. The ability to perform two tasks concurrently is a stable characteristic of the individual, and will be manifested in different combinations of tasks.

W.J. Hoyer and Plude (1980) referred to this study as one of the clearest examples of a divided-attention deficit in aging (i.e., the energy metaphor), while Kirchner himself emphasized the importance of speed (i.e., the time metaphor) as a factor responsible for reduced ability to organize the continuous interchange of incoming and outgoing information.

There is also an assortment of speculations about how the different metaphorical interpretations of processing resources may be interrelated. For example, Talland (1968) suggested that impairments in divided attention might be a consequence of slowness in alternating between processes, and Craik (1968a) speculated that reductions in attention would lead to increased delays between successive processing operations, or, effectively, slower processing. Slower rates of processing have additionally been linked to reduced capacity of working memory because information must be retained longer in the temporary store (Clay, 1954; Rabbitt, 1977; Welford, 1958), or because the early information is lost during the processing of other information (Anders & Fozard, 1973; Baddeley, 1986; Birren, 1955, 1964; G. Cohen, 1988; Fozard & J.C. Thomas, 1975; Salthouse, 1985b). Finally, the possibility that a smaller working memory capacity could contribute to slower processing was discussed by Salthouse (1985a).

One implication of the apparent interdependence of the various resource conceptualizations is that it may not be particularly meaningful to attempt to distinguish among the different versions of the processing resources perspective. If the categorizations in terms of speed of processing, capacity of working memory, and divided attention ability are somewhat arbitrary because they are all interrelated, then at a certain level they can be presumed to be equivalent. Whether this should be considered encouraging (because the interdependencies imply that a fundamental construct is involved), or discouraging (because it may be impossible to identify the specific nature of a processing resource) is probably a matter of personal judgment. Nevertheless, recognition of the close connections among the different conceptualizations of processing resources suggests that the concept of processing resources may be somewhat broader, and possibly even more general, than commonly assumed.

EVALUATION OF THE PROCESSING RESOURCES PERSPECTIVE

The processing resources perspective is based on the simple but appealing idea that a small number of factors may be responsible for many of the age differences observed in measures of cognitive functioning. Moreover, this view offers the promise of an integrative, yet still proximal, interpretation of age differences in cognition. These characteristics have contributed to considerable interest in concepts such as resources and capacity, and discussion sections in many cognitive aging articles are replete with speculations about the causes of observed age differences couched in resource and capacity terminology.

The amount of empirical evidence relevant to the processing resources perspective is currently limited, although some results do appear consistent with the idea that there may be a few relatively general determinants of the age differences in measures of cognitive functioning. For example, the age-complexity phenomenon seems convincing in suggesting that general factors may be involved in many of the age-related cognitive differences. Furthermore, several of the outcomes of statistical control procedures imply that simple resource-like constructs may contribute to at least some of the observed age differences in cognitive performance.

An objective appraisal at the present time, however, would undoubtedly have to conclude that the processing resources perspective is based more on speculation than on compelling empirical evidence. Several methods have been used to investigate the processing resources perspective, but few definitive conclusions are possible because of lack of knowledge about mechanisms (in the simulation and minimization-of-influence strategies), and weak assessment of theoretical constructs and small sample sizes (in the statistical control procedures). Additional research with these methods, and with new techniques that remain to be developed, is clearly needed before the viability of the processing resources perspective can be fairly evaluated.

The processing resources perspective is similar to other theoretical perspectives in that it is basically a set of ideas at the framework level, but it has not yet been formulated in sufficient detail to be considered a true theory or model. As it currently stands, the processing resources perspective attempts to specify the most appropriate level (i.e., specific or general) for characterizing *what* the age differences are, but it provides little indication of the source of the hypothesized reduction in resources, or of the mechanisms by which fewer resources contribute to impaired cognition. It therefore leaves unanswered the fundamental questions of *why* the reduction in resources occurs, and *how* that reduction results in lower levels of cognitive performance.

9 Final Words and Future Directions

It is often remarked that the study of adult age changes has but a short history and that one should therefore expect emphasis to be placed upon descriptive studies as a means of building the necessary foundation of empirical data. At least twenty years have passed, however, since the first important cross-sectional studies of the adult life span reached publication, but research emphasis has changed very little. It is timely, therefore, to look for theoretical models which will help integrate the wealth of research data now available.
—Schaie (1962, pp. 129-130)

It is 30 years since Schaie wrote the words quoted above, and, if it was timely to look for theoretical models of age-related phenomena then, it is even more so now. Research results have continued to accumulate, but as indicated in the previous chapters of this book, it is still possible to reach only very weak and general conclusions about the likely contribution of different classes of determinants of cognitive aging phenomena. Despite the fact that most of the developmental determinants currently assumed to be plausible were recognized over 70 years ago (e.g., Foster & G.A. Taylor, 1920), unequivocal answers to the important questions of the exact nature of the factors contributing to cognitive aging phenomena, when and how they operate, and what variables serve to moderate their impact still are not available.

There are undoubtedly many reasons the field seems to remain in the position of being able to offer only vague and tentative speculations instead of precise and definitive conclusions. Complete and accurate identification of all these reasons would probably require thorough analyses of the historical contexts of past research, and would not necessarily contribute to greater progress in the future. What may be productive, however, is an analysis of the perceived limitations of theoretical and empirical efforts in cognitive aging, and a discussion of what might be the most promising directions for future research. This final chapter is therefore written more in the style of a discussant or a commentator rather than, as was the goal in the preceding chapters, of a probing reporter. Although the following observations and recommendations are inevitably subjective, and quite possibly idiosyncratic, they are offered because of a belief that commentaries of this kind can often play an important role in highlighting central issues, and perhaps in stimulating reasoned debate about how those issues might best be resolved.

OBSERVATIONS AND RECOMMENDATIONS

Observations

Some initial observations concern the strengths and weaknesses of the five major theoretical perspectives. The following remarks are not based on a detailed accounting or systematic evaluation, but instead reflect general impressions of the current viability of each perspective.

The changing environment perspective is based on the assumption that some age differences are artifacts of progressively improving environmental conditions. This view is supported by the well-documented, positive time-lag effects on an assortment of cognitive measures. However, the findings that age-related trends similar to those reported in humans are evident in animals raised in unchanging environments makes it unlikely that this perspective can account for all age differences in cognition. Moreover, vagueness in the specification of when and how changes in the external environment exert their influences on cognitive functioning has made it difficult to identify, and hence to investigate, explicit predictions from the environmental change perspective. Both the concept of environmental change, and the related concept of a cohort, need to be decomposed, and critical variables isolated, before the environmental change perspective can be thoroughly appraised.

The idea that disuse contributes to adult age differences in cognitive functioning is intuitively plausible because cognitive performance often decreases as a function of time since learning, and as people grow older the interval from original learning increases for many activities. Despite the attractiveness of this simple idea, it seems to have little convincing empirical support at the present time. Moderate to large age differences are frequently found in tasks presumed to resemble familiar activities, the magnitude of the age differences appears to be nearly the same for people regardless of their experiential histories, and the benefit from added experience with cognitive activities seems similar for people of all ages. Although the existing evidence is largely inconsistent with the disuse perspective, essential information concerning the frequencies with which relevant cognitive processes are used in the daily lives of adults of any age is not yet available. Speculations about the frequencies of particular activities must be replaced by objective counts of the occurrence of constituent processes in order for the disuse perspective to be adequately evaluated.

The qualitative difference perspective has primarily been investigated with weak and indirect procedures because theorists favoring qualitative or structural changes have generally failed to specify testable implications of this position. Most of the relevant evidence is negative, with little or no age differences: (a) in the magnitude of the gap between performance and competence; (b) in the manner in which verbal information is organized in memory; and (c) in the pattern of correlations among cognitive variables. The evidence is more equivocal concerning possible age differences in strategies or aspects of metacognition, at least in part because of ambiguity associated with the meaning, and methods of assessment, of these constructs. However, there appears to be little evidence at present to suggest that age differences in these styles or modes of processing, if they exist, are responsible for many of the age differences in measures of cognitive functioning.

Much of the current research focus in cognitive aging falls within what was classified as the localization perspective because a goal of many researchers is to identify the specific aspects of processing that are most affected by increased age. These research efforts have produced a large collection of empirical observations, but there are reasons to question whether the attempts at isolation or localization of the source of age differences in cognitive tasks have been successful. Numerous taxonomies for classifying cognitive tasks according to the degree of age-related effects have been explored, but exceptions are apparent in most of them when tasks are categorized according to the presence or absence of age differences. One of the problems with the localization approach is that the various aspects of the human cognitive system are highly interrelated, and thus it is difficult to isolate the contribution of a single component to the performance of a complex task. This is particularly true when the primary means of localizing age-related effects to specific processes is the presence or absence of analysis-of-variance interactions. Another weakness inherent in the localization perspective is that the focus on the analysis of specific tasks provides little basis for integration of the results across different tasks.

It was partly this last limitation of the localization approach that led to the development of the reduced processing resources perspective. That is, this perspective is primarily an attempt to identify integrative concepts or principles that might underlie many of the age differences observed across different cognitive tasks. Evidence in support of the processing resources perspective is currently limited, and largely consists of two kinds of demonstrations. The first is that the magnitude of age differences appears to be related to how much processing is required, and not just the specific type of processing required (i.e., the age-complexity effect). The second category of evidence consistent with the reduced resources perspective is that removing the linear effects of certain, presumably basic, cognitive measures reduces the magnitude of the age effects on other cognitive measures (i.e., results from the statistical control procedure). The major limitations of the processing resources perspective at the present time are lack of knowledge about the exact nature of processing resources, and about the mechanisms by which reductions in processing resources contribute to lower levels of cognitive performance.

It is apparent that most of the existing theoretical perspectives within the field of cognitive aging are more at the level of theoretical frameworks rather than the level of theories or models. That is, the changing environment (chapter 3), disuse (chapter 4), qualitative difference (chapter 5), and processing resources (chapter 8) perspectives tend to consist of a few basic concepts that are so vague and poorly related to one another that they do not appear to qualify as true, or at least as complete, theories. Research inspired by the localization approach (chapters 6 and 7) is often more precise with respect to what has changed as a function of age, but it seldom addresses the issues of either the source of, or the mechanisms responsible for, those changes. The localization approach can therefore be characterized as moderately strong at the model level, but weak at the theory and framework levels where major concepts in the perspective are usually integrated. Although not treated as distinct theoretical perspectives in this volume, the research literature also contains a sizable number of descriptive generalizations that are sometimes considered to be theoretical statements. These taxonomies are also inadequate as theories of cognitive aging because they primarily appear to be systems for classifying phenomena, and not true attempts to indicate why or how the observed age differences originated.

The lack of more complete or integrative theories is unfortunate because phenomena as complex as the relations between age and cognitive functioning will almost certainly require multiple levels of explanation. In other words, explanations of the source (i.e., the why) of the differences are needed just as much as descriptions of the nature (i.e., the what) of those differences, and both kinds of theorizing need to be supplemented with proposals about the mechanisms (i.e., the how) by which the differences are manifested.

It is not yet obvious how the rapprochement between framework and model, or the conversion of descriptive generalizations to theory, can best be accomplished to yield a more complete and comprehensive form of explanation. At least three alternative possibilities can be imagined. One is that a theorist could focus on a very specific phenomenon, such as the relation between age and performance on a particular cognitive test. This phenomenon might be interpreted in terms of a model indicating which aspects of processing were responsible for the observed age differences, and a developmental theory could then be constructed to specify how and why those processing deficiencies emerged as a function of increased age. In order to assess the generality of the theory, it would naturally have to be extended to other cognitive tests or tasks, and re-evaluated with respect to additional empirical evidence. A key issue in this bottom-up approach is when one decides that it is appropriate to shift one's focus from the model of a specific task to a more general theory of cognitive aging phenomena. On the one hand, questions will always remain concerning the accuracy or completeness of any model. On the other hand, attempting to resolve all possible questions concerned with a specific task could result in the infinite postponement of the developmental theory.

An alternative approach to the establishment of more complete theories might consist of attempting to identify linkages between the broad and general concepts at the framework level, and measures of performance on specific cognitive tasks. That is, the initial emphasis might be on broad concepts, but relations between the concepts could be formulated at the theory level, and the concepts then defined in an operational fashion to allow empirical investigation of the postulated interrelations at the level of observable variables. Of course, the crucial aspect in this top-down approach is that the concepts must be defined broadly enough to do justice to the theoretical constructs, and yet explicitly enough to be amenable to empirical investigation.

What could be considered an intermediate approach might involve selecting a prototypical cognitive task, and then administering it, in several different versions and across a variety of stimulus materials, to people of a wide range of ages. The construct represented by these multiple measures might then serve as the focus of several different kinds of theoretically motivated research. For example, the target construct could be the object of investigations of distal determinants such as experiential influences, or it could be analyzed into proximal determinants by decomposing it into presumably more fundamental components. The familiar paired-associate task may be an ideal prototypical task in research on cognitive aging because of the following characteristics: (a) The ability to form associations appears fundamental to many cognitive activities; (b) age differences in the efficiency of paired associate tasks have been well documented; (c) performance on paired associate tasks is easily and objectively measured, and (d) the task appears subject to analytical decomposition. The major disadvantage of this particular task is that many contemporary researchers do not find it very interesting, perhaps because of its legacy as the primary task in the now unpopular associationism framework.

Regardless of whether one begins at the model level, the framework level, or somewhere else, all three levels of framework, theory, and model ultimately need to be addressed in order to have complete theories. The most intriguing concepts at the framework level, and the most elegant characterization of a task at the model level, are insufficient if there is no linkage of the developmental forces, the why, to the observed differences, the what, by means of a theory of how.

Recommendations

Although there is no way to ensure progress in resolving theoretical issues, some tentative guidelines may prove useful. The following recommendations are therefore offered as best guesses about the kind of research that might be expected to result in the greatest progress in understanding the causes of age-related differences in cognitive functioning.

One recommendation for future research is that greater attention be devoted to what participants in research projects bring to the assessment situation. Three particularly important kinds of additional information from the research participants concern their biological characteristics (including various indicators of health status), details about their experiential history, and their performance on variables representing other cognitive abilities.

As noted in chapter 1, an individual's level of cognitive functioning is necessarily mediated by biological processes, irrespective of whether the distal causes of the current states of those processes were endogenous or exogenous. Even if one is convinced that the distal causes of developmental phenomena are exogenous or extrinsic and that the biological processes are merely the "carriers" of the changes, therefore, the importance of determining the relation between proximal neurological or physiological characteristics and age differences in cognitive variables should be recognized. The biological factors could be specified in terms of a variety of health-related symptoms, or in terms of the values of theoretically relevant neurological and physiological variables. In either case, the specification should be precise enough to allow investigation of whether those factors might be proximal mediators of the age differences in cognitive functioning. Only when more information of this type becomes available will it be possible to be specific about the anatomical locus, or biochemical basis, of the age-related differences observed in measures of cognitive behavior.

Experiential factors also need to be investigated much more thoroughly than in the past in order to be able to reach definitive conclusions about the importance of extrinsic determinants of age differences in cognition. The topic of the relations between age and experience as determinants of cognitive functioning is one in which there are currently strong opinions but weak evidence. That is, although it has frequently been claimed that increased experience may attenuate age-related declines in cognitive functioning (Charness, 1985b; Gilbert, 1935, 1952; W.J. Hoyer, 1987; R.A. McFarland, 1956; R.A. McFarland & O'Doherty, 1959; W.R. Miles, 1942; W.R. Miles & Shriver, 1953; Murrell, 1973; Murrell & Griew, 1965; Perlmutter, 1988; Perlmutter, et al., 1990; Salthouse, 1982, 1987b, 1987c; Welford, 1958, 1962, 1983, 1985), the research reviewed in chapter 4 indicates that there is still little convincing support for this interpretation.

More conclusive evidence concerning the influence of experiential factors in age-cognition relations may be obtained if researchers were to explore explicit hypotheses about what kinds of experiences (e.g., educational, occupational, etc.), in what particular patterns (e.g., gradually accumulated over many years, intensive over a short but recent period, etc.), affect which specific aspects of cognition (e.g., rote memory, judgment). As noted earlier, this will probably require much more detailed analyses of the processes involved in both daily activities and cognitive tasks. It may also be desirable to broaden the aspects of cognitive functioning to be investigated. For example, many researchers have speculated that certain high-level decision-making or managerial skills are highly dependent upon various kinds of knowledge acquired through experience (Botwinick, 1967; Bray & A. Howard, 1983; Bromley, 1974; Gilbert, 1935, 1952; Guilford, 1969; Lawton, 1943; Salthouse, 1982, 1990; E.H. Schludermann, et al., 1983; Singleton, 1983; Wechsler, 1952). A potentially productive direction for future research, therefore, might be investigation of the interrelations among age, and measures of experience, knowledge, and decision-making or managerial effectiveness. These latter characteristics may be difficult to evaluate, particularly in realistic situations (Bromley, 1969, 1974, although see Dulewicz & Fletcher, 1982, and H.H. Meyer, 1970, for examples of the assessment of managerial performance in relation to age), but the efforts would probably be justified because results of such research are likely to have considerable theoretical and practical importance.

There are two basic reasons for recommending that research participants should be assessed on variables representing more than one theoretical construct. One reason is that the sample of research participants can be characterized more precisely when the individuals can be classified according to their performance on known variables (see the discussion of standard tasks in Salthouse, 1985b; Salthouse & Kausler, 1985; Salthouse, et al., 1988a). That is, the more information available about the participants in research projects, the easier it is to evaluate the possibility that any differences in results across studies were attributable to differences associated with the samples of participants, as opposed to methodological or procedural variations.

The second, and theoretically more interesting, reason for recommending the assessment of multiple constructs in future research is that the availability of measures of several different constructs allows their interrelations to be investigated. This kind of information can be used to evaluate generality because, if the relevant construct is unrelated to other important cognitive constructs, then the generality of the findings may be quite limited. Information from multiple constructs would also be useful in determining the extent to which hypothesized processing components identified in localization perspectives are independent of one another (as discussed in chapter 7), and in assessing the interrelations among cognitive constructs and processing resources constructs (as discussed in chapter 8).

Another practice that seems desirable in future research is to examine age-related effects across the entire distribution of individuals at each age range, and not simply in terms of the average performance at each age level. It is conceivable, for example, that age-related influences are more pronounced among the poorer-performing members of the population, perhaps because they are more vulnerable to a variety of factors contributing to impairments in performance. Information about age trends in the entire distribution may also help establish the generality of the results by demonstrating that the performance pattern of interest is not restricted to comparisons in particular regions of the measurement scale (see the discussion of discriminating power in the appendix of chapter 7).

One relatively simple method of examining distribution effects involves dividing the research participants at each age level into two groups on the basis of their score on a relevant dependent variable (Salthouse & D.R. Mitchell, 1989). This post-hoc ability factor can then be entered in an analysis of variance to investigate the possibility of age-by-ability interactions. Of course, the main effects in this type of analysis would not be informative because the age effect would merely duplicate that in the original analysis, and the ability effect would not be meaningful because the ability factor was created post-hoc on the basis of the observed scores. However, tests of the interactions should be interesting because they could indicate whether the magnitude of the age differences among individuals of low levels of ability is significantly different than those among individuals of high ability levels. This particular method may not be optimal, but it is important that procedures be explored to allow analyses of age-related effects across the entire distribution of ability levels.

The discouraging lack of consistency in the pattern of results across different studies, even when the same task or paradigm was used, suggests that certain procedural changes in the way research is conducted in cognitive aging should also be considered. That is, one possible reason for some of the discrepancies evident in past research is that the research methods may have been too weak to have yielded reliable, and hence replicable results. If adopted, the following suggestions might not only improve the robustness of the research results, but would probably also allow more powerful data analysis techniques (Hertzog, 1987; Schaie & Hertzog, 1985) than those generally possible in the past.

Research is always specific, but the results of the research can have general implications by focusing on important theoretical issues, and emphasizing powerful assessment at the construct, rather than the variable, level. The importance of the question being asked can be argued to be the major factor influencing the quality of research. The question must naturally be formulated in a manner that allows an unambiguous answer, but adequate methodology is only necessary, and not sufficient, to ensure high-quality research. In order to be important, the research question should address issues fundamental to the understanding of the major phenomenon. This implies that the researcher should be able to indicate at the outset of the research what outcomes will require what types of modifications of major theoretical interpretations. Not all research can be expected to have substantial impact, but the research may not even be worth doing if it is impossible to identify possible consequences of the research for what is presumably the primary issue of interest—which in the present context is how age differences in cognitive functioning are to be interpreted. In other words, little progress can be anticipated if no outcome of the research will place constraints on the nature of explanations of cognitive aging phenomena.

An implication of the emphasis on constructs rather than variables is that, whenever feasible, researchers should obtain multiple indicators of the important theoretical constructs. Although almost all researchers acknowledge that they are primarily concerned with relations among theoretical constructs rather than relations among particular empirical variables, there often seems to be a lack of appreciation of the idea that all variables can be assumed to be composed of construct variance, unique or method-specific variance, and error variance. Because the important variance is that associated with the theoretical construct, research with single variables may therefore confound, or at least obscure, the relations of greatest interest. The use of multiple measures or indicators of the theoretical constructs minimizes this problem because a composite or aggregate of the measures will tend to emphasize the general or common determinants, and average out the theoretically less interesting influences associated with method-specific and error factors. Assessment based on multiple measures also tends to be more reliable than that derived from single measures because more observations contribute to the measurement of the construct. Therefore both the reliability and the validity of the measurement are likely to be enhanced when theoretical constructs are investigated with multiple measures (Rushton, Brainerd, & Pressley, 1983;

J.L. Sullivan & Feldman, 1979).

As Garner, Hake, and Eriksen (1956) pointed out in a classic article, reliance on multiple converging operations to define theoretical constructs is not at all inconsistent with principles of operationism. In fact, multiple operations are needed to ensure that one's concepts are reasonably general and not restricted to particular methods of assessment. This point was elaborated by J.L. Horn (1979) in a discussion of the limitations of what he referred to as manifest variable focus:

> ... [R]esearchers often treat a particular operational definition as if that, in itself, should be a focus of research, without regard to the fact that usually very many such variables have been studied and no one of them can be regarded as any more than an indicant of a concept ... One result of manifest variable focus is that we simply accumulate results from many studies ... but acquire very little understanding. (p. 309)

Still another practice desirable in future research is to increase the size of the samples used in age-comparative investigations. Research in cognitive aging is reaching the stage where the questions are becoming more subtle and refined, and the interest is shifting to quantitative outcomes rather than qualitative patterns. Furthermore, there is growing interest in establishing the stability (or absence of age differences) of certain phenomena across the adult years, and not merely in demonstrating the existence of age differences. Finally, recognition that cognitive performance can be influenced by other individual difference characteristics besides age heightens awareness that research based on small samples may be highly susceptible to selection artifacts. For all these reasons, it is essential that the sample sizes in studies of cognitive aging are sufficiently large to provide sensitive and generalizable tests of the primary research questions.

It is impossible to specify an absolute minimum sample size for age-comparative research, but some useful guidelines can be extracted from J. Cohen's (1988) discussion of power analyses. For example, according to Cohen (p. 31), the sample size needed to have moderate power (power of .8) to detect a medium difference (equivalent to .5 standard deviation units) between two groups with a t-test (one-tailed) at the .05 significance level is 50 individuals per group. Equivalent power to detect a correlation coefficient of .3 as significantly greater than zero requires a total of 66 pairs of observations (p. 87). And finally, the number of paired observations required in each group to have .8 power to detect a medium difference between two correlations (i.e., q = .3, corresponding to differences between correlations of, for example, .62 and .40) is 140 (p. 134). These are clearly much larger sample sizes than those typically used in research on cognitive aging phenomena, and therefore at least some of the inconsistency evident in the results of previous research may be a consequence of the low power to detect small or moderate differences. That is, if the probability of detecting a significant difference is only .5 (as it would be with an effect size of .5 standard deviation units, and sample sizes of 22 per group), then one should not be surprised if 50% of the studies fail to replicate a finding of a significant age difference.

One final point related to sample size concerns the apparent assumption on the part of some researchers that small sample sizes can be compensated for by either greater amounts of, or more precise, information from each research participant. Although increasing the precision of the information from each individual will provide a better estimate of his or her true level of performance, it does not necessarily increase the sensitivity of tests of group differences. It may be easier to understand this point by considering that tests of group differences are based on ratios of between-group variance to within-group variance, and that within-group variance is in turn composed of both between-individual and within-individual variance. Increasing the precision of measurement can therefore be expected to reduce the within-individual variance, but it is unlikely either to decrease the variance across people within the same group, or to increase the variance across groups. The ratio of between-group to within-group variance will therefore not change substantially unless the initial within-individual variance was large relative to the other sources of variance. Moreover, generalizability is always a concern with small samples unless special care is taken to ensure the representativeness of the individuals in each group.

It is unrealistic to expect all of these recommendations to be adopted. Furthermore, it is probably not even desirable that all research concerned with age differences in cognition adhere to these guidelines. However, it does seem likely that certain changes in the normative mode of doing research (e.g., multiple measures of several constructs, and minimum samples sizes of approximately 50 adults per age group), would contribute to more reliable, and probably more consistent, results than those available in the past.

CONCLUSION

It has become a cliche for the phrase "further research is needed" to be included in the discussion or conclusion section of scientific articles. Unfortunately, there is no denying the accuracy of the expression with respect to understanding why increased age is associated with lower levels of performance in many measures of cognitive functioning. It is hoped that the discussion in this book has contributed to sharpening and clarification of the theoretical issues so that future research, possibly incorporating some of the recommendations discussed in this chapter, will eventually lead to their resolution, and to a definitive answer to the question of why increased age is associated with a decline in certain measures of cognitive functioning.

REFERENCES

Abbenhuis, M.A., Raaijmakers, W.G.M., Raaijmakers, J.G.W., & van Woerden, G.J.M. (1990). Episodic memory in dementia of the Alzheimer type and in normal ageing: Similar impairment in automatic processing. *Quarterly Journal of Experimental Psychology, 42A*, 569-583.

Adam, J. (1977). Statistical bias in cross-sequential studies of aging. *Experimental Aging Research, 3*, 325-333.

Adamowicz, J.K. (1976). Visual short-term memory and aging. *Journal of Gerontology, 31*, 39-46.

Adamowicz, J.K., & Hudson, B.R. (1978). Visual short-term memory, response delay and age. *Perceptual and Motor Skills, 46*, 267-270.

Adams, C., Labouvie-Vief, G., Hobart, C.J., & Dorosz, M. (1990). Adult age group differences in story recall style. *Journal of Gerontology: Psychological Sciences, 45*, P17-P25.

Adams, C.C., & Rebok, G.W. (1982-83). Planfulness and problem solving in older adults. *International Journal of Aging and Human Development, 16*, 271-282.

Aftanas, M.S., & Royce, J.R. (1969). Analysis of brain damage tests administered to normal subjects with factor score comparisons across ages. *Multivariate Behavioral Research, 4*, 459-481.

Akiyama, M.M., Akiyama, H., & Goodrich, C.C. (1985). Spatial development across the life span. *International Journal of Aging and Human Development, 21*, 175-185.

Albert, M.S. (1988). Cognitive function. In M.S. Albert & M.B. Moss (Eds.), *Geriatric neuropsychology* (pp. 33-53). New York: Guilford Press.

Albert, M.S., Duffy, F.H., & Naeser, M. (1987). Nonlinear changes in cognition with age and their neuropsychologic correlates. *Canadian Journal of Psychology, 41*, 141-157.

Albert, M.S., & Heaton, R.K. (1988). Intelligence testing. In M.S. Albert & M.B. Moss (Eds.), *Geriatric neuropsychology* (pp. 13-32). New York: Guilford Press.

Albert, M.S., Heller, H.S., & Milberg, W. (1988). Changes in naming ability with age. *Psychology and Aging, 3*, 173-178.

Albert, M.S., Wolfe, J., & Lafleche, G. (1990). Differences in abstraction ability with age. *Psychology and Aging, 5*, 94-100.

Alpaugh, P.K., & Birren, J.E. (1977). Variables affecting creative contributions across the adult life span. *Human Development, 20*, 240-248.

Alpaugh, P.K., Parham, I.A., Cole, K.D., & Birren, J.E. (1982). Creativity in adulthood and old age: An exploratory study. *Educational Gerontology, 8*, 101-116.

Anastasi, A. (1958). *Differential psychology*. New York: MacMillan.

Anders, T.R., & Fozard, J.L. (1973). Effects of age upon retrieval from primary and secondary memory. *Developmental Psychology, 9*, 411-415.

Anders, T.R., Fozard, J.L., & Lillyquist, T.D. (1972). Effects of age upon retrieval from short-term memory. *Developmental Psychology, 6,* 214-217.

Anderson, A.M. (1982). The great Japanese IQ increase. *Nature, 297,* 180-181.

Anderson, J.E. (1956a). The assessment of aging: Background in theory and experiment. In J.E. Anderson (Ed.), *Psychological aspects of aging* (pp. 75-80). Washington, DC: American Psychological Association.

Anderson, J.E. (1956b). Research problems in aging. In J.E. Anderson (Ed.), *Psychological aspects of aging* (pp. 267-289). Washington, DC: American Psychological Association.

Anderson, J.E. (1958). A development model for aging. *Vita Humana, 1,* 1-18.

Anooshian, L.J., Mammarella, S.L., & Hertel, P.T. (1989). Adult age differences in the knowledge of retrieval processes. *International Journal of Aging and Human Development, 29,* 39-52.

Arbuckle, T.Y., Gold, D., & Andres, D. (1986). Cognitive functioning of older people in relation to social and personality variables. *Psychology and Aging, 1,* 55-62.

Arbuckle, T.Y., Vanderleck, V.F., Harsany, M., & Lapidus, S. (1990). Adult age differences in memory in relation to availability and accessibility of knowledge-based schemas. *Journal of Experimental Psychology: Learning, Memory, and Cognition, 16,* 305-315.

Ardila, A., & Rosselli, M. (1989). Neuropsychological characteristics of normal aging. *Developmental Neuropsychology, 5,* 307-320.

Arenberg, D. (1967). Age differences in retroaction. *Journal of Gerontology, 22,* 88-91.

Arenberg, D. (1968a). Retention of time judgment in young and old adults. *Journal of Gerontology, 23,* 35-40.

Arenberg, D. (1968b). Concept problem solving in young and old adults. *Journal of Gerontology, 23,* 279-282.

Arenberg, D. (1974). A longitudinal study of problem solving in adults. *Journal of Gerontology, 29,* 650-654.

Arenberg, D. (1976). The effects of input condition on free recall in young and old adults. *Journal of Gerontology, 31,* 551-555.

Arenberg, D. (1977). The effects of auditory augmentation on visual retention for young and old adults. *Journal of Gerontology, 32,* 192-195.

Arenberg, D. (1978). Differences and changes with age in the Benton Visual Retention Test. *Journal of Gerontology, 33,* 534-540.

Arenberg, D. (1982a). Changes with age in problem solving. In F.I.M. Craik & S. Trehub (Eds.), *Aging and cognitive processes* (pp. 221-235). New York: Plenum.

Arenberg, D. (1982b). Estimates of age changes on the Benton Visual Retention Test. *Journal of Gerontology, 37,* 87-90.

Arenberg, D. (1987). A note on differences and changes in memory with age. In M.W. Riley, J.D. Matarazzo, & A. Baum (Eds.), *Perspectives in behavioral medicine: The aging dimension* (pp. 39-47). Hillsdale, NJ: Lawrence Erlbaum Associates.

Arenberg, D. (1988). Analysis and synthesis in problem solving and aging. In M.L. Howe & C.J. Brainerd (Eds.), *Cognitive development in adulthood* (pp. 161-183). New York: Springer-Verlag.

Arenberg, D., & Robertson-Tchabo, E.A. (1977). Learning and aging. In J.E. Birren & K.W. Schaie (Eds.), *Handbook of the psychology of aging* (pp. 421-449). New York: Van Nostrand Reinhold.

Arenberg, D., & Robertson-Tchabo, E.A. (1985). Adult age differences in memory and linguistic integration revisited. *Experimental Aging Research, 11,* 187-191.

Arvey, R.D., & Mussio, S.J. (1973). Test discrimination, job performance and age. *Industrial Gerontology,* 22-29.

Attig, M., & Hasher, L. (1980). The processing of frequency of occurrence information by adults. *Journal of Gerontology, 35,* 66-69.

Avolio, B.J., & Waldman, D.A. (1987). Personnel aptitude test scores as a function of age, education and job type. *Experimental Aging Research, 13,* 109-113.

Avolio, B.J., & Waldman, D.A. (1990). An examination of age and cognitive test performance across job complexity and occupational types. *Journal of Applied Psychology*, *75*, 43-50.

Avorn, J. (1982). Studying cognitive performance in the elderly: A biopsychological approach. In F.I.M. Craik & S. Trehub (Eds.), *Aging and cognitive processes* (pp. 317-329). New York: Plenum.

Axelrod, S., & Cohen, L.D. (1961). Senescence and embedded figure performance in vision and touch. *Perceptual and Motor Skills*, *12*, 283-288.

Azmitia, M., & Perlmutter, M. (1988). Age differences in adults' scene memory: Knowledge and strategy interactions. *Comprehensive Gerontology: Sect. B*, *2*, 75-84.

Babcock, R.L., & Salthouse, T.A. (1990). Effects of increased processing demands on age differences in working memory. *Psychology and Aging*, *5*, 421-428.

Backman, L. (1989). Varieties of memory compensation by older adults in episodic remembering. In L.W. Poon, D.C. Rubin & B.A. Wilson (Eds.), *Everyday cognition in adulthood and late life* (pp. 509-544). Cambridge, England: Cambridge University Press.

Backman, L., Herlitz, A., & Karlsson, T. (1987). Pre-experimental knowledge facilitates episodic recall in young, young-old, and old-old adults. *Experimental Aging Research*, *13*, 89-91.

Backman, L., & Karlsson, T. (1985). The relation between level of general knowledge and feeling-of-knowing: An adult study. *Scandinavian Journal of Psychology*, *26*, 249-258.

Backman, L., & Mantyla, T. (1988). Effectiveness of self-generated cues in younger and older adults: The role of retention interval. *International Journal of Aging and Human Development*, *26*, 241-248.

Backman, L., Mantyla, T., & Erngrund, K. (1984). Optimal recall in early and late adulthood. *Scandinavian Journal of Psychology*, *25*, 306-314.

Backman, L., & Molander, B. (1986). Effects of adult age and level of skill on the ability to cope with high stress conditions in a precision sport. *Psychology and Aging*, *1*, 334-336.

Backman, L., & Nilsson, L.G. (1984). Aging effects in free recall: An exception to the rule. *Human Learning*, *3*, 53-69.

Baddeley, A. (1986). *Working memory*. Oxford: Clarendon Press.

Baddeley, A., Logie, R., Bressi, S., Della Sala, S., & Spinnler, H. (1986). Dementia and working memory. *Quarterly Journal of Experimental Psychology*, *38A*, 603-618.

Bahrick, H.P. (1979). Maintenance of knowledge: Questions about memory we forgot to ask. *Journal of Experimental Psychology: General*, *108*, 296-308.

Bahrick, H.P. (1983). The cognitive map of a city: Fifty years of learning and memory. In G.H. Bower (Ed.), *The psychology of learning and motivation* (Vol. 17, pp. 125-163). New York: Academic.

Bahrick, H.P. (1984). Semantic memory content in permastore: Fifty years of memory for Spanish learned in school. *Journal of Experimental Psychology: General*, *113*, 1-29.

Bahrick, H.P., Bahrick, P.O., & Wittlinger, R.P. (1975). Fifty years of memory for names and faces: A cross-sectional approach. *Journal of Experimental Psychology: General*, *104*, 54-75.

Balota, D.A., & Duchek, J.M. (1988). Age-related differences in lexical access, spreading activation, and simple pronunciation. *Psychology and Aging*, *3*, 84-93.

Balota, D.A., & Duchek, J.M. (1989). Spreading activation in episodic memory: Further evidence for age independence. *Quarterly Journal of Experimental Psychology,*, *41A,*, 849-876.

Balota, D.A., Duchek, J.M., & Paullin, R. (1989). Age-related differences in the impact of spacing, lag, and retention interval. *Psychology and Aging*, *4*, 3-9.

Baltes, P.B. (1968). Longitudinal and cross-sectional sequences in the study of age and generation effects. *Human Development*, *11*, 145-171.

Baltes, P.B. (1973). Prototypical paradigms and questions in life-span research on development and aging. *Gerontologist*, *13*, 458-467.

Baltes, P.B., Cornelius, S.W., & Nesselroade, J.R. (1979). Cohort effects in developmental psychology. In J.R. Nesselroade & P.B. Baltes (Eds.), *Longitudinal research in the study of behavior and development* (pp. 61-87). New York: Academic.

Baltes, P.B., Dittmann-Kohli, F., & Dixon, R.A. (1984). New perspectives on the development of intelligence in adulthood: Toward a dual-process conception and a model of selective optimization with compensation. In P.B. Baltes & O.G. Brim (Eds.), *Life-span development and behavior* (Vol. 6, pp. 33-76). New York: Academic.

Baltes, P.B., Kliegl, R., & Dittmann-Kohli, F. (1988). On the locus of training gains in research on the plasticity of fluid intelligence in old age. *Journal of Educational Psychology,*, *80*, 392-400.

Baltes, P.B., & Labouvie, G.V. (1973). Adult development of intellectual performance: Description, exploration and modification. In C. Eisdorfer & M.P. Lawton (Eds.), *The psychology of adult development and aging* (pp. 157-219). Washington, DC: American Psychological Association.

Baltes, P.B., & Lindenberger, U. (1988). On the range of cognitive plasticity in old age as a function of experience: 15 years of intervention research. *Behavior Therapy*, *19*, 283-300.

Baltes, P.B., & Reese, H.W. (1984). The life-span perspective in developmental psychology. In M.H. Bornstein & M.E. Lamb (Eds.), *Developmental psychology: An advanced textbook* (pp. 493-531). Hillsdale, NJ: Lawrence Erlbaum Associates.

Baltes, P.B., Reese, H.W., & Lipsitt, L.P. (1980). Life-span developmental psychology. *Annual Review of Psychology*, *31*, 65-110.

Baltes, P.B., Reese, H.W., & Nesselroade, J.R. (1977). *Life-span developmental psychology: Introduction to research methods.* Monterey, CA: Brooks-Cole.

Baltes, P.B., & Schaie, K.W. (1974). The myth of the twilight years. *Psychology Today*, *7*, 35-40.

Baltes, P.B., & Schaie, K.W. (1976). On the plasticity of intelligence in adulthood and old age: Where Horn and Donaldson fail. *American Psychologist*, *31*, 720-725.

Baltes, P.B., Schaie, K.W., & Nardi, A.H. (1971). Age and experimental mortality in a seven-year longitudinal study of cognitive behavior. *Developmental Psychology*, *5*, 18-26.

Baltes, P.B., & Willis, S.L. (1977). Toward psychological theories of aging and development. In J.E. Birren & K.W. Schaie (Eds.), *Handbook of the psychology of aging* (pp. 128-154). New York: Van Nostrand Reinhold.

Baltes, P.B., & Willis, S.L. (1979). The critical importance of appropriate methodology in the study of aging: The sample case of psychometric intelligence. In F. Hoffmeister & C. Muller (Eds.), *Brain function in old age: Evaluation of changes and disorders* (pp. 164-187). New York: Springer-Verlag.

Banaji, M.R., & Crowder, R.G. (1989). The bankruptcy of everyday memory. *American Psychologist*, *44*, 1185-1193.

Bandura, A. (1989). Regulation of cognitive processes through perceived self-efficacy. *Developmental Psychology*, *25*, 729-735.

Barnes, C.A. (1979). Memory deficits associated with senescence: A neurophysiological and behavioral study in the rat. *Journal of Comparative and Physiological Psychology*, *93*, 74-104.

Barnes, C.A., & McNaughton, B.L. (1985). An age comparison of the rate of acquisition and forgetting of spatial information in relation to long-term enhancement of hippocampal synapses. *Behavioral Neuroscience*, *99*, 1040-1048.

Barnes, C.A., Nadel, L., & Honig, W.K. (1980). Spatial memory deficit in senescent rats. *Canadian Journal of Psychology*, *34*, 29-39.

Baron, A., & LeBreck, D. (1987). Are older adults generally more conservative? Some negative evidence from signal detection analyses of recognition memory and sensory performance. *Experimental Aging Research*, *13*, 163-165.

Baron, J., & Treiman, R. (1980). Some problems in the study of differences in cognitive processes. *Memory and Cognition, 8*, 313-321.

Barrett, G.V., Mihal, W.L., Panek, P.E., Sterns, H.L., & Alexander, R.A. (1977). Information processing skills predictive of accident involvement for younger and older commercial drivers. *Industrial Gerontology, 4*, 173-182.

Barrett, T.R., & Watkins, S.K. (1986). Word familiarity and cardiovascular health as determinants of age-related recall differences. *Journal of Gerontology, 41*, 222-224.

Barrett, T.R., & Wright, M. (1981). Age-related facilitation in recall following semantic processing. *Journal of Gerontology, 36*, 194-199.

Bartlett, J.C., & Leslie, J.E. (1986). Aging and memory for faces versus single views of faces. *Memory and Cognition, 14*, 371-381.

Bartlett, J.C., Leslie, J.E., Tubbs, A., & Fulton, A. (1989). Aging and memory for pictures of faces. *Psychology and Aging, 4*, 276-283.

Bartlett, J.C., & Snelus, P. (1980). Lifespan memory for popular songs. *American Journal of Psychology, 93*, 551-560.

Bartlett, J.C., Till, R.E., Gernsbacher, M., & Gorman, W. (1983). Age-related differences in memory for lateral orientation of pictures. *Journal of Gerontology, 38*, 439-446.

Barton, E.M., Plemons, J.K., Willis, S.L., & Baltes, P.B. (1975). Recent findings on adult and gerontological intelligence: Changing a stereotype of decline. *American Behavioral Scientist, 19*, 224-236.

Bartus, R.T. (1979). Effects of aging on visual memory, sensory processing and discrimination learning in a nonhuman primate. In J.M. Ordy & K. Brizzee (Eds.), *Sensory systems and communication in the elderly* (pp. 85-114). New York: Raven.

Bartus, R.T., & Dean, R.L. (1979). Recent memory in aged non-human primates: Hypersensitivity to visual interference during retention. *Experimental Aging Research, 5*, 385-400.

Bartus, R.T., Dean, R.L., Goas, J.A., & Lippa, A.S. (1980). Age-related changes in passive avoidance retention: Modulation with dietary choline. *Science, 209*, 301-303.

Bashore, T.R., Osman, A., & Heffley, E.F. (1989). Mental slowing in elderly persons: A cognitive psychophysiological analysis. *Psychology and Aging, 4*, 235-244.

Basowitz, H., & Korchin, S.J. (1957). Age differences in the perception of closure. *Journal of Abnormal and Social Psychology, 54*, 93-97.

Belbin, E. (1956). The effects of propaganda on recall, recognition and behaviour. *British Journal of Psychology, 47*, 259-270.

Belbin, E., & Downs, S. (1965). Interference effects from new learning: Their relevance to the design of adult training programs. *Journal of Gerontology, 20*, 154-159.

Belbin, E., & Downs, S. (1966). Teaching paired associates: The problem of age. *Occupational Psychology, 40*, 67-74.

Bellucci, G., & Hoyer, W.J. (1975). Feedback effects on the performance and self-reinforcing behavior of elderly and young adult women. *Journal of Gerontology, 30*, 456-460.

Belmore, S.M. (1981). Age-related changes in processing explicit and implicit language. *Journal of Gerontology, 36*, 316-322.

Bennett-Levy, J., & Powell, G.E. (1980). The subjective memory questionnaire (SMQ): An investigation into the self-reporting of "real life" memory skills. *British Journal of Social and Clinical Psychology, 19*, 177-188.

Beres, C.A., & Baron, A. (1981). Improved digit symbol substitution by older women as a result of extended practice. *Journal of Gerontology, 36*, 591-597.

Berg, C., Hertzog, C., & Hunt, E. (1982). Age differences in the speed of mental rotation. *Developmental Psychology, 18*, 95-107.

Bergman, M. (1980). *Aging and the perception of speech*. Baltimore: University Park Press.

Berry, J.M., West, R.L., & Dennehey, D.M. (1989). Reliability and validity of the memory self-efficacy questionnaire. *Developmental Psychology, 25*, 701-713.

Bigler, E., Steinman, D., & Newton, J. (1981). Clinical assessment of cognitive deficit in neurologic disorder: Effects of age and degenerative disease. *Clinical Neuropsychology, 3*, 5-13.

Bilash, I., & Zubek, J.P. (1960). The effects of age on factorially "pure" mental abilities. *Journal of Gerontology, 15*, 175-182.

Bingham, W.V., & Davis, W.T. (1924). Intelligence test scores and business success. *Journal of Applied Psychology, 8*, 1-22.

Birkhill, W.R., & Schaie, K.W. (1975). The effect of differential reinforcement of cautiousness in intellectual performance among the elderly. *Journal of Gerontology, 30*, 578-583.

Birren, J.E. (1952). A factorial analysis of the Wechsler-Bellevue Scale given to an elderly population. *Journal of Consulting Psychology, 16*, 399-405.

Birren, J.E. (1955). Age changes in speed of simple responses and perception and their significance for complex behavior. In *Old age in the modern world* (pp. 235-247). London: E. & S. Livingstone.

Birren, J.E. (1956). The significance of age changes in speed of perception and psychomotor skills. In J.E. Anderson (Ed.), *Psychological aspects of aging* (pp. 97-104). Washington, DC: American Psychological Association.

Birren, J.E. (1959). Principles of research on aging. In J.E. Birren (Ed.), *Handbook of aging and the individual* (pp. 3-42). Chicago: University of Chicago Press.

Birren, J.E. (1960). Behavioral theories of aging. In N.W. Shock (Ed.), *Aging: Some social and biological aspects* (pp. 305-332). Washington, DC: American Association for the Advancement of Science.

Birren, J.E. (1964). *The Psychology of aging*, Englewood Cliffs, NJ: Prentice-Hall.

Birren, J.E. (1965). Age changes in speed of behavior: Its central nature and physiological correlates. In A.T. Welford & J.E. Birren (Eds.), *Behavior, aging and the nervous system* (pp. 191-216). Springfield, IL: Charles C Thomas.

Birren, J.E. (1968). Psychological aspects of aging: Intellectual functioning. *Gerontologist, 8*, 16-19.

Birren, J.E. (1970). Toward an experimental psychology of aging. *American Psychologist, 25*, 124-135.

Birren, J.E. (1974). Translations in gerontology - from lab to life: Psychophysiology and speed of response. *American Psychologist, 29*, 808-815.

Birren, J.E., & Cunningham, W.R. (1985). Research on the psychology of aging. In J.E. Birren & K.W. Schaie (Eds.), *Handbook of the psychology of aging*, (2nd ed., pp. 3-34). New York: Van Nostrand Reinhold.

Birren, J.E., Cunningham, W.R., & Yamamoto, K. (1983). Psychology of adult development and aging. *Annual Review of Psychology, 34*, 543-575.

Birren, J.E., & Morrison, D.F. (1961). Analysis of the WAIS subtests in relation to age and education. *Journal of Gerontology, 16*, 363-369.

Birren, J.E., & Renner, V.J. (1977). Research on the psychology of aging: Principles and experimentation. In J.E. Birren & K.W. Schaie (Eds.), *Handbook of the psychology of aging* (pp. 3-38). New York: Van Nostrand Reinhold.

Birren, J.E., & Riegel, K.F. (1962). Age differences in response speed as a function of controlled variations of stimulus condition: Lights, numbers, letters, colors, syllables, words and word relationships. In C. Tibbitts & W. Donahue (Eds.), *Social and psychological aspects of aging* (pp. 751-758). New York: Columbia University Press.

Birren, J.E., Riegel, K.F., & Morrison, D.F. (1962). Age differences in response speed as a function of controlled variations of stimulus conditions: Evidence of a general speed factor. *Gerontologia, 6*, 1-18.

Birren, J.E., & Spieth, W. (1962). Age, response speed, and cardiovascular functions. *Journal of Gerontology, 17*, 390-391.

Birren, J.E., Woods, A.M., & Williams, M.V. (1979). Speed of behavior as an indicator of age changes and the integrity of the nervous system. In F. Hoffmeister & C. Muller (Eds.), *Brain function and old age* (pp. 10-44). New York: Springer-Verlag.

Bleecker, M.L., Bolla-Wilson, U., & Heller, J.R. (1985). The effect of aging on learning curves. *Annals of the New York Academy of Sciences, 444,* 499-501.

Blum, J.E., & Jarvik, L.F. (1974). Intellectual performance of octogenarians as a function of education and initial ability. *Human Development, 17,* 364-375.

Blum, J.E., Jarvik, L.F., & Clark, E.T. (1970). Rate of change on selective tests of intelligence: A twenty-year longitudinal study of aging. *Journal of Gerontology, 25,* 171-176.

Blumenthal, J.A., & Madden, D.J. (1988). Effects of aerobic exercise training, age, and physical fitness on memory-search performance. *Psychology and Aging, 3,* 280-285.

Blusewicz, M.J., Dustman, R., Schenkenberg, T., & Beck, E. (1977). Neuropsychological correlates of chronic alcoholism and aging. *The Journal of Nervous and Mental Disease, 165,* 348-355.

Blusewicz, M.J., Schenkenberg, T., Dustman, R.E., & Beck, E.C. (1977). WAIS performance in young normal, young alcoholic, and elderly normal groups: An evaluation of organicity and mental aging indices. *Journal of Clinical Psychology, 33,* 1149-1153.

Bogard, D.A. (1974). Visual perception of static and dynamic two-dimensional objects. *Perceptual and Motor Skills, 38,* 395-398.

Bogartz, R.S. (1976). On the meaning of statistical interactions. *Journal of Experimental Child Psychology, 22,* 178-183.

Borkan, G.A., Hults, D.E., & Glynn, R.J. (1983). Role of longitudinal change and secular trend in age differences in male body dimensions. *Human Biology, 55,* 629-641.

Bornstein, R., & Smircina, M.T. (1982). The status of empirical support for the hypothesis of increased variability in aging populations. *Gerontologist, 22,* 258-260.

Borod, J.C., Goodglass, H., & Kaplan, E. (1980). Normative data on the Boston Diagnostic Aphasia Examination, Parietal Lobe Battery and the Boston Naming Test. *Journal of Clinical Neuropsychology, 2,* 209-215.

Botwinick, J. (1967). *Cognitive processes in maturity and old age.* New York: Springer.

Botwinick, J. (1969). Disinclination to venture response versus cautiousness in responding: Age differences. *Journal of Genetic Psychology, 115,* 55-62.

Botwinick, J. (1977). Intellectual abilities. In J.E. Birren & K.W. Schaie (Eds.), *Handbook of the Psychology of Aging* (pp. 580-605). New York: Van Nostrand Reinhold.

Botwinick, J. (1978). *Aging and behavior.* New York: Springer.

Botwinick, J., & Arenberg, D. (1976). Disparate time spans in sequential studies of aging. *Experimental Aging Research, 2,* 55-61.

Botwinick, J., & Birren, J.E. (1963). Cognitive processes: Mental abilities and psychomotor responses in healthy aged men. In J.E. Birren, Butler, R.N., Greenhouse, S.W., Sokoloff, L., & Yarrow, M.R. (Eds.), *Human aging: A biological and behavioral study* (pp. 97-108). Washington, DC: U.S. Government Printing Office.

Botwinick, J., & Birren, J.E. (1965). A follow-up study of card-sorting performance in elderly men. *Journal of Gerontology, 20,* 208-210.

Botwinick, J., Brinley, J.F., & Robbin, J.S. (1958). The interaction effects of perceptual difficulty and stimulus exposure time on age differences in speed and accuracy of response. *Gerontologia, 2,* 1-10.

Botwinick, J., & Storandt, M. (1974). *Memory, related functions and age.* Springfield, IL: Charles C Thomas.

Botwinick, J., & Storandt, M. (1980). Recall and recognition of old information in relation to age and sex. *Journal of Gerontology, 35,* 70-76.

Botwinick, J., West, R., & Storandt, M. (1978). Predicting death from behavioral test performance. *Journal of Gerontology, 33,* 755-762.

Bowles, N.L. (1989). Age and semantic inhibition in word retrieval. *Journal of Gerontology: Psychological Sciences, 44*, P88-P90.

Bowles, N.L., & Poon, L.W. (1981). The effect of age on speed of lexical access. *Experimental Aging Research, 7*, 417-425.

Bowles, N.L., & Poon, L.W. (1982). An analysis of the effect of aging on recognition memory. *Journal of Gerontology, 37*, 212-219.

Bowles, N.L., & Poon, L.W. (1985). Aging and retrieval of words in semantic memory. *Journal of Gerontology, 40*, 71-77.

Bowles, N.L., & Poon, L.W. (1988). Age and context effects in lexical decision: An age by context interaction. *Experimental Aging Research, 14*, 201-205.

Bowles, N.W., Williams, D., & Poon, L.W. (1983). On the use of word association norms in aging research. *Experimental Aging Research, 9*, 175-177.

Braune, R., & Wickens, C.D. (1985). The functional age profile: An objective decision criterion for the assessment of pilot performance capacities and capabilities. *Human Factors, 27*, 681-693.

Bray, D.W., & Howard, A. (1983). The AT&T longitudinal studies of managers. In K.W. Schaie (Ed.), *Longitudinal studies of adult psychological development* (pp. 266-312). New York: Guilford Press.

Brigham, M.C., & Pressley, M. (1988). Cognitive monitoring and strategy choice in younger and older adults. *Psychology and Aging, 3*, 249-257.

Brinley, J.F. (1965). Cognitive sets, speed and accuracy of performance in the elderly. In A.T. Welford & J.E. Birren (Eds.), *Behavior, aging and the nervous system* (pp. 114-149). Springfield, IL: Charles C Thomas.

Brinley, J.F., Jovick, T.J., & McLaughlin, L.M. (1974). Age, reasoning and memory in adults. *Journal of Gerontology, 29*, 182-189.

Broadbent, D.E., & Heron, A. (1962). Effects of a subsidiary task upon performance involving immediate memory by younger and older subjects. *British Journal of Psychology, 53*, 189-198.

Bromley, D.B. (1956). Some experimental tests of the effect of age on creative intellectual output. *Journal of Gerontology, 11*, 74-82.

Bromley, D.B. (1957). Some effects of age on the quality of intellectual output. *Journal of Gerontology, 12*, 318-323.

Bromley, D.B. (1958). Some effects of age on short-term learning and remembering. *Journal of Gerontology, 13*, 398-406.

Bromley, D.B. (1963). Age differences in conceptual abilities. In R.H. Williams, C. Tibbitts, & W. Donahue (Eds.), *Processes of aging* (Vol. 2, pp. 96-112). New York: Atherton.

Bromley, D.B. (1967). Age and sex differences in the serial production of creative conceptual responses. *Journal of Gerontology, 22*, 32-42.

Bromley, D.B. (1969). Studies of intellectual function in relation to age and their significance for professional and managerial functions. In A.T. Welford & J.E. Birren (Eds.), *Interdisciplinary topics in gerontology* (Vol. 4, pp. 103-126). Basel: Karger.

Bromley, D.B. (1970). An approach to theory construction in the psychology of development and aging. In L.R. Goulet & P.B. Baltes (Eds.), *Life-span developmental psychology* (pp. 71-114). New York: Academic.

Bromley, D.B. (1972). Intellectual changes in adult life and old age: A commentary on the assumptions underlying the study of adult intelligence. In H.M. van Praag (Ed.), *Ageing of the central nervous system* (pp. 76-100). Amsterdam: De Erben F. Bohn, N.V.

Bromley, D.B. (1974). *The psychology of human ageing*. Middlesex, England: Penguin.

Brown J. (1958). Some tests of the decay theory of immediate memory. *Quarterly Journal of Experimental Psychology, 10*, 12-21.

Brozek, J. (1951). Changes in sensory, motor, and intellectual functions with age. *Geriatrics, 6*, 221-226.

Bruce, P.R., Coyne, A.C., & Botwinick, J. (1982) Adult age differences in metamemory. *Journal of Gerontology, 37,* 354-357.

Bruce, P.R., & Herman, J.F. (1983). Spatial knowledge of young and elderly adults: Scene recognition from familiar and novel perspectives. *Experimental Aging Research, 9,* 169-173.

Bruce, P.R., & Herman, J.F. (1986). Adult age differences in spatial memory: Effects of distinctiveness and repeated experience. *Journal of Gerontology, 41,* 774-777.

Bruning, R.H., Holzbauer, I., & Kimberlin, C. (1975). Age, word imagery, and delay interval: Effects on short term and long term retention. *Journal of Gerontology, 30,* 312-318.

Burger, M.C., Botwinick, J., & Storandt, M. (1987). Aging, alcoholism and performance on the Luria-Nebraska Neuropsychological Battery. *Journal of Gerontology, 42,* 69-72.

Burke, D.M., & Harrold, R.M. (1988). Automatic and effortful semantic processes in old age: Experimental and naturalistic approaches. In L.L. Light & D.M.Burke (Eds.), *Language, memory and aging* (pp. 100-116). New York: Cambridge University Press.

Burke, D.M., & Light, L.L. (1981). Memory and aging: The role of retrieval processes. *Psychological Bulletin, 90,* 513-546.

Burke, D.M., & Peters, L. (1986). Word associations in old age: Evidence for consistency in semantic encoding during adulthood. *Psychology and Aging, 1,* 283-292.

Burke, D.M., White, H., & Diaz, D.L. (1987). Semantic priming in young and older adults: Evidence for age constancy in automatic and attentional processes. *Journal of Experimental Psychology: Human Perception and Performance, 13,* 79-88.

Burke, D.M., Worthley, J., & Martin, J. (1988). I'll never forget what's-her-name: Aging and tip of the tongue experiences in everyday life. In M.M. Gruneberg, P.E. Morris, & R.N. Sykes (Eds.), *Practical aspects of memory: Current research and issues* (pp. 113-118). Chichester: Wiley.

Burke, D.M., & Yee, P.L. (1984). Semantic priming during sentence processing by young and older adults. *Developmental Psychology, 20,* 903-910.

Burke, H.R. (1972). Raven's Progressive Matrices: Validity, reliability and norms. *Journal of Psychology, 82,* 253-257.

Burke, H.R. (1985). Raven's Progressive Matrices (1938): More on norms, reliability, and validity. *Journal of Clinical Psychology, 41,* 231-235.

Burton, A., & Joel, W. (1945). Adult norms for the Watson-Glaser Tests of Critical Thinking. *Journal of Psychology, 19,* 43-48.

Buschke, H. (1974). Two stages of learning by children and adults. *Bulletin of the Psychonomic Society, 2,* 392-394.

Buschke, H. (1988). Memory for details in aging and dementia. In M.M. Gruneberg, P.E. Morris, & R.N. Sykes (Eds.), *Practical aspects of memory: Current research and issues.* (p. 96-100). Chichester: Wiley.

Buschke, H., & Grober, E. (1986). Genuine memory deficits in age-associated memory impairment. *Developmental Neuropsychology, 2,* 287-307.

Buschke, H., & Macht, M.L. (1983). Explanation and conceptual memory. *Bulletin of the Psychonomic Society, 21,* 397-399.

Butterfield, E.C., Nelson, T.O., & Peck, V. (1988). Developmental aspects of the feeling of knowing. *Developmental Psychology, 24,* 654-663.

Byrd, M. (1984). Age differences in the retrieval of information from semantic memory. *Experimental Aging Research, 10,* 29-33.

Caird, W.K. (1966). Aging and short-term memory. *Journal of Gerontology, 21,* 295-299.

Cameron, D.E. (1943). Impairment at the retention phase of remembering. *Psychiatric Quarterly, 17,* 395-404.

Camp, C.J., West, R.L., & Poon, L.W. (1989). Recruitment practices for psychological research in gerontology. In M.P. Lawton & A.R. Herzog (Eds.), *Special research methods for gerontology* (pp. 163-189). Amityville, NY: Baywood.

Campbell, D.T., & Fiske, D.W. (1959). Convergent and discriminant validation by the multitrait-multimethod matrix. *Psychological Bulletin, 56*, 81-105.

Cane, V., & Gregory, R.L. (1957). Noise and the visual threshold. *Nature, 180*, 1404-1405

Canestrari, R.E. (1966). The effects of commonality on paired associate learning in two age groups. *Journal of Genetic Psychology, 108*, 3-7.

Canestrari, R.E. (1968). Age changes in acquisition. In G.A. Talland (Ed.), *Human aging and behavior* (pp. 169-188). New York: Academic.

Capitani, E., Della Sala, S., Lucchelli, F., Soave, P., & Spinnler, H. (1988). Perceptual attention in aging and dementia measured by Gottshaldt's Hidden Figure Test. *Journal of Gerontology: Psychological Sciences, 43*, P157-P163.

Capon, N., Kuhn, D., & Gurucharri, M. (1981). Consumer information-processing strategies in middle and late adulthood. *Journal of Applied Developmental Psychology, 2*, 1-12.

Carroll, J.B. (1976). Psychometric tests as cognitive tasks: A new "structure of intellect". In L.B. Resnick (Ed.), *The nature of intelligence* (pp. 27-56). Hillsdale, NJ: Lawrence Erlbaum Associates.

Cattell, R.B. (1943). The measurement of adult intelligence. *Psychological Bulletin, 40*, 153-193.

Cattell, R.B. (1970). Separating endogenous, exogenous, ecogenic, and epogenic component curves in developmental data. *Developmental Psychology, 3*, 151-162.

Cattell, R.B. (1972). *Abilities: Their structure, growth and action.* Boston: Houghton Mifflin.

Cavanaugh, J.C. (1986-87). Age differences in adults' self-reports of memory ability: It depends on how and what you ask. *International Journal of Aging and Human Development, 24*, 271-277.

Cavanaugh, J.C., Grady, J.G., & Perlmutter, M. (1983). Forgetting and use of memory aids in 20 to 70 year olds everyday life. *International Journal of Aging and Human Development, 17*, 113-122.

Cavanaugh, J.C., Kramer, D.A., Sinnott, J.D., Camp, C.J., & Markley, R.P. (1985). On missing links and such: Interfaces between cognitive research and everyday problem solving. *Human Development, 28*, 146-168.

Cavanaugh, J.C., & Murphy, N. (1986). Personality and metamemory correlates of memory performance in younger and older adults. *Educational Gerontology, 12*, 385-394.

Cavanaugh, J.C., & Poon, L.W. (1989). Metamemorial predictors of memory performance in young and older adults. *Psychology and Aging, 4*, 365-368.

Ceci, S.J., & Cornelius, S.W. (1990). Commentary on Perlmutter, et al., "Development of Adaptive Competence in Adulthood." *Human Development, 33*, 198-201.

Cerella, J. (1985). Information processing rates in the elderly. *Psychological Bulletin, 98*, 67-83.

Cerella, J. (1990). Aging and information-processing rate. In J.E. Birren & K.W. Schaie (Eds.), *Handbook of the psychology of aging* (3rd ed., pp. 201-221). San Diego: Academic.

Cerella, J., DiCara, R., Williams, D., & Bowles, N. (1986). Relations between information processing and intelligence in elderly adults. *Intelligence, 10*, 75-91.

Cerella, J., & Fozard, J.L. (1984). Lexical access and age. *Developmental Psychology, 20*, 235-243.

Cerella, J., Poon, L.W., & Fozard, J.L. (1981). Mental rotation and age reconsidered. *Journal of Gerontology, 36*, 620-624.

Cerella, J., Poon, L.W., & Williams, D.M. (1980). Age and the complexity hypothesis. In L.W. Poon (Ed.), *Aging in the 1980s* (pp. 332-340). Washington, DC: American Psychological Association.

Chapman, L.J., & Chapman, J.P. (1973). Problems in the measurement of cognitive deficit. *Psychological Bulletin, 79*, 380-385.

Chapman, L.J., & Chapman, J.P. (1978). The measurement of differential deficit. *Journal of Psychiatric Research, 14*, 303-311.

Charness, N. (1979). Components of skill in bridge. *Canadian Journal of Psychology*, *33*, 1-16.

Charness, N. (1981a). Aging and skilled problem solving. *Journal of Experimental Psychology: General*, *110*, 21-38.

Charness, N. (1981b). Visual short-term memory and aging in chess players. *Journal of Gerontology*, *36*, 615-619.

Charness, N. (1982). Problem solving and aging: Evidence from semantically rich domains. *Canadian Journal on Aging*, *1*, 21-28.

Charness, N. (1985a). Introduction. In N. Charness (Ed.), *Aging and human performance* (pp. xv-xxiii). Chichester: Wiley.

Charness, N. (1985b). Aging and problem-solving performance. In N. Charness (Ed.), *Aging and human performance* (pp. 225-259). Chichester: Wiley.

Charness, N. (1987). Component processes in bridge bidding and novel problem-solving tasks. *Canadian Journal of Psychology*, *41*, 223-243.

Charness, N. (1989). Age and expertise: Responding to Talland's challenge. In L.W. Poon, D.C. Rubin & B.A. Wilson (Eds.), *Everyday cognition in adulthood and late life* (pp. 437-456). Cambridge, England: Cambridge University Press.

Charness, N., & Campbell, J.I.D. (1988). Acquiring skill at mental calculation in adulthood: A task decomposition. *Journal of Experimental Psychology: General*, *117*, 115-129.

Cherry, K.E., & Park, D.C. (1989). Age-related differences in three-dimensional spatial memory. *Journal of Gerontology: Psychological Sciences*, *44*, P16-P22.

Chiarello, C., Church, K.L., & Hoyer, W.J. (1985). Automatic and controlled semantic priming: Accuracy, response bias and aging. *Journal of Gerontology*, *40*, 593-600.

Chiarello, C., & Hoyer, W.J. (1988). Adult age differences in implicit and explicit memory: Time course and encoding effects. *Psychology and Aging*, *3*, 358-366.

Chown, S.M. (1961). Age and the rigidities. *Journal of Gerontology*, *16*, 353-362.

Cijfer, E. (1966). An experiment on some differences in logical thinking between Dutch medical people, under and over the age of 35. *Acta Psychologica*, *25*, 159-171.

Cimbalo, R.S., & Brink, L. (1982). Aging and the Von Restorff isolation effect in short-term memory. *Journal of General Psychology*, *106*, 69-76.

Clark, E.O. (1980). Semantic and episodic memory impairment in normal and cognitively impaired elderly adults. In L.K. Obler & M.L. Albert (Eds.), *Language and communication with the elderly* (pp. 47-57). Lexington, MA: D.C. Heath.

Clark, J.W. (1960). The aging dimension: A factorial analysis of individual differences with age on psychological and physiological measurements. *Journal of Gerontology*, *15*, 183-187.

Clark, L.E., & Knowles, J.B. (1973). Age differences in dichotic listening performance. *Journal of Gerontology*, *28*, 173-178.

Clarkson-Smith, L., & Halpern, D.F. (1983). Can age-related deficits in spatial memory be attenuated through the use of verbal coding? *Experimental Aging Research*, *9*, 179-184.

Clarkson-Smith, L., & Hartley, A.A. (1989). Relationships between physical exercise and cognitive abilities in older adults. *Psychology and Aging*, *4*, 183-189.

Clay, H.M. (1954). Changes of performance with age on similar tasks of varying complexity. *British Journal of Psychology*, *45*, 7-13.

Clement, F. (1969). The relative development of several psycho-physiological and psychometric variables with different occupations and intellectual levels. *Interdisciplinary Topics in Gerontology*, *4*, 57-65.

Cobb, B.B., Lay, C.D., & Bourdet, N.M. (1971). *The relationship between chronological age and aptitude test measures of advanced-level air traffic control trainees* (FAA-AM-71-36). Oklahoma City, OK: Federal Aviation Administration.

Cockburn, J., & Smith, P.T. (1988). Effects of age and intelligence on everyday memory tasks. In M.M. Gruneberg, P.E. Morris, & R.N. Sykes (Eds.), *Practical aspects of memory: Current research and issues* (pp. 132-136). Chichester: Wiley.

Cohen, D., & Wu, S. (1980). Language and cognition during aging. *Annual Review of*

Gerontology and Geriatrics, 1, 71-96.

Cohen, G. (1979). Language comprehension in old age. *Cognitive Psychology, 11,* 412-429.

Cohen, G. (1981). Inferential reasoning in old age. *Cognition, 9,* 59-72.

Cohen, G. (1988). Age differences in memory for texts: Production deficiency or processing limitations? In L.L. Light & D.M.Burke (Eds.), *Language, memory and aging* (pp. 171-190). New York: Cambridge University Press.

Cohen, G., & Faulkner, D. (1981). Memory for discourse in old age. *Discourse Processes, 4,* 253-265.

Cohen, G., & Faulkner, D. (1983a). Age differences in performance on two information-processing tasks: Strategy selection and processing efficiency. *Journal of Gerontology, 38,* 447-454.

Cohen, G., & Faulkner, D. (1983b). Word recognition: Age differences in contextual facilitation effects. *British Journal of Psychology, 74,* 239-251.

Cohen, G., & Faulkner, D. (1984). Memory in old age: "Good in parts." *New Scientist, 104,* 49-51.

Cohen, G., & Faulkner, D. (1986). Memory for proper names: Age differences in retrieval. *British Journal of Developmental Psychology, 4,* 187-197.

Cohen, G., & Faulkner, D. (1989a). Age differences in source forgetting: Effects on reality monitoring and on eyewitness testimony. *Psychology and Aging, 4,* 10-17.

Cohen, G., & Faulkner, D. (1989b). The effects of aging on perceived and generated memories. In L.W. Poon, D.C. Rubin & B.A. Wilson (Eds.), *Everyday cognition in adulthood and late life* (pp. 222-243). Cambridge, England: Cambridge University Press.

Cohen, J. (1988). *Statistical power analysis for the behavioral sciences.* (2nd ed.), Hillsdale, NJ: Lawrence Erlbaum Associates.

Cohen, R.L., Sandler, S.P., & Schroeder, K. (1987). Aging and memory for words and action events: Effects of item repetition and list length. *Psychology and Aging, 2,* 280-285.

Conrad, H.S. (1930). General information, intelligence, and the decline of intelligence. *Journal of Applied Psychology, 14,* 592-599.

Conrad, H.S. (1956). Learning, motivation and education. In J.E. Anderson (Ed.), *Psychological aspects of aging* (pp. 177-184). Washington, DC: American Psychological Association.

Conrad, H.S., & Jones, H.E. (1929). Psychological studies of motion pictures: III. Fidelity of report as a measure of adult intelligence. *University of California Publications in Psychology, 3,* 245-276.

Conrad, H.S., Jones, H.E., & Hsiao, H.H. (1933). Sex differences in mental growth and decline. *Journal of Educational Psychology, 24,* 161-169.

Cooney, T.M., Schaie, K.W., & Willis, S.L. (1988). The relationship between prior functioning on cognitive and personality dimensions and subject attrition in longitudinal research. *Journal of Gerontology, 43,* P12-P17.

Cornelius, S.W. (1984). Classic pattern of intellectual aging: Test familiarity, difficulty and performance. *Journal of Gerontology, 39,* 201-206.

Cornelius, S.W., & Caspi, A. (1986). Self-perceptions of intellectual control and aging. *Educational Gerontology, 12,* 345-357.

Cornelius, S.W., & Caspi, A. (1987). Everyday problem solving in adulthood and old age. *Psychology and Aging, 2,* 144-153.

Correll, R.E., Rokosz, S., & Blanchard, B.M. (1966). Some correlates of WAIS performance in the elderly. *Journal of Gerontology, 21,* 544-549.

Cowart, C.A., & McCallum, R.S. (1984). Simultaneous-successive processing across the life-span: A cross-sectional examination of stability and proficiency. *Experimental Aging Research, 10,* 225-229.

Coyne, A.C. (1985). Adult age, presentation time and memory performance. *Experimental Aging Research, 11,* 147-149.

Coyne, A.C., Herman, J.F., & Botwinick, J. (1980). Age differences in acoustic and semantic recognition memory. *Perceptual and Motor Skills, 51*, 439-445.

Craik, F.I.M. (1965). The nature of the age decrement in performance on dichotic listening tasks. *Quarterly Journal of Experimental Psychology, 17*, 227-240.

Craik, F.I.M. (1968a). Short-term memory and the aging process. In G.A. Talland (Ed.), *Human aging and behavior* (pp. 131-168). New York: Academic.

Craik, F.I.M. (1968b). Two components in free recall. *Journal of Verbal Learning and Verbal Behavior, 7*, 996-1004.

Craik, F.I.M. (1971). Age differences in recognition memory. *Quarterly Journal of Experimental Psychology, 23*, 316-323.

Craik, F.I.M. (1977). Age differences in human memory. In J.E. Birren & K.W. Schaie (Eds.), *Handbook of the psychology of aging* (pp. 384-420). New York: Van Nostrand Reinhold.

Craik, F.I.M. (1982). Selective changes in encoding as a function of reduced processing capacity. In F. Klix, J. Hoffmann & E. van der Meer (Eds.), *Cognitive research in psychology* (pp. 152-161). Amsterdam: North Holland.

Craik, F.I.M. (1983). On the transfer of information from temporary to permanent memory. *Philosophical Transactions of the Royal Society of London, B302*, 341-359.

Craik, F.I.M. (1984). Age differences in remembering. In L.R. Squire & N. Butters (Eds.) *Neuropsychology of memory* (pp. 3-12). New York: Guilford.

Craik, F.I.M. (1986). A functional account of age differences in memory. In F. Klix & H. Hagendorf (Eds.), *Human memory and cognitive capabilities* (pp. 409-422). Amsterdam: North-Holland.

Craik, F.I.M., & Byrd, M. (1982). Aging and cognitive deficits: The role of attentional resources. In F.I.M. Craik & S. Trehub (Eds.), *Aging and cognitive processes* (pp. 191-211). New York: Plenum Press.

Craik, F.I.M., Byrd, M., & Swanson, J.M. (1987). Patterns of memory loss in three elderly samples. *Psychology and Aging, 2*, 79-86.

Craik, F.I.M., & Lockhart, R.S. (1972). Levels of processing: A framework for memory research. *Journal of Verbal Learning and Verbal Behavior, 11*, 671-684.

Craik, F.I.M., & Masani, P.A. (1969). Age and intelligence differences in coding and retrieval of word lists. *British Journal of Psychology, 60*, 315-319.

Craik, F.I.M., & McDowd, J.M. (1987). Age differences in recall and recognition. *Journal of Experimental Psychology: Learning, Memory and Cognition, 13*, 474-479.

Craik, F.I.M., & Rabinowitz, J.C. (1984). Age differences in the acquisition and use of verbal information: A tutorial review. In H. Bouma & D.G. Bouwhuis (Eds.), *Attention and performance X: Control of language processes* (pp. 471-499). Hillsdale, NJ: Lawrence Erlbaum Associates.

Craik, F.I.M., & Rabinowitz, J.C. (1985). The effects of presentation rate and encoding task on age-related memory deficits. *Journal of Gerontology, 40*, 309-315.

Craik, F.I.M., & Simon, E. (1980). Age differences in memory: The roles of attention and depth of processing. In L.W. Poon, J.L. Fozard, L.S. Cermak, D. Arenberg & L.W. Thompson (Eds.), *New directions in memory and aging* (pp. 95-112). Hillsdale, NJ: Lawrence Erlbaum Associates.

Cremer, R., & Zeef, E.J. (1987). What kind of noise increases with age? *Journal of Gerontology, 42*, 515-518.

Crook, M.N., Alexander, E.A., Anderson, E.M., Coules, J., Hanson, J.A., & Jeffries, N.T. (1958). *Age and form perception.* (Report No. 57-124). Randolph Air Force Base, TX: USAF School of Aviation Medicine.

Crook, T.H. (1979). Psychometric assessment in the elderly. In A. Raskin & L.F. Jarvik (Eds.), *Psychiatric symptoms and cognitive loss* (pp. 207-220). New York: Halstead.

Crook, T.H., Ferris, S., & McCarthy, M. (1979). The Misplaced Objects Task: A brief test for memory dysfunction in the aged. *Journal of the American Geriatrics Society, 27*, 284-287.

Crook, T.H., & Larrabee, G.J. (1990). A self-rating scale for evaluating memory in everyday life. *Psychology and Aging, 5*, 48-57.

Crook, T.H., Ferris, S., McCarthy, M., & Rae, D. (1980). Utility of digit recall tasks for assessing memory in the aged. *Journal of Consulting and Clinical Psychology, 48*, 228-233.

Crook, T.H., & West, R.L. (1990). Name recall performance across the adult life-span. *British Journal of Psychology, 81*, 335-349.

Crossman, E.R.F.W., & Szafran, J. (1956). Changes with age in the speed of information-intake and discrimination. *Experientia Supplementum IV. Symposium on Experimental Gerontology* (pp. 128-135). Basel: Birkhauser.

Crosson, C.W. (1984). Age and field independence among women. *Experimental Aging Research, 10*, 165-170.

Crosson, C.W., & Robertson-Tchabo, E.A. (1983). Age and preference for complexity among manifestly creative women. *Human Development, 26*, 149-155.

Crovitz, E. (1966). Reversing a learning deficit in the aged. *Journal of Gerontology, 21*, 236-238.

Crowder, R.G. (1980). Echoic memory and the study of aging memory systems. In L.W. Poon, J.L. Fozard, L.S. Cermak, D. Arenberg & L.W. Thompson (Eds.). *New directions in memory and aging* (pp. 181-204). Hillsdale, NJ: Lawrence Erlbaum Associates.

Cunningham, W.R. (1978). Principles for identifying structural differences: Some methodological issues related to comparative factor analysis. *Journal of Gerontology, 33*, 82-86.

Cunningham, W.R. (1980). Age comparative factor analysis of ability variables in adulthood and old age. *Intelligence, 4*, 133-149.

Cunningham, W.R. (1987). Intellectual abilities and age. In K.W. Schaie (Ed.), *Annual review of gerontology and geriatrics* (Vol. 7, pp. 117-134). New York: Springer.

Cunningham, W.R., & Birren, J.E. (1976). Age changes in human abilities: A 28-year longitudinal study. *Developmental Psychology, 12*, 81-82.

Cunningham, W.R., Clayton, V., & Overton, W. (1975). Fluid and crystallized intelligence in young adulthood and old age. *Journal of Gerontology, 30*, 53-55.

Cunningham, W.R., Sepkoski, C.M., & Opel, M.R. (1978). Fatigue effects on intelligence test performance in the elderly. *Journal of Gerontology, 33*, 541-545.

Danziger, W.L., & Salthouse, T.A. (1978). Age and the perception of incomplete figures. *Experimental Aging Research, 4*, 67-80.

Datan, N., Rodeheaver, D., & Hughes, F. (1987). Adult development and aging. *Annual Review of Psychology, 38*, 153-180.

Davies, A.D. (1967). Age and memory-for-designs test. *British Journal of Social and Clinical Psychology, 6*, 228-233.

Davies, D.R., & Griew, S. (1965). Age and vigilance. In A.T. Welford & J.E. Birren (Eds.), *Behavior, aging and the nervous system* (pp. 54-59). Springfield, IL: Charles C Thomas.

Dean, R.L., Scozzafava, J., Goas, J.A., Regan, B., Beer, B., & Bartus, R.T. (1981). Age-related differences in behavior across the life span of the C57Bl/6J mouse. *Experimental Aging Research, 7*, 427-451.

DeCarlo, T.J. (1974). Recreation participation patterns and successful aging. *Journal of Gerontology, 29*, 416-422.

Del Vento Bielby, D., & Papalia, D. (1975). Moral development and perceptual role-taking egocentrism: Their development and interrelationship across the life-span. *International Journal of Aging and Human Development, 6*, 293-308.

Demming, J.A., & Pressey, S.L. (1957). Tests indigenous to the adult and older years. *Journal of Counseling Psychology, 4*, 144-148.

Denney, D.R., & Denney, N.W. (1973). The use of classification for problem solving: A comparison of middle and old age. *Developmental Psychology*, *9*, 275-278.

Denney, N.W. (1979). Problem solving in later adulthood: Intervention research. In P.B. Baltes & O.G. Brim (Eds.), *Life-span development and behavior* (Vol. 2, pp. 37-66). New York: Academic.

Denney, N.W. (1980). Task demands and problem-solving strategies in middle-aged and older adults. *Journal of Gerontology*, *35*, 559-564.

Denney, N.W. (1982). Aging and cognitive changes. In B.B. Wolman (Ed.), *Handbook of developmental psychology* (pp. 807-827). Englewood Cliffs, NJ: Prentice-Hall.

Denney, N.W. (1984). A model of cognitive development across the life span. *Developmental Review*, *4*, 171-191.

Denney, N.W. (1985). A review of life-span research with the 20-question task: A study of problem-solving ability. *International Journal of Aging and Human Development*, *21*, 161-173.

Denney, N.W. (1989). Everyday problem solving: Methodological issues, research findings, and a model. In L.W. Poon, D.C. Rubin & B.A. Wilson (Eds.), *Everyday cognition in adulthood and late life* (pp. 330-351). Cambridge, England: Cambridge University Press.

Denney, N.W., & Denney, D.R. (1974). Modeling effects on the questioning strategies of the elderly. *Developmental Psychology*, *10*, 458.

Denney, N.W., & Denney, D.R. (1982). The relationship between classification and questioning strategies among adults. *Journal of Gerontology*, *37*, 190-196.

Denney, N.W., & Palmer, A.M. (1981). Adult age differences on traditional and practical problem-solving measures. *Journal of Gerontology*, *36*, 323-328.

Denney, N.W., Pearce, K.A., & Palmer, A.M. (1982). A developmental study of adults' performance on traditional and practical problem-solving tasks. *Experimental Aging Research*, *8*, 115-118.

Dennis, W. (1953). *Aging and behavior: A survey of the literature*. Randolph Field, Texas: USAF School of Aviation Medicine (Tech. Report No. 21-0202-0005-1).

Desroches, H.F., Kaiman, B.D., & Ballard, H.T. (1966). Relationships between age and recall of meaningful material. *Psychological Reports*, *18*, 920-922.

Devolder, P.A., Brigham, M.C., & Pressley, M. (1990). Memory performance awareness in younger and older adults. *Psychology and Aging*, *5*, 291-303.

Devolder, P.A., & Pressley, M. (1989). Metamemory across the adult lifespan. *Canadian Psychology*, *30*, 578-587.

Dick, M., Kean, M.L., & Sands, D. (1989). Memory for internally generated words in Alzheimer-type dementia: Breakdown in encoding and semantic memory. *Brain and Cognition*, *9*, 88-108.

Dirken, J.M. (1972). *Functional age of industrial workers: A transversal survey of ageing capacities and a method for assessing functional age*. Groningen: Wolters-Noordhoff.

Dixon, R.A., & Hultsch, D.F. (1983). Metamemory and memory for text relationships in adulthood: A cross-validation study. *Journal of Gerontology*, *38*, 689-694.

Dobbs, A.R., & Rule, B.G. (1987). Prospective memory and self-reports of memory abilities in older adults. *Canadian Journal of Psychology*, *41*, 209-222.

Dobbs, A.R., & Rule, B.G. (1989). Adult age differences in working memory. *Psychology and Aging*, *4*, 500-503.

Donahue, W. (1956). Learning, motivation and education of the aging. In J.E. Anderson (Ed.), *Psychological aspects of aging* (pp. 200-206). Washington, DC: American Psychological Association.

Donaldson, G. (1981). Letter to the editor. *Journal of Gerontology*, *36*, 634-638.

Dorfman, D., Glanzer, M., & Kaufman, J. (1986). Aging effects on recognition memory when encoding and strategy are controlled. *Bulletin of the Psychonomic Society*, *24*, 172-174.

Drachman, D.A., & Leavitt, J. (1972). Memory impairment in the aged: Storage vs. retrieval. *Journal of Experimental Psychology*, *93*, 302-308.

Droege, R.C., Crambert, A.C., & Henlein, J.B. (1963). Relationship between G.A.T.B. aptitude scores and age for adults. *Personnel and Guidance Journal, 41*, 502-508.

Dubois, P.H. (1970). *A history of psychological testing.* Boston: Allyn & Bacon.

Duchek, J.M. (1984). Encoding and retrieval differences between young and old: The impact of attentional capacity usage. *Developmental Psychology, 20*, 1173-1180.

Dulewicz, V., & Fletcher, C. (1982). The relationship between previous experience, intelligence and background characteristics of participants and their performance in an assessment centre. *Journal of Occupational Psychology, 55*, 197-202.

Dustman, R.E., & Beck, E.C. (1980). Memory-for-Designs Test: Comparison of performance of young and old adults. *Journal of Clinical Psychology, 36*, 770-774.

Dywan, J., & Jacoby, L. (1990). Effects of aging on source monitoring: Differences in susceptibility to false fame. *Psychology and Aging, 5*, 379-387.

Eckensberger, L.H., Krewer, B., & Kasper, E. (1984). Simulation of cultural change by cross-cultural research: Some metamethodological considerations. In K.A. McCluskey & H.W. Reese (Eds.), *Life-span developmental psychology: Historical and generational effects* (pp. 73-107). Orlando, FL: Academic.

Edwards, A.E., & Wine, D.B. (1963). Personality changes with age: Their dependency on concomitant intellectual decline. *Journal of Gerontology, 18*, 182-184.

Egan, D.E., & Gomez, L.M. (1985). Assaying, isolating, and accommodating individual differences in learning a complex skill. In R.F. Dillon (Ed.), *Individual differences in cognition* (Vol. 2, pp. 173-217). Orlando, FL: Academic.

Eisdorfer, C. (1969). Intellectual and cognitive changes in the aged. In E.W. Busse & E. Pfeiffer (Eds.), *Behavior and adaptation in late life* (pp. 237-250). Boston, MA: Little, Brown & Co.

Einstein, G.O., & McDaniel, M.A. (1990). Normal aging and prospective memory. *Journal of Experimental Psychology: Learning, Memory, and Cognition, 16*, 717-726.

Eisner, D.A. (1972). Life-span age differences in visual perception. *Perceptual and Motor Skills, 34*, 857-858.

Elias, C.S., & Hirasuna, N. (1976). Age and semantic and phonological encoding. *Developmental Psychology, 12*, 497-503.

Elias, M.F., Robbins, M.A., Schultz, N.R., & Pierce, T.W. (1990). Is blood pressure an important variable in research on aging and neuropsychological performance? *Journal of Gerontology: Psychological Sciences, 45*, P128-P135.

Elias, P.K., Elias, M.F., Robbins, M.A., & Gage, P. (1987). Acquisition of word-processing skills by younger, middle-age, and older adults. *Psychology and Aging, 2*, 340-348.

Ellis, N.R., Palmer, R.L., & Reeves, C.L. (1988). Developmental and intellectual differences in frequency processing. *Developmental Psychology, 24*, 38-45.

Emanuelsson, I., & Svensson, A. (1986). Does the level of intelligence decrease? A comparison between thirteen-year-olds tested in 1961, 1966, and 1980. *Scandinavian Journal of Educational Research, 30*, 25-38.

Emery, O.B. (1985). Language and aging. *Experimental Aging Research, 11*, 3-60.

Erber, J.T. (1974). Age differences in recognition memory. *Journal of Gerontology, 29*, 177-181.

Erber, J.T. (1978). Age differences in a controlled-lag recognition memory task. *Experimental Aging Research, 4*, 195-205.

Erber, J.T. (1981). Remote memory and age: A review. *Experimental Aging Research, 7*, 189-199.

Erber, J.T. (1984). Age differences in the effect of encoding congruence on incidental free and cued recall. *Experimental Aging Research, 10*, 221-223.

Erber, J.T., Abello, S., & Moninger, C. (1988). Age and individual differences in immediate and delayed effectiveness of mnemonic instructions. *Experimental Aging Research, 14*, 119-124.

Erber, J.T., Galt, D. Jr., & Botwinick, J. (1985). Age differences in the effects of contextual framework and word-familiarity on episodic memory. *Experimental Aging Research, 11,* 101-103.

Erber, J.T., Herman, T.G., & Botwinick, J. (1980). Age differences in memory as a function of depth of processing. *Experimental Aging Research, 6,* 341-348.

Erickson, R.C., Poon, L.W., & Walsh-Sweeney, L. (1980). Clinical memory testing of the elderly. In L.W. Poon, J.L. Fozard, L.S. Cermak, D. Arenberg, & L.W. Thompson (Eds.), *New directions in memory and aging* (pp. 379-402). Hillsdale, NJ: Lawrence Erlbaum Associates.

Eriksen, C.W., Hamlin, R.M., & Daye, C. (1973). Aging adults and rate of memory scan. *Bulletin of the Psychonomic Society, 1,* 259-260.

Evans, G.W., Brennan, P.L., Skorpanich, M.A., & Held, D. (1984). Cognitive mapping and elderly adults: Verbal and location memory for urban landmarks. *Journal of Gerontology, 39,* 452-457.

Eysenck, M.W. (1974). Age differences in incidental learning. *Developmental Psychology, 10,* 936-941.

Eysenck, M.W. (1975). Retrieval from semantic memory as a function of age. *Journal of Gerontology, 30,* 174-180.

Farrimond, T. (1959). Age differences in the ability to use visual cues in auditory communication. *Language and Speech, 2,* 179-192.

Farrimond, T. (1969). Age differences in speed of retrieval from memory store. *Australian Journal of Psychology, 21,* 79-83.

Feier, C.D., & Gerstman, L.J. (1980). Sentence comprehension abilities throughout the adult life span. *Journal of Gerontology, 35,* 722-728.

Ferris, S.H., Crook, T., Clark, E., McCarthy, M., & Rae, D. (1980). Facial recognition memory deficits in normal aging and senile dementia. *Journal of Gerontology, 35,* 707-714.

Ferris, S.H., Crook, T., Flicker, C., Reisberg, B., & Bartus, R.T. (1986). Assessing cognitive impairment and evaluating treatment effects: Psychometric performance tests. In L.W. Poon (Ed.), *Handbook for clinical memory assessment of older adults* (pp. 139-148). Washington, DC: American Psychological Association.

Field, D., Schaie, K.W., & Leino, E.V. (1988). Continuity in intellectual functioning: The role of self-reported health. *Psychology and Aging, 3,* 385-392.

Fillenbaum, G.G. (1979). Social context and self-assessment of health among the elderly. *Journal of Health and Social Behavior, 20,* 45-51.

Fitzhugh, K., Fitzhugh, L., & Reitan, R. (1967). Influence of age on measures of problem solving and experimental background in subjects with long-standing cerebral dysfunction. *Journal of Gerontology, 19,* 132-134.

Flavell, J.H. (1970). Cognitive changes in adulthood. In L.R. Goulet & P.B. Baltes (Eds.), *Life-span developmental psychology: Research and theory* (pp. 247-253). New York: Academic.

Flicker, C., Bartus, R.T., Crook, T.H., & Ferris, S.H. (1984). Effects of aging and dementia upon recent visuospatial memory. *Neurobiology of Aging, 5,* 275-283.

Flicker, C., Ferris, S.H., Crook, T., & Bartus, R.T. (1987). A visual recognition test for the assessment of cognitive function in aging and dementia. *Experimental Aging Research, 13,* 127-132.

Flicker, C., Ferris, S.H., Crook, T., & Bartus, R.T. (1989). Age differences in the vulnerability of facial recognition memory to proactive interference. *Experimental Aging Research, 15,* 189-194.

Flynn, J.R. (1984). The mean IQ of Americans: Massive gains 1932 to 1978. *Psychological Bulletin, 95,* 29-51.

Flynn, J.R. (1987). Massive IQ gains in 14 nations: What IQ tests really measure. *Psychological Bulletin, 101,* 171-191.

Foos, P.W. (1989). Adult age differences in working memory. *Psychology and Aging*, *4*, 269-275.

Foos, P.W. (1989). Age differences in memory for two common objects. *Journal of Gerontology: Psychological Sciences*, *44*, P178-P180.

Ford, J.M., Roth, W.T., Mohs, R.C., Hopkins, W.F., & Kopell, B.S. (1979). Event-related potentials recorded from young and old adults during a memory retrieval task. *Electroencephalography and Clinical Neurophysiology*, *47*, 450-459.

Foster, J.C., & Taylor, G.A. (1920). The applicability of mental tests to persons over 50. *Journal of Applied Psychology*, *4*, 39-58.

Foulds, G.A., & Raven, J.C. (1948). Normal changes in the mental abilities of adults as age advances. *Journal of Mental Science*, *94*, 133-142.

Fozard, J.L. (1985). Memory changes in aging. In H.K. Ulatowska (Ed.), *The aging brain: Communication in the elderly* (pp. 87-107). San Diego, CA: College-Hill Press.

Fozard, J.L., & Nuttall, R.L. (1971). General Aptitude Test Battery scores for men differing in age and socioeconomic status. *Journal of Applied Psychology*, *55*, 372-379.

Fozard, J.L., Nuttall, R.L., & Waugh, N.C. (1972). Age-related differences in mental performance. *Aging and Human Development*, *3*, 19-43.

Fozard, J.L., & Thomas, J.C. (1975). Psychology of aging: Basic findings and some psychiatric applications. In J.G. Howells (Ed.), *Modern perspectives in the psychiatry of old age* (pp. 107-169). New York: Brunner/Masel.

Fozard, J.L., & Waugh, N.C. (1969). Proactive inhibition of prompted items. *Psychonomic Science*, *17*, 67-68.

Freund, J.S., & Witte, K.L. (1986). Recognition and frequency judgments in young and elderly adults. *American Journal of Psychology*, *99*, 81-102.

Friend, C.M., & Zubek, J.P. (1958). The effects of age on critical thinking ability. *Journal of Gerontology*, *13*, 407-413.

Fullerton, A.M. (1983). Age differences in the use of imagery in integrating new and old information in memory. *Journal of Gerontology*, *38*, 326-332.

Fullerton, A.M. (1988). Adult age differences in solving series problems requiring integration of new and old information. *International Journal of Aging and Human Development*, *26*, 147-154.

Furchtgott, E., & Busemeyer, J.K. (1979). Heart rate and skin conductance during cognitive processes as a function of age. *Journal of Gerontology*, *34*, 183-190.

Furry, C.A., & Baltes, P.B. (1973). The effect of age differences in ability-extraneous performance variables on the assessment of intelligence in children, adults and the elderly. *Journal of Gerontology*, *28*, 73-80.

Furry, C.A., & Schaie, K.W. (1979). Pretest activity and intellectual performance in middle-aged and older persons. *Experimental Aging Research*, *5*, 413-421.

Gallagher, M., Bostock, E., & King, R. (1985). Effects of opiate antagonists on spatial memory in young and aged rats. *Behavioral and Neural Biology*, *44*, 374-385.

Ganzler, H. (1964). Motivation as a factor in the psychological deficit of aging. *Journal of Gerontology*, *19*, 425-429.

Gardner, E.F., & Monge, R.H. (1977). Adult age differences in cognitive abilities and educational background. *Experimental Aging Research*, *3*, 337-383.

Garfein, A.J., Schaie, K.W., & Willis, S.L. (1988). Microcomputer proficiency in later-middle-aged and older adults: Teaching old dogs new tricks. *Social Behavior*, *3*, 131-148.

Garfield, S.L., & Blek, L. (1952). Age, vocabulary level and mental impairment. *Journal of Consulting Psychology*, *16*, 395-398.

Garner, W.R., Hake, H.W., & Ericksen, C.W. (1956). Operationism and the concept of perception. *Psychological Review*, *63*, 149-159.

Gaylord, S.A., & Marsh, G.R. (1976). Age differences in the speed of a spatial cognitive process. *Journal of Gerontology*, *30*, 674-678.

Giambra, L.M. (1989). Task-unrelated-thought frequency as a function of age: A laboratory study. *Psychology and Aging, 4,* 136-143.

Giambra, L.M., & Arenberg, D. (1980). Problem-solving, concept learning and aging. In L.W. Poon (Ed.), *Aging in the 1980s* (pp. 253-259). Washington, DC: American Psychological Association.

Gick, M.L., Craik, F.I.M., & Morris, R.G. (1988). Task complexity and age differences in working memory. *Memory and Cognition, 16,* 353-361.

Gilbert, J.G. (1935). Memory efficiency in senescence. *Archives of Psychology, 27,* (Whole No. 188).

Gilbert, J.G. (1941). Memory loss in senescence. *Journal of Abnormal and Social Psychology, 36,* 73-86.

Gilbert, J.G. (1952). *Understanding old age.* New York: Ronald Press.

Gilbert, J.G., & Levee, R.T. (1971). Patterns of declining memory. *Journal of Gerontology, 26,* 70-75.

Gist, M., Rosen, B., & Schwoerer, C. (1988). The influence of training method and trainee on the acquisition of computer skills. *Personnel Psychology, 41,* 255-265.

Gladis, M., & Braun, H.W. (1958). Age differences in transfer and retroaction as a function of intertask response similarity. *Journal of Experimental Psychology, 55,* 25-30.

Glanzer, M., & Glaser, R. (1959). Cross-sectional and longitudinal results in a study of age-related changes. *Educational and Psychological Measurement, 19,* 89-101.

Glynn, S.M., Okun, M.A., Muth, K.D., & Britton, B.K. (1983). Adults' text recall: An examination of the age-deficit hypothesis. *Journal of Reading Behavior, 15,* 31-45.

Gold, P.E., McGaugh, J.L., Hankins, L.L., Rose, R.P., & Vasquez, B.J. (1982). Age-dependent changes in retention in rats. *Experimental Aging Research, 8,* 53-58.

Golden, C., & Schlutter, L. (1978). The interaction of age and diagnosis in neuropsychological test results. *International Journal of Neuroscience, 8,* 61-63.

Goldfarb, W. (1941). An investigation of reaction time in older adults. *Contributions to education (Report No. 831),* New York: Teachers College, Columbia University.

Gordon, S.K. (1975). Organization and recall of related sentences by elderly and young adults. *Experimental Aging Research, 1,* 71-80.

Gordon, S.K., & Clark, W.C. (1974). Application of signal detection theory to prose recall and recognition in elderly and young adults. *Journal of Gerontology, 29,* 64-72.

Gottsdanker, R. (1980). Aging and the maintaining of preparation. *Experimental Aging Research, 6,* 13-27.

Granick, S., & Friedman, A.D. (1967). The effect of education on the decline of psychometric test performance with age. *Journal of Gerontology, 22,* 191-195.

Granick, S., Kleban, M.H., & Weiss, A.D. (1976). Relationships between hearing loss and cognition in normally hearing aged persons. *Journal of Gerontology, 30,* 434-440.

Grant, E.A., Storandt, M., & Botwinick, J. (1978). Incentive and practice in the psychomotor performance of the elderly. *Journal of Gerontology, 33,* 413-415.

Green, R.F. (1969). Age-intelligence relationship between ages sixteen and sixty-four: A rising trend. *Developmental Psychology, 1,* 618-627.

Green, R.F., & Reimanis, G. (1970). The age-intelligence relationship: Longitudinal studies can mislead. *Industrial Gerontology, 6,* 1-16.

Greene, V.L. (1983). Age dynamic models of information processing task latency: A theoretical note. *Journal of Gerontology, 38,* 46-50

Gregory, R.L. (1957). Increase in "neurological noise" as a factor in aging. *Proceedings of the 4th Congress of the International Association of Gerontology* (pp. 314-324). Merano, Italy.

Gribbin, K., & Schaie, K.W. (1976). Monetary incentive, age and cognition. *Experimental Aging Research, 2,* 461-468.

Gribbin, K., Schaie, K.W., & Parham, I.A. (1980). Complexity of life style and maintenance of intellectual abilities. *Journal of Social Issues, 36,* 47-61.

Gruenfeld, L.W., & MacEachron, A.E. (1975). Relationship between age, socioeconomic status, and field independence. *Perceptual and Motor Skills, 41*, 449-450.

Grundvig, J.L., Ajax, E.T., & Needham, W.E. (1973). Screening organic brain impairment with the Memory-for-Designs Test: Validation of comparison of different scoring systems and exposure times. *Journal of Clinical Psychology, 29*, 350-354.

Guilford, J.P. (1969). Intellectual aspects of decision making. *Interdisciplinary Topics in Gerontology, 4*, 82-102.

Guttentag, R.E. (1985). Memory and aging: Implications for theories of memory development during childhood. *Developmental Review, 5*, 56-82.

Guttentag, R.E. (1988). Processing relational and item-specific information: Effects of aging and division of attention. *Canadian Journal of Psychology, 42*, 414-423.

Guttentag, R.E. (1989). Age differences in dual-task performance: Procedures, assumptions, and results. *Developmental Review, 9*, 146-170.

Guttentag, R.E., & Hunt, R.R. (1988). Adult age differences in memory for imagined and performed actions. *Journal of Gerontology: Psychological Sciences, 43*, P107-P108.

Guttentag, R.E., & Madden, D.J. (1987). Adult age differences in the attentional capacity demands of letter matching. *Experimental Aging Research, 13*, 93-99.

Guttentag, R.E., & Siemens, L. (1986). General and context-specific encoding: A life-span developmental study. *Canadian Journal of Psychology, 40*, 457-462.

Guttman, R. (1981). Performance on the Raven Progressive Matrices as a function of age, education and sex. *Educational Gerontology, 7*, 49-55.

Guttman, R. (1984). Performance on eight spatial ability tests as a function of age and education. *Educational Gerontology, 10*, 1-11.

Hale, S., Myerson, J., Smith, G.A., & Poon, L.W. (1988). Age, variability, and speed: Between-subjects diversity. *Psychology and Aging, 3*, 407-410.

Hale, S., Myerson, J., & Wagstaff, D. (1987). General slowing of nonverbal information processing. *Journal of Gerontology, 42*, 131-136.

Halpern, D.F. (1984). Age differences in response time to verbal and symbolic traffic signs. *Experimental Aging Research, 10*, 201-204.

Halstead, W.C. (1947). *Brain and intelligence.* Chicago: University of Chicago Press.

Hamsher, K.S., & Benton, A.L. (1978). Interactive effects of age and cerebral disease on cognitive performance. *Journal of Neurology, 217*, 195-200.

Hanley-Dunn, P., & McIntosh, J.L. (1984). Meaningfulness and recall of names by young and old adults. *Journal of Gerontology, 39*, 583-585.

Harker, J.O., & Riege, W.H. (1985). Aging and delay effects on recognition of words and designs. *Journal of Gerontology, 40*, 601-604.

Hartley, A.A. (1981). Adult age difference in deductive reasoning processes. *Journal of Gerontology, 36*, 700-706.

Hartley, A.A. (1989). The cognitive ecology of problem solving. In L.W. Poon, D.C. Rubin & B.A. Wilson (Eds.), *Everyday cognition in adulthood and late life* (pp. 300-329). Cambridge, England: Cambridge University Press.

Hartley, A.A., & Anderson, J.W. (1983a). Task complexity and problem-solving performance in younger and older adults. *Journal of Gerontology, 38*, 72-77.

Hartley, A.A., & Anderson, J.W. (1983b). Task complexity, problem representation, and problem-solving performance by younger and older adults. *Journal of Gerontology, 38*, 78-80.

Hartley, A.A., & Anderson, J.W. (1986). Instruction, induction, generation, and evaluation of strategies for solving search problems. *Journal of Gerontology, 41*, 650-658.

Hartley, A.A., Hartley, J.T., & Johnson, S.A. (1984). The older adult as computer user. In P.K. Robinson, J. Livingston, & J.E. Birren (Eds.), *Aging and technological advances* (pp. 347-348). New York: Plenum Press.

Hartley, A.A., Kieley, J.M., & Slabach, E.H. (1990). Age differences and similarities in the effects of cues and prompts. *Journal of Experimental Psychology: Human Perception and Performance, 16*, 523-537.

Hartley, J.T. (1986). Reader and text variables as determinants of discourse memory in adulthood. *Psychology and Aging, 1*, 150-158.

Hartley, J.T. (1988). Aging and individual differences in memory for written discourse. In L.L. Light & D.M. Burke (Eds.), *Language, memory and aging* (pp. 36-57). New York: Cambridge University Press.

Hartley, J.T. (1989). Memory for prose: Perspectives on the reader. In L.W. Poon, D.C. Rubin & B.A. Wilson (Eds.), *Everyday cognition in adulthood and late life* (pp. 135-156). Cambridge, England: Cambridge University Press.

Hartley, J.T., Harker, J.O., & Walsh, D.A. (1980). Contemporary issues and new directions in adult development of learning and memory. In L.W. Poon (Ed.), *Aging in the 1980s* (pp. 239-252). Washington, DC: American Psychological Association.

Hartley, J.T., & Walsh, D.A. (1980). The effect of monetary incentive on amount and rate of free recall in older and younger adults. *Journal of Gerontology, 35*, 899-905.

Harwood, E., & Naylor, G.F. (1969). Recall and recognition in elderly and young subjects. *Australian Journal of Psychology, 21*, 251-257.

Hasher, L., & Zacks, R.T. (1979). Automatic and effortful processes in memory. *Journal of Experimental Psychology: General, 108*, 356-388.

Hasher, L., & Zacks, R.T. (1988). Working memory, comprehension, and aging: A review and a new view. In G.H. Bower (Ed.), *The psychology of learning and motivation* (Vol. 22, pp. 193-225). San Diego, CA: Academic.

Hashtroudi, S., Johnson, M.K., & Chrosniak, L.D. (1989). Aging and source monitoring. *Psychology and Aging, 4*, 106-112.

Hashtroudi, S., Johnson, M.K., & Chrosniak, L.D. (1990). Aging and qualitative characteristics of memories for perceived and imagined complex events. *Psychology and Aging, 5*, 119-126.

Hashtroudi, S., Parker, E.S., Luis, J.D., & Reisen, C.A. (1989). Generation and elaboration in older adults. *Experimental Aging Research, 15*, 73-78.

Hayslip, B., & Kennelly, K.J. (1982). Short-term memory and crystallized-fluid intelligence in adulthood. *Research on Aging, 4*, 314-332.

Hayslip, B., & Sterns, H.L. (1979). Age differences in relationships between crystallized and fluid intelligences and problem solving. *Journal of Gerontology, 34*, 404-414.

Heaton, R.K., Grant, I., & Matthews, C. (1986). Differences in neuropsychological test performance associated with age, education, and sex. In I. Grant & K.M. Adams (Eds.), *Neuropsychological assessment in neuro-psychiatric disorders* (pp. 100-120). New York: Oxford University Press.

Hebb, D.O. (1942). The effect of early and late brain injury upon test scores, and the nature of normal adult intelligence. *Proceedings of the American Philosophical Society, 85*, 275-292.

Hebb, D.O. (1978). On watching myself grow old. *Psychology Today, 12*, 20-23.

Helander, J. (1967). On age and mental test behavior. *Acta Psychologia Gothoburgensia VII*, Goteborg, Sweden.

Herman, J.F., & Bruce, P.R. (1983). Adults' mental rotation of spatial information: Effects of age, sex and cerebral laterality. *Experimental Aging Research, 9*, 83-85.

Herman, J.F., & Coyne, A.C. (1980). Mental manipulation of spatial information in young and elderly adults. *Developmental Psychology, 16*, 537-538.

Heron, A., & Chown, S.M. (1967). *Age and function*. Boston: Little-Brown & Co.

Heron, A., & Craik, F.I.M. (1964). Age differences in cumulative learning of meaningful and meaningless material. *Scandinavian Journal of Psychology, 5*, 209-217.

Hertzog, C. (1985). An individual differences perspective. *Research on Aging, 7*, 7-45.

Hertzog, C. (1987). Applications of structural equation models in gerontological research. In

K.W. Schaie (Ed.), *Annual review of gerontology and geriatrics* (Vol. 7, pp. 265-293). New York: Springer.

Hertzog, C. (1989). Influences of cognitive slowing on age differences in intelligence. *Developmental Psychology, 25,* 636-651.

Hertzog, C., Dixon, R.A., & Hultsch, D.F. (1990). Relationships between metamemory, memory predictions, and memory task performance in adults. *Psychology and Aging, 5,* 215-227.

Hertzog, C., Raskind, C.L., & Cannon, C.J. (1986). Age-related slowing in semantic information processing speed: An individual differences analysis. *Journal of Gerontology, 41,* 500-502.

Hertzog, C., & Schaie, K.W. (1986). Stability and change in adult intelligence: I. Analysis of longitudinal covariance structures. *Psychology and Aging, 1,* 159-171.

Hertzog, C., & Schaie, K.W. (1988). Stability and change in adult intelligence: 2. Simultaneous analysis of longitudinal means and covariance structures. *Psychology and Aging, 3,* 122-130.

Hertzog, C., Schaie, K.W., & Gribbin, K. (1978). Cardiovascular disease and changes in intellectual functioning from middle to old age. *Journal of Gerontology, 33,* 872-883.

Herzog, A.R., & Rodgers, W.L. (1989). Age differences in memory performance and memory ratings as measured in a sample survey. *Psychology and Aging, 4,* 173-182.

Hess, T.M. (1982). Visual abstraction processes in young and old adults. *Developmental Psychology, 18,* 473-484.

Hess, T.M. (1985). Aging and context influences on recognition memory for typical and atypical script actions. *Developmental Psychology, 21,* 1139-1151.

Hess, T.M., & Arnould, D. (1986). Adult age differences in memory for explicit and implicit sentence information. *Journal of Gerontology, 41,* 191-194.

Hess, T.M., Donley, J., & Vandermaas, M.O. (1989). Aging-related changes in the processing and retention of script information. *Experimental Aging Research, 15,* 89-96.

Hess, T.M., & Slaughter, S.J. (1986). Aging effects on prototype abstraction and concept identification. *Journal of Gerontology, 41,* 214-221.

Hess, T.M., Vandermaas, M.O., Donley, J., & Snyder, S.S. (1987). Memory for sex-role consistent and inconsistent actions in young and old adults. *Journal of Gerontology, 42,* 505-511.

Hess, T.M., & Wallsten, S.M. (1987). Adult age differences in the perception and learning of artistic style categories. *Psychology and Aging, 2,* 243-253.

Heston, J.C., & Cannell, C.F. (1941). A note on the relation between age and performance of adult subjects on four familiar psychometric tests. *Journal of Applied Psychology, 25,* 415-419.

Heyman, D., & Jeffers, F. (1963). Effect of time lapse on consistency of self-health and medical evaluations of elderly persons. *Journal of Gerontology, 18,* 160-164.

Hill, R.D., Crook, T.H., Zadek, A., Sheikh, J., & Yesavage, J. (1989). The effects of age on recall of information from a simulated television news broadcast. *Educational Gerontology, 15,* 607-613.

Hirt, M. (1959). Use of the General Aptitude Test Battery to determine aptitude changes with age and to predict job performance. *Journal of Applied Psychology, 43,* 36-39.

Hochanadel, G., & Kaplan, E. (1984). Neuropsychology of normal aging. In M.L. Alpert (Ed.), *Clinical neurology of aging* (pp. 231-244). New York: Oxford University Press.

Hochla, N.A., & Parsons, O.A. (1982). Premature aging in female alcoholics: A neuropsychological study. *Journal of Nervous and Mental Disease, 170,* 241-245.

Hollingshead, A.B. (1957). *Two-Factor Index of Social Position.* (Unpublished manuscript).

Hollingworth, H.L. (1927). *Mental growth and decline.* New York: Appleton.

Holtzman, R.E., Familitant, M.E., Deptula, P., & Hoyer, W.J. (1986). Aging and the use of sentential structure to facilitate word recognition. *Experimental Aging Research, 12,* 85-88.

Hooper, F.H., Hooper, J.O., & Colbert, K.C. (1984). *Personality and memory correlates of intellectual functioning: Young adulthood to old age.* Basel: Karger.

Hooper, F.H., & Sheehan, N.W. (1977). Logical concept attainment during the aging years: Issues in the neo-Piagetian research literature. In W.F. Overton & J.M. Gallagher (Eds.), *Knowledge and development: Vol. 1. Advances in research and theory* (pp. 423-466). New York: Plenum.

Horn, J.L. (1970). Organization of data on life-span development of human abilities. In L.R. Goulet & P.B. Baltes (Eds.), *Life-span developmental psychology: Research and theory* (pp. 423-466). New York: Academic Press.

Horn, J.L. (1979). Some correctable defects in research on intelligence. *Intelligence, 3,* 307-322.

Horn, J.L. (1982). The theory of fluid and crystallized intelligence in relation to concepts of cognitive psychology and aging in adulthood. In F.I.M. Craik & S. Trehub (Eds.), *Aging and cognitive processes* (pp. 237-278). New York: Plenum.

Horn, J.L. (1986). Intellectual ability concepts. In R.J. Sternberg (Ed.), *Advances in the psychology of human intelligence* (pp. 35-75). Hillsdale, NJ: Lawrence Erlbaum Associates.

Horn, J.L., & Cattell, R.B. (1966). Age differences in primary mental ability factors. *Journal of Gerontology, 21,* 210-220.

Horn, J.L., & Donaldson, G. (1976). On the myth of intellectual decline in adulthood. *American Psychologist, 31,* 701-709.

Horn, J.L., & Donaldson, G. (1977). Faith is not enough: A response to the Baltes-Schaie claim that intelligence does not wane. *American Psychologist, 32,* 369-373.

Horn, J.L., & Donaldson, G. (1980). Cognitive development in adulthood. In O.G. Brim & J. Kagan (Eds.), *Constancy and change in human development* (pp. 445-529). Cambridge, MA: Harvard University Press.

Horn, J.L., Donaldson, G., & Engstrom, R. (1981). Apprehension, memory and fluid intelligence decline in adulthood. *Research on Aging, 3,* 33-84.

Hornblum, J.N., & Overton, W.F. (1976). Area and volume conservation among the elderly: Assessment and training. *Developmental Psychology, 12,* 68-74.

Howard, D.V. (1980). Category norms: A comparison of the Battig and Montague (1969) norms with the responses of adults between the ages of 20 and 80. *Journal of Gerontology, 35,* 225-231.

Howard, D.V. (1983). The effects of aging and degree of association on the semantic priming of lexical decisions. *Experimental Aging Research, 9,* 145-151.

Howard, D.V. (1988a). Aging and memory activation: The priming of semantic and episodic memories. In L.L. Light & D.M. Burke (Eds.), *Language, memory and aging* (pp. 77-99). New York: Cambridge University Press.

Howard, D.V. (1988b). Implicit and explicit assessment of cognitive aging. In M.L. Howe & C.J. Brainerd (Eds.), *Cognitive development in adulthood* (pp. 3-37). New York: Springer-Verlag.

Howard, D.V., Heisey, J.G., & Shaw, R.J. (1986). Aging and the priming of newly learned associations. *Developmental Psychology, 22,* 78-85.

Howard, D.V., McAndrews, M.P., & Lasaga, M.I. (1981). Semantic priming of lexical decisions in young and old adults. *Journal of Gerontology, 36,* 707-714.

Howard, D.V., Shaw, R.J., & Heisey, J.G. (1986). Aging and the time course of semantic activation. *Journal of Gerontology, 41,* 195-203.

Howe, M.L., & Hunter, M.A. (1986). Long-term memory in adulthood: An examination of the development of storage and retrieval processes at acquisition and retention. *Developmental Review, 6,* 334-364.

Howell, S.C. (1972). Familiarity and complexity in perceptual recognition. *Journal of Gerontology, 27,* 364-371.

Howes, J.L., & Katz, A.N. (1988). Assessing remote memory with an improved public events questionnaire. *Psychology and Aging, 3,* 142-150.

Hoyer, F.W., Hoyer, W.J., Treat, N.J., & Baltes, P.B. (1978-79). Training response speed in young and elderly women. *International Journal of Aging and Human Development, 9,* 247-254.

Hoyer, W.J. (1974). Aging as intraindividual change. *Developmental Psychology, 10,* 821-826.

Hoyer, W.J. (1987). Acquisition of knowledge and the decentralization of *g* in adult intellectual development. In C. Schooler & K.W. Schaie (Eds.), *Cognitive functioning and social structure throughout the life course* (pp. 120-141). Norwood, NJ: Ablex.

Hoyer, W.J., Labouvie, G.V., & Baltes, P.B. (1973). Modification of response speed deficits and intellectual performance in the elderly. *Human Development, 16,* 233-242.

Hoyer, W.J., & Plude, D.J. (1980). Attentional and perceptual processes in the study of cognitive aging. In L.W. Poon (Ed.), *Aging in the 1980s* (pp. 227-238). Washington, DC: American Psychological Association.

Hoyer, W.J., & Plude, D.J. (1982). Aging and the allocation of attentional resources in visual information processing. In R. Sekuler, D. Kline, & K. Dismukes (Eds.), *Aging and human visual function* (pp. 245-263). New York: Alan R. Liss.

Hoyer, W.J., Rebok, G.W., & Sved, S.M. (1979). Effects of varying irrelevant information on adult age differences in problem solving. *Journal of Gerontology, 34,* 553-560.

Hulicka, I.M. (1965). Age differences for intentional and incidental learning and recall scores. *Journal of the American Geriatrics Society, 13,* 639-649.

Hulicka, I.M. (1967a). Age differences in retention as a function of interference. *Journal of Gerontology, 22,* 180-184.

Hulicka, I.M. (1967b). Short-term learning and memory efficiency as a function of age and health. *Journal of the American Geriatric Society, 15,* 285-294.

Hulicka, I.M. (1982). Memory functioning in late adulthood. In F.I.M. Craik & S. Trehub (Eds.), *Aging and cognitive processes* (pp. 331-351). New York: Plenum.

Hulicka, I.M., & Grossman, J.L. (1967). Age-group comparisons for the use of mediators in paired-associate learning. *Journal of Gerontology, 22,* 46-51.

Hulicka, I.M., & Rust, L.D. (1964). Age-related retention deficit as a function of learning. *Journal of the American Geriatric Society, 11,* 1061-1065.

Hulicka, I.M., Sterns, H., & Grossman, J. (1967). Age-group comparisons of paired-associate learning as a function of paced and self-paced association and response times. *Journal of Gerontology, 22,* 274-280.

Hulicka, I.M., & Weiss, R. (1965). Age differences in retention as a function of learning. *Journal of Consulting Psychology, 29,* 125-129.

Hultsch, D.F. (1971). Organization and memory in adulthood. *Human Development, 14,* 16-29.

Hultsch, D.F. (1974). Learning to learn in adulthood. *Journal of Gerontology, 29,* 302-308.

Hultsch, D.F. (1975). Adult age differences in retrieval: Trace dependent and cue-dependent forgetting. *Developmental Psychology, 11,* 197-201.

Hultsch, D.F., & Dixon, R.A. (1983). The role of pre-experimental knowledge in text processing in adulthood. *Experimental Aging Research, 9,* 17-22.

Hultsch, D.F., & Dixon, R.A. (1984). Memory for text materials in adulthood. In P.B. Baltes & O.G. Brim (Eds.), *Life-span development and behavior* (Vol. 6, pp. 77-108). New York: Academic Press.

Hultsch, D.F., & Dixon, R.A. (1990). Learning and memory in aging. In J.E. Birren & K.W. Schaie (Eds.), *Handbook of the psychology of aging.* (3rd ed., pp. 258-274). San Diego: Academic.

Hultsch, D.F., Hertzog, C., & Dixon, R.A. (1984). Text recall in adulthood: The role of intellectual abilities. *Developmental Psychology, 20,* 1193-1209.

Hultsch, D.F., Hertzog, C., & Dixon, R.A. (1987). Age differences in metamemory: Resolving the inconsistencies. *Canadian Journal of Psychology, 41,* 193-208.

Hultsch, D.F., Hertzog, C., & Dixon, R.A. (1990). Ability correlates of memory performance in adulthood and aging. *Psychology and Aging*, *5*, 356-368.

Hultsch, D.F., Hertzog, C., Dixon, R.A., & Davidson, H. (1988). Memory self-knowledge and self-efficacy in the aged. In M.L. Howe & C.J. Brainerd (Eds.), *Cognitive development in adulthood* (pp. 65-92). New York: Springer-Verlag.

Hunt, T. (1989). Introduction: Historical perspective and current considerations. In T. Hunt & C.J. Lindley (Eds.), *Testing older adults* (pp. 1-7). Austin, TX: Pro-Ed.

Hybertson, E.D., Perdue, J., & Hybertson, D. (1982). Age differences in information acquisition strategies. *Experimental Aging Research*, *8*, 109-113.

Inglis, J., & Ankus, M.N. (1965). Effects of age on short-term storage and serial rote learning. *British Journal of Psychology*, *56*, 183-195.

Inglis, J., & Caird, W.K. (1963). Age differences in successive responses to simultaneous stimulation. *Canadian Journal of Psychology*, *17*, 98-105.

Ingram, D.K., London, E.D., & Goodrick, C.L. (1981). Age and neurochemical correlates of radial maze performance in rats. *Neurobiology of Aging*, *2*, 41-47.

Inman, V.W., & Parkinson, S.R. (1983). Differences in Brown-Peterson recall as a function of age and retention interval. *Journal of Gerontology*, *38*, 58-64.

Jacewicz, M.M., & Hartley, A.A. (1979). Rotation of mental images by young and old college students: The effects of familiarity. *Journal of Gerontology*, *34*, 396-403.

Jacewicz, M.M., & Hartley, A.A. (1987). Age differences in the speed of cognitive operations: Resolution of inconsistent findings. *Journal of Gerontology*, *42*, 86-88.

Jackson, J.L., Bogers, H., & Kersholt, J. (1988). Do memory aids aid the elderly in their day to day remembering? In M.M. Gruneberg, P.E. Morris, & R.N. Sykes (Eds.), *Practical aspects of memory: Current research and issues* (pp. 137-142). Chichester: Wiley.

James, W. (1893). *Principles of psychology*. New York: Holt.

Jamieson, G.H. (1971). Learning and retention: A comparison between programmed and discovery learning at two age levels. *Programmed Learning*, *8*, 34-40.

Jarvik, L.F. (1988). Aging of the brain: How can we prevent it? *The Gerontologist*, *28*, 739-747.

Jennings, J.R., Nebes, R.D., & Yovetich, N.A. (1990). Aging increases the energetic demands of episodic memory: A cardiovascular analysis. *Journal of Experimental Psychology: General*, *119*, 77-91.

Jerome, E.A. (1962). Decay of heuristic processes in the aged. In C. Tibbitts & W. Donahue (Eds.), *Social and psychological aspects of aging* (pp. 808-823). New York: Columbia University Press.

Johnson, M.M.S. (1990). Age differences in decision making: A process methodology for examining strategic information processing. *Journal of Gerontology: Psychological Sciences*, *45*, P75-P78.

Jones, H.E. (1955). Age changes in mental abilities. In *Old age and the modern world* (pp. 267-279). London: E. & S. Livingstone.

Jones, H.E. (1956). Problems of aging in perceptual and intellective functions. In J.E. Anderson (Ed.), *Psychological aspects of aging* (pp. 135-139). Washington, DC: American Psychological Association.

Jones, H.E. (1959). Intelligence and problem solving. In J.E. Birren (Ed.), *Handbook of aging and the individual* (pp. 700-738). Chicago: University of Chicago Press.

Jones, H.E., & Conrad, H. (1933). The growth and decline of intelligence: A study of a homogeneous group between the ages of ten and sixty. *Genetic Psychological Monographs*, *13*, 223-298.

Jones, H.E., Conrad, H., & Horn, A. (1928). Psychological studies of motion pictures: II. Observation and recall as a function of age. *University of California Publications in Psychology*, *3*, 225-243.

Jones, H.E., & Kaplan, O.J. (1945). Psychological aspects of mental disorders in later life.

In O.J. Kaplan (Ed.), *Mental disorders in later life* (pp. 69-115). Stanford, CA: Stanford University Press.

Kamin, L.J. (1957). Differential changes in mental abilities in old age. *Journal of Gerontology, 12*, 66-70.

Kaplan, G.A., & Camacho, T. (1983). Perceived health and mortality: A nine-year follow-up of the human population laboratory cohort. *American Journal of Epidemiology, 117*, 292-304.

Kaszniak, A.W., Poon, L.W., & Riege, W. (1986). Assessing memory deficits: An information-processing approach. In L.W. Poon (Ed.), *Handbook for clinical memory assessment of older adults* (pp. 168-188). Washington, D.C.: American Psychological Association.

Kaufman, A.S., Reynolds, C.R., & McLean, J.E. (1989). Age and WAIS-R intelligence in a national sample of adults in the 20-to-74-year age range: A cross-sectional analysis with educational level controlled. *Intelligence, 13*, 235-253.

Kausler, D.H. (1982). *Experimental psychology and human aging.* New York: Wiley & Sons.

Kausler, D.H. (1985). Episodic memory: Memorizing performance. In N. Charness (Ed.), *Aging and human performance* (pp. 101-141). Chichester: Wiley.

Kausler, D.H. (1989a). Comments on aging memory and its everyday operations. In L.W. Poon, D.C. Rubin & B.A. Wilson (Eds.), *Everyday cognition in adulthood and late life* (pp. 483-495). Cambridge: Cambridge University Press.

Kausler, D.H. (1989b). Impairment in normal memory aging: Implications of laboratory evidence. In G.C. Gilmore, P.J. Whitehouse, & M.L. Wykle (Eds.), *Memory, aging, and dementia: Theory, assessment and treatment* (pp. 41-73). New York: Springer.

Kausler, D.H., & Hakami, M.K. (1982). Frequency judgments by young and elderly adults for relevant stimuli with simultaneously present irrelevant stimuli. *Journal of Gerontology, 37*, 438-442.

Kausler, D.H., & Hakami, M.K. (1983). Memory for topics of conversation: Adult age differences and intentionality. *Experimental Aging Research, 9*, 153-157.

Kausler, D.H., Hakami, M.K., & Wright, R.E. (1982). Adult age differences in frequency judgments of categorical representations. *Journal of Gerontology, 37*, 365-371.

Kausler, D.H., & Lair, C.V. (1965). R-S (backward) paired-associate learning in elderly subjects. *Journal of Gerontology, 20*, 29-31.

Kausler, D.H., & Lair, C.V. (1966). Associative strength and paired associate learning in elderly subjects. *Journal of Gerontology, 21*, 278-280.

Kausler, D.H., & Lair, C.V. (1968). Informative feedback conditions and verbal-discrimination learning in elderly subjects. *Psychonomic Science, 10*, 193-194.

Kausler, D.H., & Lichty, W. (1988). Memory for activities: Rehearsal-independence and aging. In M.L. Howe & C.J. Brainerd (Eds.), *Cognitive development in adulthood* (pp. 93-131). New York: Springer-Verlag.

Kausler, D.H., Lichty, W., & Davis, R.T. (1985). Temporal memory for performed activities: Intentionality and age differences. *Developmental Psychology, 21*, 1132-1138.

Kausler, D.H., Lichty, W., & Freund, J.S. (1985). Adult age differences in recognition memory and frequency judgments for planned versus performed activities. *Developmental Psychology, 21*, 647-654.

Kausler, D.H., Lichty, W., & Hakami, M.K. (1984). Frequency judgments for distractor items in a short-term memory task: Instructional variation and adult age differences. *Journal of Verbal Learning and Verbal Behavior, 23*, 660-668.

Kausler, D.H., Lichty, W., Hakami, M.K., & Freund, J.S. (1986). Activity duration and adult age differences in memory for activity performance. *Psychology and Aging, 1*, 80-81.

Kausler, D.H., & Phillips, P.L. (1988). Instructional variation and adult age differences in activity memory. *Experimental Aging Research, 14*, 195-199.

Kausler, D.H., & Puckett, J.M. (1980). Frequency judgments and correlated cognitive abilities in young and elderly adults. *Journal of Gerontology*, *35*, 376-382.

Kausler, D.H., Salthouse, T.A., & Saults, J.S. (1987). Frequency-of-occurrence memory over the adult life span. *Experimental Aging Research*, *13*, 159-161.

Kausler, D.H., Salthouse, T.A., & Saults, J.S. (1988). Temporal memory over the adult life span. *American Journal of Psychology*, *101*, 207-215.

Kausler, D.H., Wright, R., & Hakami, M.K. (1981). Variation in task complexity and adult age differences in frequency-of-occurrence judgments. *Bulletin of the Psychonomic Society*, *18*, 195-197.

Kay, H. (1951). Learning of a serial task by different age groups. *Quarterly Journal of Experimental Psychology*, *3*, 166-183.

Kay, H. (1955). Some experiments on adult learning. In *Old Age in the Modern World* (pp. 259-267). London: E. & S. Livingstone.

Kay, H. (1959). Theories of learning and aging. In J.E. Birren (Ed.), *Handbook of aging and the individual* (pp. 614-654). Chicago: University of Chicago Press.

Kear-Colwell, J.J., & Heller, M. (1978). A normative study of the Wechsler Memory Scale. *Journal of Clinical Psychology*, *34*, 437-442.

Keevil-Rogers, P., & Schnore, M.M. (1969). Short-term memory as a function of age in persons of above average intelligence. *Journal of Gerontology*, *24*, 184-188.

Keitz, S.M., & Gounard, B.R. (1976). Age differences in adults' free recall of pictorial and word stimuli. *Educational Gerontology*, *1*, 237-241.

Kellogg, R.T. (1983). Age differences in hypothesis testing and frequency processing in concept learning. *Bulletin of the Psychonomic Society*, *21*, 101-104.

Kemper, S. (1986). Imitation of complex syntactic constructions by elderly adults. *Applied Psycholinguistics*, *7*, 277-288.

Kemper, S. (1987a). Life-span changes in syntactic complexity. *Journal of Gerontology*, *42*, 323-328.

Kemper, S. (1987b). Syntactic complexity and elderly adults' recall. *Experimental Aging Research*, *13*, 47-52.

Kemper, S. (1990). Adults' diaries: Changes made to written narratives across the life span. *Discourse Processes*, *13*, 207-223.

Kemper, S., & Rash, S. (1988). Speech and writing across the life-span. In M.M. Gruneberg, P.E. Morris, & R.N. Sykes (Eds.), *Practical aspects of memory: Current research and issues* (pp. 107-112). Chichester: Wiley.

Kendall, B.S. (1962). Memory-for-designs performance in the seventh and eighth decades of life. *Perceptual and Motor Skills*, *14*, 399-405.

Kesler, M.S., Denney, N.W., & Whitely, S.E. (1976). Factors influencing problem-solving in middle-aged and elderly adults. *Human Development*, *19*, 310-320.

Kinsbourne, M. (1974). Cognitive deficit and the aging brain: A behavioral analysis. *International Journal of Aging and Human Development*, *5*, 41-49.

Kinsbourne, M. (1980). Attentional dysfunctions and the elderly: Theoretical models and research perspectives. In L.W. Poon, J.L. Fozard, L.S. Cermak, D. Arenberg, & L.W. Thompson (Eds.), *New directions in memory and aging* (pp. 113-129). Hillsdale, NJ: Lawrence Erlbaum Associates.

Kirasic, K.C. (1989). The effects of age and environmental familiarity on adults' spatial problem-solving performance: Evidence of a hometown advantage. *Experimental Aging Research*, *15*, 181-187.

Kirasic, K.C., & Allen, G.L. (1985). Aging, spatial performance and spatial competence. In N. Charness (Ed.), *Aging and human performance* (pp. 191-223). Chichester: Wiley.

Kirchner, W.K. (1958). Age differences in short-term retention of rapidly changing information. *Journal of Experimental Psychology*, *55*, 352-358.

Klatzky, R.L. (1988). Theories of information processing and theories of aging. In L.L. Light & D.M. Burke (Eds.), *Language, memory and aging* (pp. 1-16). New York: Cambridge

University Press.

Kleemeier, R.W. (1962). Intellectual changes in the senium. *Proceedings of the American Statistical Association: Social Statistics*, *1*, 290-295.

Klein, H.A., & Shaffer, K. (1986). Aging and memory in skilled language performance. *Journal of Genetic Psychology*, *146*, 389-397.

Kleinman, J.M., & Brodzinsky, D.M. (1978). Haptic exploration in young, middle-aged and elderly adults. *Journal of Gerontology*, *33*, 521-527.

Kliegl, R., Smith, J., & Baltes, P.B. (1986). Testing-the-limits, expertise, and memory in adulthood and old age. In F. Klix & H. Hagendorf (Eds.), *Human memory and cognitive capabilities* (pp. 395-407). Amsterdam: North-Holland.

Kliegl, R., Smith, J., & Baltes, P.B. (1989). Testing-the-limits and the study of adult age differences in cognitive plasticity of a mnemonic skill. *Developmental Psychology*, *25*, 247-256.

Kline, D.W., Culler, M.P., & Sucec, J. (1977). Differences in inconspicuous word identification as a function of age and reversible-figure training. *Experimental Aging Research*, *3*, 203-213.

Kline, D.W., Hogan, P.M., & Stier, D.L. (1980). Age and the identification of inconspicuous words. *Experimental Aging Research*, *6*, 137-147.

Klodin, V.M. (1976). The relationship of scoring treatment and age in perceptual-integrative performance. *Experimental Aging Research*, *2*, 303-313.

Knopf, M., & Neidhardt, E. (1989). Aging and memory for action events: The role of familiarity. *Developmental Psychology*, *25*, 780-786.

Kohn, M.L., & Schooler, C. (1978). The reciprocal effects of the substantive complexity of work and intellectual flexibility: A longitudinal assessment. *American Journal of Sociology*, *84*, 24-52.

Kohn, M.L., & Schooler, C. (1983). *Work and personality*. Norwood, NJ: Ablex.

Koriat, A., Ben-Zur, H., & Sheffer, D. (1988). Telling the same story twice: Output monitoring and age. *Journal of Memory and Language*, *27*, 23-39.

Kosloski, K. (1986). Isolating, age, period and cohort effects in developmental research. *Research on Aging*, *8*, 460-479.

Kosnik, W., Winslow, L., Kline, D., Rasinski, K., & Sekuler, R. (1988). Visual changes in daily life throughout adulthood. *Journal of Gerontology: Psychological Sciences*, *43*, P63-P70.

Kraus, J., Chalker, S., & Macindoe, I. (1967). Vocabulary and chronological age as predictors of "abstraction" on the Shipley-Hartford Retreat Scale. *Australian Journal of Psychology*, *19*, 133-135.

Krauss, I.K. (1980). Between- and within-group comparisons in aging research. In L.W. Poon (Ed.), *Aging in the 1980s* (pp. 542-551). Washington, DC: American Psychological Association.

Kriauciunas, R. (1968). The relationship of age and retention-interval activity in short-term memory. *Journal of Gerontology*, *23*, 169-173.

Kuhlen, R.G. (1963). Age and intelligence: The significance of cultural change in longitudinal vs. cross-sectional findings. *Vita Humana*, *6*, 113-124.

Kuhn, D., Pennington, N., & Leadbeater, B. (1983). Adult thinking in developmental perspective. In P.B. Baltes & O.G. Brim (Eds.), *Life-span development and behavior* (Vol. 5, pp. 157-195). New York: Academic.

Kynette, D., & Kemper, S. (1986). Aging and the loss of grammatical forms: A cross-sectional study of language performance. *Language and Communication*, *6*, 65-72.

Labouvie, G.V. (1973). Implications of geropsychological theories for intervention: The challenge for the seventies. *Gerontologist*, *13*, 10-14.

Labouvie-Vief, G. (1976). Toward optimizing cognitive competence. *Educational Gerontology*, *1*, 75-92.

Labouvie-Vief, G. (1977). Adult cognitive development: In search of alternative interpretations. *Merrill-Palmer Quarterly, 23*, 228-264.

Labouvie-Vief, G. (1980). Adaptive dimensions of adult cognition. In N. Datan & N. Lohmann (Eds.), *Transitions of aging* (pp. 3-26). New York: Academic.

Labouvie-Vief, G. (1981). Proactive and reactive aspects of constructivism: Growth and aging in life-span perspective. In R. Lerner (Ed.), *Individuals as producers of their own development* (pp. 197-230). New York: Academic.

Labouvie-Vief, G. (1982). Individual time, social time and intellectual aging. In T.K. Hareven & K.J. Adams (Es.), *Aging and the life course transitions: An interdisciplinary perspective* (pp. 151-182). New York: Guilford.

Labouvie-Vief, G. (1985). Intelligence and Cognition. In J.E. Birren & K.W. Schaie (Eds), *Handbook of the psychology of aging.* (2nd ed., pp. 500-530). New York: Van Nostrand Reinhold.

Labouvie-Vief, G., & Blanchard-Fields, F. (1982). Cognitive ageing and psychological growth. *Ageing and Society, 2*, 183-209.

Labouvie-Vief, G., & Chandler, M.J. (1978). Cognitive development and life-span developmental theory: Idealistic versus contextual perspectives. In P.B. Baltes (Ed.), *Life-span development and behavior* (Vol. 1, pp. 181-210). New York: Academic.

Labouvie-Vief, G., & Gonda, J.N. (1976). Cognitive strategy and intellectual performance in the elderly. *Journal of Gerontology, 31*, 327-332.

Labouvie-Vief, G., Hoyer, W.F., Baltes, M.M., & Baltes, P.B. (1974). An operant analysis of intelligence in old age. *Human Development, 17*, 259-272.

Labouvie-Vief, G., & Schell, D.A. (1982). Learning and memory in later life. In B.B. Wolman (Ed.), *Handbook of developmental psychology* (pp. 828-846). Englewood Cliffs, NJ: Prentice-Hall.

Lachman, J.L., Lachman, R., & Thronesberry, C. (1979). Metamemory through the adult life span. *Developmental Psychology, 15*, 543-551.

Lachman, M.E. (1983). Perceptions of intellectual aging: Antecedent or consequence of intellectual functioning? *Developmental Psychology, 19*, 482-498.

Lachman, M.E., & Jelalian, E. (1984). Self-efficacy and attributions for intellectual performance in young and elderly adults. *Journal of Gerontology, 39*, 577-582.

Lachman, M.E., & Leff, R. (1989). Perceived control and intellectual functioning in the elderly: A 5-year longitudinal study. *Developmental Psychology, 25*, 722-728.

Lachman, R., & Lachman, J.L. (1980). Age and the actualization of world knowledge. In L.W. Poon, J.L. Fozard, L.S. Cermak, D. Arenberg & L.W. Thompson (Eds.), *New directions in memory and aging* (pp. 285-311). Hillsdale, NJ: Lawrence Erlbaum Associates.

Lachman, R., Lachman, J.L., & Taylor, D.W. (1982). Reallocation of mental resources over the productive lifespan: Assumptions and task analyses. In F.I.M. Craik & S. Trehub (Eds.), *Aging and cognitive processes* (pp. 279-308). New York: Plenum.

Lair, C.V., Moon, W.H., & Kausler, D.H. (1969). Associative interference in the paired associate learning of middle aged and old subjects. *Developmental Psychology, 9*, 548-552.

Lakatos, I. (1970). Falsification and the methodology of scientific research programmes. In I. Lakatos & A. Musgrave (Eds.), *Criticism and the growth of knowledge* (pp. 91-196). London: Cambridge University Press.

Landauer, T.K. (1989). Some bad and some good reasons for studying memory and cognition in the wild. In L.W. Poon, D.C. Rubin, & B.A. Wilson (Eds.), *Everyday cognition in adulthood and late life* (pp. 116-125). New York: Cambridge University Press.

LaRue, A., Bank, L., Jarvik, L., & Hetland, M. (1979). Health in old age: How do physicians' ratings and self-ratings compare? *Journal of Gerontology, 34*, 687-691.

LaRue, A., & D'Elia, L.F. (1985). Anxiety and problem solving in middle-aged and elderly adults. *Experimental Aging Research, 11*, 215-220.

Laurence, M.W. (1966). Age differences in performance and subjective organization in the free recall learning of pictorial material. *Canadian Journal of Psychology, 20*, 388-399.

Laurence, M.W. (1967). Memory loss with age: A test of two strategies for its retardation. *Psychonomic Science, 9*, 209-210.

Laux, L.F., & Lane, D.M. (1985). Information processing components of substitution test performance. *Intelligence, 9*, 111-136.

Lawton, G. (1943). Aging mental abilities and their preservation. In G. Lawton (Eds.), *New goals for old age* (pp. 11-33). New York: Columbia University Press.

LeBreck, D.B., & Baron, A. (1987). Age and practice effects in continuous recognition memory. *Journal of Gerontology, 42*, 89-91.

Lee, J.A., & Pollack, R.A. (1978). The effects of age on perceptual problem-solving strategies. *Experimental Aging Research, 4*, 37-54.

Lehman, E.B., & Mellinger, J.C. (1984). Effects of aging on memory for presentation modality. *Developmental Psychology, 20*, 1210-1217.

Lehman, E.B., & Mellinger, J.C. (1986). Forgetting rates in modality memory for young, mid-life and older women. *Psychology and Aging, 1*, 178-179.

Lesser, R. (1976). Verbal and non-verbal memory components in the token test. *Neuropsychologia, 14*, 79-85.

Liang, J. (1986). Self-reported physical health among aged adults. *Journal of Gerontology, 41*, 248-260.

Lichty, W., Bressie, S., & Krell, R. (1988). When is a fork not a fork: Recall of performed activities as a function of age, generation, and bizarreness. In M.M. Gruneberg, P.E. Morris, & R.N. Sykes (Eds.), *Practical aspects of memory: Current research and issues* (pp. 506-511). Chichester: Wiley.

Lichty, W., Kausler, D.H., & Martinez, D.R. (1986). Adult age differences in memory for motor versus cognitive activities. *Experimental Aging Research, 12*, 227-230.

Light, L.L. (1988). Language and aging: Competence versus performance. In J.E. Birren & V.L. Bengston (Eds.), *Emergent theories of aging* (pp. 177-213). New York: Springer.

Light, L.L. (1990). Interactions between memory and language in old age. In J.E. Birren & K.W. Schaie (Eds.), *Handbook of the psychology of aging* (3rd ed., pp. 275-290). San Diego: Academic.

Light, L.L., & Albertson, S.A. (1988). Comprehension of pragmatic implications in young and older adults. In L.L. Light & D.M. Burke (Eds.), *Language, memory and aging* (pp. 133-153). New York: Cambridge University Press.

Light, L.L., & Albertson, S.A. (1989). Direct and indirect tests of memory for category exemplars in young and older adults. *Psychology and Aging, 4*, 487-492.

Light, L.L., & Anderson, P.A. (1983). Memory for scripts in young and older adults. *Memory and Cognition, 11*, 435-444.

Light, L.L., & Anderson, P.A. (1985). Working-memory capacity, age and memory for discourse. *Journal of Gerontology, 40*, 737-747.

Light, L.L., & Burke, D.M. (1988). Patterns of language and memory in old age. In L.L. Light & D.M. Burke (Eds.), *Language, memory and aging* (pp. 244-277). New York: Cambridge University Press.

Light, L.L., & Capps, J.L. (1986). Comprehension of pronouns in young and older adults. *Developmental Psychology, 22*, 580-585.

Light, L.L., & Singh, A. (1987). Implicit and explicit memory in young and older adults. *Journal of Experimental Psychology: Learning, Memory, and Cognition, 13*, 531-541.

Light, L.L., Singh, A., & Capps, J.L. (1986). The dissociation of memory and awareness in young and older adults. *Journal of Clinical and Experimental Neuropsychology, 8*, 62-74.

Light, L.L., & Zelinski, E.M. (1983). Memory for spatial information in young and old adults. *Developmental Psychology, 19*, 901-906.

Light, L.L., Zelinski, E.M., & Moore, M.M. (1982). Adult age differences in reasoning from new information. *Journal of Experimental Psychology: Learning, Memory, and Cognition*, *8*, 435-447.

Linn, B.S., & Linn, M.W. (1980). Objective and self-assessed health in the old and very old. *Social Science and Medicine*, *14A*, 311-315.

Lockhart, R.S., & Craik, F.I.M. (1990). Levels of processing: A retrospective commentary on a framework for memory research. *Canadian Journal of Psychology*, *44*, 87-112.

Loftus, G.R. (1978). On the interpretation of interactions. *Memory and Cognition*, *6*, 312-319.

Loftus, G.R., Truax, P.E., & Nelson, W.W. (1987). In C. Schooler & K.W. Schaie (Eds.), *Cognitive functioning and social structure over the life course* (pp. 59-77). Norwood, NJ: Ablex.

Looft, W., & Charles, D.C. (1971). Egocentrism and social interaction in young and old adults. *International Journal of Aging and Human Development*, *2*, 21-28.

Lorge, I. (1936). The influence of the test upon the nature of mental decline as a function of age. *Journal of Educational Psychology*, *27*, 100-110.

Lorge, I. (1956). Aging and intelligence. *Journal of Chronic Diseases*, *412*, 131-139.

Lorge, I. (1957). Methodology of the study of intelligence and emotion in ageing. *Ciba Foundation Colloquia on Ageing*, *3*, 170-182.

Lorsbach, T.C. (1990). Buildup of proactive inhibition as a function of temporal spacing and adult age. *American Journal of Psychology*, *103*, 21-36.

Lorsbach, T.C., & Simpson, G.B. (1984). Age differences in the rate of processing in short-term memory. *Journal of Gerontology*, *39*, 309-314.

Lorsbach, T.C., & Simpson, G.B. (1988). Dual-task performance as a function of adult age and task complexity. *Psychology and Aging*, *3*, 210-212.

Lovelace, E.A., & Cooley, S. (1982). Free association of older adults to single words and conceptually related word triads. *Journal of Gerontology*, *37*, 432-437.

Lovelace, E.A., & Marsh, G.R. (1985). Prediction and evaluation of memory performance by young and old adults. *Journal of Gerontology*, *40*, 192-197.

Ludwig, T.E. (1982). Age differences in mental synthesis. *Journal of Gerontology*, *37*, 182-189.

Luszcz, M.A., Roberts, T.H., & Mattiske, J. (1990). Use of relational and item-specific information in remembering by older and younger adults. *Psychology and Aging*, *5*, 242-249.

Lynn, R., & Hampson, S. (1986). The rise of national intelligence: Evidence from Britain, Japan and the USA. *Personality and Individual Differences*, *7*, 23-32.

Lynn, R., Hampson, S.L., & Mullineux, J.C. (1987). A long-term increase in the fluid intelligence of English children. *Nature*, *328*, 797.

Macht, M.L., & Buschke, H. (1983). Age differences in cognitive effort in recall. *Journal of Gerontology*, *38*, 695-700.

Macht, M.L., & Buschke, H. (1984). Speed of recall in aging. *Journal of Gerontology*, *39*, 439-443.

Mack, J.L., & Carlson, N.J. (1978). Conceptual deficits and aging: The category test. *Perceptual and Motor Skills*, *46*, 123-128.

Mackay, H.A., & Inglis, J. (1963). The effects of age on short-term auditory storage processes. *Gerontologia*, *8*, 193-200.

Madden, D.J. (1982). Age differences and similarities in the improvement of controlled search. *Experimental Aging Research*, *8*, 91-98.

Madden, D.J. (1983). Aging and distraction by highly familiar stimuli during visual search. *Developmental Psychology*, *19*, 499-507.

Madden, D.J. (1984). Data-driven and memory-driven selective attention in visual search. *Journal of Gerontology*, *39*, 72-78.

Madden, D.J. (1986a). Adult age differences in the attentional capacity demands of visual search. *Cognitive Development*, *1*, 335-363.

Madden, D.J. (1986b). Adult age differences in visual word recognition: Semantic encoding and episodic retention. *Experimental Aging Research, 12*, 71-78.

Madden, D.J. (1987). Aging, attention, and the use of meaning during visual search. *Cognitive Development, 2*, 201-216.

Madden, D.J. (1988). Adult age differences in the effects of sentence context and stimulus degradation during visual word recognition. *Psychology and Aging, 3*, 167-172.

Madden, D.J. (1989). Visual word identification and age-related slowing. *Cognitive Development, 4*, 1-29.

Madden, D.J., Blumenthal, J.A., Allen, P.A., & Emery, C.F. (1989). Improving aerobic capacity in healthy older adults does not necessarily lead to improved cognitive performance. *Psychology and Aging, 4*, 307-320.

Madden, D.J., & Nebes, R.D. (1980). Aging and the development of automaticity in visual search. *Developmental Psychology, 16*, 377-384.

Maddox, G.L. (1962). Some correlates of differences in self-assessments of health status among the elderly. *Journal of Gerontology, 17*, 180-185.

Maddox, G.L. (1964). Self-assessment of health status *Journal of Chronic Disease, 17*, 449-460.

Maddox, G.L., & Douglass, E. (1973). Self-assessment of health: A longitudinal study of elderly subjects. *Journal of Health and Social Behavior, 14*, 87-93.

Maddox, G.L., & Douglass, E. (1974). Aging and individual differences: A longitudinal analysis of social, psychological, and physiological indicators. *Journal of Gerontology, 29*, 555-563.

Manstead, A.S.R., & Lee, J.S. (1979). The effectiveness of two types of witness appeal signs. *Ergonomics, 22*, 1125-1140.

Marsh, G.R. (1975). Age differences in evoked potential correlates of a memory scanning process. *Experimental Aging Research, 1*, 3-16.

Marshall, P.H., Elias, J.W., Webber, S.M., Gist, B.A., Winn, F.J., King, P., & Moore, S.A. (1978). Age differences in verbal mediation: A structural and functional analysis. *Experimental Aging Research, 4*, 175-193.

Martin, M. (1986). Aging and patterns of change in everyday memory and cognition. *Human Learning, 5*, 63-74.

Mason, C.F., & Ganzler, H. (1964). Adult norms for the Shipley Institute of Living Scale and Hooper Visual Organization Test based on age and education. *Journal of Gerontology, 19*, 419-424.

Mason, S.E. (1979). Effects of orienting tasks on the recall and recognition performance of subjects differing in age. *Developmental Psychology, 15*, 467-469.

Mason, S.E. (1986). Age and gender as factors in facial recognition and identification. *Experimental Aging Research, 12*, 151-154.

Mason, S.E., & Smith, A.D. (1977). Imagery in the aged. *Experimental Aging Research, 3*, 17-32.

Matarazzo, J.D. (1976). *Wechsler's measurement and appraisal of intelligence.* Baltimore, MD: Williams & Witkins.

Maule, A.J., & Sanford, A.J. (1980). Adult age differences in multi-source selection behavior with partially predictable signals. *British Journal of Psychology, 71*, 69-81.

Maylor, E.A. (1990). Age, blocking and the tip-of-the-tongue state. *British Journal of Psychology, 81*, 123-134.

McCarthy, M., Ferris, S.H., Clark, E., & Crook, T. (1981). Acquisition of retention of categorized material in normal aging and senile dementia. *Experimental Aging Research, 7*, 127-135.

McCarty, S.M., Siegler, I.C., & Logue, P.E. (1982). Cross-sectional and longitudinal patterns of three Wechsler Memory Scale subtests. *Journal of Gerontology, 37*, 169-175.

McCormack, P.D. (1981). Temporal coding by young and elderly adults: A test of the Hasher-

Zacks model. *Developmental Psychology, 17,* 509-515.

McCormack, P.D. (1982). Coding of spatial information by young and elderly adults. *Journal of Gerontology, 37,* 80-86.

McCrae, R.R., Arenberg, D., & Costa, P.T. (1987). Declines in divergent thinking with age: Cross-sectional, longitudinal and cross-sequential analyses. *Psychology and Aging, 2,* 130-137.

McDaniel, M.A., Ryan, E.B., & Cunningham, C.J. (1989). Encoding difficulty and memory enhancement for young and older readers. *Psychology and Aging, 4,* 333-338.

McDowd, J.M. (1986). The effects of age and extended practice on divided attention performance. *Journal of Gerontology, 41,* 764-769.

McDowd, J.M., & Botwinick, J. (1984). Rote and gist memory in relation to type of information, sensory mode, and age. *Journal of Genetic Psychology, 145,* 167-178.

McDowd, J.M., & Craik, F.I.M. (1988). Effects of aging and task difficulty on divided attention performance. *Journal of Experimental Psychology: Human Perception and Performance, 14,* 267-280.

McFarland, C.E. Jr., Warren, L.R., & Crockard, J. (1985). Memory for self-generated stimuli in young and old adults. *Journal of Gerontology, 40,* 205-207.

McFarland, R.A. (1956). Functional efficiency, skills and employment. In J.E. Anderson (Ed.), *Psychological aspects of aging* (pp. 227-235). Washington, DC: American Psychological Association.

McFarland, R.A., & O'Doherty, B.M. (1959). Work and occupational skills. In J.E. Birren (Ed.), *Handbook of aging and the individual* (pp. 452-500). Chicago, IL: University of Chicago Press.

McIntyre, J.S., & Craik, F.I.M. (1987). Age differences in memory for item and source information. *Canadian Journal of Psychology, 41,* 175-192.

McNamara, M.C., Benignus, V.A., Benignus, G., & Miller, A.T. (1977). Active and passive avoidance in rats as a function of age. *Experimental Aging Research, 3,* 3-16.

McNulty, J.A., & Caird, W.K. (1966). Memory loss with age: Retrieval or storage. *Psychological Reports, 19,* 229-230.

McNulty, J.A., & Caird, W.K. (1967). Memory loss with age: An unsolved problem. *Psychological Reports, 20,* 283-288.

Medin, D.L. (1969). Form perception and pattern reproduction by monkeys. *Journal of Comparative and Physiological Psychology, 68,* 412-419.

Medin, D.L., O'Neal, P., Smeltz, E., & Davis, R.T. (1973). Age differences in retention of concurrent discrimination problems in monkeys. *Journal of Gerontology, 28,* 63-67.

Mergler, N.L., Dusek, J.B., & Hoyer, W.J. (1977). Central/incidental recall and selective attention in young and elderly adults. *Experimental Aging Research, 3,* 49-60.

Mergler, N.L., & Hoyer, W.J. (1981). Effects of training on dimensional classification abilities: Adult age comparisons. *Educational Gerontology, 6,* 135-145.

Meyer, B.J. (1987). Reading comprehension and aging. In K.W. Schaie (Ed.), *Annual review of gerontology and geriatrics* (Vol. 7, pp. 93-115). New York: Springer.

Meyer, B.J., & Rice, G.E. (1989). Prose processing in adulthood: The text, the reader, and the task. In L.W. Poon, D.C. Rubin & B.A. Wilson (Eds.), *Everyday cognition in adulthood and late life* (pp. 157-174). Cambridge, England: Cambridge University Press.

Meyer, B.J., Young, C.J., & Bartlett, B.J. (1989). *Memory improved: Reading and memory enhancement across the lifespan through strategic text structures.* Hillsdale, NJ: Lawrence Erlbaum Associates.

Meyer, H.H. (1970). The validity of the in-basket test as a measure of managerial performance. *Personnel Psychology, 23,* 297-307.

Miles, C.C. (1934). Influence of speed and age on intelligence scores of adults. *Journal of Genetic Psychology, 10,* 208-210.

Miles, C.C., & Miles, W.R. (1932). The correlation of intelligence scores and chronological age from early to late maturity. *American Journal of Psychology, 44*, 44-78.

Miles, W.R. (1931). Correlation of reaction and coordination speed with age in adults. *American Journal of Psychology, 43*, 377-391.

Miles, W.R. (1933). Age and human ability. *Psychological Review, 40*, 99-123.

Miles, W.R. (1935). Training, practice, and mental longevity. *Science, 81*, 79-87.

Miles, W.R. (1942). Psychological aspects of ageing. E.W. Cowdry (Ed.), *Problems of ageing* (pp. 756-784). Baltimore, MD: Williams & Wilkins.

Miles, W.R., & Miles, C.C. (1943). Principal mental changes with normal aging. In E.J. Stieglitz (Ed.), *Geriatric medicine* (pp. 99-117). Philadelphia: W.B. Saunders.

Miles, W.R., & Shriver, B.M. (1953). Aging in Air Force pilots. *Journal of Gerontology, 8*, 185-190.

Miller, K.A., & Kohn, M.L. (1983). The reciprocal effects on job conditions and the intellectuality of leisure-time activities. In M.L. Kohn & C. Schooler (Eds.), *Work and personality* (pp. 217-241). Norwood, NJ: Ablex.

Mistler-Lachman, J.L. (1977). Spontaneous shift in encoding dimensions among elderly subjects. *Journal of Gerontology, 32*, 68-72.

Mitchell, D.B. (1989). How many memory systems? Evidence from aging. *Journal of Experimental Psychology: Learning, Memory, and Cognition, 15*, 31-49.

Mitchell, D.B., Brown, A.S., & Murphy, D.R. (1990). Dissociations between procedural and episodic memory: Effects of time and aging. *Psychology and Aging, 5*, 264-276.

Mitchell, D.B., Hunt, R.R., & Schmitt, F.A. (1986). The generation effect and reality monitoring: Evidence from dementia and normal aging. *Journal of Gerontology, 41*, 79-84.

Mitchell, D.B., & Perlmutter, M. (1986). Semantic activation and episodic memory: Age similarities and differences. *Developmental Psychology, 22*, 86-94.

Moenster, P.A. (1972). Learning and memory in relation to age. *Journal of Gerontology, 27*, 361-363.

Monge, R.H. (1969). Learning in the adult years: Set or rigidity. *Human Development, 12*, 131-140.

Monge, R.H., & Gardner, E.F. (1976). Education as an aid to adaptation in the adult years. In K.F. Riegel & J.A. Meacham (Eds.), *The developing individual in a changing world* (Vol. 2, pp. 611-620). The Hague: Mouton.

Mook, D.G. (1983). In defense of external validity. *American Psychologist, 38*, 379-387.

Mook, D.G. (1989). The myth of external validity. In L.W. Poon, D.C. Rubin & B.A. Wilson (Eds.), *Everyday cognition in adulthood and late life* (pp. 25-43). Cambridge, England: Cambridge University Press.

Moore, T.E., Richards, B., & Hood, J. (1984). Aging and the coding of spatial information. *Journal of Gerontology, 39*, 210-212.

Morrell, R.W., Park, D.C., & Poon, L.W. (1989). Quality of instructions on prescription drug labels: Effects of memory and comprehension in young and old adults. *Gerontologist, 29*, 345-354.

Morrell, R.W., Park, D.C., & Poon, L.W. (1990). Effects of labeling techniques on memory and comprehension of prescription information in young and old adults. *Journal of Gerontology: Psychological Sciences, 45*, P166-P172.

Morris, R.G., Craik, F.I.M., & Gick, M.L. (1990). Age differences in working memory tasks: The role of secondary memory and the central executive system. *Quarterly Journal of Experimental Psychology, 42A*, 67-86.

Morris, R.G., Gick, M.L., & Craik, F.I.M. (1988). Processing resources and age differences in working memory. *Memory and Cognition, 16*, 362-366.

Moscovitch, M. (1982). A neuropsychological approach to perception and memory in normal and pathological aging. In F.I.M. Craik & S. Trehub (Eds.), *Aging and cognitive processes* (pp. 55-78). New York: Plenum.

Moscovitch, M., & Winocur, G. (1983). Contextual cues and release from proactive inhibition in old and young people. *Canadian Journal of Psychology*, *37*, 331-344.

Mossey, J.M., & Shapiro, E. (1982). Self-rated health: A predictor of mortality among elderly Americans. *American Journal of Public Health*, *72*, 800-808.

Mueller, J.H., Kausler, D.H., & Faherty, A. (1980). Age and access time for different memory codes. *Experimental Aging Research*, *6*, 445-450.

Mueller, J.H., Kausler, D.H., Faherty, A., & Oliveri, M. (1980). Reaction time as a function of age, anxiety and typicality. *Bulletin of the Psychonomic Society*, *16*, 473-476.

Mueller, J.H., Rankin, J.L., & Carlomusto, M. (1979). Adult age differences in free recall as a function of basis of organization and method of presentation. *Journal of Gerontology*, *34*, 375-380.

Mueller, J.H., & Ross, M.J. (1984). Uniqueness of the self-concept across the life span. *Bulletin of the Psychonomic Society*, *22*, 83-86.

Muhs, P.J., Hooper, E.H., & Papalia-Finlay, D. (1979-80). Cross-sectional analysis of cognitive functioning across the life-span. *International Journal of Aging and Human Development*, *10*, 311-333.

Murphy, M.D., Sanders, R.E., Gabriesheski, A.S., & Schmitt, F.A. (1981). Metamemory in the aged. *Journal of Gerontology*, *36*, 185-193.

Murphy, M.D., Schmitt, F.A., Caruso, M.J., & Sanders, R.E. (1987). Metamemory in older adults: The role of monitoring in serial recall. *Psychology and Aging*, *2*, 331-339.

Murrell, K.F.H. (1973). Review of *Functional Age of Industrial Workers*. *Occupational Psychology*, *47*, 93-94.

Murrell, K.F.H., & Griew, S. (1965). Age, experience and speed of response. In A.T. Welford & J.E. Birren (Eds.), *Behavior, aging and the nervous system* (pp. 60-66). Springfield, IL: Charles C Thomas.

Myerson, J., Hale, S., Wagstaff, D., Poon, L.W., & Smith, G.A. (1990). The information-loss model: A mathematical theory of age-related cognitive slowing. *Psychological Review*, *97*, 475-487.

Naveh-Benjamin, M. (1987). Coding of spatial location information: An automatic process? *Journal of Experimental Psychology: Learning, Memory, and Cognition*, *13*, 595-605.

Neale, J.G., Toye, M.H., & Belbin, E. (1968). Adult training: The use of programmed instruction. *Occupational Psychology*, *42*, 23-32.

Nebes, R.D., & Andrews-Kulis, M.E. (1976). The effect of age on the speed of sentence formation and incidental learning. *Experimental Aging Research*, *2*, 315-332.

Nebes, R.D., Boller, F., & Holland, A. (1986). Use of semantic context by patients with Alzheimer's disease. *Psychology and Aging*, *1*, 261-269.

Nehrke, M.F. (1972). Age, sex and educational differences in syllogistic reasoning. *Journal of Gerontology*, *27*, 466-470.

Nesselroade, J.R. (1977). Issues in studying developmental change from a multivariate perspective. In J.E. Birren & K.W. Schaie (Eds.), *Handbook of the psychology of aging* (pp. 59-69). New York: Van Nostrand Reinhold.

Nesselroade, J.R., & Labouvie, E.W. (1985). Experimental design in research on aging. In J.E. Birren & K.W. Schaie (Eds.), *Handbook of the psychology of aging* (2nd ed., pp. 35-60). New York: Van Nostrand Reinhold.

Nestor, P.G., Parasuraman, R., & Haxby, J.V. (1989). Attentional costs of mental operations in young and old adults. *Developmental Neuropsychology*, *5*, 141-158.

Newell, A., & Simon, H.A. (1972). *Human problem solving*. Englewood Cliffs, NJ: Prentice-Hall.

Nichols, M., Obler, L., Albert, M., & Goodglass, H. (1985). Lexical retrieval in healthy aging. *Cortex*, *21*, 596-606.

Niederehe, G., & Yoder, C. (1989). Metamemory perceptions in depressions of young and older adults. *Journal of Nervous and Mental Disease*, *177*, 4-14.

Nolan, J.D., Havemeyer, E., & Vig, S. (1978). Mature and young adult women's recall of textbook material. *Journal of Educational Psychology, 70*, 695-700.

Offenbach, S.I. (1974). A developmental study of hypothesis testing and cue selection strategies. *Developmental Psychology, 10*, 484-490.

Ohta, R.J. (1983). Spatial orientation in the elderly: The current status of understanding. In H.L. Pick, Jr. & L.P. Acvedolo (Eds.), *Spatial orientation: Theory, research and application* (pp. 105-124). New York: Plenum Press.

Ohta, R.J., Walsh, D.A., & Krauss, I.K. (1981). Spatial perspective-taking ability in young and elderly adults. *Experimental Aging Research, 7*, 45-63.

Okun, M.A. (1976). Adult age and cautiousness in decision: A review of the literature. *Human Development, 19*, 220-233.

Okun, M.A., & Elias, C.S. (1977). Cautiousness in adulthood as function of age and payoff structure. *Journal of Gerontology, 32*, 451-455.

Okun, M.A., & Siegler, I.C. (1976). Relation between preference for intermediate risk and adult age in men: A cross-cultural validation. *Developmental Psychology, 12*, 565-566.

Okun, M.A., Siegler, I.C., & George, L.K. (1978). Cautiousness and verbal learning in adulthood. *Journal of Gerontology, 33*, 94-97.

Okun, M.A., Stock, W.A., & Ceurvorst, R.W. (1980). Risk taking through the adult life span. *Experimental Aging Research, 6*, 463-474.

Orme, J.E. (1957). Non-verbal and verbal performance in normal old age, senile dementia, and elderly depression. *Journal of Gerontology, 12*, 408-413.

Owens, W.A. (1956). Research on age and mental abilities. In J.E. Anderson (Ed.), *Psychological aspects of aging* (pp. 155-157). Washington, DC: American Psychological Association.

Owens, W.A. (1966). Age and mental abilities: A second adult follow-up. *Journal of Educational Psychology, 57*, 311-325.

Pacaud, S., & Welford, A.T. (1989). Performance in relation to age and educational level: A monumental research. *Experimental Aging Research, 15*, 123-136.

Padgett, R.J., & Ratner, H.H. (1987). Older and younger adults' memory for structured and unstructured events. *Experimental Aging Research, 13*, 133-139.

Panek, P.E. (1985). Age differences in field- dependence/-independence. *Experimental Aging Research, 11*, 97-99.

Panek, P.E., Barrett, G.V., Sterns, H.L., & Alexander, R.A. (1978). Age differences in perceptual style, selective attention, and perceptual motor reaction time. *Experimental Aging Research, 4*, 377-387.

Panek, P.E., & Stoner, S.B. (1980). Age differences on Raven's Coloured Progressive Matrices. *Perceptual and Motor Skills, 50*, 977-978.

Park, D.C. (1988). Everyday memories in and out of context. *Gerontology Review, 1*, 43-50.

Park, D.C., Cherry, K.E., Smith, A.D., & Lafranza, V.N. (1990). Effects of distinctive context on memory for objects and their locations in young and elderly adults. *Psychology and Aging, 5*, 250-255.

Park, D.C., & Puglisi, J.T. (1985). Older adults' memory for the color of pictures and words. *Journal of Gerontology, 40*, 198-204.

Park, D.C., Puglisi, J.T., & Lutz, R. (1982). Spatial memory in older adults: Effects of intentionality. *Journal of Gerontology, 37*, 330-335.

Park, D.C., Puglisi, J.T., & Smith, A.D. (1986). Memory for pictures: Does an age-related decline exist? *Psychology and Aging, 1*, 11-17.

Park, D.C., Puglisi, J.T., Smith, A.D., & Dudley, W.N. (1987). Cue utilization and encoding specificity in picture recognition by older adults. *Journal of Gerontology, 42*, 423-425.

Park, D.C., Puglisi, J.T., & Sovacool, M. (1983). Memory for pictures, words and spatial location in older adults: Evidence for pictorial superiority. *Journal of Gerontology, 38*, 582-588.

Park, D.C., Royal, D., Dudley, W.N., & Morrell, R. (1988). Forgetting of pictures over a long retention interval in young and older adults. *Psychology and Aging, 3*, 94-95.

Park, D.C., Smith, A.D., Dudley, W.N., & Lafranza, V.N. (1989). Effects of age and a divided attention task presented during encoding and retrieval on memory. *Journal of Experimental Psychology: Learning, Memory, and Cognition, 15*, 1185-1191.

Park, D.C., Smith, A.D., Morrell, R.W., Puglisi, J.T., & Dudley, W.N. (1990). Effects of contextual integration on recall of pictures by older adults. *Journal of Gerontology: Psychological Sciences, 45*, P52-P57.

Parker, K.C. (1983). Factor analysis of the WAIS-R at nine age levels between 16 and 74 years. *Journal of Consulting and Clinical Psychology, 51*, 302-308.

Parker, K.C. (1986). Changes with age, year-of-birth cohort, age by year-of-birth cohort interaction and standardization of the Wechsler adult intelligence tests. *Human Development, 29*, 209-222.

Parkinson, S.R. (1982). Performance deficits in short-term memory tasks: A comparison of amnesic Korsakoff patients and the aged. In L.S. Cermak (Ed.), *Human memory and amnesia* (pp. 77-96). Hillsdale, NJ: Lawrence Erlbaum Associates.

Parkinson, S.R., Inman, V.W., & Dannenbaum, S.E. (1985). Adult age differences in short-term forgetting. *Acta Psychologica, 60*, 83-101.

Parkinson, S.R., Lindholm, J.M., & Inman, V.W. (1982). An analysis of age differences in immediate recall. *Journal of Gerontology, 37*, 425-431.

Parks, C.W., Mitchell, D.B., & Perlmutter, M. (1986). Cognitive and social functioning across adulthood: Age or student status differences? *Psychology and Aging, 1*, 248-254.

Peak, D.T. (1968). Changes in short-term memory in a group of aging community residents. *Journal of Gerontology, 23*, 9-16.

Peak, D.T. (1970). A replication study of changes in short-term memory in a group of aging community residents. *Journal of Gerontology, 25*, 316-319.

Perlmutter, M. (1978). What is memory aging the aging of? *Developmental Psychology, 14*, 330-345.

Perlmutter, M. (1979). Age differences in the consistency of adult's associative responses. *Experimental Aging Research, 5*, 549-553.

Perlmutter, M. (1980). An apparent paradox about memory aging. In L.W. Poon, J.L. Fozard, L.S. Cermak, D. Arenberg, & L.W. Thompson (Eds.), *New directions in memory and aging* (pp. 345-353). Hillsdale, NJ: Lawrence Erlbaum Associates.

Perlmutter, M. (1988). Cognitive potential throughout life. In J.E. Birren & V.L. Bengston (Eds.), *Emergent theories of aging* (pp. 247-268). New York: Springer.

Perlmutter, M., Adams, C., Berry, J., Kaplan, M., Person, D., & Verdonik, F. (1987). Aging and memory. In K.W. Schaie (Ed.), *Annual review of gerontology and geriatrics*, (Vol. 7., pp. 57-92). New York: Springer.

Perlmutter, M., Kaplan, M., & Nyquist, L. (1990). Development of adaptive competence in adulthood. *Human Development, 33*, 185-197.

Perlmutter, M., & List, J.A. (1982). Learning in later adulthood. In T.M. Field, A. Huston, H.C. Quay, L. Troll & G.E. Finley (Eds.), *Review of human development* (pp. 551-568). New York: Wiley & Sons.

Perlmutter, M., Metzger, R., Miller, K., & Nezworski, T. (1980). Memory of historical events. *Experimental Aging Research, 6*, 47-60.

Perlmutter, M., Metzger, R., Nezworski, T., & Miller, K. (1981). Spatial and temporal memory in 20 and 60 year olds. *Journal of Gerontology, 36*, 59-65.

Perlmutter, M., & Mitchell, D.B. (1982). The appearance and disappearance of age differences in adult memory. In F.I.M. Craik & S. Trehub (Eds.), *Aging and cognitive processes* (pp. 127-144). New York: Plenum Press.

Perlmutter, M., & Nyquist, L. (1990). Relationships between self-reported physical and mental health and intelligence performance across adulthood. *Journal of Gerontology: Psychological Sciences, 45*, P145-P155.

Persaud, G. (1987). Sex and age differences on the Raven's Matrices. *Perceptual and Motor Skills, 65*, 45-46.

Peterson, L.R., & Peterson, M.J. (1959). Short-term retention of individual verbal items. *Journal of Experimental Psychology, 58*, 193-198.

Petros, T.V., Zehr, H.D., & Chabot, R.J. (1983). Adult age differences in accessing and retrieving information from long-term memory. *Journal of Gerontology, 38*, 589-592.

Pezdek, K. (1983). Memory for items and their spatial locations by young and elderly adults. *Developmental Psychology, 19*, 895-900.

Pfau, H.D., & Murphy, M.D. (1988). Role of verbal knowledge in chess skill. *American Journal of Psychology, 101*, 73-86.

Pfeiffer, E. (1970). Survival in old age: Physical, psychological, and social correlates of longevity. *Journal of the American Geriatric Society, 18*, 273-285.

Pfeiffer, E., & Davis, G.C. (1971). The use of leisure time in middle life. *The Gerontologist, 11*, 187-195.

Pierce, K., & Storandt, M. (1987). Similarities in visual imagery ability in young and old women. *Experimental Aging Research, 13*, 209-211.

Pierce, T.W., Elias, M.F., Keohane, P.J., Podraza, A.M., Robbins, M.A., & Schultz, N.R. (1989). Validity of a short form of the Category Test in relation to age, education, and gender. *Experimental Aging Research, 15*, 137-141.

Pilpel, D., Carmel, S., & Galinsky, D. (1988). Self-rated health among the elderly. *Comprehensive Gerontology, Sect. B, 2*, 110-116.

Plemons, J.K., Willis, S.L., & Baltes, P.B. (1978). Modifiability of fluid intelligence in aging: A short-term longitudinal training approach. *Journal of Gerontology, 33*, 224-231.

Plude, D.J., & Hoyer, W.J. (1981). Adult age differences in visual search as a function of stimulus mapping and processing load. *Journal of Gerontology, 36*, 598-604.

Plude, D.J., & Hoyer, W.J. (1985). Attention and performance: Identifying and localizing age deficits. In N. Charness (Ed.), *Aging and human performance* (pp. 47-99). Chicester: Wiley.

Plude, D.J., Hoyer, W.J., & Lazar, J. (1982). Age, response complexity, and target consistency in visual search. *Experimental Aging Research, 8*, 99-102.

Plude, D.J., Kaye, D.B., Hoyer, W.J., Post, T.A., Saynisch, M.J., & Hahn, M.V. (1983). Aging and visual search under consistent and varied mapping. *Developmental Psychology, 19*, 508-512.

Poitrenaud, J., Malbezin, M., & Guez, D. (1989). Self-rating and psychometric assessment of age-related changes in memory among young-elderly managers. *Developmental Neuropsychology, 5*, 285-294.

Ponds, R.W.H.M., Brouwer, W.H., & van Wolfelaar, P.C. (1988). Age differences in divided attention in a simulated driving task. *Journal of Gerontology: Psychological Sciences, 43*, P151-P156.

Poon, L.W. (1985). Differences in human memory with aging: Nature, causes, and clinical implications. In J.E. Birren & K.W. Schaie (Eds.), *Handbook of the psychology of aging* (2nd ed., pp. 427-462). New York: Van Nostrand Reinhold.

Poon, L.W., & Fozard, J.L. (1978). Speed of retrieval from long-term memory in relation to age, familiarity, and datedness of information. *Journal of Gerontology, 33*, 711-717.

Poon, L.W., & Fozard, J.L. (1980). Age and word frequency effects in continuous recognition memory. *Journal of Gerontology, 35*, 77-86.

Poon, L.W., Fozard, J.L., Paulshock, D.R., & Thomas, J.C. (1979). A questionnaire assessment of age differences in retention of recent and remote events. *Experimental Aging Research, 5*, 401-411.

Poon, L.W., Fozard, J.L., & Treat, N.J. (1978). From clinical and research findings on memory to intervention programs. *Experimental Aging Research, 4*, 235-253.

Poon, L.W., Gurland, B.J., Eisdorfer, C., Crook, T., Thompson, L.W., Kaszniak, A.W., &

Davis, K.L. (1986). Integration of experimental and clinical precepts in memory assessment: A tribute to George Talland. In L.W. Poon (Ed.), *Handbook for clinical memory assessment of older adults* (pp. 3-10). Washington, DC: American Psychological Association.

Poon, L.W., Krauss, I.K., & Bowles, N.L. (1984). On subject selection in cognitive aging research. *Experimental Aging Research, 10,* 43-49.

Poon, L.W., & Walsh-Sweeney, L. (1981). Effects of bizarre and interacting imagery on learning and retrieval of the aged. *Experimental Aging Research, 7,* 65-70.

Potvin, A.R., Syndulko, K., Tourtellote, W.W., Goldberg, Z., Potvin, J.H., & Hansch, E.C. (1981). Quantitative evaluation of normal age-related changes in neurologic function. In F.J. Pirozzolo & G.J. Maletta (Eds.), *Behavioral assessment and psychopharmacology* (pp. 13-57). New York: Praeger.

Potvin, A.R., Tourtellotte, W.W., Pew, R.W., Albers, J.W., Henderson, W.G., & Snyder, D.N. (1973). The importance of age effects on performance in the assessment of clinical trials. *Journal of Chronic Diseases, 26,* 699-717.

Powell, R.R., & Pohndorf, R.H. (1971). Comparison of adult exercisers and non-exercisers on fluid intelligence and selected physiological variables. *Research Quarterly, 42,* 70-77.

Price, B. (1933). The grasping of spoken directions as an age function in adults. *Psychological Bulletin, 30,* 588-590.

Prigatano, G.P., & Parsons, O.A. (1976). Relationship of age and education to Halstead test performance in different patient populations. *Journal of Consulting and Clinical Psychology, 44,* 527-533.

Proctor, R.A. (1873). Growth and decay of mind. *Cornhill Magazine, 28,* 541-555.

Prohaska, T.R., Leventhal, E.A., Leventhal, H., & Keller, M.L. (1985). Health practices and illness cognition in young, middle-aged, and elderly adults. *Journal of Gerontology, 40,* 569-578.

Prohaska, T.R., Parham, I.A., & Teitelman, J. (1984). Age differences in attribution to causality: Implications for intellectual assessment. *Experimental Aging Research, 10,* 111-117.

Puckett, J.M., & Lawson, W.M. (1989). Absence of adult age differences in forgetting in the Brown-Peterson task. *Acta Psychologica, 72,* 159-175.

Puckett, J.M., & Stockburger, D.W. (1988). Absence of age-related proneness to short-term retroactive interference in the absence of rehearsal. *Psychology and Aging, 3,* 342-347.

Puglisi, J.T. (1980). Semantic encoding in older adults as evidenced by release from proactive inhibition. *Journal of Gerontology, 35,* 743-745.

Puglisi, J.T. (1986). Age-related slowing in memory search for three-dimensional objects. *Journal of Gerontology, 41,* 72-78.

Puglisi, J.T., & Morrell, R.W. (1986). Age-related slowing in mental rotation of three-dimensional objects. *Experimental Aging Research, 12,* 217-220.

Puglisi, J.T., & Park, D.C. (1987). Perceptual elaboration and memory in older adults. *Journal of Gerontology, 42,* 160-162.

Puglisi, J.T., Park, D.C., & Smith, A.D. (1987). Picture associations among old and young adults. *Experimental Aging Research, 13,* 115-116.

Puglisi, J.T., Park, D.C., Smith, A.D., & Dudley, W.N. (1988). Age differences in encoding specificity. *Journal of Gerontology: Psychological Sciences, 43,* P145-P150.

Puglisi, J.T., Park, D.C., Smith, A.D., & Hill, G.W. (1985). Memory for two types of spatial location: Effects of instructions, age and format. *American Journal of Psychology, 98,* 101-118.

Quattlebaum, L.F., & White, W.F. (1969). Relationships among the Quick test, two measures of psychomotor functioning, and age. *Perceptual and Motor Skills, 29,* 824-826.

Query, W.T., & Megran, J. (1983). Age-related norms for AVLT in a male patient population. *Journal of Clinical Psychology, 39,* 136-138.

Rabbitt, P. (1977). Changes in problem solving ability in old age. In J.E. Birren & K.W. Schaie (Eds.), *Handbook of the psychology of aging* (pp. 606-625). New York: Van Nostrand Reinhold.

Rabbitt, P. (1981). Human ageing and disturbances of memory control processes underlying "intelligent" performance of some cognitive tasks. In M.P. Friedman, J.P. Das & N. O'Connor (Eds.), *Intelligence and learning* (pp. 427-439). New York: Plenum Press.

Rabbitt, P. (1982). How do old people know what to do next? In F.I.M. Craik & S. Trehub (Eds.), *Aging and cognitive processes* (pp. 79-98). New York: Plenum.

Rabbitt, P. (1983). How can we tell whether human performance is related to chronological age? In D. Samuel, S. Algeri, S. Gershon, V.E. Grimm & G. Toffano (Eds.), *Aging of the brain* (pp. 9-18). New York: Raven Press.

Rabbitt, P. (1984). How old people prepare themselves for events which they expect. In H. Buoma & D.G. Bouwhuis (Eds.), *Attention and performance X: Control of language processes* (pp. 515-527). Hillsdale, NJ: Lawrence Erlbaum Associates.

Rabbitt, P. (1989). Inner-city decay? Age changes in structure and process in recall of familiar topographical information. In L.W. Poon, D.C. Rubin & B.A. Wilson (Eds.), *Everyday cognition in adulthood and late life* (pp. 284-299). Cambridge, England: Cambridge University Press.

Rabbitt, P. (1990). Applied cognitive gerontology: Some problems, methodologies and data. *Applied Cognitive Psychology, 4*, 225-246.

Rabbitt, P., & Abson, V. (1990). "Lost and found": Some logical and methodological limitations of self-report questionnaires as tools to study cognitive ageing. *British Journal of Psychology, 81*, 1-16.

Rabbitt, P., & McInnis, L. (1988). Do clever old people have earlier and richer first memories? *Psychology and Aging, 3*, 338-341.

Rabinowitz, J.C. (1984). Age and recognition failure. *Journal of Gerontology, 39*, 65-71.

Rabinowitz, J.C. (1986). Priming in episodic memory. *Journal of Gerontology, 41*, 204-213.

Rabinowitz, J.C. (1989a). Judgments of origin and generation effects: Comparisons between young and elderly adults. *Psychology and Aging, 4*, 259-268.

Rabinowitz, J.C. (1989b). Age deficits in recall under optimal study conditions. *Psychology and Aging, 4*, 378-380.

Rabinowitz, J.C., & Ackerman, B.P. (1982). General encoding of episodic events by elderly adults. In F.I.M. Craik & S. Trehub (Eds.), *Aging and cognitive processes* (pp. 145-154). New York: Plenum Press.

Rabinowitz, J.C., Ackerman, B.P., Craik, F.I.M., & Hinchley, J.L. (1982). Aging and metamemory: The roles of relatedness and imagery. *Journal of Gerontology, 37*, 688-695.

Rabinowitz, J.C., & Craik, F.I.M. (1986). Prior retrieval effects in young and old adults. *Journal of Gerontology, 41*, 368-375.

Rabinowitz, J.C., Craik, F.I.M., & Ackerman, B.P. (1982). A processing resource account of age differences in recall. *Canadian Journal of Psychology, 36*, 325-344.

Radvansky, G.A., Gerard, L.D., Zacks, R.T., & Hasher, L. (1990). Younger and older adults' use of mental models as representations for text materials. *Psychology and Aging, 5*, 209-214.

Ramalingaswami, P. (1975). *Measurement of intelligence among adult indians.* New Delhi: National Council of Educational Research and Training.

Randt, C.T., Brown, E.R., & Osborne, D.P. (1980). A memory test for longitudinal measurement of mild to moderate deficits. *Clinical Neuropsychology, 2*, 184-194.

Rankin, J.L., & Collins, M. (1985). Adult age differences in memory elaboration. *Journal of Gerontology, 40*, 451-458.

Rankin, J.L., & Collins, M. (1986). The effects of memory elaboration on adult age differences in incidental recall. *Experimental Aging Research, 12*, 231-234.

Rankin, J.L., & Firnhaber, S. (1986). Adult age differences in memory: Effects of distinctive and common encodings. *Experimental Aging Research, 12,* 141-146.

Rankin, J.L., & Hinrichs, J.V. (1983). Age, presentation rate, and the effectiveness of structural and semantic recall cues. *Journal of Gerontology, 38,* 593-596.

Rankin, J.L., & Hyland, T.P. (1983). The effects of orienting tasks on adult age differences in recall and recognition. *Experimental Aging Research, 9,* 159-164.

Rankin, J.L., Karol, R., & Tuten, C. (1984). Strategy use, recall and recall organization in young, middle-aged, and elderly adults. *Experimental Aging Research, 10,* 193-196.

Rankin, J.L., & Kausler, D.H. (1979). Adult age differences in false recognitions. *Journal of Gerontology, 34,* 58-65.

Ratner, H.H., Padgett, R.J., & Bushey, N. (1988). Old and young adults' recall of events. *Developmental Psychology, 24,* 664-671.

Ratner, H.H., Schell, D.A., Crimmins, A., Mittelman, D., & Baldinelli, L. (1987). Changes in adults' prose recall: Aging or cognitive demands? *Developmental Psychology, 23,* 521-525.

Raven, J.C. (1948). The comparative assessment of intellectual ability. *British Journal of Psychology, 39,* 12-19.

Raven, J., & Court, H. (1989). *Manual for Raven's Progressive Matrices and Vocabulary Scales: Research Supplement No. 4.* London: H.K. Lewis & Co.

Read, D.E. (1987). Neuropsychological assessment of memory in the elderly. *Canadian Journal of Psychology, 41,* 158-174.

Rebok, G.W. (1981). Age effects in problem solving in relation to irrelevant information, dimensional preferences, and feedback. *Experimental Aging Research, 7,* 393-403.

Rebok, G.W., & Balcerak, L.J. (1989). Memory self-efficacy and performance differences in young and old adults: The effect of mnemonic training. *Developmental Psychology, 25,* 714-721.

Rebok, G.W., Offermann, L.R., Wirtz, P.W., & Montaglione, C.J. (1986). Work and intellectual aging: The psychological concomitants of social-organizational conditions. *Educational Gerontology, 12,* 359-374.

Reder, L.M., Wible, C., & Martin, J. (1986). Differential memory changes with age: Exact retrieval versus plausible inference. *Journal of Experimental Psychology: Learning, Memory, and Cognition, 12,* 72-81.

Reed, H.B., & Reitan, R.M. (1963). Changes in psychological test performance associated with the normal aging process. *Journal of Gerontology, 18,* 271-274.

Reese, H.W. (1973). Models of memory and models of development. *Human Development, 16,* 397-416.

Reese, H.W., & Rodeheaver, D. (1985). Problem solving and complex decision making. In J.E. Birren & K.W. Schaie (Eds.), *Handbook of the psychology of aging.* (2nd ed., pp. 474-499). New York: Van Nostrand Reinhold.

Reitan, R.M. (1962). The comparative psychological significance of aging in groups with and without organic brain damage. In C. Tibbitts & W. Donahue (Eds.), *Social and psychological aspects of aging* (pp. 880-887). New York: Columbia University Press.

Rice, G.E. (1986a). The everyday activities of adults: Implications for prose recall - Part I. *Educational Gerontology, 12,* 173-186.

Rice, G.E. (1986b). The everyday activities of adults: Implications for prose recall - Part II. *Educational Gerontology, 12,* 187-198.

Rice, G.E., & Meyer, B.J. (1985). Reading behavior and prose recall performance of young and older adults with high and average verbal ability. *Educational Gerontology, 11,* 57-72.

Rice, G.E., & Meyer, B.J. (1986). Prose recall: Effects of aging, verbal ability, and reading behavior. *Journal of Gerontology, 41,* 469-480.

Rice, G.E., Meyer, B.J.F., & Miller, D.C. (1988). Relation of everyday activities of adults to their prose recall performance. *Educational Gerontology, 14,* 147-158.

Rice, G.E., Meyer, B.J.F., & Miller, D.C. (1989). Using text structure to improve older adults' recall of important medical information. *Educational Gerontology, 15*, 527-542.

Riege, W.H. (1983). Self-report and tests of memory aging. *Clinical Gerontologist, 1*, 23-36.

Riege, W.H., & Inman, V. (1981). Age differences in nonverbal memory tasks. *Journal of Gerontology, 36*, 51-58.

Riege, W.H., Kelly, K., & Klane, L.T. (1981). Age and error differences on Memory-for-Designs. *Perceptual and Motor Skills, 52*, 507-513.

Riegel, K.F., Riegel, R.M., & Meyer, G. (1967). A study of the dropout rates of longitudinal research on aging and the prediction of death. *Journal of Personality and Social Psychology, 5*, 342-348.

Rimoldi, H., & Vander Woude, K. W. (1969). Aging and problem solving. *Archives of General Psychiatry, 20*, 215-225.

Rissenberg, M., & Glanzer, M. (1986). Picture superiority in free recall: The effects of normal aging and primary degenerative dementia. *Journal of Gerontology, 41*, 64-71.

Rissenberg, M., & Glanzer, M. (1987). Free recall and word finding ability in normal aging and senile dementia of the Alzheimer's type: The effect of item concreteness. *Journal of Gerontology, 42*, 318-322.

Roberts, P. (1983). Memory strategy instruction with the elderly: What should memory training be the training of? In M. Pressley & J.R. Levin (Ed.), *Cognitive Strategy Research: Psychological foundations* (pp. 75-100). New York: Springer-Verlag.

Robertson, J.P. (1957). Age, vocabulary, anxiety, and brain damage as factors in verbal learning. *Journal of Consulting Psychology, 21*, 179-182.

Robertson-Tchabo, E.A., & Arenberg, D. (1976). Age differences in cognition in healthy educated men: A factor analysis of experimental measures. *Experimental Aging Research, 2*, 75-89.

Robertson-Tchabo, E.A., & Arenberg, D. (1989). Assessment of memory in older adults. In T. Hunt & C.J. Lindley (Eds.), *Testing older adults* (pp. 200-231). Austin, TX: Pro-Ed.

Rose, A.M. (1980). Information-processing abilities. In R.E. Snow, P. Federico, & W.E. Montague (Eds.), *Aptitude, learning and instruction: Vol. 1: Cognitive process analyses of aptitude* (pp. 65-86). Hillsdale, NJ: Lawrence Erlbaum Associates.

Rose, C.L. (1965). Representativeness of volunteer subjects in a longitudinal aging study. *Human Development, 8*, 152-156.

Rose, T.L., & Yesavage, J.A. (1983). Differential effects of a list-learning mnemonic in three age groups. *Gerontology, 29*, 293-298.

Rose, T.L., Yesavage, J.A., Hill, R.D., & Bower, G.H. (1986). Priming effects and recognition memory in young and elderly adults. *Experimental Aging Research, 12*, 31-37.

Rosenthal, R. (1990). How are we doing in soft psychology? *American Psychologist, 45*, 775-777.

Rosow, I. (1978). What is a cohort and why? *Human Development, 21,*, 65-75.

Ross, E. (1968). Effects of challenging and supportive instructions on verbal learning in older persons. *Journal of Educational Psychology, 59*, 261-266.

Rowe, E.J., & Schnore, M.M. (1971). Item concreteness and reported strategies in paired-associate learning as a function of age. *Journal of Gerontology, 24*, 470-475.

Royce, J.R. (1965). Pebble picking versus boulder building. *Psychological Reports, 16*, 447-450.

Royer, F.L., Gilmore, G.C., & Gruhn, J.J. (1984). Stimulus parameters that produce age differences in block design performance. *Journal of Clinical Psychology, 40*, 1474-1484.

Rubin, K.H. (1974). The relationship between spatial and communicative egocentrism in children and young and old adults. *Journal of Genetic Psychology, 125*, 295-301.

Ruch, F.L. (1934). The differentiative effects of age upon human learning. *Journal of General Psychology, 11*, 261-285.

Ruff, R.M., Light, R.H., & Evans, R.W. (1987). The Ruff Figural Fluency Test: A normative study with adults. *Developmental Neuropsychology, 3*, 37-51.

Rushton, J.P., Brainerd, C.J., & Pressley, M. (1983). Behavioral development and construct validity: The principle of aggregation. *Psychological Bulletin, 94*, 18-38.

Ruth, J., & Birren, J.E. (1985). Creativity in adulthood and old age: Relations to intelligence, sex and mode of testing. *International Journal of Behavioral Development, 8*, 99-109.

Ryan, E., & Butters, N. (1980). Learning and memory impairments in young and old alcoholics: Evidence for the premature-aging hypothesis. *Alcoholism: Clinical and Experimental Research, 4*, 288-293.

Rybarczyk, B.D., Hart, R.P., & Harkins, S.W. (1987). Age and forgetting rate with pictorial stimuli. *Psychology and Aging, 2*, 404-406.

Rybash, J.M., Hoyer, W.J., & Roodin, P.A. (1986). *Adult cognition and aging*. New York: Pergamon Press.

Salthouse, T.A. (1978a). *Age and speed: The nature of the relationship*. Unpublished manuscript.

Salthouse, T.A. (1978b). The role of memory in the age decline in digit-symbol substitution performance. *Journal of Gerontology, 33*, 232-238.

Salthouse, T.A. (1980). Age and memory: Strategies for localizing the loss. In L.W. Poon, J.L. Fozard, L. Cermak, D. Arenberg & L.W. Thompson (Eds.), *New directions in memory and aging* (pp. 47-65). Hillsdale, NJ: Lawrence Erlbaum Associates.

Salthouse, T.A. (1982). *Adult cognition: An experimental psychology of human aging*. New York: Springer-Verlag.

Salthouse, T.A. (1984). Effects of age and skill in typing. *Journal of Experimental Psychology: General, 113*, 345-371.

Salthouse, T.A. (1985a). Speed of behavior and its implications for cognition. In J.E. Birren & K.W. Schaie (Eds.), *Handbook of the psychology of aging* (2nd. ed., pp. 400-426). New York: Van Nostrand Reinhold.

Salthouse, T.A. (1985b). *A theory of cognitive aging*. Amsterdam: North-Holland.

Salthouse, T.A. (1987a). Adult age differences in integrative spatial ability. *Psychology and Aging, 2*, 254-260.

Salthouse, T.A. (1987b). Age, experience, and compensation. In C. Schooler & K.W. Schaie (Eds.), *Cognitive functioning and social structure throughout the life course* (pp. 142-157). Norwood, NJ: Ablex.

Salthouse, T.A. (1987c). The role of experience in cognitive aging. In K.W. Schaie (Ed.), *Annual Review of Gerontology* (Vol. 7, pp. 135-158). New York: Springer.

Salthouse, T.A. (1987d). The role of representations in age differences in analogical reasoning. *Psychology and Aging, 2*, 357-362.

Salthouse, T.A. (1987e). Sources of age-related individual differences in block design tasks. *Intelligence, 11*, 245-262.

Salthouse, T.A. (1988a). The complexity of age X complexity functions: Comment on Charness and Campbell. *Journal of Experimental Psychology: General, 117*, 425-428.

Salthouse, T.A. (1988b). Effects of aging on verbal abilities: An examination of the psychometric literature. In L.L. Light & D.M. Burke (Eds.), *Language and memory in old age* (pp. 17-35). New York: Cambridge University Press.

Salthouse, T.A. (1988c). Initializing the formalization of theories of cognitive aging. *Psychology and Aging, 3*, 1-16.

Salthouse, T.A. (1988d). Resource-reduction interpretations of cognitive aging. *Developmental Review, 8*, 238-272.

Salthouse, T.A. (1988e). The role of processing resources in cognitive aging. In M.L. Howe & C.J. Brainerd (Eds.), *Cognitive development in adulthood* (pp. 185-239). New York: Springer-Verlag.

Salthouse, T.A. (1989a). Age-related changes in basic cognitive processes. In M. Storandt & G.R. VandenBos (Eds.), *The adult years: Continuity and change* (pp. 9-40). Washington, DC: American Psychological Association.

Salthouse, T.A. (1989b). Training = controlled social structure? In K.W. Schaie & C. Schooler (Eds.), *Social structure and aging: Psychological processes* (pp. 121-128). Hillsdale, NJ: Lawrence Erlbaum Associates.

Salthouse, T.A. (1990). Cognitive competence and expertise in aging. In J.E. Birren & K.W. Schaie (Eds.), *Handbook of the psychology of aging* (3rd ed., pp. 310-319). San Diego: Academic.

Salthouse, T.A., & Babcock, R.L. (in press). Decomposing adult age differences in working memory. *Developmental Psychology.*

Salthouse, T.A., Babcock, R.L., Mitchell, D.R., Skovronek, E., & Palmon, R. (1990). Age and experience effects in spatial visualization. *Developmental Psychology, 26,* 128-136.

Salthouse, T.A., & Kail, R. (1983). Memory development throughout the lifespan: The role of processing rate. In P.B. Baltes & O.G. Brim (Eds.), *Life-span development and behavior* (Vol. 5, pp. 89-116). New York: Academic Press.

Salthouse, T.A., & Kausler, D.H. (1985). Memory methodology in maturity. In C.J. Brainerd & M. Pressley (Eds.), *Basic processes in memory development* (pp. 279-311). New York: Springer-Verlag.

Salthouse, T.A., Kausler, D.H., & Saults, J.S. (1988a). Investigation of student status, background variables, and the feasibility of standard tasks in cognitive aging research. *Psychology and Aging, 3,* 29-37.

Salthouse, T.A., Kausler, D.H., & Saults, J.S. (1988b). Utilization of path analytic procedures to investigate the role of processing resources in cognitive aging. *Psychology and Aging, 3,* 158-166.

Salthouse, T.A., Kausler, D.H., & Saults, J.S. (1990). Age, self-assessed health status, and cognition. *Journal of Gerontology, 45,* P156-P160.

Salthouse, T.A., Legg, S., Palmon, R., & Mitchell, D.R. (1990). Memory factors in age-related differences in simple reasoning. *Psychology and Aging, 5,* 9-15.

Salthouse, T.A., & Lichty, W. (1985). Tests of the neural noise hypothesis of age-related cognitive change. *Journal of Gerontology, 40,* 443-450.

Salthouse, T.A., & Mitchell, D.R. (1989). Structural and operational capacities in integrative spatial ability. *Psychology and Aging, 4,* 18-25.

Salthouse, T.A., & Mitchell, D.R. (1990). Effects of age and naturally occurring experience on spatial visualization performance. *Developmental Psychology, 26,* 845-854.

Salthouse, T.A., Mitchell, D.R., & Palmon, R. (1989). Memory and age differences in spatial manipulation ability. *Psychology and Aging, 4,* 480-486.

Salthouse, T.A., Mitchell, D.R., Skovronek, E., & Babcock, R.L. (1989). Effects of adult age and working memory on reasoning and spatial abilities. *Journal of Experimental Psychology: Learning, Memory, and Cognition, 15,* 507-516.

Salthouse, T.A., & Prill, K.A. (1987). Inferences about age impairments in inferential reasoning. *Psychology and Aging, 2,* 43-51.

Salthouse, T.A., & Prill, K.A. (1988). Effects of aging on perceptual closure. *American Journal of Psychology, 101,* 217-238.

Salthouse, T.A., Rogan, J.D., & Prill, K.A. (1984). Division of attention: Age differences on a visually presented memory task. *Memory and Cognition, 12,* 613-620.

Salthouse, T.A., & Saults, J.S. (1987). Multiple spans in transcription typing. *Journal of Applied Psychology, 22,* 187-196.

Salthouse, T.A., & Somberg, B.L. (1982a). Isolating the age deficit in speeded performance. *Journal of Gerontology, 37,* 59-63.

Salthouse, T.A., & Somberg, B.L. (1982b). Skilled performance: The effects of adult age and experience on elementary processes. *Journal of Experimental Psychology: General, 111,* 176-207.

Sanders, J.A., Sterns, H.L., Smith, M., & Sanders, R.E. (1975). Modification of concept identification performance in older adults. *Developmental Psychology, 11,* 824-829.

Sanders, R.E., Murphy, M.D., Schmitt, F.A., & Walsh, K.K. (1980). Age differences in free recall rehearsal strategies. *Journal of Gerontology, 35*, 550-558.

Sanders, R.E., Wise, J.L., Liddle, C.L., & Murphy, M.D. (1990). Adult age comparisons in the processing of event frequency information. *Psychology and Aging, 5*, 172-177.

Sands, L.P., Terry, H., & Meredith, W. (1989). Change and stability in adult intellectual functioning assessed by Wechsler item responses. *Psychology and Aging, 4*, 79-87.

Sanford, A.J. (1973). Age-related differences in strategies for locating hidden targets. *Gerontologia, 19*, 16-21.

Schaffer, G., & Poon, L.W. (1982). Individual variability in memory training with the elderly. *Educational Gerontology, 8*, 217-229.

Schaie, K.W. (1959). Cross-sectional methods in the study of psychological aspects of aging. *Journal of Gerontology, 14*, 208-215.

Schaie, K.W. (1962). A field-theory approach to age changes in behavior. *Vita Humana, 5*, 129-141.

Schaie, K.W. (1965). A general model for the study of developmental problems. *Psychological Bulletin, 64*, 92-107.

Schaie, K.W. (1967). Age changes and age differences. *Gerontologist, 7*, 128-132.

Schaie, K.W. (1970). A reinterpretation of age-related changes in cognitive structure and functioning. In L.R. Goulet & P.B. Baltes (Eds.), *Life-span developmental psychology: Research and theory* (pp. 485-507). New York: Academic.

Schaie, K.W. (1973). Methodological problems in descriptive developmental research on adulthood and aging. In J.R. Nesselroade & H.W. Reese (Eds.), *Life-span developmental Psychology: Methodological issues* (pp. 253-280). New York: Academic.

Schaie, K.W. (1974). Translations in gerontology - from lab to life: Intellectual functioning. *American Psychologist, 29*, 802-807.

Schaie, K.W. (1975). Age changes in adult intelligence. In D.S. Woodruff & J.E. Birren (Eds.), *Aging: Scientific perspectives and social issues* (pp. 111-124). New York: Van Nostrand Reinhold.

Schaie, K.W. (1977-78). Toward a stage theory of adult cognitive development. *International Journal of Aging and Human Development, 8*, 129-138.

Schaie, K.W. (1979). The primary mental abilities in adulthood: An exploration in the development of psychometric intelligence. In P.B. Baltes & O.G. Brim (Eds.), *Life-span development and behavior* (Vol. 2, pp. 67-115). New York: Academic.

Schaie, K.W. (1980a). Age changes in intelligence. In R.L. Sprott (Ed.), *Age, learning ability and intelligence* (pp. 41-77). New York: Van Nostrand Reinhold.

Schaie, K.W. (1980b). Intelligence and problem solving. In J.E. Birren & R.B. Sloane (Eds.), *Handbook of mental health and aging* (pp. 262-284). New York: Prentice-Hall.

Schaie, K.W. (1983). The Seattle longitudinal study: A 21-year exploration of psychometric intelligence in adulthood. In K.W. Schaie (Ed.), *Longitudinal studies of adult psychological development* (pp. 64-135). New York: Guilford Press.

Schaie, K.W. (1984a). Historical time and cohort effects. In K.A. McCluskey & H.W. Reese (Eds.), *Life-span developmental psychology: Historical and generational effects* (pp. 1-15). New York: Academic.

Schaie, K.W. (1984b). Midlife influences upon intellectual functioning in old age. *International Journal of Behavioral Development, 7*, 463-478.

Schaie, K.W. (1985). *Manual for the Schaie-Thurstone Adult Mental Abilities Test (STAMAT)*. Palo Alto, CA: Consulting Psychologists Press.

Schaie, K.W. (1986). Beyond calendar definitions of age, time, and cohort: The general developmental model revisited. *Developmental Review, 6*, 252-277.

Schaie, K.W. (1987). Applications of psychometric intelligence to the prediction of everyday competence in the elderly. In C. Schooler & K.W. Schaie (Eds.), *Cognitive functioning and social structure over the life course* (pp. 50-58). Norwood, NJ: Ablex.

Schaie, K.W. (1988). Variability in cognitive functioning in the elderly: Implications for societal participation. In A.D. Woodhead, M.A. Bender, & R.C. Leonard (Eds.), *Phenotypic variation in populations: Relevance to risk assessment* (pp. 191-212). New York: Plenum.

Schaie, K.W. (1989a). The hazards of cognitive aging. *The Gerontologist, 29,* 484-493.

Schaie, K.W. (1989b). Individual differences in rate of cognitive change in adulthood. In V.L. Bengston & K.W. Schaie (Eds.), *The course of later life: Research and reflections* (pp. 65-85). New York: Springer.

Schaie, K.W. (1989c). Perceptual speed in adulthood: Cross-sectional and longitudinal studies. *Psychology and Aging, 4,* 443-453.

Schaie, K.W. (1990a). Correction to Schaie. *Psychology and Aging, 5,* 171.

Schaie, K.W. (1990b). Intellectual development in adulthood. In J.E. Birren & K.W. Schaie (Eds.), *Handbook of the psychology of aging.* (3rd ed., pp. 291-309). San Diego: Academic.

Schaie, K.W., & Baltes, P.B. (1975). On sequential strategies in developmental research and the Schaie-Baltes controversy: Description or explanation? *Human Development, 18,* 384-390.

Schaie, K.W., Baltes, P.B., & Strother, C.R. (1964). A study of auditory sensitivity in advanced age. *Journal of Gerontology, 19,* 453-457.

Schaie, K.W., & Gribbin, K. (1975). Adult development and aging. *Annual Review of Psychology, 26,* 65-96.

Schaie, K.W., & Hertzog, C. (1982). Longitudinal methods. In B.B. Wolman (Ed.), *Handbook of developmental psychology* (pp. 91-115). Englewood Cliffs, NJ: Prentice-Hall.

Schaie, K.W., & Hertzog, C. (1983). Fourteen-year cohort-sequential analyses of adult intellectual development. *Developmental Psychology, 19,* 531-543.

Schaie, K.W., & Hertzog, C. (1985). Measurement in the psychology of adulthood and aging. In J.E. Birren & K.W. Schaie (Eds.), *Handbook of the psychology of aging.* (2nd ed., pp. 61-92). New York: Van Nostrand Reinhold.

Schaie, K.W., & Hertzog, C. (1986). Toward a comprehensive model of adult intellectual development: Contributions of the Seattle Longitudinal Study. In R. Sternberg (Ed.), *Advances in human intelligence* (pp. 79-118). Hillsdale, NJ: Lawrence Erlbaum Associates.

Schaie, K.W., Labouvie, G.V., & Barrett, T.J. (1973). Selective attrition effects in a fourteen-year study of adult intelligence. *Journal of Gerontology, 28,* 328-334.

Schaie, K.W., Labouvie, G.V., & Buech, B.V. (1973). Generational and cohort-specific differences in adult cognitive functioning: A fourteen-year study of independent samples. *Developmental Psychology, 9,* 151-166.

Schaie, K.W., & Labouvie-Vief, G. (1974). Generational versus ontogenetic components of change in adult cognitive behavior: A fourteen-year cross-sequential study. *Developmental Psychology, 10,* 305-320.

Schaie, K.W., Rosenthal, F., & Perlman, R.M. (1953). Differential mental deterioration of factorially "pure" functions in later maturity. *Journal of Gerontology, 8,* 191-196.

Schaie, K.W., & Strother, C.R. (1968a). Cognitive and personality variables in college graduates of advanced age. In G.A. Talland (Ed.), *Human behavior and aging: Recent advances in research and theory* (pp. 281-308). New York: Academic.

Schaie, K.W., & Strother, C.R. (1968b). A cross-sequential study of age changes in cognitive behavior. *Psychological Bulletin, 70,* 671-680.

Schaie, K.W., & Strother, C.R. (1968c). The effects of time and cohort differences on the interpretation of age changes in cognitive behavior. *Multivariate Behavioral Research, 3,* 259-294.

Schaie, K.W., & Strother, C.R. (1968d). Limits of optimal functioning in superior old adults. In S.M. Chown & K.F. Riegel (Eds.), *Psychological functioning in the normal aging and the senile aged* (Vol. 1, pp. 132-150). Basel: Karger.

Schaie, K.W., & Willis, S.L. (1986). Can decline in adult intellectual functioning be reversed? *Developmental Psychology*, *22*, 223-232.

Schaie, K.W., Willis, S.L., Jay, G., & Chipuer, H. (1989). Structural invariance of cognitive abilities across the adult life span: A cross-sectional study. *Developmental Psychology*, *25*, 652-662.

Schaie, K.W., & Zelinski, E. (1979). Psychometric assessment of dysfunction in learning and memory. In F. Hoffmeister & C. Muller (Eds.), *Brain function in old age* (pp. 134-150). New York: Springer-Verlag.

Schear, J.M., & Nebes, R.D. (1980). Memory for verbal and spatial information as a function of age. *Experimental Aging Research*, *6*, 271-282.

Scheidt, R.J. (1981). Ecologically valid inquiry: Fait accompli? *Human Development*, *24*, 225-228.

Schludermann, E.H., Schludermann, S.M., Merryman, P.W., & Brown, B.W. (1983). Halstead's studies in the neuropsychology of aging. *Archives of Gerontology and Geriatrics*, *2*, 49-172.

Schmidt, F.L., Hunter, J.E., & Outerbridge, A.N. (1986). Impact of job experience and ability on job knowledge, work sample performance, and supervisory ratings of job performance. *Journal of Applied Psychology*, *71*, 432-439.

Schmitt, F.A., Murphy, M.D., & Sanders, R.E. (1981). Training older adult free recall rehearsal strategies. *Journal of Gerontology*, *36*, 329-337.

Schonfield, A.E.D. (1972). Theoretical nuances and practical old questions: The psychology of aging. *Canadian Psychologist*, *13*, 252-266.

Schonfield, A.E.D. (1974). Translations in gerontology - from lab to life: Utilizing Information *American Psychologist*, *29*, 796-801.

Schonfield, A.E.D. (1980). Learning, memory, and aging. In J.E. Birren & R.B. Sloane (Eds.), *Handbook of mental health and aging* (pp. 214-244). New York: Prentice-Hall.

Schonfield, A.E.D., Davidson, H., & Jones, H. (1983). An example of age-associated interference in memorizing. *Journal of Gerontology*, *38*, 204-210.

Schonfield, A.E.D., & Robertson, E.A. (1966). Memory storage and aging. *Canadian Journal of Psychology*, *20*, 228-236.

Schonfield, A.E.D., & Stones, M.J. (1979). Remembering and aging. In J.F. Kihlstrom & F.J. Evans (Eds.), *Functional disorders of memory* (pp. 103-139). Hillsdale, NJ: Lawrence Erlbaum Associates.

Schultz, N.R., Kaye, D.B., & Hoyer, W.J. (1980). Intelligence and spontaneous flexibility in adulthood and old age. *Intelligence*, *4*, 219-231.

Schultz, N.R., Hoyer, W.J., & Kaye, D.B. (1980). Trait anxiety, spontaneous flexibility, and intelligence in young and elderly adults. *Journal of Consulting and Clinical Psychology*, *48*, 289-291.

Schwartz, D.W., & Karp, S.A. (1967). Field dependence in a geriatric population. *Perceptual and Motor Skills*, *24*, 495-504.

Schwartzman, A.E., Gold, D., Andres, D., Arbuckle, T.Y., & Chaikelson, J. (1987). Stability of intelligence: A 40-year follow-up. *Canadian Journal of Psychology*, *41*, 244-256.

Scialfa, C.T., & Margolis, R.B. (1986). Age differences in the commonality of free associations. *Experimental Aging Research*, *12*, 95-98.

Shaps, L.P., & Nilsson, L.G. (1980). Encoding and retrieval operations in relation to age. *Developmental Psychology*, *16*, 636-643.

Sharps, M.J., & Gollin, E.S. (1987). Memory for object locations in young and elderly adults. *Journal of Gerontology*, *42*, 336-341.

Shaw, R.J., & Craik, F.I.M. (1989). Age differences in predictions and performance on a cued recall task. *Psychology and Aging*, *4*, 131-135.

Shelton, M.D., Parsons, O.A., & Leber, W.R. (1982). Verbal and visuospatial performance and aging: A neuropsychological approach. *Journal of Gerontology*, *37*, 336-341.

Shepard, R.N., & Metzler, J. (1971). Mental rotation of three-dimensional objects. *Science*, *171*, 701-703.

Shichita, K., Hatano, S., Ohashi, Y., Shibata, H., & Matuzaki, T. (1986). Memory changes in the Benton Visual Retention Test between ages 10 and 75. *Journal of Gerontology*, *41*, 385-386.

Shipley, W.C. (1986). *Shipley Institute for Living Scale*. Los Angeles: Western Psychological Services.

Siegler, I.C. (1983). Psychological aspects of the Duke longitudinal studies. In K.W. Schaie (Ed.), *Longitudinal studies of adult psychological development* (pp. 136-190). New York: Guilford.

Siegler, I.C., & Botwinick, J. (1979). A long-term longitudinal study of intellectual ability of older adults: The matter of selective subject attrition. *Journal of Gerontology*, *34*, 242-245.

Simon, E. (1979). Depth and elaboration of processing in relation to age. *Journal of Experimental Psychology: Human Learning and Memory*, *5*, 115-124.

Singer, E., Garfinkel, R., Cohen, S.M., & Srole, L. (1976). Mortality and mental health: Evidence from the midtown Manhattan restudy. *Social Science and Medicine*, *10*, 517-525.

Singleton, W.T. (1983). Age, skill, and management. *International Journal of Aging and Human Development*, *17*, 15-23.

Sinnott, J.D. (1975). Everyday thinking and Piagetian operativity in adults. *Human Development*, *18*, 430-443.

Sinnott, J.D. (1986). Prospective/intentional and incidental everyday memory: Effects of age and passage of time. *Psychology and Aging*, *1*, 110-116.

Sinnott, J.D. (1989). Prospective/intentional memory and aging: Memory as adaptive action. In L.W. Poon, D.C. Rubin & B.A. Wilson (Eds.), *Everyday cognition in adulthood and late life* (pp. 352-369). Cambridge, England: Cambridge University Press.

Sinnott, J.D., & Guttmann, D. (1978). Dialectics of decision making in older adults. *Human Development*, *21*, 190-200.

Slater, P. (1947). The association between age and score in the Progressive Matrices Test. *British Journal of Psychology Statistical Section*, *1*, 64-69.

Smith, A.D. (1974). Response interference with organized recall in the aged. *Developmental Psychology*, *10*, 867-870.

Smith, A.D. (1975a). Aging and interference with memory. *Journal of Gerontology*, *30*, 319-325.

Smith, A.D. (1975b). Partial learning and recognition memory in the aged. *International Journal of Aging and Human Development*, *6*, 359-365.

Smith, A.D. (1976). Aging and the total presentation time hypothesis. *Developmental Psychology*, *12*, 87-88.

Smith, A.D. (1977). Adult age differences in cued recall. *Developmental Psychology*, *13*, 326-331.

Smith, A.D. (1979). The interaction between age and list length in free recall. *Journal of Gerontology*, *34*, 375-380.

Smith, A.D. (1980). Age differences in encoding, storage, and retrieval. In L.W. Poon, J.L. Fozard, L.S. Cermak, D. Arenberg & L.W. Thompson (Eds.), *New directions in memory and aging* (pp. 23-45). Hillsdale, NJ: Lawrence Erlbaum Associates.

Smith, A.D., & Winograd, E. (1978). Age differences in recognizing faces. *Developmental Psychology*, *14*, 443-444.

Smith, J., & Baltes, P.B. (1990). Wisdom-related knowledge: Age/cohort differences in response to life-planning problems. *Developmental Psychology*, *26*, 494-505.

Soffie, M., & Giurgea, C. (1988). Age-related memory impairments in rats: Potential paradigms for pharmacological modulation. In M.M. Gruneberg, P.E. Morris, & R.N. Sykes (Eds.), *Practical aspects of memory: Current research and issues* (pp. 143-148). Chichester: Wiley.

Somberg, B., & Salthouse, T.A. (1982). Divided attention abilities in young and old adults. *Journal of Experimental Psychology: Human Perception and Performance, 8*, 651-663.

Sorenson, H. (1933). Mental ability over a wide range of adult ages. *Journal of Applied Psychology, 17*, 729-741.

Sorenson, H. (1938). *Adult abilities.* Minneapolis: University of Minnesota Press.

Spearman, C. (1927). *The abilities of man.* London: MacMillan.

Spieth, W. (1964). Cardiovascular health status, age, and psychological performance. *Journal of Gerontology, 19*, 277-284.

Spieth, W. (1965). Slowness of task performance and cardiovascular disease. In A.T. Welford & J.E. Birren (Eds.), *Behavior, aging and the nervous system* (pp. 366-400). Springfield, IL: Charles C Thomas.

Spilich, G.J. (1985). Discourse comprehension across the span of life. In N. Charness (Ed.), *Aging and Human Performance* (pp. 144-190). Chichester: Wiley.

Squire, L.R. (1974). Remote memory as affected by aging. *Neuropsychologia, 12*, 429-435.

Squire, L.R. (1989). On the course of forgetting in very long-term memory. *Journal of Experimental Psychology: Learning, Memory and Cognition, 15*, 241-245.

Stein, C.I. (1962). The G.A.T.B.: The effect of age on intersample variations. *Personnel Guidance Journal, 60*, 779-785.

Sternberg, R., & Berg, C. (1987). What are theories of adult intellectual development theories of? In C. Schooler & K.W. Schaie (Eds.), *Cognitive functioning and social structure over the life course* (pp. 3-23). Norwood, NJ: Ablex.

Sterne, D.M. (1973). The Hooper Visual Organization Test and Trail Making Tests as discriminants of brain injury. *Journal of Clinical Psychology, 29*, 212-213.

Sterns, H.L., & Sanders, R.E. (1980). Training and education of the elderly. In R.R. Turner & H.W. Reese (Eds.), *Life-span developmental psychology: Intervention* (pp. 307-330). New York: Academic.

Stevens, J.C., Cain, W.S., & Demarque, A. (1990). Memory and identification of simulated odors in elderly and young persons. *Bulletin of the Psychonomic Society, 28*, 293-296.

Stine, E.L. (1990). On-line processing of written text by younger and older adults. *Psychology and Aging, 5*, 68-78.

Stine, E.L., & Wingfield, A. (1987). Levels upon levels: Predicting age differences in text recall. *Experimental Aging Research, 13*, 179-183.

Stine, E.L., Wingfield, A., & Myers, S.D. (1990). Age differences in processing information from television news: The effects of bisensory augmentation. *Journal of Gerontology: Psychological Sciences, 45*, P9-P16.

Stine, E.L., Wingfield, A., & Poon, L.W. (1986). How much and how fast: Rapid processing of spoken language in later adulthood. *Psychology and Aging, 1*, 303-311.

Storandt, M. (1977). Age, ability level, and method of administering and scoring the WAIS. *Journal of Gerontology, 32*, 175-178.

Storandt, M., & Futterman, A. (1982). Stimulus size and performance on two subtests of the Wechsler Adult Intelligence Scale by younger and older adults. *Journal of Gerontology, 37*, 602-603.

Storandt, M., Grant, E.A., & Gordon, B.C. (1978). Remote memory as a function of age and sex. *Experimental Aging Research, 4*, 365-375.

Strayer, D.L., Wickens, C.D., & Braune, R. (1987). Adult age differences in the speed and capacity of information processing: 2. An electrophysiological approach. *Psychology and Aging, 2*, 99-110.

Stricker, L.J., & Rock, D.A. (1987). Factor structure of the GRE General Test in Young and Middle Adulthood. *Developmental Psychology, 23*, 526-536.

Stuart-Hamilton, I., Perfect, T., & Rabbitt, P. (1988). Remembering who was who. In M.M. Gruneberg, P.E. Morris, & R.N. Sykes (Eds.), *Practical aspects of memory: Current research and issues* (pp. 169-174). Chichester: Wiley.

Suchman, E.A., Phillips, B.S., & Streib, G.F. (1958). An analysis of the validity of health questionnaires. *Social Forces, 36*, 223-232.

Suci, G.H., Davidoff, M.D., & Brown, J.C. (1962). Interference in short-term retention as a function of age. In C. Tibbitts & W. Donahue (Eds.), *Social and psychological aspects of aging* (pp. 770-773). New York: Columbia University Press.

Sullivan, E.V., & Corkin, S. (1984). Selective subject attrition in a longitudinal study of head-injured veterans. *Journal of Gerontology, 39*, 718-720.

Sullivan, J.L., & Feldman, S. (1979). *Multiple indicators: An introduction.* Sage University Paper Series on Quantitative Applications in the Social Sciences, Series No. 07-015. Beverly Hills, CA: Sage.

Sunderland, A., Harris, J.E., & Baddeley, A.D. (1984). Assessing everyday memory after severe head injury. In J.E. Harris & P.E. Morris (Eds.), *Everyday memory, actions and absent-mindedness* (pp. 191-206). London: Academic.

Surber, J.R., Kowalski, A.H., & Pena-Paez, A. (1984). Effects of aging on the recall of extended expository prose. *Experimental Aging Research, 10*, 25-28.

Sward, K. (1945). Age and mental ability in superior men. *American Journal of Psychology, 58*, 443-479.

Szafran, J. (1970). The effects of ageing on professional pilots. In J.H. Price (Ed.), *Modern trends in Psychological Medicine II* (pp. 24-52). New York: Appleton-Century Crofts.

Talland, G.A. (1962). The effect of age on speed of simple manual skill. *Journal of Genetic Psychology, 100*, 69-76.

Talland, G.A. (1967). Age and the immediate memory span. *Gerontologist, 7*, 4-9.

Talland, G.A. (1968). Age and the span of immediate recall. In G.A. Talland (Ed.), *Human aging and behavior* (pp. 93-129). New York: Academic.

Tamkin, A.S., & Jacobsen, R. (1984). Age-related norms for the Hooper Visual Organization Test. *Journal of Clinical Psychology, 40*, 1459-1463.

Taub, H.A. (1966). Visual short-term memory as a function of age, rate of presentation, and schedule of presentation. *Journal of Gerontology, 21*, 388-391.

Taub, H.A. (1968a). Age differences in memory as a function of rate of presentation, order of report, and stimulus organization. *Journal of Gerontology, 23*, 159-164.

Taub, H.A. (1968b). Aging and free recall. *Journal of Gerontology, 23*, 466-468.

Taub, H.A. (1973). Memory span, practice and aging. *Journal of Gerontology, 28*, 335-338.

Taub, H.A. (1975). Mode of presentation, age and short-term memory. *Journal of Gerontology, 30*, 56-59.

Taub, H.A. (1979). Comprehension and memory of prose materials by young and old adults. *Experimental Aging Research, 5*, 3-13.

Taub, H.A., & Grieff, S. (1967). Effects of age on organization and recall of two sets of stimuli. *Psychonomic Science, 7*, 53-54.

Taub, H.A., & Kline, G.E. (1978). Recall of prose as a function of age and input modality. *Journal of Gerontology, 33*, 725-730.

Taub, H.A., & Long, M.K. (1972). The effects of practice on short-term memory of young and old subjects. *Journal of Gerontology, 27*, 494-499.

Teasdale, T.W., & Owen, D.R. (1989). Continuing secular increases in intelligence and a stable prevalence of high intelligence levels. *Intelligence, 13*, 255-262.

Tenney, Y.T. (1984). Aging and the misplacing of objects. *British Journal of Developmental Psychology, 2*, 43-50.

Thomas, J.C., Fozard J.L., & Waugh, N.C. (1977). Age-related differences in naming latency. *American Journal of Psychology, 90*, 499-509.

Thomas, J.C., Waugh, N.C., & Fozard, J.L. (1978). Age and familiarity in memory scanning. *Journal of Gerontology, 33*, 528-533.

Thomas, J.L. (1985). Visual memory: Adult age differences in map recall and learning strategies. *Experimental Aging Research, 11*, 93-95.

Thomas, J.M., & Charles, D.C. (1964). Effects of age and stimulus size on perception. *Journal of Gerontology, 19*, 447-450.

Thorndike, E.L., Bregman, E.O., Tilton, J.W., & Woodyard, E. (1928). *Adult learning*. New York: MacMillan.

Thurstone, L.L., & Thurstone, T.G. (1941). *Factorial studies of intelligence*. Chicago: University of Chicago Press.

Thurstone, L.L., & Thurstone, T.G. (1949). *Examiner manual for the Primary Mental Abilities Test (Form 11-17)*. Chicago: Science Research Associates.

Till, R.E. (1985). Verbatim and inferential memory in young and elderly adults. *Journal of Gerontology, 40*, 316-323.

Tissue, T. (1972). Another look at self-rated health among the elderly. *Journal of Gerontology, 27*, 91-94.

Todd, M., Davis, K.E., & Cofferty, T.P. (1983-84). Who volunteers for adult development research? Research findings and practical steps to reach low volunteering groups. *International Journal of Aging and Human Development, 18*, 177-184.

Trahan, D.E., Larrabee, G.J., & Levin, H.S. (1986). Age-related differences in recognition memory for pictures. *Experimental Aging Research, 12*, 147-150.

Traxler, A.J. (1973). Retroactive and proactive inhibition in young and elderly adults using an unpaced modified free recall task. *Psychological Reports, 32*, 215-222.

Treat, N., & Reese, H.W. (1976). Age, pacing and imagery in paired-associate learning. *Developmental Psychology, 12*, 119-124.

Treat, N.J., Poon, L.W., & Fozard, J.L. (1981). Age, imagery and practice in paired-associate learning. *Experimental Aging Research, 7*, 337-342.

Trembly, D., & O'Connor, J. (1966). Growth and decline of natural and acquired intellectual characteristics. *Journal of Gerontology, 21*, 9-12.

Trites, D.K., & Cobb, B.B. (1964). Problems in air traffic management: IV. Comparison of pre-employment, job-related experience with aptitude tests as predictors of training and job performance of air traffic control specialists. *Aerospace Medicine, 35*, 428-436.

Tubi, N., & Calev, A. (1989). Verbal and visuospatial recall by younger and older subjects: Use of matched tasks. *Psychology and Aging, 4,*, 493-495.

Tuddenham, R.D. (1948). Soldier intelligence in World Wars I and II. *American Psychologist, 3*, 54-56.

Tulving, E. (1972). Episodic and semantic memory. In E. Tulving & W. Donaldson (Eds.), *Organization of memory* (pp. 381-403). New York: Academic.

Tulving, E. (1983). *Elements of Episodic Memory*. Oxford, England: Clarendon.

Tulving, E. & Arbuckle, T.Y. (1966). Input and output interference in short-term associative memory. *Journal of Experimental Psychology, 72*, 145-150.

Tun, P.A. (1989). Age differences in processing expository and narrative text. *Journal of Gerontology: Psychological Sciences, 44*, P9-P15.

Ulatowska, H.K., Cannito, M.P., Hayashi, M.M., & Fleming, S.G. (1985). Language abilities in the elderly. In H.K. Vlatowska (Ed.), *The aging brain: Communication in the elderly* (pp. 125-139). San Diego, CA: College-Hill Press.

Underwood, G. (1976). *Attention and memory*. New York: Pergamon.

Vega, A., & Parsons, O.A. (1967). Cross-validation of the Halstead-Reitan Tests for brain damage. *Journal of Consulting Psychology, 31*, 619-625.

Verhage, F. (1965). Intelligence and age in a Dutch sample. *Human Development, 8*, 238-245.

Vernon, P.E. (1947). The variations of intelligence with occupation, age and locality. *British Journal of Psychology Statistical Section, 1*, 52-63.

Verville, E., & Cameron, N. (1946). Age and sex differences in the perception of incomplete pictures by adults. *Journal of Genetic Psychology, 68*, 149-157.

Waddell, K.J., & Rogoff, B. (1981). Effect of contextual organization on spatial memory of middle-aged and older women. *Developmental Psychology, 17*, 875-885.

Waddell, K.J., & Rogoff, B. (1987). Contextual organization and intentionality in adults' spatial memory. *Developmental Psychology*, *23*, 514-520.

Wallace, J.E., Krauter, E.E., & Campbell, B.A. (1980). Animal models of declining memory in the aged: Short-term and spatial memory in the aged rat. *Journal of Gerontology*, *35*, 355-363.

Wallace, J.G. (1956). Some studies of perception in relation to age. *British Journal of Psychology*, *47*, 283-297.

Walsh, D.A. (1982). The development of visual information processes in adulthood and old age. In F.I.M. Craik & S. Trehub (Eds.), *Aging and cognitive processes* (pp. 99-125). New York: Plenum.

Walsh, D.A., & Baldwin, M. (1977). Age differences in integrated semantic memory. *Developmental Psychology*, *13*, 509-514.

Walsh, D.A., Baldwin, M., & Finkle, T.J. (1980). Age differences in integrated semantic memory for abstract sentences. *Experimental Aging Research*, *6*, 431-444.

Warren, L.R., & Mitchell, S.A. (1980). Age differences in judging the frequency of events. *Developmental Psychology*, *16*, 116-120.

Warrington, E.K., & Sanders, H.I. (1971). The fate of old memories. *Quarterly Journal of Experimental Psychology*, *23*, 432-442.

Wasserstein, J., Zappulla, R., Rosen, J., Gerstman, L., & Rock, D. (1987). In search of closure: Subjective contour illusions, gestalt completion tests, and implications. *Brain and Cognition*, *6*, 1-14.

Waugh, N.C., & Barr, R.A. (1980). Memory and mental tempo. In L.W. Poon, J.L. Fozard, L.S. Cermak, D. Arenberg & L.W. Thompson (Eds.), *New directions in memory and aging* (pp. 251-260). Hillsdale, NJ: Lawrence Erlbaum Associates.

Waugh, N.C., & Barr, R.A. (1982). Encoding deficits in aging. In F.I.M. Craik & S. Trehub (Eds.), *Aging and cognitive processes* (pp. 183-190). New York: Plenum.

Waugh, N.C., & Barr, R.A. (1989). Does retention of order require verbal labeling? *Experimental Aging Research*, *15*, 111-121.

Wechsler, D. (1952). *The range of human capacities*. Baltimore, MD: Williams & Wilkins.

Wechsler, D. (1955). *Manual for the Wechsler scale*. New York: The Psychological Corporation.

Wechsler, D. (1958). *Measurement of adult intelligence*. Baltimore, MD: Williams & Wilkins.

Wechsler, D. (1981). *Manual for the Wechsler Adult Intelligence Scale - Revised*. New York: The Psychological Corporation.

Wechsler, D. (1987). *Manual for Wechsler Memory Scale - Revised*. New York: The Psychological Corporation.

Weinert, F., Schneider, W., & Knopf, M. (1988). Individual differences in memory development across the life span. In P.B. Baltes, D.L. Featherman, & R.M. Lerner (Eds.), *Life-Span Development and Behavior* (Vol. 9, pp. 39-85). Hillsdale, NJ: Lawrence Erlbaum Associates.

Weisenburg, T., Roe, A., & McBride, K.E. (1936). *Adult intelligence*. New York: The Commonwealth Fund.

Welford, A.T. (1956). Age and learning: Theory and needed research. In F. Verzar (Ed.), *Experimental research on aging* (pp. 136-144). Basel: Birkhauser Verlag.

Welford, A.T. (1957). Methodological problems in the study of changes in human performance with age. In G.E. Wolstenholme & C.M. O'Connor (Eds.), *Ciba Foundation colloquia on ageing* (Vol. 3, pp. 149-169). London: Churchill.

Welford, A.T. (1958). *Ageing and human skill*. London: Oxford University Press.

Welford, A.T. (1959). Psychomotor performance. In J.E. Birren (Ed.), *Handbook of aging and the individual* (pp. 562-613). Chicago: University of Chicago Press.

Welford, A.T. (1962). On changes of performance with age. *Lancet*, *17*, 335-339.

Welford, A.T. (1966). Industrial work suitable for older people: Some British studies.

Gerontologist, *6*, 4-9.

Welford, A.T. (1976). Thirty years of psychological research on age and work. *Journal of Occupational Psychology*, *49*, 129-138.

Welford, A.T. (1980). Memory and age: A perspective view. In L.W. Poon, J.L. Fozard, L.S. Cermak, D. Arenberg, & L.W. Thompson (Eds.), *New directions in memory and aging* (pp. 1-17). Hillsdale, NJ: Lawrence Erlbaum Associates.

Welford, A.T. (1983). Perception, memory and motor performance in relation to age. In J.E. Birren, J.M. Munnichs, H. Thomae & M. Marois (Eds.), *Aging: A challenge to science and society* (Vol. 3, pp. 297-311). Oxford: Oxford University Press.

Welford, A.T. (1985). Changes of performance with age: An overview. In N. Charness (Ed.), *Aging and human performance* (pp. 333-369). Chichester: Wiley.

Wentworth-Rohr, I., Mackintosh, R.M., & Fialkoff, B.S. (1974). The relationship of Hooper VOT score to sex, education, intelligence and age. *Journal of Clinical Psychology*, *30*, 73-75.

West, R.L. (1989). Planning practical memory training for the aged. In L.W. Poon, D.C. Rubin & B.A. Wilson (Eds.), *Everyday cognition in adulthood and late life* (pp. 573-597). Cambridge, England: Cambridge University Press.

West, R.L., Odom, R.D., & Aschkenasy, J.R. (1978). Perceptual sensitivity and conceptual coordination in children and younger and older adults. *Human Development*, *21*, 334-345.

Wetherick, N.E. (1966). The responses of normal adult subjects to the matrices test. *British Journal of Psychology*, *57*, 297-300.

Wetherick, N.E. (1975). Age, short-term memory capacity and the higher mental functions. In D.B. Lumsden & R.H. Sherron (Eds.), *Experimental studies in adult learning and memory* (pp. 115-126). Washington, DC: Hemisphere Publications.

Whitbourne, S.K., & Slevin, A.G. (1978). Imagery and sentence retention in elderly and young adults. *Journal of Genetic Psychology*, *133*, 287-298.

White, N., & Cunningham, W.R. (1982). What is the evidence for retrieval problems in the elderly? *Experimental Aging Research*, *8*, 169-171.

White, N., & Cunningham, W.R. (1987). The age comparative construct validity of speeded cognitive factors. *Multivariate Behavioral Research*, *22*, 249-265.

Wickelgren, W.A. (1975). Age and storage dynamics in continuous recognition memory. *Developmental Psychology*, *11*, 165-169.

Wickens, C.D., Braune, R., & Stokes, A. (1987). Age differences in the speed and capacity of information processing: I. A dual-task approach. *Psychology and Aging*, *2*, 70-78.

Williams, M. (1960). The effect of past experience on mental performance in the elderly. *British Journal of Medical Psychology*, *33*, 215-221.

Willis, S.L. (1985). Toward an educational psychology of the older adult learner: Intellectual and cognitive bases. In J.E. Birren & K.W. Schaie (Eds.), *Handbook of the Psychology of Aging.* (2nd ed., pp. 818-847). New York: Van Nostrand Reinhold.

Willis, S.L. (1987). Cognitive training and everyday competence. In K.W. Schaie (Ed.), *Annual Review of Gerontology and Geriatrics* (Vol. 7, pp. 159-188). New York: Springer.

Willis, S.L. (1989a). Cohort differences in cognitive aging: A sample case. In K.W. Schaie & C. Schooler (Eds.), *Social structure and aging: Psychological processes* (pp. 95-112). Hillsdale, NJ: Lawrence Erlbaum Associates.

Willis, S.L. (1989b). Improvement with cognitive training: Which old dogs learn what tricks? In L.W. Poon, D.C. Rubin & B.A. Wilson (Eds.), *Everyday cognition in adulthood and late life* (pp. 545-569). Cambridge, England: Cambridge University Press.

Willis, S.L., & Baltes, P.B. (1980). Intelligence in adulthood and aging: Contemporary issues. In L.W. Poon (Ed.), *Aging in the 1980s* (pp. 260-272). Washington, DC: American Psychological Association.

Willis, S.L., & Baltes, P.B. (1981). Letter to the editor. *Journal of Gerontology*, *36*, 636-638.

Willis, S.L., Blieszner, R., & Baltes, P.B. (1981). Training research in aging: Modification of performance on the fluid ability of figural relations. *Journal of Educational Psychology*, *73*, 41-50.

Willis, S.L., Cornelius, S.W., Blow, F.C., & Baltes, P.B. (1983). Training research in aging: Attentional processes. *Journal of Educational Psychology*, *75*, 257-270.

Willis, S.L., & Schaie, K.W. (1986a). Practical intelligence in later adulthood. In R.J. Sternberg & R.K. Wagner (Eds.), *Practical intelligence* (pp. 236-268). New York: Cambridge University Press.

Willis, S.L., & Schaie, K.W. (1986b). Training the elderly on the ability factors of spatial orientation and inductive reasoning. *Psychology and Aging*, *1*, 239-247.

Willis, S.L., & Schaie, K.W. (1988). Gender differences in spatial ability in old age: Longitudinal and intervention findings. *Sex Roles*, *18*, 189-203.

Willoughby, R.R. (1927). Family similarities in mental test abilities (with a note on the growth and decline of these abilities). *Genetic Psychological Monograph*, *2*, 235-277.

Willoughby, R.R. (1929). Incidental learning. *Journal of Educational Psychology*, *20*, 671-682.

Willoughby, R.R. (1930). Incidental learning. *Journal of Educational Psychology*, *21*, 12-23.

Wilson, J.R., DeFries, J.G., McClearn, G.E., Vandenberg, S.G., Johnson, R.C., & Rashad, M.N. (1975). Cognitive abilities: Use of family data as a control to assess sex and age differences in two ethnic groups. *International Journal of Aging and Human Development*, *6*, 261-276.

Wilson, T.R. (1963). Flicker fusion frequency, age and intelligence. *Gerontologia*, *7*, 200-208.

Wimer, R.E. (1960). A supplementary report on age differences in retention over a twenty-four hour period. *Journal of Gerontology*, *15*, 417-418.

Wimer, R.E., & Wigdor, B.T. (1958). Age differences in retention of learning. *Journal of Gerontology*, *13*, 291-295.

Winer, B.J. (1971). *Statistical principles in experimental design* (2nd ed.). New York: McGraw-Hill.

Wingfield, A. (1980). Attention, levels of processing, and state-dependent recall. In L.W. Poon, J.L. Fozard, L.S. Cermak, D. Arenberg, & L.W. Thompson (Eds.), *New directions in memory and aging* (pp. 135-141). Hillsdale, NJ: Lawrence Erlbaum Associates.

Wingfield, A., Poon, L.W., Lombardi, L., & Lowe, D. (1985). Speed of processing in normal aging: Effects of speech rate, linguistic structure and processing time. *Journal of Gerontology*, *40*, 579-585.

Wingfield, A., & Sandoval, A.W. (1980). Perceptual processing for meaning. In L.W. Poon, J.L. Fozard, L.S. Cermak, D. Arenberg, & L.W. Thompson (Eds.), *New directions in memory and aging* (pp. 205-238). Hillsdale, NJ: Lawrence Erlbaum Associates.

Wingfield, A., & Stine, E.A.L. (1989). Modeling memory processes: Research and theory on memory and aging. In G.C. Gilmore, P.J. Whitehouse, & M.L. Wykle (Eds.), *Memory, aging, and dementia: Theory, assessment and treatment* (pp. 4-40). New York: Springer.

Wingfield, A., Stine, E.A.L., Lahar, C.J., & Aberdeen, J.S. (1988). Does the capacity of working memory change with age? *Experimental Aging Research*, *14*, 103-107.

Winn, F.J., Elias, J.W., & Marshall, P.H. (1976). Meaningfulness and interference as factors in paired-associate learning with the aged. *Educational Gerontology*, *1*, 297-306.

Winocur, G. (1988). Long-term memory loss in senescent rats: Neuropsychological analysis of interference and context effects. *Psychology and Aging*, *3*, 273-279.

Winocur, G., & Moscovitch, M. (1983). Paired-associate learning in institutionalized old people: An analysis of interference and context effects. *Journal of Gerontology*, *38*, 455-464.

Winograd, E., Smith, A.D., & Simon, E.W. (1982). Aging and the picture superiority effect in recall. *Journal of Gerontology*, *37*, 70-75.

Witt, S.J., & Cunningham, W.R. (1979). Cognitive speed and subsequent intellectual development: A longitudinal investigation. *Journal of Gerontology*, *34*, 540-546.

Witte, K.L., & Freund, J.S. (1976). Paired-associate learning in young and old adults as related to stimulus concreteness and presentation method. *Journal of Gerontology, 31*, 186-192.

Witte, K.L., Freund, J.S., & Sebby, R.A. (1990). Age differences in free recall and subjective organization. *Psychology and Aging, 5*, 307-309.

Wittels, I. (1972). Age and stimulus meaningfulness in paired-associate learning. *Journal of Gerontology, 27*, 372-375.

Wohlwill, J.F. (1970). Methodology and research strategy in the study of developmental change. In L.R. Goulet & P.B. Baltes (Eds.), *Life-span developmental psychology: Research and theory* (pp. 149-191). New York: Academic Press.

Wohlwill, J.F. (1973). *The study of behavioral development.* New York: Academic Press.

Wood, L.E., & Pratt, J.D. (1987). Pegword mnemonic as an aid to memory in the elderly: A comparison of four age groups. *Educational Gerontology, 13*, 325-339.

Worden, P.E., & Meggison, D.L. (1984). Aging and the category-recall relationship. *Journal of Gerontology, 39*, 322-324.

Worden, P.E., & Sherman-Brown, S. (1983). A word-frequency cohort effect in young versus elderly adults' memory for words. *Developmental Psychology, 19*, 521-530.

Wright, R.E. (1981). Aging, divided attention, and processing capacity. *Journal of Gerontology, 36*, 605-614.

Wright, R.E. (1982). Adult age similarities in free recall output order and strategies. *Journal of Gerontology, 37*, 76-79.

Yarmey, A.D., & Bull, M.P. (1978). Where were you when President Kennedy was assassinated? *Bulletin of the Psychonomic Society, 11*, 133-135.

Yarmey, A.D., & Kent, J. (1980). Eyewitness identification by elderly and young adults. *Law and Human Behavior, 4*, 359-371.

Yerkes, R.M. (1921). Psychological examining in the United States Army. *Memoirs of the National Academy of Sciences, 15*, 1-877.

Yesavage, J.A., Lapp, D., & Sheikh, J. (1989). Mnemonics as modified for use by the elderly. In L.W. Poon, D.C. Rubin & B.A. Wilson (Eds.), *Everyday cognition in adulthood and late life* (pp. 598-611). Cambridge, England: Cambridge University Press.

Yesavage, J.A., & Rose, T.L. (1984). The effects of a face-name mnemonic in young, middle-aged, and elderly adults. *Experimental Aging Research, 10*, 55-57.

Young, M.L. (1966). Problem-solving performance in two age groups. *Journal of Gerontology, 21*, 505-509.

Zacks, R.T. (1982). Encoding strategies used by young and elderly adults in a keeping track task. *Journal of Gerontology, 37*, 203-211.

Zacks, R.T., & Hasher, L. (1988). Capacity theory and the processing of inferences. In L.L. Light & D.M. Burke (Eds.), *Language, memory and aging* (pp. 154-170). New York: Cambridge University Press.

Zacks, R.T., Hasher, L., Doren, B., Hamm, V., & Attig, M.S. (1987). Encoding and memory of explicit and implicit information. *Journal of Gerontology, 42*, 418-422.

Zandri, E., & Charness, N. (1989). Training older and younger adults to use software. *Educational Gerontology, 15*, 615-631.

Zaretsky, H., & Halberstam, J.L. (1968). Age differences in paired-associate learning. *Journal of Gerontology, 23*, 165-168.

Zelinski, E.M., & Gilewski, M.J. (1988). Memory for prose and aging: A meta-analysis. In M.L. Howe & C.J. Brainerd (Eds.), *Cognitive development in adulthood* (pp. 133-158). New York: Springer-Verlag.

Zelinski, E.M., Gilewski, M.J., & Thompson, L.W. (1980). Do laboratory memory tests relate to everyday remembering and forgetting? In L.W. Poon, J.L. Fozard, L.S. Cermak, D. Arenberg & L.W. Thompson (Eds.), *New directions in memory and aging* (pp. 519-544). Hillsdale, NJ: Lawrence Erlbaum Associates.

Zelinski, E.M., & Light, L.L. (1988). Young and older adults' use of context in spatial memory *Psychology and Aging*, *3*, 99-101.

Zelinski, E.M., & Miura, S.A. (1988). Effects of thematic information on script memory in young and old adults. *Psychology and Aging*, *3*, 292-299.

Zelinski, E.M., Walsh, D.A., & Thompson, L.W. (1978). Orienting task effects on EDR and free recall in three age groups. *Journal of Gerontology*, *33*, 239-245.

Zivian, M.T., & Darjes, R.W. (1983). Free recall by in-school and out-of-school adults: Performance and metamemory. *Developmental Psychology*, *19*, 513-520.

Zornetzer, S.F., Thompson, R.F., & Rogers, J. (1982). Rapid forgetting in aged rats. *Behavioral and Neural Biology*, *36*, 49-60.

Author Index

Page Numbers in **bold** refer to reference pages

Subject Index

This book may be kept